The Major International
Treaties 1914–1973. *A*
history and guide
with texts

The Major International Treaties 1914–1973. *A history and guide with texts*

J. A. S. Grenville

STEIN AND DAY / Publishers / New York

First published in the United States of America by
Stein and Day/*Publishers* in 1974
Copyright © 1974 by J.A.S. Grenville
Library of Congress Catalog Card No. 75-163352
All rights reserved
Printed in the United States of America
Stein and Day/*Publishers*/Scarborough House, Briarcliff Manor, N.Y. 10510
ISBN 0-8128-1654-4

Contents

Page references in *italic* lettering refer to the commentary,
and those in **bold** to the texts of the treaties

XIX · THE MAJOR INTERNATIONAL CONFLICTS, TREATIES AND AGREEMENTS OF 1973 *528*

Maps

Preface

This book is intended for students and the general reader concerned with international affairs. It provides a short history and analysis of the major treaties and agreements since 1914, together with the texts of the most important of them. A firm grasp of the major international treaties is fundamental to an understanding of international affairs and recent history. Most monographs and general books on diplomatic history assume their knowledge, although the treaties themselves are not easily available to students. They are scattered through many volumes; few libraries possess even the most important collections and only a handful would be able to trace the text of every treaty in this book.

Many years of teaching modern international history have convinced me of the urgent need to provide a *usable* collection of such treaties in one volume. It proved a formidable task that has taken several years to complete. A selection had to be made from the more than 20,000 treaties and agreements concluded since 1914. From the point of view of the historian seeking to understand the course of events, the distinction made by international lawyers between multi-national and bilateral treaties is not relevant. Nevertheless Manley O. Hudson's *International Legislation. A Collection of Texts of Multipartite International Instruments of General Interest*, in nine volumes covering the period from 1920 to 1945 (Washington, D.C., Carnegie Endowment for International Peace, 1931–50), and the Harvard *Index to Multilateral Treaties . . . from the Sixteenth Century through 1963* . . . (ed. Vaclav Mostecky and Francis R. Doyle, Cambridge, Mass., 1965) will remain landmarks in the indexing and assembly of multilateral treaties. The great collection of *Documents* and the *Survey* of the Royal Institute of International Affairs is another useful tool, though some caution has to be exercised since the volumes were generally written close to the events described. Even treaties 'chang ?' as subsequent secret clauses come to light and the records of the negotiations leading to them are revealed.

There exist already a number of exceptionally good collections of treaties each dealing with a specific aspect of international relations. L. Shapiro's *Soviet Treaties, 1917–1939* (Washington, D.C., Georgetown University Press, 1950–5, 2 vols.) is a model of its kind; J. C. Hurewitz, *Diplomacy in the Near and Middle East. A Documentary Record* (Princeton, N.J., Van Nostrand, and London, Macmillan, 1956, 2 vols.) is another masterly survey; Keesing's *Treaties and Alliances of the World* (Bristol, Keesing's Publications Ltd, 1968) provides an excellent analysis of international treaties actually in force in the year 1968, though in the last five years a number of important treaties have been concluded; Ian Brownlie has edited treaties and documents on African affairs and other important subjects. These are only a few of the lawyers, political scientists and historians who since 1945 have made important specialist contributions. Government collections also exist on various international problems. But for the student who does not intend to specialize in a short period or in any one region, but who wishes to gain a general grasp, the task of studying all available specialist volumes and relating them to each other is formidable and usually beyond practical realization. It is also entirely beyond a student's financial means.

There is no one volume which can be referred to where the period 1914 to 1973 is treated as a whole. The basic research for this volume had to be done by patiently working through the many hundred volumes of the *League of Nations Treaty Series* and the *United Nations Treaty Series*. I would like to express my especial thanks to J. K. Nielsen and to the staff of the Dag Hammarskjöld Library of the United Nations in New York who in so many ways assisted this work. The treaties not to be found in these two great series may be discovered in national treaty series or specialist works. I found them partly in the United Nations Library in New York, also in the Library of the Royal Institute of International Affairs, in the Library of the Institute of Historical Research (University of London) and in the London Library. To the staff of these libraries I am much indebted for their expert and courteous assistance. I am grateful to Her Majesty's Stationery Office for permission to reprint treaties, and also to the National Archives, Washington.

The actual selection and editing of these treaties has been undertaken in the light of our present understanding of the diplomatic history of the last fifty years. The question may be asked, why edit the treaties at all? A study of the actual texts soon reveals that they contain much formal material which can be dispensed with. Secondly, to make the treaties usable it is helpful to focus attention on the important articles and where necessary to summarize the remainder.

Finally, even in their edited form, the major treaties fill a sizeable volume. To have printed all the treaties discussed in this book in full would have required at least twenty volumes and would have defeated my purpose, which is to highlight the significant and to bring the major treaties within one manageable volume. In editing these treaties I have kept in mind the student whose time for studying the subject is limited, but the references to the original printed texts of the treaties at the end of the book will guide those researchers who may require a particular treaty in full. The choice of treaties is difficult and bound to be subjective; I have kept in mind the use to which such a volume may be put.

This work is not meant to be a diplomatic history; it is intended for use with such histories. The treaties and introductions have been arranged to provide an historical framework to clarify their relationship to each other. I am most grateful to Methuen & Co., especially Peter Wait, and to Stein & Day for their general support while I was preparing the manuscript for publication. To my third year 'special subject' students I am also much indebted for their kind additional help in checking for errors at a time when they were very busy with their own work. For any faults or slips I alone must take responsibility; for constant encouragement and patience beyond the call of duty I have to thank Betty Anne, my wife.

December 1973   John A. S. Grenville
                                                              Birmingham University

The Major International
Treaties 1914–1973. *A*
history and guide
with texts

Introduction: International treaties

The role of treaties

International treaties have frequently turned out to be no stronger than the paper on which they are written, yet during the twenty years after the Second World War more multilateral treaties – some 2,500 – were concluded than during the whole of the previous 350 years. The inflation in the sheer number of treaties has been accompanied since the First World War by the conclusion of treaties of increasing complexity and length; some, like the treaty establishing the European Economic Community in 1957, fill a single volume; others, such as the peace settlements following the First World War, run through several volumes; and still others with accompanying amendments, as for instance the General Agreement on Tariffs and Trade signed in Geneva in 1947, fill several shelves.

There are some obvious explanations for the increase in the number and length of treaties. There exist now more sovereign nations than ever before; there has also been a spectacular growth of international organizations which sign treaties in the same way as single States; treaties since 1919 have more-over been increasingly concerned with economic and social questions. The one explanation that cannot be seriously advanced is that mutual faith in the honourable behaviour of countries party to a treaty has been noticeably strengthened over the years. The solemn undertakings and promises, the general intentions of friendship and cooperation embedded in the language of the treaties, do not by themselves carry more conviction now than they did in times past; they are no guarantee of observance. Nor has there developed any effective way of bringing to justice a treaty violator by an international tribunal backed by effective international sanction, especially when the offending nation is a powerful one. That morality as the basis of international dealings has not been strengthened in the twentieth century even the least cynical observer has to admit.

International lawyers have not had an easy time attempting to reconcile the realities of policy with the notion of the rule of law in international affairs. Ultimately there has to be some moral foundation to law and this is difficult to demonstrate as a fundamental consideration in the formation of national policies the world over. There has indeed been an interesting shift in the way in which international lawyers and diplomats have looked upon treaties during the last fifty years. A standard work on diplomatic practice was compiled by Sir Ernest Satow half a century ago (*A Guide to Diplomatic Practice*, 2 vols., London, Longmans, 1917). The chapters dealing with treaties in the edition of 1922 were based on the principle of the absolute sanctity of treaties once signed; they could not be altered or abandoned by one party to them without the agreement of the others, national necessities notwithstanding. This Satow was able to assume. By the time a new 1957 edition was prepared by Sir Nevile Bland, who had served in the Treaty Department of the British Foreign Office, the whole question of whether or not treaties could be unilaterally terminated without violating the normal practice of international law required lengthy discussion. The world meantime had witnessed the disregard of treaty obligations by Hitler, Stalin, Mussolini and the Japanese in the 1930s. Certain questions now had to be posed even if they could not be answered satisfactorily. Is a country bound by the provisions of a treaty even when the conditions prevailing when the treaty was made have greatly changed? Can there ever be permanent treaties in a rapidly changing world? One distinguished international lawyer replied a little obscurely with a double negative: 'There is nothing juridically impossible in the existence of a treaty creating obligations which are incapable of termination except by agreement of all parties ... [there is thus a] general presumption against unilateral termination.' Another authority on international law concluded that a commercial treaty could 'always be dissolved after notice, although such notice be not expressly provided for', and he extended this possibility to alliance treaties. There is in fact no agreement among international lawyers. The late Professor Hersch Lauterpacht, one of the most distinguished lawyers, used to ask his students whether international law was law properly so called. International law is 'incomplete' and in a 'state of transition' he concluded. Although a body of customary international law is developing, international law among nations in our own time remains far removed from the rule of law as generally recognized and practised by civilized communities within their own borders. There are judicial international institutions such as the International Court of Justice of the United Nations, the successor of the Permanent Court of International Justice set up after the First World War, but the power of such courts to reach enforceable judgements in serious international disputes is limited. The possibility of international sanctions based on a legal judgement is thus unlikely to prove a serious deterrent.

There have in any case always been opportunities for avoiding, without appearing to violate, the obligations of a treaty. Bismarck was a past master at wording treaties so that the irreconcilable seemed to be reconciled. But at least before 1914 the plain meaning of words was rarely in dispute. The ideological conflict in the world has since 1917 added another hazard with the breakdown of a common diplomatic vocabulary. There can be the widest divergence as to what constitutes 'interference in the internal affairs of another country', 'subversion', 'indirect aggression', 'spying', 'propaganda' and so on. There is therefore no reason to suppose that more reliance can be placed on the observance of treaties than before.

Nor is time on the side of treaty observance. The longer a treaty is intended to last the more chance is there that it will cease to correspond to national interests and international conditions. On this the most diverse of men who have guided national policies in the twentieth century are agreed. This was one of Lord Salisbury's objections to the proposal to conclude an Anglo-German alliance at the turn of the century: 'the British Government cannot undertake to declare war, for any purpose, unless it is a purpose of which the electors of this country would approve . . . I do not see how, in conscious honesty, we could invite other nations to rely upon our aids in a struggle, which must be formidable and probably supreme, when we have no means whatsoever of knowing what may be the humour of our people in circumstances which cannot be foreseen.' He concluded that national honour as well as good principles of policy required that future decisions should not be mortgaged by treaty obligations. By way of contrast, Hitler regarded morality, good faith and principles of international law, as decadent democratic weaknesses. He wrote in *Mein Kampf*: 'No consideration of foreign policy can proceed from any other criterion than this: Does it benefit our nationality now or in the future, or will it be injurious to it? . . . Partisan, religious, humanitarian and all other criteria in general are completely irrelevant.' The conclusion and violation of treaties was a decision of policy, and other States could be, and were, misled by Hitler's repeatedly proclaimed readiness to conclude and abide by the agreements he signed; for he broke them without the slightest scruple.

After the Second World War, Dean Acheson, the American Secretary of State, grappled with the dilemma of whether treaty obligations could be relied on when the passage of time had changed international circumstances. When negotiating the North Atlantic Treaty Organization Acheson asked himself, 'What was this sovereign – the United States of America – and how could it insure faith in promised future conduct?' Acheson recognized, as Salisbury himself had done half a century earlier, that the fundamental problem did not affect only a Government dependent on representative institutions. 'In reality,' wrote Acheson, 'the problem was general and insoluble, lying in inescapable change of circumstances and of national leadership and in the weakness of words to bind, especially when the juice of continued purpose is squeezed out of them and their husks analyzed to a dryly logical extreme.'

Important treaties have been and still are signed with much ceremony, with film and television cameras ensuring some public involvement. Such displays of cooperation may make a temporary impression on public opinion but are discounted by the professional diplomat. The trappings are forgotten long before a violation may occur. With the archives of the Foreign Office in London, of the Ministry of Foreign Affairs in Moscow, of the State Department in Washington and every other capital full of broken treaties, how can treaties be viewed other than in a cynical and negative way? If the behaviour of the policy-makers is rational – even if, according to the opinion of historians, sometimes misguided – why are scores of new treaties negotiated and signed every year?

For this there are good reasons too. Even when there is no expectation that a country will remain faithful to its treaty obligations in perpetuity, calculations of national self-interest may make it probable that treaty provisions will be kept for a forseeable future period of time. At least one of the parties has to believe that, whatever the secret plans of the other, or no agreement would be reached. Should there be a presumption that treaty obligations might be broken then there still has to be the possibility in the mind of one of the signatories that they will not be. The claim has been made for Chamberlain's foreign policy that he signed the Munich Agreement with Hitler on 29 September 1938 to test Hitler's good faith; but even so, Chamberlain must have thought that there was a worthwhile chance that Hitler would keep the undertakings of Munich. An open breach of treaty, such as Hitler's violation of this settlement, can still serve one important purpose in helping to rally public opinion and reluctant allies.

Not many treaties are as cynically or immediately broken as the Munich Agreement. An international treaty can be viewed as a bargain or contract. There are three inducements for keeping treaty provisions which are generally more important than any other: firstly, the positive one that a treaty contains a balance of advantages and the country which violates a treaty must expect to lose its advantages. At the simplest level, for example, when one country expels a foreign diplomat a reciprocal expulsion often follows. More important is the fact that a serious violation of a treaty may end it. Sometimes a violation is not easy to establish. Treaties on arms limitations are for this reason especially difficult to negotiate; control of armaments has not proved easy to reconcile with national sovereignty. The second inducement for keeping a treaty is the deterrent element it may contain. A Soviet occupation of West Berlin, for instance, may lead to war. Before acting political leaders have to decide whether the violation of a treaty is worth the risk of the possible countermeasures taken by the aggrieved State or States. A third inducement is that a Government has to consider its international credibility; failure to fulfil a treaty may well weaken the defaulting country's international position as other States calculate whether treaties still in force with it will be honoured, and whether new agreements can any longer usefully be concluded.

Treaties are landmarks which guide nations in their relations with each other. They express intentions, promises and normally appear to contain reciprocal advantages. Treaties represent attempts to reduce the measure of uncertainty inherent in the conduct of international affairs. In a world of growing interdependence, economic, political and strategic, where relations have become exceedingly complex and where no nation can prosper and feel secure in complete isolation from all its neighbours, the endeavour to reach agreements is an attempt to safeguard at least some vital interests.

It must be remembered that the signing of the actual treaty is only the starting point of the relationship it purports to establish. Cooperation and further detailed agreements based on the principles of the original treaty, as for instance is the case with the European Economic Community, may strengthen it. On the other hand a treaty may be drained of its effectiveness by disuse or mutual suspicions long before it is actually broken or abandoned. Despite appearances the treaty does not 'freeze' relationships; they remain fluid, and the treaty may become more meaningful or just a form of words. No one would judge the strength of a marriage by the form of vows exchanged at a ceremony. So it is with treaties; they may prosper and encompass an increasingly wider range of agreements as time passes or they may end in disillusionment. The contents of the treaty may indeed be less important than the relationship that is established as the result of agreement.

The Anglo-French *entente* of April 1904 is an interesting example of an agreement which only contained promises of limited diplomatic support, yet Anglo-French relations developed into what virtually became a close military alliance. On the other hand, the Triple Alliance between Germany, Italy and Austria-Hungary, despite its far reaching military commitments, proved itself in the end no stronger than a paper chain. Nevertheless it is important to study the actual treaty provisions. They represent a measurable standard of intent with which the relationships that later develop can be compared. They may also form the starting point, as did the Anglo-French *entente*, of a relationship not wholly foreseen when the treaty was signed.

Some political scientists have recently spoken of the 'treaty trap' – the false hope of basing foreign policy on the expectation that the legal requirements of a treaty will be fulfilled. When measured against historical evidence this reliance is seen to be a 'trap'. Such a trap only exists, however, for those who divorce the signing of a treaty from the necessary continuous vigilance over the relations that develop after its signature. Careful assessment has to be made of how the 'national interests' are viewed by the leaders of other countries, the personalities of the leaders and future leaders, and all the likely influences including public opinion which can affect their policies, because it is against this 'total' policy background that the continuing strength of a treaty, once signed, has to be judged. When this is neglected, or when serious miscalculations are made, then one party is taken totally by surprise by the other's breach of a treaty, as was Stalin when, in spite of the Nazi–Soviet Pact of 1939, Hitler invaded the Soviet Union in the spring of 1941. No practising diplomat can sensibly view a treaty merely from a juridical point of view, in a kind of legal vacuum separated from all those influences which actually shape the conduct of foreign policies. The treaty may be one of the very important influences on that policy; it can never be the sole consideration.

The alternative to imperfect agreements is either anarchy or complete uncertainty. Treaties do not by themselves assure peace and security, but far more often than not they have contributed to stability for a measurable and worthwhile period of years. The spectacular instances where they have become instruments of aggression should therefore not blind us to the utility of treaties in general. Even the most revolutionary States have discovered that there are advantages in joining a society of nations they may earlier have despised. Thus in 1971 the Chinese People's Republic accepted the manifold treaty obligations of the United Nations in order to enjoy the benefits of membership.

The form and structure of treaties

The technical and legal aspects of treaties have over the years received much learned and scholarly attention. Here it may be useful to summarize those points which are especially important to the historian of international relations. But there are no hard and fast rules.

Definition

International treaties are concluded between sovereign States and presuppose their existence. There have been a few exceptions to this simple working definition: States under the suzerainty of another State have sometimes concluded international treaties; the degree of a State's sovereignty may be in dispute, as for instance in the case of the two Boer Republics, the Transvaal and the Orange Free State, which in 1899 went to war with Britain to assert their complete independence. There are other exceptions, but the overwhelming number of treaties are concluded between sovereign States; in the twentieth century they are also concluded between an organization of States such as the European Economic Community and another State. Here the organization of States acts in a collective capacity as one party to a treaty.

The treaties of main concern to the international historian are those which are intended to create legal rights and obligations between the countries which are party to them. Whether there can be 'treaties' properly so called which do not create such rights and obligations depends on definition. The Atlantic Charter of 14 August 1941 was a 'Joint Declaration' by Roosevelt and Churchill setting out certain agreed principles of policy; no legal obligations were incurred by Britain and the United States, though Churchill's signature as Prime Minister had been approved by the War Cabinet. Was it a genuine treaty or a press communiqué? The point need not be laboured; usually only those treaties which are formally drawn up and concluded and which create legal rights and obligations concern the student of international affairs.

In the nineteenth century and earlier, treaties were always concluded between the Heads of State, whether Monarchs or Presidents. This still remains true for many treaties. But equally important treaties may be concluded between Governments rather than Heads of State, as was the North Atlantic Treaty of 4 April 1949 and the Peace Treaty with Italy of 10 February 1947. Treaties are generally drawn up in the languages of the countries party to a treaty, more than one text often being declared authentic. The Treaty of Versailles of 1919 was declared authentic both in the English and French texts, though not in German.

It is generally accepted that unless there are contrary provisions laid down by the signatories of a treaty not inconsistent with overriding principles of international law, all questions concerning the interpretation and execution of treaties, their validity and how they may be ended, are governed by international custom and where appropriate by general principles of law recognized by civilized nations.

FORM

What is in a name? Less when it comes to a treaty than in almost anything else. What a treaty is called may be a matter of chance or design but it is not significant by itself. The obligations and rights have to be studied in each case with equal care: for example, an 'alliance' may not create the relationship and obligations which the common meaning of the word would lead one to expect. The Alliance for Progress of 1961 is quite a different kind of treaty to the Austro-Hungarian–German Alliance of 1879. It is therefore not possible to distinguish treaties or the rights or obligations arising from them, or their relative importance, by their particular form or heading. One has to work from 'the other end' and disentangle from the contents of the treaty the precise obligations and rights. This is a point of great importance in the understanding of international relations. The historian, for instance, will be especially concerned to discover whether a treaty contains commitments to go to war, or merely promises support in more general terms avoiding any automatic commitment to go to war in conditions specified by the treaty. Whether the treaty is called an 'Alliance Treaty' or a 'Declaration' makes no difference. Treaties have been called by many other names and each type of treaty is usually cast in its own conventional form. Some of the more common types of treaties are headed Convention, *Acte Final*, Pact, Agreement, Protocol, Exchange of Notes, *Modus Vivendi*, or Understanding, as well as Treaty, with some prefix such as alliance, boundary, etc.; and this list is not comprehensive. It also has to be noted that until the actual contents of a document are examined it cannot be assumed that any legal rights or obligations do in fact arise, and so the document may not be a treaty at all despite appearances. The historian thus has to exercise extreme caution in distinguishing between the 'content' and the 'form' or 'packaging' of diplomatic agreements.

THE VALIDITY OF TREATIES AND THEIR RATIFICATION

There is a wide range of choice as to the means by which a country may assume treaty obligations. There is no one answer to the question of what needs to be done before a treaty becomes binding and precisely when this moment occurs. If the treaty is in the form of an exchange of notes it usually comes into force as soon as the documents have been signed, and only rarely is additional ratification provided for. The number of treaty agreements under this heading has become large. In Britain during the years 1951–2 about half the treaties signed were in this form. Such treaties are not necessarily confined to questions of a technical nature or of minor importance. Exchanges of notes may deal with questions of major importance, as was the case in the Anglo-German Treaty of 18 June 1935 concerning limitations of naval armaments.

Treaties may always be concluded which expressly stipulate that they come into force at the moment of signature and require no ratification; an important example is the Anglo-Polish Treaty of Alliance of 25 August 1939; the same was true of many treaties concluded during the Second World War.

A Government in practice has to choose how it will assume treaty obligations. Even where a country has a written constitution which requires the submission and consent of a representative assembly to a treaty, as is the case in the United States where Senate is required to approve treaties by a two-thirds majority, means may be found to circumvent the powers of such assemblies. Senator William Fulbright, the Chairman of the Senate Foreign Relations Committee, has observed that since 1940, 'the beginning of this age of crisis', 'the Senate's constitutional powers of advice and consent have atrophied into what is widely regarded as, though never asserted to be, a duty to give prompt consent with a minimum of advice'. Presidents have resorted to executive agreements at times when the consent of Senate to a treaty appeared doubtful. The important Anglo-American Agreement embodying the destroyers bases deal of September 1940 was concluded in this form. In the United States the Senate may ratify a treaty but can only do so with amendments; this in effect changes the treaty into a new one which may not be acceptable to the other signatories.

A treaty is concluded when signed, but where ratification is necessary becomes binding when ratified. Traditionally ratification signified the consent of the Sovereign to a treaty negotiated by the Sovereign's plenipotentiary, who might have no means of consulting the Sovereign when negotiating in distant countries. In modern times speed of communication has made it possible to submit the actual text of a treaty to the Government before it is signed. The practical importance of ratification now lies in the need to secure the consent of a Parliament or other elected assembly before the Government is ready to advise ratification of a treaty. In Britain, though treaty-making powers are vested in the Sovereign, the real decision lies with the Government and, where legislation is required to adapt British law to bring it into line with that required by the treaty, also with Parliament, for the necessary enabling legislation must first be passed by Parliament before the treaty can be ratified 'by the Sovereign' on the advice of the Government. The legislative and treaty-making process of Britain's adhesion to the European Economic Community provides a good example. It is the practice in Britain for the texts of all treaties requiring ratification to lie on the Table of the House of Commons for twenty-one days before ratification by the Sovereign. In France, the 1946 constitution, though vesting in the President treaty-making power, required that a wide range of treaties did not become valid unless embodied in a law passed by the French Parliament. The precise powers of representative assemblies differ widely and the constitution and practice of each country has to be considered separately.

Ratification is therefore not always a formality; important treaties by one means or another may be submitted to the approval of elected assemblies before the Government of the State concerned is able to give its consent to the treaty becoming binding. This may be due to constitutional custom or constitutional requirement, or to a Government's desire to retain the support of a majority of the elected representatives in order to continue in power.

The drafting of treaties

By this stage it will have become clear that there are no hard and fast rules as to how a treaty has to be drawn up. This is entirely a question on which the participants have free choice. But it is possible to speak of some widely adopted conventions which tend to give treaties certain common forms. Many diplomats in the world's various Foreign Ministries are employed in treaty drafting: their task is to put the intentions of the parties of a treaty in acceptable professional legal phraseology, which can at times strike the reader as rather stylized and even archaic. By way of example, a treaty between Heads of State is here considered.

Such a treaty commences with a *descriptive title*, as for instance the 'Treaty of Mutual Cooperation and Security between the United States of America and Japan'. Then follows the *preamble*, beginning with the names or description of the High Contracting Parties as 'The United States of America and Japan'; next the general purpose is set out, 'Desiring to strengthen the bonds of peace and friendship traditionally existing between them etc. . . . Having resolved to conclude a treaty of mutual cooperation and security, therefore agree as follows. . . .' The preamble often includes also, though not in the particular treaty here cited, the names and designation of the plenipotentiaries who have produced their full powers, which have been found in good order, and have agreed as follows. . . . Next follow the substantive articles each with a numeral, I, II, III, etc. which constitute the objectives, the obligations and the rights of the signatories; these articles are frequently arranged beginning with the more general and leading to the more specific. Where appropriate, an article follows which sets out the provisions for other States who may wish to accede to the treaty. Next follows an article (or articles) concerning ratification where this is provided for, the duration of the treaty and provisions for its renewal. Finally a clause is added stating 'in witness whereof' the undersigned plenipotentiaries have signed this treaty; the place where the treaty is signed is given, together with a statement as to the authentic languages of the treaty texts; and last the date is written in, followed by the seals and the signatures of the plenipotentiaries. *Conventions*, *Protocols* and other types of treaties each have their own customary form.

The vocabulary of treaties

Some terms used in treaty-making – a few of them in French and Latin – have special meanings.

Accession or *adhesion:* these terms are interchangeably used to describe the practice where a State which is not a party to a treaty later on joins such a treaty. No State has a right to accede to a treaty; the possibility and method of accession are often contained in a clause of the treaty as signed by the original parties to it.

Aggression: the common meaning of the term is an unjustified attack, and efforts have been made to define aggression by means of treaties. For example, a convention was signed in July 1933 between Russia, Afghanistan, Estonia, Poland, Rumania and Turkey which defined aggression as having been committed by the State which first (*a*) declares war on another State, (*b*) invades with its armed forces another State, (*c*) attacks with its armed forces the territory, naval vessels or aircraft of another State, (*d*) initiates a naval blockade of coasts or ports of another State; and (*e*), most interestingly of all, aggression was defined as 'aid to armed bands formed on the territory of a State and invading the territory of another State, or refusal, despite demands on the part of the State subjected to attack, to take all possible measures on its own territory to deprivate said bands of any aid and protection'. Despite the existence of such treaties, however, in the last resort each State or international tribunal has to judge on the merits of the facts before it whether particular actions constitute aggression or not.

Bilateral treaties are those between two States; *multilateral* treaties are concluded between three or more States.

Casus foederis is literally the case contemplated by the treaty, usually one of alliance; it is the event which when it occurs imposes the duty on one or more of the allies to render the assistance promised in the treaty to the other; *casus belli* has a slightly different meaning though frequently confused with *casus foederis*; *casus belli* is the provocative action by one State, which in the opinion of the injured State justifies it in declaring war.

Delimitation and *demarcation* of boundaries: boundaries of State territories are the lines drawn to divide the sovereignties of adjoining States. They form the frontiers of each respective country. Concern for frontiers is the basis of the majority of political treaties and the cause of many conflicts and wars. When a boundary can be drawn on a map and it is accepted by the States which are divided by it, even though the boundary has not actually been physically marked out on the ground by frontier posts, then it is said to have been *delimited*. The frontier is also *demarcated* when it actually has been physically set out on the ground and not only marked on a map. European frontiers have all been both delimited and demarcated. The same is not true of all boundary lines in the world especially in difficult and unpopulated regions. The distinction between delimitation and demarcation is an important one. There are no settled principles of demarcation though there are certain common practices such as to draw boundary lines through the middle of land-locked seas and rivers where they lie between two States. Estuaries and mountain ranges, however, cause more difficulty. In the absence of specific agreements the demarcation of an actual frontier based on a general boundary treaty signed much earlier – quite possibly when the state of geographical knowledge was imperfect – can become a matter of serious dispute. To avoid such disputes countries sometimes sign treaties setting out how a boundary is to be demarcated; an example is the boundary treaty between Great Britain and the United States of 11 April 1908 respecting the demarcation of the boundary between Canada and the United States. In other cases of dispute the two nations may resort to arbitration by a third party; finally a commission of two States or an international commission may have the power to demarcate boundaries. It is, however, helpful to be reminded by Professor Alistair Lamb that there are still boundaries which have been neither delimited nor demarcated; instead there is a *de facto* line. This is true of many stretches of boundaries in Asia, for example much of the Sino-Indian border, and the western end of the boundary between Chinese Sinkiang and the Soviet Union. Sometimes boundaries have been arbitrarily drawn by cartographers over country so difficult that it has not been surveyed and mapped with complete accuracy.

Demilitarization is an agreement between two or more States by treaty not to fortify or station troops in a particular zone of territory; such zones are known as *demilitarized zones*.

High Contracting Parties or *Contracting Parties*: when treaties are concluded between Heads of States they are referred to as the High Contracting Parties; when treaties are concluded between States or Governments the phrase used to describe them is usually Contracting Parties.

Modus vivendi: usually refers to a temporary or provisional agreement which it is intended shall later be replaced by a more permanent and detailed treaty.

Most-favoured-nation clause: many commercial treaties between countries contain this clause, the effect of which is that any commercial advantages either State has granted in the past to other nations, or may grant in the future, have to be granted also to the signatories of a treaty which contains a most-favoured-nation clause. The intent is therefore that the commercial advantages of two States who have signed a treaty with this provision shall never be less than those of any third State which is not a signatory. The United States has not recognized quite so unconditional an operation of this clause.

Procès-verbal: is the official record or minutes of the daily proceedings of a conference and of any conclusions arrived at, and is frequently signed by the participants; a *Protocol* is sometimes used in the same sense but more accurately is a document which constitutes an international agreement.

Sine qua non: describes a condition or conditions that have to be accepted by another party to a proposed agreement; it implies that without such acceptance the agreement cannot be proceeded with.

Status quo: the common meaning is the state of affairs existing, but an agreement can refer specifically to a previous state of affairs as for instance in the phrase *status quo ante bellum* which means the state existing before the war began, for example as relating to frontiers.

Treaties imposed by force

How can any system of law admit that right is based on might? This is what is involved if in the relations between States international law accepts that the stronger nation may impose its terms on the weaker nation by war or by threat of force.

Before 1914, war and the use of force were accepted as legitimate means of securing national interests when diplomacy failed to achieve the desired objects. Two Great Powers of Europe, Germany and Italy, owed their very unity and existence to war. Indeed, the 1914 frontiers of the continental States of Europe were based on treaties concluded by the victorious Powers. The colonial empires of Britain and other Powers, moreover, had all been acquired mainly by conquest. Might was right in the sense that the mighty rarely admit to wrongdoing.

The League of Nations was to usher in a new era of international relations, based on the acceptance of the League Covenant which limited the right to go to war. Henceforth there would be two kinds of war, illegal wars waged in breach of the League Covenant and 'legal' wars which were not in breach of treaty engagements. The Pact of Paris of 1928 and the United Nations Charter extended the limitations of the signatories to threaten or to use force. International lawyers since then have wrestled with the problem of whether treaties imposed by countries who have used force in breach of their treaty engagements are valid. In the 1930s there evolved the principle of 'non-recognition' whereby other States refused to recognize the rights of States derived from the illegal use of force. But, as one distinguished international lawyer put it, the attitude of other States 'may, after a prolonged period of time, be adjusted to the requirements of international peace and stability'. More recently, the United Nations' *Vienna Conference on the Law of Treaties* in 1969 declared, after some seventeen years of preparatory work, that 'A treaty is void if its conclusion has been procured by the threat of force in violation of the principles of international law embodied in the Charter of the United Nations' (Article 52). But even this clear statement was made conditional; Article 75 of the same Convention appears to mean that an aggressor State cannot claim this safeguard if other States acting in conformity with the Charter use force against the aggressor and then impose a treaty related to the aggression. The *Vienna Convention* in any case will only apply when thirty-five States have ratified it, and then usually only to treaties signed after it has come into force.

As long as individual States or international organizations of States apply and interpret the law, political considerations will remain a strong, even a predominant influence. Progress in the codification of international law is made. Yet today we are far from a position where international and general agreement on how to apply it regulates international conduct on issues where nations wish to use force. Important national interests will induce States to recognize many rights 'illegally' secured, and this will remain true so long as it is believed that legal and moral precepts cannot alone determine foreign policy.

I · Secret agreements and treaties of the First World War

The outbreak of the First World War in August 1914 violated more than Belgian neutrality. The majority of the great territorial settlements of the nineteenth century, embodied in international treaties since 1815, were jeopardized. During the war international treaties ceased to be respected and the belligerents engaged in fierce bargaining to gain allies and to assure for themselves a favourable territorial settlement when the war was won. Each of the Powers at war had vague and shifting 'war aims' often motivated by immediate military needs. Diplomacy in wartime was designed to support the military effort, to strengthen existing alliances and to make new allies. Secret agreements and undertakings between several allies or between one State and another were made throughout the war. They were sometimes inconsistent and could not all be reconciled with each other when the war ended, leaving a bitter legacy of dispute to the post-war world. Nor did any one State have full knowledge of the secret bargains that had been struck.

In the actual declaration of war (as opposed to mobilizations) the Central Powers took the initiative. Austria-Hungary declared war on Serbia on 28 July 1914. Germany declared war on Russia on 1 August, and on France on 3 August. The German invasion of Belgium on 4 August was followed by a British ultimatum and a British declaration of war on Germany on 4 August 1914.

Austria-Hungary remained at peace with Russia after Germany's declaration of war and was only prevailed upon to declare war on Russia on 6 August 1914. It was France and Britain who declared war on Austria-Hungary on 12 August 1914. Portugal declared its adherence to the British alliance in the autumn of 1914 and commenced military operations against Germany. Thus only in mid-August were the Central Powers – Austria-Hungary and Germany – at war with all the Allied Entente Powers – France, Britain and Russia.

1 Europe, 1914

Japan did not join the Grand Alliance of Russia, Britain and France. It sent its own ultimatum to Germany on 15 August 1914 and declared war when it expired, basing its action on the Anglo-Japanese alliance. Japan did share one treaty in common with all the Allied Entente Powers when the Japanese Government on 19 October 1915 signed the *Declaration of London*, which had been concluded between Russia, France and Britain on 5 September 1914. This declaration stipulated that none of the signatories would conclude peace separately or demand conditions of peace without the previous agreement of the other signatories.

Italy, with Germany and Austria-Hungary, was a member of the Triple Alliance (last renewed in 1912) but declared its neutrality on 3 August 1914. Italy's obligations according to Articles 2 and 3 of the Triple Alliance required Italy to fight in case of unprovoked aggression by France on Germany. This, the Italian Government concluded, had not occurred. Moreover, in August 1914 the Italian Government claimed that Austria-Hungary had not acted in accordance with Article 7 of the Triple Alliance treaty when deciding to attack Serbia, for this article required previous consultation and agreement between Italy and Austria-Hungary based on reciprocal compensations.

The Central Powers, 1914–18

Germany secured a hasty secret alliance with *Turkey on 2 August 1914* (p. 24). It stipulated that the two Powers would remain neutral in the conflict between Austria-Hungary and Serbia; but that if Russia intervened with active military measures Germany would intervene on the side of Austria-Hungary and the alliance with Turkey would become active. The German military mission was to exercise in the event of war an 'effective influence' over the Turkish army, and Germany undertook to defend Ottoman territory if it were threatened. Turkey did not enter the war straight away but took a number of steps against the Entente Powers: two German warships were sheltered and transferred to the Turkish navy in August, and on 26 September the Straits were closed thus cutting the supply route to Russia. By the end of October 1914 Turkey actively entered the war on the side of Germany and Austria-Hungary and began operations against Russia. A new alliance was signed by Turkey and Germany in January 1915 and Austria-Hungary adhered to it in March 1915.

Bulgaria was induced in September 1915 to join the war on the side of Germany and Austria-Hungary by the promise of large territorial gains including Serbian Macedonia and a substantial grant of money. On *6 September 1915*

Bulgaria signed a military agreement and an alliance treaty with Germany and Austria-Hungary to join in a military offensive against Serbia, and in mid-October 1915 Bulgaria started fighting in accordance with this treaty.

The Allied and Associated Powers, 1914–18

Despite Italy's treaty engagement as a member of the Triple Alliance to remain benevolently neutral and not make alliances with the enemies of Germany and Austria-Hungary, Italy accepted the inducements of the Allies to join the war on their side. The promises of territorial expansion after the war held out to Italy were contained in the secret *Treaty of London, 26 April 1915* (p. 24). Italy was promised territory at the expense of the Austrian-Hungarian Empire, the Trentino, the South Tyrol, Istria and a third of Dalmatia, the sovereignty of the Dodecanese Islands which Italy already occupied, as well as a 'just share' of the Ottoman Empire in Asia in the event of its partial or total partition, taking into account Italy's special position in the province of Adalia. Italy was also promised compensation for British and French gains at the expense of Germany's colonies. On 23 May 1915 Italy declared war on Austria-Hungary.

Rumania, despite its treaty relations with Germany and Austria-Hungary before the war, also changed sides and abandoned neutrality in favour of joining the Allies. By *a secret treaty between Rumania, Britain, France, Italy and Russia signed on 17 August 1916* Rumania undertook to declare war and to attack Austria-Hungary and not to conclude a separate peace. Rumania was promised portions of Austria-Hungary, Transylvania, the Bukovina and Banat. But the value of these promises was made doubtful by a secret exchange of notes between Russia, Italy, France and Britain that Rumania's promised territorial gains would be granted only so far as the general situation at the end of the war allowed. In the event, the Allies were spared embarrassment for by Rumania's separate peace signed at Bucharest on 7 May 1917 Rumania forfeited alliance claims.

The most important of the 'Associated Powers' entering the war during the first week of April 1917, side by side with the Allied Powers, was the United States. Germany resumed unrestricted submarine warfare on 1 February 1917. President Wilson asked Congress on 2 April 1917 to formally recognize that a state of war existed between the United States and Germany. The House of Representatives passed a resolution for war and the Senate also on 6 April 1917. The United States declared war on Austria-Hungary several months later on 7 December 1917. In Europe, Greece was finally brought into the war by the Allies on their side on 2 July 1917 after they had blockaded the Greek coast and forced the abdication of King Constantine. China declared a state of war with Germany and Austria-Hungary in August 1917, thus complicating the intended settlement of Japanese claims at the expense of China.

The Ottoman Empire

The Allied Powers jointly and individually concluded a number of wartime treaties, agreements and understandings concerning the future of the Ottoman Empire. They proved impossible to reconcile when the war ended. Russia was promised Constantinople and the Straits at the time of the negotiations with Italy which had led to the *Treaty of London, 26 April 1915* (p. 24). An exchange of several diplomatic notes between Russia, Britain and France during March and April 1915 set out the attitude of the Allies: a Russian note in the *Russian Circular Telegram to France and Britain, 4 March 1915* (p. 27) contained extensive Russian demands for the annexation by Russia of Constantinople, the Straits, part of southern Thrace and part of the Adriatic shore. British replies in two *aides-mémoire*, both dated 12 March 1915, agreed in principle to the Russian acquisition of Constantinople and the Straits but made this dependent on a number of conditions, including some counter-concessions to Britain in the Ottoman Empire and Persia. The French reply in a note on 10 April 1915 agreed to the Russian proposal 'relating to Constantinople and the Straits', provided war was fought until victory and France and Britain realized their plans in the East and elsewhere. These conditional promises to Russia lapsed as Allied obligations when Russia concluded a separate armistice and peace with Germany in December 1917 and March 1918.

In the Ottoman Empire in Asia and the Middle East the Allies had made a number of promises to various factions, and came to agreements with each other which laid Britain and France open to charges of bad faith when engaged in peace-making from 1919 to 1923 (pp. 48, 51). Irreconcilable claims were embittered further when each party attempted to rely on wartime promises and undertakings. In April 1915 the secret *Treaty of London* between Italy, France, Russia and Britain (pp. 25–6), as it applied to the Ottoman Empire, promised Italy the Dodecanese Islands and a share of the Mediterranean region of Anatolia adjacent to and including the province of Adalia. From *July 1915 to March 1916, Sir Henry McMahon, High Commissioner in Egypt, exchanged ten letters with the Sherif of Mecca* (p. 29) to encourage an Arab revolt against Ottoman rule; in return McMahon promised that the British would recognize and support the independence of the Arabs in all regions demanded by the Sherif of Mecca, with some major reservations – the Mediterranean coastal strip west of Damascus, Hama, Homs and Aleppo (later Lebanon and the coastal region of

French-mandated Syria) – and only in those areas where Britain was free to act without detriment to the interests of her ally, France. British interests required the Arabs to recognize Britain's special position in the provinces of Baghdad and Basra. The correspondence left the political area of Arab independence indefinite and ambiguous. Certain regions were excluded with some precision by their special mention, but Palestine was not specifically mentioned. In other regions the Arabs could assume support for independence, but the proviso that French interests would be taken into account by Britain left a very elastic loophole. Since Palestine did not become a region of French interest, the correspondence would lead the Arabs to suppose that Palestine would form part of the territory of Arab independence. But the promise to the Zionists contained in the *Balfour Declaration, 2 November 1917* (p. 34) of a 'national home for the Jewish people' could not easily be reconciled with Arab sovereignty in Palestine.

A tripartite agreement for the partition of the Ottoman Empire in Asia was worked out between France, Britain and Russia in exchanges of notes from April to October 1916, and is known as the *Sykes–Picot Agreement* (p. 30). The agreement created French and British spheres of interest; an 'independent' Arab State was foreseen as falling within French and British spheres of interest. In other specified regions more direct French and British administration was foreseen. Palestine became an international sphere of interest. The Russians sanctioned the Anglo-French partition, and in return France and Britain permitted Russian annexation in Turkish Armenia and Kurdistan. The secret Sykes–Picot Agreement was published by the Bolshevik Government after the Revolution. The tripartite British, French, Italian *Agreement at St Jean de Maurienne, 19–21 April 1917* (p. 33) assigned to Italy a large region including Adalia and Smyrna for Italian administration, and a further zone of Italian influence to the north. This agreement, subject to Russia's consent, could only have been enforced on a completely prostrate Turkey and was incompatible with Greek and French ambitions in Asia Minor (p. 49). In fact no effort was made to enforce it after 1919.

China, Japan and the Pacific

In August 1914 British policy vacillated on the desirability of invoking the Anglo-Japanese alliance and so ensuring Japan's entry into the war. Japan was expected to press its claims to take over the German lease of the port of Kiaochow and rights in the province of Shantung. Japan also sought possession of the German island colonies in the Pacific. Their future was of especial concern to two British Dominions, Australia and New Zealand, as well as to the

United States. Japan decided the issue by declaring war on Germany after the expiration of its ultimatum of 15 August 1914. *Agreement between Japan and Britain was not finally reached until February 1917*, when Britain secretly agreed to support Japanese claims to those German islands which lay north of the Equator, the Marianas, Carolines and Marshalls, as well as to German concessions in Shantung; whilst Japan promised to support British claims south of the Equator, that is, for German Samoa, German New Guinea and Nauru. The French and Italian Governments shortly after entered into similar agreements with Japan.

Japan was determined to strengthen and extend her interests and influence in China. Following the military occupation of Kiaochow Bay, Japan on 18 January 1915 presented to China *Twenty-One Demands*. They included the following: China was to give full assent to any agreement Japan might eventually make with Germany about the lease of Kiaochow and German rights in the province of Shantung; the Japanese were to be allowed to build an additional railway in the province and no land in it was to be alienated to any other country; an extension for a further ninety-nine years of the Japanese lease of Port Arthur and Dairen was to be granted; certain towns were to be opened to foreign trade; Japan demanded a recognition of her predominant position in southern Manchuria and eastern Inner Mongolia; China was not to cede or lease to any other Power any harbour, bay or island along the China coast; finally, 'seven wishes' comprised group V of the demands, including the proposal that the Chinese Government should employ Japanese political, military and financial advisers. After delivery of an ultimatum by Japan, *China and Japan signed two treaties and thirteen notes on 25 May 1915* based on the Twenty-One Demands, but the 'wishes' comprising group V were dropped. China, who had declared war on Germany in August 1917, later at the peace conference refused to accept the validity of the agreements, declaring they had been signed under threat of coercion, and left without signing the Treaty of Versailles.

Japan's ally, Britain, and the neutral United States attempted to exercise a moderating influence on Japan in 1915. The United States was still committed to upholding the 'Open Door' and China's political and territorial integrity, but the U.S. Secretary of State, Bryan, in a note to the Japanese Ambassador in Washington of 13 March 1915, had stated that the 'United States frankly recognizes that territorial contiguity creates special relations between Japan' with regard to Shantung, south Manchuria and east Mongolia. This attitude was confirmed by the *Lansing–Ishii Agreement, 2 November 1917*. The United States tried to reconcile a recognition of Japan's special interests in China with China's territorial and political integrity.

In pursuing a forceful Chinese policy, Japan had acted in concert with

Russia. Russia and Japan concluded four secret treaties and conventions between 1907 and 1916. The last of the treaties was the most extensive in scope. The *Russo-Japanese Treaty, 3 July 1916*, of two articles made public and an additional secret convention, stated that the two signatories had 'vital interests in China' and that they would cooperate to prevent China falling under the political influence of a 'third power which entertains a hostile feeling against Japan and Russia'. The secret treaty was published and repudiated some eighteen months later by the Soviet Russian leaders after the Revolution. The secret treaty is notable for extending the interest of Japan to the whole of China and for being presumably directed against the United States.

The Treaty of Brest-Litovsk: Eastern and Central Europe, 1917–18

The Europe of the inter-war years began to take shape in the spring of 1918 with the victory of the Central Powers over Russia and Rumania. The signature on *3 March 1918 of the Treaty of Brest-Litovsk* (p. 34) was of lasting importance, even though the treaty itself was formally abrogated after the defeat of the Central Powers (the abandonment of Brest-Litovsk had been one of the conditions of the Allied armistice on 11 November 1918).

The peace of Brest-Litovsk marked the break-up of the Russian Empire, the first of the three pre-war multinational empires to collapse (the Hapsburg Monarchy and the Ottoman Empire were the others). During the war the Germans had encouraged nationalism as a weapon against the Tsarist Russian Empire and had supported non-Russian ethnic groups as a means of limiting Soviet Russian power. The Ukraine was recognized as an independent State by the Central Powers in February 1918, but German and Austro-Hungarian armies under the Supreme Command remained in occupation of the 'border' territories from the Baltic to the Caucasus, and occupied the Ukraine defeating the advancing Bolshevik forces. At the request of the Finnish Government, German armed forces in April and May 1918 helped the White Finns achieve victory over the Bolsheviks in the Finnish Civil War. Towards the independence of the Baltic States and Poland, Germany maintained a reserved and equivocal attitude. The defeat of Tsarist Russia had been the first condition of the independence of the Russian borderlands; the subsequent defeat of Germany was the second condition; and before some of these States attained independence during the inter-war years, the defeat of Soviet Russia in 1919 and 1920 had become just as necessary (see pp. 129–30).

Rumania also accepted defeat and concluded the *Peace of Bucharest on 7 May 1918* with the Central Powers. The treaty deprived Rumania of the southern part of the Dobruja which was incorporated in Bulgaria; Rumania also lost territory to Hungary but retained Bessarabia. Bessarabia had only been incorporated in Rumania in April 1918, a month before the Peace of Bucharest. Bessarabia was beyond the control of the Bolsheviks in 1917 and 1918; it had been proclaimed by its leaders independent and later voted for incorporation with Rumania on 8 April 1918. This was recognized by the Central Powers but not by Soviet Russia. With the Allied victory, Rumania regained the southern Dobruja and much more than the territory lost to Hungary; Rumania also kept Bessarabia (p. 114).

For Lenin and the Bolshevik leaders, Brest-Litovsk was a bitter peace. Russia was deprived of one-third of her population and her expansion during the last three centuries was lost. But what was far more important, as Lenin understood, was that Bolshevik power had survived and was consolidated in the heart of Russia. The Bolsheviks survived by only a narrow margin and could not have withstood Germany's determination to destroy them. But the Germans, desiring peace with some established Government and fearing that the opponents of the Bolsheviks might fight on, had been keen to preserve Bolshevik control in Petrograd. Lenin had bought time. Russia's losses he regarded as temporary. They would last until the war among the imperialist Powers had been turned into an international class war with the spread of revolution outward from Russia.

The armistice and peace negotiations of Brest-Litovsk lasted from December 1917 to March 1918 and were conducted at the German headquarters of the Eastern Front. Broken off by Trotsky early in February 1918, the Russian Soviets found themselves in an even more disastrous position when they were resumed as *the Germans had by then signed a separate peace with the Ukraine on 9 February 1918*. A week later the German and Austrian armies resumed the military offensive and penetrated deeply into Russia. Eventually, on 3 March 1918, the Russians signed the treaty of peace with Germany and Lenin secured its ratification. Thereby imperial Germany became the first State to accord *de jure* recognition to the Russian Soviet Government.

The Russians had broken their undertaking to their Allies not to conclude a separate peace. From this undertaking they had not been released. Yet their sacrifices for the Allied cause had exceeded that of any other single nation. During the armistice negotiations a vain attempt had also been made by the Russians to stipulate that no German troops should be transferred to the Western Front; but the Russians were powerless to prevent such transfers. Even so, a large German army remained in the East until November 1918, regarded by the German High Command as too unreliable or ill-equipped for use on the Western Front.

Secret Treaty of Alliance between Germany and the Ottoman Empire, 2 August 1914

Article 1. The two Contracting Powers undertake to observe strict neutrality in the present conflict between Austria-Hungary and Serbia.

Article 2. In the event that Russia should intervene with active military measures and thus should create for Germany a *casus foederis* with respect to Austria-Hungary, this *casus foederis* would also come into force for Turkey.

Article 3. In the event of war, Germany will leave its Military Mission at the disposal of Turkey.

The latter, for its part, assures the said Military Mission effective influence over the general conduct of the army, in conformity with what has been agreed upon directly by His Excellency the Minister of War and His Excellency the Chief of the Military Mission.

Article 4. Germany obligates itself, by force of arms if need be, to defend Ottoman territory in case it should be threatened.

Article 5. This Agreement, which has been concluded with a view to protecting the two Empires from the international complications which may result from the present conflict, enters into force at the time of its signing by the above-mentioned plenipotentiaries and shall remain valid, with any analogous mutual agreements, until 31 December 1918.

• • •

[*Article 8.* The treaty to be secret unless signatories agree otherwise.]

Agreement between France, Russia, Britain and Italy (Treaty of London), 26 April 1915

Article 1. A military convention shall be immediately concluded between the General Staffs of France, Great Britain, Italy and Russia. This convention shall settle the minimum number of military forces to be employed by Russia against Austria-Hungary in order to prevent that Power from concentrating all its strength against Italy, in the event of Russia deciding to direct her principal effort against Germany.

This military convention shall settle question of armistices, which necessarily comes within the scope of the Commanders-in-chief of the Armies.

Article 2. On her part, Italy undertakes to use her entire resources for the purpose of waging war jointly with France, Great Britain and Russia against all their enemies.

Article 3. The French and British fleets shall render active and permanent assistance to Italy until such time as the Austro-Hungarian fleet shall have been destroyed or until peace shall have been concluded.

A naval convention shall be immediately concluded to this effect between France, Great Britain and Italy.

Article 4. Under the Treaty of Peace, Italy shall obtain the Trentino, Cisalpine Tyrol with its geographical and natural frontier (the Brenner frontier), as well as Trieste, the counties of Gorizia and

Gradisca, all Istria as far as the Quarnero and including Volosca and the Istrian islands of Cherso and Lussin, as well as the small islands of Plavnik, Unie, Canidole, Palazzuoli, San Pietro di Nembi, Asinello, Gruica, and the neighbouring islets. . . . [frontier details]

Article 5. Italy shall also be given the province of Dalmatia within its present administrative boundaries, including to the north . . . [frontier details]

NOTE: The following Adriatic territory shall be assigned by the four Allied Powers to Croatia, Serbia and Montenegro:

In the Upper Adriatic, the whole coast from the bay of Volosca on the borders of Istria as far as the northern frontier of Dalmatia, including the coast which is at present Hungarian and all the coast of Croatia, with the port of Fiume and the small ports of Novi and Carlopago, as well as the islands of Veglia, Pervichio, Gregorio, Goli and Arbe. And, in the Lower Adriatic (in the region interesting Serbia and Montenegro) the whole coast from Cape Planka as far as the River Drin, with the important harbours of Spalato, Ragusa, Cattaro, Antivari, Dulcigno and St Jean de Medua and the islands of Greater and Lesser Zirona, Bua, Solta, Brazza, Jaclian and Calamotta. The port of Durazzo to be assigned to the independent Moslem State of Albania.

Article 6. Italy shall receive full sovereignty over Valona, the island of Saseno and surrounding territory of sufficient extent to assure defence of these points . . . [frontier details]

Article 7. Should Italy obtain the Trentino and Istria in accordance with the provisions of Article 4, together with Dalmatia and the Adriatic islands within the limits specified in Article 5, and the Bay of Valona (Article 6), and if the central portion of Albania is reserved for the establishment of a small autonomous neutralized State, Italy shall not oppose the division of Northern and Southern Albania between Montenegro, Serbia and

Greece, should France, Great Britain and Russia so desire. The coast from the southern boundary of the Italian territory of Valona (see Article 6) up to Cape Stylos shall be neutralized.

Italy shall be charged with the representation of the State of Albania in its relations with foreign Powers.

Italy agrees, moreover, to leave sufficient territory in any event to the east of Albania to ensure the existence of a frontier line between Greece and Serbia to the west of Lake Ochrida.

Article 8. Italy shall receive entire sovereignty over the Dodecanese Islands which she is at present occupying.

Article 9. Generally speaking, France, Great Britain and Russia recognize that Italy is interested in the maintenance of the balance of power in the Mediterranean and that, in the event of the total or partial partition of Turkey in Asia, she ought to obtain a just share of the Mediterranean region adjacent to the province of Adalia, where Italy has already acquired rights and interests which formed the subject of an Italo-British convention. The zone which shall eventually be allotted to Italy shall be delimited, at the proper time, due account being taken of the existing interests of France and Great Britain.

The interests of Italy shall also be taken into consideration in the event of the territorial integrity of the Turkish Empire being maintained and of alterations being made in the zones of interest of the Powers.

If France, Great Britain and Russia occupy any territories in Turkey in Asia during the course of the war, the Mediterranean region bordering on the Province of Adalia within the limits indicated above shall be reserved to Italy, who shall be entitled to occupy it.

Article 10. All rights and privileges in Libya at present belonging to the Sultan by virtue of the Treaty of Lausanne are transferred to Italy.

Article 11. Italy shall receive a share of any eventual war indemnity corresponding to her efforts and her sacrifices.

Article 12. Italy declares that she associates herself in the declaration made by France, Great Britain and Russia to the effect that Arabia and the Moslem Holy Places in Arabia shall be left under the authority of an independent Moslem Power.

Article 13. In the event of France and Great Britain increasing their colonial territories in Africa at the expense of Germany, those two Powers agree in principle that Italy may claim some equitable compensation, particularly as regards the settlement in her favour of the questions relative to the frontiers of the Italian colonies of Eritrea, Somaliland and Libya and the neighbouring colonies belonging to France and Great Britain.

Article 14. Great Britain undertakes to facilitate the immediate conclusion, under equitable conditions, of a loan of at least £50,000,000, to be issued on the London market.

Article 15. France, Great Britain and Russia shall support such opposition as Italy may make to any proposal in the direction of introducing a representative of the Holy See in any peace negotiations or negotiations for the settlement of questions raised by the present war.

Article 16. The present arrangement shall be held secret. The adherence of Italy to the Declaration of the 5th September 1914 shall alone be made public, immediately upon declaration of war by or against Italy.

After having taken act of the foregoing memorandum the representatives of France, Great Britain and Russia, duly authorized to that effect, have concluded the following agreement with the representative of Italy, also duly authorized by his Government:

France, Great Britain and Russia give their full assent to the memorandum presented by the Italian Government.

With reference to Articles 1, 2, and 3 of the memorandum which provide for military and naval cooperation between the four Powers, Italy declares that she will take the field at the earliest possible date and within a period not exceeding one month from the signature of these present ...

[Signed] E. GREY, IMPERIALI, BENCKENDORFF, PAUL CAMBON.

Declaration by which France, Great Britain, Italy and Russia undertake not to conclude a separate peace during the course of the present European war

The Italian Government, having decided to participate in the present war with the French, British and Russian Governments, and to accede to the Declaration made at London, the 5th September 1914, by the three above-named Governments,

The undersigned, being duly authorized by their respective Governments, make the following declaration:

The French, British, Italian and Russian Governments mutually undertake not to conclude a separate peace during the course of the present war.

The four Governments agree that, whenever there may be occasion to discuss the terms of peace, none of the Allied Powers shall lay down any conditions of peace without previous agreement with each of the other Allies.

Declaration

The Declaration of the 26th April 1915, whereby France, Great Britain, Italy and Russia undertake not to conclude a separate peace during the present European war, shall remain secret.

After the declaration of war by or against Italy, the four Powers shall sign a new declaration in identical terms, which shall thereupon be made public.

Secret Agreements between Russia, France and Britain concerning the Straits and Constantinople, 4 March–10 April 1915

Russian Memorandum to French and British Governments, 4 March 1915

The course of recent events leads His Majesty Emperor Nicholas to think that the question of Constantinople and of the Straits must be definitively solved, according to the time-honoured aspirations of Russia.

Every solution will be inadequate and precarious if the city of Constantinople, the western bank of the Bosphorus, of the Sea of Marmara and of the Dardanelles, as well as southern Thrace to the Enez-Midye line, should henceforth not be incorporated into the Russian Empire.

Similarly, and by strategic necessity, that part of the Asiatic shore that lies between the Bosphorus, the Sakarya River and a point to be determined on the Gulf of Izmit, and the islands of the Sea of Marmara, the Imbros Islands and the Tenedos Islands must be incorporated into the [Russian] Empire.

The special interests of France and of Great Britain in the above region will be scrupulously respected.

The Imperial Government entertains the hope that the above considerations will be sympathetically received by the two Allied Governments. The said Allied Governments are assured similar understanding on the part of the Imperial Government for the realization of plans which they may frame with reference to other regions of the Ottoman Empire or elsewhere.

British Memorandum to Russian Government, 12 March 1915

Subject to the war being carried on and brought to a successful conclusion, and to the desiderata of Great Britain and France in the Ottoman Empire and elsewhere being realized, as indicated in the Russian communication herein referred to, His Majesty's Government will agree to the Russian Government's *aide-mémoire* relative to Constantinople and the Straits, the text of which was communicated to His Britannic Majesty's Ambassador by his Excellency M. Sazonof on February 19th/March 4th instant.

British Memorandum (a comment on earlier memorandum) to Russian Government, 12 March 1915

His Majesty's Ambassador has been instructed to make the following observations with reference to the *aide-mémoire* which this Embassy had the honour of addressing to the Imperial Government on February 27/March 12, 1915.

The claim made by the Imperial Government in their *aide-mémoire* of February 19/March 4, 1915, considerably exceeds the desiderata which were foreshadowed by M. Sazonof as probable a few weeks ago. Before His Majesty's Government have had time to take into consideration what their own desiderata elsewhere would be in the final terms of peace, Russia is asking for a definite promise that her wishes shall be satisfied with regard to what is in fact the richest prize of the entire war. Sir Edward Grey accordingly hopes that M. Sazonof will realize that it is not in the power of His Majesty's Government to give a greater proof of friendship than that which is afforded by the terms of the above-mentioned *aide-mémoire*. That document involves a complete reversal of the traditional policy of His Majesty's Government, and is in direct opposition to the opinions and sentiments at one time universally held in England and which have still by no means died out. Sir Edward Grey therefore trusts that the Imperial Government will recognize that the recent general assurances given to M. Sazonof have been most loyally and amply fulfilled. In presenting the *aide-mémoire* now, His Majesty's Government believe and hope that a lasting friendship between Russia and Great Britain will be assured as soon as the proposed settlement is realized.

From the British *aide-mémoire* it follows that the desiderata of His Majesty's Government, however important they may be to British interests in other parts of the world, will contain no condition which could impair Russia's control over the territories described in the Russian *aide-mémoire* of February 19/March 4, 1915.

In view of the fact that Constantinople will always remain a trade *entrepôt* for South-Eastern Europe and Asia Minor, His Majesty's Government will ask that Russia shall, when she comes into possession of it, arrange for a free port for goods in transit to and from non-Russian territory. His Majesty's Government will also ask that there shall be commercial freedom for merchant ships passing through the Straits, as M. Sazonof has already promised.

Except in so far as the naval and military operations on which His Majesty's Government are now engaged in the Dardanelles may contribute to the common cause of the Allies, it is now clear that these operations, however successful, cannot be of any advantage to His Majesty's Government in the final terms of peace. Russia alone will, if the war is successful, gather the direct fruits of these operations. Russia should therefore, in the opinion of His Majesty's Government, not now put difficulties in the way of any Power which may, on reasonable terms, offer to cooperate with the Allies. The only Power likely to participate in the operations in the Straits is Greece. Admiral Carden has asked the Admiralty to send him more destroyers, but they have none to spare. The assistance of a Greek flotilla, if it could have been secured, would thus have been of inestimable value to His Majesty's Government.

To induce the neutral Balkan States to join the Allies was one of the main objects which His Majesty's Government had in view when they undertook the operations in the Dardanelles. His Majesty's Government hope that Russia will spare no pains to calm the apprehensions of Bulgaria and Roumania as to Russia's possession of the Straits and Constantinople being to their disadvantage. His Majesty's Government also hope that Russia will do everything in her power to render the cooperation of these two States an attractive prospect to them.

Sir E. Grey points out that it will obviously be necessary to take into consideration the whole question of the future interests of France and Great Britain in what is now Asiatic Turkey; and, in formulating the desiderata of His Majesty's Government with regard to the Ottoman Empire, he must consult the French as well as the Russian Government. As soon, however, as it becomes known that Russia is to have Constantinople at the conclusion of the war, Sir E. Grey will wish to state that throughout the negotiations, His Majesty's Government have stipulated that the Mussulman Holy Places and Arabia shall under all circumstances remain under independent Mussulman dominion.

Sir E. Grey is as yet unable to make any definite proposal on any point of the British desiderata; but one of the points of the latter will be the revision of the Persian portion of the Anglo-Russian Agreement of 1907 so as to recognize the present neutral sphere as a British sphere.

Until the Allies are in a position to give to the Balkan States, and especially to Bulgaria and Roumania, some satisfactory assurance as to their prospects and general position with regard to the territories contiguous to their frontiers to the possession of which they are known to aspire; and until a more advanced stage of the agreement as to the French and British desiderata in the final peace terms is reached, Sir E. Grey points out that it is most desirable that the understanding now arrived at between the Russian,

French, and British Governments should remain secret.

French Note Verbal to Russian Government, 10 April 1915

The Government of the [French] Republic will give its agreement to the Russian aide-mémoire addressed by M. Isvolsky to M. Delcassé on 6 March last, relating to Constantinople and the Straits, on condition that war shall be prosecuted until victory and that France and Great Britain realize their plans in the Orient as elsewhere, as it is stated in the Russian aide-mémoire.

Correspondence between Sir Henry McMahon and Sherif Hussayn: letter to Hussayn, 24 October 1915

... I regret that you should have received from my last letter the impression that I regarded the question of the limits and boundaries with coldness and hesitation; such was not the case ... I have realized, however, from your last letter that you regard this question as one of vital and urgent importance. I have, therefore, lost no time in informing the Government of Great Britain of the contents of your letter, and it is with great pleasure that I communicate to you on their behalf [i.e. that of the British Government] the following statement, which I am confident you will receive with satisfaction:

The two districts of Mersina and Alexandretta and portions of Syria lying to the west of the districts of Damascus, Homs, Hama and Aleppo cannot be said to be purely Arab, and should be excluded from the limits demanded.

With the above modification, and without prejudice to our existing treaties with Arab chiefs, we accept those limits.

As for those regions lying within those frontiers wherein Great Britain is free to act without detriment to the interests of her ally, France, I am empowered in the name of the Government of Great Britain to give the following assurances and make the following reply to your letter:

1. Subject to the above modifications, Great Britain is prepared to recognize and support the independence of the Arabs in all the regions within the limits demanded by the Sherif of Mecca.

2. Great Britain will guarantee the Holy Places against all external aggression and will recognize their inviolability.

3. When the situation admits, Great Britain will give to the Arabs her advice and will assist them to establish what may appear to be the most suitable forms of government in those various territories.

4. On the other hand, it is understood that the Arabs have decided to seek the advice and guidance of Great Britain only, and that such European advisers and officials as may be required for the formation of a sound form of administration will be British.

5. With regard to the vilayets of Baghdad and Basra, the Arabs will recognize that the established position and interests of Great Britain necessitate special administrative arrangements in order to secure these territories from foreign aggression, to promote the welfare of the local populations and to safeguard our mutual economic interests.

I am convinced that this declaration will assure you beyond all possible doubt of the sympathy of Great Britain towards the aspirations of her friends the Arabs and will result in a firm and lasting alliance, the immediate results of which will be the expulsion of the Turks from the Arab countries and the freeing of the Arab peoples from the Turkish yoke, which for so many years has pressed heavily upon them. . . .

Tripartite (Sykes–Picot) Agreement for the partition of the Ottoman Empire by Britain, France and Russia, 26 April–23 October 1916

Grey to Cambon, French Ambassador in London, 16 May 1916

I have the honour to acknowledge the receipt of your Excellency's note of the 9th instant, stating that the French Government accept the limits of a future Arab State, or Confederation of States, and of those parts of Syria where French interests predominate, together with certain conditions attached thereto, such as they result from recent discussions in London and Petrograd on the subject.

I have the honour to inform your Excellency in reply that the acceptance of the whole project, as it now stands, will involve the abdication of considerable British interests, but, since His Majesty's Government recognize the advantage to the general cause of the Allies entailed in producing a more favourable internal political situation in Turkey, they are ready to accept the arrangement now arrived at, provided that the cooperation of the Arabs is secured, and that the Arabs fulfil the conditions and obtain the towns of Homs, Hama, Damascus, and Aleppo.

It is accordingly understood between the French and British Governments:

1. That France and Great Britain are prepared to recognize and protect ['protect' changed in August 1916 to 'uphold'] an independent Arab State or a Confederation of Arab States in the areas (A) and (B) marked on the annexed map, under the suzerainty of an Arab chief. That in area (A) France, and in area (B) Great Britain, shall have priority of right of enterprise and local loans. That in area (A) France, and in area (B) Great Britain, shall alone supply advisers or foreign functionaries at the request of the Arab State or Confederation of Arab States.

2. That in the blue area France, and in the red area Great Britain, shall be allowed to establish such direct or indirect administration or control as they desire and as they may think fit to arrange with the Arab State or Confederation of Arab States.

3. That in the brown area there shall be established an international administration, the form of which is to be decided upon after consultation with Russia, and subsequently in consultation with the other Allies, and the representatives of the Shereef of Mecca.

4. That Great Britain be accorded (1) the ports of Haifa and Acre, (2) guarantee of a given supply of water from the Tigris and Euphrates in area (A) for area (B). His Majesty's Government, on their part, undertake that they will at no time enter into negotiations for the cession of Cyprus to any third Power without the previous consent of the French Government.

5. That Alexandretta shall be a free port as regards the trade of the British Empire, and that there shall be no discrimination in port charges or facilities as regards British shipping and British goods; that there shall be freedom of transit for British goods through Alexandretta and by railway through the blue

area, whether those goods are intended for or originate in the red area, or (B) area, or area (A); and there shall be no discrimination, direct or indirect, against British goods on any railway or against British goods or ships at any port serving the areas mentioned.

That Haifa shall be a free port as regards the trade of France, her dominions and protectorates, and there shall be no discrimination in port charges or facilities as regards French shipping and French goods. There shall be freedom of transit for French goods through Haifa and by the British railway through the brown area, whether those goods are intended for or originate in the blue area, area (A), or area (B), and there shall be no discrimination, direct or indirect, against French goods on any railway, or against French goods or ships at any port serving the areas mentioned.

6. That in area (A) the Bagdad Railway shall not be extended southwards beyond Mosul, and in area (B) northwards beyond Samarra, until a railway connecting Bagdad with Aleppo via the Euphrates Valley has been completed, and then only with the concurrence of the two Governments.

7. That Great Britain has the right to build, administer, and be sole owner of a railway connecting Haifa with area (B), and shall have a perpetual right to transport troops along such a line at all times.

It is to be understood by both Governments that this railway is to facilitate the connection of Bagdad with Haifa by rail, and it is further understood that, if the engineering difficulties and expense entailed by keeping this connecting line in the brown area only make the project unfeasible, the French Government shall be prepared to consider that the line in question may also traverse the polygon Banias-Keis Marib-Salkhad Tell Otsda-Mesmie before reaching area (B).

8. For a period of twenty years the existing Turkish customs tariff shall remain in force throughout the whole of the blue and red areas, as well as in areas (A) and (B), and no increase in the rates of duty or conversion from *ad valorem* to specific rates shall be made except by agreement between the two powers.

There shall be no interior custom barriers between any of the above-mentioned areas. The customs duties leviable on goods destined for the interior shall be collected at the port of entry and handed over to the administration of the area of destination.

9. It shall be agreed that the French Government will at no time enter into any negotiations for the cession of their rights and will not cede such rights in the blue area to any third Power, except the Arab State or Confederation of Arab States, without the previous agreement of His Majesty's Government, who, on their part, will give a similar undertaking to the French Government regarding the red area.

10. The British and French Governments, as the protectors of the Arab State ['protectors of the Arab State' deleted August 1916], shall agree that they will not themselves acquire and will not consent to a third Power acquiring territorial possessions in the Arabian peninsula, or consent to a third Power installing a naval base either on the east coast, or on the islands, of the Red Sea. This, however, shall not prevent such adjustment of the Aden frontier as may be necessary in consequence of recent Turkish aggression.

11. The negotiations with the Arabs as to the boundaries of the Arab State or Confederation of Arab States shall be continued through the same channel as heretofore on behalf of the two Powers.

12. It is agreed that measures to control the importation of arms into the Arab territories will be considered by the two Governments.

I have further the honour to state that, in order to make the agreement complete, His Majesty's Government are proposing to the Russian Government to exchange notes analogous to those exchanged by the latter and your Excellency's Government on the 26th April last. Copies of these notes will be communicated to your Excellency as soon as exchanged.

I would also venture to remind your Excellency that the conclusion of the present agreement raises, for practical consideration, the question of the claims of Italy to a share in any partition or rearrangement of Turkey in Asia, as formulated in Article 9 of the agreement of the 26th April, 1915, between Italy and the Allies.

His Majesty's Government further consider that the Japanese Government should be informed of the arrangements now concluded.

Grey to Benckendorff, Russian Ambassador in London, 23 May 1916

I have received from the French Ambassador in London copies of the notes exchanged between the Russian and French Governments on the 26th ultimo, by which your Excellency's Government recognize, subject to certain conditions, the arrangement made between Great Britain and France, relative to the constitution of an Arab State or a Confederation of Arab States, and to the partition of the territories of Syria, Cilicia, and Mesopotamia, provided that the cooperation of the Arabs is secured.

His Majesty's Government take act with satisfaction that your Excellency's Government concur in the limits set forth in that arrangement, and I have now the honour to inform your Excellency that His Majesty's Government, on their part, in order to make the arrangement complete, are also prepared to recognize the conditions formulated by the Russian Government and accepted by the French Government in the notes exchanged at Petrograd on the 26th ultimo.

In so far, then, as these arrangements directly affect the relations of Russia and Great Britain, I have the honour to invite the acquiescence of your Excellency's Government in an agreement on the following terms:

1. That Russia shall annex the regions of Erzeroum, Trebizond, Van, and Bitlis, up to a point subsequently to be determined on the littoral of the Black Sea to the west of Trebizond.

2. That the region of Kurdistan to the south of Van and of Bitlis between Mush, Sert, the course of the Tigris, Jezireh-ben-Omar, the crest-line of the mountains which dominate Amadia, and the region of Merga Var, shall be ceded to Russia; and that starting from the region of Merga Var, the frontier of the Arab State shall follow the crest-line of the mountains which at present divide the Ottoman and Persian Dominions. These boundaries are indicated in a general manner and are subject to modifications of detail to be proposed later by the Delimitation Commission which shall meet on the spot.

3. That the Russian Government undertake that, in all parts of the Ottoman territories thus ceded to Russia, any concessions accorded to British subjects by the Ottoman Government shall be maintained. If the Russian Government express the desire that such concessions should later be modified in order to bring them into harmony with the laws of the Russian Empire, this modification shall only take place in agreement with the British Government.

4. That in all parts of the Ottoman territories thus ceded to Russia, existing British rights of navigation and development, and the rights and privileges of any British religious, scholastic, or medical institutions shall be maintained. His Majesty's Government, on their part, undertake that similar Russian rights and privileges shall be maintained in those regions which, under the conditions of this agreement, become entirely British, or in which British interests are recognized as predominant.

5. The two Governments admit in principle that every State which annexes any part of the Ottoman Empire is called upon to participate in the service of the Ottoman Debt.

Tripartite (St Jean de Maurienne) Agreement for the partition of the Ottoman Empire by Britain, France and Italy, 19 April–27 September 1917

The Agreement, London, 18 August 1917

Subject to Russia's assent.

1. The Italian Government adheres to the stipulations contained in Articles 1 and 2 of the Franco-British [Sykes–Picot] agreements of 9 and 16 May 1916. For their part, the Governments of France and of Great Britain cede to Italy, under the same conditions of administration and of interests, the green and 'C' zones as marked on the attached map . . .

2. Italy undertakes to make Smyrna a free port for the commerce of France, its colonies and its protectorates, and for the commerce of the British Empire and its dependencies. Italy shall enjoy the rights and privileges that France and Great Britain have reciprocally granted themselves in the ports of Alexandretta, of Haifa, and of St Jean d'Acre, in accordance with Article 5 of the said agreements. Mersina shall be a free port for the commerce of Italy, its colonies and its protectorates, and there shall be neither difference of treatment nor advantages in port rights which may be refused to the navy or the merchandise of Italy. There shall be free transit through Mersina, and by railroad across the *vilayet* of Adana, for Italian merchandise bound to and from the Italian zone. There shall be no difference of treatment, direct or indirect, at the expense of Italian merchandise or ships in any port along the coast of Cilicia serving the Italian zone.

3. The form of international administration in the yellow zone [same as Sykes–Picot brown zone] mentioned in Article 3 of the said agreements of 9 and 16 May shall be decided together with Italy.

4. Italy, in so far as she is concerned, approves the provisions on the ports of Haifa and of Acre contained in Article 4 of the same agreements.

5. Italy adheres, in that which relates to the green zone and zone 'C', to the two paragraphs of Article 8 of the Franco-British agreements concerning the customs régime that shall be maintained in the blue and red zones, and in zones 'A' and 'B'.

6. It is understood that the interests that each Power possesses in the zones controlled by the other Powers shall be scrupulously respected, but that the Powers concerned with these interests shall not use them as means for political action.

7. The provisions contained in Articles 10, 11 and 12 of the Franco-English agreements, concerning the Arabian Peninsula and the Red Sea, shall be considered as fully binding on Italy as if that Power were named in the articles with France and Great Britain as a Contracting Party.

8. It is understood that if, at the conclusion of peace, the advantages embodied in the agreements contracted among the allied Powers regarding the allocation to each of a part of the Ottoman Empire cannot be entirely assured to one or more of the said Powers, then in whatever alteration or arrangement of provinces of the Ottoman Empire resulting from the war the maintenance of equilibrium in the Mediterranean shall be given equitable consideration, in conformity with Article 9 of the London agreement of 26 April 1915.

9. It has been agreed that the present memorandum shall be communicated to the Russian Government, in order to permit it to make its views known.

The Balfour Declaration (letter from Balfour to Lord Rothschild), 2 November 1917

I have much pleasure in conveying to you, on behalf of His Majesty's Government, the following declaration of sympathy with Jewish Zionist aspirations which has been submitted to, and approved by, the Cabinet:

His Majesty's Government view with favour the establishment in Palestine of a national home for the Jewish people, and will use their best endeavours to facilitate the achievement of this object, it being clearly understood that nothing shall be done which may prejudice the civil and religious rights of existing non-Jewish communities in Palestine, or the rights and political status enjoyed by Jews in any other country.

I should be grateful if you would bring this declaration to the knowledge of the Zionist Federation.

Peace Treaty between Russia and Germany, Austria-Hungary, Bulgaria and Turkey (Treaty of Brest-Litovsk), 3 March 1918

Article I. Germany, Austria-Hungary, Bulgaria, and Turkey, for the one part, and Russia for the other part, declare that the state of war between them has ceased. They are resolved to live henceforth in peace and amity with one another.

Article II. The Contracting Parties will refrain from any agitation or propaganda against the Government or the public and military institutions of the other party. In so far as this obligation devolves upon Russia, it holds good also for the territories occupied by the Powers of the Quadruple Alliance.

Article III. The territories lying to the west of the line agreed upon by the Contracting Parties which formerly belonged to Russia, will no longer be subject to Russian sovereignty; the line agreed upon is traced on the map submitted as an essential part of this Treaty of Peace (Annex I). The exact fixation of the line will be established by a Russo-German Commission.

No obligations whatever toward Russia shall devolve upon the territories referred to, arising from the fact that they formerly belonged to Russia.

Russia refrains from all interference in the internal relations of these territories. Germany and Austria-Hungary purpose to determine the future status of these territories in agreement with their population.

Article IV. As soon as a general peace is concluded and Russian demobilization is carried out completely, Germany will evacuate the territory lying to the east of the line designated in paragraph 1 of Article III in so far as Article VI does not determine otherwise.

Russia will do all within her power to ensure the immediate evacuation of the provinces of Eastern Anatolia and their lawful return to Turkey.

The districts of Ardahan, Kars, and Batum will likewise and without delay be cleared of Russian troops. Russia will not interfere in the reorganization of the national and international relations of these districts, but leave it to the population of these districts to carry out this reorganization in agreement with the neighbouring States, especially with Turkey.

Article V. Russia will, without delay, carry out the full demobilization of her army inclusive of those units recently organized by the present Government.

Furthermore, Russia will either bring her warships into Russian ports and there detain them until the day of the conclusion of a general peace, or disarm them forthwith. Warships of the States which continue in a state of war with the Powers of the Quadruple Alliance, in so far as they are within Russian sovereignty, will be treated as Russian warships....

Article VI. Russia obligates herself to conclude peace at once with the Ukrainian People's Republic and to recognize the treaty of peace between that State and the Powers of the Quadruple Alliance. The Ukrainian territory will, without delay, be cleared of Russian troops and the Russian Red Guard. Russia is to put an end to all agitation or propaganda against the Government or the public institutions of the Ukrainian People's Republic.

Estonia and Livonia will likewise, without delay, be cleared of Russian troops and the Russian Red Guard. The eastern boundary of Estonia runs, in general, along the river Narva. The eastern boundary of Livonia crosses, in general, lakes Peipus and Pskov, to the south-western corner of the latter, then across Lake Luban in the direction of Livenhof on the Dvina. Estonia and Livonia will be occupied by a German police force until security is ensured by proper national institutions and until public order has been established. Russia will liberate at once all arrested or deported inhabitants of Estonia and Livonia, and ensures the safe return of all deported Estonians and Livonians.

Finland and the Aaland Islands will immediately be cleared of Russian troops and the Russian Red Guard, and the Finnish ports of the Russian fleet and of the Russian naval forces. So long as the ice

prevents the transfer of warships into Russian ports, only limited forces will remain on board the warships. Russia is to put an end to all agitation or propaganda against the Government or the public institutions of Finland.

The fortresses built on the Aaland Islands are to be removed as soon as possible. As regards the permanent non-fortification of these islands as well as their further treatment in respect to military and technical navigation matters, a special agreement is to be concluded between Germany, Finland, Russia, and Sweden; there exists an understanding to the effect that, upon Germany's desire, still other countries bordering upon the Baltic Sea would be consulted in this matter.

Article VII. In view of the fact that Persia and Afghanistan are free and independent States, the Contracting Parties obligate themselves to respect the political and economic independence and the territorial integrity of these States.

Article VIII. The prisoners of war of both parties will be released to return to their homeland. The settlement of the questions connected therewith will be effected through the special treaties provided for in Article XII.

Article IX. The Contracting Parties mutually renounce compensation for their war expenses, i.e. of the public expenditures for the conduct of the war, as well as compensation for war losses, i.e. such losses as were caused them and their nationals within the war zones by military measures, inclusive of all requisitions effected in enemy country.

Article X. Diplomatic and consular relations between the Contracting Parties will be resumed immediately upon the ratification of the Treaty of Peace. As regards the reciprocal admission of consuls, separate agreements are reserved.

Article XI. As regards the economic relations between the Powers of the Quadruple Alliance and Russia the regulations contained in Appendices II–V are determinative, namely Appendix II for the Russo-German, Appendix III for the Russo-Austro-Hungarian, Appendix IV for the Russo-Bulgarian, and Appendix V for the Russo-Turkish relations.

Supplementary Treaty of Peace between Russia and the Central Powers, Berlin, 27 August 1918

Guided by the wish to solve certain political questions which have arisen in connection with the Peace Treaty of March 3–7, 1918, between Germany, Austria-Hungary, Bulgaria, and Turkey, for the one part, and Russia, for the other part, in the spirit of friendly understanding and mutual conciliation, and, in so doing, to promote the restoration of good and confidential relations between the two Empires, for which a way was paved by the conclusion of peace, the German Imperial Government and the Government of the Russian Socialist Federal Soviet Republic have agreed to conclude a supplementary treaty to the Peace Treaty with this object, and have ... agreed to the following provisions:

[*Article 1*. Demarcation of frontiers.]

[*Article 2*. Frontier commission.]

Article 3. Germany will evacuate the territory occupied by her east of Beresina, even before the conclusion of general peace, in proportion as Russia makes the cash payments stipulated in Article 2 of the Russo-German Financial Agreement of this date; further provisions as to this, particularly the fixing of the individual sectors to be evacuated, are left to the Commission referred to in Article 2, paragraph 1, of this Supplementary Treaty.

The Contracting Parties reserve the right to make further agreements with regard to the effecting of the evacuation of the occupied territory west of the Beresina before the conclusion of general peace, in accordance with the fulfilment by Russia of the remaining financial obligations undertaken by her.

Part II · Separatist movements in the Russian Empire

Article 4. In so far as is not otherwise prescribed in the Peace Treaty or in this Supplementary Treaty, Germany will in no wise interfere in the relations between the Russian Empire and parts of its territory, and will thus in particular neither cause nor support the formation of independent States in those territories.

Part III · North Russian territory

Article 5. Russia will at once employ all the means at her disposal to expel the Entente forces from North Russian territory in observance of her neutrality.

Germany guarantees that during these operations there shall be no Finnish attack of any kind on Russian territory, particularly on St Petersburg.

Article 6. When the Entente forces shall have evacuated North Russian territory, the local Russian coast shipping within the three-mile limit from the north coast, and the fishing boats within a stretch of thirty miles along this coast shall be relieved of the barred zone menace. The German naval command shall have an opportunity, in a way to be further agreed upon, of convincing itself that this concession shall not be taken advantage of to forward contraband goods.

Part IV · Estonia, Livonia, Courland, and Lithuania

Article 7. Russia, taking account of the condition at present existing in Estonia and Livonia, renounces sovereignty over these regions, as well as all interference in their internal affairs. Their future fate shall be decided in agreement with their inhabitants. . . .

[*Article 13.* Recognition of Georgia's independence.]

[In a Financial Agreement concluded at the same time, Russia agreed to pay Germany 6,000 million marks as compensation for losses to Germany caused by Russian measures.]

Decree of the All-Russian Central Executive Committee of the Soviets on the cancellation of the Brest-Litovsk Treaty, 13 November 1918

To all peoples of Russia, to the population of all occupied regions and territories:

The All-Russian Central Executive Committee of the Soviets hereby declares solemnly that the conditions of peace with Germany signed at Brest on March 3, 1918, are null and void. The Brest-Litovsk treaty (and equally the annexed agreement signed at Berlin on August 27, and ratified by the All-Russian Central Executive Committee on September 6, 1918), in their entirety and in all their articles, are herewith declared as annulled. All obligations assumed under the Brest-Litovsk treaty and dealing with the payment of contributions or the cession of territory or regions, are declared void. . . .

II · The peace settlements and the League of Nations, 1919–23

The armed conflict of the First World War came to an end with the separate signatures of armistices between the belligerents. Turkey signed an armistice at Mudros on 30 October 1918, Austria-Hungary on 3 November 1918 and Germany on 11 November 1918.

In the West the armistice conditions of 11 November 1918 between the Allies and Germany provided for an orderly withdrawal of the German army from occupied territories and also from the right and left banks of the Rhine. But the conditions of the German armistice did not provide for the German evacuation of all occupied Tsarist territory. Territories in Central and Eastern Europe that had once formed part of the Tsarist Russian Empire of 1914 were not to be evacuated by German troops, according to Article 12 of the armistice, until 'the Allies think the moment suitable, having regard to the internal situation of these territories'. Thus the Allies enlisted German help to prevent the spread of Bolshevism until they were ready to intervene; Article 16 reserved to the Allies 'free access to the territories evacuated by the Germans on their eastern frontier, either through Danzig or by the Vistula, in order to convey supplies to the population of these territories or for the purpose of maintaining order'. Similarly anti-Bolshevik terms had been included in the Austro-Hungarian armistice of 3 November 1918. In the Turkish armistice the Allies assured themselves of strategic access to the Black Sea; they asserted their right to occupy the forts of the Dardanelles and Bosphorus and provided for an Allied occupation of Batum and Baku; they also claimed the general right to occupy any strategic point 'in the event of a situation arising which threatens the security of the Allies'. In December 1918 and January 1919 the Allies, referring to Article 12 of the German armistice, strenuously objected to German withdrawals in southern Russia, the Ukraine and from Estonia.

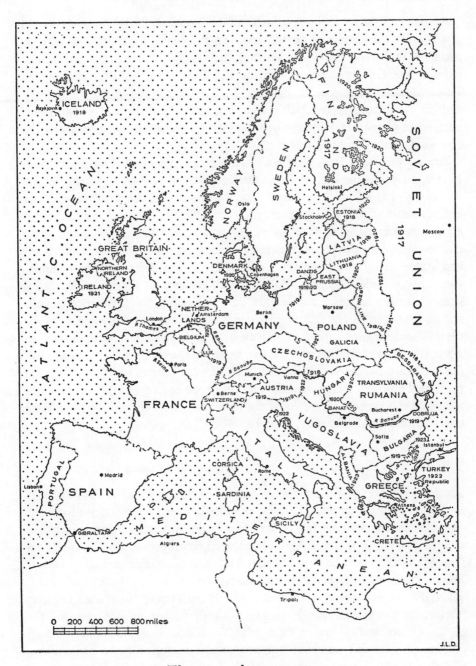

2 The peace settlements, 1919–23

'Livonia and Courland' (Latvia, Lithuania). The Allies feared that they would not be able to reinforce German and anti-Bolshevik forces fast enough to maintain their *cordon sanitaire*. During the course of 1918 the provisional independent Governments of Estonia and Latvia were reorganized by the Allies though under foreign occupation. The Allies attempted to stop the Bolshevik advance in the Baltic and in Central Europe, and as the peace conference opened in January 1919 the Germans assisted by despatching the *Free Corps* troops to the Baltic.

During the *Paris Peace Conference* four of the five Great Powers, Britain, France, Italy and the United States (but not Japan) in their negotiations and discussions ranged over the international problems of the whole world, but did not settle all the world's problems; only the Covenant of the League of Nations was intended to be of universal application. The frontiers and peace treaties settled by the peace conference were those that concerned the Allied and Associated Powers on the one hand and the defeated enemy States, Germany, Austria, Hungary, Bulgaria and Turkey, on the other. Excluded from the territorial peace settlements were Russia and the frontiers of Russia and its neighbours. The failure of Allied intervention and the outcome of the Civil War determined the fate of Russia. Russia's frontiers were dealt with separately in negotiations and treaties between Russia on the one hand, and Finland, Estonia, Latvia, Lithuania, Poland and Turkey on the other, after continued fighting in Eastern and Central Europe during 1919 and 1920. Thus the territorial peace settlements of the Allied and Associated Powers did not cover the whole of Europe.

THE ORGANIZATION OF THE PARIS PEACE CONFERENCE

The Peace Conference of Paris opened on 18 January 1919 and officially ended on 21 January 1920. Thirty-two nations, enemies of Germany or one of its allies, sent plenipotentiaries; included were five Latin American States which had severed diplomatic relations with Germany. The following States were represented: United States; Britain; Canada; Australia; South Africa; New Zealand; India; France; Italy; Japan; Belgium; Bolivia; Brazil; China; Cuba; Czechoslovakia; Ecuador; Greece; Guatemala; Haiti; the Hejaz; Honduras; Liberia; Nicaragua; Panama; Peru; Portugal; Poland; Rumania; Kingdom of the Serbs, Croats and Slovenes (Yugoslavia); Siam; Uruguay. The Council of Ten (see below) accepted separate representation for the Dominions, Canada, South Africa, Australia, New Zealand and India. Much expert research had been undertaken on the subjects with which the peace conference would have to deal, but little thought had been given to the actual organization and procedure of the conference itself. The order in which issues were to be raised and resolved was never settled, or rather the approach adopted was pragmatic; issues were decided as and when they should prove ready for discussion. Consequently the major political settlements were reached in detail by a piecemeal process and not according to an overall design and plan. The second Plenary Session of the conference established the main special commissions to examine specific issues. The crucial bargaining, however, was not conducted by all the participating nations, but only by the 'Big Five', Britain, France, Italy, Japan and the United States, which with two plenipotentiaries each formed the Council of Ten. This Great Power directorate promised to consult the smaller States when their interests were affected and established a large number of expert territorial commissions to deal with frontier questions.

After 24 March 1919 the Council of Ten gave way to a smaller, more informal, Council of Four of Wilson, Lloyd George, Clemenceau and Orlando. In the fourth week of April when Fiume was not awarded to Italy, Orlando left the Council of Four in protest, so the decisions were then left to the remaining three. The Treaty of Versailles, 28 June 1919, formally concluded the League of Nations and the German aspects of the peace settlements, and Wilson returned to the United States. Negotiations continued on the other peace treaties, with the United States playing a decreasing role after the rejection of them by the Senate on 19 November 1919 and 19 March 1920. The United States concluded separate peace treaties with Germany, Austria and Hungary in August 1921.

The Treaty of Versailles: the peace settlement with Germany

THE ARMISTICE

Germany did not 'surrender unconditionally' in November 1918. On 4 October 1918 Prime Minister Max von Baden, the German Chancellor, sought an armistice on the basis of the Fourteen Points in an appeal to President Wilson. Only after exchanging three notes with the German Government did Wilson, on 23 October, formally consult the Allies, who meantime were alarmed at the prospect of bilateral US–German negotiations for peace. The biggest obstacle did not prove to be the Fourteen Points as far as they applied to Germany, but American insistence of 'absolute freedom of navigation upon the seas, outside territorial waters' in time of peace and war. Britain strenuously resisted and maintained her national right to blockade and interruption in 1918 as she had done in 1812. Agreement was finally reached between the United States and the Allies on 4 November which accepted peace on the Fourteen Points, together with Wilson's subsequent addresses and pronouncements of principles and two further provisos, one concerning reparations, the other leaving open the question of the freedom of the seas for the peace conference. This marked the first official acceptance of Wilson's unilateral proclamation of war aims in *the Fourteen Points, 8 January 1918* (p. 57) which he had delivered in his address to a joint session of Congress. Independently, in a speech three days earlier on 5 January 1918, Lloyd George had defined British war aims, which were closely similar to all but one of Wilson's Fourteen Points, namely the second point on the freedom of the seas. Germany accepted the terms agreed by the Allies and the United States together with the military terms decided upon by the commander in the field; the armistice was signed on 11 November 1918.

THE TERRITORIAL TERMS

In the West, Alsace-Lorraine was returned to France and Germany's request for a plebiscite was rejected; the Saar was placed under an International Commission of the League and it was agreed that a plebiscite would be held at the end of fifteen years (in 1935 the Saar opted for Germany with Germany then able to repurchase mines); the mines of the Saar passed into French ownership as part of the reparations for damage to French mines; three small territories became Belgian – Moresnet, Eupen and Malmedy.

French demands for the strategic frontier of the Rhine caused a crisis among the Big Four in March and April 1919. France only acquiesced to German sovereignty continuing over the territories of both banks of the Rhine on two conditions agreed to by the Allies and the United States. Firstly, Allied troops were to occupy German territory west of the Rhine and some bridgeheads across the Rhine in three zones, to be evacuated at five-year intervals provided Germany fulfilled the treaty conditions of Versailles. In June 1919, a concession was made to Germany that if it gave proof of goodwill and satisfactory guarantees of fulfilling its obligations, the projected fifteen-year occupation might be shortened; the German territory west of the Rhine, moreover, was demilitarized (no troops or fortifications permitted in the demilitarized zone) as well as a strip of territory running 50 kilometres east of the Rhine. Secondly, France received a *Treaty of Guarantee* from the United States and Britain of military support if Germany attacked France. The *Treaties of Guarantee were signed on 28 June 1919* (p. 71), at the same time as the Treaty of Versailles, but the coming into force of the British treaty depended on the prior ratification by the Senate of the United States. Thus when Senate rejected the Versailles Treaty, the U.S. Treaty of Guarantee with France and the British Treaty of Guarantee with France lapsed also.

In the North, on the Danish–German frontier, it was agreed that a new frontier would be fixed according to a plebiscite of the population of Schleswig; the predominantly Danish-speaking northern part of Schleswig chose to join Denmark in 1920, and southern Schleswig stayed in Germany.

In the East, Germany lost large territories to the new Polish State. To allow Poland an outlet to the sea the Polish 'corridor' was created which separated Germany from the east Prussian territories. The province of Posen (Poznan) was also placed under Polish sovereignty together with Upper Silesia; the German-speaking town of Danzig was made a Free City under the supervision of the League, but with Poland enjoying special rights, a customs union and control of foreign affairs. German protests in June 1919 modified the final terms of the German eastern frontier significantly in that the final disposition of Upper Silesia was to be dependent on plebiscites held in that region. In July 1920 the territory of East Prussia was considerably enlarged southwards as a result of plebiscites in the Allenstein and Marienwerder zones; in March 1921 about two-thirds of the area of Upper Silesia voted for Germany, and only about one-third became Polish though it contained the greater mineral wealth. The settlement of the Polish–German frontier in 1920 and 1921 left a German minority of more than one million in Poland and a Polish minority in excess of half a million in Germany. Germany lost Memel and its district with its half German-speaking and half Lithuanian population, which Lithuania seized in 1923. Germany also lost a small piece of Silesian territory to Czechoslovakia.

Germany was obliged to give up all her colonies. The African colonies were divided in the form of different classes of mandates under the League of Nations between Britain, South Africa, France and Belgium (except for some small areas annexed by France and Portugal); Australia, New Zealand, Britain and Japan took over the Pacific territories. Japanese insistence on acquiring Germany's special privileges in the Chinese province of Shantung caused great difficulty at the peace conference as China was an ally that had declared war on Germany; but secret British, French and Italian wartime promises secured Japan the necessary support at the peace conference. China thereupon refused to sign the Treaty of Versailles.

REPARATIONS

The question of reparations proved among the most contentious issues of the peace conference. Too large a sum might lead the Germans to refuse to sign the treaty, and a sum likely to prove within Germany's reasonable capacity to pay would not satisfy public opinion in France and Britain, on which the British and French Prime Ministers negotiating in Paris were dependent. No total sum was stated in the treaty nor any limit to the years of payment; instead a Reparations Commission was set up to determine by 1 May 1921 the total of Germany's obligations. The inability to fix a relatively moderate sum made the earlier hard-won agreement secured by Wilson that Germany should only pay for civilian damage, not the whole of the war costs, of little practical importance. The famous War Guilt clause (Article 231) came to symbolize the injustices of the Treaty of Versailles. The wording was ill-considered and in subsequent years helped to undermine credibility in the treaty. It was not intended to be considered by itself, but was the first article in the reparations section; in Article 232 German liability was limited and 'complete reparation for all such loss and damage', that is the whole of the war costs, would not be demanded. To make the concession of requiring reparations only for civilian damage (and pensions) more palatable, it was agreed that the Allies should assert, and Germany should be obliged to accept, German responsibility with its allies for 'all the loss and damage . . . as a consequence of the war imposed upon them by the aggression of Germany and her allies'.

FOOD SUPPLIES AND THE BLOCKADE

A loosely coordinated Allied relief effort under Herbert Hoover as Director-General began to function early in 1919, and brought food and relief to the peoples of Eastern Europe facing starvation. The bulk of food supplies and services came from the United States, and Britain also made a major contribution, but Germany was excluded from the relief grants. The blockade was maintained against Germany, a later potent propaganda plank used by the Nazis to discredit all the proceedings of Versailles. The French demanded immediate reparations payments and the handing over of the German merchant fleet. This was made an additional condition of renewing the armistice on 16 January 1919. At first Germany refused, but Allied agreement was eventually reached, in Brussels on 14 March 1919, on German payments in foreign securities for food and the surrender of the German merchant fleet; before the end of the month food supplies began to reach the Germans. The blockade was relaxed but not finally raised until 12 July 1919, after the German ratification of the peace treaty.

MILITARY LIMITATIONS

The provisions of the treaty made Germany virtually defenceless; her armed forces were sufficient only for the internal preservation of law and order. The German army was limited to 100,000 men, and to prevent the training of more men a conscript army was forbidden; the period of service was set for twelve years for all but officers, who would have to serve twenty-five years. The German navy was limited and permitted no submarines; Germany was permitted no military air force, and the armaments industry was placed under the severest restraint and Allied control and inspection. The demilitarization and occupation of the Rhineland completed Germany's military impotence in facing French military strength. To make these clauses more palatable to Germany, the intention of general disarmament among all the Powers was expressed in the treaty.

OTHER PROVISIONS

Among the many other provisions of the treaty the more important were those concerning Russia; Germany had to renounce the Treaty of Brest-Litovsk and the Treaty of Bucharest, and acknowledge the right to independence of all the territories of the Russian Empire as it existed on 1 August 1914; Russia retained rights to reparations from Germany. Germany also had to recognize the frontiers and accept all treaties the Allies might conclude with present and future States, existing or coming into existence, whose territories had once formed part of the Russian Empire of 1914 (Articles 116 and 117). But the provisions for the trial of 'war criminals', including the Kaiser, proved largely inoperative. The rights of the German minority in Poland were safeguarded not in the Treaty of Versailles itself but in a treaty signed the same day, *the Minorities Treaty between the Allied and Associated Powers and Poland, 28 June 1919* (p. 72). It served as the model for treaties dealing with German and other minorities in Czechoslovakia, Yugoslavia, Rumania and Greece.

The draft peace treaty was presented to the German representatives, who were summoned for this purpose to the Trianon Palace, on 7 May 1919. After German written protests had been considered, and a few amendments made, the most significant being the plebiscite in Upper Silesia, *the Treaty of Peace was signed at Versailles on 28 June 1919* (p. 59).

Peace treaties with Austria, Bulgaria and Hungary, 1919–20

The crucial decisions affecting the territorial distributions of Central and Eastern Europe had been taken before the signature of the Versailles Treaty, indeed in many cases before the peace conference opened in Paris. Thus the Allies and the United States were committed to confirming the new multi-national succession States of the Austro-Hungarian Empire, which had broken up in the aftermath of defeat: these were Czechoslovakia and Yugoslavia. Military action too, either against the defeated forces of Austria and Hungary or to fill the vacuum left by their departure, created a number of situations by force which later proved completely or partially irrevocable and were recognized by the Allies. The Hungarian *Banat* was occupied after the armistice with Hungary by Serbian troops in November 1918, and Rumania claimed the whole region at the peace conference in vain. The Rumanians in turn occupied the whole of Transylvania and even Budapest during the spring and summer of 1919. The Italians seized disputed Fiume in September 1919, and the Czechoslovaks in the previous autumn occupied the whole of historic Bohemia and Moravia, including large German-speaking minorities. The Poles and Czechs clashed in the district of Teschen and the Poles occupied the mainly Ukrainian–Ruthenian ethnic region of eastern Galicia, which had formed part of Austria. The actual boundaries contained in the peace treaties with Austria, Hungary and Bulgaria were thus drawn largely as a result of territorial awards eventually made to the neighbouring States, of territory for the most part already occupied by them, after investigation by the Territorial Claims Commissions set up by the Council of Ten.

The Treaty of St Germain with Austria, 10 September 1919, was modelled on the Treaty of Versailles, as were the other peace treaties. The Covenant of the League of Nations was integrally included in the peace treaties, and the war responsibility and reparations clauses were similar in form to the German treaty. Austria was limited militarily and permitted a conscript army of no more than 30,000 officers and men. Austria was expressly forbidden union with Germany. The South Tyrol, with a German-speaking population of some 240,000, was handed over to Italy, giving Italy the Brenner pass frontier promised in the Allied *Treaty of London, April 1915* (p. 24); Bohemia and Moravia merged into Czechoslovakia; Bukovina was acquired by Rumania. Owing to disputes among the Allies, other areas were ceded by Austria to the Allies for disposition by them; these regions included the northern Adriatic and Galicia. In the Klagenfurth district of Carinthia a plebiscite in October 1920 decided for Austria against Yugoslavia. Austria received a small area from Hungary, and most of the 'Burgenland', but in a smaller part of 'Burgenland' a plebiscite favoured Hungary. Apart from these small areas, populations were transferred and frontiers redrawn without benefit of plebiscites. These cessions of territory left independent Austria with little more than a quarter of the territory that had formed the Austrian half of the pre-war Dual Monarchy.

The Treaty of Trianon with Hungary, 4 June 1920, was only signed several months after the formal end of the Paris Peace Conference. Peacemaking was in part delayed by the revolution and setting up of the Bolshevik Government of Béla Kun from March 1919 to August 1919. The Kun régime collapsed after attacking and being defeated by the Rumanians who were occupying western Hungary (Transylvania) and now advanced to occupy Budapest; the

Rumanians could not be induced to withdraw from some of the territory until the autumn of 1919. Historic Hungary had in practice been dismembered before the presentation of the peace treaty to the Hungarian delegates. Almost one-third of the Hungary of 1918, Transylvania and two-thirds of Banat, was ceded to Rumania, and this demarcation left about two million Magyars, mainly in south-east Transylvania, as a minority in post-war Rumania; Croatia–Slavonia and one-third of the Banat were ceded to Yugoslavia; Slovakia, Ruthenia and the region of Pressburg (Bratislava) with some 700,000 Magyars to Czechoslovakia; Fiume eventually to Italy; the greater part of the Burgenland to Austria; and finally to Poland and Czechoslovakia the small areas of Ostrava and Spis in northern Slovakia. Altogether Hungary lost rather more than two-thirds of its territory. Apart from the plebiscites permitted in two small regions, the transfer of population in Hungary was also decided upon without plebiscites. Hungary was limited to a professional army of 35,000 officers and men, and in common with the other peace treaties, the League Covenant and other clauses such as war responsibility and reparations were included. An unusual feature of the treaty was an accompanying letter from the French Prime Minister, Millerand, promising that if the Treaty contained any injustice which it would be in the general interest to remove, the Frontier Delimitation Commission might suggest revisions to the League of Nations. This as it turned out raised Hungarian hopes in vain.

The Treaty of Neuilly with Bulgaria, 27 November 1919. By the armistice terms Bulgaria had to withdraw its troops to the pre-war frontier. The territorial terms required Bulgaria to return the southern Dobruja to Rumania regardless of ethnic considerations; and to cede to Yugoslavia most of the four small regions occupied by Serbia in 1918. To the Allies, Bulgaria had to cede nearly the whole of western Thrace thus losing Bulgaria's Aegean littoral; the Allies transferred this territory to Greece by treaty on 10 August 1920, and at the same time a treaty was signed with Turkey. Reparations were required and the Bulgarian army was limited to 33,000 professionals.

Allied disputes and settlements

The peace treaties of St Germain, Neuilly and Trianon, whilst they settled the reduced frontiers of Austria, Bulgaria and Hungary, did not determine the final division of all the ceded territories among the various Allies. The principal disputes occurred over:

1. FIUME

Italy was scarcely reconciled to a compact Yugoslav State along the Adriatic which would prove an obstacle to Italian Balkan ambitions. In addition to the

Italian-speaking Trieste region, a part of Austrian domains of the Dual Monarchy, Italy also claimed Fiume, once part of Hungary, which the Yugoslavs desired as their major seaport. Italy had been excluded from Fiume in the Treaty of London, and Orlando's claim was resisted by the others in the Council of Four, causing an Allies crisis in April 1919 and the departure for a time of the Italians from the Peace Conference of Paris. In September 1919 d'Annuncio with Italian 'volunteers' seized the city and drove out the inter-Allied force of occupation. Allied efforts secured no agreement. Eventually by the *Yugoslav–Italian Treaty of Rapallo, 12 November 1920*, the Italian–Yugoslav frontier dispute was settled and Fiume made a Free City; Italy finally acquired Fiume together with a small strip of territory so that Fiume and the rest of Italy were contiguous.

2. THE BANAT

This territory ceded by Hungary had been promised by the Allies in a secret treaty to Rumania in 1916, but Rumania's separate peace treaty with the Central Powers at Bucharest in 1918 had voided the Allied promise. In November 1918 the Serbians occupied the Banat. The Allied decision in June 1919 to partition the Banat between Yugoslavia and Rumania was rejected by Rumania until Allied pressure forced Rumania to give way in December 1919.

3. ALBANIA

Italy and Greece desired Albanian territory and planned its partition in 1919 and 1920. Yugoslavia too made territorial claims. Long drawn-out negotiations ended in the recognition of Albanian independence, though Albania's frontiers were not finally agreed until 1926.

4. TESCHEN

The *Teschen* dispute was resolved largely in Czechoslovakia's favour, the incorporation of Galicia in Poland was finally acknowledged and the still uncertain frontier between Austria and Hungary settled by plebiscites.

The Allies, Turkey and Greece, 1920–3

The Allies planned the partition of Turkey at the peace conference. Not only were the subject national groups to be taken from the Ottoman Empire, but Turkey proper was to be placed under the tutelage of the Western Powers. In the Middle East, the wartime inter-Allied agreements and promises to the Arabs and Zionists made the disposition of this part of the Ottoman Empire the subject of protracted negotiations. The problems of Asia Minor were only considered intermittently at Paris during the spring of 1919. It was decided at Paris to internationalize the Straits and to assist and encourage autonomous

Governments among the liberated subject peoples. The mandate system was devised to reconcile autonomous national development and Great Power influence and supervision both in the Middle East and in respect to the German colonies. France claimed the mandate for the whole of Syria. Lloyd George wished to restrict the French mandate to the coastal region as determined in the *Sykes-Picot Agreement* of 1916 (p. 30). A mandate for Armenia and the Straits was offered at Paris to the United States, but Wilson could give no decision before his return to Washington in June 1919, and Congress did not formally refuse the mandate until a year later. The peace settlement was further delayed by the claims of Italy and Greece. In April 1919, the Italians had landed troops in Antalya (Adalia) in Asia Minor, and in May 1919 the Greeks landed troops in Izmir (Smyrna). An Allied force had been in occupation of the Straits in accordance with the terms of the Armistice of Mudros, 30 October 1918, and in March 1920 occupied Constantinople. The peace terms were presented to the practically captive Sultan's Government in May 1920 and the Sultan's Government concluded the *Treaty of Sèvres with the Allies on 10 August 1920*. In European Turkey, eastern Thrace was ceded to Greece and most of the Aegean islands; the Straits were left under nominal Turkish sovereignty, but the waterway was internationalized, demilitarized and was to be open to all merchant ships and warships in peace and in war (a reversal of the régime established by the Straits Convention of 1841); it was to be run by a Commission of ten Powers under the League of Nations framework. Smyrna and district in western Anatolia was to be administered by Greece for five years, followed by a plebiscite. In eastern Anatolia, Armenia was granted independence and its frontiers were to be decided later; Kurdistan was permitted autonomy; Turkey lost Syria which became a French mandate, Palestine and Mesopotamia which became British mandates, and the Arabian peninsula which was granted independence as the Kingdom of Hejaz. Turkish finances were placed under British, French and Italian supervision.

These onerous terms were signed by the Sultan's Government which was increasingly losing control of the country to the Turkish Nationalists led by Mustafa Kemal. Kemal and the Nationalist Assembly in Ankara rejected the terms. Kemal and the reorganized Turkish army concluded *a treaty with Bolshevik Russia on 16 March 1921* (p. 77), and crushed Armenia. The Moscow treaty with Soviet Russia settled Turkey's eastern frontier without reference to the Allies and rejected the validity of any treaty imposed on Turkey.

Kemal's growing strength decided the Allies against attempting to enforce the Treaty of Sèvres by force. The United States had withdrawn its support altogether. In June 1921 Italy began to evacuate Asia Minor. France and Turkey concluded the *Treaty of Ankara, 20 October 1921*. Hostilities between

France and Kemal's troops ceased; a new frontier was drawn between Syria and Turkey more favourable to Turkey than that of Sèvres. France recognized Kemal's Government of the Grand National Assembly. By the treaty Allied unity and the Treaty of Sèvres was shattered as France concluded a separate peace.

The Greek army in Asia Minor was decisively defeated in August 1922 and Kemal's troops entered Izmir on 9 September. In the Straits Allied unity had crumbled when French and Italian garrisons were withdrawn in September 1922. The British remained alone guarding the Straits at Chanak with the Turks in October 1922 determined to regain control. The consequent Chanak crisis was resolved by negotiation and the *Armistice of Mudanya* between Turkey, Italy, France and Britain on *11 October 1922* (on 14 October the Greeks acceded to it): by the terms of the armistice eastern Thrace as far as the Maritsa river and Adrianople was handed by the Greeks to the Nationalist Turks, and Turkish sovereignty over Istanbul (Constantinople) and the Straits was recognized.

The final settlement was worked out at the *Conference of Lausanne, 21 November 1922–4 February 1923 and 23 April–24 July 1923*. The ambiguous position of the Turkish Nationalists and the Sultan was resolved by the abolition of the Sultanate on 1 November 1922. During the course of the conference agreement was reached in January 1923 on a compulsory exchange of Greek and Turkish minorities and a convention signed to this effect by *Greece and Turkey, 30 January 1923*. After protracted negotiations the conference ended with the signature by Turkey of the *Treaty of Lausanne, 24 July 1923* (p. 79). Many of the onerous terms of the Treaty of Sèvres were abandoned. Turkey alone among ex-enemy States was not required to pay reparations. The special legal privileges which the 'civilized' Western nations had enjoyed in their dealings with the Ottoman Empire, known as the capitulations, were abolished. Few restrictions on national Turkish sovereignty remained. The treaty settled the boundaries of Turkey, and, with the restoration of eastern Thrace, Turkey's frontier in Europe was restored to what it had been in 1914 (with the exception of a small piece of territory ceded to Bulgaria). Greece retained all but two of the former Turkish Aegean islands, which were near the mouth of the Dardanelles and which were returned to Turkey. (The Dodecanese Islands were retained by Italy.) British sovereignty over Cyprus was confirmed. The frontier between British-mandated Iraq and Turkey was not finally settled; the key region of Mosul had been left for later settlement, eventually reached in 1926 when Mosul was given to Iraq.

The question of the Straits was settled by the *Straits Convention* (p. 80) which formed an annex to the treaty. A demilitarized zone was established on both the Asian and European shores, but the Turks were permitted to garrison

Istanbul; the security of the Straits and the demilitarized zones and free navigation was guaranteed by the signatories of the convention and more especially by France, Britain, Italy and Japan; the Soviet Union signed but did not ratify the convention. The passage of merchant vessels was guaranteed through the Straits in time of peace or war, and if Turkey itself was at war; the passage of warships in time of peace was limited by tonnage and number, and to a maximum force for each country not exceeding 'the most powerful fleet of the littoral Powers of the Black Sea', at such a time. In time of war, Turkey being neutral, warships of belligerents could pass the Straits without practical limitations (this marked the great change of rule from that established by the Straits Convention of 1841). In time of war, *Turkey being a belligerent*, the passage of neutral warships was permitted, limited by the same provision as for warships in time of peace.

The rule of the Straits established by the Treaty of Lausanne lasted until 1936 when it was replaced by the *Montreux Convention, 20 July 1936* (p. 83). This treaty restored Turkish sovereignty over the Straits, subject to certain conditions. It permitted the Black Sea powers *in time of peace* to send warships through the Straits subject to certain restrictions (Articles 11–14); other naval Powers could pay courtesy visits to Turkish ports in the Straits (Article 17). The total tonnage any Black Sea Power could have in the Black Sea was limited by Article 18, but the limitations were only relative and flexible. Thus the Black Sea States, including the Soviet Union, enjoyed considerable advantages of egress denied to the other Powers desiring to enter the Black Sea. In time of war, Turkey being neutral, warships of belligerents were *not* permitted to pass through the Straits unless assisting the victim of aggression within the framework of the League of Nations (Article 19). If Turkey itself were at war, or threatened with war, the passage of warships was left to its discretion (Articles 20 and 21). Turkish control of the Straits was restored; the International Straits Commission's work was handed over to the Turkish Government (Article 24) and the demilitarized zones abolished, allowing Turkey to guard the Straits (this was done by omitting the relevant articles of the Treaty of Lausanne).

The settlement in the Middle East

The settlement of the territories of the former Ottoman Empire outside the Asian frontiers of Turkey was modified by the *Treaty of Lausanne in 1923* (p. 79) which made the full application of the secret inter-Allied wartime agreements of Italian, French and British spheres of influence in Anatolia and Asia Minor impossible to fulfil. At the *Conference of San Remo, April 1920*, the

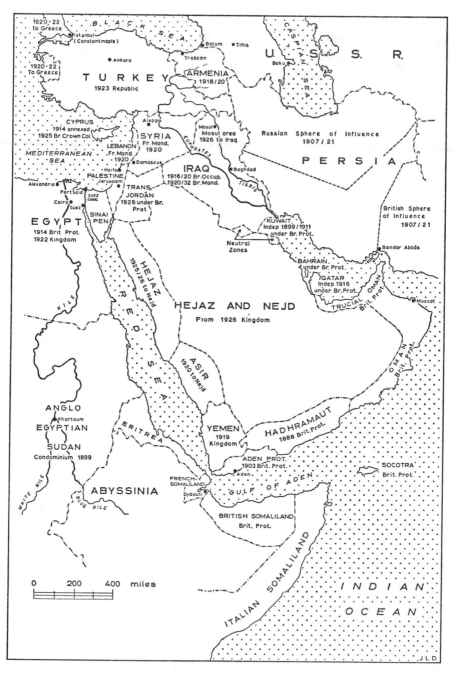

3 The Middle East, 1926

former Ottoman province of Syria was divided between French and British mandates and the Arabian peninsula proper permitted independent Arab government. The outcome of the various Allied decisions and actions for the Middle East was as follows.

1. *Under British influence and/or jurisdiction.* Palestine, where Britain was given full control by the mandate; Transjordan granted its own government by a treaty with Britain in 1928, with British influence over finance, foreign policy and defence. Britain received the mandate for Mesopotamia, renamed Iraq; Iraq became a kingdom in 1921, and gained independence by the *Anglo-Iraq Alliance Treaty, 30 June 1930*, which terminated the British mandate; but Britain retained special rights for the defence of Iraq as well as air bases. Iraq was admitted to the League of Nations in October 1932. Egypt was pronounced independent by Britain on 1 March 1922, but here too Britain retained special rights including the presence of British troops to defend Egypt and the Suez Canal; Britain also reserved to itself the continuing control of the Sudan. A new *Anglo-Egyptian Alliance Treaty, 26 August 1936*, brought the British military occupation of Egypt to an end, but Britain was permitted to continue stationing forces in 'Egyptian territory in the vicinity of the Canal' to defend the Canal. Iran (Persia) was an independent State, but British influence was exerted through controlling interests in the oil industry. Britain had special treaty arrangements with Sheiks in the Persian Gulf. Britain also concluded the *Jedda Treaty, 20 May 1927*, with the independent kingdom of Hejaz and Nejd (renamed Saudi Arabia after 1932). Aden was a Crown colony and British influence predominated over the Aden Protectorate.

2. *Under French influence.* The history of these territories before 1939 is in this sense simpler in that the French mandate was maintained. France had received the mandate of Syria, which the French did not confine to the coastal regions but extended to the interior by military action in July 1920. The French divided their mandate into the State of Syria (1924) and the Lebanon (1920). Draft alliance treaties between France and Syria, 9 September 1936, making provisions for the ending of the mandates but preserving special French rights were not signed owing to the fall of the French Government that had negotiated the treaty. The independent States of Syria and Lebanon were proclaimed by the 'Free French' in 1941 after replacing the Vichy Authorities during the Second World War. The admission of Syria and Lebanon to the U.N., at the foundation of the organization, internationally confirmed the end of the French mandates, and French troops withdrew in 1946.

China, Japan and the Pacific: the Washington Conference, 1921–2

The Paris Peace Conference had assigned to Japan mandates of Germany's Pacific island colonies north of the Equator; Japan had also secured German rights in Shantung. Apart from thus disposing of German assets, no general settlement between the Powers concerning their future relationships in China and the Pacific was reached in Paris. These problems were the subject of the negotiations at the *Washington Conference, November 1921–February 1922*. Of the Powers with interests in the Pacific only Soviet Russia was not invited. Three major treaties were concluded. A treaty on the *limitation of naval armaments, 6 February 1922, between the British Empire, France, Italy, Japan and the United States* (p. 87) limited and set proportions between the signatories of warships of the largest tonnage, mainly battleships, as follows: Britain – 5, United States – 5, Japan – 3, France – 1·7, and Italy – 1·7. A ten-year 'naval holiday' on the construction of capital ships apart from specific exceptions was to be followed by only limited construction until 1936. The disadvantage of the proportions to Japan was counterbalanced by an agreement in the treaty limiting the construction of new naval bases or the expansion of existing bases in the Pacific, but excluding Hawaii. A *Nine Power Treaty concerning China was signed on 6 February 1922 by the British Empire, France, Italy, Japan, the United States, China, Netherlands, Belgium and Portugal* (p. 90). Its purpose was to bolster up the integrity and independence of China, particularly threatened by the special rights demanded by Japan during the First World War. Japan made some concessions in Shantung and the signatories promised to respect the sovereignty and integrity of China and the 'Open Door', but China did not secure the withdrawal of Japanese troops from Manchuria or the recognition of Chinese sovereignty over Manchuria. Nor was China's unequal status abolished. The foreign Powers maintained special rights; by a separate treaty the Chinese were permitted to raise their customs tariff over whose rates the foreign Powers retained control. The Powers were unwilling to give up their existing rights, and only promised not to extend them. The third treaty to be signed was the *Four Power Treaty relating to insular possessions and insular dominions in the Pacific Ocean between the British Empire, France, the United States and Japan, 13 December 1921* (p. 91). This Four Power Treaty replaced the alliance relationship between Britain and Japan (last renewed in 1911). The four Powers undertook to respect the rights of each other in their 'insular possessions and insular dominions in the region of the Pacific Ocean', whereby any American recognition of Japan's position in China and Siberia was avoided. The treaty also contained provision for conferences between the signatories to resolve disputes and frank exchanges if the rights of the signatories were threatened by other Powers.

The League of Nations

The devastation of two great European wars encouraged the victors on both occasions to try to find a better way of conducting diplomacy. After the Napoleonic Wars, the Vienna settlement of 1815 was accompanied by the cooperation of the Great Powers known as the 'Concert of Europe', and the First World War led in 1920 to the *League of Nations* (p. 59) whose aim it was to allow States great and small to find security with justice. Within ten years of the foundation of the League it could be seen that these high hopes were unlikely to be fulfilled. Britain, France and the United States were not willing to check aggression by risking war in the 1930s; no one else could. The League had been weakened at the outset by the Senate's rejection of the peace treaties which meant that the United States could not become a member. But this was not the cause of its failure since the U.S. was frequently ready to cooperate.

The League provided both the rules of conduct between nations and new diplomatic machinery intended to ensure that these rules would be observed. The strength of the League ultimately depended on its members and not on the procedures written into the Covenant. But the will to uphold and strengthen the purposes of the League was lacking when the State to be disciplined was a Great Power. The sacrifices required of the other Great Powers in such a situation were not made. Support for the principles and rules of the League came second when weighed against individual national interests.

The immediate origins of the League are to be found in the advocacy of English and American statesmen, notably the former President Taft, President Wilson, Lord Robert Cecil and Sir Edward Grey. Organized groups of private citizens advocating a new international order after the war were influential in persuading the British and American leaders at Paris that the creation of an international organization was likely to win strong political support in their own countries.

Various drafts reflecting the French, American and British points of view on how to best 'organize' peace were considered at Paris in January and February 1919 by the League Commission, and the text of a completed draft of the Covenant was submitted to the Plenary Session of the peace conference on 14 February 1919. President Wilson then explained to the members of that session that *the Covenant* was based on two principles: (1) that 'no nation shall go to war with any other nation until every other possible means of settling the dispute shall have been full and fairly tried'; and (2) that 'under no circumstances shall any nation seek forcibly to disturb the territorial settlement to be arrived at as the consequence of this peace or to interfere with the political independence of any of the States of the world'.

The League came into existence when the Treaty of Versailles entered into force on 10 January 1920, and was an association of States each retaining its sovereignty. The institutions of the League provided the machinery for working out agreed policies. Its two major purposes were the achievement of international security through collective action, and international cooperation for social and economic welfare. The following articles of the Covenant should be especially noted. In Article 10 members subscribed to a mutual guarantee of the political independence and territorial integrity of all Member States. This was really no more than a declaration of intent, a moral commitment; military support for a victim of aggression was not automatic. The drafting of Article 10 was ambiguous. Any military obligations which might have arisen were in any case made optional when in 1923 an interpretive resolution of Article 10 was adopted by the League which left it to each State to decide how far it was bound to contribute military force to fulfil its obligations.

Articles 12 to 17 provided the League with fact-finding and some arbitral functions. Here too are to be found the sanctions which could be adopted against the aggressor. These sanctions emphasized economic pressure which it was believed would be effective and left the ultimate military obligations of Member States obscure.

The Geneva Protocol of 1924 attempted to strengthen the League by filling in the 'gaps' of the existing Covenant. The Covenant as it stood did not cover all possible situations of aggression and victimization. If the Council of the League, for instance, should fail to reach unanimous agreement on its report on a dispute, or if for any reason that seemed sufficient to it the Council did not report on a dispute, then League sanctions could not be invoked and one State could make war on another with impunity. In any case an individual State desiring to go to war was obliged only to observe a three-month cooling-off period; thereafter the Council was not bound to impose sanctions if the two States involved in a conflict refused to accept the report of the Council, or the decision of the Court of Arbitrators. The Geneva Protocol sought to ensure that all disputes would be settled by some means other than war. Sanctions would, according to the Geneva Protocol, be imposed on any State resorting to war. Without the adoption of the Protocol sanctions could only be imposed when a State was found to be at war in breach of the Covenant. Although the Geneva Protocol was agreed to and recommended to members by the League, the British Conservative Government in 1925 rejected it as it was unwilling to accept a widening of obligations.

The League was ineffective during the decade of aggression 1931-41, but its record of promoting international and social collaboration through such bodies as the Health Organization, World Economic Conferences and the International Labour Organizations was notable. Through the League was devised the mandate system for providing a period of European 'tutelage' over emerging non-European nations or former colonies. The League also sought to ensure the rights of minorities and to carry out humanitarian work for refugees.

By November 1920 there were forty-two members of the League, ten more than the Allied States originally signatories of the treaties of peace. But the United States never became a member. Germany was admitted in 1926 and the U.S.S.R. in 1934. Those Great Powers who planned or carried out aggression left the League one by one in the 1930s: Nazi Germany in 1933, Japan in the same year, Italy in 1937 and the U.S.S.R. was expelled in December 1939 after its attack on Finland. In April 1946, after the establishment of the United Nations, the League was dissolved by resolution of the U.N. Assembly which, however, provided for the continuation of some of its functions.

President Wilson's Fourteen Points, 8 January 1918

We entered this war because violations of right had occurred which touched us to the quick and made the life of our own people impossible unless they were corrected and the world secure once for all against their recurrence. What we demand in this war, therefore, is nothing peculiar to ourselves. It is that the world be made fit and safe to live in; and particularly that it be made safe for every peace-loving nation which, like our own, wishes to live its own life, determine its own institutions, be assured of justice and fair dealing by the other peoples of the world as against force and selfish aggression. All the peoples of the world are in effect partners in this interest, and for our own part we see very clearly that unless justice be done to others it will not be done to us. The programme of the world's peace, therefore, is our programme; and that programme, the only possible programme, as we see it, is this:

I. Open covenants of peace, openly arrived at, after which there shall be no private international understandings of any kind but diplomacy shall proceed always frankly and in the public view.

II. Absolute freedom of navigation upon the seas, outside territorial waters, alike in peace and in war, except as the seas may be closed in whole or in part by international action for the enforcement of international covenants.

III. The removal, so far as possible, of all economic barriers, and the establishment of an equality of trade conditions among all the nations consenting to the peace and associating themselves for its maintenance.

IV. Adequate guarantees given and taken that national armaments will be reduced to the lowest point consistent with domestic safety.

V. A free, open-minded, and absolutely impartial adjustment of all colonial claims, based upon a strict observance of the principle that in determining all such questions of sovereignty the interests of the populations concerned must have equal weight with the equitable claims of the Government whose title is to be determined.

VI. The evacuation of all Russian territory and such a settlement of all questions affecting Russia as will secure the best and freest cooperation of the other nations of the world in obtaining for her an unhampered and unembarrassed opportunity for the independent determination of her own political development and national policy and assure her of a sincere welcome into the society of free nations under institutions of her own choosing; and, more than a welcome, assistance also of every kind that she may need and may herself desire. The treatment accorded Russia by her sister nations in the months to come will be the acid test of their good will, of their comprehension of her needs as distinguished from their own interests, and of their intelligent and unselfish sympathy.

VII. Belgium, the whole world will agree, must be evacuated and restored, without any attempt to limit the sovereignty which she enjoys in common with all other free nations. No other single act will serve as this will serve to restore confidence among the nations in the laws which they have themselves set and determined for the government of their relations with one another. Without this healing act the whole structure and validity of international law is forever impaired.

VIII. All French territory should be freed and the invaded portions restored, and the wrong done to France by Prussia in 1871 in the matter of Alsace-Lorraine, which has unsettled the peace of the world for nearly fifty years, should be righted, in order that peace may once more be made secure in the interest of all.

IX. A readjustment of the frontiers of Italy should be effected along clearly recognizable lines of nationality.

X. The peoples of Austria-Hungary, whose place among the nations we wish to see safeguarded and assured, should be accorded the freest opportunity of autonomous development.

XI. Rumania, Serbia, and Montenegro should be evacuated; occupied territories restored; Serbia accorded free and secure access to the sea; and the relations of the several Balkan States to one another determined by friendly counsel along historically established lines of allegiance and nationality; and international guarantees of the political and economic independence and territorial integrity of the several Balkan States should be entered into.

XII. The Turkish portions of the present Ottoman Empire should be assured a secure sovereignty, but the other nationalities which are now under Turkish rule should be assured an undoubted security of life and an absolutely unmolested opportunity of autonomous development, and the Dardanelles should be permanently opened as a free passage to the ships and commerce of all nations under international guarantees.

XIII. An independent Polish State should be erected which should include the territories inhabited by indisputably Polish populations, which should be assured a free and secure access to the sea, and whose political and economic independence and territorial integrity should be guaranteed by international covenant.

XIV. A general association of nations must be formed under specific covenants for the purpose of affording mutual guarantees of political independence and territorial integrity to great and small States alike.

In regard to these essential rectifications of wrong and assertions of right we feel ourselves to be intimate partners of all the Governments and peoples associated together against the Imperialists. We cannot be separated in interest or divided in purpose. We stand together until the end. . . .

Treaty of Peace between the Allied and Associated Powers and Germany (Treaty of Versailles), 28 June 1919

Part I · The Covenant of the League of Nations

THE HIGH CONTRACTING PARTIES,

In order to promote international co-operation and to achieve international peace and security

by the acceptance of obligations not to resort to war,

by the prescription of open, just and honourable relations between nations,

by the firm establishment of the understandings of international law as the actual rule of conduct among Governments, and

by the maintenance of justice and a scrupulous respect for all treaty obligations in the dealings of organized peoples with one another,

Agree to this Covenant of the League of Nations.

Article 1. The original Members of the League of Nations shall be those of the Signatories which are named in the Annex to this Covenant and also such of those other States named in the Annex as shall accede without reservation to this Covenant. Such accession shall be effected by a declaration deposited with the Secretariat within two months of the coming into force of the Covenant. Notice thereof shall be sent to all other Members of the League.

Any fully self-governing State, Dominion or Colony not named in the Annex may become a Member of the League if its admission is agreed to by two-thirds of the Assembly, provided that it shall give effective guarantees of its sincere intention to observe its international obligations, and shall accept such regulations as may be prescribed by the League in regard to its military, naval and air forces and armaments.

Any Member of the League may, after two years' notice of its intention so to do, withdraw from the League, provided that all its international obligations and all its obligations under this Covenant shall have been fulfilled at the time of its withdrawal.

Article 2. The action of the League under this Covenant shall be effected through the instrumentality of an Assembly and of a Council, with a permanent Secretariat.

Article 3. The Assembly shall consist of Representatives of the Members of the League.

The Assembly shall meet at stated intervals and from time to time as occasion may require at the Seat of the League or at such other place as may be decided upon.

The Assembly may deal at its meetings with any matter within the sphere of action of the League or affecting the peace of the world.

At meetings of the Assembly each Member of the League shall have one vote, and may have not more than three Representatives.

Article 4. The Council shall consist of Representatives of the Principal Allied and Associated Powers, together with Representatives of four other Members of the League. These four Members of the League shall be selected by the Assembly from time to time in its discretion. Until the appointment of the Representatives of the four Members of the League first selected by the Assembly, Representatives of Belgium, Brazil, Spain and Greece shall be members of the Council.

With the approval of the majority of the Assembly, the Council may name additional Members of the League whose Representatives shall always be members of the Council; the Council with like approval may increase the number of

Members of the League to be selected by the Assembly for representation on the Council.

The Council shall meet from time to time as occasion may require, and at least once a year, at the Seat of the League, or at such other place as may be decided upon.

The Council may deal at its meetings with any matter within the sphere of action of the League or affecting the peace of the world.

Any Member of the League not represented on the Council shall be invited to send a Representative to sit as a member at any meeting of the Council during the consideration of matters specially affecting the interests of that Member of the League.

At meetings of the Council, each Member of the League represented on the Council shall have one vote, and may have not more than one Representative.

Article 5. Except where otherwise expressly provided in this Covenant or by the terms of the present Treaty, decisions at any meeting of the Assembly or of the Council shall require the agreement of all the Members of the League represented at the meeting.

All matters of procedure at meetings of the Assembly or of the council, including the appointment of Committees to investigate particular matters, shall be regulated by the Assembly or by the Council and may be decided by a majority of the Members of the League represented at the meeting.

The first meeting of the Assembly and the first meeting of the Council shall be summoned by the President of the United States of America.

Article 6. The permanent Secretariat shall be established at the Seat of the League. The Secretariat shall comprise a Secretary-General and such secretaries and staff as may be required.

The first Secretary-General shall be the person named in the Annex; thereafter the Secretary-General shall be appointed by the Council with the approval of the majority of the Assembly.

The secretaries and staff of the Secretariat shall be appointed by the Secretary-General with the approval of the Council.

The Secretary-General shall act in that capacity at all meetings of the Assembly and of the Council.

The expenses of the Secretariat shall be borne by the Members of the League in accordance with the apportionment of the expenses of the International Bureau of the Universal Postal Union.

Article 7. The Seat of the League is established at Geneva.

The Council may at any time decide that the Seat of the League shall be established elsewhere.

Article 8. The Members of the League recognize that the maintenance of peace requires the reduction of national armaments to the lowest point consistent with national safety and the enforcement by common action of international obligations.

The Council, taking account of the geographical situation and circumstances of each State, shall formulate plans for such reduction for the consideration and action of the several Governments ...

[*Article 9.* Permanent Commission to be set up to advise Council on the execution of Articles 1–8.]

Article 10. The Members of the League undertake to respect and preserve as against external aggression the territorial integrity and existing political independence of all Members of the League. In case of any such aggression or in case of any threat or danger of such aggression the Council shall advise upon the means by which this obligation shall be fulfilled.

Article 11. Any war or threat of war, whether immediately affecting any of the Members of the League or not, is hereby declared a matter of concern to the whole League, and the League shall take any action that may be deemed wise and effectual to safeguard the peace of nations. In case any such emergency should arise the Secretary-General shall on the request of any Member of the League forthwith summon a meeting of the Council.

It is also declared to be the friendly right of each Member of the League to bring to the attention of the Assembly or of the Council any circumstance whatever affecting international relations which threatens to disturb international peace or the good understanding between nations upon which peace depends.

Article 12. The Members of the League agree that if there should arise between them any dispute likely to lead to a rupture, they will submit the matter either to arbitration or to inquiry by the Council, and they agree in no case to resort to war until three months after the award by the arbitrators or the report by the Council.

In any case under this Article the award of the arbitrators shall be made within a reasonable time, and the report of the Council shall be made within six months after the submission of the dispute.

Article 13. The Members of the League agree that whenever any dispute shall arise between them which they recognize to be suitable for submission to arbitration and which cannot be satisfactorily settled by diplomacy, they will submit the whole subject-matter to arbitration.

Disputes as to the interpretation of a treaty, as to any question of international law, as to the existence of any fact which if established would constitute a breach of any international obligation, or as to the extent and nature of the reparation to be made for any such breach, are declared to be among those which are generally suitable for submission to arbitration.

For the consideration of any such dispute the court of arbitration to which the case is referred shall be the court agreed on by the parties to the dispute or stipulated in any convention existing between them.

The Members of the League agree that they will carry out in full good faith any award that may be rendered, and that they will not resort to war against a Member of the League which complies therewith. In the event of any failure to carry out such an award, the Council shall propose what steps should be taken to give effect thereto.

Article 14. The Council shall formulate and submit to the Members of the League for adoption plans for the establishment of a Permanent Court of International Justice. The Court shall be competent to hear and determine any dispute of an international character which the parties thereto submit to it. The Court may also give an advisory opinion upon any dispute or question referred to it by the Council or by the Assembly.

Article 15. If there should arise between Members of the League any dispute likely to lead to a rupture, which is not submitted to arbitration in accordance with Article 13, the Members of the League agree that they will submit the matter to the Council. Any party to the dispute may effect such submission by giving notice of the existence of the dispute to the Secretary-General, who will make all necessary arrangements for a full investigation and consideration thereof.

For this purpose the parties to the dispute will communicate to the Secretary-General, as promptly as possible, statements of their case, with all the relevant facts and papers, and the Council may forthwith direct the publication thereof.

The Council shall endeavour to effect a settlement of the dispute, and if such efforts are successful, a statement shall be made public giving such facts and explanations regarding the dispute and the terms of settlement thereof as the Council may deem appropriate.

If the dispute is not thus settled, the Council either unanimously or by a majority vote shall make and publish a report containing a statement of the facts of the dispute and the recommendations which are deemed just and proper in regard thereto.

Any Member of the League represented on the Council may make public a statement of the facts of the dispute and of its conclusions regarding the same.

If a report by the Council is unanimously agreed to by the members thereof other than the Representatives of one or more of the parties to the dispute, the Members of the League agree that they will not go to war with any party to the dispute which complies with the recommendations of the report.

If the Council fails to reach a report which is unanimously agreed to by the members thereof, other than the Representatives of one or more of the parties to the dispute, the Members of the League reserve to themselves the right to take such action as they shall consider necessary for the maintenance of right and justice.

If the dispute between the parties is claimed by one of them, and is found by the Council, to arise out of a matter which by international law is solely within the domestic jurisdiction of that party, the Council shall so report, and shall make no recommendation as to its settlement.

The Council may in any case under this Article refer the dispute to the Assembly. The dispute shall be so referred at the request of either party to the dispute, provided that such request be made within fourteen days after the submission of the dispute to the Council.

In any case referred to the Assembly, all the provisions of this Article and of Article 12 relating to the action and powers of the Council shall apply to the action and powers of the Assembly, provided that a report made by the Assembly, if concurred in by the Representatives of those Members of the League represented on the Council and of a majority of the other Members of the League, exclusive in each case of the Representatives of the parties to the dispute, shall have the same force as a report by the Council concurred in by all the members thereof other than the Representatives of one or more of the parties to the dispute.

Article 16. Should any Member of the League resort to war in disregard of its covenants under Articles 12, 13 or 15, it shall *ipso facto* be deemed to have committed an act of war against all other Members of the League, which hereby undertake immediately to subject it to the severance of all trade or financial relations, the prohibition of all intercourse between their nationals and the nationals of the covenant-breaking State, and the prevention of all financial, commercial or personal intercourse between the nationals of the covenant-breaking State and the nationals of any other State, whether a Member of the League or not.

It shall be the duty of the Council in such case to recommend to the several Governments concerned what effective military, naval or air force the Members of the League shall severally contribute to the armed forces to be used to protect the covenants of the League.

The Members of the League agree, further, that they will mutually support one another in the financial and economic measures which are taken under this Article, in order to minimize the loss and inconvenience resulting from the above measures, and that they will mutually support one another in resisting any special measures aimed at one of their number by the covenant-breaking State, and that they will take the necessary steps to afford passage through their territory to the forces of any of the Members of the League which are cooperating to protect the covenants of the League.

Any Member of the League which has violated any covenant of the League may be declared to be no longer a Member of the League by a vote of the Council concurred in by the Representatives of all the other Members of the League represented thereon.

Article 17. In the event of a dispute between a Member of the League and a State which is not a Member of the League, or between States not Members of the League, the State or States not Members of the League shall be invited to accept the obligations of Membership in the League for the purposes of such dispute, upon such conditions as the Council may deem just. If such invitation is accepted, the provisions of Articles 12 to 16 inclusive shall be applied . . .

Article 18. Every treaty or international engagement entered into hereafter by any Member of the League shall be forthwith registered with the Secretariat and shall as soon as possible be published by it. No such treaty or international engagement shall be binding until so registered.

Article 19. The Assembly may from time to time advise the reconsideration by Members of the League of treaties which have become inapplicable and the consideration of international conditions whose continuance might endanger the peace of the world.

Article 20. The Members of the League severally agree that this Covenant is accepted as abrogating all obligations or understandings *inter se* which are inconsistent with the terms thereof, and solemnly undertake that they will not hereafter enter into any engagements inconsistent with the terms thereof.

In case any Member of the League shall, before becoming a Member of the League, have undertaken any obligations inconsistent with the terms of this Covenant, it shall be the duty of such Member to take immediate steps to procure its release from such obligations.

Article 21. Nothing in this Covenant shall be deemed to affect the validity of international engagements, such as treaties of arbitration or regional understandings like the Monroe Doctrine, for securing the maintenance of peace.

Article 22. To those colonies and territories which as a consequence of the late war have ceased to be under the sovereignty of the States which formerly governed them and which are inhabited by peoples not yet able to stand by themselves under the strenuous conditions of the modern world, there should be applied the principle that the well-being and development of such peoples form a sacred trust of civilization and that

securities for the performance of this trust should be embodied in this Covenant.

The best method of giving practical effect to this principle is that the tutelage of such peoples should be entrusted to advanced nations who by reason of their resources, their experience or their geographical position can best undertake this responsibility, and who are willing to accept it, and that this tutelage should be exercised by them as Mandatories on behalf of the League.

The character of the mandate must differ according to the stage of the development of the people, the geographical situation of the territory, its economic conditions and other similar circumstances.

Certain communities formerly belonging to the Turkish Empire have reached a stage of development where their existence as independent nations can be provisionally recognized subject to the rendering of administrative advice and assistance by a Mandatory until such time as they are able to stand alone. The wishes of these communities must be a principal consideration in the selection of the Mandatory.

Other peoples, especially those of Central Africa, are at such a stage that the Mandatory must be responsible for the administration of the territory under conditions which will guarantee freedom of conscience and religion, subject only to the maintenance of public order and morals, the prohibition of abuses such as the slave trade, the arms traffic and the liquor traffic, and the prevention of the establishment of fortifications or military and naval bases and of military training of the natives for other than police purposes and the defence of territory, and will also secure equal opportunities for the trade and commerce of other Members of the League.

There are territories, such as Southwest Africa and certain of the South Pacific Islands, which, owing to the sparseness of their population, or their small size, or their remoteness from the centres of civilization, or their geographical contiguity to the territory of the Mandatory, and other circumstances, can be best administered under the laws of the Mandatory as integral portions of its territory, subject to the safeguards above mentioned in the interests of the indigenous population.

In every case of mandate, the Mandatory shall render to the Council an annual report in reference to the territory committed to its charge.

The degree of authority, control, or administration to be exercised by the Mandatory shall, if not previously agreed upon by the Members of the League, be explicitly defined in each case by the Council.

A permanent Commission shall be constituted to receive and examine the annual reports of the Mandatories and to advise the Council on all matters relating to the observance of the mandates.

Article 23. Subject to and in accordance with the provisions of international conventions existing or hereafter to be agreed upon, the Members of the League:

(*a*) will endeavour to secure and maintain fair and humane conditions of labour for men, women, and children, both in their own countries and in all countries to which their commercial and industrial relations extend, and for that purpose will establish and maintain the necessary international organizations;

(*b*) undertake to secure just treatment of the native inhabitants of territories under their control;

(*c*) will entrust the League with the general supervision over the execution of agreements with regard to the traffic in women and children, and the traffic in opium and other dangerous drugs;

(*d*) will entrust the League with the general supervision of the trade in arms and ammunition with the countries in which the control of this traffic is necessary in the common interest;

(*e*) will make provision to secure and maintain freedom of communications and of transit and equitable treatment for the commerce of all Members of the League. In this connection, the special necessities of the regions devastated during the war of 1914–1918 shall be borne in mind;

(*f*) will endeavour to take steps in matters of international concern for the prevention and control of disease.

[*Article 24.* International bureaux to be placed under League if parties consent.]

[*Article 25.* Encouragement of Red Cross.]

Article 26. Amendments to this Covenant will take effect when ratified by the Members of the League whose Representatives compose the Council and by a majority of the Members of the League whose Representatives compose the Assembly.

No such amendment shall bind any Member of the League which signifies its dissent therefrom, but in that case it shall cease to be a Member of the League.

Part II · Boundaries of Germany

Article 27. The boundaries of Germany will be determined as follows ... [see map on p. 39]

Part III · Political clauses for Europe

SECTION I · BELGIUM

Article 31. Germany, recognizing that the Treaties of April 19, 1839, which established the status of Belgium before the war, no longer conform to the requirements of the situation, consents to the abrogation of the said treaties and undertakes immediately to recognize and to observe whatever conventions may be entered into by the Principal Allied and Associated Powers, or by any of them, in concert with the Governments of Belgium and of the Netherlands, to replace the said Treaties of 1839. If her formal adhesion should be required to such conventions or to any of their stipulations, Germany undertakes immediately to give it.

Article 32. Germany recognizes the full sovereignty of Belgium over the whole of the contested territory of Moresnet (called *Moresnet neutre*).

...

[*Article 40.* Germany renounces all rights in Luxembourg.]

SECTION III · LEFT BANK OF THE RHINE

Article 42. Germany is forbidden to maintain or construct any fortifications either on the left bank of the Rhine or on the right bank to the west of a line drawn 50 kilometres to the east of the Rhine.

Article 43. In the area defined above the maintenance and the assembly of armed forces, either permanently or temporarily, and military manœuvres of any kind, as well as the upkeep of all permanent works for mobilization, are in the same way forbidden.

Article 44. In case Germany violates in any manner whatever the provisions of Articles 42 and 43, she shall be regarded as committing a hostile act against the Powers signatory of the present Treaty and as calculated to disturb the peace of the world.

SECTION IV · SAAR BASIN

Article 45. As compensation for the destruction of the coal mines in the north of France and as part payment towards the total reparation due from Germany for the damage resulting from the war, Germany cedes to France in full and absolute possession, with exclusive rights of exploitation, unencumbered and free from all debts and charges of any kind, the coal mines situated in the Saar Basin as defined in Article 48.

...

Article 49. Germany renounces in favour of the League of Nations, in the capacity of trustee, the government of the territory defined above.

At the end of fifteen years from the coming into force of the present Treaty the inhabitants of the said territory shall be called upon to indicate the sovereignty under which they desire to be placed.

SECTION V · ALSACE-LORRAINE

The HIGH CONTRACTING PARTIES, recognizing the moral obligation to redress the wrong done by Germany in 1871 both to the rights of France and to the wishes of the population of Alsace and Lorraine, which were separated from their country in spite of the solemn protest of their representatives at the Assembly of Bordeaux,

Agree upon the following Articles:

Article 51. The territories which were ceded to Germany in accordance with the Preliminaries of Peace signed at Versailles on February 26, 1871, and the Treaty of Frankfurt of May 10, 1871, are restored to French sovereignty as from the date of the Armistice of November 11, 1918.

The provisions of the Treaties establishing the delimitation of the frontiers before 1871 shall be restored.

...

SECTION VI · AUSTRIA

Article 80. Germany acknowledges and will respect strictly the independence of Austria, within the frontiers which may be fixed in a Treaty between that State and the Principal Allied and Associated Powers; she agrees that this independence shall be inalienable, except with the consent of the Council of the League of Nations.

SECTION VII · CZECHO-SLOVAK STATE

Article 81. Germany, in conformity with the action already taken by the Allied and Associated Powers, recognizes the complete independence of the Czecho-Slovak State which will include the autonomous territory of the Ruthenians to the south of the Carpathians. Germany hereby recognizes the frontiers of this State as determined by the Principal Allied and Associated Powers and the other interested States.

...

SECTION VIII · POLAND

Article 87. Germany, in conformity with the action already taken by the Allied and Associated Powers, recognizes the complete independence of Poland, and renounces in her favour all rights and title over the territory bounded by the Baltic Sea, the eastern frontier of Germany as laid down in Article 27 of Part II (Boundaries of Germany) of the present Treaty up to a point situated about 2 kilometres to the east of Lorzendorf, then a line to the acute angle which the northern boundary of Upper Silesia makes about 3 kilometres north-west of Simmenau, then the boundary of Upper Silesia to its meeting point with the old frontier between Germany and Russia, then this frontier to the point where it crosses the course of the Niemen, and then the northern frontier of East Prussia as laid down in Article 28 of Part II aforesaid.

The provisions of this Article do not, however, apply to the territories of East Prussia and the Free City of Danzig, as defined in Article 28 of Part II (Boundaries of Germany) and in Article 100 of Section XI (Danzig) of this Part.

The boundaries of Poland not laid down in the present Treaty will be subsequently determined by the Principal Allied and Associated Powers. . . .

Article 89. Poland undertakes to accord freedom of transit to persons, goods, vessels, carriages, wagons and mails in transit between East Prussia and the rest of Germany over Polish territory, including territorial waters, and to treat them at least as favourably as the persons, goods, vessels, carriages, wagons and mails respectively of Polish or of any other more favoured nationality, origin, importation, starting point, or ownership as regards facilities, restrictions and all other matters.

Goods in transit shall be exempt from all customs or other similar duties.

Freedom of transit will extend to telegraphic and telephonic services under the conditions laid down by the conventions referred to in Article 98.

. . .

Article 93. Poland accepts and agrees to embody in a Treaty with the Principal Allied and Associated Powers such provisions as may be deemed necessary by the said Powers to protect the interests of inhabitants of Poland who differ from the majority of the population in race, language or religion.

Poland further accepts and agrees to embody in a Treaty with the said Powers such provisions as they may deem necessary to protect freedom of transit and equitable treatment of the commerce of other nations.

Section IX · East Prussia

Article 94. In the area between the southern frontier of East Prussia, as described in Article 28 of Part II (Boundaries of Germany) of the present Treaty, and the line described below, the inhabitants will be called upon to indicate by a vote the State to which they wish to belong. . . .

Section X · Memel

Article 99. Germany renounces in favour of the Principal Allied and Associated Powers all rights and title over the territories included between the Baltic, the north-eastern frontier of East Prussia as defined in Article 28 of Part II (Boundaries of Germany) of the present Treaty and the former frontier between Germany and Russia.

Germany undertakes to accept the settlement made by the Principal Allied and Associated Powers in regard to these territories, particularly in so far as concerns the nationality of the inhabitants.

Section XI · Free City of Danzig

Article 100. Germany renounces in favour of the Principal Allied and Associated Powers all rights and title over the territory comprised within the following limits. . . .

Article 102. The Principal Allied and Associated Powers undertake to establish the town of Danzig, together with the rest of the territory described in Article 100, as a Free City. It will be placed under the protection of the League of Nations.

Article 103. A constitution for the Free City of Danzig shall be drawn up by the duly appointed representatives of the Free City in agreement with a High Commissioner to be appointed by the League of Nations. This constitution shall be placed under the guarantee of the League of Nations.

The High Commissioner will also be entrusted with the duty of dealing in the first instance with all differences arising beween Poland and the Free City of Danzig in regard to this Treaty or any arrangements or agreements made thereunder.

The High Commissioner shall reside at Danzig.

Article 104. The Principal Allied and Associated Powers undertake to negotiate a Treaty between the Polish Government and the Free City of Danzig, which shall come into force at the same time as the establishment of the said Free City, with the following objects:

(1) To effect the inclusion of the Free City of Danzig within the Polish customs frontiers, and to establish a free area in the port;

(2) To ensure to Poland without any restriction the free use and service of all waterways, docks, basins, wharves and other works within the territory of the Free City necessary for Polish imports and exports;

(3) To ensure to Poland the control and administration of the Vistula and of the whole railway system within the Free City, except such street and other railways as serve primarily the needs of the Free City, and of postal, telegraphic and telephonic communication between Poland and the port of Danzig;

(4) To ensure to Poland the right to develop and improve the waterways, docks, basins, wharves, railways and other works and means of communication mentioned in this Article, as well as to lease or purchase through appropriate processes such land and other property as may be necessary for these purposes;

(5) To provide against any discrimination within the Free City of Danzig to the detriment of citizens of Poland and other persons of Polish origin or speech;

(6) To provide that the Polish Government shall undertake the conduct of the foreign relations of the Free City of Danzig as well as the diplomatic protection of citizens of that city when abroad.

SECTION XIV · RUSSIA AND RUSSIAN STATES

Article 116. Germany acknowledges and agrees to respect as permanent and inalienable the independence of all the territories which were part of the former Russian Empire on August 1, 1914.

In accordance with the provisions of Article 259 of Part IX (Financial Clauses) and Article 292 of Part X (Economic Clauses) Germany accepts definitely the abrogation of the Brest-Litovsk Treaties and of all other treaties, conventions and agreements entered into by her with the Maximalist Government in Russia.

The Allied and Associated Powers formally reserve the rights of Russia to obtain from Germany restitution and reparation based on the principles of the present Treaty.

Article 117. Germany undertakes to recognize the full force of all treaties or agreements which may be entered into by the Allied and Associated Powers with States now existing or coming into existence in future in the whole or part of the former Empire of Russia as it existed on August 1, 1914, and to recognize the frontiers of any such States as determined therein.

Part IV · German rights and interests outside Germany

Article 118. In territory outside her European frontiers as fixed by the present Treaty, Germany renounces all rights, titles and privileges whatever in or over territory which belonged to her or to her allies, and all rights, titles and privileges whatever their origin which she held as against the Allied and Associated Powers.

Germany hereby undertakes to recognize and to conform to the measures which may be taken now or in the future by the Principal Allied and Associated Powers, in agreement where necessary with third Powers, in order to carry the above stipulation into effect.

In particular Germany declares her acceptance of the following Articles relating to certain special subjects.

SECTION I · GERMAN COLONIES

Article 119. Germany renounces in favour of the Principal Allied and Associated Powers all her rights and titles over her oversea possessions. . . .

[*Article 128.* Germany renounces all rights acquired in 1901 in China.]

[*Article 138.* Germany renounces all rights in Liberia.]

[*Article 141.* Germany renounces all rights in Morocco.]

[*Article 147.* Germany renounces all rights in Egypt.]

SECTION VIII · SHANTUNG

Article 156. Germany renounces, in favour of Japan, all her rights, title and privileges – particularly those concerning the territory of Kiaochow, railways, mines and submarine cables – which she acquired in virtue of the Treaty concluded by her with China on March 6, 1898, and of all other arrangements relative to the Province of Shantung. . . .

Part V · Military, naval and air clauses

In order to render possible the initiation of a general limitation of the armaments of all nations, Germany undertakes strictly to observe the military, naval and air clauses which follow.

SECTION I · MILITARY CLAUSES

Chapter I: Effectives and cadres of the German army

Article 159. The German military forces shall be demobilized and reduced as prescribed hereinafter.

Article 160. 1. By a date which must not be later than March 31, 1920, the German army must not comprise more than seven divisions of infantry and three divisions of cavalry.

After that date the total number of effectives in the army of the States constituting Germany must not exceed one hundred thousand men, including officers and establishments of depots. The army shall be devoted exclusively to the maintenance of order within the territory and to the control of the frontiers.

. . .

Chapter II: Armament, munitions and material

Article 164. Up till the time at which Germany is admitted as a member of the League of Nations the German army must not possess an armament greater than the amounts fixed in Table No. II annexed to this Section. . . .

Article 173. Universal compulsory military service shall be abolished in Germany.

The German army may only be constituted and recruited by means of voluntary enlistment.

Article 174. The period of enlistment for non-commissioned officers and privates must be twelve consecutive years. . . .

Article 175. The officers who are retained in the army must undertake the obligation to serve in it up to the age of forty-five years at least. . . .

Chapter IV: Fortifications

Article 180. All fortified works, fortresses and field works situated in German territory to the west of a line drawn 50 kilometres to the east of the Rhine shall be disarmed and dismantled. . . .

[*Article 181.* Naval limitation to six battleships and thirty smaller warships; no submarines.]

[*Article 198.* No military or naval air force.]

Section IV · Inter-Allied Commissions of Control

Article 203. All the military, naval and air clauses contained in the present Treaty, for the execution of which a time limit is prescribed, shall be executed by Germany under the control of Inter-Allied Commissions specially appointed for this purpose by the Principal Allied and Associated Powers. . . .

Part VIII · Reparation

Section I · General provisions

Article 231. The Allied and Associated Governments affirm and Germany accepts the responsibility of Germany and her allies for causing all the loss and damage to which the Allied and Associated Governments and their nationals have been subjected as a consequence of the war imposed upon them by the aggression of Germany and her allies.

Article 232. The Allied and Associated Governments recognize that the resources of Germany are not adequate, after taking into account permanent diminutions of such resources which will result from other provisions of the present Treaty, to make complete reparation for all such loss and damage.

The Allied and Associated Governments, however, require, and Germany undertakes, that she will make compensation for all damage done to the civilian population of the Allied and Associated Powers and to their property during the period of the belligerency of each as an Allied or Associated Power against Germany by such aggression by land, by sea and from the air, and in general all damage as defined in Annex I hereto.

In accordance with Germany's pledges, already given, as to complete restoration for Belgium, Germany undertakes, in addition to the compensation for damage elsewhere in this Part provided for, as a consequence of the violation of the Treaty of 1839, to make reimbursement of all sums which Belgium has borrowed from the Allied and Associated Governments up to November 11, 1918, together with interest at the rate of five per cent (5%) per annum on such sums. This amount shall be determined by the Reparation Commission. . . .

Article 233. The amount of the above damage for which compensation is to be made by Germany shall be determined by an Inter-Allied Commission, to be called the *Reparation Commission* and constituted in the form and with the powers set forth hereunder and in Annexes II to VII inclusive hereto.

This Commission shall consider the claims and give to the German Government a just opportunity to be heard.

The findings of the Commission as to the amount of damage defined as above shall be concluded and notified to the German Government on or before May 1, 1921, as representing the extent of that Government's obligations.

The Commission shall concurrently draw up a schedule of payments prescribing the time and manner for securing and discharging the entire obligation within a period of thirty years from May 1, 1921. If, however, within the period mentioned, Germany fails to discharge her obligations, any balance remaining unpaid may, within the discretion of the Commission, be postponed for settlement in subsequent years, or may be handled otherwise in such manner as the Allied and Associated Governments, acting in accordance with the procedure laid down in this Part of the present Treaty, shall determine.

Part IX · Financial clauses

Article 248. Subject to such exceptions as the Reparation Commission may approve, a first charge upon all the assets and revenues of the German Empire and its constituent States shall be the cost of reparation and all other costs arising under the present Treaty or any treaties or agreements supplementary thereto or under arrangements concluded between

Germany and the Allied and Associated Powers during the Armistice or its extensions. . . .

Article 249. There shall be paid by the German Government the total cost of all armies of the Allied and Associated Governments in occupied German territory from the date of the signature of the Armistice of November 11, 1918, including the keep of men and beasts, lodging and billeting, pay and allowances, salaries and wages, bedding, heating, lighting, clothing, equipment, harness and saddlery, armament and rolling stock, air services, treatment of sick and wounded, veterinary and remount services, transport service of all sorts (such as by rail, sea or river, motor lorries), communications and correspondence, and in general the cost of all administrative or technical services the working of which is necessary for the training of troops and for keeping their numbers up to strength and preserving their military efficiency.

The cost of such liabilities under the above heads so far as they relate to purchases or requisitions by the Allied and Associated Governments in the occupied territories shall be paid by the German Government to the Allied and Associated Governments in marks at the current or agreed rate of exchange. All other of the above costs shall be paid in gold marks.

Part XIV · Guarantees

Section I · Western Europe

Article 428. As a guarantee for the execution of the present Treaty by Germany, the German territory situated to the west of the Rhine, together with the bridgeheads, will be occupied by Allied and Associated troops for a period of fifteen years from the coming into force of the present Treaty.

Article 429. If the conditions of the present Treaty are faithfully carried out by Germany, the occupation referred to in Article 428 will be successively restricted as follows:

(i) At the expiration of five years there will be evacuated: the bridgehead of Cologne and the territories north of a line running along the Ruhr, then along the railway Jülich, Düren, Euskirchen, Rheinbach, thence along the road Rheinbach to Sinzig, and reaching the Rhine at the confluence with the Ahr; the roads, railways and places mentioned above being excluded from the area evacuated.

(ii) At the expiration of ten years there will be evacuated: the bridgehead of Coblenz and the territories north of a line to be drawn from the intersection between the frontiers of Belgium, Germany and Holland, running about 4 kilometres south of Aix-la-Chapelle, then to and following the crest of Forst Gemünd, then east of the railway of the Urft Valley, then along Blankenheim, Valdorf, Dreis, Ulmen to and following the Moselle from Bremm to Nehren, then passing by Kappel and Simmern, then following the ridge of the heights between Simmern and the Rhine and reaching this river at Bacharach; all the places, valleys, roads and railways mentioned above being excluded from the area evacuated.

(iii) At the expiration of fifteen years there will be evacuated: the bridgehead of Mainz, the bridgehead of Kehl and the remainder of the German territory under occupation.

If at that date the guarantees against unprovoked aggression by Germany are not considered sufficient by the Allied and Associated Governments, the evacuation of the occupying troops may be delayed to the extent regarded as necessary for the purpose of obtaining the required guarantees.

Article 430. In case either during the occupation or after the expiration of the fifteen years referred to above the Reparation Commission finds that Germany refuses to observe the whole or part of her obligations under the present Treaty with regard to reparation, the whole or part of the areas specified in Article 429 will be reoccupied immediately by the Allied and Associated forces.

Article 431. If before the expiration of the period of fifteen years Germany complies with all the undertakings resulting from the present Treaty, the occupying forces will be withdrawn immediately.

Article 432. All matters relating to the occupation and not provided for by the present Treaty shall be regulated by subsequent agreements, which Germany hereby undertakes to observe.

SECTION II · EASTERN EUROPE

Article 433. As a guarantee for the execution of the provisions of the present Treaty, by which Germany accepts definitely the abrogation of the Brest-Litovsk Treaty, and of all treaties, conventions and agreements entered into by her with the Maximalist Government in Russia, and in order to ensure the restoration of peace and good government in the Baltic Provinces and Lithuania, all German troops at present in the said territories shall return to within the frontiers of Germany as soon as the Governments of the Principal Allied and Associated Powers shall think the moment suitable, having regard to the internal situation of these territories. These troops shall abstain from all requisitions and seizures and from any other coercive measures, with a view to obtaining supplies intended for Germany, and shall in no way interfere with such measures for national defence as may be adopted by the Provisional Governments of Estonia, Latvia and Lithuania.

No other German troops shall, pending the evacuation or after the evacuation is complete, be admitted to the said territories.

Part XV · Miscellaneous provisions

Article 434. Germany undertakes to recognize the full force of the Treaties of Peace and Additional Conventions which may be concluded by the Allied and Associated Powers with the Powers who fought on the side of Germany and to recognize whatever dispositions may be made concerning the territories of the former Austro-Hungarian Monarchy, of the Kingdom of Bulgaria and of the Ottoman Empire, and to recognize the new States within their frontiers as there laid down.

Treaty between France and Great Britain (Treaty of Guarantee), 28 June 1919

Assistance to France in the event of unprovoked aggression by Germany

Article 1. In case the following stipulations relating to the Left Bank of the Rhine contained in the Treaty of Peace with Germany signed at Versailles the 28th day of June, 1919, by the British Empire, the French Republic, and the United States of America among other Powers:

ARTICLE 42. Germany is forbidden to maintain or construct any fortifications either on the left bank of the Rhine or on the right bank to the west of a line drawn 50 kilometres to the east of the Rhine.

ARTICLE 43. In the area defined above the maintenance and assembly of armed forces, either permanently, or temporarily, and military manœuvres of any kind, as well as the upkeep of all permanent works for mobilization, are in the same way forbidden.

ARTICLE 44. In case Germany violates in any manner whatsoever the provisions of Articles 42 and 43, she shall be regarded as committing a hostile act against the Powers signatory of the present Treaty and as calculated to disturb the peace of the world.

may not at first provide adequate security and protection to France, Great Britain agrees to come immediately to her assistance in the event of any unprovoked movement of aggression against her being made by Germany.

Article 2. The present Treaty, in similar terms with the Treaty of even date for the same purpose concluded between the French Republic and the United States of America, a copy of which Treaty is annexed hereto, will only come into force when the latter is ratified.

Article 3. The present Treaty must be submitted to the Council of the League of Nations and must be recognized by the Council, acting if need be by a majority, as an engagement which is consistent with the Covenant of the League; it will continue in force until on the application of one of the Parties to it the Council, acting if need be by a majority, agree that

the League itself affords sufficient protection.

Article 4. The present Treaty shall before ratification by His Majesty be submitted to Parliament for approval.

It shall before ratification by the President of the French Republic be submitted to the French Chambers for approval.

Article 5. The present Treaty shall impose no obligation upon any of the Dominions of the British Empire unless and until it is approved by the Parliament of the Dominion concerned.

The present Treaty shall be ratified, and shall, subject to Articles 2 and 4, come into force at the same time as the Treaty of Peace with Germany of even date comes into force for the British Empire and the French Republic.

In Faith Whereof the above-named plenipotentiaries have signed the present Treaty, drawn up in the English and French languages.

Done in duplicate at Versailles, on the twenty-eighth day of June, 1919.

(Seal) D. LLOYD GEORGE
(Seal) ARTHUR JAMES BALFOUR
(Seal) G. CLEMENCEAU
(Seal) S. PICHON

Treaty between the Allied and Associated Powers and Poland on the protection of minorities, 28 June 1919

Article 2. Poland undertakes to assure full and complete protection of life and liberty to all inhabitants of Poland without distinction of birth, nationality, language, race or religion.

All inhabitants of Poland shall be entitled to the free exercise, whether public or private, of any creed, religion or belief, whose practices are not inconsistent with public order or public morals.

Article 3. Poland admits and declares to be Polish nationals *ipso facto* and with-

out the requirement of any formality German, Austrian, Hungarian or Russian nationals habitually resident at the date of the coming into force of the present Treaty in territory which is or may be recognized as forming part of Poland, but subject to any provisions in the Treaties of Peace with Germany or Austria respectively relating to persons who became resident in such territory after a specified date.

Nevertheless, the persons referred to above, who are over eighteen years of age will be entitled under the conditions contained in the said Treaties to opt for any other nationality which may be open to them. Option by a husband will cover his wife and option by parents will cover their children under eighteen years of age....

Article 7. All Polish nationals shall be equal before the law and shall enjoy the same civil and political rights without distinction as to race, language or religion.

Differences of religion, creed or confession shall not prejudice any Polish national in matters relating to the enjoyment of civil or political rights, as for instance admission to public employments, functions and honours, or exercise of professions and industries.

No restriction shall be imposed on the free use by any Polish national of any language in private intercourse, in commerce, in religion, in the press or in publications of any kind, or at public meetings....

Article 8. Polish nationals who belong to racial, religious or linguistic minorities shall enjoy the same treatment and security in law and in fact as the other Polish nationals. In particular they shall have an equal right to establish, manage and control at their own expense charitable, religious and social institutions, schools and other educational establishments, with the right to use their own language and to exercise their religion freely therein.

Article 9. Poland will provide in the public educational system in towns and districts in which a considerable proportion of Polish nationals of other than Polish speech are residents adequate facilities for ensuring that in the primary schools the instruction shall be given to the children of such Polish nationals through the medium of their own language. This provision shall not prevent the Polish Government from making the teaching of the Polish language obligatory in the said schools.

• • •

Article 11. Jews shall not be compelled to perform any act which constitutes a violation of their Sabbath, nor shall they be placed under any disability by reason of their refusal to attend courts of law or to perform any legal business on their Sabbath. This provision however shall not exempt Jews from such obligations as shall be imposed upon all other Polish citizens for the necessary purposes of military service, national defence or the preservation of public order....

Treaty of Peace between the Allied and Associated Powers and Turkey (Treaty of Sèvres), 10 August 1920

[Part I · Covenant of the League of Nations]

Part II · Frontiers of Turkey

Article 27. I. In Europe, the frontiers of Turkey will be laid down as follows:

1. *The Black Sea:* From the entrance of the Bosphorus to the point described below.

2. *With Greece:* From a point to be chosen on the Black Sea near the mouth of the Biyuk Dere, situated about 7 kilometres north-west of Podima, south-westwards to the most north-westerly point of the limit of the basin of the Istranja Dere (about 8 kilometres north-west of Istranja),

a line to be fixed on the ground passing through Kapilja Dagh and Uchbunar Tepe;

thence south-south-eastwards to a point to be chosen on the railway from Chorlu to Chatalja about 1 kilometre west of the railway station of Sinekli,

a line following as far as possible the western limit of the basin of the Istranja Dere;

thence south-eastwards to a point to be chosen between Fener and Kurfali on the watershed between the basins of those rivers which flow into Biyuk Chekmeje Geul, on the north-east, and the basin of those rivers which flow direct into the Sea of Marmora on the south-west,

a line to be fixed on the ground passing south of Sinekli;

thence south-eastwards to a point to be chosen on the Sea of Marmora about 1 kilometre south-west of Kalikratia,

a line following as far as possible this watershed.

3. *The Sea of Marmora:* From the point defined above to the entrance of the Bosphorus.

II. In Asia, the frontier of Turkey will be laid down as follows:

1. *On the West and South:* From the entrance of the Bosphorus into the Sea of Marmora to a point described below, situated in the eastern Mediterranean Sea in the neighbourhood of the Gulf of Alexandretta near Karatash Burun,

the Sea of Marmora, the Dardanelles, and the Eastern Mediterranean Sea; the islands of the Sea of Marmora, and those which are situated within a distance of 3 miles from the coast, remaining Turkish, subject to the provisions of Section IV and Articles 84 and 122, Part III (Political Clauses).

2. *With Syria:* From a point to be chosen on the eastern bank of the outlet of the Hassan Dede, about 3 kilometres north-west of Karatash Burun, north-eastwards to a point to be chosen on the Djaihun Irmak about 1 kilometre north of Babeli,

a line to be fixed on the ground passing north of Karatash;

thence to Kesik Kale,

the course of the Djaihun Irmak upstream;

thence north-eastwards to a point to be chosen on the Djaihun Irmak about 15 kilometres east-southeast of Karsbazar,

a line to be fixed on the ground passing north of Kara Tepe;

thence to the bend in the Djaihun Irmak situated west of Duldul Dagh,

the course of the Djaihun Irmak upstream;

thence in a general south-easterly direction to a point to be chosen on Emir Musi Dagh about 15 kilometres south-south-west of Giaour Geul,

a line to be fixed on the ground at a distance of about 18 kilometres from the railway, and leaving Duldul Dagh to Syria;

thence eastwards to a point to be chosen about 5 kilometres north of Urfa,

a generally straight line from west to east to be fixed on the ground passing north of the roads connecting the towns of Baghche, Aintab, Biridjik, and Urfa and leaving the last three named towns to Syria;

thence eastwards to the south-western extremity of the bend in the Tigris about 6 kilometres north of Azekh (27 kilometres west to Djezire-ibn-Omar),

a generally straight line from west to east to be fixed on the ground leaving the town of Mardin to Syria;

thence to a point to be chosen on the Tigris between the point of confluence of the Khabur Su with the Tigris and the bend in the Tigris situated about 10 kilometres north of this point,

the course of the Tigris downstream, leaving the island on which is situated the town of Djezire-ibn-Omar to Syria.

3. *With Mesopotamia:* Thence in a general easterly direction to a point to be chosen on the northern boundary of the *vilayet* of Mosul,

a line to be fixed on the ground;

thence eastwards to the point where it meets the frontier between Turkey and Persia,

the northern boundary of the *vilayet*

of Mosul, modified, however, so as to pass south of Amadia.

4. *On the East and the North-east:* From the point above defined to the Black Sea, the existing frontier between Turkey and Persia, then the former frontier between Turkey and Russia, subject to the provisions of Article 89.

5. *The Black Sea.*

Part III · Political clauses

SECTION I · CONSTANTINOPLE

Article 36. Subject to the provisions of the present Treaty, the High Contracting Parties agree that the rights and title of the Turkish Government over Constantinople shall not be affected, and that the said Government and His Majesty the Sultan shall be entitled to reside there and to maintain there the capital of the Turkish State.

Nevertheless, in the event of Turkey failing to observe faithfully the provisions of the present Treaty, or of any treaties or conventions supplementary thereto, particularly as regards the protection of the rights of racial, religious or linguistic minorities, the Allied Powers expressly reserve the right to modify the above provisions, and Turkey hereby agrees to accept any dispositions which may be taken in this connection.

SECTION II · STRAITS

Article 37. The navigation of the Straits, including the Dardanelles, the Sea of Marmora and the Bosphorus, shall in future be open, both in peace and war, to every vessel of commerce or of war and to military and commercial aircraft, without distinction of flag.

These waters shall not be subject to blockade, nor shall any belligerent right be exercised nor any act of hostility be committed within them, unless in pursuance of a decision of the Council of the League of Nations.

Article 38. The Turkish Government recognizes that it is necessary to take further measures to ensure the freedom of navigation provided for in Article 37, and accordingly delegates, so far as it is concerned, to a Commission to be called the 'Commission of the Straits', and hereinafter referred to as 'the Commission', the control of the waters specified in Article 39.

The Greek Government, so far as it is concerned, delegates to the Commission the same powers and undertakes to give it in all respects the same facilities.

Such control shall be exercised in the name of the Turkish and Greek Governments respectively, and in the manner provided in this Section.

Article 39. The authority of the Commission will extend to all the waters between the Mediterranean mouth of the Dardanelles and the Black Sea mouth of the Bosphorus, and to the waters within three miles of each of these mouths.

This authority may be exercised on shore to such extent as may be necessary for the execution of the provisions of this Section.

Article 40. The Commission shall be composed of representatives appointed respectively by the United States of America (if and when that Government is willing to participate), the British Empire, France, Italy, Japan, Russia (if and when Russia becomes a member of the League of Nations), Greece, Roumania, and Bulgaria and Turkey (if and when the two latter States become members of the League of Nations). Each Power shall appoint one representative. The representatives of the United States of America, the British Empire, France, Italy, Japan and Russia shall each have two votes. The representatives of Greece, Roumania, and Bulgaria and Turkey shall each have one vote. Each Commissioner shall be removable only by the Government which appointed him.

Article 42. The Commission will exercise the powers conferred on it by the present Treaty in complete independence of the local authority. It will have its own flag, its own budget and its separate organization.

Article 43. Within the limits of its jurisdiction as laid down in Article 39 the Commission will be charged with the following duties:

(*a*) the execution of any works considered necessary for the improvement of the channels or the approaches to harbours;

(*b*) the lighting and buoying of the channels;

(*c*) the control of pilotage and towage;

(*d*) the control of anchorages;

(*e*) the control necessary to assure the application in the ports of Constantinople and Haidar Pasha of the régime prescribed in Articles 335 to 344, Part XI (Ports, Waterways and Railways) of the present Treaty;

(*f*) the control of all matters relating to wrecks and salvage;

(*g*) the control of lighterage.

Article 44. In the event of the Commission finding that the liberty of passage is being interfered with, it will inform the representatives at Constantinople of the Allied Powers providing the occupying forces provided for in Article 178. These representatives will thereupon concert with the naval and military commanders of the said forces such measures as may be deemed necessary to preserve the freedom of the Straits. Similar action shall be taken by the said representatives in the event of any external action threatening the liberty of passage of the Straits.

...

Article 48. In order to facilitate the execution of the duties with which it is entrusted by this Section, the Commission shall have power to organize such a force of special police as may be necessary. This force shall be drawn so far as possible from the native population of the zone of the Straits and islands referred to in Article 178, Part V (Military, Naval and Air Clauses), excluding the islands of Lemnos, Imbros, Samothrace, Tenedos and Mitylene. The said force shall be commanded by foreign police officers appointed by the Commission.

[Provision for autonomy, and later on, if people were considered ready, independence.]

SECTION IV · SMYRNA

Article 65. The provisions of this Section will apply to the city of Smyrna and the adjacent territory defined in Article 66, until the determination of their final status in accordance with Article 83.

Article 66. The geographical limits of the territory adjacent to the city of Smyrna will be laid down as follows....

[*Articles 69–71.* The city of Smyrna and territory defined in Article 66 to remain under Turkish sovereignty. Turkey however transfers to the Greek Government the exercise of her rights over these territories. Greek Government will be responsible for administration and will maintain such military forces necessary for order and public security.]

[*Article 72.* A local parliament to be set up; electoral system to ensure proportional representation of all sections of the population including linguistic, racial and religious minorities.]

...

Article 83. When a period of five years shall have elapsed after the coming into force of the present Treaty the local parliament referred to in Article 72 may, by a majority of votes, ask the Council of the League of Nations for the definitive incorporation in the Kingdom of Greece of the city of Smyrna and the territory defined in Article 66. The Council may require, as a preliminary, a plebiscite under conditions which it will lay down.

In the event of such incorporation as a result of the application of the foregoing paragraph, the Turkish sovereignty referred to in Article 69 shall cease. Turkey hereby renounces in that event in favour of Greece all rights and title over the city of Smyrna and the territory defined in Article 66.

SECTION V · GREECE

Article 84. Without prejudice to the frontiers of Bulgaria laid down by the Treaty of Peace signed at Neuilly-sur-Seine on November 27, 1919, Turkey renounces in favour of Greece all rights and title over the territories of the former Turkish Empire in Europe situated outside the frontiers of Turkey as laid down by the present Treaty.

The islands of the Sea of Marmora are not included in the transfer of sovereignty effected by the above paragraph.

Turkey further renounces in favour of Greece all her rights and title over the islands of Imbros and Tenedos. . . .

Treaty of Friendship between Russia and Turkey, 16 March 1921

The Government of the Russian Socialist Federal Soviet Republic and the Government of the Grand National Assembly of Turkey, sharing as they do the principles of the liberty of nations, and the right of each nation to determine its own fate, and taking into consideration, moreover, the common struggle undertaken against imperialism, foreseeing that the difficulties arising for the one would render worse the position of the other, and inspired by the desire to bring about lasting good relations and uninterrupted sincere friendship between themselves, based on mutual interests, have decided to sign an agreement to assure amicable and fraternal relations between the two countries. . . .

Article I. Each of the Contracting Parties agrees not to recognize any peace treaty or other international agreement imposed upon the other against its will. The Government of the R.S.F.S.R. agrees not to recognize any international agreement relating to Turkey which is not recognized by the National Government of Turkey, at present represented by the Grand National Assembly.

The expression 'Turkey' in the present Treaty is understood to mean the territories included in the Turkish National Pact on the 28th January 1920, eleborated and proclaimed by the Ottoman Chamber of Deputies in Constantinople, and communicated to the press and to all foreign Governments.

The north-east frontier of Turkey is fixed as follows: [frontier definition]

Article II. Turkey agrees to cede to Georgia the right of suzerainty over the town and the port of Batum, and the territory situated to the north of the frontier mentioned in Article I, which formed a part of the district of Batum, on the following conditions:

(a) The population of the localities specified in the present Article shall enjoy a generous measure of autonomy, assuring to each community its cultural and religious rights, and allowing them to enact agrarian laws in accordance with the wishes of the population of the said districts.

(b) Turkey will be granted free transit for all Turkish imports and exports through the port of Batum, without payment of taxes and customs duties and without delays. The right of making use of the port of Batum without special expenses is assured to Turkey.

Article III. Both Contracting Parties agree that the Nakhichevan district, with the boundaries shown in Annex 1 (C) to the present Treaty, shall form an autonomous territory under the protection of Azerbaijan, on condition that the latter cannot transfer this protectorate to any third State. . . .

Article IV. The Contracting Parties, establishing contact between the national movement for the liberation of the Eastern peoples and the struggle of the workers of Russia for a new social order, solemnly recognize the right of these nations to freedom and independence, also their right to choose a form of government according to their own wishes.

Article V. In order to assure the opening of the Straits to the commerce of all nations, the Contracting Parties agree to entrust the final elaboration of an international agreement concerning the Black Sea to a conference composed of delegates of the littoral States, on condition that the decisions of the above-mentioned conference shall not be of such a nature as to diminish the full sovereignty of Turkey or the security of Constantinople, her capital.

Article VI. The Contracting Parties agree that the treaties concluded heretofore between the two countries do not correspond with their mutual interests, and therefore agree that the said treaties shall be considered as annulled and abrogated.

The Government of the R.S.F.S.R. declares that it considers Turkey to be liberated from all financial and other liabilities based on agreements concluded between Turkey and the Tsarist Government.

Article VII. The Government of the R.S.F.S.R., holding that the Capitulations régime is incompatible with the full exercise of sovereign rights and the national development of any country, declares this régime and any rights connected therewith to be null and void.

Article VIII. The Contracting Parties undertake not to tolerate in their respective territories the formation and stay of organizations or associations claiming to be the Government of the other country or of a part of its territory and organizations whose aim is to wage warfare against the other State.

Russia and Turkey mutually accept the same obligation with regard to the Soviet Republic of the Caucasus.

'Turkish territory', within the meaning of this Article, is understood to be territory under the direct civil and military administration of the Government of the Grand National Assembly of Turkey.

Article IX. To secure uninterrupted communication between the two countries, both Contracting Parties undertake to carry out urgently, and in agreement one with the other, all necessary measures for the security and development of the railway lines, telegraph and other means of communication, and to assure free movement of persons and goods between the two countries. It is agreed that the regulations in force in each country shall be applied as regards the movement, entry and exit of travellers and goods.

Article X. The nationals of the Contracting Parties residing on the territory of the other shall be treated in accordance with the laws in force in the country of their residence, with the exception of those connected with national defence, from which they are exempt....

Article XI. The Contracting Parties agree to treat the nationals of one of the parties residing in the territory of the other in accordance with the most-favoured-nation principles.

This Article will not be applied to citizens of the Soviet Republics allied with Russia, nor to nationals of Mussulman States allied with Turkey.

Article XII. Any inhabitant of the territories forming part of Russia prior to 1918, and over which Turkish sovereignty has been acknowledged by the Government of the R.S.F.S.R., in the present Treaty, shall be free to leave Turkey and to take with him all his goods and possessions or the proceeds of their sale. The population of the territory of Batum, sovereignty over which has been granted to Georgia by Turkey, shall enjoy the same right.

Article XIII. Russia undertakes to return, at her own expense within three months, to the north-east frontier of Turkey all

Turkish prisoners of war and interned civilians in the Caucasus and in European Russia, and those in Asiatic Russia within six months, dating from the signature of the present Treaty....

Article XIV. The Contracting Parties agree to conclude in as short a time as possible a consular agreement and other arrangements regulating all economic, financial and other questions which are necessary for the establishment of friendly relations between the two countries, as set forth in the preamble to the present Treaty.

Article XV. Russia undertakes to take the necessary steps with the Transcaucasian Republics with a view to securing the recognition by the latter, in their agreement with Turkey, of the provisions of the present Treaty which directly concern them.

[*Article XVI.* Ratification.]

Treaty of Peace with Turkey (Treaty of Lausanne), 24 July 1923

The British Empire, France, Italy, Japan, Greece, Roumania and the Serb-Croat-Slovene State,

of the one part,

and Turkey,

of the other part;

Being united in the desire to bring to a final close the state of war which has existed in the East since 1914 ... have agreed as follows:

Part I · Political clauses

Article 1. From the coming into force of the present Treaty, the state of peace will be definitely re-established between the British Empire, France, Italy, Japan, Greece, Roumania and the Serb-Croat-Slovene State of the one part, and Turkey of the other part, as well as between their respective nationals....

SECTION I · TERRITORIAL CLAUSES

Article 2. From the Black Sea to the Ægean the frontier of Turkey is laid down as follows....

[*Article 3.* The frontier from the Mediterranean to the frontier of Persia.]

[*Articles 4–11.* Frontier delimitation, work of the Boundary Commission.]

[*Article 12.* Greek sovereignty over islands in Eastern Mediterranean confirmed. Unless provision to contrary, Turkey to retain sovereignty over islands less than 3 miles from Asiatic coast.]

[*Article 13.* Greece undertakes not to fortify Mytilene, Chios, Samos and Nikaria.]

...

Article 15. Turkey renounces in favour of Italy all rights and title over the following islands: Stampalia (Astrapalia), Rhodes (Rhodos), Calki (Kharki), Scarpanto, Casos (Casso), Piscopis (Tilos), Misiros (Nisyros), Calimnos (Kalymnos), Leros, Patmos, Lipsos (Lipso), Simi (Symi), and Cos (Kos), which are now occupied by Italy, and the islets dependent thereon, and also over the island of Castellorizzo....

Article 16. Turkey hereby renounces all rights and title whatsoever over or respecting the territories situated outside the frontiers laid down in the present Treaty and the islands other than those over which her sovereignty is recognized by the said Treaty, the future of these territories and islands being settled or to be settled by the parties concerned.

The provisions of the present Article do

not prejudice any special arrangements arising from neighbourly relations which have been or may be concluded between Turkey and any limitrophe countries.

Article 17. The renunciation by Turkey of all rights and titles over Egypt and over the Soudan will take effect as from the 5th November 1914.

...

Article 20. Turkey hereby recognizes the annexation of Cyprus proclaimed by the British Government on the 5th November 1914.

...

[*Article 22.* Turkey renounces rights in Libya.]

...

[*Article 28.* Abolition of Capitulations is accepted.]

SECTION III · PROTECTION OF MINORITIES

Article 37. Turkey undertakes that the stipulations contained in Articles 38 to 44 shall be recognized as fundamental laws, and that no law, no regulation, nor

official action shall conflict or interfere with these stipulations, nor shall any law, regulation, nor official action prevail over them.

Article 38. The Turkish Government undertakes to assure full and complete protection of life and liberty to all inhabitants of Turkey without distinction of birth, nationality, language, race or religion.

[*Articles 39–44.* Non-Moslem Turkish citizens to enjoy equal political and civil rights as Moslem Turkish citizens.]

[*Article 45.* The same rights as in Articles 39 to 44 to be enjoyed by Moslem majority in Greece.]

Part II · Financial clauses

[*Articles 46–58.* These deal with the Ottoman Public Debt. Article 58 states that Turkey and the Allied Powers, except Greece, renounce all financial claims arising from war and conflict since 1 August 1914.]

Convention regarding the régime of the Straits (Lausanne Convention), 24 July 1923

Article 1. The High Contracting Parties agree to recognize and declare the principle of freedom of transit and of navigation by sea and by air in the Strait of the Dardanelles, the Sea of Marmora and the Bosphorus, hereinafter comprised under the general term of the 'Straits'.

Article 2. The transit and navigation of commercial vessels and aircraft, and of war vessels and aircraft in the Straits in time of peace and in time of war shall henceforth be regulated by the provisions of the attached Annex.

Annex · *Rules for the Passage of Commercial Vessels and Aircraft, and of War Vessels and Aircraft through the Straits...*

1. MERCHANT VESSELS, INCLUDING HOSPITAL SHIPS, YACHTS AND FISHING VESSELS AND NON-MILITARY AIRCRAFT

[In time of peace: freedom of passage. In time of war, Turkey being neutral: freedom of passage. In time of war, Turkey being belligerent: freedom of passage for neutrals, Turkey being permitted the right of search of contraband. Turkey may take whatever measures regarded as necessary to prevent use of Straits by enemy ships.]

2. WARSHIPS, INCLUDING FLEET AUXILIARIES, TROOPSHIPS, AIRCRAFT CARRIERS AND MILITARY AIRCRAFT

(a) *In time of peace.* Complete freedom of passage by day and by night under any flag, without any formalities, or tax, or charge whatever, but subject to the following restrictions as to the total force:

The maximum force which any one Power may send through the Straits into the Black Sea is not to be greater than that of the most powerful fleet of the littoral Powers of the Black Sea existing in that sea at the time of passage; but with the proviso that the Powers reserve to themselves the right to send into the Black Sea, at all times and under all circumstances, a force of not more than three ships, of which no individual ship shall exceed 10,000 tons.

Turkey has no responsibility in regard to the number of war vessels which pass through the Straits.

In order to enable the above rule to be observed, the Straits Commission provided for in Article 10 will, on the 1st January and 1st July of each year, enquire of each Black Sea littoral Power the number of each of the following classes of vessel which such Power possesses in the Black Sea: battleships, battle-cruisers, aircraft carriers, cruisers, destroyers, submarines, or other types of vessels as well as naval aircraft; distinguishing between the ships which are in active commission and the ships with reduced complements, the ships in reserve and the ships undergoing repairs or alterations.

The Straits Commission will then inform the Powers concerned that the strongest naval force in the Black Sea comprise: battleships, battle-cruisers, aircraft carriers, cruisers, destroyers, submarines, aircraft and units of other types which may exist. The Straits Commission will also immediately inform the Powers concerned when, owing to the passage into or out of the Black Sea of any ship of the strongest Black Sea force, any alteration in that force has taken place.

The naval force that may be sent through the Straits into the Black Sea will be calculated on the number and type of the ships of war in active commission only.

(b) *In time of war, Turkey being neutral.* Complete freedom of passage by day and by night under any flag, without any formalities, or tax, or charge whatever, under the same limitations as in paragraph 2 (a).

However, these limitations will not be applicable to any belligerent Power to the prejudice of its belligerent rights in the Black Sea.

The rights and duties of Turkey as a neutral Power cannot authorize her to take any measures liable to interfere with navigation through the Straits, the waters of which, and the air above which, must remain entirely free in time of war, Turkey being neutral, just as in time of peace.

Warships and military aircraft of belligerents will be forbidden to make any capture, to exercise the right of visit and search, or to carry out any other hostile act in the Straits.

As regards revictualling and carrying out repairs, war vessels will be subject to the terms of the Thirteenth Hague Convention of 1907, dealing with maritime neutrality.

Military aircraft will receive in the Straits similar treatment to that accorded under the Thirteenth Hague Convention of 1907 to warships, pending the conclusion of an international convention establishing the rules of neutrality for aircraft.

(c) *In time of war, Turkey being belligerent.* Complete freedom of passage for neutral warships, without any formalities, or tax, or charge whatever, but under the same limitations as in paragraph 2 (a).

The measures taken by Turkey to prevent enemy ships and aircraft from using the Straits are not to be of such a nature as to prevent the free passage of neutral ships and aircraft, and Turkey agrees to provide the said ships and aircraft with either the necessary instructions or pilots for the above purpose.

Neutral military aircraft will make the passage of the Straits at their own risk and peril, and will submit to investigation as to their character. For this purpose aircraft are to alight on the ground or on the sea in such areas as are specified and prepared for this purpose by Turkey.

3. (a) The passage of the Straits by submarines of the Powers at peace with Turkey must be made on the surface....

(c) The right of military and nonmilitary aircraft to fly over the Straits, under the conditions laid down in the present rules, necessitates for aircraft:

(i) Freedom to fly over a strip of territory of 5 kilometres wide on each side of the narrow parts of the Straits;

(ii) Liberty, in the event of a forced landing, to alight on the coast or on the sea in the territorial waters of Turkey.

...

Article 3. With a view to maintaining the Straits free from any obstacle to free passage and navigation, the provisions contained in Articles 4 to 9 will be applied to the waters and shores thereof as well as to the islands situated therein, or in the vicinity.

Article 4. The zones and islands indicated below shall be demilitarized:

1. Both shores of the Straits of the Dardanelles and the Bosphorus over the extent of the zones delimited below [*Dardanelles; Bosphorus*].

2. All the islands in the Sea of Marmora, with the exception of the island of Emir Ali Adasi.

3. In the Ægean Sea, the islands of Samothrace, Lemnos, Imbros, Tenedos and Rabbit Islands.

Article 5. A Commission composed of four representatives appointed respectively by the Governments of France, Great Britain, Italy and Turkey shall meet within 15 days of the coming into force of the present Convention to determine on the spot the boundaries of the zone laid down in Article 4 (1)....

Article 6. Subject to the provisions of Article 8 concerning Constantinople, there shall exist, in the demilitarized zones and islands, no fortifications, no permanent artillery organization, no submarine engines of war other than submarine vessels, no military aerial organization, and no naval base.

No armed forces shall be stationed in the demilitarized zones and islands except the police and *gendarmerie* forces necessary for the maintenance of order....

Article 7. No submarine engines of war other than submarine vessels shall be installed in the waters of the Sea of Marmora.

The Turkish Government shall not install any permanent battery or torpedo tubes, capable of interfering with the passage of the Straits, in the coastal zone of the European shore of the Sea of Marmora or in the coastal zone on the Anatolian shore situated to the east of the demilitarized zone of the Bosphorus as far as Darije.

Article 8. At Constantinople, ... there may be maintained for the requirements of the capital, a garrison with maximum strength of 12,000 men....

Article 9. If, in case of war, Turkey, or Greece, in pursuance of their belligerent rights, should modify in any way the provisions of demilitarization prescribed above, they will be bound to re-establish as soon as peace is concluded the régime laid down in the present Convention.

Article 10. There shall be constituted at Constantinople an International Commission composed in accordance with Article 12 and called the 'Straits Commission'.

Article 11. The Commission will exercise its functions over the waters of the Straits.

Article 12. The Commission shall be composed of a representative of Turkey, who shall be President, and representatives of France, Great Britain, Italy, Japan, Bulgaria, Greece, Roumania, Russia, and the Serb-Croat-Slovene State, in so far as these Powers are signatories of the present Convention, each of these Powers being entitled to representation as from its ratification of the said Convention.

The United States of America, in the event of their acceding to the present Convention, will also be entitled to have one representative on the Commission.

Under the same conditions any independent littoral States of the Black Sea which are not mentioned in the first paragraph of the present Article will possess the same right.

[*Articles 14–16.* Duties of Commission to see provisions of treaties are observed.]

Article 17. The terms of the present Convention will not infringe the right of Turkey to move her fleet freely in Turkish waters.

Article 18. The High Contracting Parties, desiring to secure that the demilitarization of the Straits and of the contiguous zones shall not constitute an unjustifiable danger to the military security of Turkey, and that no act of war should imperil the freedom of the Straits or the safety of the demilitarized zones, agree as follows:

Should the freedom of navigation of the Straits or the security of the demilitarized zones be imperilled by a violation of the provisions relating to freedom of passage, or by a surprise attack or some act of war or threat of war, the High Contracting Parties, and in any case France, Great Britain, Italy and Japan, acting in conjunction, will meet such violation, attack, or other act of war or threat of war, by all the means that the Council of the League of Nations may decide for this purpose.

So soon as the circumstance which may have necessitated the action provided for in the preceding paragraph shall have ended, the régime of the Straits as laid down by the terms of the present Convention shall again be strictly applied.

The present provision, which forms an integral part of those relating to the demilitarization and to the freedom of the Straits, does not prejudice the rights and obligations of the High Contracting Parties under the Covenant of the League of Nations.

Convention regarding the régime of the Straits (Montreux Convention), 20 July 1936

Article 1. The High Contracting Parties recognize and affirm the principle of freedom of transit and navigation by sea in the Straits.

The exercise of this freedom shall henceforth be regulated by the provisions of the present Convention.

SECTION I · MERCHANT VESSELS

Article 2. In time of peace, merchant vessels shall enjoy complete freedom of transit and navigation in the Straits, by day and by night, under any flag and with any kind of cargo, without any formalities, except as provided in Article 3 below. No taxes or charges other than those authorized by Annex I to the present Convention shall be levied by the Turkish authorities on these vessels when passing in transit without calling at a port in the Straits. . . .

[*Article 3.* Sanitary regulations.]

Article 4. In time of war, Turkey not being belligerent, merchant vessels, under any flag or with any kind of cargo, shall enjoy freedom of transit and navigation in the Straits subject to the provisions of Articles 2 and 3.

Pilotage and towage remain optional.

Article 5. In time of war, Turkey being belligerent, merchant vessels not belonging to a country at war with Turkey shall enjoy freedom of transit and navigation in the Straits on condition that they do not in any way assist the enemy.

Such vessels shall enter the Straits by day and their transit shall be effected by the route which shall in each case be indicated by the Turkish authorities.

Article 6. Should Turkey consider herself to be threatened with imminent danger of war, the provisions of Article 2 shall nevertheless continue to be applied except that vessels must enter the Straits by day and that their transit must be effected by the route which shall, in each case, be indicated by the Turkish authorities. . . .

SECTION II · VESSELS OF WAR

Article 11. Black Sea Powers may send through the Straits capital ships of a tonnage greater than that laid down in the first paragraph of Article 14, on condition that these vessels pass through the Straits singly, escorted by not more than two destroyers.

Article 12. Black Sea Powers shall have the right to send through the Straits, for the purpose of rejoining their base, submarines constructed or purchased outside the Black Sea, provided that adequate notice of the laying down or purchase of such submarines shall have been given to Turkey.

Submarines belonging to the said Powers shall also be entitled to pass through the Straits to be repaired in dockyards outside the Black Sea on condition that detailed information on the matter is given to Turkey.

In either case, the said submarines must travel by day and on the surface, and must pass through the Straits singly.

[*Article 13.* Details of notification to Turkish authorities of transit of warships.]

Article 14. The maximum aggregate tonnage of all foreign naval forces which may be in course of transit through the Straits shall not exceed 15,000 tons, except in the cases provided for in Article 11 . . .

The forces specified in the preceding paragraph shall not, however, comprise more than nine vessels.

Vessels, whether belonging to Black Sea or non-Black Sea Powers, paying visits to a port in the Straits, in accordance with the provisions of Article 17, shall not be included in this tonnage.

Neither shall vessels of war which have suffered damage during their passage through the Straits be included in this tonnage; such vessels, while undergoing repair, shall be subject to any special provisions relating to security laid down by Turkey.

[*Article 15.* Prohibition against use of aircraft by warships in transit.]

[*Article 16.* Except in case of damage, transit to be accomplished without delay.]

Article 17. Nothing in the provisions of the preceding Articles shall prevent a naval force of any tonnage or composition from paying a courtesy visit of limited duration to a port in the Straits, at the invitation of the Turkish Government. Any such force must leave the Straits by the same route as that by which it entered, unless it fulfils the conditions required for passage in transit through the Straits as laid down by Articles 10, 14 and 18.

Article 18. 1. The aggregate tonnage which non-Black Sea Powers may have in that sea in time of peace shall be limited as follows:

(a) Except as provided in paragraph (b) below, the aggregate tonnage of the said Powers shall not exceed 30,000 tons;

(b) If at any time the tonnage of the

strongest fleet in the Black Sea shall exceed by at least 10,000 tons the tonnage of the strongest fleet in that sea at the date of the signature of the present Convention, the aggregate tonnage of 30,000 tons mentioned in paragraph (a) shall be increased by the same amount, up to a maximum of 45,000 tons. For this purpose, each Black Sea Power shall, in conformity with Annex IV to the present Convention, inform the Turkish Government, on the 1st January and the 1st July of each year, of the total tonnage of its fleet in the Black Sea; and the Turkish Government shall transmit this information to the other High Contracting Parties and to the Secretary General of the League of Nations;

(c) The tonnage which any one non-Black Sea Power may have in the Black Sea shall be limited to two-thirds of the aggregate tonnage provided for in paragraphs (a) and (b) above;

(d) In the event, however, of one or more non-Black Sea Powers desiring to send naval forces into the Black Sea, for a humanitarian purpose, the said forces, which shall in no case exceed 8,000 tons altogether, shall be allowed to enter the Black Sea without having to give the notification provided for in Article 13 of the present Convention, provided an authorization is obtained from the Turkish Government . . .

2. Vessels of war belonging to non-Black Sea Powers shall not remain in the Black Sea more than twenty-one days, whatever be the object of their presence there.

Article 19. In time of war, Turkey not being belligerent, warships shall enjoy complete freedom of transit and navigation through the Straits under the same conditions as those laid down in Articles 10 to 18.

Vessels of war belonging to belligerent Powers shall not, however, pass through the Straits except in cases arising out of the application of Article 25 of the present Convention, and in cases of assistance rendered to a State victim of aggression in virtue of a treaty of mutual assistance binding Turkey, concluded within the framework of the Covenant of the League of Nations, and registered and published in accordance with the provisions of Article 18 of the Covenant.

In the exceptional cases provided for in the preceding paragraph, the limitations laid down in Articles 10 to 18 of the present Convention shall not be applicable.

Notwithstanding the prohibition of passage laid down in paragraph 2 above, vessels of war belonging to belligerent Powers, whether they are Black Sea Powers or not, which have become separated from their bases, may return thereto.

Vessels of war belonging to belligerent Powers shall not make any capture, exercise the right of visit and search, or carry out any hostile act in the Straits.

Article 20. In time of war, Turkey being belligerent, the provisions of Articles 10 to 18 shall not be applicable; the passage of warships shall be left entirely to the discretion of the Turkish Government.

Article 21. Should Turkey consider herself to be threatened with imminent danger of war she shall have the right to apply the provisions of Article 20 of the present Convention.

Vessels which have passed through the Straits before Turkey has made use of the powers conferred upon her by the preceding paragraph, and which thus find themselves separated from their bases, may return thereto. It is, however, understood that Turkey may deny this right to vessels of war belonging to the State whose attitude has given rise to the application of the present Article.

Should the Turkish Government make use of the powers conferred by the first paragraph of the present Article, a notification to that effect shall be addressed to the High Contracting Parties and to the Secretary-General of the League of Nations.

If the Council of the League of Nations decide by a majority of two-thirds that the measures thus taken by Turkey are not justified, and if such should also be the opinion of the majority of the High Contracting Parties signatories to the present Convention, the Turkish Government undertakes to discontinue the measures in question as also any measures which may have been taken under Article 6 of the present Convention.

Protocol

At the moment of signing the Convention bearing this day's date, the undersigned plenipotentiaries declare for their respective Governments that they accept the following provisions:

1. Turkey may immediately remilitarize the zone of the Straits as defined in the Preamble to the said Convention.

2. As from the 15th August, 1936, the Turkish Government shall provisionally apply the régime specified in the said Convention.

3. The present Protocol shall enter into force as from this day's date.

SECTION III · AIRCRAFT

[*Article 23*. Turkish Government to indicate routes for civil aircraft between Mediterranean and Black Sea.]

Article 24. The functions of the International Commission set up under the Convention relating to the régime of the Straits of the 24th July 1923, are hereby transferred to the Turkish Government.

The Turkish Government undertake to collect statistics and furnish information concerning the application of Articles 11, 12, 14 and 18 of the present Convention.

They will supervise the execution of all the provisions of the present Convention relating to the passage of vessels of war through the Straits.

As soon as they have been notified of the intended passage through the Straits of a foreign naval force the Turkish Government shall inform the representatives at Angora of the High Contracting Parties of the composition of that force, its tonnage, the date fixed for its entry into the Straits, and, if necessary, the probable date of its return.

The Turkish Government shall address to the Secretary-General of the League of Nations and to the High Contracting Parties an annual report giving details regarding the movements of foreign vessels of war through the Straits and furnishing all information which may be of service to commerce and navigation, both by sea and by air, for which provision is made in the present Convention.

Article 25. Nothing in the present Convention shall prejudice the rights and obligations of Turkey, or of any of the other High Contracting Parties members of the League of Nations, arising out of the Covenant of the League of Nations.

SECTION V · FINAL PROVISIONS

Article 26. The present Convention shall be ratified as soon as possible. . . .

[*Article 27*. After entry into force, Convention open to accession by any signatory of Treaty of Lausanne, 1923.]

Article 28. The present Convention shall remain in force for twenty years from the date of its entry into force.

The principle of freedom of transit and navigation affirmed in Article 1 of the present Convention shall however continue without limit of time.

If, two years prior to the expiry of the said period of twenty years, no High Contracting Party shall have given notice of denunciation to the French Government the present Convention shall continue in force until two years after such notice shall have been given. Any such notice shall be communicated by the French Government to the High Contracting Parties.

In the event of the present Convention being denounced in accordance with the provisions of the present Article, the High Contracting Parties agree to be represented at a conference for the purpose of concluding a new Convention.

Article 29. At the expiry of each period of five years from the date of the entry into force of the present Convention each of the High Contracting Parties shall be entitled to initiate a proposal for amending one or more of the provisions of the present Convention. . . .

Should it be found impossible to reach an agreement on these proposals through the diplomatic channel, the High Contracting Parties agree to be represented at a conference to be summoned for this purpose.

Such a conference may only take decisions by a unanimous vote, except as regards cases of revision involving Articles 14 and 18, for which a majority of three-quarters of the High Contracting Parties shall be sufficient.

The said majority shall include three-quarters of the High Contracting Parties which are Black Sea Powers, including Turkey. . . .

Treaty between the United States, the British Empire, France, Italy and Japan limiting naval armament, 6 February 1922

The United States of America, the British Empire, France, Italy and Japan;

Desiring to contribute to the maintenance of the general peace, and to reduce the burdens of competition in armament . . .

Have agreed as follows:

Chapter I: General provisions relating to the limitation of naval armament

Article I. The Contracting Powers agree to limit their respective naval armament as provided in the present Treaty.

Article II. The Contracting Powers may retain respectively the capital ships which are specified in Chapter II, Part 1. On the coming into force of the present Treaty, but subject to the following provisions of this Article, all other capital ships, built or building, of the United States, the British Empire and Japan shall be disposed of as prescribed in Chapter II, Part 2.

In addition to the capital ships specified in Chapter II, Part 1, the United States may complete and retain two ships of the *West Virginia* class now under construction. On the completion of these two ships the *North Dakota* and *Delaware* shall be disposed of as prescribed in Chapter II, Part 2.

The British Empire may, in accordance with the replacement table in Chapter II, Part 3, construct two new capital ships not exceeding 35,000 tons (35,560 metric tons) standard displacement each. On the completion of the said two ships the *Thunderer, King George V, Ajax* and *Centurion* shall be disposed of as prescribed in Chapter II, Part 2.

Article III. Subject to the provisions of Article II, the Contracting Powers shall abandon their respective capital ship building programmes, and no new capital ships shall be constructed or acquired by any of the Contracting Powers except replacement tonnage which may be constructed or acquired as specified in Chapter II, Part 3.

Ships which are replaced in accordance with Chapter II, Part 3, shall be disposed of as described in Part 2 of that Chapter.

Article IV. The total capital ship replacement tonnage of each of the Contracting Powers shall not exceed in standard displacement, for the United States 525,000 tons (533,400 metric tons); for the British Empire 525,000 tons (533,400 metric tons); for France 175,000 tons (177,800 metric tons); for Italy 175,000 tons (177,800 metric tons); for Japan 315,000 tons (320,040 metric tons).

Article V. No capital ship exceeding 35,000 tons (35,560 metric tons) standard displacement shall be acquired by, or constructed by, for, or within the jurisdiction of, any of the Contracting Powers.

Article VI. No capital ship of any of the Contracting Powers shall carry a gun with a calibre in excess of 16 inches (406 millimetres).

Article VII. The total tonnage for aircraft carriers of each of the Contracting Powers shall not exceed in standard displacement, for the United States 135,000 tons (137,160 metric tons); for the British Empire 135,000 tons (137,160 metric tons); for France 60,000 tons (60,960 metric tons); for Italy 60,000 tons (60,960 metric tons); for Japan 81,000 tons (82,296 metric tons).

Article VIII. The replacement of aircraft carriers shall be effected only as prescribed in Chapter II, Part 3, provided, however, that all aircraft carrier tonnage in existence or building on November 12, 1921, shall be considered experimental, and may be replaced, within the total tonnage limit prescribed in Article VII, without regard to its age.

Article IX. No aircraft carrier exceeding 27,000 tons (27,432 metric tons) standard displacement shall be acquired by, or constructed by, for or within the jurisdiction of, any of the Contracting Powers.

However, any of the Contracting Powers may, provided that its total tonnage allowance of aircraft carriers is not thereby exceeded, build not more than two aircraft carriers, each of a tonnage of not more than 33,000 tons (33,528 metric tons) standard displacement, and in order to effect economy any of the Contracting Powers may use for this purpose any two of their ships, whether constructed or in course of construction, which would otherwise be scrapped under the provisions of Article II ... [limitation on armament].

[*Article X.* Armament limitation: calibre of guns.]

Article XI. No vessel of war exceeding 10,000 tons (10,160 metric tons) standard displacement, other than a capital ship or aircraft carrier shall be acquired by, or constructed by, for, or within the jurisdiction of, any of the Contracting Powers. Vessels not specifically built as fighting ships nor taken in time of peace under government control ... shall not be within the limitations of this Article.

...

Article XV. No vessel of war constructed within the jurisdiction of any of the Contracting Powers for a non-Contracting Power shall exceed the limitations as to displacement and armament prescribed by the present Treaty for vessels of a similar type which may be constructed by or for any of the Contracting Powers; provided, however, that the displacement for aircraft carriers constructed for a non-Contracting Power shall in no case exceed 27,000 tons (27,432 metric tons) standard displacement.

Article XIX. The United States, the British Empire and Japan agree that the *status quo* at the time of the signing of the present Treaty, with regard to fortifications and naval bases, shall be maintained in their respective territories and possessions specified hereunder:

(1) The insular possessions which the United States now holds or may hereafter acquire in the Pacific Ocean, except (a) those adjacent to the coast of the United States, Alaska and the Panama Canal Zone, not including the Aleutian Islands, and (b) the Hawaiian Islands;

(2) Hongkong and the insular possessions which the British Empire now holds or may hereafter acquire in the Pacific Ocean, east of the meridian 110° east longitude, except (a) those adjacent to the coast of Canada, (b) the Commonwealth of Australia and its Territories, and (c) New Zealand;

(3) The following insular territories and possessions of Japan in the Pacific Ocean, to wit: the Kurile Islands, the Bonin Islands, Amami-Oshima, the Loochoo Islands, Formosa and the Pescadores,

and any insular territories or possessions in the Pacific Ocean which Japan may hereafter acquire.

The maintenance of the *status quo* under the foregoing provisions implies that no new fortifications or naval bases shall be established in the territories and possessions specified, that no measures shall be taken to increase the existing naval facilities for the repair and maintenance of naval forces, and that no increase shall be made in the coast defences of the territories and possessions above specified. This restriction, however, does not preclude such repair and replacement of worn-out weapons and equipment as is customary in naval and military establishments in time of peace.

Article XX. The rules for determining tonnage displacement prescribed in Chapter II, Part 4, shall apply to the ships of each of the Contracting Powers.

Chapter III: Miscellaneous provisions

Article XXI. If during the term of the present Treaty the requirements of the national security of any Contracting Power in respect of naval defence are, in the opinion of that Power, materially affected by any change of circumstances, the Contracting Powers will, at the request of such Power, meet in conference with a view to the reconsideration of the provisions of the Treaty and its amendment by mutual agreement.

In view of possible technical and scientific developments, the United States, after consultation with the other Contracting Powers, shall arrange for a conference of all the Contracting Powers which shall convene as soon as possible after the expiration of eight years from the coming into force of the present Treaty to consider what changes, if any, in the Treaty may be necessary to meet such developments.

Article XXII. Whenever any Contracting Power shall become engaged in a war which in its opinion affects the naval defence of its national security, such Power may after notice to the other Contracting Powers suspend for the period of hostilities its obligations under the present Treaty other than those under Articles XIII and XVII, provided that such Power shall notify the other Contracting Powers that the emergency is of such a character as to require such suspension.

The remaining Contracting Powers shall in such case consult together with a view to agreement as to what temporary modifications if any should be made in the Treaty as between themselves. Should such consultation not produce agreement, duly made in accordance with the constitutional methods of the respective Powers, any one of said Contracting Powers may, by giving notice to the other Contracting Powers, suspend for the period of hostilities its obligations under the present Treaty, other than those under Articles XIII and XVII.

On the cessation of hostilities the Contracting Powers will meet in conference to consider what modifications, if any, should be made in the provisions of the present Treaty.

Article XXIII. The present Treaty shall remain in force until December 31, 1936, and in case none of the Contracting Powers shall have given notice two years before that date of its intention to terminate the Treaty, it shall continue in force until the expiration of two years from the date on which notice of termination shall be given by one of the Contracting Powers, whereupon the Treaty shall terminate as regards all the Contracting Powers. . . .

[*Article XXIV.* Ratification.]

Treaty between the United States, Belgium, the British Empire, China, France, Italy, Japan, the Netherlands and Portugal (Nine Power Treaty) concerning China, 6 February 1922

The United States of America, Belgium, the British Empire, China, France, Italy, Japan, the Netherlands and Portugal:

Desiring to adopt a policy designed to stabilize conditions in the Far East, to safeguard the rights and interests of China, and to promote intercourse between China and the other Powers upon the basis of equality of opportunity ...

Have agreed as follows:

Article I. The Contracting Powers, other than China, agree:

1. To respect the sovereignty, the independence, and the territorial and administrative integrity of China;

2. To provide the fullest and most unembarrassed opportunity to China to develop and maintain for herself an effective and stable government;

3. To use their influence for the purpose of effectually establishing and maintaining the principle of equal opportunity for the commerce and industry of all nations throughout the territory of China;

4. To refrain from taking advantage of conditions in China in order to seek special rights or privileges which would abridge the rights of subjects or citizens of friendly States, and from countenancing action inimical to the security of such States.

Article II. The Contracting Powers agree not to enter into any treaty, agreement, arrangement, or understanding, either with one another, or individually or collectively, with any Power or Powers, which would infringe or impair the principles stated in Article I.

Article III. With a view to applying more effectually the principles of the Open Door or equality of opportunity in China for the trade and industry of all nations, the Contracting Powers, other than China, agree that they will not seek, nor support their respective nationals in seeking:

(a) Any arrangement which might purport to establish in favour of their interests any general superiority of rights with respect to commercial or economic development in any designated region of China;

(b) Any such monopoly or preference as would deprive the nationals of any other Power of the right of undertaking any legitimate trade or industry in China, or of participating with the Chinese Government, or with any local authority, in any category of public enterprise, or which by reason of its scope, duration or geographical extent is calculated to frustrate the practical application of the principle of equal opportunity.

It is understood that the foregoing stipulations of this Article are not to be so construed as to prohibit the acquisition of such properties or rights as may be necessary to the conduct of a particular commercial, industrial, or financial undertaking or to the encouragement of invention and research.

China undertakes to be guided by the principles stated in the foregoing stipulations of this Article in dealing with applications for economic rights and privileges from Governments and nationals of all foreign countries, whether parties to the present Treaty or not.

Article IV. The Contracting Powers agree not to support any agreements by their respective nationals with each other designed to create Spheres of Influence or to provide for the enjoyment of mutually exclusive opportunities in designated parts of Chinese territory.

Article V. China agrees that, throughout the whole of the railways in China, she will not exercise or permit unfair discrimination of any kind. . . .

Article VI. The Contracting Powers, other than China, agree fully to respect China's rights as a neutral in time of war to which China is not a party; and China declares that when she is a neutral she will observe the obligations of neutrality.

Article VII. The Contracting Powers agree that, whenever a situation arises which in the opinion of any one of them involves the application of the stipulations of the present Treaty, and renders desirable discussion of such application, there shall be full and frank communication between the Contracting Powers concerned.

Article VIII. Powers not signatory to the present Treaty, which have Government ments recognized by the signatory Powers and which have treaty relations with China, shall be invited to adhere to the present Treaty. To this end the Government of the United States will make the necessary communications to non-signatory Powers and will inform the Contracting Powers of the replies received. Adherence by any Power shall become effective on receipt of notice thereof by the Government of the United States.

[*Article IX.* Ratification.]

Declaration by China

China, upon her part, is prepared to give an undertaking not to alienate or lease any portion of her territory or littoral to any Power.

Treaty between the United States, the British Empire, France and Japan (Four Power Treaty) relating to their insular possessions and insular dominions in the Pacific Ocean, 13 December 1921

The United States of America, the British Empire, France and Japan,

With a view to the preservation of the general peace and the maintenance of their rights in relation to their insular possessions and insular dominions in the region of the Pacific Ocean, have determined to conclude a Treaty to this effect and have agreed as follows:

Article I. The High Contracting Parties agree as between themselves to respect their rights in relation to their insular possessions and insular dominions in the region of the Pacific Ocean.

If there should develop between any of the High Contracting Parties a controversy arising out of any Pacific question and involving their said rights which is not satisfactorily settled by diplomacy and is likely to affect the harmonious accord now happily subsisting between them, they shall invite the other High Contracting Parties to a joint conference to which the whole subject will be referred for consideration and adjustment.

Article II. If the said rights are threatened by the aggressive action of any other Power, the High Contracting Parties shall communicate with one another fully and frankly in order to arrive at an understanding as to the most efficient measures to be taken, jointly or separately, to meet the exigencies of the particular situation.

Article III. This Treaty shall remain in force for ten years from the time it shall take effect, and after the expiration of said period it shall continue to be in force subject to the right of any of the High Contracting Parties to terminate it upon twelve months' notice.

Article IV. This Treaty shall be ratified as soon as possible in accordance with the constitutional methods of the High Contracting Parties ...

[In ratifying this Treaty the United States resolved ... 'The United States understands that under the statement in the preamble or under the terms of this Treaty there is no commitment to armed force, no alliance, no obligation to join in any defense.']

Declaration accompanying the Treaty

In signing the Treaty this day between the United States of America, the British Empire, France and Japan, it is declared to be the understanding and intent of the signatory Powers:

1. That the Treaty shall apply to the mandated islands in the Pacific Ocean; provided, however, that the making of the Treaty shall not be deemed to be an assent on the part of the United States of America to the mandates and shall not preclude agreements between the United States of America and the Mandatory Powers respectively in relation to the mandated islands.

2. That the controversies to which the second paragraph of Article I refers shall not be taken to embrace questions which according to principles of international law lie exclusively within the domestic jurisdiction of the respective Powers.

Supplementary Agreement

... The term 'insular possessions and insular dominions' used in the aforesaid Treaty shall, in its application to Japan, include only Karafuto (or the southern portion of the island of Sakhalin), Formosa and the Pescadores, and the islands under the mandate of Japan ...

III · France, Britain, Italy and Germany, 1921–33

Within six years of the signature of the Treaty of Versailles the relationship of Germany and the victorious Western Powers who had dictated the peace terms to Germany had profoundly changed. The terms imposed on Germany were being significantly changed and softened. The question of reparations bedevilled Germany's relations with the West. The huge total sum demanded in 1921 was progressively abandoned during the decade of the 1920s. The treaties of Locarno of 1925 established a new relationship and signified the practical abandonment of the policy of imposing the terms of Versailles by military sanction. The Rhineland was evacuated completely five years ahead of time in June 1930 and effective means of supervising German armaments by Allied control were abandoned in 1927. The Pact of Paris in 1928 symbolized the idealistic and optimistic side of Great Power diplomacy in this era, but the reservations added to it indicate an underlying sense of realism. By the end of the decade and the beginning of the 1930s disarmament had become largely a question of which powers were to disarm and which to *rearm*. The 1930s became increasingly dominated by Hitler, but the abandonment of parts of the Versailles settlement had already occurred before he came to power.

The reparations question

German 'reparations' in theory were intended to make good the civilian damage caused by Germany in France, Belgium, Britain and elsewhere and were expected to burden the German people for more than half a century. In the event the burden lasted only a decade and brought no benefit to those who received these sums. No sensible settlement of post-war finance was politically possible in the early 1920s. The debt the Allies owed each other was huge, as

93

was the debt of some 11,000 million dollars the Allied nations owed the United States. To be in a position to pay their debts the Allies created 'credits' by imposing reparations plans on the defeated Germans; France and Britain had to collect reparations if the debts to the United States were to be paid. But the Allied nations were not allowing Germany such conditions of international trade as would have permitted the Germans to make sustained large payments from surpluses earned by exports. Largely private loans to German industry and the German Government totalling more than 5,000 million dollars provided a means to pay the reparations of almost 4,700 million dollars, and these payments enabled the Allies to service the debts to the United States. (Note: to convert the dollar amount to pounds sterling divide by five.) The Allies' other 'creditor' was Soviet Russia whose leaders were pressed at the Genoa Conference and elsewhere to honour the debts of the Tsarist Empire. In turn the Soviet leaders were promised, as part of a deal, a share in German reparations according to Article 116 of the Treaty of Versailles. In the event the threats and counterthreats to collect debts and enforce reparations payments brought the Germans and Russians together and they concluded the *Treaty of Rapallo* (p. 139).

The Treaty of Versailles had empowered the Reparations Commission to collect 5,000 million dollars before 1 May 1921 and then to announce the total amount Germany would have to meet. Disputes on this liability led to an Allied ultimatum in March 1921 and an extension of Allied occupation to Düsseldorf and two other German towns, and subsequently the declaration that Germany was in default. The Reparations Commission finally worked out the German bill at about 33,000 million dollars, a huge and unrealistic sum. More important were the details of the annual payment plan worked out at the *Second London Conference, 30 April–5 May 1921*, involving reparations at an annual rate of about 500 million dollars, and in addition an amount equivalent to 26 per cent of German exports. A little over a year later, on 31 August 1922, Germany's inability to pay was recognized by the Allies. The policy of meeting Allied claims, the declared intention of the German Foreign Minister, Walter Rathenau, proved impossible to realize as far as reparations were concerned.

Under the London payment plan of 1921 Germany had paid a total of about 3,000 million gold marks in gold and goods (the Germans claimed that they had paid all that was due) and then made no further payment. The response of France and Belgium was to occupy the Ruhr, the centre of German industry, in January 1923. Some financial order was restored in 1924 by the *Dawes Plan* (p. 100) which began with a loan and called for payments rising annually to 2,500 million Reichsmarks. In May and June 1930, just after the *Young Plan* (p. 101) came into force, the occupation of the last zone of the Rhineland was ended prematurely. The Young Plan scaled down Germany's repayments to 1,900 million Reichsmarks. Under the Young Plan the ultimate total payment would have worked out to about a third of the original total fixed in 1921. In 1931, a year of deepening economic depression, President Hoover proposed and gained acceptance of a one-year moratorium of all inter-Government debts including Germany's reparation payments. Finally at the *Lausanne Conference, June–July 1932*, German reparations were reduced to a nominal sum, more important psychologically than financially.

Of the total reparations fixed by the Reparations Commission in 1921 as 132,000 million gold marks (33,000 million dollars) the Germans had 'paid' a little more than a tenth (the precise figures remain in dispute), and during the same period had obtained foreign loans attracted by a high interest rate well in excess of the payments made in reparation; the loans had been subscribed by American and Allied investors; Hitler in 1934 repudiated them. The huge total sum arrived at in 1921 was intended more as a political gesture to appease public opinion than as the kind of reparations the experts had the slightest expectations of ever collecting. Reality brought the reparations chapter to a virtual close in 1932–3 amid worldwide depression. Hitler's version of the history of reparations served Nazi propaganda in the years that followed.

The treaties of Locarno, 16 October 1925

France had emerged a victorious ally in 1918, but physically Germany remained potentially the preponderant Power in Europe. At the peace conference the French had only been prevailed upon to abandon plans of detaching large parts of Germany by the promise of a guarantee of security and the alliance offered to France by the United States and Britain. This treaty never came into force for the Senate repudiated Wilson's policy of global involvement (p. 41). Then the League of Nations' security procedures were hedged by so many qualifications that the French never placed undue faith in them. When the clarification and stiffening of measures against aggression embodied in the *Geneva Protocol of 1924* (p. 56) was abandoned in 1925, the writing was on the wall. In a Great Power conflict the League was unlikely to prove effective. What France desired above all was a British alliance, but British support could only be secured conditionally. This the French had to accept as better than nothing. The attraction to France of a German proposal for a security pact to cover the Rhine area was that Britain promised to support such a settlement. On French insistence the scope of the treaties was enlarged to include some arrangements for Eastern Europe. The British Government favoured the treaties signed at Locarno as they appeared to solve a number of problems simultaneously:

France would be promised support only conditionally on following a defensive policy in Europe; the reduction of Franco-German tension would contribute to general pacification, yet British commitments would remain strictly limited whilst allowing her the diplomatic initiative. But the Dominions were not bound and the British Government signed on behalf of the United Kingdom alone, not for the British Empire. In Anglo-French relations the Locarno relationship remained important until the eve of the Second World War. The architects of the Locarno complex of treaties were Aristide Briand, Austen Chamberlain and Gustav Stresemann.

For the German Government of the Weimar Republic, Locarno represented the exchange of a German undertaking to accept the Versailles territorial settlement in the West for the concrete advantages that a growing sense of French security would lead to the recovery of German sovereignty, to the relaxation of Allied control over German armaments, and above all, to the early evacuation of all the parts of the Rhineland occupied by the Allies. But Germany was not reconciled to the 1922 frontier with Poland. An alignment with Soviet Russia had been established at *Rapallo* (p. 139) and was maintained after the signature of the Locarno treaties, with the *Treaty of Berlin* (p. 142). Germany made it clear that when it entered the League of Nations and took its permanent seat on the Council as promised at Locarno, and achieved in the autumn of 1926, Article 16 would not bind Germany to fight Soviet Russia or oblige the German Government to permit armed forces passing across German territory to aid the victim of aggression. Germany had no intention of protecting 'Versailles' Poland. Nor would Germany guarantee its own eastern frontiers with Poland and Czechoslovakia as being permanent; only an arbitration agreement between these States and Germany in case of dispute was concluded. Its enforcement was not guaranteed by Britain and Italy; there was no reference in their preamble to the Treaty of Mutual Guarantee.

There were altogether five *Locarno treaties concluded on 16 October 1925* (p. 101): the Treaty of Mutual Guarantee and four arbitration treaties between Germany, Poland, Czechoslovakia, Belgium and France. The *Treaty of Mutual Guarantee* (p. 102) was signed by Britain, France, Germany, Belgium and Italy. These Powers guaranteed the territorial *status quo* resulting from the frontiers between France and Germany and Germany and Belgium. They also guaranteed the demilitarization of the Rhine as provided in Articles 42 and 43 of the Treaty of Versailles. Germany, France and Belgium mutually undertook not to invade each other or to resort to force (Article 2). But this stipulation did not apply 'to a flagrant breach of Articles 42 or 43 of the said Treaty of Versailles, if such breach constitutes an unprovoked act of aggression and by reason of the assembly of armed forces in the demilitarized zone immediate action is necessary': in such a case France could resort to force. If France, Belgium or Germany claimed a violation of the treaty had been committed, or a breach of Articles 42 or 43 of the Treaty of Versailles had been or was being committed, the question was to be brought to the League of Nations; and if the League found a violation to have been committed, the Guaranteeing Powers (Britain and Italy) would each come to the assistance of the victim. But the Guaranteeing Powers would anticipate the League decision and come to the immediate assistance of the victim in a case of 'flagrant violation' of Article 2, or if Germany 'flagrantly' violated Articles 42 and 43 concerning the demilitarized Rhineland, and the Guaranteeing Powers (Britain and Italy) were satisfied 'that this violation constitutes an unprovoked act of aggression and that by reason either of the crossing of the frontier or of the outbreak of hostilities or of the assembly of the armed forces in the demilitarized zone immediate action is necessary' (Article 4). Articles 2 and 4 had been very carefully worded and were the subject of lengthy negotiation. The actual commitment of Britain and Italy remained imprecise and would depend on their own decision whether the treaty had merely been violated or 'flagrantly' violated. There was thus no automatic commitment to go to war. There was no doubt Britain would do so if Germany actually invaded or attacked France. For French security the demilitarized Rhineland was of capital importance. The Versailles treaty regarded *any* violation as an 'hostile act'. The new treaty only promised the help of Britain and Italy if their view of the violation was flagrant. The diplomatic discussions preceding the Locarno treaty indicated that Britain would not regard Germany taking some military defensive measures as a 'flagrant violation' though they clearly were a violation of Versailles. Britain's view appears to have been that only if a German military build-up in the Rhineland was clearly an offensive step leading to the invasion of France or Belgium would the case of 'flagrant violation' be made out. The result for France was therefore a weakening of the terms imposed on Germany at Versailles, but also a strengthening of security in that military help was promised by Britain in certain circumstances without having to await the doubtful processes of the League of Nations. This undertaking was the substitute for the failed *Treaty of Guarantee of 1919* (p. 71). The French still retained another guarantee – the Allies remained in occupation of the three Rhineland zones, and would evacuate only one zone, the Cologne zone, towards the end of the year 1926.

Besides the Treaty of Mutual Guarantee, Germany signed *Arbitration Treaties with France and Belgium* (p. 104). These in turn were guaranteed by the Treaty of Mutual Guarantee. Germany also signed an *Arbitration Treaty with Poland and with Czechoslovakia* (p. 107) virtually identical in wording with the

German–French and German–Belgian arbitration treaties, but vitally different in that these two treaties were not related to or covered by the Treaty of Mutual Guarantee. This meant not only that Britain and Italy would not guarantee to come to the aid of the victim by reason of a violation of the arbitration clauses, but it also meant that there was no undertaking by Germany to accept the frontiers as settled in 1922, so that any violation of that frontier would not automatically place Germany in the wrong. Further, although Germany undertook not to resort to force from the start but to accept arbitration, the Germans made it clear at the time that this did not mean that under certain conditions force would not be employed eventually. France had been unable to secure an extension of a guarantee of the *status quo* in the East. France signed new alliance treaties with Czechoslovakia and Poland on the same day as the Locarno treaties, but it was clear that these alliances did not fall within the multinational framework of the latter. The French ability to fulfil its commitments to Poland and Czechoslovakia had in fact been weakened (p. 113).

The Pact of Paris, 27 August 1928

A treaty attempting to 'outlaw' war was first drafted by France and the United States on the initiative of Briand. This draft, the *Briand–Kellogg Pact*, fifteen nations were invited to sign on *27 August 1928* under its official title of the *Pact of Paris* (p. 108). Other nations quickly adhered and by 1933 sixty-five Governments had pledged themselves to observe its provisions.

During the course of negotiations the French Government, generally followed by other States, made four reservations: (1) the treaty was not to be effective unless it secured universal adherence or until some special further agreement had been reached; (2) each country retained the right of legitimate defence; (3) if one country violated its pledge then the others would be automatically released from theirs; (4) the treaty was not to interfere with French treaty obligations under the League, Locarno or her neutrality treaties. Specifically, in respect to Article 1 Britain reserved her right to act in the Empire and would not allow interference in these regions of the world. The U.S. Foreign Relations Committee understood that by the treaty the right of self defence was not curtailed nor the right to maintain the Monroe Doctrine. The Soviet Union sent a long protest at its exclusion from the discussions, but together with the Baltic States signed a declaration adhering to the treaty. The reservations undermined the credibility of the Pact of Paris.

The treaty was a self-denying undertaking containing no sanctions against countries in breach of it. The aggressors of the 1930s, Japan, Italy, Germany and the Soviet Union, were not restrained by it though they were all signatories. The treaty was based on the hope that the forces of moral diplomacy and the weight of world public opinion were powerful influences restraining the use of force. The events of the next two decades falsified that hope.

The Four Power Pact, 7 June 1933

In a speech at Turin in October 1932, Mussolini proposed a Four Power Pact between the four great European Powers, Italy, France, Germany and Britain. Its main purpose was to be the consideration of the revision of the peace treaties in a way agreed to by the four Powers, who would then 'induce' other countries to 'adopt the same policy of peace'. Germany would have been the principal beneficiary. It was intended that the revision of the treaties, such as gradual rearmament, would be brought about through agreement and not unilaterally by Hitler's Germany. The Little Entente Powers had most to lose from any revision of the peace treaties and they objected violently. The Four Power Pact was only signed on 7 June 1933 after France had secured substantial amendment to the original draft. The pact was never ratified and in its emasculated form proved of little influence even in the immediate months after its signature.

Disarmament

As an essential part of the general post-war settlement the Allies and Associated Powers worked for a reduction of armaments and the diminution of armament rivalries on land and on the sea. In accordance with Articles 8 and 9 of the Covenant a Permanent Advisory Commission of the League was set up in May 1920. In the following year the *Naval Limitation Treaty* was negotiated at the *Washington Conference, 1921–2* (p. 54). Little other progress was made, but with the signature of the Locarno treaties the Council of the League took a fresh initiative in setting up a Preparatory Commission in December 1925, which it was intended should be followed by a Disarmament Conference. Progress was frustrated by national assessments of security needs. Eventually in 1930 *the London Naval Conference led to a Naval Treaty, 22 April 1930*, which extended to other than capital ships the provisions of the naval limitations of the Washington treaty of 1922. But only three groups of Powers ratified the treaty: Britain and the Dominions, Japan, and the United States. Italian claims for parity with France frustrated the intention of including these two European States. The general Disarmament Conference sponsored by the Council of the League did not meet until February 1932. The various phases of the conference revealed the growing international conflicts and produced only one tangible result, the banning of chemical and bacteriological warfare. In October 1933 Nazi Germany withdrew from the conference; thereafter it dragged on a few months longer to its inevitable practical failure and adjournment in May 1934.

Japan gave notice of termination of the Washington treaty of 6 February 1922, and this treaty as well as provisions in the Naval Treaty of 22 April 1930 concerning naval limitation expired on 31 December 1936. A Naval Conference as provided by the treaty of 1930 met in London in December 1935, but Japan withdrew. A *Naval Treaty was signed between the United States, France, Great Britain and the Dominions on 25 March 1936* which provided for little more than consultation. In December 1938, subject to certain provisions, Italy acceded, but with the outbreak of war in September 1939 the treaty was suspended. In practice the naval conference of 1936 marked the end of the search for disarmament which had been pursued during the inter-war years.

Agreement between the Reparations Commission and the German Government (Dawes Plan), 9 August 1924

The Contracting Parties

Being desirous of carrying into effect the plan for the discharge of reparation obligations and other pecuniary liabilities of Germany under the Treaty of Versailles proposed to the Reparation Commission on April 9, 1924, by the First Committee of Experts appointed by the Commission (which plan is referred to in this agreement as the Experts' [Dawes] Plan) and of facilitating the working of the Experts' Plan by putting into operation such additional arrangements as may hereafter be made between the German Government and the Allied Governments at the Conference now being held in London, in so far as the same may lie within the respective spheres of action of the Reparation Commission and the German Government;

And the Reparation Commission acting in virtue not only of the powers conferred upon it by the said treaty but also of the authority given to it by the Allied Governments represented at the said Conference in respect of all payments by Germany dealt with in the Experts' Plan but not comprised in Part VIII of the said treaty;

Hereby agree as follows:

1. The German Government undertakes to take all appropriate measures for carrying into effect the Experts' Plan and for ensuring its permanent operation....

Protocol concerning approval in principle of Report of Experts on Reparations (Young Plan), 31 August 1929

The representatives of Germany, Belgium, France, Great Britain, Italy and Japan, meeting at Geneva on the 16 September 1928, expressed their determination to make a complete and final settlement of the question of reparations and, with a view to attaining this object, provided for the constitution of a Committee of Financial Experts.

With this object the Experts met at Paris and their report was made on the 7 June 1929. Approval in principle was given to this report by The Hague Protocol of the 31 August 1929....

Article 1. The Experts' Plan of the 7 June 1929, together with this present Agreement and the Protocol of the 31 August 1929 (all of which are hereinafter described as the New Plan) is definitely accepted as a complete and final settlement, so far as Germany is concerned, of the financial questions resulting from the war. By their acceptance the signatory Powers undertake the obligations and acquire the rights resulting for them respectively from the New Plan.

The German Government gives the creditor Powers the solemn undertaking to pay the annuities for which the New Plan provides in accordance with the stipulations contained therein.

...

Article 8. With a view to facilitating the successful working of the New Plan the German Government declares spontaneously that it is firmly determined to make every possible effort to avoid a declaration of postponement and not to have recourse thereto until it has come to the conclusion in good faith that Germany's exchange and economic life may be seriously endangered by the transfer in part or in full of the postponable portion of the annuities. It remains understood that Germany alone has authority to decide whether occasion has arisen for declaring a postponement as provided by the New Plan.

[In Annex III, Germany undertook to make annual payments beginning in 1929 and ending in 1988; these varied each year but averaged about 1,700 million Reichsmarks.]

Pact of Locarno, 16 October 1925

Final Protocol of the Locarno Conference, 1925

The representatives of the German, Belgian, British, French, Italian, Polish, and Czechoslovak Governments, who have met at Locarno from the 5th to 16th October 1925, in order to seek by common agreement means for preserving their respective nations from the scourge of war and for providing for the peaceful settlement of disputes of every nature which might eventually arise between them,

Have given their approval to the draft treaties and conventions which respectively affect them and which, framed in the course of the present conference, are mutually interdependent:

Treaty between Germany, Belgium, France, Great Britain, and Italy (Annex A).

Arbitration Convention between Germany and Belgium (Annex B).

Arbitration Convention between Germany and France (Annex C).

Arbitration Treaty between Germany and Poland (Annex D).

Arbitration Treaty between Germany and Czechoslovakia (Annex E).

These instruments, hereby initialed *ne varietur*, will bear today's date, the representatives of the interested parties agreeing to meet in London on the 1st December next, to proceed during the course of a single meeting to the formality of the signature of the instruments which affect them.

The Minister for Foreign Affairs of France states that as a result of the draft arbitration treaties mentioned above, France, Poland, and Czechoslovakia have also concluded at Locarno draft agreements in order reciprocally to assure to themselves the benefit of the said treaties. These agreements will be duly deposited at the League of Nations, but M. Briand holds copies forthwith at the disposal of the Powers represented here.

The Secretary of State for Foreign Affairs of Great Britain proposes that, in reply to certain requests for explanations concerning Article 16 of the Covenant of the League of Nations presented by the Chancellor and the Minister for Foreign Affairs of Germany, a letter, of which the draft is similarly attached (Annex F) should be addressed to them at the same time as the formality of signature of the above-mentioned instruments takes place. This proposal is agreed to.

The representatives of the Governments represented here declare their firm conviction that the entry into force of these treaties and conventions will contribute greatly to bring about a moral relaxation of the tension between nations, that it will help powerfully towards the solution of many political or economic problems in accordance with the interests and sentiments of peoples, and that, in strengthening peace and security in Europe, it will hasten on effectively the disarmament provided for in Article 8 of the Covenant of the League of Nations.

They undertake to give their sincere cooperation to the work relating to disarmament already undertaken by the League of Nations and to seek the realization thereof in a general agreement.

[Signed] Luther, Stresemann, Vandervelde, Briand, Chamberlain, Mussolini, Skrzynski, Benes.

Treaty of Mutual Guarantee between the United Kingdom, Belgium, France, Germany and Italy, Locarno, 16 October 1925

The Heads of State of Germany, Belgium, France, Britain, and Italy . . .

Anxious to satisfy the desire for security and protection which animates the peoples upon whom fell the scourge of the war of 1914–18;

Taking note of the abrogation of the treaties for the neutralization of Belgium, and conscious of the necessity of ensuring peace in the area which has so frequently been the scene of European conflicts;

Animated also with the sincere desire of giving to all the signatory Powers concerned supplementary guarantees within the framework of the Covenant of the League of Nations and the treaties in force between them;

Have determined to conclude a Treaty

with these objects, and have ... agreed as follows:

Article 1. The High Contracting Parties collectively and severally guarantee, in the manner provided in the following Articles, the maintenance of the territorial *status quo* resulting from the frontiers between Germany and Belgium and between Germany and France and the inviolability of the said frontiers as fixed by or in pursuance of the Treaty of Peace signed at Versailles on the 28th June 1919, and also the observance of the stipulations of Articles 42 and 43 of the said treaty concerning the demilitarized zone.

Article 2. Germany and Belgium, and also Germany and France, mutually undertake that they will in no case attack or invade each other or resort to war against each other.

This stipulation shall not, however, apply in the case of:

1. The exercise of the right of legitimate defence, that is to say, resistance to a violation of the undertaking contained in the previous paragraph or to a flagrant breach of Articles 42 or 43 of the said Treaty of Versailles, if such breach constitutes an unprovoked act of aggression and by reason of the assembly of armed forces in the demilitarized zone immediate action is necessary.

2. Action in pursuance of Article 16 of the Covenant of the League of Nations.

3. Action as the result of a decision taken by the Assembly or by the Council of the League of Nations or in pursuance of Article 15, paragraph 7, of the Covenant of the League of Nations, provided that in this last event the action is directed against a State which was the first to attack.

Article 3. In view of the undertakings entered into in Article 2 of the present Treaty, Germany and Belgium and Germany and France undertake to settle by peaceful means and in the manner laid down herein all questions of every kind which may arise between them and which it may not be possible to settle by the normal methods of diplomacy:

Any question with regard to which the parties are in conflict as to their respective rights shall be submitted to judicial decision, and the parties undertake to comply with such decision.

All other questions shall be submitted to a Conciliation Commission. If the proposals of this commission are not accepted by the two parties, the question shall be brought before the Council of the League of Nations, which will deal with it in accordance with Article 15 of the Covenant of the League.

The detailed arrangements for effecting such peaceful settlement are the subject of special agreements signed this day.

Article 4. 1. If one of the High Contracting Parties alleges that a violation of Article 2 of the present Treaty or a breach of Articles 42 or 43 of the Treaty of Versailles has been or is being committed, it shall bring the question at once before the Council of the League of Nations.

2. As soon as the Council of the League of Nations is satisfied that such violation or breach has been committed, it will notify its findings without delay to the Powers signatory of the present Treaty, who severally agree that in such case they will each of them come immediately to the assistance of the Power against whom the act complained of is directed.

3. In case of a flagrant violation of Article 2 of the present Treaty or of a flagrant breach of Articles 42 or 43 of the Treaty of Versailles by one of the High Contracting Parties, each of the other Contracting Parties hereby undertakes immediately to come to the help of the party against whom such a violation or breach has been directed as soon as the said Power has been able to satisfy itself that this violation constitutes an unprovoked act of aggression and that by reason either of the crossing of the frontier or of the outbreak of hostilities or of the assembly of armed forces in the demilitarized zone immediate action is necessary.

Nevertheless, the Council of the League of Nations, which will be seized of the question in accordance with the first paragraph of this Article, will issue its findings, and the High Contracting Parties undertake to act in accordance with the recommendations of the Council provided that they are concurred in by all the members other than the representatives of the parties which have engaged in hostilities.

Article 5. The provisions of Article 3 of the present Treaty are placed under the guarantee of the High Contracting Parties as provided by the following stipulations:

If one of the Powers referred to in Article 3 refuses to submit a dispute to peaceful settlement or to comply with an arbitral or judicial decision and commits a violation of Article 2 of the present Treaty or a breach of Articles 42 or 43 of the Treaty of Versailles, the provisions of Article 4 shall apply.

Where one of the Powers referred to in Article 3 without committing a violation of Article 2 of the present Treaty or a breach of Articles 42 or 43 of the Treaty of Versailles, refuses to submit a dispute to peaceful settlement or to comply with an arbitral or judicial decision, the other party shall bring the matter before the Council of the League of Nations, and the Council shall propose what steps shall be taken; the High Contracting Parties shall comply with these proposals.

Article 6. The provisions of the present Treaty do not affect the rights and obligations of the High Contracting Parties under the Treaty of Versailles or under arrangements supplementary thereto, including the agreements signed in London on the 30th August 1924.

Article 7. The present Treaty, which is designed to ensure the maintenance of peace, and is in conformity with the Covenant of the League of Nations, shall not be interpreted as restricting the duty of the League to take whatever action may be deemed wise and effectual to safeguard the peace of the world.

Article 8. The present Treaty shall be registered at the League of Nations in accordance with the Covenant of the League. It shall remain in force until the Council, acting on a request of one or other of the High Contracting Parties notified to the other signatory Powers three months in advance, and voting at least by a two-thirds majority, decides that the League of Nations ensures sufficient protection to the High Contracting Parties; the Treaty shall cease to have effect on the expiration of a period of one year from such decision.

Article 9. The present Treaty shall impose no obligation upon any of the British Dominions, or upon India, unless the Government of such Dominion, or of India, signifies its acceptance thereof.

Article 10. The present Treaty shall be ratified as soon as possible.

It shall enter into force as soon as all the ratifications have been deposited and Germany has become a member of the League of Nations....

Arbitration Convention between Germany and France, 16 October 1925

[An identical Arbitration Convention was concluded between Germany and Belgium.]

The undersigned duly authorized,

Charged by their respective Governments to determine the methods by which, as provided in Article 3 of the Treaty concluded this day between Germany, Belgium, France, Great Britain, and Italy, a peaceful solution shall be attained of all questions which cannot be settled amicably between Germany and Belgium,

Have agreed as follows:

Part I

Article 1. All disputes of every kind between Germany and France with regard to which the parties are in conflict as to their respective rights, and which it may not be possible to settle amicably by the normal methods of diplomacy, shall be submitted for decision either to an arbitral tribunal or to the Permanent Court of International Justice, as laid down hereafter. It is agreed that the disputes referred to above include in particular those mentioned in Article 13 of the Covenant of the League of Nations.

This provision does not apply to disputes arising out of events prior to the present Convention and belonging to the past.

Disputes for the settlement of which a special procedure is laid down in other conventions in force between Germany and France shall be settled in conformity with the provisions of those conventions.

Article 2. Before any resort is made to arbitral procedure or to procedure before the Permanent Court of International Justice, the dispute may, by agreement between the parties, be submitted, with a view to amicable settlement, to a permanent international commission styled the Permanent Conciliation Commission, constituted in accordance with the present Convention.

Article 3. In the case of a dispute the occasion of which, according to the municipal law of one of the parties, falls within the competence of the national courts of such party, the matter in dispute shall not be submitted to the procedure laid down in the present Convention until a judgement with final effect has been pronounced, within a reasonable time, by the competent national judicial authority.

Article 4. The Permanent Conciliation Commission mentioned in Article 2 shall be composed of five members, who shall be appointed as follows, that is to say: the German Government and the French Government shall each nominate a commissioner chosen from among their respective nationals, and shall appoint, by common agreement, the three other commissioners from among the nationals of third Powers; these three commissioners must be of different nationalities, and the German and French Governments shall appoint the president of the Commission from among them.

The commissioners are appointed for three years, and their mandate is renewable. Their appointment shall continue until their replacement and, in any case, until the termination of the work in hand at the moment of the expiry of their mandate....

Article 5. The Permanent Conciliation Commission shall be constituted within three months from the entry into force of the present Convention....

Article 6. The Permanent Conciliation Commission shall be informed by means of a request addressed to the president by the two parties acting in agreement or, in the absence of such agreement, by one or other of the parties.

The request, after having given a summary account of the subject of the dispute, shall contain the invitation to the Commission to take all necessary measures with a view to arrive at an amicable settlement.

If the request emanates from only one of the parties, notification thereof shall be made without delay to the other party.

Article 7. Within fifteen days from the date when the German Government or the French Government shall have brought a dispute before the Permanent Conciliation Commission either party may, for the examination of the particular dispute, replace its commissioner by a person possessing special competence in the matter....

Article 8. The task of the Permanent Conciliation Commission shall be to elucidate questions in dispute, to collect with that object all necessary information by means of inquiry or otherwise, and to endeavour to bring the parties to an agreement. It may, after the case has been examined, inform the parties of the terms of settlement which seem suitable to it, and lay down a period within which they are to make their decision.

At the close of its labours the Commission shall draw up a report stating, as the case may be, either that the parties have come to an agreement and, if need arises, the terms of the agreement, or that it has been impossible to effect a settlement.

The labours of the Commission must, unless the parties otherwise agree, be terminated within six months from the day on which the Commission shall have been notified of the dispute.

[*Article 9.* Commission shall lay down its own procedure failing any provision to the contrary.]

[*Article 10.* President chooses meeting place in absence of agreement by parties to the contrary.]

[*Article 11.* Work of Permanent Conciliation Commission not public unless agreement by parties to the contrary.]

[*Article 12.* The parties shall be represented by agents before the Commission; agents may be assisted by experts; Commission may obtain oral evidence from agents, experts and with the consent of their Government from any person they regard as useful.]

Article 13. Unless otherwise provided in the present Convention, the decisions of the Permanent Conciliation Commission shall be taken by a majority.

Article 14. The German and French Governments undertake to facilitate the labours of the Permanent Conciliation Commission ... to allow it to proceed in their territory and in accordance with their law to the summoning and hearing of witnesses or experts, and to visit the localities in question.

[*Article 15.* Salary of Commissioners.]

Article 16. In the event of no amicable agreement being reached before the Permanent Conciliation Commission the dispute shall be submitted by means of a special agreement either to the Permanent Court of International Justice under the conditions and according to the procedure laid down by its statute or to an arbitral tribunal under the conditions and according to the procedure laid down by the Hague Convention of the 18th October 1907, for the Pacific Settlement of International Disputes.

If the parties cannot agree on the terms of the special arrangement after a month's notice one or other of them may bring the dispute before the Permanent Court of International Justice by means of an application.

Part II

Article 17. All questions on which the German and French Governments shall differ without being able to reach an amicable solution by means of the normal methods of diplomacy the settlement of which cannot be attained by means of a judicial decision as provided in Article 1 of the present Convention, and for the settlement of which no procedure has been laid down by other conventions in force between the parties, shall be submitted to the Permanent Conciliation Commission, whose duty it shall be to propose to the parties an acceptable solution and in any case to present a report.

The procedure laid down in Articles 6–15 of the present Convention shall be applicable.

Article 18. If the two parties have not reached an agreement within a month from the termination of the labours of the Permanent Conciliation Commission the question shall, at the request of either party, be brought before the Council of the League of Nations, which shall deal with it in accordance with Article 15 of the Covenant of the League.

GENERAL PROVISION

Article 19. In any case, and particularly if the question on which the parties differ arises out of acts already committed or on the point of commission, the Conciliation Commission or, if the latter has not been notified thereof, the arbitral tribunal or the Permanent Court of International Justice, acting in accordance with Article 41 of its statute, shall lay down within the shortest possible time the provisional measures to be adopted. It shall similarly be the duty of the Council of the League of Nations, if the question is brought before it, to ensure that suitable provisional measures are taken. The German and French Governments undertake respectively to accept such measures, to abstain from all measures likely to have a reper-cussion prejudicial to the execution of the decision or to the arrangements proposed by the Conciliation Commission or by the Council of the League of Nations, and in general to abstain from any sort of action whatsoever which may aggravate or extend the dispute.

Article 20. The present Convention continues applicable as between Germany and France even when other Powers are also interested in the dispute.

Article 21. The present Convention shall be ratified. Ratifications shall be deposited at Geneva with the League of Nations at the same time as the ratifications of the treaty concluded this day between Germany, Belgium, France, Great Britain, and Italy.

It shall enter into and remain in force under the same conditions as the said treaty. . . .

Arbitration Treaty between Germany and Poland, 16 October 1925

[An identical treaty was concluded between Germany and Czechoslovakia.

The terms of this treaty are the same as the Arbitration Convention with two exceptions. Article 22 states that the treaty is in conformity with the Covenant and does not affect the rights of members of the League. But the crucial difference lies in the preamble which does not refer to the Treaty of Mutual Guarantee. This link with the four Guaranteeing Powers is absent; compare with the preamble of the German–French Arbitration Convention.]

Preamble

The President of the German Empire and the President of the Polish Republic;

Equally resolved to maintain peace between Germany and Poland by assuring the peaceful settlement of differences which might arise between the two countries;

Declaring that respect for the rights established by treaty or resulting from the law of nations is obligatory for international tribunals;

Agreeing to recognize that the rights of a State cannot be modified save with its consent;

And considering that sincere observance of the methods of peaceful settlement of international disputes permits of resolving, without recourse to force, questions which may become the cause of division between States;

Have decided to embody in a treaty their common intentions in this respect, and have named as their plenipotentiaries the following . . .

Who, having exchanged their full powers, found in due and good form, are agreed upon the following Articles . . .

Collective Note to Germany regarding Article 16 of the Covenant of the League of Nations

The German delegation has requested certain explanations in regard to Article 16 of the Covenant of the League of Nations.

We are not in a position to speak in the name of the League, but in view of the discussions which have already taken place in the Assembly and in the commissions of the League of Nations, and after the explanations which have been exchanged between ourselves, we do not hesitate to inform you of the interpretation which, in so far as we are concerned, we place upon Article 16.

In accordance with that interpretation the obligations resulting from the said Article on the Members of the League must be understood to mean that each State Member of the League is bound to cooperate loyally and effectively in support of the Covenant and in resistance to any act of aggression to an extent which is compatible with its military situation and takes its geographical position into account.

Pact of Paris (Briand–Kellogg Pact), 27 August 1928

[The Heads of State of the United States, Belgium, Czechoslovakia, Britain, Germany, Italy, Japan and Poland....]

Deeply sensible of their solemn duty to promote the welfare of mankind; persuaded that the time has come when a frank renunciation of war as an instrument of national policy should be made, to the end that the peaceful and friendly relations now existing between their peoples may be perpetuated;

Convinced that all changes in their relations with one another should be sought only by pacific means and be the result of a peaceful and orderly process, and that any signatory Power which shall hereafter seek to promote its national interests by resort to war should be denied the benefits furnished by this Treaty;

Hopeful that, encouraged by their example, all the other nations of the world will join in this humane endeavour and, by adhering to the present Treaty as soon as it comes into force, bring their peoples within the scope of its beneficent provisions, thus uniting the civilized nations of the world in a common renunciation of war as an instrument of their national policy;

Have decided to conclude a treaty, ... and ... have agreed upon the following Articles:

Article I. The High Contracting Parties solemnly declare, in the names of their respective peoples, that they condemn recourse to war for the solution of international controversies and renounce it as an instrument of national policy in their relations with one another.

Article II. The High Contracting Parties agree that the settlement or solution of all disputes or conflicts, of whatever nature or of whatever origin they may be, which may arise among them, shall never be sought except by pacific means.

[*Article III.* Ratification] ...

This Treaty shall, when it has come into effect as prescribed in the preceding paragraph, remain open as long as may be necessary for adherence by all the other Powers of the world....

Protocol concluded between the Soviet Union, Estonia, Latvia, Poland and Rumania on 9 February 1929, giving effect to the treaty renouncing war

The Government of the Estonian Republic, the President of the Latvian Republic, the President of the Polish Republic, His Majesty the King of Rumania and the Central Executive Committee of U.S.S.R.; animated by the desire to contribute to the maintenance of the existing peace between their countries and for the purpose of putting into force without delay, between the peoples of those countries, the Treaty for the Renunciation of War as an Instrument of National Policy, signed at Paris on August 27, 1928; have decided to achieve this purpose by means of the present Protocol and have ... agreed as follows:

Article I. The Treaty for the Renunciation of War as an Instrument of National Policy, signed at Paris on August 27, 1928, a copy of which is attached to the present Protocol as an integral part of this instrument, shall come into force between the Contracting Parties after the ratification of the said Treaty of Paris of 1928 by the competent legislative bodies of the respective Contracting Parties.

Article II. The entry into force, in virtue of the present Protocol of the Treaty of Paris of 1928 in the reciprocal relations between the parties to the present Protocol shall be valid independently of the entry into force of the Treaty of Paris of 1928 as provided in Article III of the last-named Treaty.

Article III. The present Protocol shall be ratified by the competent legislative bodies of the Contracting Parties, in conformity with the requirements of their respective constitutions ...

Treaty between Britain and Dominions, France, Italy, Japan and the United States for the limitation and reduction of naval armament, London, 22 April 1930

...

Desiring to prevent the dangers and reduce the burdens inherent in competitive armaments, and

Desiring to carry forward the work begun by the Washington Naval Conference and to facilitate the progressive realization of general limitation and reduction of armaments,

Have resolved to conclude a Treaty for the limitation and reduction of naval armament, and have accordingly appointed as their plenipotentiaries ...

Part I

Article 1. The High Contracting Parties agree not to exercise their rights to lay down the keels of capital ship replacement tonnage during the years 1931–1936 inclusive as provided in Chapter II, Part 3, of the Treaty for the Limitation of Naval Armament signed between them at Washington on the 6th February 1922, and referred to in the present Treaty as the Washington Treaty.

This provision is without prejudice to the disposition relating to the replacement of ships accidentally lost or destroyed contained in Chapter II, Part 3, Section I, paragraph (c) of the said Treaty.

France and Italy may, however, build the replacement tonnage which they were entitled to lay down in 1927 and

1929 in accordance with the provisions of the said Treaty.

Article 2. 1. The United States, the United Kingdom of Great Britain and Northern Ireland and Japan shall dispose of the following capital ships as provided in this Article. . . .

[U.S. – 3, U.K. – 5, and Japan – 1 named ship.]

2. Subject to any disposal of capital ships which might be necessitated, in accordance with the Washington Treaty, by the building by France or Italy of the replacement tonnage referred to in Article 1 of the present Treaty, all existing capital ships mentioned in Chapter II, Part 3, Section II of the Washington Treaty and not designated above to be disposed of may be retained during the term of the present Treaty.

[*Articles 3 and 4*. Definition of aircraft carrier; no aircraft carrier to be constructed of less than 10,000 tons.]

[*Article 5*. Restriction on armament of aircraft carriers.]

[*Article 7*. Limitation on submarine construction.]

. . .

Part III

The President of the United States of America, His Majesty the King of Great Britain, Ireland and the British Dominions beyond the Seas, Emperor of India, and His Majesty the Emperor of Japan, have agreed as between themselves to the provisions of this Part III:

Article 14. The naval combatant vessels of the United States, the British Commonwealth of Nations and Japan, other than capital ships, aircraft carriers and all vessels exempt from limitation under Article 8, shall be limited during the term of the present Treaty as provided in this Part III, and, in the case of special vessels, as provided in Article 12.

Article 15. For the purpose of this Part III the definition of the cruiser and destroyer categories shall be as follows. . . .

Article 16. 1. The completed tonnage in the cruiser, destroyer and submarine categories which is not to be exceeded on the 31st December 1936, is given in the following table. . . .

2. Vessels which cause the total tonnage in any category to exceed the figures given . . . [*Cruisers*: U.S. tonnage, 323,500 tons; British Commonwealth, 339,000 tons; Japan, 208,850 tons. *Destroyers*: U.S. tonnage, 150,000 tons; British Commonwealth, 150,000 tons; Japan, 105,500 tons. *Submarines*: U.S. tonnage, 52,700 tons; British Commonwealth, 52,700 tons; Japan, 52,700 tons] shall be disposed of gradually during the period ending on the 31st December 1936.

3. The maximum number of cruisers of sub-category (a) shall be as follows: for the United States, 18; for the British Commonwealth of Nations, 15; for Japan, 12. . . .

Article 21. If, during the term of the present Treaty, the requirements of the national security of any High Contracting Party in respect of vessels of war limited by Part III of the present Treaty are in the opinion of that Party materially affected by new construction of any Power other than those who have joined in Part III of this Treaty, that High Contracting Party will notify the other Parties to Part III as to the increase required to be made in its tonnages within one or more of the categories of such vessels of war, . . . and shall be entitled to make such increase. Thereupon the other Parties to Part III of this Treaty shall be entitled to make a proportionate increase in the category or categories specified . . .

Part IV

[Accepted rules of international law.]

[*Article 23*. Treaty shall remain in force until 31 December 1936. New Conference to meet in 1935.]

Four Power Pact between Italy, Britain, France and Germany, Rome, 7 June 1933

[This was not ratified and did not enter into force.]

...

Article 1. The High Contracting Parties will consult together as regards all questions which appertain to them. They undertake to make every effort to pursue, within the framework of the League of Nations, a policy of effective cooperation between all Powers with a view to the maintenance of peace.

Article 2. In respect of the Covenant of the League of Nations, and particularly Articles 10, 16 and 19, the High Contracting Parties decide to examine between themselves and without prejudice to decisions which can only be taken by the regular organs of the League of Nations, all proposals relating to methods and procedure calculated to give due effect to these Articles.

Article 3. The High Contracting Parties undertake to make every effort to ensure the success of the Disarmament Conference and, should questions which particularly concern them remain in suspense on the conclusion of that Conference, they reserve the right to re-examine these questions between themselves in pursuance of the present Agreement with a view to ensuring their solution through the appropriate channels.

Article 4. The High Contracting Parties affirm their desire to consult together as regards all economic questions which have a common interest for Europe and particularly for its economic restoration, with a view to seeking a settlement within the framework of the League of Nations. ...

[*Article 5.* Agreement concluded for ten years.]

[*Article 6.* Ratification.]

IV · France and her Eastern Allies, 1921–39

Even at the time of victory in January 1919, when the French Premier Georges Clemenceau became host to the peace conference and Paris was the centre of world diplomacy, the French never lost sight of the fact that France was in a position of fundamental weakness in post-war Europe. With more than 4 million dead and maimed and a huge debt of 34,000 million gold francs, as well as the physical destruction of much of northern France, French statesmen did not face the future with much confidence. The recovery of a Germany that contained 20 million more Germans than Frenchmen as well as the capacity of the industrial Ruhr basin could once more place France internationally on the defensive, contemplating the possibility of a third German invasion. French foreign policy was thus designed to fulfil two complementary objectives: to find a way of permanently reducing Germany's future power and to retain and gain new allies to ensure a preponderance of strength over a revived Germany. The League of Nations was the third prop, but successive French Governments were loath to place much reliance on it.

The search for firm alliances in the West, that is with Britain and the United States, proved elusive during the years 1919–24; only in the Locarno peace framework could France in 1925 secure British promises of help (p. 95). In the East the position had totally changed with Imperial Russia's defeat and the Bolshevik Revolution. At the end of the war the Czechs were in a good position to occupy and claim all the lands which were to become the Republic of Czechoslovakia.

French alliances with Czechoslovakia and Poland, 1921–5

The Czechs looked to the French as their allies. The position of the Polish frontiers, on the other hand, remained unsettled in the east and the west; what is more, the Poles were in bitter dispute over the Teschen territory with the Czechs. For the French there appeared to be the alternative policy of making a revived Russia France's major ally. As long as the Civil War continued in Russia and the overthrow of the Bolshevik Russian forces remained a possibility, France would not back Poland's policy of annexing more Russian territory as this would have earned France the enmity of the White Russians. And so Poland owed its national survival in the war with Bolshevik Russia (1920–1) to its own strength rather than to French help.

With the *Treaty of Riga, 18 March 1921* (p. 137) which settled the Russian–Polish frontier, and with the consolidation of Soviet power, the French reviewed their Eastern policy during the winter of 1920–1. The French Government now in 1921 concluded that a strong Poland linked in military alliance with France would prove a barrier to Bolshevik Russia and the best check on Germany. The alternative of attempting to gain the alliance of Soviet Russia was not adopted in the 1920s. Franco-Polish cooperation was seen by France as making an essential contribution to post-war European stability. *On 19 February 1921 Poland and France signed an Alliance Treaty, and on 21 February a secret Military Convention* (p. 116). These two agreements were coupled with a secret Polish–French economic agreement, not finally concluded until 6 February 1922, which provided that in return for a French loan of 400 million francs Poland would purchase all its war materials in France. The commercial agreements also gave France preferential treatment in bilateral trade, especially in the Polish oil industry.

At the time of concluding the alliance there remained widespread French misgivings on the extensive commitments assumed. By limiting the *casus foederis* to unprovoked aggression the French hoped to guard against an 'adventurous' Polish policy at the expense of Russia. The military commitment was nevertheless far reaching.

The Czechs felt themselves more secure than the Poles. When the *Franco-Czechoslovak Alliance was signed on 25 January 1924* (p. 117) it was the Czechs not the French who refused an additional secret military convention. The Czech Government wished to retain freedom of action and to follow an independent foreign policy in the Danubian regions. The Franco-Czech alliance was thus much more imprecise and flexible than the Franco-Polish treaties, and Franco-Czech military consultation and cooperation was provided for only by a secret exchange of letters and not by treaty.

Revised alliance treaties with Poland and Czechoslovakia were signed by France on 16 October 1925, at the time of the conclusion of the *Locarno Treaties* (p. 119). To reconcile French obligations under the Locarno treaties with commitments to Poland and Czechoslovakia, France's Eastern allies, was difficult even though the new alliance treaties did not supersede the old. France could no longer act in defence of Poland by invading Germany from the west. Poland and Czechoslovakia would first have to turn to the League of Nations. In practice France was tying its hands to the views taken by Britain and Italy, the Locarno guarantors of the Franco-German frontier. In practice too, Poland and Czechoslovakia followed, perhaps realistically, independent foreign policies and did not rely for sole support on the French alliance. In 1925, with the signature of the Locarno treaties, the French alliances and the Balkan alignments the European diplomatic pattern of the inter-war years was emerging from the uncertainties of the years immediately following Germany's collapse in 1918.

The Little Entente States and the Polish–Rumanian Alliance, 1920–39

The peace settlements did not mark an end to the frontier problems of the States of the Danube region. The diplomatic relations of the nations were largely influenced by three sometimes contradictory considerations.

1. The 'Successor States' carved out of the Austro-Hungarian Monarchy, namely Czechoslovakia and Yugoslavia together with Rumania, which had acquired much former Hungarian territory as well as Bulgarian territory, stood for the maintenance of the peace treaties, and tended to combine against Germany, Hungary, Austria and Bulgaria, countries that might desire to 'revise' these settlements. 2. Soviet Russia was not only feared by Rumania, which had received formerly Russian Bessarabia; for ideological reasons the spread of revolution was feared by all the States on its borders, and they tended to combine against the Bolsheviks. The Czechs were the most friendly to Soviet Russia. 3. Finally, just as before 1914 the smaller States of the Balkans were bound to react to the ambitions of those Great Powers who pursued an active Balkan policy during the inter-war period, especially France, Italy, and in the 1930s, Germany.

It was the uncertainty of French policy in the Balkans and French advances to Hungary in 1920 which first led some of the Balkan States to band together in a joint defence of their interests. Yugoslavia, Czechoslovakia and Rumania began in the summer of 1920 to negotiate the series of treaties which formed the *Little Entente: a defensive alliance between Czechoslovakia and Yugoslavia, 14 August 1920*, directed against Hungarian revisionist plans; a *treaty between Czechoslovakia and Rumania, 5 June 1921*, aimed at preventing Hungarian and Bulgarian revisionism, based on a *convention* directed only against Hungary of *23 April 1921*; finally a *treaty between Yugoslavia and Rumania, 7 June 1921*, directed against both Bulgaria and Hungary (pp. 121–2). Thus the basis of the

Little Entente was the determination to maintain the Treaty of Neuilly (p. 47) and the Treaty of Trianon (p. 46).

The Polish Government was not well disposed to the Little Entente, which tended to give diplomatic leadership to the Czechs. No lasting friendship and cooperation could be established between the Czechs and Poles during the inter-war years. The Rumanians, however, were not only afraid of Hungarian and Bulgarian irredentism (hence their partnership in the *Little Entente*) but also of Russian hostility over the loss of Bessarabia. As the Little Entente was not directed against Russia, *the Poles and Rumanians signed a separate Alliance Treaty, 3 March 1921* (p. 122), providing for help if either State was attacked by Russia. This treaty was renewed and extended by the *Treaty of Guarantee, 26 March 1926*, which stipulated immediate help to the ally in the event of unprovoked attack contrary to Articles 12, 13 and 15 of the Covenant of the League of Nations (p. 122).

The Little Entente States and Rumania and Poland wished by their alignments to create a stable and strong Central and Danubian Europe. They were prepared to make agreements with Great Power neighbours France, Italy, Germany and even the Soviet Union, in order to strengthen their security and independence. Thus the inter-war period saw the conclusion not only of treaties with France but also between *Italy and Yugoslavia* (January 1924), *Czechoslovakia and Italy* (July 1924), *France and Rumania* (January 1926), *Italy and Rumania* (September 1926) and *France and Yugoslavia* (November 1927).

These agreements had their effects on the relations of the Danubian States and Poland in the inter-war period, but from the moment of crisis in the autumn of 1938 onwards they counted for very little. Czechoslovakia was not preserved by the Little Entente in 1938–9, nor did Poland receive aid from Rumania in September 1939 when invaded by Germany and Russia. Yugoslavia was invaded by Germany in April 1941 and was left to fend for itself; Rumania, with Greece the recipient of a unilateral *Anglo-French Guarantee of March 1939* (p. 189), joined the Germans in their war against the Soviet Union in 1941. Though France had been the principal Great Power seeking allies in Eastern and Central Europe in the 1920s, the majority of French leaders came to look upon the Eastern connections in the 1930s as more of a liability and obstacle to effective 'appeasement' than a source of strength.

Political Agreement between France and Poland, 19 February 1921

The Polish Government and the French Government, both desirous of safeguarding, by the maintenance of the Treaties which both have signed or which may in future be recognized by both Parties, the peace of Europe, the security of their territories and their common political and economic interests, have agreed as follows:

1. In order to coordinate their endeavours towards peace, the two Governments undertake to consult each other on all questions of foreign policy which concern both States, so far as those questions affect the settlement of international relations in the spirit of the Treaties and in accordance with the Covenant of the League of Nations.

2. In view of the fact that economic restoration is the essential preliminary condition of the re-establishment of international order and peace in Europe, the two Governments shall come to an understanding in this regard, with a view to concerted action and mutual support.

They will endeavour to develop their economic relations, and for this purpose will conclude special agreements and a Commercial Treaty.

3. If, notwithstanding the sincerely peaceful views and intentions of the two Contracting States, either or both of them should be attacked without giving provocation, the two Governments shall take concerted measures for the defence of their territory and the protection of their legitimate interests, within the limits specified in the preamble.

4. The two Governments undertake to consult each other before concluding new agreements which will affect their policy in Central and Eastern Europe.

5. The present Agreement shall not come into force until the commercial agreements now in course of negotiation have been signed.

Secret Military Convention between France and Poland, 21 February 1921

[This summary is based on the reconstruction of this military treaty from manuscript sources by Piotr S. Wandycz, *France and her Eastern Allies 1919–1925*, Minneapolis, University of Minnesota Press, 1962, pp. 394–5.]

[*Article 1.* If the situation of Germany should become menacing to the extent that there is a threat of war against one of the two signatories, and especially if Germany mobilizes or if the maintenance of the Treaty of Versailles necessitates joint action by the signatories, then the two signatories undertake to strengthen their military preparations in such a way as to be in a position to provide effective and speedy assistance to each other and to act in common. If Germany attacks one of the two countries they are bound to afford assistance to each other following an agreement between them.

Article 2. If Poland is threatened or attacked by Soviet Russia, France undertakes to hold Germany in check by action as necessary on land and sea and to aid Poland in defence against the Soviet army as detailed below.

Article 3. If the eventualities foreseen in Articles 1 and 2 arise, direct French help to Poland will consist of sending to Poland war equipment and a technical mission, but not French troops, and securing the lines of sea communication between France and Poland.

...

Article 5. Poland undertakes with French help to develop its war indemnity according to a particular plan so as to be able to equip the Polish army as necessary.

Article 6. Provision for continuous consultations between the general staffs of the two countries to fulfil the provisions of this treaty.

Article 7. Measures to be taken to ensure the effectiveness of the French military mission in Poland.

Article 8. This Agreement will only come into force when the commercial agreement is concluded.]

Treaty of Alliance between France and Czechoslovakia, 25 January 1924

The President of the French Republic and the President of Czechoslovak Republic,

Being earnestly desirous of upholding the principle of international agreements which was solemnly confirmed by the Covenant of the League of Nations,

Being further desirous of guarding against any infraction of the peace, the maintenance of which is necessary for the political stability and economic restoration of Europe,

Being resolved for this purpose to ensure respect for the international juridical and political situation created by the Treaties of which they were both signatories,

And having regard to the fact that, in order to attain this object, certain mutual guarantees are indispensable for security against possible aggression and for the protection of their common interests,

Have appointed as their plenipotentiaries:

For the President of the French Republic:

M. Raymond Poincaré, *President of the Council, Minister for Foreign Affairs*;

For the President of the Czechoslovak Republic:

M. Edvard Benes, *Minister for Foreign Affairs*,

Who, after examining their full powers, which were found in good and due form, have agreed to the following provisions:

Article 1. The Governments of the French Republic and of the Czechoslovak Republic undertake to concert their action in all matters of foreign policy which may threaten their security or which may tend to subvert the situation created by the Treaties of Peace of which both parties are signatories.

Article 2. The High Contracting Parties shall agree together as to the measures to be adopted to safeguard their common interests in case the latter are threatened.

Article 3. The High Contracting Parties, being fully in agreement as to the importance, for the maintenance of the world's peace, of the political principles laid down in Article 88 of the Treaty of Peace of St Germain-en-Laye of September 10, 1919, and in the Protocols of Geneva dated October 4, 1922, of which instruments they both are signatories, undertake to consult each other as to the measures to be taken in case there should be any danger of an infraction of these principles.

Article 4. The High Contracting Parties, having special regard to the declarations made by the Conference of Ambassadors on February 3, 1920, and April 1, 1921, on which their policy will continue to be based, and to the declaration made on November 10, 1921, by the Hungarian Government to the Allied diplomatic representatives, undertake to consult each other in case their interests are threatened by a failure to observe the principles laid down in the aforesaid declarations.

Article 5. The High Contracting Parties solemnly declare that they are in complete agreement as to the necessity, for the maintenance of peace, of taking common action in the event of any attempt to restore the Hohenzollern dynasty in Germany, and they undertake to consult each other in such a contingency.

Article 6. In conformity with the principles laid down in the Covenant of the League of Nations, the High Contracting Parties agree that if in future any dispute should arise between them which cannot be settled by friendly agreement and through diplomatic channels, they will submit such dispute either to the Permanent Court of International Justice or to such other arbitrator or arbitrators as they may select.

Article 7. The High Contracting Parties undertake to communicate to each other all agreements affecting their policy in Central Europe which they may have previously concluded, and to consult one another before concluding any further agreements. They declare that, in this matter, nothing in the present Treaty is contrary to the above agreements, and in particular to the Treaty of Alliance between France and Poland, or to the Conventions and Agreements concluded by Czechoslovakia with the Federal Republic of Austria, Roumania, the Kingdom of the Serbs, Croats and Slovenes, or to the Agreement effected by an exchange of notes on February 8, 1921, between the Italian Government and the Czechoslovak Government.

Article 8. The present Treaty shall be communicated to the League of Nations in conformity with Article 18 of the Covenant.

The present Treaty shall be ratified and the instruments of ratification shall be exchanged at Paris as soon as possible.

In faith whereof the respective plenipotentiaries, being duly empowered for this purpose, have signed the present Treaty and have thereto affixed their seals.

Done at Paris, in duplicate, on January 25, 1924.

[Signed] R. POINCARÉ, DR EDVARD BENES

Treaty of Understanding between France and Yugoslavia, 11 November 1927

[This treaty is similar in text to the Treaty of Friendship between France and Rumania, 10 June 1926. Rumania also signed a Treaty of Friendship with Italy, 16 September 1926.]

• • •

Article 1. France and the Kingdom of the Serbs, Croats and Slovenes reciprocally undertake to refrain from all attacks or invasions directed against one another and in no circumstances to resort to war against one another ... [unless in virtue of League obligations]

[*Article 2.* Pacific settlement of disputes.]

• • •

Article 5. The High Contracting Parties agree to take counsel together in the event of any modification, or attempted modification, of the political status of European countries and, subject to any resolutions which may be adopted in such case by the Council or Assembly of the League of Nations, to come to an understanding as to the attitude which they should respectively observe in such an eventuality.

Article 6. The High Contracting Parties declare that nothing in this Treaty is to be interpreted as contradicting the stipulations of the treaties at present in force which have been signed by France or the Kingdom of the Serbs, Croats and Slovenes, and which concern their policy in Europe. They undertake to exchange views on questions affecting European policy in order to coordinate their efforts in the cause of peace, and for this purpose to communicate to each other henceforward any treaties or agreements which they may conclude with third Powers on the same subject. Such treaties or agreements shall invariably be directed to aims which are compatible with the maintenance of peace.

Treaty of Mutual Guarantee between France and Poland, Locarno, 16 October 1925

[This treaty is identical in text to the Treaty of Mutual Guarantee between France and Czechoslovakia, 16 October 1925.]

The President of the French Republic and the President of the Polish Republic;

Equally desirous to see Europe spared from war by a sincere observance of the undertakings arrived at this day with a view to the maintenance of general peace,

Have resolved to guarantee their benefits to each other reciprocally by a treaty concluded within the framework of the Covenant of the League of Nations and of the treaties existing between them . . . and . . . have agreed on the following provisions:

Article 1. In the event of Poland or France being injured by a failure to observe the undertakings arrived at this day between them and Germany with a view to the maintenance of general peace, France, and reciprocally Poland, acting in application of Article 16 of the Covenant of the League of Nations, undertake to lend each other immediately aid and assistance, if such a failure is accompanied by an unprovoked resort to arms.

In the event of the Council of the League of Nations, when dealing with a question brought before it in accordance with the said undertakings, being unable to succeed in making its report accepted by all its members other than the representatives of the parties to the dispute, and in the event of Poland or France being attacked without provocation, France, or reciprocally Poland, acting in application of Article 15, paragraph 7, of the Covenant of the League of Nations, will immediately lend aid and assistance.

Article 2. Nothing in the present Treaty shall affect the rights and obligations of the High Contracting Parties as members of the League of Nations, or shall be interpreted as restricting the duty of the League to take whatever action may be deemed wise and effectual to safeguard the peace of the world.

Article 3. The present Treaty shall be registered with the League of Nations, in accordance with the Covenant.

Article 4. The present Treaty shall be ratified. The ratifications will be deposited at Geneva with the League of Nations at the same time as the ratification of the Treaty concluded this day between Germany, Belgium, France, Great Britain, and Italy, and the ratification of the Treaty concluded at the same time between Germany and Poland.

It will enter into force and remain in force under the same conditions as the said Treaties. ...

Alliance between Yugoslavia and Czechoslovakia, 14 August 1920

Firmly resolved to maintain the peace obtained by so many sacrifices, and provided for by the Covenant of the League of Nations, as well as the situation created by the Treaty concluded at Trianon on June 4, 1920, between the Allied and Associated Powers on the one hand, and Hungary on the other, the President of the Czechoslovak Republic and His Majesty the King of the Serbs, Croats, and Slovenes have agreed to conclude a defensive Convention ... and have agreed as follows:

Article 1. In case of an unprovoked attack on the part of Hungary against one of the High Contracting Parties, the other party agrees to assist in the defence of the party attacked, in the manner laid down by the arrangement provided for in Article 2 of the present Convention.

Article 2. The competent Technical Authorities of the Czechoslovak Republic and the Kingdom of the Serbs, Croats, and Slovenes shall decide, by mutual agreement, upon the provisions necessary for the execution of the present Convention.

Article 3. Neither of the High Contracting Parties shall conclude an alliance with a third Power without preliminary notice to the other.

Article 4. The present Convention shall be valid for two years from the date of the exchange of ratifications. On the expiration of this period, each of the Contracting Parties shall have the option of denouncing the present Convention. It shall, however, remain in force for six months after the date of denunciation.

Alliance between Rumania and Czechoslovakia, 23 April 1921

Firmly resolved to maintain the peace obtained by so many sacrifices, and provided for by the Covenant of the League of Nations, as well as the situation created by the Treaty concluded at Trianon on June 4, 1920, between the Allied and Associated Powers on the one hand, and Hungary on the other, the President of the Czechoslovak Republic and His Majesty the King of Rumania, have agreed to conclude a defensive Convention ... and have agreed as follows:

Article 1. In case of an unprovoked attack on the part of Hungary against one of the High Contracting Parties, the other party agrees to assist in the defence of the party attacked, in the manner laid down by the arrangement provided for in Article 2 of the present Convention.

Article 2. The competent Technical Authorities of the Czechoslovak Republic and Rumania shall decide by mutual agreement and in a Military Convention to be concluded, upon the provisions necessary for the execution of the present Convention.

Article 3. Neither of the High Contracting Parties shall conclude an alliance with a third Power without preliminary notice to the other.

Article 4. For the purpose of coordinating their efforts to maintain peace, the two Governments undertake to consult together on questions of foreign policy concerning their relations with Hungary.

Article 5. The present Convention shall be valid for two years from the date of the exchange of ratifications. On the expiration of this period, each of the Contracting Parties shall have the option of denouncing the present Convention. It shall, however, remain in force for six months after the date of denunciation.

Alliance between Yugoslavia and Rumania, 7 June 1921

Firmly resolved to maintain the peace obtained by so many sacrifices, and the situation created by the Treaty concluded at Trianon on June 4, 1920, between the Allied and Associated Powers on the one hand, and Hungary on the other, as well as the Treaty concluded at Neuilly on November 27, 1919, between the same Powers and Bulgaria, His Majesty the King of the Serbs, Croats, and Slovenes and His Majesty the King of Rumania have agreed to conclude a defensive Convention ... and have concluded the following Articles:

Article 1. In case of an unprovoked attack on the part of Hungary or of Bulgaria, or of these two Powers, against one of the two High Contracting Parties, with the object of destroying the situation created by the Treaty of Trianon or the Treaty of Neuilly, the other Party agrees to assist in the defence of the Party attacked, in the manner laid down by Article 2 of this Convention.

Article 2. The Technical Authorities of the Kingdom of the Serbs, Croats, and Slovenes and of the Kingdom of Rumania shall decide by mutual agreement, in a Military Convention to be concluded as soon as possible, upon the provisions necessary for the execution of the present Convention.

Article 3. Neither of the High Contracting Parties shall conclude an alliance with a third Power without preliminary notice to the other.

Article 4. With the object of associating their efforts to maintain peace, the two Governments bind themselves to consult together on questions of foreign policy concerning their relations with Hungary and Bulgaria.

Alliance between Poland and Rumania, 3 March 1921

Being firmly resolved to safeguard a peace which was gained at the price of so many sacrifices, the Chief of the State of the Polish Republic and His Majesty the King of Rumania have agreed to conclude a Convention for a defensive alliance....

Article 1. Poland and Rumania undertake to assist each other in the event of their being the object of an unprovoked attack on their present eastern frontiers.

Accordingly, if either State is the object of an unprovoked attack, the other shall consider itself in a state of war and shall render armed assistance.

Article 2. In order to coordinate their efforts to maintain peace, both Governments undertake to consult together on such questions of foreign policy as concern their relations with their eastern neighbours.

Article 3. A military Convention shall determine the manner in which either country shall render assistance to the other should the occasion arise.

This Convention shall be subject to the same conditions as the present Convention as regards duration and denunciation.

Article 4. If, in spite of their efforts to maintain peace, the two States are compelled to enter on a defensive war under the terms of Article 1, each undertakes not to negotiate nor to conclude an armistice or a peace without the participation of the other State.

Article 5. The duration of the present Convention shall be five years from the date of its signature, but either Government shall be at liberty to denounce it after two years, on giving the other State six months' notice.

Article 6. Neither of the High Contracting Parties shall be at liberty to conclude an alliance with a third Power without having previously obtained the assent of the other party.

Alliances with a view to the maintenance of treaties already signed jointly by both Poland and Rumania are excepted from this provision.

Such alliances must, however, be notified.

The Polish Government hereby declares that it is acquainted with the agreements entered into by Rumania with other States with a view to upholding the Treaties of Trianon and Neuilly, which agreements may be transformed into treaties of alliance.

The Rumanian Government hereby declares that it is acquainted with the agreements entered into by Poland with the French Republic.

Treaty of Guarantee between Poland and Rumania, 26 March 1926

The President of the Polish Republic and His Majesty the King of Rumania, noting with satisfaction the consolidation of the guarantees for the general peace of Europe, and anxious to satisfy the desire for peace by which the peoples are animated, desirous of seeing their country spared from war, and animated also with the sincere desire of giving to their peoples supplementary guarantees within the framework of the Covenant of the League of Nations and of the treaties of which they are signatories, have determined to conclude a Treaty with this object....

Article 1. Poland and Rumania undertake each to respect and preserve against external aggression the territorial integrity and existing political independence of the other.

Article 2. In the event of Poland or Rumania, contrary to the undertakings imposed by Articles 12, 13, and 15 of the Covenant of the League of Nations, being attacked without provocation, Poland and reciprocally Rumania, acting in application of Article 16 of the Covenant of the League of Nations, undertake to lend each other immediately aid and assistance.

In the event of the Council of the League of Nations, when dealing with a question brought before it in accordance with the provisions of the Covenant of the League of Nations, being unable to secure the acceptance of its report by all its Members other than the representatives of the parties to the dispute, and in the event of Poland or Rumania being attacked without provocation, Poland or reciprocally Rumania, acting in application of Article 15, paragraph 7, of the Covenant of the League of Nations, will immediately lend aid and assistance to the other country.

Should a dispute of the kind provided for in Article 17 of the Covenant of the League of Nations arise, and Poland or Rumania be attacked without provocation, Poland and reciprocally Rumania undertake to lend each other immediately aid and assistance.

The details of application of the above provisions shall be settled by technical agreements.

Article 3. If, in spite of their efforts to maintain peace, the two States are compelled to enter on a defensive war under the terms of Articles 1 and 2, each undertakes not to negotiate or conclude an armistice or a peace without the participation of the other State.

Article 4. In order to coordinate their efforts to maintain peace, both Governments undertake to consult together on such questions of foreign policy as concern both Contracting Parties.

Article 5. Neither of the High Contracting Parties shall be at liberty to conclude an alliance with a third Power without having previously consulted the other party.

Alliances with a view to the maintenance of treaties already signed jointly by both Poland and Rumania are excepted from this provision.

Such alliances must, however, be notified.

Article 6. The High Contracting Parties undertake to submit all disputes which may arise between them or which it may not have been possible to settle by the ordinary methods of diplomacy, to conciliation or arbitration. The details of this procedure of pacific settlement shall be laid down in a special convention to be concluded as soon as possible.

Article 7. The present Treaty shall remain in force for five years from the date of its signature, but either of the two Governments shall be entitled to denounce it after two years, upon giving six months' notice.

[*Article 8.* Ratification.]

Protocol

The Convention of Defensive Alliance which expires on April 3, 1926, being recognized to have had results beneficial to the cause of peace, the undersigned plenipotentiaries, holding full powers, found in good and due form, from the President of the Polish Republic and from His Majesty the King of Rumania, respectively, have agreed to conclude a Treaty of Guarantee for a further period of five years....

[The Treaty of Guarantee was concluded again on 15 January 1931.]

Supplementary Agreement to the Treaties of Friendship and Alliance between the States of the Little Entente, 27 June 1930

[Czechoslovakia, Rumania and Yugoslavia ...]

Being desirous of strengthening still further the ties of friendship and alliance which exist between the States of the Little Entente,

Wishing to supplement the organization of the political cooperation and of the defence of the common interests of their three States by means of a fixed procedure,

Have resolved to confirm the present practice and the present procedure of close cooperation between their States by defining them with greater precision....

Article I. The Ministers for Foreign Affairs of the Little Entente shall meet whenever circumstances make it necessary. They shall in any case meet at least once a year. Compulsory ordinary meetings shall be held, in turn, in each of the three States at a place selected beforehand. There shall also be an optional ordinary meeting at Geneva during the Assemblies of the League of Nations.

Article II. The compulsory meeting shall be presided over by the Minister for Foreign Affairs of the State in which it is held. That Minister is responsible for fixing the date and selecting the place of the meeting. He draws up its agenda and is responsible for the preparatory work connected with the decisions to be taken.

Until the regular meeting of the following year he is considered as President for the time being.

Article III. In all the questions which are discussed and in all the measures which are taken in regard to the relations of the States of the Little Entente between themselves, the principle of the absolute equality of the three States shall be rigorously respected. That principle shall also be respected more particularly in the relations of these States with other States or with a group of States, or with the League of Nations.

Article IV. According to the necessities of the situation, the three Ministers for Foreign Affairs may decide, by common agreement, that in regard to any particular question the representation or the defence of the point of view of the States of the Little Entente shall be entrusted to a single delegate or to the delegation of a single State.

Article V. An extraordinary meeting may be convened by the President for the time being when the international situation or an international event requires it.

Article VI. The present Agreement shall enter into force immediately. It shall be ratified and the exchange of ratifications shall take place at Prague as soon as possible....

Pact of Organization of the Little Entente, 16 February 1933

... Desirous of maintaining and organizing peace;

Firmly determined to strengthen economic relations with all States without distinction and with the Central European States in particular,

Anxious that peace shall be safeguarded in all circumstances, that progress in the direction of the real stabilization of conditions in Central Europe shall be assured and that the common interests of their three countries shall be respected,

Determined, with this object, to give an organic and stable basis to the relations of friendship and alliance existing between the three States of the Little Entente, and,

Convinced of the necessity of bringing about such stability on the one hand by the complete unification of their general policy and on the other by the creation of a directing organ of this common policy, namely, the group of the three States of the Little Entente, thus forming a higher international unit, open to other States under conditions to be agreed upon in each particular case ...

Article 1. A Permanent Council of the States of the Little Entente, composed of the Ministers for Foreign Affairs of the three respective countries or of the special delegates appointed for the purpose, shall be constituted as the directing organ of the common policy of the group of the three States. Decisions of the Permanent Council shall be unanimous.

Article 2. The Permanent Council, apart from its normal intercourse through the diplomatic channel, shall be required to meet at least three times a year. One obligatory annual meeting shall be held in the three States in turn, and another shall be held at Geneva during the Assembly of the League of Nations.

Article 3. The President of the Permanent Council shall be the Minister for Foreign Affairs of the State in which the obligatory annual meeting is held. He shall take the initiative in fixing the date and the place of meeting, shall arrange its agenda and shall draw up the questions to be decided. He shall continue to be President of the Permanent Council until the first obligatory meeting of the following year.

Article 4. In all questions that may be discussed, as in all decisions that may be reached, whether in regard to the relations of the States of the Little Entente among themselves or in regard to their relations with other States, the principle of the absolute equality of the three States of the Little Entente shall be rigorously respected.

Article 5. According to the exigencies of the situation, the Permanent Council may decide that in any given question the representation or the defence of the point of view of the States of the Little Entente shall be entrusted to a single delegate or to the delegation of a single State.

Article 6. Every political treaty of any one State of the Little Entente, every unilateral act changing the existing political situation of one of the States of the Little Entente in relation to an outside State, and every economic agreement involving important political consequences shall henceforth require the unanimous consent of the Council of the Little Entente.

The existing political treaties of each State of the Little Entente with outside States shall be progressively unified as far as possible.

Article 7. An Economic Council of the States of the Little Entente shall be constituted for the progressive coordination of the economic interests of the three States, whether among themselves or in their relations with other States. It shall be composed of specialists and experts in economic, commercial and financial matters and shall act as an auxiliary advisory organ of the Permanent Council in regard to its general policy.

Article 8. The Permanent Council shall be empowered to establish other stable or temporary organs, commissions or committees for the purpose of studying and preparing the solution of special questions or groups of questions for the Permanent Council.

Article 9. A Secretariat of the Permanent Council shall be created. Its headquarters shall be established in each case for one year in the capital of the President in office of the Permanent Council. A section of the Secretariat shall function permanently at the seat of the League of Nations at Geneva.

Article 10. The common policy of the Permanent Council shall be inspired by the general principles embodied in all the great international instruments relating to post-war policy, such as the Covenant of the League of Nations, the Pact of Paris, the General Act of Arbitration, any Conventions concluded in regard to disarmament, and the Locarno Pacts. Furthermore, nothing in the present Pact shall be construed as contrary to the principles or provisions of the Covenant of the League of Nations.

Article 11. The Conventions of Alliance between Roumania and Czechoslovakia of April 23, 1921, between Roumania and Yugoslavia of June 7, 1921, and between Czechoslovakia and Yugoslavia of August 31, 1922, which were extended on May 21, 1929, and are supplemented by the provisions of the present Pact, as well as the Act of Conciliation, Arbitration and Judicial Settlement signed by the three States of the Little Entente at Belgrade on May 21, 1929, are hereby renewed for an indefinite period.

Article 12. The present Pact shall be ratified and the exchange of ratifications shall take place at Prague not later than the next obligatory meeting. . . .

Pact of Balkan Entente between Turkey, Greece, Rumania and Yugoslavia, 9 February 1934

Article 1. Greece, Roumania, Turkey and Yugoslavia mutually guarantee the security of each and all of their Balkan frontiers.

Article 2. The High Contracting Parties undertake to concert together in regard to the measures to be taken in contingencies liable to affect their interests as defined by the present Agreement. They undertake not to embark upon any political action in relation to any other Balkan country not a signatory of the present Agreement without previous mutual consultation, nor to incur any political obligation to any other Balkan country without the consent of the other Contracting Parties.

Article 3. The present Agreement shall come into force on the date of its signature by the Contracting Parties . . .

Protocol: Annex of the Pact, 9 February 1954

In proceeding to sign the Pact of Balkan Entente, the four Ministers for Foreign Affairs of Greece, Roumania, Yugoslavia, and Turkey have seen fit to define as follows the nature of the undertakings assumed by their respective countries, and to stipulate explicitly that the said definitions form an integral part of the Pact.

1. Any country committing one of the acts of aggression to which Article 2 of the London Conventions of July 3rd and 4th, 1933, relates shall be treated as an aggressor.

2. The Pact of Balkan Entente is not directed against any Power. Its object is to guarantee the security of the several Balkan frontiers against any aggression on the part of any Balkan State.

3. Nevertheless, if one of the High Contracting Parties is the victim of aggression on the part of any other non-Balkan Power, and a Balkan State associates itself with such aggression, whether at the time or subsequently, the Pact of Balkan Entente shall be applicable in its entirety in relation to such Balkan State.

4. The High Contracting Parties undertake to conclude appropriate Conven-

tions for the furtherance of the objects pursued by the Pact of Balkan Entente. The negotiation of such Conventions shall begin within six months.

5. As the Pact of Balkan Entente does not conflict with previous undertakings, all previous undertakings and all Conventions based on previous treaties shall be applicable in their entirety, the said undertakings and the said treaties having all been published.

6. The words 'Firmly resolved to ensure the observance of the contractual obligations already in existence', in the Preamble to the Pact, shall cover the observance by the High Contracting Parties of existing treaties between Balkan States, to which one or more of the High Contracting Parties is a signatory party.

7. The Pact of Balkan Entente is a defensive instrument; accordingly, the obligations on the High Contracting Parties which arise out of the said Pact shall cease to exist in relation to a High Contracting Party becoming an aggressor against any other country within the meaning of Article 2 of the London Conventions.

8. The maintenance of the territorial situation in the Balkans as at present established is binding definitively on the High Contracting Parties. The duration of the obligations under the Pact shall be fixed by the High Contracting Parties in the course of the two years following the signature of the Pact, or afterwards. During the two years in question the Pact cannot be denounced. The duration of the Pact shall be fixed at not less than five years, and may be longer. If, two years after the signature of the same, no duration has been fixed, the Pact of Balkan Entente shall *ipso facto* remain in force for five years from the expiry of the two years after the signature thereof. On the expiry of the said five years, or of the period on which the High Contracting Parties have agreed for its duration, the Pact of Balkan Entente shall be renewed automatically by tacit agreement for the period for which it was previously in force, failing denunciation by any one of the High Contracting Parties one year before the date of its expiry; provided always that no denunciation or notice of denunciation shall be admissible, whether in the first period of the Pact's validity (namely, seven or more than seven years) or in any subsequent period fixed automatically by tacit agreement, before the year preceding the date on which the Pact expires.

9. The High Contracting Parties shall inform each other as soon as the Pact of Balkan Entente is ratified in accordance with their respective laws.

Balkan Entente between Turkey, Greece, Rumania and Yugoslavia, 9 February 1934, and Bulgaria, 31 July 1938

Whereas Bulgaria is an adherent of the policy of consolidation of peace in the Balkans, and is desirous of maintaining relations of good neighbourhood and full and frank collaboration with the Balkan States, and

Whereas the States of the Balkan Entente are animated by the same pacific spirit in relation to Bulgaria and the same desire of cooperation,

Now therefore the undersigned:

His Excellency Monsieur Georges KIOSSÉIVANOV, President of the Council of Ministers, Bulgarian Minister for Foreign Affairs and Public Worship, of the one part, and

His Excellency Monsieur Jean METAXAS, President of the Council of Ministers, Greek Minister for Foreign Affairs, acting in his capacity as President in Office of the Permanent Council of the Balkan Entente, in the name of all the Members of the Balkan Entente, of the other part,

Hereby declare, on behalf of the States which they represent, that the said States undertake to abstain in their relations with one another from any resort to force, in accordance with the agreements to which they have severally subscribed in respect of non-aggression, and are agreed to waive the application in so far as they are concerned of the provisions contained in Part IV (Military, Naval and Air clauses) of the Treaty of Neuilly, as also of the provisions contained in the Convention respecting the Thracian Frontier, signed at Lausanne, July 24th, 1923.

V · The Soviet Union and her neighbours, 1919–37

The years from 1918 to 1921 saw an astonishing transformation of Bolshevik Russia's fortunes. In the spring of 1918 the control of the Bolsheviks over Russia's territory had shrunk to only a shadow of the former empire. Russia was occupied on the one hand by the Germans who could still advance at will, and also by Allied 'intervention'. But even after Germany's collapse in November 1918, Soviet Russia's troubles were far from over. Allied 'intervention' continued; Soviet Russia simultaneously fought and survived both the Civil War and the Polish War.

The first task facing the Soviet leaders was to achieve settled frontiers and to secure Soviet power within them. Taking advantage of Russia's weakness, the Poles early in 1919 had occupied as much territory eastwards as they could, whilst from Siberia, Admiral Kolchak's anti-Bolshevik forces were pushing into European Russia. Kolchak was defeated but the Poles could not be simultaneously resisted. That autumn of 1919 Yudenich advanced from his Baltic base and threatened Moscow. But early in 1920 the Red Army defeated the White Russian forces and Wrangel's last stand in the Crimea during 1920–1 proved but an epilogue to the Civil War. Allied intervention, never effective, ceased for all practical purposes. During the spring of 1920 the Poles, led by Marshal Joseph Pilsudski, posed the greatest threat to Russia. In April 1920 Pilsudski negotiated an agreement with the hard pressed anti-Bolshevik régime of what remained of the independent State of the Ukraine. The Poles advanced and reached Kiev in May 1920. The Russian counter-attack came within reach of Warsaw in August, but Pilsudski was able to counter-attack in turn and to force the Red Army to withdraw. In October 1920 an armistice brought the war to an end, and the *Treaty of Riga, 18 March 1921* (p. 137), settled the frontiers of the two States until 1939. That same year,

1920, Soviet Russia recognized the independence of the three Baltic Republics, Estonia, Latvia and Lithuania, and also of Finland. With Finland Russia concluded the *Treaty of Dorpat, 14 October 1920* (p. 136). Not until the spring of 1921 did Soviet Russia win a measure of international recognition with the signature of the *Anglo-Soviet Trade Agreement, 16 March 1921* (p. 140). Soviet foreign policy was designed to achieve two complementary objectives: to strengthen and broaden the Soviet base and to weaken the 'capitalist' opposition.

Soviet treaties, 1921–7

Soviet treaties fall into distinctive groups: treaties of peace with Russia's neighbours, Poland, the Baltic Republics and Finland, all formerly part of the Russian Tsarist Empire and now recognized as independent States with mutually agreed and delimited frontiers.

The need for recognition and trade led Soviet Russia to make a number of treaties and agreements with the West. The first breakthrough came with the signature of the *Anglo-Soviet Trade Agreement, 16 March 1921* (p. 140), whereby Soviet Russia secured *de facto* recognition from the world's most important 'capitalist State'. Soviet Russia gradually gained international recognition throughout the world including the United States (1933). While the Russian Soviet Government on the one hand signed treaties in which conditions were to be created for normalizing relations between the Soviet Union and its neighbours, the Russian Communist Party on the other sought to organize world revolution with the help of the Comintern.

The First Congress of the Third International held in Moscow in March 1919 served Lenin's purpose in that it created an organization around which could be grouped a worldwide international socialist movement under the control of the Russian Communist Party. Its aim was to promote revolution abroad. The Second Congress met in July 1920, and during its course Lenin laid down the conditions which had to be met before a communist group could be admitted to the Third International. By the time of the meeting of the Third Congress (June–July 1921) it had become evident that world revolution was no longer imminent, but the efforts to promote it were not abandoned: revolution was merely delayed.

Alliances and treaties with anti-colonial and nationalist movements were concluded by *Soviet Russia and Iran on 26 February 1921* which, as one Soviet historian recently wrote, 'struck a powerful blow at imperialism and its colonial system'. Two days later came the signature of a *Soviet Treaty with Afghanistan, 28 February 1921*, whereby the Soviets intended to weaken the British position in India; and a month later the remarkable Soviet coup was completed with the signature of the *Soviet–Turkish Treaty of Friendship, 16 March 1921* (p. 77). These treaties were confirmed by the signatures of the *Soviet–Turkish Treaty of Non-Aggression and Neutrality, 17 December 1925*, and similar treaties with *Afghanistan, 31 August 1926*, and *Iran, 1 October 1927*.

Relations between the Soviet Union and Germany

Germany and Russia, once in the relationship of victor and vanquished when Brest-Litovsk was signed, had both become defeated Powers after November 1918. The war had gravely weakened the two countries. Nevertheless Russia and Germany remained potentially Great Powers. Thus despite their entirely different political complexions there was a community of interest which brought Russia and Germany together in the 1920s. Their collaboration involved some limited secret military cooperation and limited economic assistance for Russia; joint enmity towards Poland within its post-war frontiers was the basis. In 1922 the *Genoa Conference* of major European Powers met to reconstruct the economy of Europe and to revive world trade. It proved abortive. The most important result was that two of the participants, Soviet Russia and Germany, unable to persuade the Western Powers to make sufficient concessions, signed a treaty with each other at the neighbouring resort of Rapallo. The significance of the *Treaty of Rapallo, 16 April 1922* (p. 139) lay in the fact that both Soviet Russia and Germany broke out of diplomatic isolation. Their cooperation was based not on an identity of views or genuine friendship but on self-interest. The Locarno reconciliation with the West and Germany's entry into the League of Nations in 1926 was carefully dovetailed by Stresemann to harmonize with Germany's undertakings to Soviet Russia. Thus Germany would not be automatically obliged to join in any action against Russia under Article 16, because it need only do so to an extent that was compatible with its military situation and geographical location, a phrase that left Germany the decision. Weimar Germany reaffirmed its relationship with Soviet Russia by the *Treaty of Berlin, 24 April 1926* (p. 142); but the relative position of the two countries had changed. Locarno meant that Germany was no longer exclusively reliant on the Soviet Union for support (p. 96). The Soviet Union attempted to extend the principle of neutrality and non-aggression treaties to the Baltic States. All these efforts failed except for a *treaty with Lithuania, 28 September 1926*. On *25 January 1929, Germany and the Soviet Union concluded a Conciliation Convention* (pp. 144, 145).

The consequences of the world depression of 1929 ended the collaboration between the Weimar Republic and Soviet Russia. From 1930 to 1933 the German Communists combined with the Nazis to undermine the Weimar Republic. In this they succeeded.

A NOTE ON SECRET GERMAN–SOVIET MILITARY COOPERATION

Several secret military agreements were concluded between the German industrialists, the German army (with the knowledge of some ministers of the Weimar Government) and the Soviet Union. The first of these was a provisional agreement, 15 March 1922, which provided the finance for Junkers to build an aeroplane factory in the Soviet Union. German troops were sent for training to the Soviet Union in 1922; munitions and poison gas were manufactured in Russia. The agreements were not formal treaties, but nevertheless were concrete arrangements to further what were then regarded by the German military as the mutual and parallel interests of Germany and the Soviet Union; they both looked on post-Versailles Poland as the enemy. By 1926 relatively little was actually achieved in providing Germany with armaments. The most important advantage for Germany was the provision of training facilities for German pilots. After 1929 a tank school trained some German troops in the Soviet Union; there were some joint German–Soviet poison gas experiments, and a number of German officers participated in Soviet manœuvres. These agreements broke the military terms of the Versailles treaty. They were, however, much more limited than the rumoured 'secret treaties' of extensive military cooperation, which did not exist.

Treaties of non-aggression and mutual assistance in Europe, 1926–36

The years after 1926 mark a new stage in Soviet policy. Within the Soviet Union, Stalin emerged as sole dictator and the organs of the State were transformed to a fully totalitarian system. Stalin embarked on a policy of industrialization, on collectivization of agriculture regardless of human life, and on a policy of terror against all probable and improbable opponents. Internationally the Soviet Union, despite its recognition and entry into the League of Nations in 1934, felt itself increasingly isolated and in danger. All was now subordinated to the security of the State. The virulent hatred of the Nazis for the Bolsheviks cut the links between the Soviet Union and Germany. These had been weakening since Locarno.

The Soviet Union engaged in vigorous diplomatic activity to assure its safety from attack and to prevent a hostile coalition of Powers coming into being. From 1926 to 1937 the Soviet Union concluded a large number of non-aggression treaties. Stalin acquiesced for the time being in the existence of the 'Buffer States', Poland, the Baltic States and Finland. The most important *non-aggression treaty was that concluded with Poland, 25 July 1932* (p. 145); similar treaties were concluded with *France, 29 November 1932* (p. 148), and *Finland, 21 January 1932* (p. 149), *Latvia, 5 February 1932, Estonia, 4 May 1932, and Lithuania in 1926* (p. 144).

The failure to obtain an Eastern Locarno, whereby France and Russia would have guaranteed the independence of the Buffer States, led the Russians to sign with France a *Treaty of Mutual Assistance, 2 May 1935* (p. 152). Although the clauses of the treaty suggest a complete and effective alliance, appearances are misleading. The obligation to go to war was not automatic; the League of Nations had first to recognize the fact of aggression under Article 16 of the Covenant. There were no detailed military provisions; geography ensured that since Russia and Germany lacked a common frontier, Russia could not help France as long as Germany and Russia respected Polish and Baltic neutrality; similarly France could not 'attack' Germany without a breach of Locarno. The treaty was not ratified for almost a year and entered into force on 27 March 1936. The *Soviet Union also signed a Mutual Assistance Treaty with Czechoslovakia, 16 May 1935* (p. 154), but it contained the provision that it would only become operative if France first came to the help of the Czechs. Once more geography denied Soviet Russia the possibility of giving direct military help without passing through hostile Poland or Rumania. Despite these agreements Czechoslovakia was sacrificed to Hitler at Munich in September 1938 (without Soviet participation at the conference but also without any real chance of Soviet help for Czechoslovakia during the crisis).

Soviet treaties in eastern Asia

In 1919 in the Far East, Soviet Russia felt itself threatened by Allied and Japanese intervention, by occupation and by support given to anti-Bolshevik forces. Attempts to win over China by denouncing Tsarist imperialism were not very successful. The Chinese, taking advantage of Russian impotence, had regained control of the Chinese Eastern Railway and over autonomous Outer Mongolia. By April 1920 the Soviet position improved. Only the Japanese remained a strong foreign force on Russian soil. A Soviet-supported revolution brought Outer Mongolia back under Soviet protection. Russo-Chinese relations in the 1920s varied from normalization, advanced by the *Agreement of 31 May 1924 concerning the Chinese Eastern Railway*, to the all but declared war in 1929 as a result of Soviet attempts to establish Soviet influence in China. In the 1920s good relations were established between Russia and Japan, marked especially by the *Convention between Japan and the Soviet Union concerning their general relationship, 20 January 1925* (p. 156).

But the 1930s saw a reversal of Russia's Far Eastern policies. With Japanese aggression in China and Japan's growing expansionism, the Soviet Union gave support to China. The change in this relationship with China is marked by the signature of a *Treaty of Non-Aggression between the U.S.S.R. and the Republic of China, 21 August 1937* (p. 160). Despite the agreement reached between the Soviet Union with Japan's puppet state of Manchukuo for the sale of the *Chinese Eastern Railway, 23 March 1935* (p. 159), Soviet–Japanese relations remained very strained. With the *Mongolian People's Republic the Soviet Union concluded a Mutual Assistance Treaty, 12 March 1936* (p. 159).

Treaty of Peace between Latvia and Soviet Russia, 11 August 1920

[Similar treaties were concluded with the other Baltic States.]

Russia on the one hand, and Latvia on the other, being strongly desirous of bringing to an end the present state of war between them, and of bringing about a final settlement of all the questions arising from the former subjection of Latvia to Russia, have decided to commence negotiations for peace and to conclude as soon as possible a lasting, honourable and just peace ... and have agreed on the following terms:

Article I. The state of war between the Contracting Parties shall cease from the date of the coming into force of the present Treaty.

Article II. By virtue of the principle proclaimed by the Federal Socialist Republic of the Russian Soviets, which establishes the right of self-determination for all nations, even to the point of total separation from the States with which they have been incorporated, and in view of the desire expressed by the Latvian people to possess an independent national existence, Russia unreservedly recognizes the independence and sovereignty of the Latvian State and voluntarily and irrevoc-ably renounces all sovereign rights over the Latvian people and territory which formerly belonged to Russia under the then existing constitutional law as well as under international treaties, which, in the sense here indicated, shall in future cease to be valid. The previous status of subjection of Latvia to Russia shall not entail any obligation towards Russia on the part of the Latvian people or territory.

Article III. The State frontier between Russia and Latvia shall be fixed as follows: ... [for details of frontiers, see map on p. 39].

Article IV. The two Contracting Parties undertake:

1. To forbid any army to remain on either territory except their own army or that of friendly States with which one of the Contracting Parties has concluded a military convention, but which are not in a *de facto* state of war with either Contracting Party; and also to forbid, within the limits of their respective territory, the mobilization and recruiting of any personnel intended for the armies of States, organizations or groups, for purposes of armed conflict against the other Contracting Party. ...

2. Not to permit the formation or residence in their territory of organizations or groups of any kind claiming to represent the Government of all or part of the territory of the other Contracting Party; or of representatives or officials of organizations or groups having as their object the overthrow of the Government of the other Contracting Party.

3. To forbid Governments in a *de facto* state of war with the other party, and organizations and groups having as their object military action against the other Contracting Party, to transport through their ports or their territory anything which might be used for military purposes against the other Contracting Party, in particular, military forces belonging to these States, organizations or groups; material of war; technical military stores belonging to artillery, supply services, engineers or air services.

4. To forbid, except in cases provided for by international law, passage through or navigation in their territorial waters of all warships, gunboats, torpedo boats, etc., belonging either to organizations and groups whose object is military action against the other Contracting Party, or to Governments which are in state of war with the other Contracting Party and which aim at military action against the other Contracting Party. This provision shall come into force as soon as such intentions are known to the Contracting Party to whom the said territorial waters and ports belong.

Article V. The two parties mutually undertake not to claim the expenses of the war from each other. By this is understood the expenses incurred by the State for the conduct of the war, and likewise any compensations for losses occasioned by the war, that is, losses occasioned to themselves or to their subjects by military operations, including all kinds of requisitions made by one of the Contracting Parties in the territory of the other.

Article VI. In view of the fact that it is necessary to apportion in an equitable manner among the States of the world the obligation to make good the damages caused by the World War of 1914-17 to States that have been ruined, or to portions of States on whose territory military operations have taken place, the two Contracting Parties undertake to do all in their power to secure an agreement among all States in order to establish an international fund, which would be used to cover the sums intended for the reparation of damages due to the war.

Independently of the creation of this international fund, the Contracting Parties consider it necessary that Russia and all new States constituting independent Republics in what was formerly Russian territory should render each other, as far as possible, mutual support to make good from their own resources the damage caused by the World War, and undertake to do all in their power to secure this agreement between the above-mentioned Republics.

Article VII. Prisoners of war of both parties shall be repatriated as soon as possible. The method of exchange of prisoners is laid down in the Annex to this present Article.
Note: All captives who are not serving voluntarily in the army of the Government which has made them prisoners shall be considered as prisoners of war.

ANNEX TO ARTICLE VII

1. Prisoners of the two Contracting Parties shall be repatriated unless, with the consent of the Government on whose territory they are, they express the desire to remain in the country in which they are or to proceed to any other country. . . .

Treaty of Peace between Finland and Soviet Russia (Treaty of Dorpat), 14 October 1920

Whereas Finland declared its independence in 1917, and Russia has recognized the independence and the sovereignty of Finland within the frontiers of the Grand Duchy of Finland,

The Government of the Republic of Finland, and the Government of the Federal Socialist Republic of Soviet Russia,

Actuated by a desire to put an end to the war which has arisen between their States, to establish mutual and lasting peace relations and to confirm the situation which springs from the ancient political union of Finland and Russia,

Have resolved to conclude a Treaty with this object in view, and have agreed on the following provisions:

Article I. From the date upon which this Treaty shall come into force, a state of war shall cease to exist between the Contracting Powers, and the two Powers shall mutually undertake to maintain, for the future, an attitude of peace and goodwill towards one another.

Article II. The frontier between the States of Russia and of Finland shall be as follows ... [for frontier details see map on p. 4].

...

Article VI. 1. Finland guarantees that she will not maintain, in the waters contiguous to her seaboard in the Arctic Ocean, warships or other armed vessels, other than armed vessels of less than 100 tons displacement, which Finland may keep in these waters in any number, and of a maximum number of fifteen warships and other armed vessels, each with a maximum displacement of 400 tons.

Finland also guarantees that she will not maintain, in the above-mentioned waters, submarines or armed airplanes.

2. Finland also guarantees that she will not establish on the coast in question

naval ports, bases or repairing stations of greater size than are necessary for the vessels mentioned in the preceding paragraph and for their armament.

...

Article VIII. 1. The right of free transit to and from Norway through the territory of Pechenga shall be guaranteed to the State of Russia and to its nationals....

...

Article XII. The two Contracting Powers shall on principle support the neutralization of the Gulf of Finland and of the whole Baltic Sea, and shall undertake to cooperate in the realization of this object.

Article XIII. Finland shall militarily neutralize the following of her islands in the Gulf of Finland: Sommaro (Someri), Nervo (Narvi), Seitskar (Seiskari), Peninsaari, Lavansaari, Stora Tyterskar (Suuri Tytarsaari), Lilla Tyterskar (pieni Tytarsaari) and Rodskar....

Article XIV. As soon as this Treaty comes into force, Finland shall take measures for the military neutralization of Hogland under an international guarantee....

...

Article XVI. ... Russia shall, however, have the right to send Russian war vessels into the navigable waterways of the interior by the canals along the southern bank of Ladoga and even, should the navigation of these canals be impeded, by the southern part of Ladoga.

2. Should the Gulf of Finland and the Baltic Sea be neutralized, the Contracting Powers mutually undertake to neutralize Ladoga also.

...

Article XXIV. The Contracting Powers will exact no indemnity whatsoever from one another for war expenses.

Finland will take no share in the expenses incurred by Russia in the World War of 1914–1918.

Article XXV. Neither of the Contracting Powers is responsible for the public debts and other obligations of the other Power.

Article XXVI. The debts and other obligations of the Russian State and of Rus- sian governmental institutions towards the State of Finland and the Bank of Finland, and, similarly, the debts and obligations of the State of Finland and Finnish governmental institutions towards the Russian State and its governmental institutions, shall be regarded as mutually liquidated. . . .

Treaty of Peace between Poland and Soviet Russia (Treaty of Riga), 18 March 1921

Poland of the one hand and Russia and the Ukraine of the other, being desirous of putting an end to the war and of concluding a final, lasting and honourable peace based on a mutual understanding and in accordance with the peace preliminaries signed at Riga on October 12, 1920, have decided to enter into negotiations and have appointed for this purpose as plenipotentiaries ... and have agreed to the following provisions:

Article I. The two Contracting Parties declare that a state of war has ceased to exist between them.

Article II. The two Contracting Parties, in accordance with the principle of national self-determination, recognize the independence of the Ukraine and of White Ruthenia and agree and decide that the eastern frontier of Poland, that is to say, the frontier between Poland on the one hand, and Russia, White Ruthenia and the Ukraine on the other, shall be as follows ... [details].

Article III. Russia and the Ukraine abandon all rights and claims to the territories situated to the west of the frontier laid down by Article II of the present Treaty. Poland, on the other hand, abandons in favour of the Ukraine and of White Ruthenia all rights and claims to the territory situated to the east of this fron-tier. The two Contracting Parties agree that, in so far as the territory situated to the west of the frontier fixed in Article II of the present Treaty includes districts which form the subject of a dispute between Poland and Lithuania, the question of the attribution of these districts to one of those two States is a matter which exclusively concerns Poland and Lithuania.

Article IV. Poland shall not, in view of the fact that a part of the territories of the Polish Republic formerly belonged to the Russian Empire, be held to have incurred any debt or obligation towards Russia, except as provided in the present Treaty.

Similarly, no debt or obligation shall be regarded as incurred by Poland towards White Ruthenia or the Ukraine and vice versa except as provided in the present Treaty, owing to the fact that these countries formerly belonged to the Russian Empire.

Article V. Each of the Contracting Parties mutually undertakes to respect in every way the political sovereignty of the other party, to abstain from interference in its internal affairs, and particularly to refrain from all agitation, propaganda or interference of any kind, and not to encourage any such movement,

Each of the Contracting Parties undertakes not to create or protect organizations which are formed with the object of encouraging armed conflict against the other Contracting Party or of undermining its territorial integrity, or of subverting by force its political or social institutions, nor yet such organizations as claim to be the Government of the other party or of a part of the territories of the other party. The Contracting Parties therefore, undertake to prevent such organizations, their official representatives and other persons connected therewith, from establishing themselves on their territory, and to prohibit military recruiting and the entry into their territory and transport across it of armed forces, arms, munitions and war material of any kind destined for such organizations.

Article VI. 1. All persons above the age of 18 who, at the date of the ratification of the present Treaty are within the territory of Poland and on August 1, 1914 were nationals of the Russian Empire and are, or have the right to be, included in the registers of the permanent population of the former Kingdom of Poland, or have been included in the registers of an urban or rural commune, or of one of the class organizations in the territories of the former Russian Empire which formed part of Poland, shall have the right of opting for Russian or Ukrainian nationality. A similar declaration by nationals of the former Russian Empire of all other categories who are within Polish territory at the date of the ratification of the present Treaty shall not be necessary.

2. Nationals of the former Russian Empire above the age of 18 who at the date of the ratification of the present Treaty are within the territory of Russia and of the Ukraine and are, or have the right to be, included in the register of the permanent population of the former Kingdom of Poland, or have been included in the registers of an urban or rural commune, or of one of the class organizations in the territories of the former Russian Empire which formed part of Poland, shall be considered as Polish citizens if they express such a desire in accordance with the system of opting laid down in this Article. Persons above the age of 18 who are within the territory of Russia and of the Ukraine shall also be considered as Polish citizens if they express such a desire, in accordance with the system of opting laid down in this Article, and if they provide proofs that they are descendants of those who took part in the Polish struggle for independence between 1830 and 1865, or that they are descendants of persons who have for at least three generations been continuously established in the territory of the former Polish Republic, or if they show that they have by their actions, by the habitual use of the Polish language and by their method of educating their children, given effective proof of their attachment to Polish nationality....

Article VII. 1. Russia and the Ukraine undertake that persons of Polish nationality in Russia, the Ukraine and White Ruthenia shall, in conformity with the principles of the equality of peoples, enjoy full guarantees of free intellectual development, the use of their national language and the exercise of their religion. Poland undertakes to recognize the same rights in the case of persons of Russian, Ukrainian and White Ruthenian nationality in Poland....

...

3. The churches and religious associations in Russia, the Ukraine and White Ruthenia, of which Polish nationals are members, shall, so far as is in conformity with the domestic legislation of these countries, have the right of independent self-administration in domestic matters....

Article VIII. The two Contracting Parties mutually abandon all claims to the repayment of war expenses, that is to say all the expenses incurred by the State during the war, and of the indemnities for damages caused by the war, that is to say, for damages caused to them or to their nationals in the theatre of war as a result of the war or of military measures taken during the Polish-Russian-Ukrainian War.

Treaty between Germany and Soviet Russia (Treaty of Rapallo) regarding the solution of general problems, 16 April 1922

The German Government, represented by Reichsminister Dr Walther Rathenau, and the Government of R.S.F.S.R., represented by People's Commissar Chicherin, have agreed upon the following provisions:

Article I. The two Governments agree that all questions resulting from the state of war between Germany and Russia shall be settled in the following manner:

(a) Both Governments mutually renounce repayment for their war expenses and for damages arising out of the war, that is to say, damages caused to them and their nationals in the zone of the war operations by military measures, including all requisitions effected in a hostile country. They renounce in the same way repayment for civil damages inflicted on civilians, that is to say, damages caused to the nationals of the two countries by exceptional war legislation or by violent measures taken by any authority of the State of either side.

(b) All legal relations concerning questions of public or private law resulting from the state of war, including the question of the treatment of merchant ships which fell into the hands of the one side or the other during the war, shall be settled on the basis of reciprocity.

(c) Germany and Russia mutually renounce repayment of expenses incurred for prisoners of war. The German Government also renounces repayment of expenses for soldiers of the Red Army interned in Germany. The Russian

Government, for its part, renounces repayment of the sums Germany has derived from the sale of Russian army material brought into Germany by these interned troops.

Article II. Germany renounces all claims resulting from the enforcement of the laws and measures of the Soviet Republic as it has affected German nationals or their private rights or the rights of the German State itself, as well as claims resulting from measures taken by the Soviet Republic or its authorities in any other way against subjects of the German State or their private rights, provided that the Soviet Republic shall not satisfy similar claims by any third State.

Article III. Consular and diplomatic relations between Germany and the Federal Soviet Republic shall be resumed immediately. The admission of consuls to both countries shall be arranged by special agreement.

Article IV. Both Governments agree, further, that the rights of the nationals of either of the two parties on the other's territory as well as the regulation of commercial relations shall be based on the most-favoured-nation principle. This principle does not include rights and facilities granted by the Soviet Government to another Soviet State or to any State that formerly formed part of the Russian Empire.

Article V. The two Governments undertake to give each other mutual assistance for the alleviation of their economic difficulties in the most benevolent spirit. In the event of a general settlement of this question on an international basis, they undertake to have a preliminary exchange of views. The German Government declares itself ready to facilitate, as far as possible, the conclusion and the execution of economic contracts between private enterprises in the two countries.

Article VI. Article I, paragraph (b), and Article IV of this agreement will come into force after the ratification of this document. The other Articles will come into force immediately.

Trade Agreement between Britain and the Soviet Union, London, 16 March 1921

Whereas it is desirable in the interests both of Russia and of the United Kingdom that peaceful trade and commerce should be resumed forthwith between these countries, and whereas for this purpose it is necessary pending the conclusion of a formal general Peace Treaty between the Governments of these countries by which their economic and political relations shall be regulated in the future that a preliminary Agreement should be arrived at between the Government of the United Kingdom and the Government of the Russian Socialist Federal Soviet Republic, hereinafter referred to as the Russian Soviet Government.

The aforesaid parties have accordingly entered into the present Agreement for the resumption of trade and commerce between the countries.

The present Agreement is subject to the fulfilment of the following conditions, namely:

(a) That each party refrains from hostile action or undertakings against the other and from conducting outside of its own borders any official propaganda direct or indirect against the institutions of the British Empire or the Russian Soviet Republic respectively, and more particularly that the Russian Soviet Government refrains from any attempt by military or diplomatic or any other form of action or propaganda to encourage any of the peoples of Asia in any form of hostile action against British interests or the British Empire, especially in India and in the Independent State of Afghanistan. The British Government gives a similar particular undertaking to the Russian Soviet Government in respect of the countries which formed part of the former Russian Empire and which have now become independent.

(b) That all British subjects in Russia are immediately permitted to return home, and that all Russian citizens in Great Britain or other parts of the British Empire who desire to return to Russia are similarly released.

It is understood that the term 'conducting any official propaganda' includes the giving by either party of assistance or encouragement to any propaganda conducted outside its own borders.

The parties undertake to give forthwith all necessary instructions to their agents and to all persons under their authority to conform to the stipulations undertaken above.

Article I. Both parties agree not to impose or maintain any form of blockade against each other and to remove forthwith all obstacles hitherto placed in the way of the resumption of trade between the United Kingdom and Russia in any commodities which may be legally exported from or imported into their respective territories to or from any other foreign country, and do not exercise any discrimination against such trade, as compared with that carried on with any other foreign country or to place any impediments in the way of banking, credit and financial operations for the purpose of such trade, but subject always to legislation generally applicable in the respective countries. It is understood that nothing in this Article shall prevent either party from regulating the trade in arms and ammunition under general provisions of law which are applicable to the import of arms and ammunition from, or their export to foreign countries. . . .

. . .

Article IV. Each party may nominate such number of its nationals as may be agreed from time to time as being reasonably necessary to enable proper effect to be given to this Agreement, having regard to the conditions under which trade is carried on in its territories, and the other party shall permit such persons to enter its territories, and to sojourn and carry on trade there, provided that either party may restrict the admittance of any such persons into any specified areas, and may refuse admittance to or sojourn in its territories to any individual who is *persona non grata* to itself, or who does not comply with this Agreement or with the conditions precedent thereto. . . .

. . .

Article XIII. The present Agreement shall come into force immediately and both parties shall at once take all necessary measures to give effect to it. It shall continue in force unless and until replaced by the Treaty contemplated in the preamble so long as the conditions laid down both in the Articles of the Agreement and in the preamble are observed by both sides. Provided that at any time after the expiration of twelve months from the date on which the

Agreement comes into force either party may give notice to terminate the provisions of the preceding Articles, and on the expiration of six months from the date of such notice those Articles shall terminate accordingly. . . .

Provided also that in the event of the infringement by either party at any time of any of the provisions of this Agreement or of the conditions referred to in the preamble, the other party shall immediately be free from the obligations of the Agreement. Nevertheless it is agreed that before taking any action inconsistent with the Agreement the aggrieved party shall give the other party a reasonable opportunity of furnishing an explanation or remedying the default. . . .

Declaration of Recognition of Claims

At the moment of signature of the preceding Trade Agreement both parties declare that all claims of either party or of its nationals against the other party in respect of property or rights or in respect of obligations incurred by the existing or former Governments of either country shall be equitably dealt with in the formal general Peace Treaty referred to in the preamble.

In the meantime and without prejudice to the generality of the above stipulation the Russian Soviet Government declares that it recognizes in principle that it is liable to pay compensation to private persons who have supplied goods or services to Russia for which they have not been paid. The detailed mode of discharging this liability shall be regulated by the Treaty referred to in the preamble.

The British Government hereby makes a corresponding declaration.

It is clearly understood that the above declarations in no way imply that the claims referred to therein will have preferential treatment in the aforesaid Treaty as compared with any other classes of claims which are to be dealt with in that Treaty.

Treaty of Berlin between the Soviet Union and Germany, Berlin, 24 April 1926

The German Government and the Government of the Union of Socialist Soviet Republics, being desirous of doing all in their power to promote the maintenance of general peace,

And being convinced that the interests of the German people and of the peoples of the Union of Socialist Soviet Republics demand constant and trustful cooperation,

Having agreed to strengthen the friendly relations existing between them by means of a special Treaty ... have agreed upon the following provisions:

Article 1. The relations between Germany and the Union of Socialist Soviet Republics shall continue to be based on the Treaty of Rapallo.

The German Government and the Government of the Union of Socialist Soviet Republics will maintain friendly contact in order to promote an understanding with regard to all political and economic questions jointly affecting their two countries.

Article 2. Should one of the Contracting Parties, despite its peaceful attitude, be attacked by one or more third Powers, the other Contracting Party shall observe neutrality for the whole duration of the conflict.

Article 3. If on the occasion of a conflict of the nature mentioned in Article 2, or at a time when neither of the Contracting Parties is engaged in warlike operations, a coalition is formed between third Powers with a view to the economic or financial boycott of either of the Contracting Parties, the other Contracting Party undertakes not to adhere to such coalition.

Article 4. The present Treaty shall be ratified and the instruments of ratification shall be exchanged at Berlin.

It shall enter into force on the date of the exchange of the instruments of ratification and shall remain in force for five years. The two Contracting Parties shall confer in good time before the expiration of this period with regard to the future development of their political relations.

In faith whereof the plenipotentiaries have signed the present Treaty.

Exchange of Notes, 24 April 1926

(a) HERR STRESEMANN TO M. KRESTINSKI

With reference to the negotiations upon the Treaty signed this day between the German Government and the Government of the Union of Socialist Soviet Republics, I have the honour, on behalf of the German Government, to make the following observations:

(1) In the negotiation and signature of the Treaty, both Governments have taken the view that the principle laid down by them in Article 1, paragraph 2, of the Treaty, of reaching an understanding on all political and economic questions affecting the two countries, will contribute considerably to the maintenance of peace. In any case the two Governments will in their deliberations be guided by the need for the maintenance of the general peace.

(2) In this spirit also the two Governments have approached the fundamental questions which are bound up with the entry of Germany into the League of Nations. The German Government is convinced that Germany's membership of the League cannot constitute an obstacle to the friendly development of the relations between Germany and the Union of Socialist Soviet Republics. According to its basic idea, the League of Nations is designed for the peaceful and equitable settlement of international disputes. The German Government is determined to cooperate to the best of its ability in the realization of this idea. If, however, though the German Government does

not anticipate this, there should at any time take shape within the League, contrary to that fundamental idea of peace, any efforts directed exclusively against the Union of Socialist Soviet Republics, Germany would most energetically oppose such efforts.

(3) The German Government also proceeds upon the assumption that this fundamental attitude of German policy towards the Union of Socialist Soviet Republics cannot be adversely influenced by the loyal observance of the obligations, arising out of Articles 16 and 17 of the Covenant of the League and relating to the application of sanctions, which would devolve upon Germany as a consequence of her entry into the League of Nations. By the terms of these Articles, the application of sanctions against the Union of Socialist Soviet Republics would come into consideration, in the absence of other causes, only if the Union of Socialist Soviet Republics entered upon a war of aggression against a third State. It is to be borne in mind that the question whether the Union of Socialist Soviet Republics is the aggressor in the event of a conflict with a third State could only be determined with binding force for Germany with her own consent; and that, therefore, an accusation to this effect levelled by other Powers against the Union of Socialist Soviet Republics and regarded by Germany as unjustified, would not oblige Germany to take part in measures of any kind instituted on the authority of Article 16. With regard to the question whether, in a concrete case, Germany would be in a position to take part in the application of sanctions at all, and to what extent, the German Government refers to the Note of December 1, 1925, on the interpretation of Article 16 addressed to the German Delegation on the occasion of the signing of the Treaties of Locarno.

(4) In order to create a secure basis for disposing without friction of all questions arising between them, the two Governments regard it as desirable that they should immediately embark upon negotiations for the conclusion of a general treaty for the peaceful solution of any conflicts that may arise between them, when special attention shall be given to the possibilities of the procedure of arbitration and conciliation.

I avail myself of this opportunity to renew to Your Excellency the assurance of my highest consideration.

(b) M. KRESTINSKI TO HERR STRESEMANN

... I have the honour, on behalf of the Union of Socialist Soviet Republics, to make the following reply:

(1) In the negotiation and signature of the Treaty, both Governments have taken the view that the principle laid down by them in Article 1, paragraph 2, of the Treaty, of reaching an understanding on all political and economic questions jointly affecting the two countries, will contribute considerably to the maintenance of peace. In any case the two Governments will in their deliberations be guided by the need for the maintenance of the general peace.

(2) The Government of the Union of Socialist Soviet Republics takes note of the explanation contained in Sections 2 and 3 of your Note concerning the fundamental questions connected with Germany's entry into the League of Nations.

(3) In order to create a secure basis for disposing without friction of all questions arising between them, the two Governments regard it as desirable that they should immediately embark upon negotiations for the conclusion of a general treaty for the peaceful solution of any conflicts that may arise between them, when special attention shall be given to the possibilities of the procedure of arbitration and conciliation ...

Treaty of Non-Aggression concluded between the Soviet Union and Lithuania, 28 September 1926

• • •

Article 1. The relations between the Union of Socialist Soviet Republics and the Lithuanian Republic shall continue to be based on the Treaty of Peace between Lithuania and Russia, concluded at Moscow on July 12, 1920, all provisions of which shall retain their force and inviolability.

Article 2. The Lithuanian Republic and the Union of Socialist Soviet Republics undertake to respect in all circumstances each other's sovereignty and territorial integrity and inviolability.

Article 3. Each of the two Contracting Parties undertakes to refrain from any act of aggression whatsoever against the other party.

Should one of the Contracting Parties, despite its peaceful attitude, be attacked by one or several third Powers, the other Contracting Party undertakes not to support the said third Power or Powers against the Contracting Party attacked.

Article 4. If, on the occasion of a conflict of the type mentioned in Article 3, second paragraph, or at a time when neither of the Contracting Parties is engaged in warlike operations, a political agreement directed against one of the Contracting Parties is concluded between third Powers, or a coalition is formed between third Powers with a view to the economic or financial boycott of either of the Contracting Parties, the other Contracting Party undertakes not to adhere to such agreement or coalition.

Article 5. Should a dispute arise between them, the Contracting Parties undertake to appoint conciliation commissions if it should not prove possible to settle the dispute by diplomatic means.

The composition of the said commissions, their rights and the procedure they shall observe shall be settled in virtue of a separate agreement to be concluded between the two parties.

• • •

Conciliation Convention between Germany and the Soviet Union, 25 January 1929

The Central Executive Committee of U.S.S.R. and the President of the German Reich, animated by a desire further to strengthen the friendly relations which exist between the two countries, have decided, in execution of the Agreement reached in the Exchange of Notes of April 24, 1926, to conclude an Agreement for a procedure of conciliation, and ... have agreed upon the following terms:

Article I. Disputes of all kinds, particularly differences of opinion which arise regarding the interpretation of the bilateral treaties which exist between the two Contracting Parties or regarding past or future agreements concerning their elucidation or execution, shall, in the event of difficulties arising over their solution through diplomatic channels, be submitted to a procedure of conciliation in accordance with the following provisions.

Article II. The procedure of conciliation shall be before a Conciliation Commission.

The Conciliation Commission shall not be permanent, but shall be formed expressly for each meeting. It shall meet once a year in the middle of the year, in ordinary session, the exact date of which shall be arranged each year by agreement between the two Governments.

There shall be extraordinary sessions whenever in the opinion of the two Governments special need arises.

The meetings of the Conciliation Commission shall be held alternately in Moscow and Berlin. The place of the first meeting shall be decided by lot.

A session shall ordinarily last not longer than fourteen days.

...

Article V. The task of the Conciliation Commission shall be to submit to the two Governments a solution of the questions laid before it which shall be fair and acceptable to both parties, with special regard to the avoidance of possible future differences of opinion between the two parties on the same question.

Should the Conciliation Commission in the course of a session fail to agree upon a recommendation regarding any question on the agenda, the question shall be laid before an extraordinary session of the Conciliation Commission, which must, however, meet not later than four months after the first meeting. Otherwise the matter shall be dealt with through diplomatic channels.

The results of each session of the Conciliation Commission shall be submitted to the two Governments for approval in the form of a report.

The report, or parts of it, shall be published only by agreement between the two Governments.

...

[In an additional Protocol, it was stated that the Soviet Union could not accept any provision for the appointment of a Chairman; the possibility was not excluded in special cases.]

[NOTE: This Convention and the Agreement of Neutrality and Non-Aggression of 24 April 1926 were prolonged by a Protocol concluded 24 June 1931.]

Pact of Non-Aggression between the Soviet Union and Poland, 25 July 1932

The President of the Polish Republic of the one part, and the Central Executive Committee of U.S.S.R. of the other part; desirous of maintaining the present state of peace between their countries and convinced that the maintenance of peace between them constitutes an important factor in the work of preserving universal peace; considering that the Treaty of Peace of March 18, 1921 constitutes, now as in the past, the basis of their reciprocal relations and undertakings; convinced that the peaceful settlement of international disputes and the exclusion of all that might be contrary to the normal condition of relations between States are the surest means of arriving at the goal desired; declaring that none of the obligations hitherto assumed by either of the parties stands in the way of peaceful development of their mutual relations or is incompatible with the present Pact; have decided to conclude the present Pact with the object of amplifying and completing the Pact for the Renunciation of War signed at Paris on August 27, 1928, and put into force by the Protocol signed at Moscow on February 9, 1929; ... and have agreed on the following provisions:

Article I. The two Contracting Parties, recording the fact that they have renounced war as an instrument of national policy in their mutual relations, reciprocally undertake to refrain from taking any aggressive action against or invading the territory of the other party, either alone or in conjunction with other Powers.

Any act of violence attacking the integrity and inviolability of the territory or the political independence of the other Contracting Party shall be regarded as contrary to the undertakings contained in the present Article, even if such acts are committed without declaration of war and avoid all warlike manifestations as far as possible.

Article II. Should one of the Contracting Parties be attacked by a third State or by a group of other States, the other Contracting Party undertakes not to give aid or assistance, either directly or indirectly, to the aggressor State during the whole period of the conflict.

Should one of the Contracting Parties commit an act of aggression against a third State, the other Contracting Party shall have the right to denounce the present Pact without notice.

Article III. Each of the Contracting Parties undertakes not to be a party to any agreement openly hostile to the other party from the point of view of aggression.

Article IV. The undertakings provided for in Articles I and II of the present Pact shall in no case limit or modify the international rights and obligations of each Contracting Party under agreements concluded by it before the coming into force of the present Pact, so far as the said agreements contain no aggressive elements.

Article V. The two Contracting Parties, desirous of settling and solving, exclusively by peaceful means, any disputes and differences, of whatever nature or origin, which may arise between them, undertake to submit questions at issue, which it has not been possible to settle within a reasonable period by diplomacy, to a procedure of conciliation, in accordance with the provisions of the Convention for the application of the procedure of conciliation which constitutes an integral part of the present Pact and shall be signed separately and ratified as soon as possible simultaneously with the Pact of Non-Aggression.

Article VI. The present Pact shall be ratified as soon as possible, and the instruments of ratification shall be exchanged at Warsaw within thirty days following the ratification by Poland and U.S.S.R., after which the Pact shall come into force immediately.

Article VII. The Pact is concluded for three years. If it is not denounced by one of the Contracting Parties, after previous notice of not less than six months before the expiry of that period, it shall be automatically renewed for a further period of two years.

Article VIII. The present Pact is drawn up in Polish and Russian, both texts being authentic.

Protocol of Signature (I)

The Contracting Parties declare that Article VII of the Pact of July 25, 1932 may not be interpreted as meaning that the expiry of the time limit of denunciation before the expiry of the time period under Article VII could have as a result the limitation or cancellation of the obligations arising out of the Pact of Paris of 1928.

Protocol of Signature (II)

On signing the Pact of Non-Aggression this day, the two parties, having exchanged their views on the draft Conciliation Convention submitted by the Soviet Party, declare that they are convinced that there is no essential difference of opinion between them.

Protocol prolonging the Pact of Non-Aggression, 25 July 1932, with Final Protocol, 5 May 1934

The Central Executive Committee of U.S.S.R. and the President of the Republic of Poland; being desirous of providing as firm a basis as possible for the development of the relations between their countries; being desirous of giving each other fresh proof of the unchangeable character and solidity of the pacific and friendly relations happily established between them; moved by the desire to contribute to the consolidation of world peace and to the stability and peaceful development of international relations in Eastern Europe; noting that the conclusion on July 25, 1932 at Moscow of the Treaty between U.S.S.R. and the Republic of Poland has had a beneficial influence on the development of their relations and on the solution of the above-mentioned problems; have decided to sign the present Protocol and have ... agreed on the following provisions:

Article I. In modification of the provisions of Article VII of the Treaty of Non-Aggression concluded at Moscow on July 25, 1932 between U.S.S.R. and the Republic of Poland concerning the date and manner in which that Treaty shall cease to have effect, the two Contracting Parties decide that it shall remain in force until December 31, 1945.

Each of the High Contracting Parties shall be entitled to denounce the Treaty by giving notice to that effect six months before the expiry of the above-mentioned period. If the Treaty is not denounced by either of the Contracting Parties, its period of validity shall be automatically prolonged for two years; similarly, the Treaty shall be regarded as prolonged on each occasion for a further period of two

years, if it is not denounced by either of the Contracting Parties in the manner provided for in the present Article.

Article II. The present Protocol is drawn up in duplicate, each copy being in the Russian and Polish languages and both texts being equally authentic.

The present Protocol shall be ratified as soon as possible, and the instruments of ratification shall be exchanged between the Contracting Parties at Warsaw.

The present Protocol shall come into force on the date of the exchange of the instruments of ratification.

Final Protocol

In connection with the signature on this date of the Protocol prolonging the Treaty of Non-Aggression between the U.S.S.R. and the Republic of Poland of July 25, 1932, each of the High Contracting Parties, having again examined all the provisions of the Peace Treaty concluded at Riga on March 18, 1921, which constitutes the basis of their mutual relations, declares that it has no obligations and is not bound by any declarations inconsistent with the provisions of the said Peace Treaty in particular of Article III thereof.

Consequently, the Government of U.S.S.R. confirms that the Note from the People's Commissar, G. V. Chicherin, of September 28, 1926, to the Lithuanian Government cannot be interpreted to mean that that Note implied any intention on the part of the Soviet Socialist Government to interfere in the settlement of the territorial questions mentioned therein.

Joint Soviet–Polish Statement, 26 November 1938

A series of conversations recently held between the U.S.S.R. People's Commissar for Foreign Affairs, M. Litvinov, and the Polish Ambassador in Moscow, M. Grzybowski, has led to the following statement:

1. Relations between the Polish Republic and U.S.S.R. are and will continue to be based to the fullest extent on all the existing Agreements, including the Polish–Soviet Pact of Non-Aggression dated July 25, 1932. This Pact, concluded for five years and extended on May 5, 1934 for a further period ending December 31, 1945, has a basis wide enough to guarantee the inviolability of peaceful relations between the two States.

2. Both Governments are favourable to the extension of their commercial relations.

3. Both Governments agree that it is necessary to settle a number of current and longstanding matters that have arisen in connection with the various Agreements in force and, in particular, to dispose of the various frontier incidents that have recently been occurring.

Protocol of Signature
...

2. The High Contracting Parties declare that subsequent denunciation of the present Treaty before its termination or annulment shall neither cancel nor restrict the undertakings arising from the Pact for the Renunciation of War signed at Paris on August 27, 1928.

Pact of Non-Aggression between the Soviet Union and France, 29 November 1932

[A Conciliation Convention was signed at the same time.]

The President of the French Republic and the Central Executive Committee of U.S.S.R.; animated by the desire to consolidate peace; convinced that it is in the interests of both High Contracting Parties to improve and develop relations between the two countries; mindful of the international undertakings which they have previously assumed and none of which, they declare, constitutes an obstacle to the pacific development of their mutual relations or is inconsistent with the present Treaty; desirous of confirming and defining, so far as concerns their respective relations, the General Pact of August 27, 1928 for the renunciation of war; ... have agreed on the following provisions:

Article I. Each of the High Contracting Parties undertakes with regard to the other not to resort in any case, whether alone or jointly with one or more third Powers, either to war or to any aggression by land, sea or air against that other party, and to respect the inviolability of the territories which are placed under the party's sovereignty or which it represents in external relations or for whose administration it is responsible.

Article II. Should either High Contracting Party be the object of aggression by one or more third Powers, the other High Contracting Party undertakes not to give aid or assistance, either directly or indirectly, to the aggressor or aggressors during the period of the conflict.

Should either High Contracting Party resort to aggression against a third Power, the other High Contracting Party may denounce the present Treaty without notice.

Article III. The undertakings set forth in Articles I and II above shall in no way limit or modify the rights or obligations of each Contracting Party under agreements concluded by it before the coming into force of the present Treaty, each Party hereby declaring further that it is not bound by any agreement involving an obligation for it to participate in aggression by a third State.

Article IV. Each of the High Contracting Parties undertakes, for the duration of the present Treaty, not to become a party to any international agreement of which the effect in practice would be to prevent the purchase of goods from or the sale of goods or the granting of credits to the other party, and not to take any measure which would result in the exclusion of the other party from any participation in its foreign trade.

Article V. Each of the High Contracting Parties undertakes to respect in every connection the sovereignty or authority of the other party over the whole of that party's territories as defined in Article I of the present Treaty, not to interfere in any way in its internal affairs, and to abstain more particularly from action of any kind calculated to promote or encourage agitation, propaganda or attempted intervention designed to prejudice its territorial integrity or to transform by force the political or social régime of all or part of its territories.

Each of the High Contracting Parties undertakes in particular not to create, protect, equip, subsidize or admit in its territory either military organizations for the purpose of armed combat with the other party or organizations assuming the role of government or representing all or part of its territories.

Article VI. The High Contracting Parties having already recognized, in the General Pact of August 27, 1928 for the renunciation of war, that the settlement or solution of all disputes or conflicts, of whatever nature or of whatever origin they may be, which may arise among them, shall never be sought except by pacific means, confirm that provision, and, in order to give effect to it, annex to the present Treaty a Convention relating to conciliation procedure.

Article VII. The present Treaty, of which the French and Russian texts shall both be authentic, shall be ratified, and the ratifications thereof shall be exchanged at Moscow. It shall enter into effect on the date of the said exchange and shall remain in force for the period of one year as from the date on which either High Contracting Party shall have notified the other of its intention to denounce it. Such notification may not, however, be given before the expiry of a period of two years from the date of the entry into force of the present Treaty.

Treaty of Non-Aggression between the Soviet Union and Finland, 21 January 1932

The Central Executive Committee of U.S.S.R. on the one part, and the President of the Republic of Finland on the other part, actuated by the desire to contribute to the maintenance of general peace; being convinced that the conclusion of the undertakings mentioned below and the pacific settlement of any dispute whatsoever between U.S.S.R. and the Republic of Finland is in the interests of both High Contracting Parties and will contribute towards the development of friendly and neighbourly relations between the two countries; declaring that none of the international obligations which they have hitherto assumed debars the pacific development of their mutual relations or is incompatible with the present Treaty; being desirous of confirming and completing the General Pact of August 27, 1928 for the renunciation of war; have resolved to conclude the present Treaty ... and have agreed upon the following provisions:

Article I. 1. The High Contracting Parties mutually guarantee the inviolability of the frontiers existing between U.S.S.R. and the Republic of Finland, as fixed by the Treaty of Peace concluded at Dorpat on October 14, 1920, which shall remain the firm foundation of their relations, and reciprocally undertake to refrain from any act of aggression directed against each other.

2. Any act of violence attacking the integrity and inviolability of the territory or the political independence of the other High Contracting Party shall be regarded as an act of aggression, even if it is committed without declaration of war and avoids warlike manifestations.

PROTOCOL TO ARTICLE I. In conformity with the provisions of Article IV of the present Treaty, the Agreement of June 1, 1922 regarding measures ensuring the inviolability of the frontiers shall not be affected by the provisions of the present Treaty and shall continue to remain fully in force.

Article II. 1. Should either High Contracting Party be the object of aggression on the part of one or more third Powers, the other High Contracting Party undertakes to maintain neutrality throughout the duration of the conflict.

2. Should either High Contracting Party resort to aggression against a third Power, the other High Contracting Party may denounce the present Treaty without notice.

Article III. Each of the High Contracting Parties undertakes not to become a party to any treaty, agreement or convention which is openly hostile to the other party or contrary, whether formally or in substance, to the present Treaty.

Article IV. The obligations mentioned in the preceding Articles of the present Treaty may in no case affect or modify the international rights or obligations of the High Contracting Parties under agreements concluded or undertakings assumed before the coming into force of the present Treaty, in so far as such agreements contain no elements of aggression within the meaning of the present Treaty.

Article V. The High Contracting Parties declare that they will always endeavour to settle in a spirit of justice any disputes of whatever nature or origin which may arise between them, and will resort exclusively to pacific means of settling such disputes. For this purpose, the High Contracting Parties undertake to submit any disputes which may arise between them after the signature of the present Treaty, and which it may not have been possible to settle through diplomatic proceedings within a reasonable time, to a procedure of conciliation before a joint conciliation commission whose powers, composition and working shall be fixed by a special supplementary Convention, which shall form an integral part of the present Treaty and which the High Contracting Parties undertake to conclude as soon as possible and in any event before the present Treaty is ratified. Conciliation procedure shall also be applied in the event of any dispute as to the application or interpretation of a Convention concluded between the High Contracting Parties, and particularly the question whether the mutual undertaking as to non-aggression has or has not been violated.

[*Articles VI and VII*. Ratification.]

[*Article VIII*. Treaty concluded for three years, automatically renewed for a further two years unless six months' notice of termination is given.]

Convention concluded between the Soviet Union, Afghanistan, Estonia, Latvia, Persia, Poland and Rumania regarding the definition of aggression, 3 July 1933

[A similar Convention was concluded by the Soviet Union, Rumania, Turkey and Yugoslavia on 4 July 1933.]

...

Article II. Accordingly, the aggressor in an international conflict shall, subject to the agreement in force between the parties to the dispute, be considered to be that State which is the first to commit any of the following actions:

1. Declaration of war upon another State;

2. Invasion by its armed forces, with or without a declaration of war, of the territory of another State;

3. Attack by its land, naval or air forces, with or without a declaration of war, on the territory, vessels or aircraft of another State;

4. Naval blockade of the coasts or ports of another State;

5. Provision of support to armed bands formed in its territory which have invaded the territory of another State, or refusal, notwithstanding the request of the invaded State, to take in its own territory all the measures in its power to deprive those bands of all assistance or protection.

No political, military, economic or other considerations may serve as an excuse or justification for the aggression referred to in Article II. (For examples, see Annex.)

Annex

The High Contracting Parties signatories of the Convention relating to the definition of aggression; desiring, subject to the express reservation that the absolute validity of the rule laid down in Article III of that Convention shall be in no way restricted, to furnish certain indications for determining the aggressor; declare that no act of aggression within the meaning of Article II of that Convention can be justified on either of the following grounds, among others:

A. The internal condition of a State: e.g. its political, economic or social structure; alleged defects in its administration; disturbances due to strikes, revolutions, counter-revolutions or civil war.

B. The international conduct of a State: e.g. the violation or threatened violation of the material or moral rights or interests of a foreign State or its nationals; the rupture of diplomatic or economic relations; economic or financial boycotts; disputes relating to economic, financial or other obligations towards foreign States; frontier incidents not forming any of the cases of aggression specified in Article II.

The High Contracting Parties further agree to recognize that the present Convention can never make legitimate any violations of international law that may be implied in the circumstances comprised in the above list.

Baltic Entente between Lithuania, Estonia and Latvia, 3 November 1934

Article 1. In order to coordinate their efforts in the cause of peace, the three Governments undertake to confer together on questions of foreign policy which are of common concern and to afford one another mutual political and diplomatic assistance in their international relations.

Article 2. For the purpose set forth in Article 1, the High Contracting Parties hereby decide to institute periodical conferences of the Ministers for Foreign Affairs of the three countries, to take place at regular intervals, at least twice a year, in the territories of each of the three States in turn. At the request of one of the High Contracting Parties and by joint agreement, extraordinary conferences may be held in the territory of one of the three States or elsewhere. . . .

Article 3. The High Contracting Parties recognize the existence of the specific problems which might make a concerted attitude with regard to them difficult. They agree that such problems constitute an exception to the undertakings laid down in Article 1 of the present Treaty.

Article 4. The High Contracting Parties shall endeavour to settle amicably and in a spirit of justice and equity any questions in respect of which their interests may clash and also to do so in the shortest possible time. . . .

Treaty of Mutual Assistance between the Soviet Union and France, 2 May 1935

The Central Executive Committee of U.S.S.R. and the President of the French Republic, being desirous of strengthening peace in Europe and of guaranteeing its benefits to their respective countries by securing a fuller and stricter application of those provisions of the Covenant of the League of Nations which are designed to maintain the national security, territorial integrity and political independence of States; determined to devote their efforts to the preparation and conclusion of a European agreement for that purpose and in the meantime to promote, as far as lies in their power, the effective application of the provisions of the Covenant of the League of Nations; have resolved to conclude a Treaty to this end and have appointed as their plenipotentiaries . . . and have agreed upon the following provisions:

Article I. In the event of France or U.S.S.R. being threatened with or in danger of aggression on the part of any European State, U.S.S.R. and reciprocally France undertake mutually to proceed to an immediate consultation as regards the measures to be taken for the observance of the provisions of Article X of the Covenant of the League of Nations.

Article II. Should, in the circumstances specified in Article XV, paragraph 7, of the Covenant of the League of Nations, France or U.S.S.R. be the object, notwithstanding the sincerely peaceful intentions of both countries, of an unprovoked aggression on the part of a European State, U.S.S.R. and reciprocally France shall immediately come to each other's aid and assistance.

Article III. In consideration of the fact that under Article XVI of the Covenant of the League of Nations any member of the League which resorts to war in disregard of its covenants under Articles XII, XIII or XV of the Covenant is *ipso facto* deemed to have committed an act of war against all other members of the League, France and reciprocally U.S.S.R. undertake, in the event of one of them being the object, in these conditions and notwithstanding the sincerely peaceful intentions of both countries, of an unprovoked aggression on the part of a European State, immediately to come to each other's aid and assistance in application of Article XVI of the Covenant.

The same obligation is assumed in the event of France or U.S.S.R. being the object of an aggression on the part of a European State in the circumstances specified in Article XVII, paragraphs 1 and 3, of the Covenant of the League of Nations.

Article IV. The undertakings stipulated above being consonant with the obligations of the High Contracting Parties as members of the League of Nations, nothing in the present Treaty shall be interpreted as restricting the duty of the latter to take any action that may be deemed wise and effectual to safeguard the peace of the world, or as restricting the obligations resulting for the High Contracting Parties from the Covenant of the League of Nations.

[*Article V*. Ratification to be exchanged as soon as possible. Treaty to remain in force for five years unless denounced by either party giving at least one year's notice; at end of five years the Treaty to continue indefinitely, each party being at liberty to terminate it with one year's notice.]

Protocol of Signature

Upon proceeding to the signature of the Franco-Soviet Treaty of Mutual Assistance of today's date the plenipotentiaries have signed the following Protocol, which shall be included in the exchange of ratifications of the Treaty.

1. It is agreed that the effect of Article III is to oblige each Contracting Party immediately to come to the assistance of the other by immediately complying with the recommendations of the Council of the League of Nations as soon as they have been issued in virtue of Article XVI of the Covenant. It is further agreed that the two Contracting Parties will act in concert to insure that the Council shall issue the said recommendations with all the speed required by the circumstances, and that should the Council nevertheless, for whatever reason, issue no recommendation or fail to reach a unanimous decision, effect shall none the less be given to the obligation to render assistance. It is also agreed that the undertakings to render assistance mentioned in the present Treaty refer only to the case of an aggression committed against either Contracting Party's own territory.

2. It being the common intention of the two Governments in no way to contradict, by the present Treaty, undertakings previously assumed toward third States by France and by U.S.S.R. in virtue of published treaties, it is agreed that effect shall not be given to the provisions of the said Treaty in a manner which, being incompatible with treaty obligations assumed by one of the Contracting Parties, would expose that party to sanctions of an international character.

3. The two Governments, deeming it desirable that a regional agreement should be concluded aiming at organizing security between Contracting States, and which might moreover embody or be accompanied by pledges of mutual assistance, recognize their right to become parties by mutual consent, should

occasion arise, to similar agreements in any form, direct or indirect, that may seem appropriate, the obligations under these various agreements to take the place of those assumed under the present Treaty.

4. The two Governments place on record the fact that the negotiations which have resulted in the signature of the present Treaty were originally undertaken with a view to supplementing a security agreement embracing the countries of north-eastern Europe, namely, U.S.S.R., Germany, Czechoslovakia, Poland and the Baltic States which are neighbours of U.S.S.R.; in addition to that agreement, there was to have been concluded a treaty of assistance between U.S.S.R. and France and Germany, by which each of those three States was to have undertaken to come to the assistance of any one of them which might be the object of aggression on the part of any other of those three States. Although circumstances have not hitherto permitted the conclusion of those agreements, which both parties continue to

regard as desirable, it is nonetheless the case that the undertakings stipulated in the Franco-Soviet Treaty of Assistance are to be understood as intended to apply only within the limits contemplated in the three-party agreement previously planned. Independently of the obligations assumed under the present Treaty, it is further recalled that, in accordance with the Franco-Soviet Pact of Non-Aggression signed on November 29, 1932, and moreover, without affecting the universal character of the undertakings assumed in the Pact, in the event of either party becoming the object of aggression by one or more third European Powers not referred to in the above-mentioned three-party agreement, the other Contracting Party is bound to abstain, during the period of the conflict, from giving any aid or assistance, either direct or indirect, to the aggressor or aggressors, each party declaring further that it is not bound by any assistance agreement which would be contrary to this undertaking.

Treaty of Mutual Assistance between the Soviet Union and Czechoslovakia, 16 May 1935

The President of the Czechoslovak Republic and the Central Executive Committee of the U.S.S.R.; being desirous of strengthening peace in Europe and of guaranteeing its benefits to their respective countries by securing a fuller and stricter application of those provisions of the Covenant of the League of Nations which are designed to maintain the national security, territorial integrity and political independence of States; determined to devote their efforts to the preparation and conclusion of a European agreement for that purpose, and in the meantime to promote, as far as lies in their power, the effective application

of the provisions of the Covenant of the League of Nations; have resolved to conclude a Treaty to this end and have appointed as their plenipotentiaries:

The President of the Czechoslovak Republic: Eduard Benes, Minister for Foreign Affairs;

The Central Executive Committee of U.S.S.R.: Sergei Alexandrovsky, Envoy Extraordinary and Minister Plenipotentiary of the U.S.S.R.;

... and have agreed upon the following provisions:

Article I. In the event of the Czechoslovak Republic or U.S.S.R. being threatened with, or in danger of, aggression on the part of any European State, U.S.S.R. and reciprocally the Czechoslovak Republic undertake mutually to proceed to an immediate consultation as regards the measures to be taken for the observance of the provisions of Article X of the Covenant of the League of Nations.

Article II. Should, in the circumstances specified in Article XV, paragraph 7, of the Covenant of the League of Nations, the Czechoslovak Republic or U.S.S.R. be the object, notwithstanding the sincerely peaceful intentions of both countries, of an unprovoked aggression on the part of a European State, U.S.S.R. and reciprocally the Czechoslovak Republic shall immediately come to each other's aid and assistance.

Article III. In consideration of the fact that under Article XVI of the Covenant of the League of Nations any member of the League which resorts to war in disregard of its covenants under Articles XII, XIII or XV of the Covenant is *ipso facto* deemed to have committed an act of war against all other members of the League, the Czechoslovak Republic and reciprocally U.S.S.R. undertake, in the event of one of them being the object, in these conditions and notwithstanding the sincerely peaceful intentions of both countries, of an unprovoked aggression on the part of a European State, immediately to come to each other's aid and assistance in application of Article XVI of the Covenant.

The same obligation is assumed in the event of the Czechoslovak Republic or U.S.S.R. being the object of an aggression on the part of a European State in the circumstances specified in Article XVII, paragraphs 1 and 3, of the Covenant of the League of Nations.

Article IV. Without prejudice to the preceeding provisions of the present Treaty, it is stipulated that should either of the High Contracting Parties become the object of an aggression on the part of one or more third Powers in conditions not giving ground for aid or assistance within the meaning of the present Treaty, the other High Contracting Party undertakes not to lend, for the duration of the conflict, aid or assistance, either directly or indirectly, to the aggressor or aggressors. Each High Contracting Party further declares that it is not bound by any other agreement for assistance which is incompatible with the present undertaking.

Article V. The undertakings stipulated above being consonant with the obligations of the High Contracting Parties as members of the League of Nations, nothing in the present Treaty shall be interpreted as restricting the duty of the latter to take any action that may be deemed wise and effectual to safeguard the peace of the world or as restricting the obligations resulting for the High Contracting Parties from the Covenant of the League of Nations.

Article VI. The present Treaty, both the Czechoslovak and the Russian texts whereof shall be equally authentic, shall be ratified and the instruments of ratification shall be exchanged at Moscow as soon as possible. It shall be registered with the Secretariat of the League of Nations.

It shall take effect as soon as the ratifications have been exchanged and shall remain in force for five years. If it is not denounced by either of the High Contracting Parties giving notice thereof at least one year before the expiry of that period, it shall remain in force indefinitely, each of the High Contracting Parties being at liberty to terminate it at a year's notice by a declaration to that effect.

Protocol of Signature

Upon proceeding to the signature of the Treaty of Mutual Assistance between the Czechoslovak Republic and U.S.S.R. of today's date, the plenipotentiaries have signed the following Protocol, which shall be included in the exchange of ratifications of the Treaty.

I. It is agreed that the effect of Article III is to oblige each Contracting Party immediately to come to the assistance of the other by immediately complying with the recommendations of the Council of the League of Nations as soon as they have been issued in virtue of Article XVI of the Covenant. It is further agreed that the two Contracting Parties will act in concert to ensure that the Council shall issue the said recommendations with all the speed required by the circumstances and that, should the Council nevertheless, for whatever reason, issue no recommendation or fail to reach a unanimous decision, effect shall none the less be given to the obligation to render assistance. It is also agreed that the undertakings to render assistance mentioned in the present Treaty refer only to the case of an aggression committed against either Contracting Party's own territory. •

II. The two Governments declare that the undertakings laid down in Articles I, II and III of the present Treaty, concluded with a view to promoting the establishment in Eastern Europe of a regional system of security, inaugurated by the Franco-Soviet Treaty of May 2, 1935, will be restricted within the same limits as were laid down in paragraph 4 of the Protocol of signature of the said Treaty. At the same time, the two Governments recognize that the undertakings to render mutual assistance will operate between them only in so far as the conditions laid down in the present Treaty may be fulfilled and in so far as assistance may be rendered by France to the party victim of the aggression.

III. The two Governments, deeming it desirable that a regional agreement should be concluded aiming at organizing security between Contracting States, and which might moreover embody or be accompanied by pledges of mutual assistance, recognize their right to become parties by mutual consent, should occasion arise, to similar agreements in any form, direct or indirect, that may seem appropriate; the obligations under these various agreements to take the place of those resulting from the present Treaty.

Convention between Japan and the Soviet Union, Peking, 20 January 1925

Japan and U.S.S.R., desiring to promote relations of good neighbourhood and economic cooperation between them, have resolved to conclude a Convention embodying basic rules in regulation of such relations and, to that end, have agreed as follows:

Article I. The High Contracting Parties agree that with the coming into force of the present Convention, diplomatic and consular relations shall be established between them.

Article II. U.S.S.R. agrees that the Treaty of Portsmouth of September 5, 1905, shall remain in force.

It is agreed that the treaties, conventions and agreements other than the said Treaty of Portsmouth, which were concluded between Japan and Russia prior to November 7, 1917, shall be re-examined at a conference to be subsequently held between the Governments of the High Contracting Parties and are liable to revision or annulment as altered circumstances may require.

Article III. The Governments of the High Contracting Parties agree that upon the coming into force of the present Convention, they shall proceed to the revision of the Fishery Convention of 1907, taking into consideration such changes as may have taken place in the general conditions since the conclusion of the said Fishery Convention.

Pending the conclusion of a convention so revised, the Government of U.S.S.R. shall maintain the practice established in 1924 relating to the lease of fishery lots to Japanese subjects.

Article IV. The Governments of the High Contracting Parties agree that upon the coming into force of the present Convention, they shall proceed to the conclusion of a treaty of commerce and navigation in conformity with the principles hereunder mentioned, and that, pending the conclusion of such a treaty, the general intercourse between the two countries shall be regulated by those principles. . . .

Article V. The High Contracting Parties solemnly affirm their desire and intention to live in peace and amity with each other, scrupulously to respect the undoubted right of a State to order its own life within its own jurisdiction in its own way, to refrain and to restrain all persons in any governmental service for them, and all organizations in receipt of any financial assistance from them, from any act overt or covert liable in any way whatsoever to endanger the order and security in any part of the territories of Japan or U.S.S.R.

It is further agreed that neither Contracting Party shall permit the presence in the territories under its jurisdiction : (a) of organizations or groups pretending to be the Government for any part of the territories of the other party, or (b) of alien subjects or citizens who may be found to be actually carrying on political activities for such organizations or groups.

Article VI. In the interest of promoting economic relations between the two countries, and taking into consideration the needs of Japan with regard to natural resources, the Government of U.S.S.R. is willing to grant to Japanese subjects, companies and associations, concessions for the exploitation of minerals, forests and other natural resources in all the territories of U.S.S.R.

[*Article VII.* Ratification.]

Protocol A

Japan and U.S.S.R., in proceeding this day to the signature of the Convention embodying basic rules of the relations between them, have deemed it advisable to regulate certain questions in relation to the said Convention, and have, through their respective plenipotentiaries, agreed upon the following stipulations :

Article I. Each of the High Contracting Parties undertakes to place in the possession of the other party the movable and immovable property belonging to the embassy under consulates of such other party and actually existing within its own territories. . . .

Article II. It is agreed that all questions of the debts due to the Government of subjects of Japan on account of public loans and treasury bills issued by the former Russian Governments, to wit, by the Imperial Government of Russia and the Provisional Government which succeeded it, are reserved for adjustment at subsequent negotiations between the Government of Japan and the Government of U.S.S.R.: provided that in the adjustment of such question, the Government or subjects of Japan shall not, all other conditions being equal, be placed in any position less favourable than that which the Government of U.S.S.R. may accord to the Government or nationals of any other country on similar questions.

It is also agreed that all questions relating to claims of the Government of either party to the Government of the other, or of the nationals of either party to the Government of the other, are reserved for adjustment at subsequent negotiations between the Government of Japan and the Government of U.S.S.R.

Article III. In view of climatic conditions in Northern Sakhalin preventing the immediate homeward transportation of

Japanese troops now stationed there, these troops shall be completely withdrawn from the said region by May 15, 1925.

Such withdrawal shall be commenced as soon as climatic conditions will permit, and any and all districts in Northern Sakhalin so evacuated by Japanese troops shall immediately thereupon be restored in full sovereignty to the proper authorities of U.S.S.R. . . .

Article IV. The High Contracting Parties mutually declare that there actually exists no treaty or agreement of military alliance nor any other secret agreement which either of them has entered into with any third party and which constitutes an infringement upon, or a menace to, the sovereignty, territorial rights or national safety of the other Contracting Party.

Article V. The present Protocol is to be considered as ratified with the ratification of the Convention embodying basic rules of the relations between Japan and U.S.S.R., signed under the same date.

Protocol B

The High Contracting Parties have agreed upon the following as the basis for the concession contracts to be concluded within five months from the date of the complete evacuation of Northern Sakhalin by Japanese troops, as provided for in Article III of Protocol A signed this day between the plenipotentiaries of Japan and of U.S.S.R.

Article 1. The Government of U.S.S.R. agrees to grant to Japanese concerns recommended by the Government of Japan the concession for the exploitation of 50 per cent, in area, of the oil fields in Northern Sakhalin which are mentioned in the Memorandum submitted to the representative of the Union by the Japanese representative on August 29, 1924. . . .

Article 2. The Government of U.S.S.R. also agrees to authorize Japanese concerns recommended by the Government of Japan to prospect oil fields, for a period of from five to ten years, on the eastern coast of Northern Sakhalin over an area

of one thousand square versts to be selected within one year after the conclusion of the concession contracts, and in case oil fields shall have been established in consequence of such prospecting by the Japanese, the concession for the exploitation of 50 per cent, in area, of the oil fields so established shall be granted to the Japanese.

Article 3. The Government of U.S.S.R. agrees to grant to Japanese concerns recommended by the Government of Japan the concession for the exploitation of coal fields on the western coast of Northern Sakhalin over a specific area which shall be determined in the concession contracts.

The Government of U.S.S.R. further agrees to grant to such Japanese concerns the concession regarding coal fields in the Doue district over a specific area to be determined in the concession contracts.

With regard to the coal fields outside the specific areas mentioned in the preceding two paragraphs, it is also agreed that should the Government of U.S.S.R. decide to offer them for foreign concession, Japanese concerns shall be afforded equal opportunity in the matter of such concession.

Article 4. The period of the concession for the exploitation of oil and coal fields stipulated in the preceding paragraphs shall be from forty to fifty years.

Article 5. As royalty for the said concessions, the Japanese concessionaires shall make over annually to the Government of U.S.S.R., in case of coal fields, from 5 to 8 per cent of their gross output and, in case of oil fields, from 5 to 15 per cent of their gross output. . . .

Declaration

In proceeding this day to the signature of the Convention embodying basic rules of the relations between U.S.S.R. and Japan, the undersigned plenipotentiary of U.S.S.R. has the honour to declare that the recognition by the Government of

U.S.S.R. of the validity of the Treaty of Portsmouth of September 5, 1905 does not in any way signify that the Government of the Union shares with the former Tsarist Government the political responsibility for the conclusion of the said Treaty.

. . .

Agreement on the sale of Chinese Eastern Railway to Manchukuo, Tokyo, 23 March 1935

Manchukuo and U.S.S.R., being desirous of settling the question of the North Manchuria Railway (Chinese Eastern Railway) and thus to contribute to the safeguarding of peace in the Far East, have resolved to conclude an Agreement for the cession to Manchukuo of the rights of U.S.S.R. concerning the North Manchuria Railway (Chinese Eastern Railway), and have . . . agreed upon the following Articles:

Article I. The Government of U.S.S.R. will cede to the Government of Manchukuo all the rights it possesses over the North Manchuria Railway (Chinese Eastern Railway), in consideration of which the Government of Manchukuo will pay to the Government of U.S.S.R. the sum of one hundred and forty million (140,000,000) yen in Japanese currency.

Article II. All the rights of the Government of U.S.S.R. concerning the North Manchuria Railway (Chinese Eastern Railway) will pass to the Government of Manchukuo upon the coming into force of the present Agreement, and at the same time the North Manchuria Railway (Chinese Eastern Railway) will be placed under the complete occupation and the sole management of the Government of Manchukuo.

Article III. 1. Upon the coming into force of the present Agreement, the senior members of the administration of the North Manchuria Railway (Chinese Eastern Railway) who are citizens of U.S.S.R. will be released from their duties. The said senior members of the administration of the railway will hand over all the archives, records, papers and documents of whatever description in their charge to their respective successors in the new administration of the railway . . . [administrative and financial details].

Protocol of Mutual Assistance between the Mongolian People's Republic and the Soviet Union, Ulan Bator, 12 March 1936

The Governments of U.S.S.R. and the Mongolian People's Republic, taking into consideration the unalterable friendship that has existed between their countries since the liberation of the territory of the Mongolian People's Republic in 1921, with the support of the Red Army, from the White Guard detachments and the military forces with which the latter were connected and which invaded Soviet Territory, and desirous of supporting the cause of peace in the Far East and further strengthening the friendly relations between their countries, have decided to set forth in the form of the present Protocol the gentlemen's agreement existing between them since November 27, 1934, providing for mutual assistance in every possible manner in the matter of averting and preventing the danger of military attack and for support in the event of an attack by any third party on U.S.S.R. or the Mongolian People's Republic, and for these purposes have signed the present Protocol.

Article I. In the event of the threat of an attack on the territory of the Mongolian or Soviet Socialist Republics by a third country, the Governments of U.S.S.R. and the Mongolian People's Republic undertake to confer immediately regarding the situation and to adopt all measures that may be necessary for the protection and safety of their territories.

Article II. The Governments of U.S.S.R. and the Mongolian People's Republic undertake, in the event of a military attack on one of the Contracting Parties, to render each other every assistance, including military assistance.

Article III. The Governments of U.S.S.R. and the Mongolian People's Republic are in full understanding that the troops of either country will be sent into the territory of the other in accordance with a mutual agreement and in accordance with Articles I and II of this Protocol, and will immediately be withdrawn from that territory as soon as the period of necessity is over, as took place in 1925 when Soviet troops retired from the territory of the Mongolian People's Republic.

...

Treaty of Non-Aggression between China and the Soviet Union, Moscow, 21 August 1937

The National Government of the Republic of China and the Government of U.S.S.R., animated by the desire to contribute to the maintenance of general peace, to consolidate the amicable relations now existing between them on a firm and lasting basis, and to confirm in a more precise manner the obligations mutually undertaken under the Treaty for the Renunciation of War, signed in Paris on August 27, 1928, have resolved to conclude the present Treaty and have ... agreed on the following Articles:

Article I. The two High Contracting Parties solemnly reaffirm that they condemn recourse to war for the solution of international controversies, and that they renounce it as an instrument of national policy in their relations with each other, and, in pursuance of this pledge, they undertake to refrain from any aggression against each other either individually or jointly with one or more other Powers.

Article II. In the event that either of the High Contracting Parties should be subjected to aggression on the part of one or more third Powers, the other High Contracting Party obligates itself not to render assistance of any kind, either directly or indirectly to such third Power or Powers at any time during the entire conflict, and also to refrain from taking any action or

entering into any agreement which may be used by the aggressor or aggressors to the disadvantage of the parties subjected to aggression.

Article III. The provisions of the present Treaty shall not be so interpreted as to affect or modify the rights and obligations arising, in respect of the High Contracting Parties, out of bilateral or multilateral treaties or agreements to which the High Contracting Parties are signatories and which were concluded prior to the entering into force of the present Treaty,

Article IV. The present Treaty is drawn up in duplicate in English. It comes into force on the day of signature by the above-mentioned plenipotentiaries and shall remain in force for a period of five years. Either of the High Contracting Parties may inform the other six months before the expiration of the period of its desire to terminate the Treaty. In case both parties fail to do so in time, the Treaty shall be considered as being automatically extended for a period of two years after the expiration of the first period. Should neither of the High Contracting Parties inform the other six months before the expiration of the two-year period of its desire to terminate the Treaty, it shall continue in force for another period of two years, and so on successively.

VI · The collapse of the territorial settlements of Versailles, 1931–8

The security of post-Versailles Europe rested on certain assumptions: a military balance that favoured France and Britain, and the maintenance of the provisions of the Versailles treaty. The Germany of the Weimar Republic had already succeeded in weakening the control and constraints imposed by the Versailles treaty. By 1930, the Allies had evacuated the Rhineland ahead of time, German armaments were no longer closely controlled and Germany was no longer diplomatically isolated. But all this had been achieved by Governments which were determined to avoid another collision with France and Britain and which did not openly flout the provisions of the Versailles treaty. With the coming to power of Hitler, German policy was set on a revolutionary Nazi course. Hitler rejected pre-1914 concepts of the successful National State expanding through piecemeal territorial conquests. To re-establish Germany as an equal Great Power, to 'rectify' the eastern frontier – these were not just ends he had in view; for Hitler they were stepping stones to creating a new European order, and beyond that a new world order based on race with the German 'Aryan' race at its apex.

From 1933 to 1938 Hitler laid the foundation for his wars of conquest: he openly defied the disarmament restrictions of Versailles, he remilitarized the Rhineland in 1936, and prepared the way for undermining the independence of Austria and Czechoslovakia through support of local Nazi movements. The ambitions of Japan in Asia and Italy in Africa, and the international division caused by the Spanish Civil War, Italy's conquest of Abyssinia, Western suspicion of Soviet ideological policies, and the effect of economic depression, all provided Hitler with opportunities for ruthless exploitation. The creditability of the League of Nations was shattered in the 1930s: it could not check aggression by the adoption of 'procedures' when the European Powers and the

United States lacked either the will or the means to do so. Such was the case when Japan decided to dominate Manchuria by force.

War in Manchuria, 1931–3: the League, China and Japan

Manchuria played an important role in the Great Power rivalries of eastern Asia during the first half of the twentieth century. No Chinese Central Government was able to gain complete control over this great region before the 1950s. From 1900 to 1904 Russia exerted predominant control; after the Russo-Japanese war, Japan secured what were formerly Russian privileges in the south, whilst Russian influence remained in the north. Even when in 1925, after the death of Sun Yat-sen, Chiang Kai-shek successfully asserted control over the greater part of China, the warlord Chang Hsueh-liang was able to maintain his power and local autonomy in Manchuria. The warlord also tried to lessen Soviet and Japanese influence by regaining control over the railway lines (the Soviet, Chinese Eastern Railway and the Japanese South Manchurian railway) running through the province. The Japanese reacted forcefully. Japanese troops in Manchuria took matters into their own hands. During the night of *18–19 September 1931 the Mukden incident* marked the beginning of the Japanese military occupation of southern Manchuria and fighting spread to the north. In September 1932 Japan signed a treaty giving *de jure* recognition to a puppet state, Manchukuo, which had been set up the previous February.

The Chinese appealed on 21 September 1931 to the League under Article 11. But at the League Palace of Nations in Geneva, effective action, it was believed, would depend on securing the practical cooperation of the United States against Japan. This the United States would not contemplate. Secretary of State Stimson, in a Note of 7 January 1932, would go no further than enunciating an American doctrine of non-recognition of situations created in defiance of specific treaty engagements.

The conflict in China spread to Shanghai in January 1932. The Chinese now also invoked Articles 10 and 15 of the League Covenant, which in the event of a breach being found would bring the sanction article (19) into force (p. 59).

The League was unable to bring about a Japanese withdrawal in compliance with a League resolution and so break the deadlock, and on 21 November 1931 it accepted a Japanese proposal to send to Manchuria a Commission of Enquiry. Lord Lytton headed the commission, which left in February 1932. On 11 March 1932 the League issued a Declaration similar to the non-recognition doctrine first formulated by Stimson. But the League did not proceed to sanctions. Instead of sanctions, it postponed concrete action by deciding to wait for the report of the Lytton Commission. The Lytton Report, when finally laid before the League on 1 October 1932, found that Japan had no valid reason for invading Manchuria and envisaged as a solution some form of Manchurian autonomy under Chinese sovereignty. To achieve a solution Lytton recommended a League effort at conciliation. While the League attempted to find a way out along these lines, the Japanese in January 1933 extended their aggression against China. In February 1933 at Geneva, meantime, the principles of the Lytton Report were accepted. The only action the League took against Japanese aggression was juridical in that it refused to recognize the State of Manchukuo. In protest, on 27 March 1933 the Japanese announced their intention of leaving the League. Soon after, China, abandoning all hope of practical help, acknowledged defeat. *On 31 May 1933 the Chinese and Japanese concluded the Tangku Truce* which provided for Chinese withdrawal from a demilitarized zone of 5,000 square miles on the Chinese side of the Great Wall. The League had thus failed to preserve one of its members from aggression by another member, which was a Great Power. Collective security in the face of aggression had proved ineffective.

Japan in the 1930s moved away from her traditional alignment with Britain and began to turn to Nazi Germany. As a further step to gain ascendancy over China, and also in order to warn off the Soviet Union, Japan signed the German-inspired *Anti-Comintern Pact, 25 November 1936* (p. 168).

Germany's military revival, 1933–6

The coming to power of Hitler as Chancellor on 30 January 1933 marked the beginning of a German policy that destroyed the European territorial settlements of Versailles in the West, the East and Central Europe within the space of eight years, and substituted for these settlements the continental hegemony of Germany. The years from 1933 to the spring of 1939 are therefore more notable for the breach of treaties than for the conclusion of new ones. Hitler utilized the Disarmament Conference to further his plan to rearm while others disarmed and, unable to gain the approval of Britain and France, withdrew from the conference and the *League of Nations on 14 October 1933.* He followed this by proclaiming his peaceful intentions towards Poland and towards any frontier revisions in the East, and a *German–Polish Treaty was concluded on 26 January 1934* (p. 169) renouncing the use of force for ten years. An Austrian Nazi coup, involving the assassination of the Austrian Chancellor Dolfuss on 25 July 1934, failed. Mussolini was still acting as the protector of Austrian independence.

In January 1935 a plebiscite was held in the Saar which voted to return to Germany;

this was Germany's first, albeit legal, increase of territory since the peace settlements. In the spring of 1935 Hitler risked the open repudiation of the military clauses of the Versailles treaty, announcing on 9 March 1935 that a German air force was in existence, and a week later on 16 March he declared that Germany would resume complete freedom in establishing offensive forces and announced the introduction of conscription. At the *Stresa Conference, 11–14 April 1935*, Britain, France and Italy condemned Germany's unilateral repudiation of her Versailles obligations, and their resolution to this effect was carried unanimously by the League Council. But three months later Britain agreed to German naval rearmament, though the British Government hoped it would be limited by the terms of the *Anglo-German Naval Agreement, 18 June 1935* (p. 166). Meantime *France and the Soviet Union had signed the Pact of Mutual Assistance, 2 May 1935* (p. 152). The Franco-Soviet treaty was ratified by the French Chamber of Deputies almost a year later on 27 February 1936; this gave Hitler the pretext to make a crucial breach in the Versailles military limitations on Germany, and on 7 March 1936 he remilitarized the Rhineland. He justified his action by a *Note on 7 March 1936* denouncing the Locarno pact as incompatible with the Franco-Soviet pact; that denunciation was coupled with proposals for various new peace pacts.

The formation of the Rome–Berlin Axis: Abyssinia, Spain and Austria, 1935–8

Mussolini planned to dominate Abyssinia as a first step on the road to making Italy a World Power. The Duce prepared the way by seeking agreement with France. On *7 January 1935* Laval, the French Foreign Minister, and Mussolini signed a *secret agreement in Rome* intended to settle Italian–French colonial disputes and designed to facilitate the united front against Germany. The Stresa Conference in April 1935 was the public affirmation of this unity of purpose. It was shortlived. The Anglo-German Naval Agreement of 18 June 1935 (p. 166) shattered Anglo-French solidarity. The French paid a price: the Franco-Italian understanding of 7 January 1935 was interpreted by Mussolini as giving him practically a free hand in his dealings with Abyssinia as far as France was concerned. After months of tension, *Italy invaded Abyssinia on 3 October 1935*. The League Council on 7 October 1935 in its report condemned Italy for aggression. Member States were now obliged to apply the sanctions of Article 16. But the League followed a 'double policy': economic sanctions were gradually applied, but France and Britain were encouraged to seek a settlement of the Abyssinian–Italian conflict, it being understood this would involve the loss of some Abyssinian territory. In December 1935 the British

Foreign Secretary, Sir Samuel Hoare, and Pierre Laval agreed on a plan to end the conflict, to be put to the belligerents. The Hoare–Laval plan envisaged widespread concessions to Italy at Abyssinia's expense, but it was received with such disapproval by public opinion in Britain that Prime Minister Baldwin had to disavow it. Conciliation efforts were dead. Mussolini proceeded with the conquest of Abyssinia. On 5 May 1936 Addis Ababa fell and Italy proclaimed the annexation of Abyssinia. Meantime sanctions were not effectively applied by the League. A decision on oil sanctions was constantly postponed – the one sanction that might have hurt Italy's military effort – and the Suez Canal was not closed to Italy. Collective security through the adoption of sanctions in the face of aggression had completely failed.

The *de jure* recognition of Italy's conquest of Abyssinia by the most important of the Western democracies, Britain, followed some two years later when on 16 November 1938 the British Government brought into force an *Anglo-Italian Agreement, concluded on 16 April 1938* and concerned with Italian intervention in Spain where another war – the Civil War – was being fought. In accordance with the agreement, Italy promised to withdraw her troops from Spain, but only when the war was over; then the agreement would come into force.

The Civil War had begun in mid-July 1936 with a military revolt led by General Franco against the Spanish Government. The Italians provided substantial help for General Franco through 'volunteer' troops, planes and armaments, with the Germans supplying armaments and the fighters and bombers that formed the 'Condor Legion', which fought under German command. Russia sent arms and planes to Republican Spain. An International Brigade of some 18,000, including large volunteer contingents from France, Italy, Germany, Austria and Britain fought for the Republic. Officially, Britain, France, as well as Italy, Germany and Russia accepted a policy of neutrality and non-intervention in the Spanish Civil War by the end of August 1936. During the months it functioned, the ban was openly flouted by Italy, Germany and the Soviet Union. But two Anglo-Italian agreements were concluded: on 2 January 1937, in the so-called 'Gentleman's Agreement', Italy and Britain disclaimed any desire to see modified the *status quo* as regards national sovereignty of territories in the Mediterranean region; and an agreement in March 1937 provided for the withdrawal of volunteers and the setting-up of an international blockade to report on breaches of the agreements reached on non-intervention. The policy of non-intervention was a failure. But when 'pirate' submarines, actually Italian submarines aiding Franco, attacked neutral ships including British ones, a conference of Mediterranean and Black Sea Powers met at Nyon, and *on 14 September 1937 signed the Agreement of Nyon* (p. 171) to defend neutral ships by sinking at sight suspicious submarines. The Governments effectively defended their own ships and interests. The Italians were Franco's main ally and helped him to win the Civil War by the spring of 1939.

March 1938 marked the demise of Austria, a member of the League of Nations, as a result of a German military invasion and a German proclamation of Anschluss or union with Germany. The way to Nazi dominance had been prepared by the *Austro-German Agreement, 11 July 1936* (p. 172). It committed Germany to a promise of respecting Austrian independence, but the Austrian Government was gravely weakened by having to admit Nazi sympathizers into the Government itself, by opening Austria to Nazi propaganda, and by conceding that Austrian foreign policy would be based on the principle that Austria was a 'German State'.

Austrian independence had rested partly on Italian support. The growing intimacy of Germany and Italy, partly the consequence of Italy's Abyssinian and Spanish policies, undermined Austria's independence. Italian–German cooperation was first set out in the *October Protocol, 1936*, on a number of issues. On 1 November 1936 in a speech at Milan, Mussolini referred to the existence of a Rome–Berlin axis. The treaty ties between Italy and Germany were drawn closer when Italy *on 6 November 1937 joined the Anti-Comintern Pact signed a year earlier by Germany and Japan* (p. 174) and they culminated in an *Italian–German alliance, The Pact of Steel, 22 May 1939* (p. 193). Between the signatures by Italy of the Anti-Comintern Pact and the Pact of Steel occurred the loss of Austrian independence, and this time without Italian protest.

Anglo-German Naval Agreement, 18 June 1935 (Exchange of Notes)

Your Excellency,

1. During the last few days the representatives of the German Government and His Majesty's Government in the United Kingdom have been engaged in conversations, the primary purpose of which has been to prepare the way for the holding of a general conference on the subject of the limitation of naval armaments. I have now much pleasure in notifying your Excellency of the formal acceptance by His Majesty's Government in the United Kingdom of the proposal of the German Government discussed at those conversations that the future strength of the German navy in relation to the aggregate naval strength of the Members of the British Commonwealth of Nations should be in the proportion of 35 : 100. His Majesty's Government in the United Kingdom regard this proposal as a contribution of the greatest importance to the cause of future naval limitation. They further believe that the agreement which they have now reached with the German Government, and which they regard as a permanent and definite agreement as from today between the two Govern-

ments, will facilitate the conclusion of a general agreement on the subject of naval limitation between all the naval Powers of the world.

2. His Majesty's Government in the United Kingdom also agreed with the explanations which were furnished by the German representatives in the course of the recent discussions in London as to the method of application of this principle. These explanations may be summarized as follows:

(a) The ratio of 35 : 100 is to be a permanent relationship, i.e. the total tonnage of the German fleet shall never exceed a percentage of 35 of the aggregate tonnage of the naval forces, as defined by treaty, of the Members of the British Commonwealth of Nations, or, if there should in future be no treaty limitations of this tonnage, a percentage of 35 of the aggregate of the actual tonnages of the Members of the British Commonwealth of Nations.

(b) If any future general treaty of naval limitation should not adopt the method of limitation by agreed ratios between the fleets of different Powers, the German Government will not insist on the incorporation of the ratio mentioned in the preceding sub-paragraph in such future general treaty, provided that the method therein adopted for the future limitation of naval armaments is such as to give Germany full guarantees that this ratio can be maintained.

(c) Germany will adhere to the ratio 35 : 100 in all circumstances, e.g. the ratio will not be affected by the construction of other Powers. If the general equilibrium of naval armaments, as normally maintained in the past, should be violently upset by any abnormal and exceptional construction by other Powers, the German Government reserve the right to invite His Majesty's Government in the United Kingdom to examine the new situation thus created.

(d) The German Government favour, in the matter of limitation of naval armaments, that system which divides naval vessels into categories, fixing the maximum tonnage and/or armament for vessels in each category, and allocates the tonnage to be allowed to each Power by categories of vessels. Consequently, in principle, and subject to (f) below, the German Government are prepared to apply the 35 per cent ratio to the tonnage of each category of vessel to be maintained, and to make any variation of this ratio in a particular category or categories dependent on the arrangements to this end that may be arrived at in a future general treaty on naval limitation, such arrangements being based on the principle that any increase in one category would be compensated for by a corresponding reduction in others. If no general treaty on naval limitation should be concluded, or if the future general treaty should not contain provision creating limitation by categories, the manner and degree in which the German Government will have the right to vary the 35 per cent ratio in one or more categories will be a matter for settlement by agreement between the German Government and His Majesty's Government in the United Kingdom, in the light of the naval situation then existing.

(e) If, and for so long as, other important naval Powers retain a single category for cruisers and destroyers, Germany shall enjoy the right to have a single category for these two classes of vessel, although she would prefer to see these classes in two categories.

(f) In the matter of submarines, however, Germany, while not exceeding the ratio of 35 : 100 in respect of total tonnage, shall have the right to possess a submarine tonnage equal to the total submarine tonnage possessed by the Members of the British Commonwealth of Nations. The German Government, however, undertake that, except in the circumstances indicated in the immediately following sentence, Germany's submarine tonnage shall not exceed 45 per cent of the total of that possessed by the Members of the British Commonwealth of Nations. The German Government reserve the right, in the event of a situation arising which in their opinion makes it necessary for Germany to avail herself of her right to a percentage of submarine tonnage exceeding the 45 per cent above mentioned, to give notice to this effect to His Majesty's Government in the United Kingdom, and agree that the matter shall be the subject of friendly discussion before the German Government exercise that right.

(g) Since it is highly improbable that the calculation of the 35 per cent ratio should give for each category of vessels tonnage figures exactly divisible by the maximum individual tonnage permitted for ships in that category, it may be necessary that adjustments should be made in order that Germany shall not be debarred from utilizing her tonnage to the full. It has consequently been agreed that the German Government and His Majesty's Government in the United Kingdom will settle by common accord what adjustments are necessary for this purpose, and it is understood that this procedure shall not result in any substantial or permanent

departure from the ratio 35:100 in respect of total strengths.

3. With reference to sub-paragraph (c) of the explanations set out above, I have the honour to inform you that His Majesty's Government in the United Kingdom have taken note of the reservation and recognize the right therein set out, on the understanding that the 35:100 ratio will be maintained in default of agreement to the contrary between the two Governments.

4. I have the honour to request your Excellency to inform me that the German Government agree that the proposal of the German Government has been correctly set out in the preceding paragraphs of this note.

[On 10 December 1938 Germany formally exercised its option to build submarines up to the strength of the British and Commonwealth number, having in fact already laid down submarines in breach of the 1935 treaty. On 27 April 1939 Hitler denounced the treaty.]

Agreement (Anti-Comintern) between Japan and Germany, Berlin, 25 November 1936

The Imperial Government of Japan and the Government of Germany,

In cognizance of the fact that the object of the Communistic International (the so-called Komintern) is the disintegration of, and the commission of violence against, existing States by the exercise of all means at its command;

Believing that the toleration of interference by the Communistic International in the internal affairs of nations not only endangers their internal peace and social welfare, but threatens the general peace of the world;

Desiring to cooperate for defence against communistic disintegration, have agreed as follows:

Article I. The High Contracting States agree that they will mutually keep each other informed concerning the activities of the Communistic International, will confer upon the necessary measures of defence, and will carry out such measures in close cooperation.

Article II. The High Contracting States will jointly invite third States whose internal peace is menaced by the disintegrating work of the Communistic International, to adopt defensive measures in the spirit of the present Agreement or to participate in the present Agreement.

Article III. The Japanese and German texts are each valid as the original text of this Agreement. The Agreement shall come into force on the day of its signature and shall remain in force for the term of five years. The High Contracting States will, in a reasonable time before the expiration of the said term, come to an understanding upon the further manner of their cooperation. . . .

Supplementary Protocol to the Agreement guarding against the Communistic International

On the occasion of the signature this day of the Agreement guarding against the Communistic International the undersigned plenipotentiaries have agreed as follows:

(a) The competent authorities of both High Contracting States will closely cooperate in the exchange of reports on the activities of the Communistic International and on measures of information and defence against the Communistic International.

(b) The competent authorities of both High Contracting States will, within the framework of the existing law, take stringent measures against those who at home or abroad work on direct or indirect duty of the Communistic International or assist its disintegrating activities.

(c) To facilitate the cooperation of the competent authorities of the two High Contracting States as set out in (a) above, a standing committee shall be established. By this committee the further measures to be adopted in order to counter the disintegrating activities of the Communistic International shall be considered and conferred upon. . . .

Declaration of Non-Aggression between Germany and Poland, 26 January 1934

The Governments of Germany and Poland consider that the time has arrived to introduce a new phase in the political relations between Germany and Poland by a direct understanding between State and State. They have therefore decided to lay the foundation for the future development of these relations in the present Declaration.

Both Governments base their action on the fact that the maintenance and guarantee of a permanent peace between their countries is an essential condition for the general peace of Europe. They are therefore determined to base their mutual relations on the principles contained in the Pact of Paris of the 27th August 1928, and desire to define more precisely the application of these principles in so far as the relations between Germany and Poland are concerned.

In so doing each of the two Governments declares that the international obligations hitherto undertaken by it towards a third party do not hinder the peaceful development of their mutual relations, do not conflict with the present Declaration and are not affected by this Declaration. In addition both Governments state that the present Declaration does not extend to questions which, in accordance with international law, are to be regarded exclusively as internal concerns of either of the two States.

Both Governments announce their intention to reach direct understanding on questions of any nature whatsoever concerning their mutual relations. Should any disputes arise between them and agreement thereon not be reached by direct negotiations, they will in each particular case, on the basis of mutual agreement, seek a solution by other peaceful means, without prejudice to the possibility of applying, if necessary, such modes of procedure as are provided for such cases by other agreements in force between them. In no circumstances, however, will they proceed to use force in order to settle such disputes.

The guarantee of peace created by these principles will facilitate for both Governments the great task of finding for political, economic and cultural problems solutions based upon just and equitable adjustment of the interests of both parties.

Both Governments are convinced that the relations between their countries will in this manner fruitfully develop and will lead to the establishment of good neighbourly relations, contributing to the well-being not only of their two countries but also of the other nations of Europe.

The present Declaration shall be ratified and the instruments of ratification shall be exchanged at Warsaw as soon as possible. The Declaration is valid for a period of ten years, reckoned from the date of the exchange of the instruments of ratification. If it is not denounced by either of the two Governments six months before the expiration of this period, it will continue in force, but can then be denounced by either Government at any time on giving six months' notice.

Done in duplicate in the German and Polish languages.

Berlin, January 26, 1934

For the German Government:
C. FREIHERR VON NEURATH

For the Polish Government:
JÓZEF LIPSKI

Rome Protocol between Italy, Austria and Hungary, 17 March 1934

The Head of the Government of His Majesty the King of Italy,

The Federal Chancellor of the Republic of Austria,

The President of the Royal Council of Ministers of Hungary,

Being anxious to contribute to the maintenance of peace and to the economic reconstruction of Europe on the basis of respect for the independence and rights of every State;

Being convinced that cooperation in this direction between the three Governments is likely to create a genuine basis for wider cooperation with other States;

Undertake, with a view to achieving the above-mentioned purposes:

To confer together on all problems which particularly concern them, and on problems of a general character, with a view to pursuing, in the spirit of the existing treaties of friendship between Italy and Austria, Italy and Hungary and Austria and Hungary,

which are based on a recognition of the existence of numerous common interests, a concordant policy directed towards the promotion of effective cooperation between the States of Europe and particularly between Italy, Austria and Hungary.

To this end, the three Governments shall proceed to hold joint consultations whenever at least one of them deems it desirable.

[A further Protocol for the Development of Economic Relations was also concluded on 17 March 1934.]

Additional Protocol, 23 March 1936

[Reaffirmed Protocol of 17 March 1934 and specifically to consult with each other before undertaking any important negotiation on Danubian questions with any other State. A permanent organ composed of Foreign Ministers of three States was to be established for consultation.]

Nyon Agreement between Britain, Bulgaria, Egypt, France, Greece, Rumania, Turkey, U.S.S.R. and Yugoslavia, Nyon, 14 September 1937

Whereas arising out of the Spanish conflict attacks have been repeatedly committed in the Mediterranean by submarines against merchant ships not belonging to either of the conflicting Spanish parties; and

Whereas these attacks are violations of the rules of international law referred to in Part IV of the Treaty of London of April 22, 1930 with regard to the sinking of merchant ships and constitute acts contrary to the most elementary dictates of humanity, which should be justly treated as acts of piracy; and

Whereas without in any way admitting the right of either party to the conflict in Spain to exercise belligerent rights or to interfere with merchant ships on the high seas even if the laws of warfare at sea are observed and without prejudice to the right of any participating Power to take such action as may be proper to protect its merchant shipping from any kind of interference on the high seas or to the possibility of further collective measures being agreed upon subsequently, it is necessary in the first place to agree upon certain special collective measures against piratical acts by submarines:

In view thereof the undersigned, being authorized to this effect by their respective Governments, have met in conference at Nyon between the 9th and the 14th September 1937, and have agreed upon the following provisions which shall enter immediately into force:

I. The participating Powers will instruct their naval forces to take the action indicated in paragraphs II and III below with a view to the protection of all merchant ships not belonging to either of the conflicting Spanish parties.

II. Any submarine which attacks such a ship in a manner contrary to the rules of international law referred to in the International Treaty for the Limitation and Reduction of Naval Armaments signed in London on April 22, 1930, and confirmed in the Protocol signed in London on November 6, 1936, shall be counterattacked and, if possible, destroyed.

III. The instruction mentioned in the preceding paragraph shall extend to any submarine encountered in the vicinity of a position where a ship not belonging to either of the conflicting Spanish parties has recently been attacked in violation of the rules referred to in the preceding paragraph in circumstances which give valid grounds for the belief that the submarine was guilty of the attack.

IV. In order to facilitate the putting into force of the above arrangements in a practical manner, the participating Powers have agreed upon the following arrangements:

1. In the western Mediterranean and in the Malta Channel, with the exception of the Tyrrhenean Sea, which may form the subject of special arrangements, the British and French fleets will operate both on the high seas and in the territorial waters of the participating Powers, in accordance with the division of the area agreed upon between the two Governments.

2. In the eastern Mediterranean:

(a) Each of the participating Powers will operate in its own territorial waters;

(b) On the high seas with the exception of the Adriatic Sea, the British and French fleets will operate up to the entrance to the Dardanelles, in those areas where there is reason to apprehend danger to shipping in accordance with the division of the area agreed upon between the two Governments. The other participating Governments possessing a sea border on the Mediterranean, undertake, within the limit of their resources, to furnish these fleets any assistance that may be asked for; in particular, they will permit them to take action in their territorial waters and to use such of their ports as they shall indicate.

3. It is further understood that the limits of the zones referred to in sub-paragraphs 1 and 2 above, and their allocation shall be subject at any time to revision by the participating Powers in order to take account of any change in the situation.

V. The participating Powers agree that, in order to simplify the operation of the above-mentioned measures, they will for their part restrict the use of their submarines in the Mediterranean in the following manner:

(a) Except as stated in (b) and (c) below, no submarine will be sent to sea within the Mediterranean.

(b) Submarines may proceed on passage after notification to the other participating Powers, provided that they proceed on the surface and are accompanied by a surface ship.

(c) Each participating Power reserves for purposes of exercises certain areas defined in Annex I hereto in which its submarines are exempt from the restrictions mentioned in (a) or (b).

The participating Powers further undertake not to allow the presence in their respective territorial waters of any foreign submarines except in case of urgent distress, or where the conditions prescribed in sub-paragraph (b) above are fulfilled.

VI. The participating Powers also agree that, in order to simplify the problem involved in carrying out the measures above described, they may severally advise their merchant shipping to follow certain main routes in the Mediterranean agreed upon between them and defined in Annex II hereto.

VII. Nothing in the present Agreement restricts the right of any participating Power to send its surface vessels to any part of the Mediterranean. . . .

'Gentlemen's' Agreement between Austria and Germany, 11 July 1936

CONFIDENTIAL!

Convinced that the mutually expressed desire for the re-establishment of normal and friendly relations between the German Reich and the Federal State of Austria requires a series of preliminary stipulations on the part of the two Governments, both Governments approve the following confidential Gentlemen's Agreement:

I · REGULATION OF THE TREATMENT OF REICH-GERMANS IN AUSTRIA AND OF AUSTRIAN NATIONALS IN THE REICH

Associations of their nationals in either country shall not be hindered in their activities so long as they comply with the policies established in their bylaws in conformity with the laws in force and do not interfere in the internal political affairs of the other country, nor, in particular, endeavour to influence citizens of the other State by means of propaganda.

II · MUTUAL CULTURAL RELATIONS

All factors decisive for the formation of public opinion of both countries shall serve the purpose of re-establishing normal and friendly relations. With the thought that both countries belong within the German cultural orbit, both parties pledge themselves immediately to renounce any aggressive utilization of radio, motion picture, newspaper, and theatrical facilities against the other party. . . .

III · THE PRESS

Both parties shall influence their respective Press to the end that it refrain from exerting any political influence on conditions in the other country and limit its objective criticism of conditions in the other country to an extent not offensive to public opinion in the other country. This obligation also applies to the *émigré* Press in both countries.

The gradual elimination of prohibitions on the importation of newspapers and printed matter of the other party is envisaged by both parties, in relation to the gradual *détente* in mutual relations aimed at in this Agreement. Newspapers admitted shall, in any criticism of the internal political situation in the other country, adhere particularly strictly to the principle enunciated in paragraph I. . . .

IV · EMIGRÉ PROBLEMS

Both parties agree in their desire to contribute by reciprocal concessions to the speediest possible satisfactory solution of the problem of the Austrian National Socialist exiles in the Reich.

The Austrian Government will proceed to the examination of this problem as soon as possible and will announce the result to a joint commission to be composed of representatives of the competent Ministries so that an agreement may be put into effect.

V · NATIONAL INSIGNIA AND NATIONAL ANTHEMS

Each of the two Governments declares that within the scope of existing laws, it will place the nationals of the other party on an equal footing with nationals of third States in regard to the display of the national insignia of their country.

The singing of national anthems shall – in addition to official occasions – be permitted to nationals of the other party at closed meetings attended by these nationals exclusively.

VI · ECONOMIC RELATIONS

The Government of the German Reich, putting aside considerations of Party policy, is prepared to open the way for normal economic relations between the German Reich and Austria, and this readiness extends to the re-establishment of routine border crossing [*der Kleine Grenzverkehr*]. Discrimination against persons and areas, if not based upon purely economic considerations will not be undertaken.

VII · TOURIST TRAFFIC

The restrictions on tourist traffic imposed by both sides because of the tension which had arisen between the two States shall be lifted. This understanding shall not affect restrictions based on the legislation of both countries for the protection of foreign exchange. . . .

VIII · FOREIGN POLICY

The Austrian Government declares that it is prepared to conduct its foreign policy in the light of the peaceful endeavours of the German Government's foreign policy. It is agreed that the two Governments will from time to time enter into an exchange of views on the problems of foreign policy affecting both of them. The Rome Protocols of 1934 and the Supplementary Protocols of 1936, as well as the position of Austria with regard to Italy and Hungary as parties to these Protocols, are not affected thereby.

IX · AUSTRIAN DECLARATION ON DOMESTIC POLICY IN RELATION TO THIS *modus vivendi*

The Federal Chancellor declares that he is prepared:

(a) To grant a far-reaching political amnesty, from which persons who have committed serious public crimes shall be excluded.

Also covered by this amnesty shall be persons who have not yet been sentenced by judicial decree or penalized by administrative process.

These provisions shall also be duly applied to *émigrés*.

(b) For the purpose of promoting a real pacification, to appoint at the appropriate moment, contemplated for the near future, representatives of the so-called 'National Opposition in Austria' to participate in political responsibility; they shall be men who enjoy the personal confidence of the Federal Chancellor and whose selection he reserves to himself. It is agreed, in this connection, that persons trusted by the Federal Chancellor shall be charged with the task of arranging, in accordance with a plan worked out with the Federal Chancellor, for the internal pacification of the National Opposition and for its participation in the shaping of the political will in Austria.

X · PROCEDURE FOR OBJECTIONS AND COMPLAINTS

For the handling of objections and complaints which may arise in connection with the above Gentlemen's Agreement, as well as in order to guarantee a progressive *détente* within the framework of the preceding agreements, there shall be established a joint commission composed of three representatives of the Foreign Ministry of each country. Its task shall be to discuss at regular meetings the operation of the Agreement as well as any supplements thereto which may be required.

SCHUSCHNIGG
Federal Chancellor

VIENNA, 11 July 1936

Protocol concluded by Italy, Germany and Japan (Anti-Comintern Pact), Rome, 6 November 1937

The Italian Government, the Government of the German Reich, and the Imperial Government of Japan,

Considering that the Communist International continues constantly to imperil the civilized world in the Occident and Orient, disturbing and destroying peace and order,

Considering that only close collaboration looking to the maintenance of peace and order can limit and remove that peril,

Considering that Italy – who with the advent of the Fascist régime has with inflexible determination combated that peril and rid her territory of the Communist International – has decided to align herself against the common enemy along with Germany and Japan, who for their part are animated by like determination to defend themselves against the Communist International,

Have, in conformity with Article II of the Agreement against the Communist International concluded at Berlin on November 25, 1936, by Germany and Japan, agreed upon the following:

Article 1. Italy becomes a party to the Agreement against the Communist International and to the Supplementary Protocol concluded on November 25, 1936, between Germany and Japan, the text of which is included in the Annex to the present Protocol.

Article 2. The three Powers signatory to the present Protocol agree that Italy will be considered as an original signatory to the Agreement and Supplementary Protocol mentioned in the preceding Article, the signing of the present Protocol being equivalent to the signature of the original text of the aforesaid Agreement and Supplementary Protocol.

Article 3. The present Protocol shall constitute an integral part of the above-mentioned Agreement and Supplementary Protocol.

Article 4. The present Protocol is drawn up in Italian, Japanese, and German, each text being considered authentic. It shall enter into effect on the date of signature.

In testimony whereof, etc....

[signed] CIANO, VON RIBBENTROPP, HOTTA.

VII · From peace to world war in Europe and Asia, 1937–41

During the short space of eighteen months, from March 1938 to September 1939, Hitler plunged Europe from one crisis to another, each time 'breaking his word' that he had made his last territorial demand. When each crisis is examined in isolation there seems some merit in Germany's arguments: why should the Austrians of the Sudeten German-speaking population of Czechoslovakia be denied the right of self-determination; the 'rectification' of Germany's eastern frontier was an objective followed by the 'European' Stresemann in the 1920s before Hitler made his demands concerning the Polish corridor and Danzig; was it not time to remove the last vestiges of discrimination against Germany imposed by the Versailles *Diktat*? Reasonable Western statesmen would surely prefer diplomatic adjustments, even some sacrifice on the part of the 'artificially' created post-Versailles States, to world war.

To begin with, Neville Chamberlain, leading the French Daladier Government, was prepared to follow the path of apparent reason in preference to the human and material destruction that another world war would entail. But the cumulative impact of Hitler's aggressions of 1938–9 and the realization that he was launched on a policy of aggression without foreseeable 'diplomatic' limits led to a fundamental change of British policy in 1939 which carried France with it. The door to diplomatic agreements for a settlement of all European questions would not be closed; Hitler should be offered all possible enticements to choose diplomacy rather than force; he would hopefully also be deterred by an alliance against Germany; but if neither inducements nor deterrents could influence him then Britain was prepared for war rather than allow Hitler the hegemony of continental Europe. But where would the Soviet Union fit into this new pattern of diplomacy? No one in Britain or Germany knew for certain until Stalin made his choice in August 1939.

In Asia, Japan had resumed fighting in China in July 1937 and an 'undeclared war' began. The sympathy of the Western democracies was with China, but the more immediate threat of Germany in Europe decided France and Britain to preserve a policy of limiting help to China to an extent that would allow peaceful relations to be preserved with Japan. The outbreak of war in Europe only strengthened this resolve. After the fall of France in June 1940, Britain agreed to the closure of the Burma supply route to China, but reopened it in October 1940. From then on, British policy followed in the wake of American policy in the Pacific. United States resistance to Japanese expansion in South-east Asia finally led to the Japanese decision to start war advantageously with the surprise attack on Pearl Harbor, 7 December 1941. For the U.S.S.R., fighting a war for survival since June 1941, the absolute need to avoid having to face a second front in Asia as well overrode all other considerations; and so it remained loyal to the Neutrality Pact it had concluded with Japan in April 1941.

Europe, 1938–9

GERMAN EXPANSION

The German proclamation of the *Austrian Anschluss on 13 March 1938* for the first time during the Nazi era extended German sovereignty by the threat and use of force. When the opportunity was offered, Hitler assumed control over the whole of Austria. With similar opportunism Hitler broke up Czechoslovakia in October 1938 by annexing the so-called mainly German-speaking Sudeten areas. In the following March he partitioned what was left of the country and created an 'independent' Puppet State of Slovakia.

The first transfer of Czech territory in October 1938 was given a semblance of international sanction at the *Four Power Conference at Munich, 29–30 September 1938*. Germany, Italy, France and Britain participated in this 'settlement'. The Czechoslovak Government was not represented and only acquiesced in the decisions of Munich in the face of the German threat of force, and since without the help of her Western ally, France, military resistance would have been hopeless. The extent of Soviet help too would have been uncertain and in any case probably ineffective. (See p. 117 for the terms of the Franco-Czech alliance and pp. 152–6 for the Franco-Soviet and Czech–Soviet treaties of 1935.) A number of documents were signed at Munich: *the Munich Four Power Agreement, 29–30 September 1938* (p. 187), which provided for the occupation of the Sudetenland in stages from 1–10 October 1938; a *conditional guarantee* for the remainder of Czechoslovakia after Polish and Hungarian claims had been settled; and an *Anglo-German Declaration* (p. 189) of pacific intent. Not to be outdone the Daladier Government concluded a *Franco-German Agreement on 6 December 1938*. It recognized mutual frontiers and thus the Germans appeared to abandon claims to Alsace-Lorraine; it promised consultations between France and Germany on questions of mutual interest, while their 'relations' with other States were not affected. The use of the word 'relations' in place of existing 'alliances' seemed to point to a French desire to play down the alliances without abandoning them.

The validity of the Four Power Agreement was challenged by the Czecho-slovak Government, in exile during the Second World War, on the grounds that Czech assent to the occupation had been obtained under duress. Of the original signatories which later declared the treaty to be invalid, the French National Committee did so in 1942 and the French Provisional Government reaffirmed this in 1944, and post-Fascist Italy declared the treaty invalid from the beginning in 1944. The wartime British Government would not repudiate the legality of the original Munich Agreements but only bound itself in 1942 to regard the treaty as no longer in force due to the Germans having broken it. The Federal German Government in 1973 is currently negotiating this ques-tion among several with the Czechoslovak Government. The Soviet Union, not a signatory of Munich, was the first Great Power to declare to the Czecho-slovak Government that it had not recognized the Munich settlement at the time or since.

The guarantee given at Munich never became operative as the British and French Governments decided that they would only honour it in the event of Hitler's aggression if Italy also did so. Despite a visit by Chamberlain to Mussolini in January 1939 there was not the slightest chance that Italy would work against her Axis partner. When a political crisis in autonomous Slovakia gave Hitler his next opportunity, he ordered German troops on 15 March 1939 to occupy the remnants of the Czech State, and set up the Protectorate of Bohemia and Moravia on 16 March 1939. *On 23 March 1939 a German–Slovak treaty* was signed which described Slovakia as an independent State but under the protection of Germany, with closely subservient Slovak policies in matters of the army, foreign policy and economic and financial affairs; Germany was given the right to station troops in Slovakia and undertook to protect the independence of its satellite.

Poland and Hungary also benefited from the break-up of Czechoslovakia (October 1938–March 1939). Poland secured the territory of Teschen, 1–2 October 1938, after the Czechoslovak Government accepted a peremptory demand for its cession. Hungary, by the *First Vienna Award, 2 November 1938*, an arbitral judgement given by Germany and Italy, re-acquired the ethnic strip of Magyar territory along the Hungarian borders with Slovakia and Ruthenia, which left the rest of Slovakia and Ruthenia autonomous. *Hungary* formally joined the Axis Powers when adhering *on 26 February 1939 to the Anti-Comintern Pact*, and two weeks later on 14–15 March 1939, with German encouragement, the Hungarians annexed Ruthenia (also known as 'Carpatho-Ukraine') at the same time as the Wehrmacht marched into Czechoslovakia.

Hitler made his first aggressive move in the Baltic the day after entering Czechoslovakia, by sending an ultimatum to Lithuania on 16 March 1939 demanding the cession of the Memelland. Lithuania accepted on 19 March 1939. Hitler entered Memel from the sea on 23 March 1939 when the treaty of cession was formally signed. His next objective was the Free City of Danzig together with an extra-territorial corridor linking East Prussia to the rest of Germany. Mussolini now sprang his surprise by *annexing Albania to Italy on 7 April 1939.*

The Anglo-French response

These sudden violent changes created great uncertainty throughout Europe. Rumania was already more in the German than Western orbit, having signed a number of economic agreements with Germany in December 1938 and on 23 March 1939; but Rumania also felt its territorial integrity threatened by Hungary, Bulgaria and Germany during the crisis of mid-March 1939. Poland was threatened by a Slovakia under German control and by Hitler's ambitions in the Baltic. Against the background of general diplomatic confusion, and fearing a complete collapse of Central and Eastern Europe to Nazi aggression, there began the British attempt, in association with France, to call a halt to further German territorial expansion by force. On *31 March 1939 Chamberlain announced a provisional Anglo-French guarantee of Poland* (p. 189). After Italy seized Albania on 7 April 1939, this guarantee was extended to the Balkans when on *13 April 1939 an Anglo-French guarantee of Greece and Rumania was announced.* Turkey was brought into the Anglo-French alignment when on 12 May 1939 the British and Turkish Governments issued a declaration that they would cooperate in the event of aggression leading to war in the Mediterranean; the two Governments also said that they would conclude a long-term treaty (for the Anglo-French-Turkish Treaty, 19 October 1939, see p. 197). The long drawn-out diplomatic exchanges and negotiations between France, Britain and the Soviet Union from March 1939 to August 1939 led to no result.

The refusal of the Polish Government to give in to the substance of German demands and Britain's determination to stand by Poland led to a more definitive alliance, the *Anglo-Polish Agreement of Mutual Assistance, 25 August 1939* (p. 190).

THE AXIS

Germany bound Italy more closely to its side when Hitler finally persuaded Mussolini to conclude a military alliance, the *Pact of Steel, 22 May 1939* (p. 193), but in a secret memorandum for Hitler a week later Mussolini stated that Italy would not be ready for war until after the end of 1942. On the eve of Germany's attack on Poland, on 25 August 1939, Mussolini replied to Hitler that he could not take military action before the end of 1942 unless sufficient arms and raw materials were provided for Italy. Hitler preferred to do without immediate Italian military help when he attacked Poland on 1 September 1939, having already purchased Soviet acquiescence. Secretly the Soviet Union negotiated with Germany in Berlin whilst simultaneously negotiating with France and Britain in Moscow. The *German–Soviet Non-Aggression Pact was signed on 23 August 1939* (p. 195), and a secret Protocol was signed the same day which outlined the German and Soviet spheres of interest and paved the way for Soviet annexations of territory in the Baltic and Central Europe (p. 199). The German invasion of Poland on 1 September 1939 was followed on 3 September 1939 by British and French ultimatums and declarations of war.

Allied diplomacy, 1939–41

In September 1939 war did not immediately engulf all of Europe. The countries which declared war on Germany were Britain and the Dominions (with the exception of Eire) and France; Poland had no choice as she was attacked by Germany without a declaration of war. But Germany's ally Italy, with Hitler's consent, remained neutral. Portugal, Britain's ally, with British consent declared its neutrality on the outbreak of war. On the Allied side the earliest effort at diplomacy in wartime was to win the support of Turkey.

TURKEY

On 19 October 1939 Britain, France and Turkey concluded a Tripartite Treaty (p. 197). Five months earlier (12 May 1939) an Anglo-Turkish declaration had foreshadowed a long-term treaty to meet aggression in the Mediterranean region. The treaty now concluded on 19 October 1939 provided for a promise of British and French help if Turkey was attacked by a European Power; the three Powers, France and Britain on the one hand and Turkey on the other, promised mutual assistance if a European Power committed an act of aggression leading to a war which involved the signatories; Turkey promised aid if Britain and France were at war in consequence of their guarantees to Greece and Rumania, but could remain benevolently neutral if a war involving Britain and France was the result of events outside the Mediterranean region, as was the case over Poland. Thus in practice the application of the alliance was limited to aggression by Germany or Italy in the Balkans; an important additional clause provided that the obligations Turkey undertook were not to have the effect of compelling her to go to war with the U.S.S.R. When Italy entered the war on 10 June 1940 during the final phase of the French collapse, Turkey disavowed the Tripartite Treaty, claiming that France could no longer fulfil it, and declared its intention to remain non-belligerent. The Italian and German attacks on Greece in 1941 did not alter Turkey's stand. After Germany's threat had lessened through military failure, Turkey broke off diplomatic relations on 2 August 1944 but did not declare war until 23 February 1945.

The United States and the European War

On 11 December 1941, four days after the Japanese attack on Pearl Harbor (7 December 1941, p. 187), Germany and Italy declared war on the United States. By a number of agreements made during the period of American neutrality (September 1939 to December 1941) the United States had provided crucial help for the Allied cause even before becoming an ally. On 4 November 1939 Roosevelt approved the revised *Neutrality Act* which repealed the embargo on the export of munitions to belligerents, though American supplies to the Allies before the fall of France were not large. The German conquests of Denmark, Norway, the Netherlands, Belgium, and France in the spring and summer of 1940 led to increasing American help and to a tremendous expansion of the American armaments industry. *The Anglo-American Destroyer–Naval Base Agreement, 2 September 1940*, gave Britain fifty American First World War destroyers in exchange for leasing to the United States naval bases in the British islands of the western Atlantic, in the Caribbean and in British Guiana. *The Lend–Lease Act, 11 March 1941*, passed Congress with the stated purpose of promoting the defence of the United States by providing all-out material aid to any country whose defence the President regarded as vital to the defence of the United States, on whatever terms the President regarded as proper. In August 1941 Churchill and Roosevelt met and set out their principles of present and future policy in the *Atlantic Charter, published on 14 August 1941* (p. 198). On 17 November 1941 Congress further revised the Neutrality Acts. American merchant ships could now carry arms to belligerent ports (British ports) and so be armed.

The German victories in Europe also raised the possibility that German aggression might expand to the Western hemisphere. Pan-American solidarity in the event of the war reaching the American Republics was strengthened at the *Panama Conference, 23 September–3 October 1939* (p. 301). This created a neutral belt of several hundred miles from the coastline of the American Republics, foreshadowed the United States revision of the neutrality legislation and affirmed the no-transfer principle. The Declaration of Panama said: In case any geographic region of America subject to the jurisdiction of a non-American State should be obliged to change its sovereignty and there should result therefrom a danger to the security of the American continent, a consultative meeting such as the one now being held will be convoked with the urgency that the case may require. With the German occupation of France, Belgium, the Netherlands, Norway and Denmark, the danger envisaged had come near and the United States Congress on 18 June 1940 affirmed that it would not acquiesce in any transfer of sovereignty from one non-American State to another of territory in the American hemisphere. The Pan-American Conference met again in Havana on 21 July 1940. The no-transfer principle was reaffirmed by resolution and the *Act of Havana, which came into force on 8 January 1942* (p. 324). It provided in case of necessity that the Republics in collective trusteeship would administer any such territory that was threatened. The Havana Conference also passed a resolution that an act of aggression against one Republic would be treated as an act of aggression against all, which would lead to consultation on measures of common defence.

New allies and the collapse of France

In 1940 Britain lost the war on the continent of Europe and gained new allies, not by their choice but because they became victims of German aggression. Germany extended the war in the West by attacking Denmark and Norway on 9 April 1940. Denmark was occupied virtually without resistance and Norway, despite Allied attempts to create a front in the central and northern regions of the country, fell a few weeks later.

Germany opened her military offensive against France a month later on 10 May 1940 by crossing three neutral frontiers, the Netherlands, Belgium and Luxembourg. All three Governments after the complete military collapse refused to sign an armistice with Germany, and transferred themselves to London to join there the Polish and Norwegian Governments in exile. After the defeat of the British and French armies Marshal Pétain formed a new

Government which sought an armistice from the Germans. The *Franco-German armistice was signed on 22 June 1940* and became effective three days later. It divided France into an occupied zone of northern France and the Atlantic coastline and an unoccupied zone. The 'Free French' under de Gaulle continued to fight on the Allied side but were not recognized as a fully-fledged Government in exile. Meantime Italy had declared war on France and Britain on 10 June 1940 during the closing stages of the German campaign in France. Italy's contribution to the growing number of Allied Powers was to follow up her short campaign in France by attacking *Greece on 28 October 1940*. Greece now joined the war against Italy. Italian military ineptitude brought about German intervention when *Germany attacked Greece on 6 April 1941*.

The Axis Powers and the Soviet Union, 1939–41: the Winter War

For Germany and Poland the Second World War began on 1 September 1939 when the Wehrmacht and the Luftwaffe crossed the Polish frontier. Just a week earlier the Soviet Union and Germany announced a *Treaty of Non-Aggression, 23 August 1939* (p. 195). After Hitler's virulent anti-Bolshevik tirades, such a treaty marked a reversal of what the public could have anticipated. Equally, communists throughout Europe were thrown into confusion. An additiona *secret protocol* marked out German and Soviet 'spheres of influence' and en-l visaged the partition of Poland and other territories within each sphere according to the convenience of each signatory. On 17 September 1939, seventeen days after Germany's attack on Poland, with the Polish armies routed but still fighting the Germans, Soviet troops crossed Poland's eastern frontier. The detailed division of Poland was laid down in the *German–Soviet Boundary and Friendship Treaty, 28 September 1939* (p. 199), to which were added one confidential and two secret Protocols. These political treaties were accompanied by German–Soviet economic agreements. The first economic agreement, the *German–Soviet Trade Agreement, was concluded on 19 August 1939* (p. 194). Six months later a comprehensive and extensive *German–Soviet Commercial Agreement was signed on 11 February 1940* (p. 200).

Having concluded these political and economic agreements which apparently ensured that Germany and the Soviet Union could count on the neutrality of one State towards the other, Germany and the Soviet Union pursued their separate expansionist policies. Germany attacked Denmark and Norway on 9 April 1940 and the Netherlands, Belgium and Luxembourg on 10 May 1940.

The Soviet Union, in accordance with the German–Soviet Boundary and Friendship Treaty on 28 September 1939, had secured German agreement that Lithuania fell within her sphere of interest. Stalin was now determined to assure Soviet predominance in the Baltic States of Lithuania, Estonia and Latvia as well as Finland. Under threat of force a *Soviet–Estonian Mutual Assistance Pact was concluded on 28 September 1939*, which, whilst formally preserving Estonian sovereignty, made military bases available to the Soviet Union in Estonia and permitted the Soviet Union to station troops in these bases. *Latvia signed a similar pact with the Soviet Union on 5 October 1939* (p. 201). *Lithuania* also was forced to sign a pact with the Soviet Union permitting the stationing of the Red Army in Lithuania, but on *10 October 1939* received a 'consolation prize': Vilna and its region was transferred from occupied Poland to Lithuania. The Soviet Government wished to control the foreign and military affairs of the Baltic to strengthen Soviet security. Independent Governments continued to function in the Baltic States until mid-June 1940. Then, after unremitting pressure and when already under Soviet control, the Baltic States 'requested' incorporation in the Soviet Union. Lithuania was accordingly 'admitted' to the Soviet Union on 1 August 1940, Latvia on 5 August 1940, Estonia on 8 August 1940, and these States became Republics of the Soviet Union. This marked the extinction of the three Baltic States as sovereign nations.

Finland in October 1939 refused Soviet demands which involved frontier changes and the abandonment of the Mannerheim line of fortifications across the Karelian isthmus. After fruitless negotiations the Soviet Union began the invasion of Finland on 30 November 1939. The Winter War lasted unexpectedly long with strong Finnish resistance, but after three months of fighting Finland was forced to sue for peace. *On 12 March 1940 a Finnish–Soviet Peace Treaty was signed* which accepted Soviet demands for frontier changes and bases.

The Soviet Union next moved to increase the security of her southern frontier by demanding from Rumania on 26 June 1940 Bessarabia and northern Bukovina. The Rumanians accepted, on German advice, and by 1 July 1940 this region had been completely occupied by Soviet troops. The Hungarians now also wished to recover territory lost after the First World War (p. 46) and threatened to use force if Rumania did not hand back Transylvania; the Bulgarians demanded from Rumania frontier concessions in the Dobruja. Hitler imposed a settlement by the *Second Vienna Award, 30 August 1940*, partitioning Transylvania, which left Rumania about three-fifths and gave Hungary the remainder. *Rumania ceded the southern Dobruja to Bulgaria on 7 September 1940*. In its new frontiers Hitler now gave a *German guarantee to Rumania* at the request of the Rumanians, who on 1 July 1940 had formally denounced the *Anglo-French guarantee of March 1939* (see p. 189). In September 1940 German troops began to occupy Rumania at 'Rumania's request', as

Hitler assured the Russians. Russo-German relations deteriorated. In November 1940 Hitler secretly prepared for war in the Balkans and an attack on Russia, Bulgaria and Greece. Meantime, not to be outdone by Germany in the Balkans Mussolini attacked Greece on 28 October 1940.

Faced with the hostile Great Powers, Italy, Germany and Russia, the still independent Balkan States attempted to strengthen their security by diplomacy and by appeasing Hitler. The Bulgarians in November 1940 promised to cooperate with the three Axis Powers, Germany, Italy and Japan who had concluded the *Tripartite Pact of 27 September 1940* (p. 202). Hungary signed a *Protocol of Adherence to the Tripartite Pact, 20 November 1940*, but according to its terms the Hungarians were left some freedom in choosing what action to take to help the Axis partners. *Rumania* adhered to the *Tripartite Pact on 23 November 1940 and Slovakia on 24 November 1940*. On *12 December 1940 the Hungarian–Yugoslav Pact* apparently reconciled these two States. On the following day, 13 December 1940, Hitler issued military directives for a German attack on Greece and on 18 December 1940 for an attack on the Soviet Union. Germany strengthened her position by securing Bulgarian acquiescence to a virtual German military occupation during February 1941. *Bulgaria* next concluded a *Non-Aggression Pact with Turkey on 17 February 1942*.

The aggressive policies of Germany and Italy had thrown the Balkan States (all of which, apart from Greece, had remained at peace) into such a state of great alarm that they vied for German friendship. On *1 March 1941 Bulgaria openly adhered to the Tripartite Pact*. Finally, *on 25 March 1941 Yugoslavia adhered to the Tripartite Pact* receiving assurances from Germany that her sovereignty and territorial integrity would be respected. This pro-Axis policy resulted in a popular uprising in Yugoslavia: the military leaders took charge, the Prince Regent was deposed, and a new Government was formed. To gain time the new Yugoslav Government forwarded to Berlin protestations of friendship for Italy and Germany. Hitler responded to the Yugoslav coup by ordering a German surprise attack on Yugoslavia and on Greece, which commenced on 6 April 1941. Three days later the Hungarians also crossed the Yugoslav frontier. On 17 April 1941 the Yugoslav army surrendered. The Government under King Peter left the country, while in Yugoslavia the struggle was continued in the mountains. By the end of May 1941 the Germans had conquered Greece and Crete.

Hitler could now dispose of the spoils of victory. Yugoslavia was partitioned between Germany, Italy, Hungary and Bulgaria; an 'independent kingdom' of Croatia was allowed to exist under Italian control; what was left of Serbia became another 'independent State' under German occupation.

Greece was deprived of western Thrace and eastern Macedonia, which was handed to Bulgaria; Italy took the Ionian Islands and enlarged Albania at the Greeks' expense. The remainder of Greece was placed under mainly Italian occupation after a formal Greek military surrender to the Germans had been signed on 23 April 1941.

Having gained complete dominance in the Balkans, Hitler was now ready to take his most momentous step in expanding the war in Europe by next launching an attack on the Soviet Union. But Yugoslavia's resistance had postponed the original time set for the attack: instead of in May, it could only begin on 22 June 1941. Hitler was joined by allies. Italy and Rumania declared war on Russia on 22 June 1941, Slovakia on 23 June 1941, Finland on 25 June 1941 and Hungary on 27 June 1941. Only Bulgaria (practically under German control) remained neutral, together with Turkey. With the onset of winter, the Soviet Union avoided the defeat predicted by the Allies and the Axis in 1941.

Asia: Japan, Russia and China, 1937–41

In July 1937 Japan resumed an 'undeclared war' against China. During the two years from the renewed invasion of China by Japan in the summer of 1937 until the outbreak of war in Europe in September 1939, fighting not only spread through China but the tension between Russia and Japan increased to the point of open fighting on the borders of Manchuria.

On 21 August 1937 the Soviet Union and China signed a Non-Aggression Pact (p. 160). But Japan's diplomatic position was strengthened when Italy in November 1937 joined the *German–Japanese Anti-Comintern Pact* (p. 168). China's appeal to the League resulted in no effective support. In 1938 the Soviet Union began to provide credit and send war supplies to free China. By the summer of 1938 fierce fighting broke out between Japanese and Soviet troops over the border, near the junction of Manchuria, Korea and the Soviet Union. Although a truce was concluded the tension continued. From May–September 1939 serious clashes occurred between Japanese and Soviet troops on the Mongolian–Manchurian border. The Soviet Union appeared encircled and threatened by two Axis Powers – Germany and Japan. The alignment of the Axis against the Soviet Union was suddenly broken by the signature of the *German–Soviet Non-Aggression Pact* in August 1939 (p. 195). The Soviet Union, while continuing in 1939 and 1940 to aid China with supplies, also sought some accommodation with Japan. Japan meanwhile strengthened her ties with Italy and Germany after Germany's military successes in France, and concluded the *Tripartite Pact on 27 September 1940* (p. 202). For Japan, Indo-China and the Dutch East Indies were assuming new importance in the autumn of 1940. This Japanese drive southwards, partly to ensure for herself the raw materials essential for war, brought her into conflict with the United States. For Japan a settlement with the Soviet Union thus became more desirable. It was achieved when *Japan and the Soviet Union concluded a Neutrality Pact on 13 April 1941.*

Asia: the United States, Britain and Japan, 1940–1

Japan extended her influence in Asia and the Pacific as Germany, the Axis partner, spread over the continent of Europe. After unrelenting Japanese military pressure the Japanese and Vichy Government reached a *Franco-Japanese Agreement on Indo-China by an exchange of notes, 30 August 1940.* France recognized Japan's predominance in the Far East, special economic privileges in Indo-China and, most important, special military facilities to enable Japan to bring the war with China to an end; Japan recognized French sovereignty over Indo-China and Indo-China's territorial integrity. After further tension leading to the brink of conflict, a *Franco-Japanese Military Agreement concerning Indo-China was signed on 22 September 1940* which permitted the Japanese the use of three airfields in Tongking and the right to station 6,000 troops on them, as well as the right to send up to 25,000 men through Tongking to attack China.

Japan also supported Thailand (Siam). Thailand began to acquire Cambodian territory in Indo-China. This local conflict was brought to a halt by Japan on terms favourable to Japanese interests. The *Thailand–Franco-Japanese treaties of 9 May 1941* gave to Thailand about one-third of Cambodia and part of Laos on the west bank of the Mekong; Japan guaranteed the French–Thailand settlement, and Thailand and the Vichy French Government in Indo-China undertook to conclude no agreements which could involve them in political, economic or military collaboration with another country against Japan. *On 29 July 1941 the Japanese extended their occupation over southern Indo-China* having extracted an agreement from Vichy France under threat of using force. Japan had further strengthened her position for moving southwards by signing the *Tripartite Pact of 27 September 1940 with Italy and Germany* (p. 202) and the *Japanese–Soviet Pact of Neutrality of 13 April 1941.* But Japanese efforts to bring the Dutch East Indies into her Greater East Asia sphere from February 1940 to December 1941 met with Dutch resistance. The Dutch authorities would not consent to allowing Japan a privileged economic position which she wanted so as to be able to assure her vital oil supplies and other minerals. Japan was also faced with strong American diplomatic and economic opposition. The extension of the Japanese occupation of southern Indo-China in July 1941 provided bases against Britain in Malaya and the

Dutch East Indies. But the alarm felt at Japanese expansion by the United States led to a number of American measures intended to hinder further Japanese expansion; the United States adopted what in practice amounted to a financial and oil embargo, and also increased military aid to China.

Though there were American–Japanese negotiations for a general settlement these were broken off by the Japanese attack at dawn on the American fleet at *Pearl Harbor on 7 December 1941*. About an hour and a half earlier, under cover of darkness, Japanese troops began landing on the British Malay coast. At 6 a.m. Japan declared war on Britain and the United States, but owing to the international dateline the day of Pearl Harbor was 8 December 1941 in Tokyo and Malaya. Japan's surprise attack was followed by a *German and Italian declaration of war on the United States on 11 December 1941*. The United States had now become a full ally of Britain and the Allied nations both in Asia and Europe.

The Munich Agreement between Germany, Britain, Italy and France, Munich, 29 September 1938

Germany, the United Kingdom, France and Italy, taking into consideration the agreement which has been already reached in principle for the cession to Germany of the Sudeten German territory, have agreed on the following terms and conditions governing the said cession and the measures consequent thereon, and by this Agreement they each hold themselves responsible for the steps necessary to secure its fulfilment:

1. The evacuation will begin on 1st October.

2. The United Kingdom, France and Italy agree that the evacuation of the territory shall be completed by 10th October without any existing installations having been destroyed, and that the Czechoslovak Government will be held responsible for carrying out the evacuation without damage to the said installations.

3. The conditions governing the evacuation will be laid down in detail by an international commission composed of representatives of Germany, the United Kingdom, France, Italy and Czechoslovakia.

4. The occupation by stages of the predominantly German territory by German troops will begin on 1st October. The four territories marked on the attached map will be occupied by German troops in the following order: the territory marked No. I on the 1st and 2nd October; the territory marked No. II on the 2nd and 3rd October; the territory marked No. III on the 3rd, 4th and 5th October; the territory marked No. IV on the 6th and 7th October. The remaining territory of preponderatingly German character will be ascertained by the aforesaid international commission forthwith and be occupied by German troops by the 10th October.

5. The international commission referred to in paragraph 3 will determine the territories in which a plebiscite is to be held. These territories will be occupied

by international bodies until the plebiscite has been completed. The same commission will fix the conditions in which the plebiscite is to be held, taking as a basis the conditions of the Saar plebiscite. The commission will also fix a date, not later than the end of November, on which the plebiscite will be held.

6. The final determination of the frontier will be carried out by the international commission. This commission will also be entitled to recommend to the four Powers – Germany, the United Kingdom, France and Italy – in certain exceptional cases minor modifications in the strictly ethnographical determination of the zones which are to be transferred without plebiscite.

7. There will be a right of option into and out of the transferred territories, the option to be exercised within six months from the date of this Agreement. A German-Czechoslovak commission shall determine the details of the option, consider ways of facilitating the transfer of population and settle questions of principle arising out of the said transfer.

8. The Czech Government will, within a period of four weeks from the date of this Agreement, release from their military and police forces any Sudeten Germans who may wish to be released, and the Czech Government will, within the same period, release Sudeten German prisoners who are serving terms of imprisonment for political offences.

Munich, September 29, 1938

Annex

His Majesty's Government in the United Kingdom and the French Government have entered into the above agreement on the basis that they stand by the offer, contained in paragraph 6 of the Anglo-French proposals of 19th September, relating to an international guarantee of the new boundaries of the Czech State against unprovoked aggression.

When the question of the Polish and Hungarian minorities in Czechoslovakia has been settled, Germany and Italy, for their part, will give a guarantee to Czechoslovakia.

Munich, September 29, 1938

Declaration

The heads of the Governments of the four Powers declare that the problems of the Polish and Hungarian minorities in Czechoslovakia, if not settled within three months by agreement between the respective Governments, shall form the subject of another meeting of the heads of the Governments of the four Powers here present.

Munich, September 29, 1938

Supplementary Declaration

All questions which may arise out of the transfer of the territory shall be considered as coming within the terms of reference of the international commission.

Munich, September 29, 1938

The four heads of Governments here present agree that the international commission provided for in the Agreement signed by them today shall consist of the Secretary of State in the German Foreign Office, the British, French and Italian Ambassadors accredited in Berlin, and a representative to be nominated by the Government of Czechoslovakia.

Munich, September 29, 1938

Anglo-German Declaration, Munich, 30 September 1938

We, the German Führer and Chancellor and the British Prime Minister, have had a further meeting today and are agreed in recognizing that the question of Anglo-German relations is of the first importance for the two countries and for Europe.

We regard the agreement signed last night and the Anglo-German Naval Agreement as symbolic of the desire of our two peoples never to go to war with one another again.

We are resolved that the method of consultation shall be the method adopted to deal with any other questions that may concern our two countries, and we are determined to continue our efforts to remove possible sources of difference and thus to contribute to assure the peace of Europe.

(Signed) A. HITLER
(Signed) NEVILLE CHAMBERLAIN

Statement by Chamberlain in the House of Commons concerning the guarantee to Poland, 31 March 1939

The Prime Minister [*Mr Chamberlain*]: The Right Hon. Gentleman the Leader of the Opposition asked me this morning whether I could make a statement as to the European situation. As I said this morning, His Majesty's Government have no official confirmation of the rumours of any projected attack and they must not, therefore, be taken as accepting them as true.

I am glad to take this opportunity of stating again the general policy of His Majesty's Government. They have constantly advocated the adjustment, by way of free negotiation between the parties concerned, of any differences that may arise between them. They consider that this is the natural and proper course where differences exist. In their opinion there should be no question incapable of solution by peaceful means, and they would see no justification for the substitution of force or threats of force for the method of negotiation.

As the House is aware, certain consultations are now proceeding with other Governments. In order to make perfectly clear the position of His Majesty's Government in the meantime before those consultations are concluded, I now have to inform the House that during that period, in the event of any action which clearly threatened Polish independence, and which the Polish Government accordingly considered it vital to resist with their national force, His Majesty's Government would feel themselves bound at once to lend the Polish Government all support in their power. They have given the Polish Government an assurance to this effect.

I may add that the French Government have authorized me to make it plain that they stand in the same position in this matter as do His Majesty's Government.

Agreement of Mutual Assistance between Britain and Poland, London, 25 August 1939

The Government of the United Kingdom of Great Britain and Northern Ireland and the Polish Government:

Desiring to place on a permanent basis the collaboration between their respective countries resulting from the assurances of mutual assistance of a defensive character which they have already exchanged;

Have resolved to conclude an Agreement for that purpose and have ... agreed on the following provisions:

Article 1. Should one of the Contracting Parties become engaged in hostilities with a European Power in consequence of aggression by the latter against that Contracting Party, the other Contracting Party will at once give the Contracting Party engaged in hostilities all the support and assistance in its power.

Article 2. 1. The provisions of Article 1 will also apply in the event of any action by a European Power which clearly threatened, directly or indirectly, the independence of one of the Contracting Parties, and was of such a nature that the party in question considered it vital to resist it with its armed forces.

2. Should one of the Contracting Parties become engaged in hostilities with a European Power in consequence of action by that Power which threatened the independence or neutrality of another European State in such a way as to constitute a clear menace to the security of that Contracting Party, the provisions of Article 1 will apply, without prejudice, however, to the rights of the other European State concerned.

Article 3. Should a European Power attempt to undermine the independence of one of the Contracting Parties by processes of economic penetration or in any other way, the Contracting Parties will support each other in resistance to such attempts. Should the European Power concerned thereupon embark on hostilities against one of the Contracting Parties, the provisions of Article 1 will apply.

Article 4. The methods of applying the undertakings of mutual assistance provided for by the present Agreement are established between the competent naval, military and air authorities of the Contracting Parties.

Article 5. Without prejudice to the foregoing undertakings of the Contracting Parties to give each other mutual support and assistance immediately on the outbreak of hostilities, they will exchange complete and speedy information concerning any development which might threaten their independence and, in particular, concerning any development which threatened to call the said undertakings into operation.

Article 6. 1. The Contracting Parties will communicate to each other the terms of any undertakings of assistance against aggression which they have already given or may in future give to other States.

2. Should either of the Contracting Parties intend to give such an undertaking after the coming into force of the present Agreement, the other Contracting Party shall, in order to ensure the proper functioning of the Agreement, be informed thereof.

3. Any new undertaking which the Contracting Parties may enter into in future shall neither limit their obligations under the present Agreement nor indirectly create new obligations between the Contracting Party not participating in these undertakings and the third State concerned.

Article 7. Should the Contracting Parties be engaged in hostilities in consequence of the application of the present Agreement, they will not conclude an armistice or treaty of peace except by mutual agreement.

Article 8. 1. The present Agreement shall remain in force for a period of five years.

2. Unless denounced six months before the expiry of this period it shall continue in force, each Contracting Party having thereafter the right to denounce it at any time by giving six months' notice to that effect.

3. The present Agreement shall come into force on signature.

In faith whereof the above-named plenipotentiaries have signed the present Agreement and have affixed thereto their seals.

Done in English in duplicate at London, the 25th August 1939. A Polish text shall subsequently be agreed upon between the Contracting Parties and both texts will then be authentic.

(L.S.)   HALIFAX
(L.S.)   EDWARD RACZYŃSKI

Secret Protocol

The Polish Government and the Government of the United Kingdom of Great Britain and Northern Ireland are agreed upon the following interpretation of the Agreement of Mutual Assistance signed this day as alone authentic and binding:

1. (a) By the expression 'a European Power' employed in the Agreement is to be understood Germany.

(b) In the event of action within the meaning of Articles 1 or 2 of the Agreement by a European Power other than Germany, the Contracting Parties will consult together on the measures to be taken in common.

2. (a) The two Governments will from time to time determine by mutual agreement the hypothetical cases of action by Germany coming within the ambit of Article 2 of the Agreement.

(b) Until such time as the two Governments have agreed to modify the following provisions of this paragraph, they will consider: that the case contemplated by paragraph 1 of Article 2 of the Agreement is that of the Free City of Danzig; and that the cases contemplated by paragraph 2 of Article 2 are Belgium, Holland, Lithuania.

(c) Latvia and Estonia shall be regarded by the two Governments as included in the list of countries contemplated by paragraph 2 of Article 2 from the moment that an undertaking of mutual assistance between the United Kingdom and a third State covering those two countries enters into force.

(d) As regards Roumania, the Government of the United Kingdom refers to the guarantee which it has given to that country; and the Polish Government refers to the reciprocal undertakings of the Roumano-Polish alliance which Poland has never regarded as incompatible with her traditional friendship for Hungary.

3. The undertakings mentioned in Article 6 of the Agreement, should they be entered into by one of the Contracting Parties with a third State, would of necessity be so framed that their execution should at no time prejudice either the sovereignty or territorial inviolability of the other Contracting Party.

4. The present Protocol constitutes an integral part of the Agreement signed this day, the scope of which it does not exceed.

In faith whereof the undersigned, being duly authorized, have signed the present Protocol.

Done in English in duplicate, at London, the 25th August 1939. A Polish text will subsequently be agreed upon between the Contracting Parties and both texts will then be authentic.

(Signed)   HALIFAX
(Signed)   EDWARD RACZYŃSKI

Protocol of Mutual Assistance between Poland and France, 4 September 1939

Article 1. The Polish Government and the French Government, desiring to assure the full efficacy of the Polish-French Alliance, and having especially in view the present situation of the League of Nations, agree to confirm that their mutual obligations of assistance in the event of aggression by a third Power continue to be founded on the Agreements of Alliance in force.

At the same time they declare that henceforth they interpret the said Agreements as embodying the following obligations: The undertaking of the two Contracting Parties mutually to render all aid and assistance in their power at once and from the outbreak of hostilities between one of the Contracting Parties and a European Power in consequence of that Power's aggression against the said Contracting Party, equally applies to the case of any action by a European Power which manifestly directly or indirectly threatens the independence of one of the Contracting Parties, and is of such a nature that the Party in question considers it vital to resist that aggression with its armed forces.

Should one of the Contracting Parties become engaged in hostilities with a European Power in consequence of action by that Power which threatened the independence or neutrality of another European State in such a way as to constitute a clear menace to the security of that Contracting Party, the provisions of Article 1 will apply, without prejudice, however, to the rights of the other European State concerned.

Article 2. The methods of applying the undertakings of mutual assistance provided for by the present Agreement are established between the competent military, naval, and air authorities of the Contracting Parties.

Article 3. 1. The Contracting Parties will communicate to each other the terms of any undertakings of assistance against aggression which they have already given or may in the future give to other States.

2. Should either of the Contracting Parties intend to give such an undertaking after the coming into force of the present Agreement, the other Contracting Party shall, in order to ensure proper functioning of the Agreement, be informed thereof.

3. Any new undertaking which the Contracting Parties may enter into in the future shall neither limit their obligations under the present Agreement nor indirectly create new obligations between the Contracting Party not participating in those undertakings and the third State concerned.

Article 4. Should the Contracting Parties be engaged in hostilities in consequence of the application of the present Agreement, they will not conclude an armistice or treaty of peace except by mutual agreement.

The present Protocol, constituting an integral part of the Polish-French Agreements of 1921 and 1925, shall remain in force as long as the said Agreements.

Alliance between Germany and Italy (Pact of Steel), 22 May 1939

The German Chancellor and His Majesty the King of Italy and Albania, Emperor of Ethiopia, deem that the time has come to strengthen the close relationship of friendship and homogeneity, existing between National Socialist Germany and Fascist Italy, by a solemn pact.

Now that a safe bridge for mutual aid and assistance has been established by the common frontier between Germany and Italy fixed for all time, both Governments reaffirm the policy, the principles and objectives of which have already been agreed upon by them, and which has proved successful, both for promoting the interests of the two countries and also for safeguarding peace in Europe.

Firmly united by the inner affinity between their ideologies and the comprehensive solidarity of their interests, the German and Italian nations are resolved in future also to act side by side and with united forces to secure their living space and to maintain peace.

Following this path, marked out for them by history, Germany and Italy intend, in the midst of a world of unrest and disintegration, to serve the task of safeguarding the foundations of European civilization.

In order to lay down these principles in a pact there have been appointed plenipotentiaries ... and they have agreed on the following terms.

Article I. The High Contracting Parties will remain in continuous contact with each other in order to reach an understanding on all questions affecting their common interests or the general European situation.

Article II. Should the common interests of the High Contracting Parties be endangered by international events of any kind whatsoever, they will immediately enter into consultations on the measures to be taken for the protection of these interests.

Should the security or other vital interests of one of the High Contracting Parties be threatened from without, the other High Contracting Party will afford the threatened party full political and diplomatic support in order to remove this threat.

Article III. If, contrary to the wishes and hopes of the High Contracting Parties, it should happen that one of them became involved in warlike complications with another Power or Powers, the other High Contracting Party would immediately come to its assistance as an ally and support it with all its military forces on land, at sea and in the air.

Article IV. In order to ensure in specific cases the speedy execution of the obligations of alliance undertaken under Article III, the Governments of the two High Contracting Parties will further intensify their collaboration in the military field, and in the field of war economy.

In the same way the two Governments will remain in continuous consultation also on other measures necessary for the practical execution of the provisions of this Pact.

For the purposes indicated in paragraphs 1 and 2 above, the two Governments will set up commissions which will be under the direction of the two Foreign Ministers.

Article V. The High Contracting Parties undertake even now that, in the event of war waged jointly, they will conclude an armistice and peace only in full agreement with each other.

Article VI. The two High Contracting Parties are aware of the significance that attaches to their common relations with Powers friendly to them. They are resolved to maintain these relations in the future also and together to shape them in accordance with the common interests which form the bonds between them and these Powers.

Article VII. This Pact shall enter into force immediately upon signature. The two High Contracting Parties are agreed in laying down that its first term of validity shall be for ten years. In good time before the expiry of this period, they will reach agreement on the extension of the validity of the Pact.

In witness whereof the plenipotentiaries have signed this Pact and affixed thereto their seals.

Done in duplicate in the German and the Italian languages, both texts being equally authoritative.

Berlin, May 22, 1939, in the XVIIth year of the Fascist Era.

JOACHIM V. RIBBENTROP
GALEAZZO CIANO

Trade Agreement between the Soviet Union and Germany, 19 August 1939

[The contents of this agreement can be derived from the German Foreign Ministry Memorandum of 29 August 1939 below.]

Memorandum

The German-Soviet Trade Agreement concluded on August 19 covers the following:

1. Germany grants the Soviet Union a merchandise credit of 200 million Reichsmarks. The financing will be done by the German Golddiskontbank ... [at an actual rate of interest of 4½ per cent].

2. The credit will be used to finance Soviet orders in Germany. The Soviet Union will make use of it to order the industrial products listed in schedule A of the Agreement. They consist of machinery and industrial installations. Machine tools up to the very largest dimensions form a considerable part of the deliveries. And armaments in the broader sense (such as optical supplies, armour plate and the like) will, subject to examination of every single item, be supplied in smaller proportion.

3. The credit will be liquidated by Soviet raw materials, which will be selected by agreement between the two Governments. The annual interest will

likewise be paid from the proceeds of Soviet merchandise, that is, from the special accounts kept in Berlin.

4. In order that we might secure an immediate benefit from the Credit Agreement, it was made a condition from the beginning that the Soviet Union bind itself to the delivery, starting immediately, of certain raw materials as current business. It was possible so to arrange these raw-material commitments of the Russians that our wishes were largely met. The Russian commitments of raw materials are contained in schedule C. They amount to 180 million Reichsmarks: half to be delivered in each of the first and second years following the conclusion of the Agreement. It is a question, in particular, of lumber, cotton, feed grain, oil cake, phosphate, platinum, raw furs, petroleum, and other goods which for us have a more or less gold value.

5. Since these Soviet deliveries made as current business are to be compensated by German counterdeliveries, certain German promises of delivery had to be made to the Russians. The German industrial products to be supplied in current business as counterdeliveries for Russian raw materials are listed in schedule B. This schedule totals 120 million Reichsmarks and comprises substantially the

same categories of merchandise as schedule A.

6. From the welter of difficult questions of detail which arose during the negotiations, the following might also be mentioned: guaranteeing of the rate of exchange of the Reichsmark. The complicated arrangement arrived at appears in the Confidential Protocol signed on August 26 of this year. In order not to jeopardize the conclusion of the Agreement on August 19 of this year, the question was laid aside and settled afterwards. The questions of the liquidation of the old credits, the shipping clause, an emergency clause for the event of inability to deliver of either party, the arbitration procedure, the price clause, etc., were settled satisfactorily despite the pressure of time.

7. The Agreement, which has come into being after extraordinary difficulties, will undoubtedly give a decided impetus to German–Russian trade. We must try to build anew on this foundation and, above all, try to settle a number of questions which could not heretofore be settled, because of the low ebb which had been reached in our trade relations. The framework now set up represents a minimum. Since the political climate is favourable, it may well be expected that it will be exceeded considerably in both directions, both in imports and exports.

8. Under the Agreement, the following movement of goods can be expected for the next few years:

Exports to the U.S.S.R.

200 million Reichsmarks credit deliveries, schedule 'A'.

120 mill. RM. deliveries as current business, schedule 'B'.

X mill. RM. unspecified deliveries on current business.

Imports from the U.S.S.R.

180 mill. RM. raw material deliveries, schedule 'C'.

200 mill. RM. repayment of 1935 credit.

approx. 100 mill. RM. capitalized interest from present and last credit.

X mill. RM. unspecified deliveries of Soviet goods under German–Soviet Trade Agreement of Dec. 19, 1938.

The movement of goods envisaged by the Agreement might therefore reach a total of more than 1 billion Reichsmarks for the next few years, not including liquidation of the present 200 million credit by deliveries of Russian raw materials beginning in 1946.

9. Apart from the economic imports of the Treaty, its significance lies in the fact that the negotiations also served to renew political contacts with Russia and that the Credit Agreement was considered by both sides as the first decisive step in the reshaping of political relations.

Treaty of Non-Aggression between Germany and the Soviet Union, Moscow, 23 August 1939

The Government of the German Reich and

The Government of the Union of Soviet Socialist Republics

Desirous of strengthening the cause of peace between Germany and the U.S.S.R., and proceeding from the fundamental provisions of the Neutrality Agreement concluded in April 1926 between Germany and the U.S.S.R., have reached the following Agreement:

Article I. Both High Contracting Parties obligate themselves to desist from any act of violence, any aggressive action, and any attack on each other, either individually or jointly with other Powers.

Article II. Should one of the High Contracting Parties become the object of belligerent action by a third Power, the other High Contracting Party shall in no manner lend its support to this third Power.

Article III. The Governments of the two High Contracting Parties shall in the future maintain continual contact with one another for the purpose of consultation in order to exchange information on problems affecting their common interests.

Article IV. Neither of the two High Contracting Parties shall participate in any grouping of Powers whatsoever that is directly or indirectly aimed at the other party.

Article V. Should disputes or conflicts arise between the High Contracting Parties over problems of one kind or another, both parties shall settle these disputes or conflicts exclusively through friendly exchange of opinion or, if necessary, through the establishment of arbitration commissions.

Article VI. The present Treaty is concluded for a period of ten years, with the proviso that, in so far as one of the High Contracting Parties does not denounce it one year prior to the expiration of this period, the validity of this Treaty shall automatically be extended for another five years.

Article VII. The present Treaty shall be ratified within the shortest possible time. The ratifications shall be exchanged in Berlin. The Agreement shall enter into force as soon as it is signed.

Secret Additional Protocol

On the occasion of the signature of the Non-Aggression Pact between the Ger-

man Reich and the Union of Socialist Soviet Republics the undersigned plenipotentiaries of each of the two parties discussed in strictly confidential conversations the question of the boundary of their respective spheres of influence in Eastern Europe. These conversations led to the following conclusions:

Article 1. In the event of a territorial and political rearrangement in the areas belonging to the Baltic States (Finland, Estonia, Latvia, Lithuania), the northern boundary of Lithuania shall represent the boundary of the spheres of influence of Germany and the U.S.S.R. In this connection the interest of Lithuania in the Vilna area is recognized by each party.

Article 2. In the event of a territorial and political rearrangement of the areas belonging to the Polish State the spheres of influence of Germany and the U.S.S.R. shall be bounded approximately by the line of the rivers Narew, Vistula, and San.

The question of whether the interests of both parties make desirable the maintenance of an independent Polish State and how such a State should be bounded can only be definitely determined in the course of further political developments.

In any event both Governments will resolve this question by means of a friendly agreement.

Article 3. With regard to south-eastern Europe attention is called by the Soviet side to its interest in Bessarabia. The German side declares its complete political disinterestedness in these areas.

Article 4. This Protocol shall be treated by both parties as strictly secret.

Moscow, August 23, 1939

For the Government
of the German Reich:
v. RIBBENTROP

Plenipotentiary of the
Government of the U.S.S.R.
V. MOLOTOV

Treaty of Mutual Assistance between Britain, France and Turkey
19 October 1939

Article 1. In the event of Turkey being involved in hostilities with a European Power in consequence of aggression by that Power against Turkey, France and the United Kingdom will cooperate effectively with Turkey and will lend her all aid and assistance in their power.

Article 2. 1. In the event of an act of aggression by a European Power leading to war in the Mediterranean area in which France and the United Kingdom are involved, Turkey will collaborate effectively with France and the United Kingdom and will lend them all aid and assistance in her power.

2. In the event of an act of aggression by a European Power leading to war in the Mediterranean area in which Turkey is involved, France and the United Kingdom will collaborate effectively with Turkey and will lend her all aid and assistance in their power.

Article 3. So long as the guarantees given by France and the United Kingdom to Greece and Roumania by their respective Declarations of the 13th April 1939 remain in force, Turkey will cooperate effectively with France and the United Kingdom and will lend them all aid and assistance in her power, in the event of France and the United Kingdom being engaged in hostilities in virtue of either of the said guarantees.

Article 4. In the event of France and the United Kingdom being involved in hostilities with a European Power in consequence of aggression committed by that Power against either of those States without the provisions of Articles 2 or 3 being applicable, the High Contracting Parties will immediately consult together.

It is nevertheless agreed that in such an eventuality Turkey will observe at least a benevolent neutrality towards France and the United Kingdom.

Article 5. Without prejudice to the provisions of Article 3 above, in the event of either:

1. Aggression by a European Power against another European State which the Government of one of the High Contracting Parties had, with the approval of that State, undertaken to assist in maintaining its independence or neutrality against such aggression, or

2. Aggression by a European Power which while directed against another European State, constituted, in the opinion of the Government of one of the High Contracting Parties, a menace to its own security,

the High Contracting Parties will immediately consult together with a view to such common action as might be considered effective.

Article 6. The present Treaty is not directed against any country, but is designed to assure France, the United Kingdom and Turkey of mutual aid and assistance in resistance to aggression should the necessity arise.

Article 7. The provisions of the present Treaty are equally binding as bilateral obligations between Turkey and each of the two other High Contracting Parties.

Article 8. If the High Contracting Parties are engaged in hostilities in consequence of the operation of the present Treaty, they will not conclude an armistice or peace except by common agreement.

Article 9. The present Treaty shall be ratified and the instruments of ratification shall be deposited simultaneously at Angora as soon as possible. It shall enter into force on the date of this deposit.

The present Treaty is concluded for a period of fifteen years. If none of the High Contracting Parties has notified the two others of its intention to terminate it six months before the expiration of the said period, the Treaty will be renewed by tacit consent for a further period of five years, and so on.

Protocol No. 1

The undersigned plenipotentiaries state that their respective Governments agree that the Treaty of today's date shall be put into force from the moment of its signature.

The present Protocol shall be considered as an integral part of the Treaty concluded today between France, the United Kingdom and Turkey.

Protocol No. 2

At the moment of signature of the Treaty between France, the United Kingdom and Turkey, the undersigned plenipotentiaries, duly authorized to this effect, have agreed as follows:

The obligations undertaken by Turkey in virtue of the above-mentioned Treaty cannot compel that country to take action having as its effect, or involving as its consequence, entry into armed conflict with the Soviet Union.

Declaration of Principles known as the Atlantic Charter, made public on 14 August 1941

Joint Declaration of the President of the United States of America and the Prime Minister, Mr Churchill, representing His Majesty's Government in the United Kingdom, being met together, deem it right to make known certain common principles in the national policies of their respective countries on which they base their hopes for a better future for the world.

First, their countries seek no aggrandizement, territorial or other;

Second, they desire to see no territorial changes that do not accord with the freely expressed wishes of the peoples concerned;

Third, they respect the right of all peoples to choose the form of government under which they will live; and they wish to see sovereign rights and self-government restored to those who have been forcibly deprived of them;

Fourth, they will endeavour, with due respect for their existing obligations, to further the enjoyment by all States, great or small, victor or vanquished, of access, on equal terms, to the trade and to the raw materials of the world which are needed for their economic prosperity;

Fifth, they desire to bring about the fullest collaboration between all nations in the economic field with the object of securing, for all, improved labour standards, economic advancement and social security;

Sixth, after the final destruction of the Nazi tyranny, they hope to see established a peace which will afford to all nations the means of dwelling in safety within their own boundaries, and which will afford assurance that all the men in all the lands may live out their lives in freedom from fear and want;

Seventh, such a peace should enable all men to traverse the high seas and oceans without hindrance;

Eighth, they believe that all of the nations of the world, for realistic as well as spiritual reasons must come to the abandonment of the use of force. Since no future peace can be maintained if land, sea or air armaments continue to be employed by nations which threaten, or may threaten, aggression outside of their frontiers, they believe, pending the establishment of a wider and permanent system of general security, that the disarmament of such nations is essential. They will likewise aid and encourage all other practicable measures which will lighten for peace-loving peoples the crushing burden of armaments.

Boundary and Friendship Treaty between the Soviet Union and Germany, Moscow, 28 September 1939

The Government of the German Reich and the Government of the U.S.S.R. consider it as exclusively their task, after the collapse of the former Polish State, to re-establish peace and order in these territories and to assure to the peoples living there a peaceful life in keeping with their national character. To this end, they have agreed upon the following:

Article I. The Government of the German Reich and the Government of the U.S.S.R. determine as the boundary of their respective national interests in the territory of the former Polish State the line marked on the attached map, which shall be described in more detail in a Supplementary Protocol.

Article II. Both parties recognize the boundary of the respective national interests established in Article I as definitive and shall reject any interference of third Powers in this settlement.

Article III. The necessary reorganization of public administration will be effected in the areas west of the line specified in Article I by the Government of the German Reich, in the areas east of this line by the Government of the U.S.S.R.

Article IV. The Government of the German Reich and the Government of the U.S.S.R. regard this settlement as a firm foundation for a progressive development of the friendly relations between their peoples.

Article V. This Treaty shall be ratified and the ratifications shall be exchanged in Berlin as soon as possible. The Treaty becomes effective upon signature.

Confidential Protocol

[Provided that Germans and people of German descent may leave territories under Soviet jurisdiction for Germany, and Ukrainians and White Russians may leave German territories for Soviet Union.]

Secret Supplementary Protocol

The undersigned plenipotentiaries declare the agreement of the Government of the German Reich and the Government of U.S.S.R. on the following:

The Secret Supplementary Protocol signed on August 23, 1939 shall be amended in Item 1 to the effect that the territory of the Lithuanian State falls in the sphere of influence of U.S.S.R., while, on the other hand, the province of Lublin and parts of the province of Warsaw fall in the sphere of influence of Germany (cf. the map attached to the Frontier and Friendship Treaty signed today). As soon as the Government of U.S.S.R. takes special measures on Lithuanian territory to protect its interests, the present German–Lithuanian frontier, for the purpose of a natural and simple frontier delineation, will be rectified in such a way that the Lithuanian territory situated to the south-west of the line marked on the attached map will fall to Germany.

Further it is declared that the Economic Agreements now in force between Germany and Lithuania will not be affected by the measures of the Soviet Union referred to above.

Secret Supplementary Protocol

The undersigned plenipotentiaries, on concluding the German–Russian Frontier and Friendship Treaty, have declared their agreement on the following:

Neither party will tolerate in its territories Polish agitation that affects the territories of the other party. Both parties will suppress in their territories all beginnings of such agitation and will inform each other concerning suitable measures for this purpose.

Declaration

After the Government of the German Reich and the Government of U.S.S.R. have, by means of the Treaty signed today, definitively settled the problems arising from the collapse of the Polish State and have thereby created a sure foundation for a lasting peace in Eastern Europe, they mutually express their conviction that it would serve the true interests of all peoples to put an end to the state of war existing at present between Germany on the one side, and England and France on the other. Both Governments will therefore direct their common efforts, jointly with other friendly Powers if occasion arises, towards attaining this goal as soon as possible.

Should, however, the efforts of the two Governments remain fruitless, this would demonstrate the fact that England and France are responsible for the continuation of the war, whereupon, in case of the continuation of the war, the Governments of Germany and of U.S.S.R. will engage in mutual consultations with regard to necessary measures.

Commercial Agreement between the Soviet Union and Germany, 11 February 1940

[Information based on German Foreign Ministry Memorandum below.]

Memorandum

The Agreement is based on the correspondence—mentioned in the Preamble —between the Reich Minister for Foreign Affairs and the Chairman of the Council of People's Commissars, Molotov, dated September 28, 1939. The Agreement represents the first great step towards the economic programme envisaged by both sides and is to be followed by others.

1. The Agreement covers a period of twenty-seven months, i.e. the Soviet deliveries, which are to be made within eighteen months, will be compensated by German deliveries in turn within twenty-seven months. The most difficult point of the correspondence of September 28, 1939, namely, that the Soviet raw material deliveries are to be compensated by German industrial deliveries over a *longer period*, is thereby settled in accordance with our wishes. . . .

2. The Soviet deliveries. According to the Agreement, the Soviet Union shall within the first twelve months deliver raw materials in the amount of approximately 500 million Reichsmarks.

In addition, the Soviets will deliver raw materials, contemplated in the Credit Agreement of August 19, 1939, for the same period, in the amount of approximately 100 million Reichsmarks.

The most important raw materials are the following:

1,000,000 tons of grain for cattle, and of legumes, in the amount of 120 million Reichsmarks

900,000 tons of mineral oil in the amount of approximately 115 million Reichsmarks

100,000 tons of cotton in the amount of approximately 90 million Reichsmarks

500,000 tons of phosphates

100,000 tons of chrome ores

500,000 tons of iron ore

300,000 tons of scrap iron and pig iron

2,400 kg of platinum

Manganese ore metals, lumber, and numerous other raw materials.

... [Stalin also promised to purchase raw materials in third countries for Germany.]

Pact of Mutual Assistance between the Soviet Union and Latvia, Moscow, 5 October 1939

[Pacts of Mutual Assistance were also concluded with Estonia, 28 September 1939, and Lithuania, 10 October 1939.] The Presidium of the Supreme Soviet of U.S.S.R. on the one hand, and the President of the Latvian Republic on the other, for the purpose of developing the friendly relations created by the Peace Treaty of August 11, 1920, which were based on the recognition of the independent statehood and non-interference in the internal affairs of the other party; recognizing that the Peace Treaty of August 11, 1920 and the Agreement of February 5, 1932 concerning non-aggression and the amicable settlement of conflicts, continue to be the firm basis of their mutual relations and obligations; convinced that a definition of the precise conditions ensuring mutual safety is in accordance with the interests of both Contracting Parties; have considered it necessary to conclude between them the following Mutual Assistance Pact ...

Article I. Both Contracting Parties undertake to render each other every assistance, including military, in the event of a direct attack, or threat of attack, on the part of any European Great Power, with respect to the sea borders of the Contracting Parties on the Baltic Sea, or their land borders through the territory of the Estonian or Latvian Republics, or also the bases referred to in Article III.

Article II. The Soviet Union undertakes to render assistance on preferential conditions to the Latvian army in the form of armaments and other war materials.

Article III. In order to ensure the safety of U.S.S.R. and to consolidate her own independence, the Latvian Republic grants to the Union the right to maintain in the cities of Liapaja (Libava) and Ventspils (Vindava) naval bases and several airfields for aviation purposes on leasehold at a reasonable rental. The locations of the bases and airfields shall be exactly specified and their boundaries determined by mutual agreement.

For the purpose of protecting the Straits of Irbe, the Soviet Union is given the right to establish on the same conditions a coast artillery base between Ventspils and Pitrags.

For the purpose of protecting the naval bases, the airfields and the coast artillery base, the Soviet Union has the right to maintain at its own expense on the areas set aside for bases and airfields a strictly limited number of Soviet land and air forces, the maximum number of which is to be fixed by special agreement.

Article IV. Both Contracting Parties undertake not to enter into any alliances or to participate in any coalitions directed against one of the Contracting Parties.

Article V. The entry into force of the present Pact must in no way affect the sovereign rights of the Contracting Parties, in particular their political structure, their economic and social system, and their military measures.

The areas set aside for the bases and airfields (Article III) remain in the territory of the Latvian Republic.

Article VI. The present Pact goes into force with the exchange of documents of ratification. The exchange of documents will take place in the City of Riga within six days after the signing of the present Pact.

The present Pact shall remain in force for a period of ten years, and in the event that one of the Contracting Parties does not consider it necessary to denounce it prior to the expiration of such period, it will automatically remain in force for the following ten years.

Treaty of Non-Aggression between Germany and Turkey, 18 June 1941

Article 1. The Turkish Republic and the German Reich undertake to respect mutually the inviolability and integrity of their territories, and to abstain from all action aimed directly or indirectly against one another.

Article 2. The Turkish Republic and the German Reich undertake to enter into friendly contact in the future in regard to all matters involving their mutual

interests with a view to reaching an agreement for their solution.

Article 3. The present Treaty which shall enter into force on the date of its signature shall be valid for a period of ten years. The High Contracting Parties shall in due time reach an agreement on the matter of its prolongation.

The present Treaty shall be ratified and the ratifications shall be exchanged in Berlin as soon as possible....

Three Powers Pact between Germany, Italy and Japan, Berlin, 27 September 1940

The Governments of Germany, Italy and Japan, considering it as the condition precedent of any lasting peace that all nations of the world be given each its own proper place, have decided to stand by and cooperate with one another in regard to their efforts in Greater East Asia and the regions of Europe respectively wherein it

is their prime purpose to establish and maintain a new order of things calculated to promote mutual prosperity and welfare of the peoples concerned.

Furthermore it is the desire of the three Governments to extend cooperation to such nations in other spheres of the world as may be inclined to put forth endeavours along lines similar to their own, in order that their ultimate aspirations for world peace may thus be realized. Accordingly the Governments of Germany, Italy and Japan have agreed as follows:

Article 1. Japan recognizes and respects the leadership of Germany and Italy in the establishment of a new order in Europe.

Article 2. Germany and Italy recognize and respect the leadership of Japan in the establishment of a new order in Greater East Asia.

Article 3. Germany, Italy and Japan agree to cooperate in their efforts on the aforesaid lines. They further undertake to assist one another with all political, economic and military means when one of the three Contracting Parties is attacked by a Power at present not involved in the European War or in the Sino-Japanese Conflict.

Article 4. With a view to implementing the present Pact, joint technical commissions the members of which are to be appointed by the respective Governments of Germany, Italy and Japan will meet without delay.

Article 5. Germany, Italy and Japan affirm that the aforesaid terms do not in any way affect the political status which exists at present as between each of the three Contracting Parties and Soviet Russia.

Article 6. The present Pact shall come into effect immediately upon signature and shall remain in force for ten years from the date of its coming into force.

At proper time before the expiration of the said term the High Contracting Parties shall, at the request of any one of them, enter into negotiations for its renewal. ...

Agreement between Germany, Italy and Japan on the joint prosecution of the war, Berlin, 11 December 1941

In their unshakeable determination not to lay down arms until the common war against the United States of America and Britain has been brought to a successful conclusion, the German Government, the Italian Government, and the Japanese Government have agreed upon the following provisions:

Article 1. Germany, Italy and Japan jointly and with every means at their disposal will pursue the war forced upon them by the United States of America and Britain to a victorious conclusion.

Article 2. Germany, Italy, and Japan undertake not to conclude an armistice or peace with the United States of Amer-

ica or Britain except in complete mutual agreement.

Article 3. After victory has been achieved Germany, Italy, and Japan will continue in closest cooperation with a view to establishing a new and just order along the lines of the Tripartite Agreement concluded by them on September 27, 1940.

Article 4. The present Agreement will come into force with its signature, and will remain valid as long as the Tripartite Pact of September 27, 1940.

The High Contracting Parties will in good time before the expiry of this term of validity enter into consultation with each other as to the future development of their cooperation, as provided under Article 3 of the present Agreement.

VIII · The Grand Alliance: Britain, the United States and the Soviet Union, 1941–5

Britain, the United States and the Soviet Union, June 1941–June 1942

In a broadcast on the evening of 22 June 1941, Winston Churchill promised help to Russians fighting for their homeland in the cause of 'free men and free people' everywhere. Military supplies from Britain and America began to reach the Soviet Union in appreciable quantities in the autumn of 1941. The Anglo-Soviet alliance against Germany was first placed on a formal basis by the brief *Anglo-Soviet Agreement of 12 July 1941*, in which the two Powers undertook to render each other assistance and support in the war against 'Hitlerite Germany', and not to negotiate an armistice or peace treaty except by mutual agreement. From the first, relations between the Soviet Union and Britain, and later the United States, were made difficult by Stalin's insistent demand that Russia's allies should engage the Germans on the continent of Europe. His call for a second front was not fully satisfied until the Allied landings in France in June 1944. As a result of Russian pressure, however, *Britain declared war on Finland, Hungary and Rumania on 6 December 1941*. Bulgaria had not joined in the German war against the Soviet Union, but to show a theoretical loyalty to the Axis declared war on Britain and the United States on 13 December 1941.

An *Anglo-Soviet–Iranian Treaty was concluded on 29 January 1942* (p. 210) which promised Britain and Russia all facilities to defend Iran from aggression, and Britain and Russia promised to respect Persian independence and integrity and to withdraw not later than six months after the war. Negotiations for a full Anglo-Soviet alliance were long drawn-out. Stalin's suspicions of Britain's resolution to relieve German military pressure in Russia, and Russian territorial demands in the post-war European settlement, were the major obstacles. Russia wished recognition of her right to the Baltic States and to

Poland up to the Curzon line, with possible minor frontier readjustments. But Britain, and later the United States, had agreed to postpone all questions of the new frontiers until after the war. Finally the Russian denial of, and Poland's insistence on, her claim to the right of restoration within her pre-1939 frontiers could not be reconciled; Britain gave support to Poland in 1941 declaring in a *Note to the Polish Government, 30 July 1941* (p. 211), that it recognized none of the changes of territory brought about in Poland by the Soviet Union or Germany since August 1939. The fundamental differences between the Allies are reflected in the difficulties the negotiators faced in attempting to reach agreement and to conclude treaties.

With Japan's attack on Pearl Harbor on 7 December 1941, and Germany's and Italy's declaration of war on the United States on 11 December 1941, Britain, the United States and Russia became allies in the war against Germany and Italy, but only Britain and the United States were allies in the war against Japan. In the drafting of a comprehensive alliance between the Powers at war this was a further cause of difficulty. Such a comprehensive alliance was first set out in negotiations in Washington and took the form of the *United Nations Declaration of 1 January 1942* (p. 212). The 'United Nations' declaration, a phrase originating with Roosevelt, was intended to circumvent the right of the United States Senate to pass by a two-thirds majority treaties of alliance negotiated with foreign Powers. The Free French did not sign despite the loophole which would have allowed 'appropriate authorities which are not Governments' to adhere. The Joint Declaration listed the Allied nations in alphabetical order but placed at the head were the United States, Britain, the U.S.S.R. and China. In this way these four nations were treated differently from the rest thus setting out their status as 'Great Powers'.

In the spring of 1942, Britain and the Soviet Union concluded the negotiation of an alliance treaty begun the previous autumn. The Soviet Union agreed to the omission of a clause defining specific frontiers, such as her rights to all territory included in Soviet Russia on 22 June 1941. The Russians at the time were anxious to hasten the opening of a 'second front' against Germany in France.

The *Anglo-Soviet Alliance of 26 May 1942* (p. 212) appeared momentous at the time because it provided a bond between the Soviet Union and Britain, a great 'capitalistic' imperial Power. The treaty was intended to outlast the German war for it was given a duration of twenty years. It repeated the undertakings of the agreement of 12 July 1941 (mutual assistance, no separate peace), but went further in a second part which set out some of the principles of post-war cooperation. The signatories envisaged an organization of States for the preservation of peace; Britain and the Soviet Union also declared that they would 'take into account' the interests of the United Nations and not seek 'territorial aggrandizement for themselves'. Stalin, of course, did not regard the incorporation in the Soviet Union of eastern Poland in 1939 and the Baltic States in 1940 as 'aggrandizement', since he claimed the populations concerned had opted for the Soviet Union. Churchill had been ready in March 1942 to go further and to breach the principle of no frontier discussions by accepting Russia's claim to her 1940 frontiers (including the Baltic States, Bessarabia, Bukovina and Finnish conquests), except for territories which had been Polish in 1939. In the event the Soviet Union accepted the treaty without territorial clauses.

Poland, Czechoslovakia and the Soviet Union, 1941-4

The Polish Government in exile in London, headed by General Wladislav Sikorski, fought uncompromisingly for Poland's pre-war frontiers. With the entry of the U.S.S.R. into the war the Polish Government with equal urgency wished to secure the release of Polish prisoners placed into camps by the Russians. Polish–Soviet diplomatic relations were resumed with the signature of the *Polish–Soviet Treaty of 30 July 1941*. Though the Soviet Union in this treaty declared that the German–Soviet treaties of 1939 relating to Polish territory had 'lost their validity' Stalin did not abandon his claim to the Polish territory then seized.

The *Anglo-Soviet Agreement of 12 July 1941* had been accompanied by a *British Note to the Polish Government of 30 July 1941* (p. 211) in which the British Government declared that, in conformity with the Anglo-Polish alliance of 1939, it had entered into no undertaking towards the U.S.S.R. affecting Polish–Soviet relations, and that His Majesty's Government did not recognize any territorial changes which had been effected in Poland since August 1939.

On *14 August 1941 a Polish–Soviet Military Agreement* was concluded providing for the organization of a Polish army in the U.S.S.R. Poles kept in camps in Russia were to be released. The U.S.S.R. was to assist in the arming of Polish units who would fight in the Soviet Union under Polish command, but this would be subordinated operationally under the High Command of the U.S.S.R. In December 1941 General Sikorski visited Moscow, and a *Polish–Soviet Declaration of Friendship and Mutual Assistance was signed on 4 December 1941*. But from 1941 to 1943 Polish–Soviet relations were embittered by Russia's claim to have irrevocably annexed the region of pre-war Poland occupied in 1939, and by Russian insistence that according to Soviet law the permanent inhabitants of those lands were Soviet citizens. The Poles were also dissatisfied with the treatment of Poles released from Russian camps, and individual cases of maltreatment. Polish officers and men continued to be missing. Soviet–Polish relations were close to breaking point when the Germans broadcast on 13 April 1943 that they had discovered a mass grave of some 10,000 Polish officers in Katyn, near Smolensk, and accused the Russians of their murder. The Polish Government requested the International Red Cross to investigate, and the Russians on 25 April 1943 severed relations with the Polish Government, declaring that the Germans had massacred the missing Polish officers and that in accusing the Russians the Polish Government in London was acting in collusion with Hitler. The problem of Poland continued to present a major difficulty in the way of Allied cooperation to the end of the war.

The Czechoslovak Government in exile chose a different course from the Polish Government in dealing with the Soviet Union. Soviet–Czech military cooperation against Germany was provided for in the *Czechoslovak–Soviet Agreement of 18 July 1941*. Benes had been disillusioned by the Munich settlement in 1938 (p. 176) and would no longer rely solely on the friendship of the Western Powers. He was determined to win Russia's friendship and to secure from all the Allies a declaration that since the Munich settlement had been imposed by threat of force on Czechoslovakia it was invalid. The British Government would only agree to declare that since the Germans had subsequently broken it, the Munich treaty was no longer binding. The Soviet Government, on the other hand, recognized the Czechoslovak Government in exile and Czechoslovakia in its 1937 frontiers, and also declared the Munich settlement as illegal and void. A *Soviet–Czechoslovak Treaty of Friendship and Alliance was signed on 12 December 1943* (p. 215). Benes, in Moscow for the signature of the treaty, was also confronted with Russian demands for aligning the post-war Czech economy with the Soviet economy, which he consented to in an additional agreement. *On 8 May 1944 a further Soviet–Czechoslovak Agreement regarding the administration of liberated Czechoslovak territories* was concluded. The Soviet advance into Czechoslovakia began in the autumn of 1944, but too late to prevent the Germans crushing a national uprising in Slovakia. Czech administrators were only permitted to function with Soviet consent and the Czechoslovak Government had to accept the 'wish' of the Ruthenians to accede to the Soviet Union. With the acquisition of this strategically vital territory together with the eastern Polish territories, the Soviet Union gained a common frontier with Hungary and Czechoslovakia.

The Allies and France, 1941-5

France and Germany signed an *armistice on 22 June 1940*. On 28 June 1940 the British Government recognized General de Gaulle as the 'Leader of all Free

Frenchmen, wherever they may be, who rally to him in support of the Allied cause'. The future of the French fleet, still in the control of the new French Government of Marshal Pétain, and of the French Colonial Empire remained in doubt, though Britain received French assurances that the fleet would not be allowed to fall into the hands of the Germans. But the British Government was not prepared to trust these assurances and there resulted the British bombardment on French warships at Mers-el-Kebir on 3 July 1940. Britain and Vichy France broke direct diplomatic links, but avoided a complete breach. The United States and Vichy France remained in complete and normal diplomatic relations after the armistice which precluded the recognition of de Gaulle's movement as the Government of France in exile. By the end of August 1940 the French African colonial territories of Chad and the Cameroons rallied to de Gaulle and became the nucleus of 'Free France'. The French Empire in North Africa and Indo-China remained loyal to Vichy France. On 8 June 1941 an Anglo-French force was sent to the French mandated territory of Syria, which remained loyal to Vichy. The Free French issued a proclamation declaring Syria and the Lebanon 'sovereign and independent peoples'. After heavy fighting *Syria* passed into Anglo-Free French wartime control with the *armistice of 14 July 1941*. In the autumn of 1941, the Free French movement was strengthened by the creation and British recognition of a Free French National Committee. But the United States continued to remain in full diplomatic relations with Vichy France after entering the war in December 1941. In July 1942 it recognized the French National Committee without breaking with Vichy, and by Allied agreement the Free French movement called itself the 'Fighting French', implying leadership of all Frenchmen fighting the Germans whether in 'Free' French territories or in metropolitan Vichy France.

Throughout 1942 the United States and Britain continued, for what appeared to be compelling military reasons, to treat Vichy France as a legitimate Government to ensure that the French fleet should remain in French hands and to avoid driving the Vichy North African territory into open opposition. In May 1942 British troops began the occupation of Vichy France Madagascar, without prior reference to General de Gaulle for fear of driving the Vichy colonial authorities into active opposition. Madagascar was a curtain raiser for North Africa where the Anglo-American allies were prepared to negotiate with the Vichy French authorities, ignoring the claims of the Free French National Committee to represent all French interests. Operation Torch was the name given to the Anglo-American invasion of French North Africa which had remained loyal to Vichy. General de Gaulle and the Free French did not participate in the landings, and the operation was kept secret from them. The

Allies pinned their hopes on General Giraud, who had escaped from a German prisoner-of-war camp in April 1942, to rally French North Africa to the Allied cause. The Allied landings began on 8 November 1942 near Algiers, Oran and Casablanca. Three days later, on 11 November, the Germans militarily occupied 'Unoccupied France', but the Vichy French commanders succeeded in scuttling the French fleet at Toulon. Contrary to expectations General Giraud had little influence. Admiral Darlan, who was visiting Algiers, as the highest ranking representative of Vichy commanded the French forces. *It was with the Vichy French administration under Darlan that the Allies reached agreement on 17 November 1942*, accepting Darlan's authority and securing the ending of French military resistance to the Allied operations. With the assassination of Darlan on 23 December 1942, Giraud assumed political leadership. Although General de Gaulle met General Giraud at the Casablanca conference in January 1943, Giraud maintained Vichy legality; *not until 3 June 1943 was an agreement signed fixing Giraud's and de Gaulle's authorities in a new French Committee of National Liberation* under their joint presidency. With the exception of the Soviet Government, Britain and the United States refused to recognize the National Committee as legitimately representing the interests of all France. The French Committee of National Liberation began to change its composition in November 1943, admitting French political parties and representatives of the Resistance and dropping Giraud step by step. On 15 May 1944 the French Committee of National Liberation changed its name to Provisional Government of the Republic of France under de Gaulle's leadership, General Giraud having resigned on 14 April 1944. But General Eisenhower, the Supreme Allied Commander, refused to recognize de Gaulle's authority before D-Day, 6 June 1944, when the Allies began their assault on German occupied France. Only on 11 July 1944 were the Americans prepared to recognize de Gaulle and his committee as the *de facto* representatives of the French people. Full recognition was awarded by Great Britain, the United States and the Soviet Union to General de Gaulle as the head of the Provisional Government of France on 23 October 1944. *An Alliance Treaty between the Soviet Union and France was concluded on 10 December 1944* (p. 216). France was invited to become a member of the European Advisory Commission and the fifth permanent member of the proposed Security Council of the United Nations organization (p. 242).

The Allies and Italy, 1943-5

The Allies landed in Sicily on 10 July 1943; on 25 July 1943 Mussolini fell from power and was replaced by Marshal Pietro Badoglio, who secretly negotiated a military armistice accepting the Allied terms of surrender on 3 September 1943. The *Italian armistice* required Italy to withdraw her armed forces from the war, established an Allied Military Government under the Allied Commander-in-Chief over all parts of Italy, and bound the Italian Government at a later time to accept the political and economic conditions demanded by the Allies. The armistice was publicly announced on *8 September 1943* to coincide with the Allied seaborne invasion of Italy at Salerno. More detailed armistice conditions were signed on *29 September 1943*. On 13 October 1943 the King of Italy declared war on Germany, and Italy was granted the status of co-belligerency. Italy became a battleground of the Allied forces and the Germans, who militarily occupied central and northern Italy over which Mussolini's Republic of Salo claimed legal control. The Italian Peace Treaty was eventually signed in February 1947, nearly two years after the German surrender in May 1945.

Alliance Treaty between Britain, the Soviet Union and Iran, 29 January 1942

Article 1. His Majesty The King of Great Britain, Ireland and the British Dominions beyond the Seas, Emperor of India, and the Union of Soviet Socialist Republics (hereinafter referred to as the Allied Powers) jointly and severally undertake to respect the territorial integrity, sovereignty and political independence of Iran.

Article 2. An alliance is established between the Allied Powers on the one hand and His Imperial Majesty The Shahinshah of Iran on the other.

Article 3. (i) The Allied Powers jointly and severally undertake to defend Iran by all means at their command from all aggression on the part of Germany or any other Power.

(ii) His Imperial Majesty The Shahinshah undertakes:

(a) To cooperate with the Allied Powers with all the means at his command and in every way possible, in order that they may be able to fulfil the above undertaking. The assistance of the Iranian forces shall, however, be limited to the mainten-ance of internal security on Iranian territory;

(b) To secure to the Allied Powers, for the passage of troops or supplies from one Allied Power to the other or for other similar purposes, the unrestricted right to use, maintain, guard and, in case of military necessity, control in any way that they may require, all means of communication throughout Iran, including railways, roads, rivers, aerodromes, ports, pipelines and telephone, telegraph and wireless installations. ...

Article 4. (i) The Allied Powers may maintain in Iranian territory land, sea and air forces in such number as they consider necessary. The location of such forces shall be decided in agreement with the Iranian Government so long as the strategic situation allows. ...

Article 5. The forces of the Allied Powers shall be withdrawn from Iranian territory not later than six months after all hostilities between the Allied Powers and Germany and her associates have been suspended by the conclusion of an armistice or armistices, or on the conclusion of peace between them, whichever date is the earlier. The expression 'associates' of Germany means all other Powers which have engaged or may in the future engage in hostilities against either of the Allied Powers.

Article 6 (i) The Allied Powers undertake in their relations with foreign countries not to adopt an attitude which is preju-dicial to the territorial integrity, sovereignty or political independence of Iran, nor to conclude treaties inconsistent with the provisions of the present Treaty. They undertake to consult the Government of His Imperial Majesty the Shahinshah in all matters affecting the direct interests of Iran.

(ii) His Imperial Majesty the Shahinshah undertakes not to adopt in his relations with foreign countries an attitude which is inconsistent with the alliance . . .

Note issued by the Foreign Office in London on non-recognition of any territorial changes in Poland since August 1939

London, 30 July 1941

1. An agreement between the Republic of Poland and the Soviet Union was signed in the Secretary of State's room at the Foreign Office on July 30. General Sikorski, Polish Prime Minister, signed for Poland; M. Maisky, Soviet Ambassador, signed for the Soviet Union. Mr Churchill and Mr Eden were present.

2. The agreement is being published.

3. After the signature of the agreement, Mr Eden handed to General Sikorski an official Note in the following terms:

On the occasion of the signature of the Polish–Soviet Agreement of today, I desire to take this opportunity of informing you that in conformity with the provision of the Agreement of Mutual Assistance between the United Kingdom and Poland of the 25th August 1939, His Majesty's Government in the United Kingdom have entered into no undertakings towards the Union of Socialist Soviet Republics which affect the relations between that country and Poland. I also desire to assure you that His Majesty's Government do not recognize any territorial changes which have been effected in Poland since August 1939.

General Sikorski handed to Mr Eden the following reply:

The Polish Government take note of your letter dated July 30 and desire to express sincere satisfaction at the statement that His Majesty's Government in the United Kingdom do not recognize any territorial changes which have been effected in Poland since August 1939. This corresponds with the view of the Polish Government which, as they have previously informed His Majesty's Government, have never recognized any territorial changes effected in Poland since the outbreak of the war.

Declaration by the United Nations, 1 January 1942

The Governments signatory hereto,

Having subscribed to a common programme of purposes and principals embodied in the Joint Declaration of the President of the United States of America and the Prime Minister of the United Kingdom of Great Britain and Northern Ireland dated August 14, 1941, known as the Atlantic Charter,

Being convinced that complete victory over their enemies is essential to defend life, liberty, independence and religious freedom, and to preserve human rights and justice in their own lands as well as in other lands, and that they are now engaged in a common struggle against savage and brutal forces seeking to subjugate the world,

Declare:

(i) Each Government pledges itself to employ its full resources, military or economic, against those members of the Tripartite Pact and its adherents with which such Government is at war.

(ii) Each Government pledges itself to cooperate with the Governments signatory hereto and not to make a separate armistice or peace with the enemies.

The foregoing Declaration may be adhered to by other nations which are, or may be, rendering material assistance and contributions in the struggle for victory over Hitlerism.

Alliance between Britain and the Soviet Union, London, 26 May 1942

His Majesty The King of Great Britain, Ireland, and the British Dominions beyond the Seas, Emperor of India, and the Presidium of the Supreme Council of the Union of Soviet Socialist Republics;

Desiring to confirm the stipulations of the Agreement between His Majesty's Government in the United Kingdom and the Government of the Union of Soviet Socialist Republics for joint action in the war against Germany, signed at Moscow on the 12th July 1941, and to replace them by a formal treaty;

Desiring to contribute after the war to the maintenance of peace and to the prevention of further aggression by Germany or the States associated with her in acts of aggression in Europe;

Desiring, moreover, to give expression to their intention to collaborate closely with one another as well as with the other United Nations at the peace settlement and during the ensuing period of reconstruction on the basis of the principles enunciated in the declaration made on the 14th August 1941 by the President of the United States of America and the Prime Minister of Great Britain to which the Government of the Union of Soviet Socialist Republics has adhered;

Desiring, finally, to provide for mutual assistance in the event of an attack upon either High Contracting Party by Germany or any of the States associated with her in acts of aggression in Europe. . . .

Have decided to conclude a Treaty for that purpose and have appointed as their plenipotentiaries:

His Majesty The King of Great Britain, Ireland, and the British Dominions beyond the Seas, Emperor of India,

For the United Kingdom of Great Britain and Northern Ireland:

The Right Honourable Anthony Eden, M.P., His Majesty's Principal Secretary of State for Foreign Affairs,

The Presidium of the Supreme Council of the Union of Soviet Socialist Republics:

M. Vyacheslav Mikhailovich Molotov, People's Commissar for Foreign Affairs,

Who, having communicated their full powers, found in good and due form, have agreed as follows:

Part I

Article I. In virtue of the alliance established between the United Kingdom and the Union of Soviet Socialist Republics the High Contracting Parties mutually undertake to afford one another military and other assistance and support of all kinds in the war against Germany and all those States which are associated with her in acts of aggression in Europe.

Article II. The High Contracting Parties undertake not to enter into any negotiations with the Hitlerite Government or any other Government in Germany that does not clearly renounce all aggressive intentions, and not to negotiate or conclude except by mutual consent any armistice or peace treaty with Germany or any other State associated with her in acts of aggression in Europe.

Part II

Article III. (1) The High Contracting Parties declare their desire to unite with other like-minded States in adopting proposals for common action to preserve peace and resist aggression in the post-war period.

(2) Pending the adoption of such proposals, they will after the termination of hostilities take all the measures in their power to render impossible a repetition of aggression and violation of the peace by Germany or any of the States associated with her in acts of aggression in Europe.

Article IV. Should one of the High Contracting Parties during the post-war period become involved in hostilities with Germany or any of the States mentioned in Article III (2) in consequence of an attack by that State against that party, the other High Contracting Party will at once give to the Contracting Party so involved in hostilities all the military and other support and assistance in his power.

This Article shall remain in force until the High Contracting Parties, by mutual agreement, shall recognize that it is superseded by the adoption of the proposals contemplated in Article III (1). In default of the adoption of such proposals, it shall remain in force for a period of twenty years, and thereafter until terminated by either High Contracting Party, as provided in Article VIII.

Article V. The High Contracting Parties, having regard to the interests of the security of each of them, agree to work together in close and friendly collaboration after the re-establishment of peace for the organization of security and economic prosperity in Europe. They will take into account the interests of the United Nations in these objects, and they will act in accordance with the two principles of not seeking territorial aggrandizement for themselves and of non-interference in the internal affairs of other States.

Article VI. The High Contracting Parties agree to render one another all possible economic assistance after the war.

Article VII. Each High Contracting Party undertakes not to conclude any alliance and not to take part in any coalition directed against the other High Contracting Party.

Article VIII. The present Treaty is subject to ratification in the shortest possible time and the instruments of ratification shall be exchanged in Moscow as soon as possible.

It comes into force immediately on the exchange of the instruments of ratification and shall thereupon replace the Agreement between the Government of the Union of Soviet Socialist Republics and His Majesty's Government in the United Kingdom, signed at Moscow on the 12th July 1941.

Part I of the present Treaty shall remain in force until the re-establishment of peace between the High Contracting Parties and Germany and the Powers associated with her in acts of aggression in Europe.

Part II of the present Treaty shall remain in force for a period of twenty years. Thereafter, unless twelve months'

notice has been given by either party to terminate the Treaty at the end of the said period of twenty years, it shall continue in force until twelve months after either High Contracting Party shall have given notice to the other in writing of his intention to terminate it.

In witness whereof the above-named plenipotentiaries have signed the present Treaty and have affixed thereto their seals.

Done in duplicate in London on the 26th day of May, 1942, in the English and Russian languages, both texts being equally authentic.

(L.S.) ANTHONY EDEN

(L.S.) V. MOLOTOV

Agreement between Poland and the Soviet Union, 30 July 1941

The Government of the Republic of Poland and the Government of the Union of Soviet Socialist Republics have concluded the present Agreement and decided as follows:

1. The Government of the Union of Soviet Socialist Republics recognizes that the Soviet-German treaties of 1939 relative to territorial changes in Poland have lost their validity. The Government of the Republic of Poland declares that Poland is not bound by any Agreement with any third State directed against the U.S.S.R.

2. Diplomatic relations will be restored between the two Governments upon the signature of this Agreement and an exchange of Ambassadors will follow immediately.

3. The two Governments mutually undertake to render one another aid and support of all kinds in the present war against Hitlerite Germany.

4. The Government of the Union of Soviet Socialist Republics expresses its consent to the formation on the territory of the Union of Soviet Socialist Republics

of a Polish army under a commander appointed by the Government of the Republic of Poland, in agreement with the Government of the Union of Soviet Socialist Republics. The Polish army on the territory of the Union of Soviet Socialist Republics will be subordinated in operational matters to the Supreme Command of the U.S.S.R. on which there will be a representative of the Polish army. All details as to command, organization and employment of this force will be settled in a subsequent agreement.

5. This Agreement will come into force immediately upon its signature and without ratification. The present Agreement is drawn up in two copies, each of them in the Russian and Polish languages. Both texts have equal force.

Secret Protocol

1. Various claims both of public and private nature will be dealt with in the course of further negotiations between the two Governments.

2. This Protocol enters into force simul-

taneously with the Agreement of the 30th of July, 1941.

Protocol

1. As soon as diplomatic relations are re-established the Government of the Union of Soviet Socialist Republics will grant amnesty to all Polish citizens who are at present deprived of their freedom on the territory of the U.S.S.R. either as prisoners of war or on other adequate grounds.

2. The present Protocol comes into force simultaneously with the Agreement of July 30, 1941.

Treaty of Friendship and Mutual Assistance and Post-War Cooperation between the Soviet Union and Czechoslovakia, Moscow, 12 December 1943

The Presidium of the Supreme Soviet of the Union of Soviet Socialist Republics and the President of the Czechoslovakian Republic, desiring to modify and supplement the Treaty of Mutual Assistance existing between the Union of Soviet Socialist Republics and the Czechoslovakian Republic and signed in Prague on May 16, 1935, and to confirm the terms of the Agreement between the Government of the Union of Soviet Socialist Republics and the Government of the Czechoslovakian Republic concerning joint action in the war against Germany, signed July 18, 1941, in London; desiring to cooperate after the war to maintain peace and to prevent further aggression on the part of Germany and to assure permanent friendship and peaceful post-war cooperation between them, have resolved to conclude for this purpose a Treaty and ... have agreed to the following:

Article 1. The High Contracting Parties, having agreed mutually to join in a policy of permanent friendship and friendly post-war cooperation, as well as of mutual assistance, engage to extend to each other military and other assistance and support of all kinds in the present war against Germany and against all those States which are associated with it in acts of aggression in Europe.

Article 2. The High Contracting Parties engage not to enter during the period of the present war into any negotiations with the Hitler Government or with any other Government in Germany which does not clearly renounce all aggressive intentions, and not to carry on negotiations and not to conclude without mutual agreement any armistice or other treaty of peace with Germany or with any other State associated with it in acts of aggression in Europe.

Article 3. Affirming their pre-war policy of peace and mutual assistance, expressed in the treaty signed at Prague on May 16, 1935, the High Contracting Parties, in case one of them in the period after the war should become involved in military action with Germany, which might resume its policy of 'Drang nach Osten', or with any other State which might join with Germany directly or in any other form in such a war, engage to extend immediately to the other Contracting Party thus involved in military action all manner of military and other support and assistance at its disposal.

Article 4. The High Contracting Parties, having regard to the security interests of each of them, agree to close and friendly cooperation in the period after the restoration of peace and agree to act in accordance with the principles of mutual respect for their independence and sovereignty, as well as of non-interference in the internal affairs of the other State. They agree to develop their economic relations to the fullest possible extent and to extend to each other all possible economic assistance after the war.

Article 5. Each of the High Contracting Parties engages not to conclude any alliance and not to take part in any coalition directed against the other High Contracting Party.

Article 6. The present Treaty shall come into force immediately after signature and shall be ratified within the shortest possible time; the exchange of ratifications will take place in Moscow as soon as possible.

The present Treaty shall remain in force for a period of twenty years from the date of signature, and if one of the High Contracting Parties at the end of this period of twenty years does not give notice of its desire to terminate the Treaty twelve months before its expiration, it will continue to remain in force for the following five years and for each ensuing five-year period unless one of the High Contracting Parties gives notice in writing twelve months before the expiration of the current five-year period of its intention to terminate it.

Protocol

On the conclusion of the Treaty of Friendship, Mutual Assistance and Post-War Cooperation between the Union of Soviet Socialist Republics and the Czechoslovakian Republic the High Contracting Parties undertake that, in the event that any third country bordering on the U.S.S.R. or the Czechoslovakian Republic and constituting in this war an object of German aggression desires to subscribe to this Treaty, it will be given the opportunity, upon the joint agreement of the Governments of the U.S.S.R. and the Czechoslovakian Republic, to adhere to this Treaty, which will thus acquire the character of a tripartite agreement.

By Authority of the Presidium of the Supreme Council of the U.S.S.R.
V. MOLOTOV

By Authority of the President of the Czechoslovakian Republic
Z. FIERLINGER

Treaty of Alliance and Mutual Assistance between the Soviet Union and the French Republic, Moscow, 10 December 1944

The Presidium of the Supreme Soviet of the Union of Soviet Socialist Republics and the Provisional Government of the French Republic, determined to prosecute jointly and to the end the war against Germany, convinced that once victory is achieved, the re-establishment of peace on a stable basis and its prolonged maintenance in the future will be conditioned upon the existence of close collaboration between them and with all the United Nations; having resolved to collaborate in the cause of the creation of an international system of security for the effective maintenance of general peace and for ensuring the harmonious development of relations between nations; desirous of confirming the mutual obligations resulting from the exchange of letters of September 20, 1941, concerning joint actions in the war against Germany; convinced that the conclusion of an alliance between the U.S.S.R. and France corresponds to the sentiments and interests of both peoples, the demands of war, and the requirements of peace and economic reconstruction in full conformity with the aims which the United Nations have set themselves, have decided to conclude a Treaty to this effect and appointed as their plenipotentiaries ...

Article I. Each of the High Contracting Parties shall continue the struggle on the side of the other party and on the side of the United Nations until final victory over Germany. Each of the High Contracting Parties undertakes to render the other party aid and assistance in this struggle with all the means at its disposal.

Article II. The High Contracting Parties shall not agree to enter into separate negotiations with Germany or to conclude without mutual consent any armistice or peace treaty either with the Hitler Government or with any other Government or authority set up in Germany for the purpose of the continuation or support of the policy of German aggression.

Article III. The High Contracting Parties undertake also, after the termination of the present war with Germany, to take jointly all necessary measures for the elimination of any new threat coming from Germany, and to obstruct such actions as would make possible any new attempt at aggression on her part.

Article IV. In the event either of the High Contracting Parties finds itself involved in military operations against Germany, whether as a result of aggression committed by the latter or as a result of the operation of the above Article III, the other party shall at once render it every aid and assistance within its power.

Article V. The High Contracting Parties undertake not to conclude any alliance and not to take part in any coalition directed against either of the High Contracting Parties.

Article VI. The High Contracting Parties agree to render each other every possible economic assistance after the war, with a view to facilitating and accelerating reconstruction of both countries, and in order to contribute to the cause of world prosperity.

Article VII. The present Treaty does not in any way affect obligations undertaken previously by the High Contracting Parties in regard to third States in virtue of published treaties.

Article VIII. The present Treaty, whose Russian and French texts are equally valid, shall be ratified and ratification instruments shall be exchanged in Paris as early as possible. It comes into force from the moment of the exchange of ratification instruments and shall be valid for twenty years. If the Treaty is not denounced by either of the High Contracting Parties at least one year before the expiration of this term, it shall remain valid for an unlimited time; each of the Contracting Parties will be able to terminate its operation by giving notice to that effect one year in advance. . . .

On the authorization of the Presidium of the Supreme Soviet of the U.S.S.R.
MOLOTOV

On the authorization of the Provisional Government of the French Republic
BIDAULT

IX · The Allied conferences and the political settlement of Europe, 1943–5

The conferences

The Allied conferences from 1943 to 1945 attempted to reconcile the wartime military policies of the Allies with an agreed programme of post-war settlements in Europe and Asia. For the sake of the maximum possible degree of military cooperation which was necessary to defeat the powerful and fanatically tenacious German war effort, fundamental Allied differences were not allowed to develop into major rifts. At the Yalta Conference the 'Great Power' interests of Britain, the United States and the Soviet Union largely determined the post-war settlements not only of defeated enemies but also of the smaller Allies. At Yalta, the Big Three displayed at least an outward show of unanimity of purpose and wartime comradeship. By the time of the Potsdam Conference a few months later the Allied differences which developed into the 'cold war' were already strongly in evidence.

The ten major Allied conferences of this period fall into two divisions: (1) predominantly Anglo-American, and (2) Three Power conferences between Russia, Britain and the United States, sometimes with other countries present. The table illustrated on pages 220–1 summarizes their sequence.

The first two important conferences of 1943 endeavoured to coordinate British and United States diplomacy and did not involve the Russians. From a political point of view the *Conference of Casablanca* (Churchill, Roosevelt, Combined Chiefs of Staff) *14–25 January 1943* was notable for the attempt made to bring together Generals Giraud and de Gaulle; also for the 'unconditional surrender' call as the only terms the Allies would offer their enemies. The phrase 'unconditional surrender' had been under discussion, but was omitted from the final communiqué, though publicly announced in a press conference given by President Roosevelt.

Research which was to lead to the making of the atomic bomb was the subject of a secret Anglo-American agreement at the *Quebec Conference of August 1943*, not disclosed until 1954. The exclusive possession of the bomb with its secrets, and the unknown possible application of atomic energy after the war, made the knowledge of the secrets one of the most prized assets of power in the war and in the post-war world. These secrets were not shared with the Soviet Union. *The Agreement on Anglo-American–Canadian collaboration and development of atomic research was signed on 19 August 1943* by Churchill and Roosevelt. It set out the policy of pooling in the United States the scientists and resources to speed the project. The two countries undertook not to use the atomic bomb against each other; they also agreed not to use it against another country without each others' consent; they agreed not to communicate any information to another country without their mutual consent. Britain disclaimed any 'post-war advantages of an industrial or commercial character' beyond what the President of the United States considered fair and just and for the welfare of the world. Allocation of materials, all policy, and interchange of information was to be the function of a Combined Policy Committee of the three American, two British and one Canadian officials. Information about large-scale plants was to become the subject of later agreements. The first atomic bomb was dropped on Hiroshima on 6 August 1945 and the second on Nagasaki on 9 August 1945. The post-war operation of this secret executive agreement caused Anglo-American differences of opinion in 1945 and 1946 after Roosevelt's death; its existence was unknown to Congress. The American desire to preserve secrecy and military nuclear monopoly led to the passing of the McMahon Act in 1946 which made the wartime agreement in practice inoperative (p. 510).

At the *Conference of Foreign Ministers at Moscow* (Molotov, Eden, Hull, Deane) *18–30 October 1943*, agreement was reached on a *Four Power Declaration of General Security* whereby the United States, Great Britain, the Soviet Union and China agreed to help establish a general international organization for the maintenance of peace and security, and to continue their collaboration in peace as in war. The conference also agreed to set up a *European Advisory Commission* with headquarters in London to consider all specific questions concerning the surrender terms and their execution; the commission was empowered to make recommendations but could exercise no mandatory authority. An *Advisory Council for Italy* was also established but exercised little influence. The Foreign Ministers agreed that Austria should be re-established as an independent State after the war. A decision on cooperating in the punishment of individuals

Date	Subjects discussed
14–25 January 1943	Reconciling 'Free French'; 'unconditional surrender' call; Far Eastern and European strategy.
August 1943	Atomic research and use of atomic bomb; 'second front' in Europe; Far Eastern strategy; Italian surrender.
18–30 October 1943	U.N.; Austria; surrender terms; war criminals.
22–26 November 1943	Japanese surrender terms; Far Eastern settlement; Far Eastern military strategy.
28 November–1 December 1943	European and Far Eastern strategy; Russia and Japan; U.N.; Turkey; Italy; Russia's eastern frontiers; Poland; Germany's eastern frontier.
21 August–28 September and 29 September–7 October 1944	U.N.
11–19 September 1944	Germany; military strategy in Europe and in war against Japan.
9–20 October 1944	Balkan 'spheres of influence'; Poland; Soviet entry into war against Japan.
30 January–3 February 1945	Military strategy; occupation zones in Germany; Italy and China.
4–11 February 1945	Post-war policies: Germany, U.N., Poland, liberated Europe, Russia, Japan and China.
25 April–26 June 1945	U.N.
1–22 July 1945	International finance and trade.
17 July–2 August 1945	Draft peace treaties; Germany; Poland; Japan.

Casablanca

Quebec (with Canada) Quadrant

Moscow Conference of Foreign Ministers

Cairo (with China)

Teheran

Dumbarton Oaks (second part with China)

Quebec (with Canada) Octagon

Anglo-Soviet discussion in Moscow, Churchill, Eden and Stalin with Harriman as 'observer'

Malta

Yalta

San Francisco (together with delegations of countries at war with Germany)

Bretton Woods (U.N. conference)

Potsdam

responsible for atrocities was also reached. At the end of the conference an official communiqué was issued together with four *Declarations on General Security, Italy, Austria, and German Atrocities, 30 October 1943.*

The Cairo Conference took place on 22–26 November 1943 (Roosevelt, Churchill, Chiang Kai-shek). The Russians would not attend since they were not at war with Japan. Besides military strategy in the Far East, the post-war settlement there was discussed. The final communiqué outlined the territorial peace terms the three Allies would impose on Japan, and promised Korea independence in due course.

Roosevelt and Churchill next flew to Persia to participate with the Russians in the *Teheran Conference* (Churchill, Roosevelt, Stalin, Eden, Hopkins, Combined Chiefs of Staff) *28 November–1 December 1943.* The military situation in Europe and the Far East was discussed. Stalin declared Russia would join in the war against Japan after victory over Germany. There were exploratory discussions concerning the future of France, Germany and Poland. Roosevelt initiated a discussion on the establishment of a post-war international organization to preserve peace and security. It was agreed that 'Overlord', the Anglo-American invasion of northern France, would take place on 1 May 1944. Turkey and Italy were discussed. No formal written agreement was reached on Russia's and Poland's western frontiers, though Churchill agreed to the Curzon line as a basis and to the acquisition by Poland of German territory east of the Oder river. A declaration promised to Iran independence and territorial integrity. A communiqué on the results of the conference was published on 6 December 1943.

More than a year elapsed after the conclusion of the Teheran Conference until Churchill, Roosevelt and Stalin met again at Yalta in February 1945. Meantime Roosevelt and Churchill and the Combined Chiefs of Staff had met at *Quebec, 11–19 September 1944* to discuss future policy towards Germany; Churchill flew to Moscow to discuss post-war spheres of influence, the Balkans and Poland, with Stalin; Harriman attended as an observer from 9–20 October 1944. Shortly before Yalta, the Combined Chiefs of Staff, Churchill, Eden and Stettinius met at *Malta, 30 January–3 February 1945*, to examine military strategy and the Anglo-American zones of occupation, and briefly discuss Italy and China.

The 'Big Three' meeting at *Yalta* (Churchill, Roosevelt, Stalin, Chiefs of Staff, Molotov, Stettinius, Eden, Hopkins) *4–11 February 1945* (p. 226) was the most crucial of the war in moulding the reconstruction of the post-war world. Roosevelt was anxious to secure a firm Russian undertaking to join in the war against Japan. He acceded to Stalin's condition that Russia should resume her old rights in China lost as a result of the Russo-Japanese war of 1904–5.

Despite the difficulties of China's rights, *a secret tripartite agreement was signed concerning Russia's participation in the war against Japan on 11 February 1945* (p. 230); this agreement was only published a year after its signature on 11 February 1946. Allied policy towards Germany led to discussions and agreements at Yalta. The European Advisory Commission had reached agreed recommendations which formed the basis of the awards at Yalta on the zones of occupation, on Berlin and on the form of Allied control. At Yalta agreement was also reached to allow the French a zone of occupation and to admit France as an equal member of the Allied Control Commission for Germany. A decision on reparations was referred to a Reparations Commission to be set up in Moscow. The decisions concerning Allied treatment of Germany reached at Yalta lacked precision and were vague, since practical details were not worked out. They were summarized in Protocols III, IV, V and VI of the Proceedings of the Conference. Protocol I set out the agreement reached on the setting up of a World Organization of the United Nations, and more especially on the voting formula for the Security Council; it was agreed to call a United Nations Conference at San Francisco on 25 April 1945 (p. 227).

The future of Poland was a most contentious and difficult issue at Yalta, and no precise conclusions were reached on post-war Polish boundaries (though the Curzon line with some small digressions in Poland's favour was referred to as Poland's eastern frontier). Nor was there agreement over the 'reconstruction' of the Polish Government. The ambiguous Declaration on Poland was embodied in Protocol VII. A number of other important post-war problems were set out in Protocols IX to XIV. Finally, the Declaration on Liberated Europe, Protocol II, is noteworthy as an attempt, on American initiative, to commit Russia to the restoration of democratic national self-government to the States occupied by the Russian armies at the close of the war.

By the time of the next Big Three meeting at Potsdam in July 1945 the war in Europe was over. Admiral Dönitz, who had succeeded Hitler, authorized the acceptance of Germany's unconditional surrender, and the instrument of surrender was signed at Eisenhower's headquarters in Rheims on 7 May 1945; Stalin insisted on a second capitulation in Berlin on 9 May 1945 a day after the fighting had ended. Before the Potsdam meeting the agreements reached at Yalta were being differently interpreted by the Allies. Russian pressure for the establishment of a communist Government on 6 March 1945 was regarded by the Western Allies as in breach of the Declaration of Liberated Europe. On 10 March 1945, Stalin assigned to Rumania the part of Transylvania which Hitler had awarded to Hungary. Allied disputes over the future Polish Government continued. On 12 April 1945 Roosevelt died and Truman was sworn in as President. Serious Allied differences over the control of Austria, deep suspicion of Russian intentions in Poland, problems in occupied Germany, hard-won agreement over the establishment of an international organization and the reparations question were all part of the diplomatic confrontation during the immediate aftermath of the end of the war in Europe. Some differences were patched up. The Charter of the United Nations was signed on 26 June 1945 (p. 247). The British and American Governments recognized a reorganized Soviet-sponsored Polish Provisional Government of National Unity on 5 July 1945. The machinery of Allied control over Germany was established, and the zones of occupation brought under the respective military control of the U.S.S.R., France, Britain and the United States. The Polish western frontier had not been finally settled at Yalta; the Russians handed over German territory as far as the rivers Oder and the western Neisse to Polish administration. The Potsdam Conference was to settle future Allied policies, to lay the foundation for definitive peace settlements and to reach agreed policies on the treatment of Germany.

The Potsdam Conference, 17 July–2 August 1945 (p. 231) – *Attlee, Churchill* (Prime Minister until 26 July when the General Election brought Attlee and the Labour Party to power), *Stalin, Truman, Bevin, Byrnes, Eden, Molotov* – appeared to get off to a good start with an agreement on an American proposal that a Council of Foreign Ministers should be set up to prepare drafts of peace treaties with the ex-enemy States in Europe and Asia (this body replaced the European Advisory Commission); London was chosen as the permanent seat of the council. The French had not been invited to Potsdam but were to be represented on the Council of Foreign Ministers. Germany's frontiers were not established with finality, though it was agreed that the frontiers of 1937 should be taken as the basis for discussion, which excluded Austria, the territory taken from Czechoslovakia at Munich, as well as German-occupied Poland. The Polish question led to acrimonious debate, particularly the extent of Polish expansion eastward at Germany's expense, the Russians and Britain and the United States differing later as to what had been settled. The agreement left under the Polish administration the territory assigned to them by the Russians, adding that it was not 'considered as part of the Soviet zone of occupation of Germany'; while the final delimitation of Poland's western frontier was reserved until the conclusion of a German peace treaty. Russian claims to about half of East Prussia including Königsberg were accepted, by Britain and the United States who undertook to support Russia when a peace conference assembled. Agreement was reached on the treatment of Austria. But Soviet insistence that immediate recognition be granted to the Soviet-sponsored Armistice Governments of Hungary, Bulgaria and Rumania proved unacceptable to the three Western Powers, as did Western insistence on supervised genuinely free elections. In practice these three countries were left in Soviet control. The Western interpretation of the Yalta Declaration on Liberated Europe could not be realized. Many questions remained unsettled, such as the Turkish Straits and the Italian colonies. On the central problem of the treatment of Germany, agreements were reached which reflected paper compromises. The idea of partitioning Germany into a number of States was dropped. Supreme authority in Germany was to be exercised by the Commanders-in-Chief of the British, French, American and Russian armed forces each in their own zones, whilst for Germany as a whole they were to act jointly as members of the Control Council. Principles governing the treatment of the whole of Germany leading to disarmament, de-Nazification and demilitarization were agreed. But policies in practice differed widely between the Russian and Western zones of occupation. Similarly, it was agreed that Germany was to be treated as a single economic unit with a living standard for the German people *not exceeding* the average of other Europeans, but again control of German industry was exercised differently in each zone, as was the collection of reparations despite agreement on general principles. The differing views of the Russians and Western Powers on reparations and the German frontiers proved amongst the most intractable problems of the conference. The decisions concerning Germany in practice undermined the general principle of treating occupied Germany as a whole, and confirmed the divisions of Germany especially as between the Russian and Western zones. A major problem was the settlement of German refugees, several million of whom were either fleeing or were being expelled from Polish-occupied Germany, from the Czech Sudetenland, East Prussia and Hungary. Their expulsion was accepted at Potsdam as necessary but it was to be carried out in an 'orderly and humane manner'.

The surrender of Japan, 14 August 1945

The British and American delegations at Potsdam agreed, on behalf of the nations at war with Japan, on a declaration calling upon Japan to submit to surrender 'unconditionally', and published the *Potsdam Declaration on 26 July 1945*. In practice this declaration outlined surrender conditions. On 6 and 9 August 1945 atomic bombs were dropped on Hiroshima and Nagasaki. On 8 August 1945 the Soviet Union declared war on Japan, to take effect the following day when the Russian armies began occupying Manchuria. On 10 August the Japanese acceptance of the conditions of the Potsdam Declaration was received by the Americans, but Japan's acceptance was conditional on the Allies agreeing that the prerogatives of the Emperor as a sovereign ruler were not prejudiced. The Americans replied on 11 August 1945 that the Emperor would be subject to the Supreme Commander and that the 'ultimate form of government of Japan shall, in accordance with the Potsdam Declaration, be established by the freely expressed will of the Japanese people'. On these conditions the Japanese surrendered on 14 August 1945. The formal instrument of surrender was signed on 2 September 1945 in Tokyo Bay. Japanese armies throughout Asia surrendered to the military Commander-in-Chief in each region. The Japanese armies in Manchuria, Korea north of the 38th parallel, the Kuriles and Sakhalin surrendered to the Russians. The Soviet Union regularized the hasty Russian invasion of Manchuria by concluding the *Sino-Soviet Treaty of Friendship on 14 August 1945* (p. 237).

Report of the Crimea Conference (Yalta Conference), 11 February 1945

For the past eight days Winston S. Churchill, Prime Minister of Great Britain, Franklin D. Roosevelt, President of the United States of America, and Marshal J. V. Stalin, Chairman of the Council of People's Commissars of the Union of Soviet Socialist Republics, have met with the Foreign Secretaries, Chiefs of Staff and other advisers in the Crimea.

In addition to the three Heads of Government, the following took part in the Conference ...

The following statement is made by the Prime Minister of Great Britain, the President of the United States of America, and the Chairman of the Council of People's Commissars of the Union of Soviet Socialist Republics, on the results of the Crimea Conference.

I · THE DEFEAT OF GERMANY

We have considered and determined the military plans of the three Allied Powers for the final defeat of the common enemy. The military staffs of the three Allied nations have met in daily meetings throughout the Conference. These meetings have been most satisfactory from every point of view and have resulted in closer coordination of the military effort

of the three Allies than ever before. The fullest information has been interchanged. The timing, scope and coordination of new and even more powerful blows to be launched by our armies and air forces into the heart of Germany from the East, West, North and South have been fully agreed and planned in detail.

Our combined military plans will be made known only as we execute them, but we believe that the very close working partnership among the three staffs attained at this Conference will result in shortening the war. Meetings of the three staffs will be continued in the future whenever the need arises.

Nazi Germany is doomed. The German people will only make the cost of their defeat heavier to themselves by attempting to continue a hopeless resistance.

II · THE OCCUPATION AND CONTROL OF GERMANY

We have agreed on common policies and plans for enforcing the unconditional surrender terms which we shall impose together on Nazi Germany after German armed resistance has been finally crushed. These terms will not be made known until the final defeat of Germany has been accomplished. Under the agreed plan, the forces of the Three Powers will each occupy a separate zone of Germany. Coordinated administration and control has been provided for under the plan through a central Control Commission consisting of the Supreme Commanders of the Three Powers with headquarters in Berlin. It has been agreed that France should be invited by the Three Powers, if she should so desire, to take over a zone of occupation, and to participate as a fourth member of the Control Commission. The limits of the French zone will be agreed by the four Governments concerned through their representatives on the European Advisory Commission.

It is our inflexible purpose to destroy German militarism and Nazism and to ensure that Germany will never again be able to disturb the peace of the world. We are determined to disarm and disband all German armed forces; break up for all time the German General Staff that has repeatedly contrived the resurgence of German militarism; remove or destroy all German military equipment; eliminate or control all German industry that could be used for military production; bring all war criminals to just and swift punishment and exact reparation in kind for the destruction wrought by the Germans; wipe out the Nazi party, Nazi laws, organizations and institutions, remove all Nazi and militarist influences from public office and from the cultural and economic life of the German people; and take in harmony such other measures in Germany as may be necessary to the future peace and safety of the world. It is not our purpose to destroy the people of Germany, but only when Nazism and militarism have been extirpated, will there be hope for a decent life for Germans, and a place for them in the comity of nations.

III · REPARATION BY GERMANY

We have considered the question of the damage caused by Germany to the Allied nations in this war and recognized it as just that Germany be obliged to make compensation for this damage in kind to the greatest extent possible. A Commission for the Compensation of Damage will be established. The Commission will be instructed to consider the question of the extent and methods for compensating damage caused by Germany to the Allied countries. The Commission will work in Moscow.

IV · UNITED NATIONS CONFERENCE

We are resolved upon the earliest possible establishment with our Allies of a general international organization to maintain peace and security. We believe that this is essential, both to prevent aggression and to remove the political, economic and social causes of war through the close and continuing collaboration of all peace-loving peoples.

The foundations were laid at Dumbarton Oaks. On the important question of voting procedure, however, agreement was not there reached. The present Conference has been able to resolve this difficulty.

We have agreed that a Conference of United Nations should be called to meet at San Francisco in the United States on the 25th April 1945, to prepare the charter of such an organization, along the lines proposed in the informal conversations at Dumbarton Oaks.

The Government of China and the Provisional Government of France will be immediately consulted and invited to sponsor invitations to the Conference jointly with the Governments of the United States, Great Britain and the Union of Soviet Socialist Republics. As soon as the consultation with China and France has been completed, the text of the proposals on voting procedure will be made public.

V · DECLARATION ON LIBERATED EUROPE

We have drawn up and subscribed to a Declaration on Liberated Europe. This Declaration provides for concerting the policies of the Three Powers and for joint action by them in meeting the political and economic problems of liberated Europe in accordance with democratic principles. The text of the Declaration is as follows:

The Premier of the Union of Soviet Socialist Republics, the Prime Minister of the United Kingdom, and the President of the United States of America have consulted with each other in the common interests of the peoples of their countries and those of liberated Europe. They jointly declare their mutual agreement to concert during the temporary period of instability in liberated Europe the policies of their three Governments in assisting the peoples liberated from the domination of Nazi Germany and the peoples of the former Axis satellite States of Europe to solve by democratic means their pressing political and economic problems.

The establishment of order in Europe and the rebuilding of national economic life must be achieved by processes which will enable the liberated peoples to destroy the last vestiges of Nazism and Fascism and to create democratic institutions of their own choice. This is a principle of the Atlantic Charter - the right of all peoples to choose the form of government under which they will live - the restoration of sovereign rights and self-government to those peoples who have been forcibly deprived of them by the aggressor nations.

To foster the conditions in which the liberated peoples may exercise those rights, the three Governments will jointly assist the people in any European liberated State or former Axis satellite State in Europe where in their judgement conditions require: (a) to establish conditions of internal peace; (b) to carry out emergency measures for the relief of distressed peoples; (c) to form interim governmental authorities broadly representative of all democratic elements in the population and pledged to the earliest possible establishment through free elections of Governments responsive to the will of the people; and (d) to facilitate where necessary the holding of such elections.

The three Governments will consult the other United Nations and provisional authorities or other Governments in Europe when matters of direct interest to them are under consideration.

When, in the opinion of the three Governments, conditions in any European liberated State or any former Axis satellite State in Europe make such action necessary, they will immediately consult together on the measures necessary to discharge the joint responsibilities set forth in this Declaration.

By this Declaration we reaffirm our faith in the principles of the Atlantic Charter, our pledge in the Declaration by the United Nations, and our determination to build in cooperation with other peace-loving nations a world order under law, dedicated to peace, security, freedom and the general well-being of all mankind.

In issuing this Declaration, the Three Powers express the hope that the Provisional Government of the French Republic may be associated with them in the procedure suggested.

VI · POLAND

We came to the Crimea Conference resolved to settle our differences about Poland. We discussed fully all aspects of the question. We reaffirm our common desire to see established a strong, free independent and democratic Poland. As a result of our discussions we have agreed on the conditions in which a new Polish Provisional Government of National Unity may be formed in such a manner as to command recognition by the three major Powers.

The agreement reached is as follows:

A new situation has been created in Poland as a result of her complete liberation by the Red Army. This calls for the establishment of a Polish Provisional Government which can be more broadly based than was possible before the recent liberation of western Poland. The Provisional Government which is now functioning in Poland should therefore be reorganized on a broader democratic basis with the inclusion of democratic leaders from Poland itself and from Poles abroad. This new Government should then be called the Polish Provisional Government of National Unity.

M. Molotov, Mr Harriman and Sir A. Clark Kerr are authorized as a Commission to consult in the first instance in Moscow with members of the present Provisional Government and with other Polish democratic leaders from within Poland and from abroad, with a view to the reorganization of the present Government along the above lines. This Polish Provisional Government of National Unity shall be pledged to the holding of free and unfettered elections as soon as possible on the basis of universal suffrage and secret ballot. In these elections all democratic and anti-Nazi parties shall have the right to take part and to put forward candidates.

When a Polish Provisional Government of National Unity has been properly formed in conformity with the above, the Government of the Union of Soviet Socialist Republics, which now maintains diplomatic relations with the present Provisional Government of Poland, and the Government of the United Kingdom and the Government of the United States will establish diplomatic relations with the new Polish Government of National Unity, and will exchange Ambassadors by whose reports the respective Governments will be kept informed about the situation in Poland.

The three Heads of Government consider that the eastern frontier of Poland should follow the Curzon line with digressions from it in some regions of 5 to 8 kilometres in favour of Poland. They recognize that Poland must receive substantial accessions of territory in the north and west. They feel that the opinion of the new Polish Provisional Government of National Unity should be sought in due course on the extent of these accessions and that the final delimitation of the western frontier of Poland should thereafter await the Peace Conference.

VII · Yugoslavia

We have agreed to recommend to Marshal Tito and Dr Subasić that the Agreement between them should be put into effect immediately, and that a new Government should be formed on the basis of that Agreement.

We also recommend that as soon as the new Government has been formed it should declare that:

(i) The Anti-Fascist Assembly of National Liberation (Avnoj) should be extended to include members of the last Yugoslav Parliament (Skupshtina) who have not compromised themselves by collaboration with the enemy, thus forming a body to be known as a temporary Parliament; and

(ii) Legislative acts passed by the Assembly of National Liberation will be subject to subsequent ratification by a Constituent Assembly.

There was also a general review of other Balkan questions.

VIII · Meetings of Foreign Secretaries

Throughout the Conference, besides the daily meetings of the Heads of Governments, and the Foreign Secretaries, separate meetings of the three Foreign Secretaries, and their advisers, have also been held daily.

These meetings have proved of the utmost value and the Conference agreed that permanent machinery should be set up for regular consultation between the three Foreign Secretaries. They will, therefore, meet as often as may be necessary, probably about every three or four months. These meetings will be held in rotation in the three capitals, the first meeting being held in London, after the United Nations Conference on World Organization.

IX · Unity for peace as for war

Our meeting here in the Crimea has reaffirmed our common determination to maintain and strengthen in the peace to come that unity of purpose and of action which has made victory possible and certain for the United Nations in this war. We believe that this is a sacred obligation which our Governments owe to our peoples and to all the peoples of the world.

Only with continuing and growing cooperation and understanding among our three countries, and among all the peace-loving nations, can the highest aspiration of humanity be realized – a secure and lasting peace which will, in the words of the Atlantic Charter 'Afford assurance that all the men in all the lands may live out their lives in freedom from fear and want'.

Victory in this war and establishment of the proposed international organization will provide the greatest opportunity in all history to create in the years to come the essential conditions of such a peace.

(Signed)

WINSTON S. CHURCHILL
FRANKLIN D. ROOSEVELT
J. V. STALIN
11th February 1945

Yalta Agreement on the Kuriles and entry of the Soviet Union in the war against Japan, 11 February 1945 (released 11 February 1946)

The leaders of the three Great Powers – the Soviet Union, the United States of America and Great Britain – have agreed that in two or three months after Germany has surrendered and the war in Europe has terminated the Soviet Union shall enter into the war against Japan on the side of the Allies on condition that:

1. The *status quo* in Outer Mongolia (The Mongolian People's Republic) shall be preserved;

2. The former rights of Russia violated by the treacherous attack of Japan in 1904 shall be restored, viz:

(a) the southern part of Sakhalin as well as all the islands adjacent to it shall be returned to the Soviet Union,

(b) the commercial port of Dairen shall be internationalized, the pre-eminent interests of the Soviet Union in this port being safeguarded and the lease of Port Arthur as a naval base of the U.S.S.R. restored,

(c) the Chinese-Eastern Railroad and the South-Manchurian Railroad which provides an outlet to Dairen shall be jointly operated by the establishment of a joint Soviet-Chinese Company, it being understood that the pre-eminent interests of the Soviet Union shall be safeguarded and that China shall retain full sovereignty in Manchuria;

3. The Kuril islands shall be handed over to the Soviet Union.

It is understood that the agreement concerning Outer Mongolia and the ports and railroads referred to above will require concurrence of Generalissimo Chiang Kai-shek. The President will take measures in order to obtain this concurrence on advice from Marshal Stalin.

The Heads of the three Great Powers have agreed that these claims of the Soviet Union shall be unquestionably fulfilled after Japan has been defeated.

For its part the Soviet Union expresses its readiness to conclude with the National Government of China a pact of friendship and alliance between the U.S.S.R. and China in order to render assistance to China with its armed forces for the purpose of liberating China from the Japanese yoke.

February 11, 1945

J. STALIN
FRANKLIN D. ROOSEVELT
WINSTON S. CHURCHILL

Potsdam Conference Protocol, 2 August 1945

The Berlin Conference of the three Heads of Government of the U.S.S.R., U.S.A., and U.K., which took place from July 17 to August 2, 1945, came to the following conclusions:

I · Establishment of a Council of Foreign Ministers

A. The Conference reached the following agreement for the establishment of a Council of Foreign Ministers to do the necessary preparatory work for the peace settlements:

1. There shall be established a Council composed of the Foreign Ministers of the United Kingdom, the Union of Soviet Socialist Republics, China, France, and the United States.

2. (i) The Council shall normally meet in London which shall be the permanent seat of the joint Secretariat which the Council will form....

3. (i) As its immediate important task, the Council shall be authorized to draw up, with a view to their submission to the United Nations, treaties of peace with Italy, Rumania, Bulgaria, Hungary and Finland, and to propose settlements of territorial questions outstanding on the termination of the war in Europe. The Council shall be utilized for the preparation of a peace settlement for Germany to be accepted by the Government of Germany when a Government adequate for the purpose is established.

(ii) For the discharge of each of these tasks the Council will be composed of the Members representing those States which were signatory to the terms of surrender imposed upon the enemy State concerned. For the purposes of the peace settlement for Italy, France shall be regarded as a signatory to the terms of surrender for Italy. Other Members will be invited to participate when matters directly concerning them are under discussion.

(iii) Other matters may from time to time be referred to the Council by agreement between the Member Governments.

4. (i) Whenever the Council is considering a question of direct interest to a State not represented thereon, such State should be invited to send representatives to participate in the discussion and study of that question.

(ii) The Council may adapt its procedure to the particular problems under consideration. In some cases it may hold its own preliminary discussions prior to the participation of other interested States. In other cases, the Council may convoke a formal conference of the States chiefly interested in seeking a solution of the particular problem.

B. It was agreed that the three Governments should each address an identical invitation to the Governments of China and France to adopt this text and to join in establishing the Council. . . .

[It was agreed to recommend that the European Advisory Commission be dissolved.]

II · The principles to govern the treatment of Germany in the initial control period

A · POLITICAL PRINCIPLES

1. In accordance with the Agreement on Control Machinery in Germany, supreme authority in Germany is exercised, on instructions from their respective Governments, by the Commanders-in-Chief of the armed forces of the United States of America, the United Kingdom, the Union of Soviet Socialist Republics, and the French Republic, each in his own zone of occupation, and also jointly, in matters affecting Germany as a whole, in their capacity as members of the Control Council.

2. So far as is practicable, there shall be uniformity of treatment of the German population throughout Germany.

3. The purposes of the occupation of Germany by which the Control Council shall be guided are:

(i) The complete disarmament and demilitarization of Germany and the elimination or control of all German industry that could be used for military production....

(ii) To convince the German people that they have suffered a total military defeat and that they cannot escape responsibility for what they have brought upon themselves, since their own ruthless warfare and the fanatical Nazi resistance have destroyed German economy and made chaos and suffering inevitable.

(iii) To destroy the National Socialist Party and its affiliated and supervised organizations, to dissolve all Nazi institutions, to ensure that they are not revived in any form, and to prevent all Nazi and militarist activity or propaganda.

(iv) To prepare for the eventual reconstruction of German political life on a democratic basis and for eventual peaceful cooperation in international life by Germany.

4. All Nazi laws which provided the basis of the Hitler régime or established discriminations on grounds of race, creed, or political opinion shall be abolished. No such discriminations, whether legal, administrative or otherwise, shall be tolerated.

5. War criminals and those who have participated in planning or carrying out Nazi enterprises involving or resulting in atrocities or war crimes shall be arrested and brought to judgement. Nazi leaders, influential Nazi supporters and high officials of Nazi organizations and institutions and any other persons dangerous to the occupation or its objectives shall be arrested and interned.

6. All members of the Nazi Party who have been more than nominal participants in its activities and all other persons hostile to Allied purposes shall be removed from public and semi-public office, and from positions of responsibility in important private undertakings. Such persons shall be replaced by persons who, by their political and moral qualities, are deemed capable of assisting in developing genuine democratic institutions in Germany.

7. German education shall be so controlled as completely to eliminate Nazi and militarist doctrines and to make possible the successful development of democratic ideas.

8. The judicial system will be reorganized in accordance with the principles of democracy, of justice under law, and of equal rights for all citizens without distinction of race, nationality or religion.

9. The administration in Germany should be directed towards the decentralization of the political structure and the development of local responsibility. To this end:

(i) local self-government shall be restored throughout Germany on democratic principles and in particular through elective councils as rapidly as is consistent with military security and the purposes of military occupation;

(ii) all democratic political parties with rights of assembly and of public discussion shall be allowed and encouraged throughout Germany;

(iii) representative and elective principles shall be introduced into regional, provincial and State (*Land*) administration as rapidly as may be justified by the successful application of these principles in local self-government;

(iv) for the time being, no central German Government shall be established. Notwithstanding this, however, certain essential central German administrative departments, headed by State Secretaries, shall be established, particularly in the fields of finance, transport, communications, foreign trade and industry. Such departments will act under the direction of the Control Council.

10. Subject to the necessity for maintaining military security, freedom of speech, press and religion shall be permitted, and religious institutions shall be respected. Subject likewise to the maintenance of military security, the formation of free trade unions shall be permitted.

B · ECONOMIC PRINCIPLES

11. In order to eliminate Germany's war potential, the production of arms, ammunition and implements of war as well as all types of aircraft and sea-going ships shall be prohibited and prevented. Production of metals, chemicals, machinery and other items that are directly necessary to a war economy shall be rigidly controlled and restricted to Germany's approved post-war peacetime needs to meet the objectives stated in paragraph 15. Productive capacity not needed for permitted production shall be removed in accordance with the reparations plan recommended by the Allied Commission on Reparations and approved by the Governments concerned or if not removed shall be destroyed.

12. At the earliest practicable date, the German economy shall be decentralized for the purpose of eliminating the present excessive concentration of economic power as exemplified in particular by cartels, syndicates, trusts and other monopolistic arrangements.

13. In organizing the German economy, primary emphasis shall be given to the development of agriculture and peaceful domestic industries.

14. During the period of occupation Germany shall be treated as a single economic unit. To this end common policies shall be established in regard to:

(a) mining and industrial production and its allocation;

(b) agriculture, forestry and fishing;

(c) wages, prices and rationing;

(d) import and export programmes for Germany as a whole;

(e) currency and banking, central taxation and customs;

(f) reparation and removal of industrial war potential;

(g) transportation and communications.

In applying these policies account shall be taken, where appropriate, of varying local conditions.

15. Allied controls shall be imposed upon the German economy but only to the extent necessary....

16. In the imposition and maintenance of economic controls established by the Control Council, German administrative machinery shall be created and the German authorities shall be required to the fullest extent practicable to proclaim and assume administration of such controls....

17. Measures shall be promptly taken:

(a) to effect essential repair of transport;

(b) to enlarge coal production;

(c) to maximize agricultural output; and

(d) to effect emergency repair of housing and essential utilities.

18. Appropriate steps shall be taken by the Control Council to exercise control and the power of disposition over German-owned external assets not already under the control of United Nations which have taken part in the war against Germany.

19. Payment of reparations should leave enough resources to enable the German people to subsist without external assistance. In working out the economic balance of Germany the necessary means must be provided to pay for imports approved by the Control Council in Germany. The proceeds of exports from current production and stocks shall be available in the first place for payment for such imports....

III · Reparations from Germany

1. Reparation claims of the U.S.S.R. shall be met by removals from the zone of Germany occupied by the U.S.S.R., and from appropriate German external assets.

2. The U.S.S.R. undertakes to settle the reparation claims of Poland from its own share of reparations.

3. The reparation claims of the United States, the United Kingdom and other countries entitled to reparations shall be met from the Western zones and from appropriate German external assets.

4. In addition to the reparations to be taken by the U.S.S.R. from its own zone of occupation, the U.S.S.R. shall receive additionally from the Western zones:

(a) Fifteen per cent of such usable and complete industrial capital equipment, in the first place from the metallurgical, chemical and machine manufacturing industries as is unnecessary for the German peace economy and should be removed from the Western zones of Germany, in exchange for an equivalent value of food, coal, potash, zinc, timber, clay products, petroleum products, and such other commodities as may be agreed upon.

(b) Ten per cent of such industrial capital equipment as is unnecessary for the German peace economy and should be removed from the Western zones, to be transferred to the Soviet Government on reparations account without payment or exchange of any kind in return.

Removals of equipment as provided in (a) and (b) above shall be made simultaneously. . . .

8. The Soviet Government renounces all claims in respect of reparations to shares of German enterprises which are located in the Western zones of Germany as well as to German foreign assets in all countries except those specified in paragraph 9 below.

9. The Governments of the U.K. and U.S.A. renounce all claims in respect of reparations to shares of German enterprises which are located in the Eastern zone of occupation in Germany, as well as to German foreign assets in Bulgaria, Finland, Hungary, Rumania and Eastern Austria. . . .

IV · Disposal of the German Navy and Merchant Marine

A. The following principles for the distribution of the German Navy were agreed:

1. The total strength of the German Surface Navy, excluding ships sunk and those taken over from Allied Nations, but including ships under construction or repair, shall be divided equally among the U.S.S.R., U.K., and U.S.A. . . .

The German Merchant Marine, surrendered to the Three Powers and wherever located, shall be divided equally among the U.S.S.R., the U.K., and the U.S.A.

V · City of Koenigsberg and the adjacent area

The Conference examined a proposal by the Soviet Government to the effect that pending the final determination of territorial questions at the peace settlement, the section of the western frontier of the Union of Soviet Socialist Republics which is adjacent to the Baltic Sea should pass from a point on the eastern shore of the Bay of Danzig to the east, north of Braunsberg-Goldap, to the meeting point of the frontiers of Lithuania, the Polish Republic and East Prussia.

The Conference has agreed in principle to the proposal of the Soviet Government concerning the ultimate transfer to the Soviet Union of the City of Koenigsberg and the area adjacent to it as described above subject to expert examination of the actual frontier.

The President of the United States and the British Prime Minister have declared that they will support the proposal of the Conference at the forthcoming peace settlement.

VI · War criminals

[Trials to begin at earliest possible date.]

VII · Austria

The Conference examined a proposal by the Soviet Government on the extension of the authority of the Austrian Provisional Government to all of Austria.

The three Governments agreed that they were prepared to examine this question after the entry of the British and American forces into the city of Vienna.

It was agreed that reparations should not be exacted from Austria.

VIII · Poland

A · DECLARATION

We have taken note with pleasure of the agreement reached among representative Poles from Poland and abroad which has made possible the formation, in accordance with the decisions reached at the Crimea Conference, of a Polish Provisional Government of National Unity recognized by the Three Powers. The establishment by the British and United States Governments of diplomatic relations with the Polish Provisional Government of National Unity has resulted in the withdrawal of their recognition from the former Polish Government in London, which no longer exists.

The British and United States Governments have taken measures to protect the interest of the Polish Provisional Government of National Unity as the recognized Government of the Polish State in the property belonging to the Polish State located in their territories and under their control, whatever the form of this property may be. They have further taken measures to prevent alienation to third parties of such property. All proper facilities will be given to the Polish Provisional Government of National Unity for the exercise of the ordinary legal remedies for the recovery of any property belonging to the Polish State which may have been wrongfully alienated.

The Three Powers are anxious to assist the Polish Provisional Government of National Unity in facilitating the return to Poland as soon as practicable of all Poles abroad who wish to go, including members of the Polish armed forces and the Merchant Marine. They expect that those Poles who return home shall be accorded personal and property rights on the same basis as all Polish citizens.

The Three Powers note that the Polish Provisional Government of National Unity, in accordance with the decisions of the Crimea Conference, has agreed to the holding of free and unfettered elections as soon as possible on the basis of universal suffrage and secret ballot in which all democratic and anti-Nazi parties shall have the right to take part and to put forward candidates, and that representatives of the Allied press shall enjoy full freedom to report to the world upon developments in Poland before and during the elections.

B · WESTERN FRONTIER OF POLAND

In conformity with the agreement on Poland reached at the Crimea Conference the three Heads of Government have sought the opinion of the Polish Provisional Government of National Unity in regard to the accession of territory in the north and west which Poland should receive. The President of the National Council of Poland and members of the Polish Provisional Government of National Unity have been received at the Conference and have fully presented their views. The three Heads of Government reaffirm their opinion that the final delimitation of the western frontier of Poland should await the peace settlement.

The three Heads of Government agree that, pending the final determination of Poland's western frontier, the former German territories east of a line running from the Baltic Sea immediately west of Swinamunde, and thence along the Oder river to the confluence of the western Neisse river and along the western Neisse to the Czechoslovak frontier, including that portion of East Prussia not placed under the administration of the Union of Soviet Socialist Republics in accordance with the understanding reached at this Conference and including the area of the former Free City of Danzig, shall be under the administration of the Polish State and for such purposes should not be considered as part of the Soviet zone of occupation in Germany.

IX · Conclusion of peace treaties and admission to the United Nations Organization

The three Governments consider it desirable that the present anomalous position of Italy, Bulgaria, Finland, Hungary and

Rumania should be terminated by the conclusion of peace treaties. They trust that the other interested Allied Governments will share these views. . . .

As regards the admission of other States into the United Nations Organization, Article 4 of the Charter of the United Nations declares that:

1. Membership in the United Nations is open to all other peace-loving States who accept the obligations contained in the present Charter and, in the judgement of the Organization, are able and willing to carry out these obligations.

2. The admission of any such State to membership in the United Nations will be effected by a decision of the General Assembly upon the recommendation of the Security Council.

The three Governments, so far as they are concerned, will support applications for membership from those States which have remained neutral during the war and which fulfil the qualifications set out above.

The three Governments feel bound however to make it clear that they for their part would not favour any application for membership put forward by the present Spanish Government, which having been founded with the support of the Axis Powers, does not, in view of its origins, its nature, its record and its close association with the aggressor States, possess the qualifications necessary to justify such membership.

X · Territorial trusteeship

The Conference examined a proposal by the Soviet Government on the question of trusteeship territories as defined in the decision of the Crimea Conference and in the Charter of the United Nations Organization.

After an exchange of views on this question it was decided that the disposition of any former Italian colonial territories was one to be decided in connection with the preparation of a peace treaty for Italy and that the question of Italian colonial territory would be considered by the September Council of Ministers of Foreign Affairs.

XI · Revised Allied Control Commission procedure in Rumania, Bulgaria and Hungary

[Revision of procedures will be undertaken.]

XII · Orderly transfer of German populations

The three Governments, having considered the question in all its aspects, recognize that the transfer to Germany of German populations, or elements thereof, remaining in Poland, Czechoslovakia and Hungary, will have to be undertaken. They agree that any transfers that take place should be effected in an orderly and humane manner. . . .

XIII · Oil equipment in Rumania

|Commission of experts to investigate.]

XIV · Iran

It was agreed that Allied troops should be withdrawn immediately from Teheran, and that further stages of the withdrawal of troops from Iran should be considered at the meeting of the Council of Foreign Ministers to be held in London in September 1945.

XV · International zone of Tangier

[Agreement to be reached.]

XVI · The Black Sea Straits

The three Governments recognized that the Convention concluded at Montreux should be revised as failing to meet present-day conditions.

It was agreed that as the next step the matter should be the subject of direct conversations between each of the three Governments and the Turkish Government.

. . .

[Signed] Stalin, Truman, Attlee.

Treaty of Friendship and Alliance between China and the Soviet Union, Moscow, 14 August 1945

I · Treaty of Friendship and Alliance

The President of the National Government of the Republic of China and the Praesidium of the Supreme Soviet of the Union of Soviet Socialist Republics,

Being desirous of strengthening the friendly relations which have always prevailed between the Republic of China and the Soviet Union, by means of an alliance and by good neighbourly post-war collaboration;

Determined to assist each other in the struggle against aggression on the part of the enemies of the United Nations in this World War and to collaborate in the common war against Japan until that country's unconditional surrender;

Expressing their unswerving resolve to collaborate in maintaining peace and security for the benefit of the peoples of both countries and of all peace-loving nations ... have agreed as follows:

Article 1. The High Contracting Parties undertake jointly with the other United Nations to prosecute the war against Japan until final victory is achieved. The High Contracting Parties mutually undertake to afford one another all necessary military and other assistance and support in this war.

Article 2. The High Contracting Parties undertake not to enter into separate negotiations with Japan or conclude, except by mutual consent, any armistice or peace treaty either with the present Japanese Government or any other Government or authority set up in Japan that does not clearly renounce all aggressive intentions.

Article 3. On the conclusion of the war against Japan, the High Contracting Parties undertake to carry out jointly all the measures in their power to render

impossible a repetition of aggression and violation of the peace by Japan.

Should either of the High Contracting Parties become involved in hostilities with Japan in consequence of an attack by the latter against that party, the other High Contracting Party will at once render to the High Contracting Party so involved in hostility all the military and other support and assistance in its power.

This Article shall remain in force until such time as, at the request of both High Contracting Parties, responsibility for the prevention of further aggression by Japan is placed upon the 'United Nations' Organization.

Article 4. Each High Contracting Party undertakes not to conclude any alliance and not to take part in any coalition directed against the other Contracting Party.

Article 5. The High Contracting Parties, having regard to the interests of the security and economic development of each of them, agree to work together in close and friendly collaboration after the re-establishment of peace and to act in accordance with the principles of mutual respect for each other's sovereignty and territorial integrity and non-intervention in each other's internal affairs.

Article 6. The High Contracting Parties agree to afford one another all possible economic assistance in the post-war period in order to facilitate and expedite the rehabilitation of both countries and to make their contribution to the prosperity of the world.

Article 7. Nothing in this Treaty should be interpreted in such a way as to prejudice the rights and duties of the High Contracting Parties as Members of the Organization of the 'United Nations'.

Article 8. The present Treaty is subject to ratification in the shortest possible time. The instruments of ratification shall be exchanged in Chungking as soon as possible.

The Treaty comes into force immediately upon ratification, and shall remain in force for thirty years. Should neither of the High Contracting Parties make, one year before the date of the Treaty's expiry, a statement of its desire to denounce it, the Treaty will remain in force for an unlimited period, provided that each High Contracting Party may invalidate it by announcing its intention to do so to the other Contracting Party one year in advance.

...

Exchange of Notes

No. 1

In connection with the signing on this date of the Treaty of Friendship and Alliance between China and the Union of Soviet Socialist Republics, I have the honour to place on record that the following provisions are understood by both Contracting Parties as follows:

1. In accordance with the spirit of the above-mentioned Treaty and to implement its general idea and its purposes, the Soviet Government agrees to render China moral support and assist her with military supplies and other material resources, it being understood that this support and assistance will go exclusively to the National Government as the Central Government of China.

2. During the negotiations on the ports of Dairen and Port Arthur and on the joint operation of the Chinese Changchun Railway, the Soviet Government regarded the Three Eastern Provinces as part of China and again affirmed its respect for the complete sovereignty of China over the Three Eastern Provinces and recognition of their territorial and administrative integrity.

3. With regard to recent events in Sinkiang, the Soviet Government confirms that, as stated in Article 5 of the Treaty of Friendship and Alliance, it has no intention of interfering in the internal affairs of China.

...

No. 3

In view of the frequently manifested desire for independence of the people of Outer Mongolia, the Chinese Government states that, after the defeat of Japan, if this desire is confirmed by a plebiscite of the people of Outer Mongolia, the Chinese Government will recognize the independence of Outer Mongolia within her existing frontiers....

II · Agreement between the Chinese Republic and the Union of Soviet Socialist Republics on the Chinese Changchun Railway, signed at Moscow on 14 August 1945

The President of the National Government of the Republic of China and the Praesidium of the Supreme Soviet of the U.S.S.R. being desirous of strengthening, on the basis of complete regard for the rights and interests of each of the two parties, friendly relations and economic ties between the two countries, have agreed as follows:

Article 1. After the expulsion of the Japanese armed forces from the Three Eastern Provinces of China, the main trunk lines of the Chinese Eastern Railway and the South Manchurian Railway leading from the station of Manchouli to the station of Pogranichnaya and from Harbin to Dairen and Port Arthur, shall be combined to form a single railway system to be known as 'Chinese Changchun Railway', and shall become the joint property of the U.S.S.R. and the Chinese Republic and be jointly exploited by them. Only such lands and branch lines shall become joint property and be jointly exploited as were constructed by the Chinese Eastern Railway while it was under Russian and joint Soviet-Chinese management, and by the South Manchurian Railway while under Russian management, and which are intended to serve the direct needs of those railways. Ancillary undertakings directly serving the needs of those railways and constructed during the above-mentioned periods shall also be included. All other railway branch lines, ancillary undertakings and lands will be the exclusive property of the Chinese Government. The joint exploitation of the above-mentioned railways shall be effected by a single administration under Chinese sovereignty as a purely commercial transport undertaking.

[*Articles 2–18*. Details of administration.]

III · Agreement on the Port of Dairen, signed at Moscow on 14 August 1945

Whereas a Treaty of Friendship and Alliance has been concluded between the Chinese Republic and the Union of Soviet Socialist Republics, and whereas the U.S.S.R. has guaranteed to respect the sovereignty of China over the Three Eastern Provinces as an inalienable part of China, the Chinese Republic, in order to protect the interests of the Union of Soviet Socialist Republics in Dairen as a port for the import and export of goods, hereby agrees:

1. To proclaim Dairen a free port, open to the trade and shipping of all countries.

2. The Chinese Government agrees to allocate docks and warehouse accommodation in the said free port to be leased to the U.S.S.R. under a separate agreement.

Protocol

1. The Government of China when requested to do so by the Soviet Union shall grant the Soviet Union, freely and without consideration, a thirty years' lease of one-half of all harbour installations and equipment, the other half of the harbour installations and equipment remaining the property of China.

...

IV · Agreement on Port Arthur, signed at Moscow on 14 August 1945

In accordance with the Sino-Soviet Treaty of Friendship and Alliance and as an addition thereto, both Contracting Parties have agreed on the following:

1. In order to strengthen the security of China and the U.S.S.R. and prevent a repetition of aggression on the part of Japan, the Government of the Chinese Republic agrees to the joint use by both Contracting Parties of Port Arthur as a naval base. ....

V · Agreement on relations between the Soviet Commander-in-Chief and the Chinese administration following the entry of Soviet forces into the territory of the three Eastern Provinces of China in connection with the present joint war against Japan, signed at Moscow on 14 August 1945

The President of the National Government of the Chinese Republic and the Praesidium of the Supreme Soviet of the Union of Soviet Socialist Republics, being desirous that after the entry of Soviet forces into the territory of the Three Eastern Provinces of China in connection with the present joint war of China and the U.S.S.R. against Japan, relations between the Soviet Commander-in-Chief and the Chinese administration conform with the spirit of friendship and alliance existing between both countries, have agreed on the following:

1. After the entry, as a result of military operations, of Soviet troops into the territory of the Three Eastern Provinces of China, the supreme authority and responsibility in the zone of military activity in all matters relating to the conduct of the war shall, during the period necessary for conducting such operations, be vested in the Commander-in-Chief of the Soviet Armed Forces.

2. A representative of the National Government of the Chinese Republic and

a staff shall be appointed in any recaptured territory, who shall:

(a) Organize and control, in accordance with the laws of China, the administration on the territory freed from the enemy;

(b) Assist in establishing cooperation in restored territories between the Chinese armed forces, whether regular or irregular, and the Soviet armed forces;

(c) Ensure the active collaboration of the Chinese administration with the Soviet Commander-in-Chief and, in particular, issue corresponding instructions to the local authorities, being guided by the requirements and desires of the Soviet Commander-in-Chief.

3. A Chinese Military Mission shall be appointed to the Headquarters of the Soviet Commander-in-Chief for the purpose of maintaining contact between the Soviet Commander-in-Chief and the representative of the National Government of the Chinese Republic.

4. In zones that are under the supreme authority of the Soviet Commander-in-Chief, the administration of the National Government of the Chinese Republic for restored territories shall maintain contact with the Soviet Commander-in-Chief through a representative of the National Government of the Chinese Republic.

5. As soon as part of a recaptured territory ceases to be a zone of direct military operations, the National Government of the Chinese Republic shall assume complete power in respect of civil affairs and shall render the Soviet Commander-in-Chief all assistance and support through its civil and military organs.

6. All members of the Soviet armed forces on Chinese territory shall be under the jurisdiction of the Soviet Commander-in-Chief. All Chinese citizens whether civil or military, shall be under Chinese jurisdiction ...

Minutes

At the fifth meeting between Generalissimo Stalin and Mr T. V. Soong, President of the Executive Yuan, which took place on 11 July 1945, the question of the evacuation of Soviet forces from Chinese territory after participation of the U.S.S.R. in the war against Japan was discussed. Generalissimo Stalin declined to include in the Agreement on the Entry of Soviet Forces into the Territory of the Three Eastern Provinces any provision for the evacuation of Soviet troops within three months following the defeat of Japan. Generalissimo Stalin stated, however, that the Soviet forces would begin to be withdrawn within three weeks after the capitulation of Japan.

Mr T. V. Soong asked how much time would be required to complete the evacuation. Generalissimo Stalin stated that in his opinion the evacuation of troops could be completed within a period of not exceeding two months. Mr T. V. Soong again asked whether the evacuation would really be completed within three months. Generalissimo Stalin stated that three months would be a maximum period sufficient for the completion of the withdrawal of troops.

X · The United Nations

With victory seemingly in Hitler's grasp, the Allies in the *London Declaration of 12 June 1941* proclaimed their intention to work together with other free peoples to establish 'a world in which, relieved of the menace of aggression, all may enjoy economic and social security'. This was expanded at Washington into the *United Nations Declaration of 1 January 1942* (p. 212). At the Allied meetings at Moscow and Teheran in the autumn of 1943 support was declared for the establishment of an international organization for the maintenance of peace and international security (pp. 219–22). Britain, the United States, Russia and China agreed to work out the functions and powers of an international world organization at a meeting in Washington to be held in two parts, with the Soviet Union, not then at war with Japan, leaving the conference to make way for a second stage where China would participate. Accordingly the *Dumbarton Oaks Conference took place in two phases from 21 August to 28 September 1944 and from 29 September to 7 October 1944.* The communiqué after the conference on 9 October 1944 published 'Proposals for the Establishment of a General International Organization', which outlined the main structure of the United Nations; but on the crucial question of whether one of the Great Powers holding a permanent seat on the Security Council could exercise a veto on a dispute involving itself, no final agreement was reached. (It was, however, agreed that a permanent member of the Security Council could exercise a veto on issues in which his country was not directly involved.) The proposals left open to later agreement three contentious issues: the voting procedures of the Security Council, the membership of the organization and the question of trusteeship and colonial territories. At the Yalta Conference in February 1945 (p. 226) the Big Three reached agreement on an American proposal for the voting procedure on the Security Council whereby the veto would not apply to every issue before it; procedural questions or the peaceful adjustments of disputes would not be subject to the veto; but the unanimity of all the permanent members, i.e. their right to a veto, would be required in all decisions involving enforcement measures. Nevertheless the wording of this agreement proved too imprecise to prevent later dispute. On the question of U.N. membership it was agreed that three Russian States would be admitted, including the Ukraine and Byelorussia. All the States that had declared war on the Axis by 1 March 1945 were also to be founder members. It was further agreed that a Drafting Conference should convene at San Francisco on 25 April 1945 and that China and France should be invited together with the Big Three.

The San Francisco Conference of 25 April–26 June 1945 was attended by the Foreign Ministers of the Great Powers and their delegations, as well as by delegations of countries at war with Germany. But the Polish Government did not attend as the Russian-sponsored Polish Government was not recognized by the Western Powers. The Soviet Union, for their part, objected unsuccessfully to the participation of Argentina.

The most bitter dispute of the conference, which even threatened the founding of an international organization, concerned the voting procedure of the proposed Security Council. This procedure was complicated by the distinction drawn between the different types of decisions the Security Council would be asked to reach.

1. It was accepted by the delegates at San Francisco that each of the permanent members, that is, the 'Five', Britain, France, China, Russia and the United States, whether a party to a dispute or not, would have to concur if any sanctions including military action were decided on to restore peace or to meet aggression. Each of the 'Big Five' thus held a 'veto' against action involving enforcement.

2. Questions merely of 'procedure' as to methods of proceeding in the event of a dispute being brought before the Security Council could be decided on by a majority of any seven members out of the original eleven (later, in 1965, nine out of the increased membership of fifteen).

3. The third category would arise when the Security Council discussed a dispute and reached and recorded conclusions about it intended to facilitate a peaceful settlement but not involving enforcement action. Such decisions or resolutions are called 'substantive' and it was agreed that they would require the unanimity of all the permanent members of the Security Council, but that any permanent members themselves involved in the dispute could not vote. In other words, a permanent member in these circumstances could only exercise a veto if his country was not involved in the dispute. The trouble was,

and remains, one of defining 'procedural', 'substantive', and what constitutes precisely 'enforcement action'. The widest interpretation of the veto held by the Soviet Union in 1945 was not in the end accepted by the conference, but the freedom of the Security Council to work for the *peaceful resolution* of disputes was also curtailed. The temporary absence of the Soviet Union, in protest at the continual presence of Nationalist China on the Security Council, created an exceptional circumstance which enabled the council to *recommend* in June 1950 that Member States furnish military help to South Korea in order to repel invasion from the north, though the absent permanent member, Russia, backed the communist State of North Korea.

The military force to be placed at the disposal of the Security Council, as envisaged in Article 43 of the Charter, does not exist for this article and has never been implemented. Consequently the Security Council cannot enforce military sanctions as intended but can only *recommend* that Member States furnish troops to preserve peace or to resist aggression. Economic sanctions can be invoked by the Security Council, and were for the first time in December 1966 against the régime of Southern Rhodesia.

The most important contribution of the San Francisco Conference was to safeguard the rights of nations to defend themselves singly or in alliance with others in the event that (as occurred) the Security Council through lack of agreement should find itself unable to act. This right is embodied in Article 51 which has justified the development of the defensive regional alliance groupings since the Second World War, such as NATO.

The Charter was unanimously adopted on 25 June 1945. By 24 October 1945, the 'Big Five' and a majority of other signatory States had ratified it and it was brought into effect. It established the United Nations Organization whose members are sovereign national States. By September 1973 the U.N. had grown to a membership of 135 from the original 51 Member States in 1945. The Federal Republic of Germany (West Germany) and the German Democratic Republic became full members in 1973. (The recently concluded German treaties, 1972, p. 295, provided for an application of both German States to membership of the U.N.) The United Nations consists of four main organs: the General Assembly to which all members belong; the Security Council built around the nucleus of the five Powers thereby defined (in the event unrealistically) as the Great Powers and a number of lesser Powers elected to the Security Council; the Secretariat under an elected Secretary-General; and an International Court of Justice. In contrast to the League of Nations, unanimity is not required in the Assembly or the Security Council of the U.N. The complex voting procedure of the Security Council has been discussed; in the Assembly 'important questions' are decided by a two-thirds majority. Under the Charter, the Security Council has special authority in all questions of peace and security. The General Assembly enjoys exclusive and ultimate authority in other fields.

The failure of the Security Council to enforce peace because of disagreement led to attempts to bypass the Security Council. Under the 'Uniting for Peace' Resolution of 2 November 1950 the General Assembly was empowered to meet within twenty-four hours if the Security Council failed in its responsibilities to maintain peace and security, and could take a number of steps *recommending* Member States to furnish armed forces for use as a U.N. unit. The Secretary-General too under Article 99 can take the initiative to bring problems to the attention of the Security Council and secure powers to maintain peace. Peacekeeping forces responsible to the Security Council were set up in the Middle East (the United Nations Truce Supervision Organization, UNTSO) to maintain the 1949 armistice between Israel and her Arab neighbours. This force has supervised the ceasefire line established after the six-day Arab–Israeli war of June 1967. In the conflict between India and Pakistan over Kashmir, a United Nations Military Observer Group for India and Pakistan (UNMOGIP) was set up in 1949. In Korea the United Nations Military Command was set up in July 1950, and since July 1953 it has supervised the armistice line between South and North Korea. United Nations forces were sent to Egypt during the Suez crisis of 1956 and in 1960 to the Congo. A United Nations Peace-Keeping Force in Cyprus (UNFICYP) was set up in March 1964 to help prevent communal strife between the Greeks and the Turks on the island. The refusal of some Powers to pay for peacekeeping operations they have not agreed to, and especially the refusal of the Soviet Union, which is assessed to pay nearly a third of the U.N. expenses, has brought the U.N. into deep financial crisis. It is a consideration inhibiting such military actions against the opposition of some permanent members of the Security Council. Whilst the success of the United Nations in its peacekeeping function has been limited, a wide variety of organs and agencies forming part of the U.N. or working with the U.N. have contributed to international cooperation in the fields of education, social welfare, human rights, health, regional economic development and international trade.

The United Nations is not a World Government. The Secretary-General is the servant of the organization, though he can play an active diplomatic role in initiating discussion and suggesting ways and means of defusing crises. But ultimately United Nations action is dependent on the willingness of its members to agree to it. In its role of maintaining peace and security the United Nations remains especially dependent on the willingness to work together of its five permanent members on the Security Council: China, France, Great

Britain, the Soviet Union and the United States. With the seating of the People's Republic of China in 1971 as a permanent member of the Security Council the ideological disagreements of members of the Council have further sub-divided.

Among United Nation activities, or activities of international organizations related to the United Nations, the following may be especially noted:

The Economic and Social Council is assigned the task of acting as a link between independent special agencies and promoting study in aspects not covered by these agencies in order to fulfil the U.N. Charter's purpose in the social and economic fields, including 'human rights'. In a complex structure sub-commissions, regional commissions and specialized agencies are responsible to ECOSOC, among them the United Nations Development Programme and the United Nations High Commission for Refugees.

The Trusteeship Council consists of representatives of Member States, as well as representatives of non-administering members of the Big Five and some members elected by the General Assembly. Its responsibilities extend not only over the mandated territories of the League but also over all non-self-governing territories, and it supervises the declaration of Chapter XI of the Charter, which sets out a code of behaviour towards inhabitants of territories which are not self-governing. The council may investigate and make recommendations.

The United Nations Educational, Scientific and Cultural Organization (UNESCO) has since 1946 promoted many international educational and cultural projects, including a campaign against illiteracy and the saving of the Abu Simbel temple sculptures. In January 1972 there were 125 Member States represented, i.e. almost all the members of the U.N. Only some small States are not members. The only large State not to be a member is South Africa.

The World Health Organization is a specialized agency to combat disease on a global scale. In January 1972 133 countries were members.

The United Nations Children's Fund (UNICEF) was founded in 1946 to aid mothers and children in need as a result of war or from other causes, especially in developing countries. It is financed by voluntary contributions.

The International Labour Organization (ILO) was originally established in 1919 with the same membership as the League; in January 1972 it had a membership of 121 countries. It is concerned internationally with establishing agreed conditions of labour and is also concerned with social security, economic planning and full employment.

The United Nations Relief and Rehabilitation Administration (UNRRA) was established in November 1943 and ceased in March 1949. Its main purpose was to provide relief, especially food, to parts of Europe and China devastated by war, and to stave off famine and collapse. Financed mainly by the United

States during the early years, UNRRA personnel and foreign aid were despatched to Italy, Greece, Poland and Yugoslavia. Foreign aid was granted to Eastern Europe including the Ukraine and Byelorussia. UNRRA had provided help for several million refugees before ceasing its operations; this work was taken over by the International Refugee Organization until 1951, and then by the High Commissioner for Refugees.

The International Atomic Energy Agency (IAEA) was set up in 1957 to promote the use of atomic energy for peace, health and prosperity, and to ensure that help under the programme is not misused for military purposes. In January 1972, 102 countries were members.

The Food and Agricultural Organization (FAO) established in 1945 was set up to raise living standards by improving production and distribution of agricultural produce.

International cooperation in world trade and finance developed from the *United Nations Monetary Conference at Bretton Woods in New Hampshire, 1-22 July 1944*, which recommended the establishment of two institutions. *The International Bank of Reconstruction and Development* was set up in December 1945 to promote the economic development of Member States by encouraging and making investments. In January 1972 there were 117 members. The U.S.S.R. and members of the Warsaw Pact alliance are not members, nor is Switzerland. Two organizations affiliated to the International Bank of Reconstruction and Development (World Bank) are, firstly, the *International Development Association* to help economic development in the less developed areas of the world. In January 1972 there were 107 members; the U.S.S.R. and its allies do not belong. Secondly, *the International Finance Corporation* (set up in 1956) is to stimulate private enterprise in less developed countries. In January 1972 there were 96 members; the U.S.S.R. and its allies are not members.

The International Monetary Fund (p. 262) exists to promote international cooperation in trade and finance and to help preserve stability in currency exchanges, which was regarded as an essential condition of expanding trade. In January 1972, 120 countries were members; but Switzerland is not one nor are any of the Warsaw Pact countries, although Rumania applied for membership in that year. In 1947 a multilateral tariff treaty known as *GATT* was negotiated to remove barriers to the growth of world trade, raise standards of living and promote the economic growth of its signatories. After 1955 it was turned into an organization by the creation of a permanent Secretariat. In January 1972 there were 80 members, including Poland, Czechoslovakia, Rumania and Switzerland, but not the U.S.S.R. One purpose of all three organizations is to ensure the liberalization of trade. This purpose has only been fulfilled imperfectly. The rules of GATT have also frequently been breached in law as well as in spirit. Nevertheless the three organizations embody principles to which member nations may work, and at critical times they have provided the negotiating forum for solving international financial crises which could threaten social and political stability. The less developed nations have set up the *United Nations Conference on Trade and Development* (UNCTAD) to combat the financial power of the richest ten nations dominating the International Money Fund.

The Food and Agricultural Organization (FAO) was founded in 1943 especially to improve food production and distribution through research and technical assistance, and so to raise living standards. In January 1972, 125 countries were members.

Though the Charter makes disarmament and the regulating of armament one of the principal concerns of the organization, and the United Nations has set up a series of commissions and committees since 1946, negotiations directly conducted under the aegis of the United Nations have largely been fruitless; but the United Nations has created a moral pressure expressed in the concern of the General Assembly. Real advances, such as the *Test Ban Treaty of 1963* (p. 515), have been negotiated by the Powers concerned at conferences set up especially for the purpose. The most important of such negotiations are those which have been in progress since November 1969 between the United States and the U.S.S.R. – SALT, the Strategic Arms Limitation Talks (p. 512).

Charter of the United Nations

We the Peoples of the United Nations determined

to save succeeding generations from the scourge of war, which twice in our lifetime has brought untold sorrow to mankind, and

to reaffirm faith in fundamental human rights, in the dignity and worth of the human person, in the equal rights of men and women and of nations large and small, and

to establish conditions under which justice and respect for the obligations arising from treaties and other sources of international law can be maintained, and

to promote social progress and better standards of life in larger freedom,

and for these ends

to practise tolerance and live together in peace with one another as good neighbours, and

to unite our strength to maintain international peace and security, and

to ensure, by the acceptance of principles and the institution of methods, that armed force shall not be used, save in the common interest, and

to employ international machinery for the promotion of the economic and social advancement of all peoples,

have resolved to combine our efforts to accomplish these aims

Accordingly, our respective Governments, through representatives assembled in the city of San Francisco, who have exhibited their full powers found to be in good and due form, have agreed to the present Charter of the United Nations and do hereby establish an international organization to be known as the United Nations.

Chapter I: Purposes and Principles

Article 1. The Purposes of the United Nations are:

1. To maintain international peace and security, and to that end: to take effective collective measures for the prevention and removal of threats to the peace, and for the suppression of acts of aggression or other breaches of the peace, and to bring about by peaceful means, and in conformity with the principles of justice and international law, adjustment or settlement of international disputes or situations which might lead to a breach of the peace;

2. To develop friendly relations among nations based on respect for the principle of equal rights and self-determination of peoples, and to take other appropriate measures to strengthen universal peace;

3. To achieve international cooperation in solving international problems of an economic, social, cultural, or humanitarian character, and in promoting and encouraging respect for human rights and for fundamental freedoms for all without distinction as to race, sex, language, or religion; and

4. To be a centre of harmonizing the actions of nations in the attainment of these common ends.

Article 2. The Organization and its Members, in pursuit of the Purposes stated in Article 1, shall act in accordance with the following Principles.

1. The Organization is based on the principle of the sovereign equality of all its Members.

2. All Members, in order to ensure to all of them the rights and benefits resulting from membership, shall fulfil in good faith the obligations assumed by them in accordance with the present Charter.

3. All Members shall settle their international disputes by peaceful means in such a manner that international peace and security, and justice, are not endangered.

4. All Members shall refrain in their international relations from the threat or use of force against the territorial integrity or political independence of any State, or in any other manner inconsistent with the Purposes of the United Nations.

5. All Members shall give the United Nations every assistance in any action it takes in accordance with the present Charter, and shall refrain from giving assistance to any State against which the United Nations is taking preventive or enforcement action.

6. The Organization shall ensure that States which are not Members of the United Nations act in accordance with these Principles so far as may be necessary for the maintenance of international peace and security.

7. Nothing contained in the present Charter shall authorize the United Nations to intervene in matters which are essentially within the domestic jurisdiction of any State or shall require the Members to submit such matters to settlement under the present Charter; but this principle shall not prejudice the application of enforcement measures under Chapter VII.

Chapter II: Membership

Article 3. The original Members of the United Nations shall be the States which, having participated in the United Nations Conference on International Organization at San Francisco, or having previously signed the Declaration by United Nations of January 1, 1942, sign the present Charter and ratify it in accordance with Article 110.

Article 4. 1. Membership in the United Nations is open to all other peace-loving States which accept the obligations contained in the present Charter and, in the judgement of the Organization, are able and willing to carry out these obligations.

2. The admission of any such State to membership in the United Nations will be effected by a decision of the General Assembly upon the recommendation of the Security Council.

Article 5. A Member of the United Nations against which preventive or enforcement action has been taken by the Security Council may be suspended from the exercise of the rights and privileges of membership by the General Assembly upon the recommendation of the Security Council. The exercise of these rights and privileges may be restored by the Security Council.

Article 6. A Member of the United Nations which has persistently violated the Principles contained in the present Charter may be expelled from the Organization by the General Assembly upon the recommendation of the Security Council.

Chapter III: Organs

Article 7. 1. There are established as the principal organs of the United Nations; a General Assembly, a Security Council, an Economic and Social Council, a Trusteeship Council, an International Court of Justice, and a Secretariat.

2. Such subsidiary organs as may be found necessary may be established in accordance with the present Charter.

Article 8. The United Nations shall place no restrictions on the eligibility of men and women to participate in any capacity and under conditions of equality in its principal and subsidiary organs.

Chapter IV: The General Assembly

COMPOSITION

Article 9. 1. The General Assembly shall consist of all the Members of the United Nations.

2. Each Member shall have not more than five representatives in the General Assembly.

FUNCTIONS AND POWERS

Article 10. The General Assembly may discuss any questions or any matter within the scope of the present Charter or relating to the powers and functions of any organs provided for in the present Charter, and, except as provided in Article 12, may make recommendations to the Members of the United Nations or to the Security Council or to both on any such questions or matters.

Article 11. 1. The General Assembly may consider the general principles of cooperation in the maintenance of international peace and security, including the principles governing disarmament and the regulation of armaments, and may make recommendations with regard to such principles to the Members or to the Security Council or to both.

2. The General Assembly may discuss any questions relating to the maintenance of international peace and security brought before it by any Member of the United Nations, or by the Security Council, or by a State which is not a Member of the United Nations in accordance with Article 35, paragraph 2, and, except as provided in Article 12, may make recommendations with regard to any such question to the State or States concerned or to the Security Council or to both. Any such question on which action is necessary shall be referred to the Security Council by the General Assembly either before or after discussion.

3. The General Assembly may call the attention of the Security Council to situations which are likely to endanger international peace and security.

4. The powers of the General Assembly set forth in this Article shall not limit the general scope of Article 10.

Article 12. 1. While the Security Council is exercising in respect of any dispute or situation the functions assigned to it in the present Charter, the General Assembly shall not make any recommendations with regard to that dispute or situation unless the Security Council so requests.

2. The Secretary-General, with the consent of the Security Council, shall notify the General Assembly at each session of any matters relative to the maintenance of international peace and security which are being dealt with by the Security Council and shall similarly notify the General Assembly, or the Members of the United Nations if the General Assembly is not in session, immediately the Security Council ceases to deal with such matters.

Article 13. 1. The General Assembly shall initiate studies and make recommendations for the purpose of:

(a) promoting international cooperation in the political field and encouraging the progressive development of international law and its codification;

(b) promoting international cooperation in the economic, social, cultural, educational, and health fields, and assisting in the realization of human rights and fundamental freedoms for all without distinction as to race, sex, language, or religion.

2. The further responsibilities, functions, and powers of the General Assembly with respect to matters mentioned in paragraph 1 (b) above are set forth in Chapters IX and X.

Article 14. Subject to the provisions of Article 12, the General Assembly may recommend measures for the peaceful adjustment of any situation, regardless of origin, which it deems likely to impair the general welfare or friendly relations among nations, including situations resulting from a violation of the provisions of the present Charter setting forth the Purposes and Principles of the United Nations.

Article 15. 1. The General Assembly shall receive and consider annual and special reports from the Security Council; these reports shall include an account of the measures that the Security Council has decided upon or taken to maintain international peace and security.

2. The General Assembly shall receive and consider reports from the other organs of the United Nations.

Article 16. The General Assembly shall perform such functions with respect to the international trusteeship system as are assigned to it under Chapters XII and XIII, including the approval of the trusteeship agreements for areas not designated as strategic.

Article 17. 1. The General Assembly shall consider and approve the budget of the Organization.

2. The expenses of the Organization shall be borne by the Members as apportioned by the General Assembly.

3. The General Assembly shall consider and approve any financial and budgetary arrangements with specialized agencies referred to in Article 57 and shall examine the administrative budgets of such specialized agencies with a view to making recommendations to the agencies concerned.

VOTING

Article 18. 1. Each member of the General Assembly shall have one vote.

2. Decisions of the General Assembly on important questions shall be made by a two-thirds majority of the members present and voting. These questions shall include: recommendations with respect to the maintenance of international peace and security, the election of the non-permanent members of the Security Council, the election of the members of the Economic and Social Council, the election of members of the Trusteeship Council in accordance with paragraph 1 (c) of Article 86, the admission of new Members to the United Nations, the suspension of the rights and privileges of membership, the expulsion of Members, questions relating to the operation of the trusteeship system, and budgetary questions.

3. Decisions on other questions, including the determination of additional categories of questions to be decided by a two-thirds majority, shall be made by a

majority of the members present and voting.

Article 19. A Member of the United Nations which is in arrears in the payment of its financial contributions to the Organization shall have no vote in the General Assembly if the amount of its arrears equals or exceeds the amount of the contributions due from it for the preceding two full years. The General Assembly may, nevertheless, permit such a Member to vote if it is satisfied that the failure to pay is due to conditions beyond the control of the Member.

PROCEDURE

Article 20. The General Assembly shall meet in regular annual sessions and in such special sessions as occasion may require. Special sessions shall be convoked by the Secretary-General at the request of the Security Council or of a majority of the Members of the United Nations.

Article 21. The General Assembly shall adopt its own rules of procedure. It shall elect its President for each session.

Article 22. The General Assembly may establish such subsidiary organs as it deems necessary for the performance of its functions.

Chapter V: The Security Council

COMPOSITION

Article 23. 1. The Security Council shall consist of fifteen Members of the United Nations. The Republic of China, France, the Union of Soviet Socialist Republics, the United Kingdom of Great Britain and Northern Ireland, and the United States of America shall be permanent members of the Security Council. The General Assembly shall elect ten other Members of the United Nations to be non-permanent members of the Security Council, due regard being specially paid, in the first instance to the contribution of Members of the United Nations to the maintenance of international peace and security and to the other purposes of the Organization, and also to equitable geographical distribution.

2. The non-permanent members of the Security Council shall be elected for a term of two years. In the first election of the non-permanent members after the increase of the membership of the Security Council from eleven to fifteen, two of the four additional members shall be chosen for a term of one year. A retiring member shall not be eligible for immediate re-election.

3. Each member of the Security Council shall have one representative.

FUNCTIONS AND POWERS

Article 24. 1. In order to ensure prompt and effective action by the United Nations, its Members confer on the Security Council primary responsibility for the maintenance of international peace and security, and agree that in carrying out its duties under this responsibility the Security Council acts on their behalf.

2. In discharging these duties the Security Council shall act in accordance with the Purposes and Principles of the United Nations. The specific powers granted to the Security Council for the discharge of these duties are laid down in Chapters VI, VII, VIII, and XII.

3. The Security Council shall submit annual and, when necessary, special reports to the General Assembly for its consideration.

Article 25. The Members of the United Nations agree to accept and carry out the decisions of the Security Council in accordance with the present Charter.

Article 26. In order to promote the establishment and maintenance of international peace and security with the least diversion for armaments of the world's human and economic resources, the Security Council shall be responsible for formulating, with the assistance of the Military Staff Committee referred to in Article 47, plans to be submitted to the Members of the United Nations for the establishment of a system for the regulation of armaments.

VOTING

Article 27. 1. Each member of the Security Council shall have one vote.

2. Decisions of the Security Council on procedural matters shall be made by an affirmative vote of nine members.

3. Decisions of the Security Council on all other matters shall be made by an affirmative vote of nine members including the concurring votes of the permanent members; provided that, in decisions under Chapter VI, and under paragraph 3 of Article 52, a party to a dispute shall abstain from voting.

PROCEDURE

Article 28. 1. The Security Council shall be so organized as to be able to function continuously. Each member of the Security Council shall for this purpose be represented at all times at the seat of the Organization.

2. The Security Council shall hold periodic meetings at which each of its members may, if it so desires, be represented by a member of the Government or by some other specially designated representative.

3. The Security Council may hold meetings at such places other than the seat of the Organization as in its judgement will best facilitate its work.

Article 29. The Security Council may establish such subsidiary organs as it deems necessary for the performance of its functions.

Article 30. The Security Council shall adopt its own rules of procedure, including the method of selecting its President.   *

Article 31. Any Member of the United Nations which is not a member of the Security Council may participate, without vote, in the discussion of any question brought before the Security Council whenever the latter considers that the interests of that Member are specially affected.

Article 32. Any Member of the United Nations which is not a member of the Security Council or any State which is not a Member of the United Nations, if it is a party to a dispute under consideration by the Security Council, shall be invited to participate, without vote, in the discussion relating to the dispute. The Security Council shall lay down such conditions as it deems just for the participation of a State which is not a Member of the United Nations.

Chapter VI: Pacific settlement of disputes

Article 33. 1. The parties to any dispute, the continuance of which is likely to endanger the maintenance of international peace and security, shall, first of all, seek a solution by negotiation, enquiry, mediation, conciliation, arbitration, judicial settlement, resort to regional agencies or arrangements, or other peaceful means of their own choice.

2. The Security Council shall, when it deems necessary, call upon the parties to settle their dispute by such means.

Article 34. The Security Council may investigate any dispute, or any situation which might lead to international friction or give rise to a dispute, in order to determine whether the continuance of the dispute or situation is likely to endanger the maintenance of international peace and security.

Article 35. 1. Any Member of the United Nations may bring any dispute, or any situation of the nature referred to in Article 34, to the attention of the Security Council or of the General Assembly.

2. A State which is not a Member of the United Nations may bring to the attention of the Security Council or of the General Assembly any dispute to which it is a party if it accepts in advance, for the purposes of the dispute, the obligations of pacific settlement provided in the present Charter.

3. The proceedings of the General Assembly in respect of matters brought to its attention under this Article will be subject to the provisions of Articles 11 and 12.

Article 36. 1. The Security Council may, at any stage of a dispute of the nature referred to in Article 33 or of a situation of like nature, recommend appropriate procedures or methods of adjustment.

2. The Security Council should take into consideration any procedures for the settlement of the dispute which have already been adopted by the parties.

3. In making recommendations under this Article the Security Council should also take into consideration that legal disputes should as a general rule be referred by the parties to the International Court of Justice in accordance with the provisions of the Statute of the Court.

Article 37. 1. Should the parties to a dispute of the nature referred to in Article 33 fail to settle it by the means indicated in that Article, they shall refer it to the Security Council.

2. If the Security Council deems that the continuance of the dispute is in fact likely to endanger the maintenance of international peace and security, it shall decide whether to take action under Article 36 or to recommend such terms of settlement as it may consider appropriate.

Article 38. Without prejudice to the provisions of Articles 33 to 37, the Security Council may, if all the parties to any dispute so request, make recommendations to the parties with a view to a pacific settlement of the dispute.

Chapter VII: Action with respect to threats to the peace, breaches of the peace, and acts of aggression

Article 39. The Security Council shall determine the existence of any threat to the peace, breach of the peace, or act of aggression and shall make recommendations, or decide what measures shall be taken in accordance with Articles 41 and 42, to maintain or restore international peace and security.

Article 40. In order to prevent an aggravation of the situation, the Security Council may, before making the recommenda-tions or deciding upon the measures provided for in Article 39, call upon the parties concerned to comply with such provisional measures as it deems necessary or desirable. Such provisional measures shall be without prejudice to the rights, claims, or position of the parties concerned. The Security Council shall duly take account of failure to comply with such provisional measures.

Article 41. The Security Council may decide what measures not involving the use of armed force are to be employed to give effect to its decisions, and it may call upon the Members of the United Nations to apply such measures. These may include complete or partial interruption of economic relations and of rail, sea, air, postal, telegraphic, radio, and other means of communication, and the sever-ance of diplomatic relations.

Article 42. Should the Security Council consider that measures provided for in Article 41 would be inadequate or have proved to be inadequate, it may take such action by air, sea, or land forces as may be necessary to maintain or restore inter-national peace and security. Such action may include demonstrations, blockade, and other operations by air, sea, or land forces of Members of the United Nations.

Article 43. 1. All Members of the United Nations, in order to contribute to the maintenance of international peace and security, undertake to make available to the Security Council, on its call and in accordance with a special agreement or agreements, armed forces, assistance, and facilities, including rights of passage, necessary for the purpose of maintaining international peace and security.

2. Such agreement or agreements shall govern the numbers and types of forces, their degree of readiness and general loca-tion, and the nature of the facilities and assistance to be provided.

3. The agreement or agreements shall be negotiated as soon as possible on the initiative of the Security Council. They shall be concluded between the Security

Council and Members or between the Security Council and groups of Members and shall be subject to ratification by the signatory States in accordance with their respective constitutional processes.

Article 44. When the Security Council has decided to use force it shall, before calling upon a Member not represented on it to provide armed forces in fulfilment of the obligations assumed under Article 43, invite that Member, if the Member so desires, to participate in the decisions of the Security Council concerning the employment of contingents of that Member's armed forces.

Article 45. In order to enable the United Nations to take urgent military measures, Members shall hold immediately available national airforce contingents for combined international enforcement action. The strength and degree of readiness of these contingents and plans for their combined action shall be determined, within the limits laid down in the special agreement or agreements referred to in Article 43, by the Security Council with the assistance of the Military Staff Committee.

Article 46. Plans for the application of armed force shall be made by the Security Council with the assistance of the Military Staff Committee.

Article 47. 1. There shall be established a Military Staff Committee to advise and assist the Security Council on all questions relating to the Security Council's military requirements for the maintenance of international peace and security, the employment and command of forces placed at its disposal, the regulation of armaments, and possible disarmament.

2. The Military Staff Committee shall consist of the Chiefs of Staff of the permanent members of the Security Council or their representatives. Any Member of the United Nations not permanently represented on the Committee shall be invited by the Committee to be associated with it when the efficient discharge of the

Committee's responsibilities requires the participation of that Member in its work.

3. The Military Staff Committee shall be responsible under the Security Council for the strategic direction of any armed forces placed at the disposal of the Security Council. Questions relating to the command of such forces shall be worked out subsequently.

4. The Military Staff Committee, with the authorization of the Security Council and after consultation with appropriate regional agencies, may establish regional sub-committees.

Article 48. 1. The action required to carry out the decisions of the Security Council for the maintenance of international peace and security shall be taken by all the Members of the United Nations or by some of them, as the Security Council may determine.

2. Such decisions shall be carried out by the Members of the United Nations directly and through their action in the appropriate international agencies of which they are members.

Article 49. The Members of the United Nations shall join in affording mutual assistance in carrying out the measures decided upon by the Security Council.

Article 50. If preventive or enforcement measures against any State are taken by the Security Council, any other State, whether a Member of the United Nations or not, which finds itself confronted with special economic problems arising from the carrying out of those measures shall have the right to consult the Security Council with regard to a solution of those problems.

Article 51. Nothing in the present Charter shall impair the inherent right of individual or collective self-defence if an armed attack occurs against a Member of the United Nations, until the Security Council has taken measures necessary to maintain international peace and security. Measures taken by Members in the exercise of this right of self-defence shall be immediately reported to the Security

Council and shall not in any way affect the authority and responsibility of the Security Council under the present Charter to take at any time such action as it deems necessary in order to maintain or restore international peace and security.

Chapter VIII: Regional arrangements

Article 52. 1. Nothing in the present Charter precludes the existence of regional arrangements or agencies for dealing with such matters relating to the maintenance of international peace and security as are appropriate for regional action, provided that such arrangements or agencies and their activities are consistent with the Purposes and Principles of the United Nations.

2. The Members of the United Nations entering into such arrangements or constituting such agencies shall make every effort to achieve pacific settlement of local disputes through such regional arrangements or by such regional agencies before referring them to the Security Council.

3. The Security Council shall encourage the development of pacific settlement of local disputes through such regional arrangements or by such regional agencies either on the initiative of the States concerned or by reference from the Security Council.

4. This Article in no way impairs the application of Articles 34 and 35.

Article 53. 1. The Security Council shall, where appropriate, utilize such regional arrangements or agencies for enforcement action under its authority. But no enforcement action shall be taken under regional arrangements or by regional agencies without the authorization of the Security Council, with the exception of measures against any Enemy State, as defined in paragraph 2 of this Article, provided for pursuant to Article 107 or in regional arrangements directed against renewal of aggressive policy on the part of any such State, until such time as the Organization may, on request of the Governments concerned, be charged with the responsibility for preventing further aggression by such a State.

2. The term Enemy State as used in paragraph 1 of this Article applies to any State which during the Second World War has been an enemy of any signatory of the present Charter.

Article 54. The Security Council shall at all times be kept fully informed of activities undertaken or in contemplation under regional arrangements or by regional agencies for the maintenance of international peace and security.

Chapter IX: International economic and social cooperation

Article 55. With a view to the creation of conditions of stability and well-being which are necessary for peaceful and friendly relations among nations based on respect for the principle of equal rights and self-determination of peoples, the United Nations shall promote:

(a) higher standards of living, full employment, and conditions of economic and social progress and development;

(b) solutions of international economic, social, health, and related problems; and international cultural and educational cooperation; and

(c) universal respect for, and observance of, human rights and fundamental freedoms for all without distinction as to race, sex, language, or religion.

Article 56. All Members pledge themselves to take joint and separate action in cooperation with the Organizatio. for the achievement of the purposes set forth in Article 55.

Article 57. 1. The various specialized agencies, established by intergovernmental agreement and having wide international responsibilities, as defined in their basic instruments, in economic, social, cultural, educational, health, and related fields, shall be brought into relationship with the United Nations in accordance with the provisions of Article 63.

2. Such agencies thus brought into re-

lationship with the United Nations are hereinafter referred to as specialized agencies.

Article 58. The Organization shall make recommendations for the coordination of the policies and activities of the specialized agencies.

Article 59. The Organization shall, where appropriate, initiate negotiations among the States concerned for the creation of any new specialized agencies required for the accomplishment of the purposes set forth in Article 55.

Article 60. Responsibility for the discharge of the functions of the Organization set forth in this Chapter shall be vested in the General Assembly and, under the authority of the General Assembly, in the Economic and Social Council, which shall have for this purpose the powers set forth in Chapter X.

Chapter X: The Economic and Social Council

COMPOSITION

Article 61. 1. The Economic and Social Council shall consist of twenty-seven Members of the United Nations elected by the General Assembly. . . .

FUNCTIONS AND POWERS

Article 62. 1. The Economic and Social Council may make or initiate studies and reports with respect to international economic, social, cultural, educational, health, and related matters and may make recommendations with respect to any such matters to the General Assembly, to the Members of the United Nations, and to the specialized agencies concerned. . . .

[*Articles 62–6.* Set out in detail these functions and powers.]

VOTING

Article 67. 1. Each member of the Economic and Social Council shall have one vote.

2. Decisions of the Economic and Social Council shall be made by a majority of the members present and voting.

[*Articles 68–72.* Set out in detail the procedure to be followed.]

Chapter XI: Declaration regarding non-self-governing territories

Article 73. Members of the United Nations which have or assume responsibilities for the administration of territories whose peoples have not yet attained a full measure of self-government recognize the principle that the interests of the inhabitants of these territories are paramount, and accept as a sacred trust the obligation to promote to the utmost, within the system of international peace and security established by the present Charter, the well-being of the inhabitants of these territories, and, to this end:

(a) to ensure, with due respect for the culture of the peoples concerned, their political, economic, social, and educational advancement, their just treatment, and their protection against abuses;

(b) to develop self-government, to take due account of the political aspirations of the peoples, and to assist them in the progressive development of their free political institutions, according to the particular circumstances of each territory and its peoples and their varying stages of advancement;

(c) to further international peace and security;

(d) to promote constructive measures of development, to encourage research, and to cooperate with one another and, when and where appropriate, with specialized international bodies with a view to the practical achievement of the social, economic, and scientific purposes set forth in this Article; and

(e) to transmit regularly to the Secretary-General for information purposes, subject to such limitation as security and constitutional considerations may require, statistical and other information of a technical nature relating to economic, social, and educational conditions in the territories for which they are respectively responsible other than those territories to which Chapters XII and XIII apply.

Article 74. Members of the United Nations also agree that their policy in respect of the territories to which this Chapter applies, no less than in respect of their metropolitan areas, must be based on the general principle of good-neighbourliness, due account being taken of the interests and well-being of the rest of the world, in social, economic, and commercial matters.

Chapter XII: International trusteeship system

Article 75. The United Nations shall establish under its authority an international trusteeship system for the administration and supervision of such territories as may be placed thereunder by subsequent individual agreements. These territories are hereinafter referred to as trust territories.

Article 76. The basic objectives of the trusteeship system, in accordance with the Purposes of the United Nations laid down in Article 1 of the present Charter, shall be:

(a) to further international peace and security;

(b) to promote the political, economic, social, and educational advancement of the inhabitants of the trust territories, and their progressive development towards self-government or independence as may be appropriate to the particular circumstances of each territory and its peoples and the freely expressed wishes of the peoples concerned, and as may be provided by the terms of each trusteeship agreement;

(c) to encourage respect for human rights and for fundamental freedoms for all without distinction as to race, sex, language, or religion, and to encourage recognition of the interdependence of the peoples of the world; and

(d) to ensure equal treatment in social, economic, and commercial matters for all Members of the United Nations and their nationals, and also equal treatment

for the latter in the administration of justice, without prejudice to the attainment of the foregoing objectives and subject to the provisions of Article 80.

Article 77. 1. The trusteeship system shall apply to such territories in the following categories as may be placed thereunder by means of trusteeship agreements:

(a) territories now held under mandate;

(b) territories which may be detached from Enemy States as a result of the Second World War; and

(c) territories voluntarily placed under the system by States responsible for their administration.

2. It will be a matter for subsequent agreement as to which territories in the foregoing categories will be brought under the trusteeship system and upon what terms.

Article 78. The trusteeship system shall not apply to territories which have become Members of the United Nations, relationship among which shall be based on respect for the principle of sovereign equality.

Article 79. The terms of trusteeship for each territory to be placed under the trusteeship system, including any alteration or amendment, shall be agreed upon by the States directly concerned, including the mandatory power in the case of territories held under mandate by a Member of the United Nations, and shall be approved as provided for in Articles 83 and 85.

Article 80. 1. Except as may be agreed upon in individual trusteeship agreements, made under Articles 77, 79, and 81, placing each territory under the trusteeship system, and until such agreements have been concluded, nothing in this Chapter shall be construed in or of itself to alter in any manner the rights whatsoever of any States or any peoples or the terms of existing international instruments to which Members of the United Nations may respectively be parties.

2. Paragraph 1 of this Article shall not be interpreted as giving grounds for delay or postponement of the negotiation and conclusion of agreements for placing mandated and other territories under the trusteeship system as provided for in Article 77.

Article 81. The trusteeship agreement shall in each case include the terms under which the trust territory will be administered and designate the authority which will exercise the administration of the trust territory. Such authority, hereinafter called the administering authority, may be one or more States or the Organization itself.

Article 82. There may be designated, in any trusteeship agreement, a strategic area or areas which may include part or all of the trust territory to which the agreement applies, without prejudice to any special agreement or agreements made under Article 43.

Article 83. 1. All functions of the United Nations relating to strategic areas, including the approval of the terms of trusteeship agreements and of their alteration or amendment, shall be exercised by the Security Council.

2. The basic objectives set forth in Article 76 shall be applicable to the people of each strategic area.

3. The Security Council shall, subject to the provisions of the trusteeship agreements and without prejudice to security considerations, avail itself of the assistance of the Trusteeship Council to perform those functions of the United Nations under the trusteeship system relating to political, economic, social, and educational matters in the strategic areas.

Article 84. It shall be the duty of the administering authority to ensure that the trust territory shall play its part in the maintenance of international peace and security. To this end the administering authority may make use of volunteer forces, facilities, and assistance from the trust territory in carrying out the obligations towards the Security Council undertaken in this regard by the administering authority, as well as for local defence and the maintenance of law and order within the trust territory.

Article 85. 1. The functions of the United Nations with regard to trusteeship agreements for all areas not designated as strategic, including the approval of the terms of the trusteeship agreements and of their alteration or amendment, shall be exercised by the General Assembly.

2. The Trusteeship Council, operating under the authority of the General Assembly, shall assist the General Assembly in carrying out these functions.

Chapter XIII: The Trusteeship Council

COMPOSITION

Article 86. 1. The Trusteeship Council shall consist of the following Members of the United Nations:

(a) those Members administering trust territories;

(b) such of those Members mentioned by name in Article 23 as are not administering trust territories; and

(c) as many other Members elected for three-year terms by the General Assembly as may be necessary to ensure that the total number of members of the Trusteeship Council is equally divided between those Members of the United Nations which administer trust territories and those which do not.

2. Each member of the Trusteeship Council shall designate one specially qualified person to represent it therein.

FUNCTIONS AND POWERS

Article 87. The General Assembly and, under its authority, the Trusteeship Council, in carrying out their functions, may:

(a) consider reports submitted by the administering authority;

(b) accept petitions and examine them in consultation with the administering authority;

(c) provide for periodic visits to the respective trust territories at times agreed upon with the administering authority; and

(d) take these and other actions in conformity with the terms of the trusteeship agreements.

Article 88. The Trusteeship Council shall formulate a questionnaire on the political, economic, social, and educational advancement of the inhabitants of each trust territory, and the administering authority for each trust territory within the competence of the General Assembly shall make an annual report to the General Assembly upon the basis of such questionnaire.

VOTING

Article 89. 1. Each member of the Trusteeship Council shall have one vote.

2. Decisions of the Trusteeship Council shall be made by a majority of the members present and voting.

PROCEDURE

Article 90. 1. The Trusteeship Council shall adopt its own rules of procedure, including the method of selecting its President....

Chapter XIV: The International Court of Justice

Article 92. The International Court of Justice shall be the principal judicial organ of the United Nations. It shall function in accordance with the annexed Statute, which is based upon the Statute of the Permanent Court of International Justice and forms an integral part of the present Charter.

Article 93. 1. All Members of the United Nations are *ipso facto* parties to the Statute of the International Court of Justice.

2. A State which is not a Member of the United Nations may become a party to the Statute of the International Court of Justice on conditions to be determined in each case by the General Assembly upon the recommendation of the Security Council.

Article 94. 1. Each Member of the United Nations undertakes to comply with the decision of the International Court of Justice in any case to which it is a party.

2. If any party to a case fails to perform the obligations incumbent upon it under a judgement rendered by the Court, the other party may have recourse to the Security Council, which may, if it deems necessary, make recommendations or decide upon measures to be taken to give effect to the judgement.

Article 95. Nothing in the present Charter shall prevent Members of the United Nations from entrusting the solution of their differences to other tribunals by virtue of agreements already in existence or which may be concluded in the future.

Article 96. 1. The General Assembly or the Security Council may request the International Court of Justice to give an advisory opinion on any legal question.

2. Other organs of the United Nations and specialized agencies, which may at any time be so authorized by the General Assembly, may also request advisory opinions of the Court on legal questions arising within the scope of their activities.

Chapter XV: The Secretariat

Article 97. The Secretariat shall comprise a Secretary-General and such staff as the Organization may require. The Secretary-General shall be appointed by the General Assembly upon the recommendation of the Security Council. He shall be the chief administrative officer of the Organization.

Article 98. The Secretary-General shall act in that capacity in all meetings of the General Assembly, of the Security Council, of the Economic and Social Council, and of the Trusteeship Council, and shall perform such other functions as are entrusted to him by these organs. The Secretary-General shall make an annual report to the General Assembly on the work of the Organization.

Article 99. The Secretary-General may bring to the attention of the Security Council any matter which in his opinion may threaten the maintenance of international peace and security.

Article 100. 1. In the performance of their duties the Secretary-General and the staff shall not seek or receive instructions from any Government or from any other authority external to the Organization. They shall refrain from any action which might reflect on their position as international officials responsible only to the Organization.

2. Each Member of the United Nations undertakes to respect the exclusively international character of the responsibilities of the Secretary-General and the staff and not to seek to influence them in the discharge of their responsibilities.

Article 101. 1. The staff shall be appointed by the Secretary-General under regulations established by the General Assembly. . . .

Chapter XVI: Miscellaneous provisions

Article 102. 1. Every treaty and every international agreement entered into by any Member of the United Nations after the present Charter comes into force shall as soon as possible be registered with the Secretariat and published by it.

2. No party to any such treaty or international agreement which has not been registered in accordance with the provisions of paragraph 1 of this Article may invoke that treaty or agreement before any organ of the United Nations.

Article 103. In the event of a conflict between the obligations of the Members of the United Nations under the present Charter and their obligations under any other international agreement, their obligations under the present Charter shall prevail.

[*Articles 104–5.* Legal privileges of the Organization and its representatives in member countries.]

Chapter XVII: Transitional security arrangements

Article 106. Pending the coming into force of such special agreements referred to in Article 43 as in the opinion of the Security Council enable it to begin the exercise of its responsibilities under Article 42, the parties to the Four Nation Declaration, signed at Moscow, October 30, 1943, and France, shall, in accordance with the provisions of paragraph 5 of that Declaration, consult with one another and as occasion requires with other Members of the United Nations with a view to such joint action on behalf of the Organization as may be necessary for the purpose of maintaining international peace and security.

Article 107. Nothing in the present Charter shall invalidate or preclude action, in relation to any State which during the Second World War has been an enemy of any signatory to the present Charter, taken or authorized as a result of that war by the Governments having responsibility for such action.

Chapter XVIII: Amendments

Article 108. Amendments to the present Charter shall come into force for all Members of the United Nations when they have been adopted by a vote of two-thirds of the members of the General Assembly and ratified in accordance with their respective constitutional processes by two-thirds of the Members of the United Nations, including all the permanent members of the Security Council.

Article 109. 1. A General Conference of the Members of the United Nations for the purpose of reviewing the present Charter may be held at a date and place to be fixed by a two-thirds vote of the members of the General Assembly and by a vote of any seven members of the Security Council. Each Member of the United Nations shall have one vote in the conference.

2. Any alteration of the present Charter recommended by a two-thirds vote of the conference shall take effect when ratified in accordance with their respective constitutional processes by two-thirds of the Members of the United Nations in-

cluding all the permanent members of the Security Council.

3. If such a conference has not been held before the tenth annual session of the General Assembly following the coming into force of the present Charter, the proposal to call such a conference shall be placed on the agenda of that session of the General Assembly, and the conference shall be held if so decided by a majority vote of the members of the General Assembly and by a vote of any seven members of the Security Council.

Chapter XIX: Ratification and signature

Article 110. 1. The present Charter shall be ratified by the signatory States in accordance with their respective constitutional processes.

2. The ratifications shall be deposited with the Government of the United States of America, which shall notify all the signatory States of each deposit as well as the Secretary-General of the Organization when he has been appointed.

3. The present Charter shall come into force upon the deposit of ratifications by the Republic of China, France, the Union of Soviet Socialist Republics, the United Kingdom of Great Britain and Northern Ireland, and the United States of America, and by a majority of the other signatory States. A Protocol of the ratifications deposited shall thereupon be drawn up by the Government of the United States of America which shall communicate copies thereof to all the signatory States.

4. The States signatory to the present Charter which ratify it after it has come into force will become original Members of the United Nations on the date of the deposit of their respective ratifications.

Article 111. The present Charter, of which the Chinese, French, Russian, English and Spanish texts are equally authentic, shall remain deposited in the archives of the Government of the United States of America. Duly certified copies thereof shall be transmitted by that Government to the Governments of the other signatory States.

IN FAITH WHEREOF the representatives of the Governments of the United Nations have signed the present Charter.

DONE at the city of San Francisco the twenty-sixth day of June, one thousand nine hundred and forty-five.

Articles of Agreement of the International Monetary Fund, Washington, 27 December 1945

The Governments on whose behalf the present Agreement is signed agree as follows:

Introductory Article. The International Monetary Fund is established and shall operate in accordance with the following provisions:

Article I: Purposes. The purposes of the International Monetary Fund are:

(I) To promote international monetary cooperation through a permanent institution which provides the machinery for consultation and collaboration on international monetary problems.

(II) To facilitate the expansion and balanced growth of international trade, and to contribute thereby to the promotion and maintenance of high levels of employment and real income and to the development of the productive resources of all members as primary objectives of economic policy.

(III) To promote exchange stability, to

maintain orderly exchange arrangements among members, and to avoid competitive exchange depreciation.

(IV) To assist in the establishment of a multilateral system of payments in respect of current transactions between members and in the elimination of foreign exchange restrictions which hamper the growth of world trade.

(V) To give confidence to members by making the Fund's resources available to them under adequate safeguards, thus providing them with opportunity to correct maladjustments in their balance of payments without resorting to measures destructive of national or international prosperity.

(VI) In accordance with the above, to shorten the duration and lessen the degree of disequilibrium in the international balances of payments of members.

The Fund shall be guided in all its decisions by the purposes set forth in this Article.

Articles of Agreement of the International Bank for Reconstruction and Development, 27 December 1945

The Governments on whose behalf the present Agreement is signed agree as follows:

Introductory Article. The International Bank for Reconstruction and Development is established and shall operate in accordance with the following provisions:

Article I: Purposes. The purposes of the Bank are:

(I) To assist in the reconstruction and development of territories of members by facilitating the investment of capital for productive purposes, including the restoration of economies destroyed or disrupted by war, the reconversion of productive facilities to peacetime needs and the encouragement of the development of productive facilities and resources in less developed countries.

(II) To promote private foreign investment by means of guarantees or participations in loans and other investments made by private investors; and when private capital is not available on reasonable terms, to supplement private investment by providing, on suitable conditions, finance for productive purposes out of its own capital, funds raised by it and its other resources.

(III) To promote the long-range balanced growth of international trade and the maintenance of equilibrium in balances of payments by encouraging international investment for the development of the productive resources of members, thereby assisting in raising productivity, the standard of living and conditions of labour in their territories.

(IV) To arrange the loans made or guaranteed by it in relation to international loans through other channels so that the more useful and urgent projects, large and small alike, will be dealt with first.

(V) To conduct its operations with due regard to the effect of international investment on business conditions in the territories of members and, in the immediate post-war years, to assist in bringing about a smooth transition from a wartime to a peacetime economy.

The Bank shall be guided in all its decisions by the purposes set forth above.

XI · The peace treaties, 1945–72

Peace treaties between some of the belligerents of the Second World War were signed, after much wrangling, within a few years after the end of the war, but the attempt to reach a final peace treaty and comprehensive settlement with Germany was tacitly abandoned for the foreseeable future and instead an interim settlement was concluded with and between the two Germanies in 1972.

The Potsdam Conference in July 1945 (p. 231) laid down the procedures to be followed to arrive at peace settlements and charged the Council of Foreign Ministers to draft peace treaties immediately with Italy, Rumania, Bulgaria, Hungary and Finland. A peace settlement for Germany was expected to take longer to conclude since in 1945 the time seemed distant and uncertain when a German Government could be re-established that could accept and sign a peace treaty with the Allies. Not all members of the Council of Foreign Ministers were to participate in the drafting of peace terms but only those representing States signatory to the terms of surrender of the enemy State concerned. China thus only had a voice in the Far Eastern settlements. France was entitled to participate in the Italian treaty and, it was understood, would participate in any eventual treaty with Germany. The United States would play no part in the treaty with Finland. The Great Powers would draft the treaties and then submit them to the other Allies for approval. The special position of the Great Powers in their peacemaking role was thus emphasized as it had been at Paris in 1919 and at Vienna in 1814–15.

Allied peacemaking: the first phase, September 1945–February 1947

For more than a year there six major rounds of Allied negotiations: the Council of Foreign Ministers in London (September–October 1945), the Foreign

Ministers Meeting of the U.S.S.R., U.S.A. and Great Britain in Moscow (December 1945), the Council of Foreign Ministers Meetings in Paris (April–May 1946 and June–July 1946), followed by the Paris Peace Conference of twenty-one nations (29 July–15 October 1946) and a final Council of Foreign Ministers Meeting in New York (4 November–12 December 1946). From these negotiations there emerged the drafts of peace treaties with Italy, Rumania, Bulgaria, Hungary and Finland. Peace treaties with these States were formally concluded in February 1947.

THE ITALIAN PEACE TREATY, 10 FEBRUARY 1947 (p. 277)

Eleven headings and seventeen annexes made up the treaty between Italy on the one hand and the Allied and Associated Powers on the other. The preamble acknowledges that the Fascist régime was overthrown not only in consequence of Allied victory but also 'with the assistance of the democratic elements of the Italian people'. Territorially Italy was re-established in its frontiers of 1 January 1938 with a number of important exceptions. The conquests of Albania and Ethiopia were annulled, the Dodecanese ceded to Greece and some Italian islands in the Adriatic were ceded to Greece and to Yugoslavia. There were territorial adjustments involving Italian cessions along the boundary between Italy and France.

It was the eastern frontier of Italy that caused the greatest diplomatic difficulties. The larger part of the Venezia Giulia peninsula including Fiume was ceded to Yugoslavia by the peace treaty. Trieste with a small hinterland, formerly Italian, was set up as the *Free Territory of Trieste* under the guarantee of the Security Council of the U.N. The Free Territory was divided into Zone A, comprising mainly the city of Trieste, to be administered by Britain and the United States, and a Zone B under Yugoslav administration. Britain and the United States after 1948 gradually handed their Trieste zone over to the Italians. By October 1954 a settlement was reached between the Four Powers (U.S.S.R., U.S., Great Britain and France), Yugoslavia and Italy whereby nearly all of Zone A reverted to Italy while Zone B, with a small addition, was ceded to Yugoslavia; Trieste retained its status as a free port and the rights of ethnic minorities were safeguarded.

The Italians continued to retain the south Tyrolean region of Bolzano which led to disturbances among some of its German-speaking population and to differences with Austria. A comprehensive Italian–Austrian settlement of these differences in principle was reached on 30 November 1969 after long negotiations.

The future of the Italian African colonies of Libya, Eritrea and Somaliland was not settled by the peace treaty. The treaty provided that if the Four

Powers failed to reach agreement within one year of the coming into force of the peace treaty, then the matter was to be referred to the General Assembly of the United Nations. Under the auspices of the U.N., Libya became independent in December 1951, an autonomous Eritrea was federated to Ethiopia in 1952 and in 1950 Somaliland became a U.N. trust territory under Italian administration, leading to the independence of Somalia in 1960 formed by unifying previously British and Italian administered Somalilands.

The Italian navy, army and air force were limited until modified 'by agreement between the Allied and Associated Powers and Italy or, after Italy becomes a member of the United Nations, by agreement between the Security Council and Italy'.

The political clauses of the Italian peace treaty included provisions for human rights and fundamental freedoms, and specifically an obligation that Fascist and other anti-democratic organizations would not be permitted to revive. The treaty also provided for the trial of war criminals. Military clauses limited Italian armaments so that Italy would not again be able to wage aggressive war, but it was, however, foreseen that the military clauses might later be relaxed in two circumstances: 'in whole or in part by agreement between the Allied and Associated Powers and Italy . . .' (Article 46), or secondly if an agreement were reached between Italy and the Security Council once Italy had been admitted to membership of the U.N. Allied troops were to be withdrawn by December 1947. Reparations were exacted and the Soviet Union was to receive some 100 million dollars over a period of seven years; other reparation payments were to be paid to Yugoslavia (125 million dollars), Greece (105 million dollars), Ethiopia (25 million dollars) and Albania (5 million dollars). France, Britain and the U.S. agreed to forgo their reparations claims.

THE PEACE TREATIES WITH RUMANIA, HUNGARY, BULGARIA AND FINLAND

These were all concluded at the same time as the Italian treaty, on 10 February 1947, and followed it in their form and structure. The political clauses of these treaties guaranteed human rights and the elimination of Fascist organizations. In 1949 Great Britain and the United States complained that the peoples of Rumania, Hungary and Bulgaria were not enjoying the fundamental freedoms so guaranteed. The military clauses placed limitations on the armed forces of the defeated States. Reparations were paid as follows: Rumania and Finland to pay 300 million dollars each to the Soviet Union; Hungary to pay 200 million dollars to the Soviet Union, and 100 million dollars each to Czechoslovakia and Yugoslavia; Bulgaria to pay 45 million dollars to Greece and 25 million dollars to Yugoslavia. The re-establishment of international control over, and freedom of, navigation along the Danube was not finally settled in the peace treaties but became a matter of serious dispute between the Soviet Union and the Western Powers. In 1950 the Soviet Union took the lead in establishing a Six Power Danube Commission excluding Austria and the Western Powers. The United States, Great Britain and France refused to recognize this commission for it deprived Greece, Britain, France and Italy and Belgium of their rights under the treaty of 1921; Austria and Germany were not represented either.

The peace treaties brought about a number of territorial changes. *Bulgaria* was recognized within its frontiers of 1 January 1941; by this settlement Bulgaria retained the southern Dobruja acquired by an earlier Axis treaty from Rumania in September 1940. But Bulgaria returned Serbian territory to Yugoslavia and Western Thrace to Greece.

Hungary was required to return northern Transylvania, acquired in the Vienna Award of August 1940 (p. 183), to Rumania. Hungary also had to return to Czechoslovakia southern Slovakia, which had been secured after the Munich Conference in 1938 (p. 176), and also to cede additional Hungarian territory across the Danube opposite Bratislava to Czechoslovakia.

Rumania: the cession of Bessarabia and northern Bukovina to the U.S.S.R., first occupied by Russia in June 1940, was now confirmed in 1947. The Soviet Union retained a special right in 1947 to maintain enough troops in Rumania and Hungary to safeguard its communications with the Red Army in the Soviet zone of Austria until the conclusion of a State treaty with Austria.

Finland confirmed the cession of three territories to the Soviet Union originally ceded in 1940: the province of Petsamo, an area along the central portion of the Soviet–Finnish frontier, and the province of the Karelian isthmus in south-eastern Finland. The Soviet Union renounced its right to the lease of the Hango Peninsula, but secured instead a fifty-year lease of the Porkkala–Udd area as a naval base to protect the entrance to the Gulf of Finland; this lease was terminated by Russia in 1955.

Allied peacemaking: the second phase, the Austrian State Treaty

More than eight years elapsed after the conclusion of the five peace treaties of 1947 before the Soviet Union, Britain, the United States and France could agree on the terms of the next treaty, that with Austria. Although the three Foreign Ministers' Meeting in Moscow in 1943 had issued a declaration that Britain, the United States and the Soviet Union wished 'to see re-established a free and independent Austria', Austria in July 1945 was placed under military occupation and administration and divided into four zones, French, American, Soviet and British, Vienna being placed under their joint administration. The road to Austrian independence proved slow. In April 1945 a provisional Austrian Government under Dr Karl Renner as Chancellor was established, with the approval of the Soviet occupation authority. Allied recognition was granted in October 1945 and elections were held in November 1945. Karl Renner became president and Leopold Figl chancellor, but Austria remained under Four Power military occupation. Austria was not required to sign a 'peace treaty' since according to Allied declarations Austria was regarded as a victim of German aggression at the time of the *Anschluss* in March 1938. The treaty completely re-establishing Austrian sovereignty was therefore referred to as a 'State Treaty'.

Three specific differences between the Soviet Union and the Western Powers led to delay in the conclusion of negotiations: the transfer to the Soviet Union and Yugoslavia of 'German' assets in Austria sufficient to meet demands for reparations (it had been agreed at Potsdam that Austria was to pay no reparations); Yugoslav claims, supported by the Soviet Union, to territorial cessions; finally, ideological disputes as to what constituted 'democracy'. More important than these specific issues were the Great Power considerations and strategy of the 'cold war'. The Soviet Union for a time hoped to link concessions over Austria with a German settlement more favourable to the Soviet interests. In 1955 a change of Soviet policy at last made the Austrian State Treaty possible. In practice the Soviet Union secured Austrian neutrality and non-participation in the NATO alliance, in return for agreeing to withdraw its occupation forces and zonal administration. Austrian neutrality was not written into the State Treaty but promulgated as a constitutional law by the Austrian Parliament on 26 October 1955. It stated that with the object of a lasting and perpetual maintenance of Austrian independence, Austria declared of her own free will her perpetual neutrality which she would defend by all means at her disposal; Austria would join no military alliances or permit foreign bases of foreign States on her territory.

The Austrian State Treaty of 15 May 1955 (p. 281) re-established Austria within the frontiers of 1 January 1938 (Article 5) as a sovereign and independent State. Germany in the peace treaty would be required to recognize Austrian independence and renounce all territorial and political claims on Austria, and Austria and Germany were prohibited from forming a political or economic union (Articles 3 and 4). The treaty contained articles guaranteeing human rights (Article 6), minority rights (Article 7), democratic institutions (Article 8), provided for the dissolution of Nazi organizations (Article 9); a number of articles prevented Austrian acquisition of special weapons, such as the atomic bomb and German and Japanese aircraft. Austria was not required to pay reparations, but was obliged to meet Soviet financial reparation claims from 'German' assets by paying 150 million dollars over six years, and by granting for thirty years extensive concessions to oilfields equivalent to 60 per cent of the extraction of oil in Austria for 1947. All the occupying forces agreed to withdraw not later than 31 December 1955. With the signature of the State Treaty with Austria, on 15 May 1955, the Soviet Union lost its right to station troops in Hungary and Rumania in accordance with the peace treaties of 1947, but the signature of the *Warsaw Pact on 14 May 1955* (p. 365) permitted the Soviet Union to continue to retain garrisons in these two countries.

The Western Peace Treaty with Japan

In August 1945, after Japan's surrender to the Allies, General Douglas MacArthur was appointed Supreme Allied Commander and American troops predominantly provided the occupation forces of Japan. The Emperor, a Japanese Government and Diet under the overall authority and supervision of the Supreme Commander governed the country. The seven Allied Powers who had been at war with Japan were represented on the *Far Eastern Commission* in Washington, which came into being in the spring of 1946 together with an Allied Council in Tokyo. In practice the United States, represented by General MacArthur, maintained its predominant influence in carrying through the occupation policies of the Allies with the broad objectives of democratizing and demilitarizing Japan. In 1946 a new constitution was promulgated for Japan. Its preamble pledged the people to maintain the high ideals of the democratic constitution, dedicated to peaceful cooperation among nations and the blessings of liberty. The Emperor's powers were limited to those of a constitutional monarch; henceforth he became only 'the symbol of the state of the unity of all the people' and his position derived 'from the will of the people with whom resides sovereign power'. In Article 9 of the constitution war was renounced and no armed forces were to be maintained. 'Aspiring sincerely to an international peace based on justice and order, the Japanese people forever renounce war as a sovereign right of the nation and the threat or use of force as means of settling territorial disputes. In order to accomplish the aim of the preceding paragraph, land, sea, and air forces, as well as other war potential, will never be maintained. The right of belligerency of the State will not be recognized.'

The surrender limited Japanese sovereignty from north to south, to the islands of Honshu, Hokkaido, Kyushu and Shikoku, together with some minor islands. The Kurile islands and southern Sakhalin were administered by the Soviet Union; in Korea, Japanese forces north of latitude 38° surrendered to the Russians and south to the Americans, thus creating two military zones. Soviet forces withdrew from North Korea in October 1948 after the establishment of a communist North Korean Government; the United States withdrew from South Korea in June 1949 where a Government was also established under U.N. auspices. Formosa and the Pescadores were handed over to China; the Ryuku Islands including Okinawa were placed under U.S. administration, and the Japanese league trusteeship of Germany's former Pacific islands became United Nations strategic trust territory under American administration. In preparing a peace treaty for Japan, the Soviet Union on the one hand and the Western Powers on the other were soon in dispute. A breach occurred over the rejection in January 1950 of the Soviet demand that the Nationalist Chinese representative on the Far Eastern Commission be replaced by the representative of the People's Republic of China, and the consequent Soviet withdrawal from the Far Eastern Commission. The years from 1949 to 1950 brought about far-reaching changes in Eastern Asia and fundamental reappraisals of Great Power diplomacy. In 1949 the Communist Chinese defeated the Nationalist Chinese, who under the leadership of Chiang Kai-shek withdrew to Taiwan (Formosa). On 25 June 1950 the Korean War began, involving the North Koreans and eventually Chinese 'volunteers' on the one side, and the South Koreans and the United States and U.N. allies, who came to the defence of South Koreans, on the other. For the United States these events led to basic important policy decisions to maintain a line of defence including Taiwan, Japan and South Korea. In the midst of the Korean War, the United States resolved to conclude a peace treaty with Japan even if Soviet approval could not be won, and to convert a defeated enemy into a willing ally. President Harry Truman sent Ambassador John Foster Dulles to America's principal allies to work out an agreed draft peace treaty. Then, on the basis of an Anglo-American draft, the United States and Britain invited the fifty nations which had declared war on Japan to a Peace Conference at San Francisco to meet in September 1951. The Soviet Union was included in the invitation, but not China, either Nationalist or Communist (the three associated States of Indo-China on the other hand received an invitation). India, Burma and Yugoslavia declined the invitation. The Soviet Union, Poland and Czechoslovakia attended, but refused to sign the treaty.

The Japanese Peace Treaty of 8 September 1951 (p. 283), negotiated substantially in advance before the San Francisco conference opened, was only signed by the majority of nations at war with Japan and not by the U.S.S.R. nor either of the Chinas. The territorial terms corresponded to the dispositions at the end of the war, and Japan renounced its rights to all territories surrendered by the armistice of 2 September 1945, and all special rights in China. But no title of possession over former Japanese territories, the Kuriles and southern Sakhalin was granted to the U.S.S.R. or over Taiwan to China. The peace treaty established that in principle Japan should pay reparations, but left amounts to later bilateral negotiations. Japan agreed to follow the principles of the U.N. Charter as well as internationally accepted fair practices in trade and commerce. Sovereignty and independence was restored to Japan, and the occupation régime was to end ninety days after the treaty became effective; but the treaty did not prevent the stationing of foreign troops in consequence of a treaty made by Japan with one or more Allied Powers. Comparing the Japanese peace treaty with the European peace treaties already negotiated, there is one marked feature of difference in the absence from the Japanese treaty of military clauses restricting the military forces of Japan. As has been noted earlier, the Japanese constitution of 1946 forbade the maintenance of any Japanese armed forces. Article 5 of the peace treaty promised Japanese assistance in action taken in accordance with the U.N. Charter (the Korean War), and the Allied Powers who were signatories confirmed Japan's 'inherent right of individual or collective self-defence' referred to in Article 51 of the Charter of the United Nations, which permitted Japan to voluntarily enter into collective security arrangements.

On the same day the peace treaty was signed, a *Japanese–United States Security Treaty, 8 September 1951* (p. 286), which came into force on ratification in April 1952 (p. 310), was concluded which allowed the United States to maintain armed forces 'in and about Japan', and at the request of the Japanese Government to use U.S. forces to put down large scale internal riots in Japan caused by the instigation or intervention of an outside Power. Japan undertook not to grant to any other country either bases or garrisons without the prior consent of the United States. This treaty was one of a number of Far Eastern treaties negotiated by the U.S. at the time.

The *Japanese–United States Security Treaty, 8 September 1951* (p. 286), was replaced by the signature of a *Treaty of Mutual Cooperation and Security between the United States and Japan on 19 January 1960* (p. 287) and entered into force on 23 June 1960. The growth and economic transformation of Japan during the decade of the 1950s, the demands for equal treatment and, as victims of the first nuclear bombs, the desire for security with minimal military involvement, made the revision of the treaty a passionate issue of Japanese politics. American troops stationed in Japan were greatly reduced. The treaty of 1960 contained important revisions: it removed all derogations of sovereignty, and acknowledged that Japanese forces could only be used in self-defence. The United States (Article 6), for the purpose of contributing to the security of Japan and the maintenance of international peace and security in the Far East, was granted the continued use of bases in Japan for its land, air and naval forces. The use of these facilities was governed by a separate exchange of notes whereby the United States agreed on prior consultation with the Japanese Government before increasing U.S. forces in Japan, making any essential change of arming its forces (nuclear weapons), and using any bases under Japanese rule outside the treaty area. On 22 June 1970 the Japanese Government announced its intention to continue the Security Treaty of 1970, which would remain in force indefinitely unless either country gave one year's notice to terminate it. Negotiations for the return of the Ryuku Islands and Okinawa were concluded by a *Japanese–United States Treaty signed on 17 June 1971*: the islands were to revert to Japan and they were returned in the spring of 1972; the Mutual Security Treaty became fully applicable to them and Japan granted continued use of bases to America on the same conditions as agreed under the Security Treaty of 1960. Meantime in 1956 the Soviet Union concluded a Fisheries Agreement with Japan and diplomatic relations were formally re-established; the Soviet Union has retained the former Japanese-governed southernmost Kurile islands as well as the southern half of Sakhalin Island.

In September 1972 Japan re-established diplomatic relations and recognized the People's Republic of China (mainland China). A nine-point joint statement on 29 September 1972 was issued by the Prime Ministers of China and Japan, Chou En-lai and Kakuei Tanaka, whose most important provisions are that Japan recognizes the Government of the People's Republic of China as the 'sole legal government of China', that 'the Government of the People's Republic of China reaffirms that Taiwan is an inalienable part of the territory of the People's Republic of China. The Government of Japan fully understands and respects this stand of the Government of China and adheres to its stand of complying with Article 8 of the Potsdam proclamation.' In conformity with the U.N. Charter all their disputes are to be settled by peaceful means; the 'normalization of relations between China and Japan is not directed against third countries. Neither of the two countries should seek hegemony in the Asia–Pacific region and each country is opposed to efforts by any other country or group of countries to establish such hegemony.' Negotiations are to be held, aimed at concluding a treaty of peace and friendship, and agreements on trade and other matters of mutual benefit are to be negotiated. On the same day the Chinese Republic (Taiwan) broke off diplomatic relations with Japan. Thus by the autumn of 1972 Japan had established normal relations with the Soviet Union and Communist China. Full peace treaties with these two States remain to be concluded; Japan desires to restore Japanese sovereignty over some of the Kurile islands, and the Soviet Union may be willing to give up the two most southernmost islands lying closest to Japan.

Towards a German settlement, 1945–72

The frontiers of the Federal Republic of Germany and the German Democratic Republic have their origins in Allied decisions reached in 1944 before the end of the war, and in the action of the Allies jointly and individually in 1945. The Moscow Conference in October 1943 had set up the European Advisory Commission, which prepared draft agreements delimiting the three zones of Germany respectively to be occupied by the U.S.S.R., the United States and Great Britain. The commission also proposed three zones of occupation for Greater Berlin, which was treated separately. To have allowed one Power (and geography would have decreed that this must be the U.S.S.R.) the sole right to occupy the capital would, in the views of the other two Powers, have allowed too much weight and prestige in Germany as a whole to the U.S.S.R. In these original agreements, based on the proposals of the European Advisory Commission dated 12 September 1944 and amended and made more specific in a supplementary agreement on 14 November 1944, the occupying forces of each zone were placed under the authority of a Commander-in-Chief of the country occupying the zone. Berlin was treated separately; the city was placed under the joint control of an Allied governing authority composed of three Commandants appointed by their respective Commanders-in-Chief. This distinction remains an important fact relating to the status of Berlin.

The Yalta Conference in February 1945 (p. 226) confirmed and expanded the agreements reached by the European Advisory Commission. The Russian, British and American zones of Germany, and the joint control and individual zones of the three Powers in Berlin, were agreed upon. Agreement was reached on inviting France to become the fourth occupying Power of Germany with equal rights. The French zone was to be formed out of the British and American zones. The Russian zone extended to the eastern frontiers of Germany of 31 December 1931. The Yalta Protocol VII, however, envisaged that territory of eastern Germany would be transferred to Poland: 'The three Heads of Government . . . recognize that Poland must receive substantial annexations of territory in the North and West. They feel that the opinion of the new Polish Provincial Government of National Unity should be sought in due course on the extent of these annexations and that the final delimitation of the western frontier of Poland should thereafter await the peace conference.' At Yalta, Protocol IV, the establishment of an Allied Control Council for

Germany, was briefly referred to in connection with inviting French membership.

On 1 June 1945 the Four Powers were still not in occupation of the precise zones assigned to them; when hostilities ended American and British troops held portions of the zone assigned to the U.S.S.R., and the respective occupation of Berlin by the Four Powers remained to be completed. On *5 June 1945* the four Commanders-in-Chief met in Berlin and signed a *Four Power Declaration on the assumption of supreme authority in Germany* (p. 290), which also set out guidelines for the behaviour of the Germans. But the Soviet Marshal Zhukov rejected the setting up of the Allied Control Council until still unsettled boundaries had been determined (French zone) and the forces of each occupying Power had withdrawn within their zonal boundaries. A joint statement was also issued on 5 June 1945 by the Allies concerning the agreements so far reached on zones of occupation and the administration of Germany. It described the function and composition of the Allied Control Council for Germany, composed of the four Commanders-in-Chief, which was to be paramount in matters affecting Germany as a whole; but the Commanders-in-Chief were the supreme authority, each in his own sphere. Berlin would be administered by the Four Powers jointly, the four appointed Commandants contributing an Allied *Komendatura* responsible to an Allied Control Council for Greater Berlin. A timetable for effecting the military withdrawals was agreed. The American and British forces were back in their zones and their garrisons in their respective Berlin sectors by 4 July 1945, and on 30 August 1945 the Allied Council proclaimed that it had begun to function. Since each Commander-in-Chief was supreme in his own zone as well, any disagreement at the Allied Control Council could only have the negative effect of preventing action on 'matters affecting Germany as a whole' without limiting the supreme authority of each Commander-in-Chief in his zone.

In the summer of 1945 a number of important issues remained to be settled. The question of U.S., British and French access to their three sectors in Berlin, embedded as they were in the Soviet zone of Germany, was first resolved in a preliminary way at a conference between the Allied Commanders in Berlin on 29 June 1945, which guaranteed the use of one main rail line, one highway and two air corridors to the three Western Powers. At meetings of the Allied Control Council these agreements were finalized and approved. A few months later, on *30 November*, the *Allied Control Council* provided three air corridors (in place of two) between Berlin and the British and American zones, and it was specifically stated that 'flight over these routes (corridors) will be conducted without previous notice being given, by aircraft of the nations governing Germany' (p. 291). An Allied Berlin Air Safety Centre was established to ensure the safety of all flights in the Berlin area. These rights of access derived from the arrangement for joint occupation and joint control of 'Greater Berlin' which France, Britain and the United States have continued to maintain.

The eastern frontier of Germany (western frontier of Poland) was one of the principal issues of the Potsdam Conference of July 1945 (p. 231). By the time the leaders of the Big Three, the U.S., U.S.S.R., and Great Britain, attended the conference, the Red Army was in occupation of the whole of its German zone of occupation, as defined in inter-Allied agreements before Yalta and confirmed at the Yalta Conference; but the Soviet authorities had already handed a part of their zone over to the Poles in unilateral fulfilment of the general promise made at Yalta that Poland 'must receive substantial annexations of territory'. The *fait accompli* was partially accepted in section VIII of the Potsdam Conference Protocol. The German territories were not annexed and did not formally become a part of Poland since the Protocol stated 'that the final delimitation of the western frontier of Poland should await the peace settlement'; the extent of German territory handed over to Poland was agreed to at Potsdam, and this territory was placed 'under the administration of the Polish State'; it was also separated from the rest of Germany by a specific reference that it did not form part of the Soviet zone of occupation. The 1972 frontier between the German Democratic Republic and Poland corresponds to the Potsdam provisional delimitation; the relevant Potsdam section VIII did not mention the German town of Stettin which lies *west* of the Oder, but an earlier Western memorandum had specifically included Stettin as falling into Polish-administered territory, and it is now Polish Szczecin.

The western frontier of the present German Federal Republic also corresponds to the western zonal boundaries that Britain and the United States confirmed at Yalta and Potsdam, with some minor adjustments in favour of the Netherlands and Belgium agreed as 'provisional rectifications' in March 1949. More important, the Saar region (a territory larger than the pre-war Saar) was for a time integrated economically with France but given autonomous status by the French from 1947 to 1956. With the adoption of the Schuman Plan in April 1951, which led to the setting up of the High Authority of the European Coal and Steel Community controlling the pooled Franco-German iron and steel production, including that of the Saar, the Saar problem as a cause of Franco-German contention lost some of its significance (p. 388). An agreement between France and Germany, leading to a plebiscite in October 1955 and elections soon after, closed the issue and the Saar region was reunited with the Federal Republic of Germany on 1 January 1957.

The creation of the Federal German Republic as an independent sovereign State on 5 May 1955 came about in a number of important stages. The gradual recovery of West German sovereignty was closely bound up both with the 'cold war' situation and the movement towards Western European unity (p. 386). Disagreements between the four Powers responsible for Germany, especially between the Soviet Union and the Western Allies, were reflected in the inability of the Council of Foreign Ministers during 1946 and 1947 to make any real progress towards a peace settlement for Germany as a whole. The breakdown of inter-Allied control of Germany in 1948 accentuated the different interpretations and applications of Allied agreements in the respective zones of the occupying Powers.

In mid-June 1948 the Soviet authorities blocked the access of France, Britain and the U.S. to Berlin by road and rail, but did not block the air corridors. The *Berlin blockade* was raised by the Soviet authorities in May 1949 and the rights of access of the three Western Powers reaffirmed. Meantime, in November 1948, the Soviet authorities set up a separate communist Municipal Government in the Soviet sector, and thus the unity of Berlin under joint Allied authority was disrupted. The Soviet authorities and the Government of the German Democratic Republic (established in the Soviet zone on 7 October 1949) increasingly prevented the movement of Germans between East and West. But a flood of refugees continued to leave the German Democratic Republic through 'Greater Berlin' by passing from the Soviet sector to one of the western sectors. The virtually complete sealing-off of the German Democratic Republic occurred on 13 August 1961 when a fortified wall was built along the Soviet sector of Berlin. The flow of East Germans leaving for West Germany was effectively stopped. While the German Democratic Republic declares that the Soviet sector of Berlin constitutes the 'capital' and an integral part of the D.D.R., the Soviet Government in the *Four Power Berlin Agreement of 3 September 1971* continues to accept responsibility for the rights of Britain, France and the United States originating in the wartime agreements, and acknowledges the links between the Federal Republic of Germany and West Berlin. France, Britain and the United States for their part, while supporting the close relations of West Berlin and the Federal Republic, continue to maintain the special status of the whole of Greater Berlin and to station military garrisons in the western sectors.

In 1969 negotiations were initiated by the Federal German Government headed by Chancellor Willy Brandt to break the deadlock over a German peace settlement. It involved on the Federal German side a willingness to accept the authority of the German Democratic Republic as a negotiating partner and as possessing some of the attributes of a State, but not recognition of the D.D.R. as a full sovereign State. The outcome of these initiatives was the formal signature of a *treaty between Poland and the Federal Republic of Germany on 7 December*

1970 (p. 294) in which both countries agreed to the existing boundary line of the Oder and the western Neisse and on the inviolability of their existing frontiers in the present and the future; they agreed to settle all disputes between them by peaceful means. *The Soviet Union and the Federal Republic of Germany signed a treaty on 12 August 1970 on the renunciation of force* (p. 293). In articles of this treaty the signatories undertook to respect the territorial integrity of all States in Europe within their existing frontiers, including the Oder–Neisse line which forms the western frontier of Poland and the frontier between the Federal German Republic and the German Democratic Republic. Chancellor Brandt made it clear that ratification of the Moscow treaty was indissolubly linked with a satisfactory Berlin settlement. Talks to reach such a settlement were begun by the four occupying Powers in March 1970, and a *Four Power Berlin Agreement was reached on 3 September 1971*. The U.S.S.R., France, the U.S. and the U.K. accepted their individual responsibilities and reaffirmed their joint rights in Berlin as unchanged. The U.S.S.R. declared that transport between the western sectors of Berlin and the Federal German Republic and the D.D.R. would be unimpeded. France, the U.K. and the U.S. declared that the ties between West Berlin and the Federal German Republic would be developed, but that their sectors did not form a constituent part of the German Federal Republic and would not be governed by it. They agreed that a Soviet Consulate-General would be established in West Berlin. The complex round of negotiations was completed by an agreement between the Federal German Republic and the D.D.R. concerning the means to be adopted in carrying out the *Four Power Berlin Agreement*. The Federal German Parliament ratified the 'eastern' treaties with Russia and Poland and an agreement concerning transport to Berlin concluded with the D.D.R. was ratified in September 1972, thereby implicitly recognizing the D.D.R. as capable of signing treaties. Finally, after lengthy negotiations the two German States signed a *Treaty on the bases of relations between the German Democratic Republic and the Federal Republic of Germany, Berlin, 21 December 1972* (p. 296). But the Federal German Government is not prepared to abandon the ultimate right of the German people to choose unity, a right which can be preserved by the continuation of Four Power responsibilities for Berlin and Germany as a whole. The Federal German Government also desires a freer movement of peoples between the two Germanies, though there are no signs in 1973 that the D.D.R. is prepared to pull down its guarded frontier or to allow all its citizens full freedom of choice regarding which Germany to make their home.

Peace Treaty between the Allies and Italy, 10 February 1947

Part I · Territorial clauses

SECTION I · FRONTIERS

Article 1. The frontiers of Italy shall, subject to the modifications set out in Articles 2, 3, 4, 11 and 22, be those which existed on January 1, 1938. These frontiers are traced on the maps attached to the present Treaty (Annex I). In case of a discrepancy between the textual description of the frontiers and the maps, the text shall be deemed to be authentic.

Article 2. The frontier between Italy and France, as it existed on January 1, 1938, shall be modified as follows:

    1. *Little St Bernard Pass* ...
    2. *Mont Cenis Plateau* ...
    3. *Mont Thabor-Chaberton* ...
    4. *Upper Valleys of the Tinée, Vesubie and Roya* ...

Article 3. The frontier between Italy and Yugoslavia shall be fixed as follows ...

SECTION V · GREECE (special clause)

Article 14. 1. Italy hereby cedes to Greece in full sovereignty the Dodecanese Islands indicated hereafter, namely Stampalia (Astropalia), Rhodes (Rhodos), Calki (Kharki), Scarpanto, Casos (Casso), Piscopis (Tilos), Misiros (Nisyros), Calimnos (Kalymnos), Leros, Patmos, Lipsos (Lipso), Simi (Symi), Cos (Kos) and Castellorizo, as well as the adjacent islets.

2. These islands shall be and shall remain demilitarized....

Part II · Political clauses

SECTION I · GENERAL clauses

Article 15. Italy shall take all measures necessary to secure to all persons under Italian jurisdiction, without distinction as to race, sex, language or religion, the enjoyment of human rights and of the fundamental freedoms, including freedom of expression, of press and publication, of religious worship, of political opinion and of public meeting.

Article 16. Italy shall not prosecute or molest Italian nationals, including members of the armed forces, solely on the ground that during the period from June 10, 1940, to the coming into force of the present Treaty, they expressed sympathy with or took action in support of the cause of the Allied and Associated Powers.

Article 17. Italy, which, in accordance with Article 30 of the Armistice Agreement, has taken measures to dissolve the Fascist organizations in Italy, shall not permit the resurgence on Italian territory of such organizations, whether political, military or semi-military, whose purpose it is to deprive the people of their democratic rights.

Article 18. Italy undertakes to recognize the full force of the Treaties of Peace with Roumania, Bulgaria, Hungary and Finland and other agreements or arrangements which have been or will be reached by the Allied and Associated Powers in respect of Austria, Germany and Japan for the restoration of peace.

SECTION III · FREE TERRITORY OF TRIESTE

Article 21. 1. There is hereby constituted the Free Territory of Trieste, consisting of the area lying between the Adriatic Sea and the boundaries defined in Articles 4 and 22 of the present Treaty. The Free Territory of Trieste is recognized by the Allied and Associated Powers and by Italy, which agree that its integrity and independence shall be assured by the Security Council of the United Nations.

2. Italian sovereignty over the area constituting the Free Territory of Trieste, as above defined, shall be terminated upon

the coming into force of the present Treaty.

3. On the termination of Italian sovereignty, the Free Territory of Trieste shall be governed in accordance with an instrument for a provisional régime drafted by the Council of Foreign Ministers and approved by the Security Council. This Instrument shall remain in force until such date as the Security Council shall fix for the coming into force of the Permanent Statute which shall have been approved by it. The Free Territory shall thenceforth be governed by the provisions of such Permanent Statute. The texts of the Permanent Statute and of the Instrument for the Provisional Régime are contained in Annexes VI and VII.

4. The Free Territory of Trieste shall not be considered as ceded territory within the meaning of Article 19 and Annex XIV of the present Treaty.

5. Italy and Yugoslavia undertake to give to the Free Territory of Trieste the guarantees set out in Annex IX.

Article 22. The frontier between Yugoslavia and the Free Territory of Trieste shall be fixed as follows ...

SECTION IV · ITALIAN COLONIES

Article 23. 1. Italy renounces all right and title to the Italian territorial possessions in Africa, i.e. Libya, Eritrea and Italian Somaliland.

2. Pending their final disposal, the said possessions shall continue under their present administration.

3. The final disposal of these possessions shall be determined jointly by the Governments of the Soviet Union, of the United Kingdom, of the United States of America, and of France within one year from the coming into force of the present Treaty, in the manner laid down in the joint declaration of February 10, 1947, issued by the said Governments, which is reproduced in Annex XI.

SECTION V · SPECIAL INTERESTS OF CHINA

Article 24. Italy renounces in favour of China all benefits and privileges resulting from the provisions of the final Protocol signed at Pekin on September 7, 1901, and all annexes, notes and documents supplementary thereto ...

SECTION VI · ALBANIA

Article 27. Italy recognizes and undertakes to respect the sovereignty and independence of the State of Albania.

Article 28. Italy recognizes that the Island of Saseno is part of the territory of Albania and renounces all claims thereto.

SECTION VII · ETHIOPIA

Article 33. Italy recognizes and undertakes to respect the sovereignty and independence of the State of Ethiopia.

Part IV · Naval, military and air clauses

SECTION I · DURATION OF APPLICATION

Article 46. Each of the military, naval and air clauses of the present Treaty shall remain in force until modified in whole or in part by agreement between the Allied and Associated Powers and Italy or, after Italy becomes a member of the United Nations, by agreement between the Security Council and Italy.

SECTION II · GENERAL LIMITATIONS

Article 47. 1. (a) The system of permanent Italian fortifications and military installations along the Franco-Italian frontier, and their armaments, shall be destroyed or removed ...

Article 48. 1. (a) Any permanent Italian fortifications and military installations along the Italo-Yugoslav frontier, and their armaments, shall be destroyed or removed ...

SECTION III · LIMITATION OF THE ITALIAN NAVY

Article 59. 3. The total standard displacement of the war vessels, other than battleships, of the Italian Navy, including vessels under construction after the date of launching, shall not exceed 67,500 tons.

4. Any replacement of war vessels by Italy shall be effected within the limit of tonnage given in paragraph 3. There shall be no restriction on the replacement of auxiliary vessels.

5. Italy undertakes not to acquire or lay down any war vessels before January 1, 1950, except as necessary to replace any vessel, other than a battleship, accidentally lost, in which case the displacement of the new vessel is not to exceed by more than 10 per cent the displacement of the vessel lost.

6. The terms used in this Article are, for the purposes of the present Treaty, defined in Annex XIII A.

Article 60. 1. The total personnel of the Italian Navy, excluding any naval air personnel, shall not exceed 25,000 officers and men....

SECTION IV · LIMITATION OF THE ITALIAN ARMY

Article 61. The Italian Army, including the Frontier Guards, shall be limited to a force of 185,000 combat, service and overhead personnel and 65,000 ...

SECTION V · LIMITATION OF THE ITALIAN AIR FORCE

Article 64. 1. The Italian Air Force, including any naval air arm, shall be limited to a force of 200 fighter and reconnaissance aircraft and 150 transport, air-sea rescue, training (school type) and liaison aircraft. These totals include reserve aircraft. All aircraft except for fighter and reconnaissance aircraft shall be unarmed. The organization and armament of the Italian Air Force as well as their deployment throughout Italy shall be designed to meet only tasks of an internal character, local defence of Italian frontiers and defence against air attack.

2. Italy shall not possess or acquire any aircraft designed primarily as bombers with internal bomb-carrying facilities.

Article 65. 1. The personnel of the Italian Air Force, including any naval air personnel, shall be limited to a total of 25,000 effectives, which shall include combat, service and overhead personnel.

SECTION VII · PREVENTION OF GERMAN AND JAPANESE REARMAMENT

Article 68. Italy undertakes to cooperate fully with the Allied and Associated Powers with a view to ensuring that Germany and Japan are unable to take steps outside German and Japanese territories towards rearmament.

Part V · Withdrawal of Allied forces

Article 73. 1. All armed forces of the Allied and Associated Powers shall be withdrawn from Italy as soon as possible and in any case not later than ninety days from the coming into force of the present Treaty.

2. All Italian goods for which compensation has not been made and which are in possession of the armed forces of the Allied and Associated Powers in Italy at the coming into force of the present Treaty shall be returned to the Italian Government within the same period of ninety days or due compensation shall be made.

3. All bank and cash balances in the hands of the forces of the Allied and Associated Powers at the coming into force of the present Treaty which have been supplied free of cost by the Italian Government shall similarly be returned or a corresponding credit given to the Italian Government.

Part VI · Claims arising out of the war

SECTION I · REPARATION

Article 74. A. *Reparation for the Union of Soviet Socialist Republics* 1. Italy shall pay the Soviet Union reparation in the amount of $100,000,000 during a period of seven years from the coming into force of the present Treaty. Deliveries from current industrial production shall not be made during the first two years.

2. Reparation shall be made from the following sources:

(a) A share of the Italian factory and tool equipment designed for the manufacture of war material, which is not required by the permitted military establishments, which is not readily susceptible of conversion to civilian purposes and which will be removed from Italy pursuant to Article 67 of the present Treaty;

(b) Italian assets in Roumania, Bulgaria and Hungary, subject to the exceptions specified in paragraph 6 of Article 79;

(c) Italian current industrial production, including production by extractive industries.

3. The quantities and types of goods to be delivered shall be the subject of agreements between the Governments of the Soviet Union and of Italy, and shall be selected and deliveries shall be scheduled in such a way as to avoid interference with the economic reconstruction of Italy and the imposition of additional liabilities on other Allied or Associated Powers. Agreements concluded under this paragraph shall be communicated to the Ambassadors in Rome of the Soviet Union, of the United Kingdom, of the United States of America, and of France.

4. The Soviet Union shall furnish to Italy on commercial terms the materials which are normally imported into Italy and which are needed for the production of these goods. Payments for these materials shall be made by deducting the value of the materials furnished from the value of the goods delivered to the Soviet Union.

5. The four Ambassadors shall determine the value of the Italian assets to be transferred to the Soviet Union.

6. The basis of calculation for the settlement provided in this Article will be the United States dollar at its gold parity on July 1, 1946, i.e. $35 for one ounce of gold.

B. *Reparation for Albania, Ethiopia, Greece and Yugoslavia.* 1. Italy shall pay reparation to the following States:

Albania in the amount of	$5,000,000
Ethiopia in the amount of	$25,000,000
Greece in the amount of	$105,000,000
Yugoslavia in the amount of	$125,000,000

These payments shall be made during a period of seven years from the coming into force of the present Treaty. Deliveries from current industrial production shall not be made during the first two years.

2. Reparation shall be made from the following sources:

(a) A share of the Italian factory and tool equipment designed for the manufacture of war material, which is not required by the permitted military establishments, which is not readily susceptible of conversion to civilian purposes and which will be removed from Italy pursuant to Article 67 of the present Treaty;

(b) Italian current industrial production, including production by extractive industries;

(c) All other categories of capital goods or services, excluding Italian assets which, under Article 79 of the present Treaty, are subject to the jurisdiction of the States mentioned in paragraph 1 above. Deliveries under this paragraph shall include either or both of the passenger vessels *Saturnia* and *Vulcania*, if, after their value has been determined by the four Ambassadors, they are claimed within ninety days by one of the States mentioned in paragraph 1 above. Such deliveries may also include seeds.

3. The quantities and types of goods and services to be delivered shall be the subject of agreements between the Governments entitled to receive reparation and the Italian Government, and shall be selected and deliveries shall be scheduled in such a way as to avoid interference with the economic reconstruction of Italy and the imposition of additional liabilities on other Allied or Associated Powers.

4. The States entitled to receive reparation from current industrial production

shall furnish to Italy on commercial terms the materials which are normally imported into Italy and which are needed for the production of these goods. Payment for these materials shall be made by deducting the value of the materials furnished from the value of the goods delivered.

5. The basis of calculation for the settlement provided in this Article will be the United States dollar at its gold parity on July 1, 1946, i.e. $35 for one ounce of gold.

6. Claims of the States mentioned in paragraph 1 of part B of this Article, in excess of the amounts of reparation specified in that paragraph, shall be satisfied out of the Italian assets subject to their respective jurisdictions under Article 79 of the present Treaty.

. . .

D. *Reparation for other States.* 1. Claims of the other Allied and Associated Powers shall be satisfied out of the Italian assets subject to their respective jurisdictions under Article 79 of the present Treaty.

2. The claims of any State which is receiving territories under the present Treaty and which is not mentioned in part B of this Article shall also be satisfied by the transfer to the said State, without payment, of the industrial installations and equipment situated in the ceded territories and employed in the distribution of water, and the production and distribution of gas and electricity, owned by any Italian company whose *siège social* is in Italy or is transferred to Italy, as well as by the transfer of all other assets of such companies in ceded territories.

3. Responsibility for the financial obligations secured by mortgages, *liens* and other charges on such property shall be assumed by the Italian Government.

E. *Compensation for property taken for reparation purposes.* The Italian Government undertakes to compensate all natural or juridical persons whose property is taken for reparation purposes under this Article.

SECTION II · RESTITUTION BY ITALY

Article 75. 1. Italy accepts the principles of the United Nations Declaration of January 5, 1943, and shall return, in the shortest possible time, property removed from the territory of any of the United Nations.

2. The obligation to make restitution applies to all identifiable property at present in Italy which was removed by force or duress by any of the Axis Powers from the territory of any of the United Nations, irrespective of any subsequent transactions by which the present holder of any such property has secured possession.

3. The Italian Government shall return the property referred to in this Article in good order and, in this connection, shall bear all costs in Italy relating to labour, materials and transport.

State Treaty for the establishment of an independent and democratic Austria, Vienna, 15 May 1955

... Whereas on 13th March 1938, Hitlerite Germany annexed Austria by force and incorporated its territory in the German Reich;

Whereas in the Moscow Declaration published on 1st November 1943 the Governments of the Union of Soviet Socialist Republics, the United Kingdom and the United States of America declared that they regarded the annexation of Austria by Germany on 13th March 1938 as null and void and affirmed their wish to see Austria re-established as a free and independent State, and the French Committee of National Liberation made a similar declaration on 16th November 1943 ...

Part I · Political and territorial clauses

Article 1. Re-establishment of Austria as a free and independent State. The Allied and Associated Powers recognize that Austria is re-established as a sovereign, independent and democratic State.

Article 2. Maintenance of Austria's independence. The Allied and Associated Powers declare that they will respect the independence and territorial integrity of Austria as established under the present Treaty.

Article 3. Recognition by Germany of Austrian independence [to be included in German peace treaty].

Article 4. Prohibition of Anschluss. 1. The Allied and Associated Powers declare that political or economic union between Austria and Germany is prohibited. Austria fully recognizes its responsibilities in this matter and shall not enter into political or economic union with Germany in any form whatsoever ... [Austria not to promote union by any means whatever].

Article 5. Frontiers of Austria. The frontiers of Austria shall be those existing on 1st January 1938.

Article 6. Human rights [guarantee of].

Article 7. Rights of the Slovene and Croat minorities [guarantee of].

Article 8. Democratic institutions. Austria shall have a democratic Government based on elections by secret ballot and shall guarantee to all citizens free, equal and universal suffrage as well as the right to be elected to public office without discrimination as to race, sex, language, religion or political opinion.

Article 9. Dissolution of Nazi organizations [measures to be taken].

[*Article 10. Special clauses on legislation.* 1. To liquidate remnants of Nazi régime and re-establish a democratic system. 2. To maintain law of 3 April 1919, concerning the House of Hapsburg–Lorraine.]

[*Article 11.* Austria to recognize all peace treaties between other belligerents of the Second World War.]

Part II · Military and air clauses

[*Articles 12–16.* Restriction on possession of weapons including prohibition of nuclear weapons; restrictions on former Nazis serving in armed services. Austria to cooperate in preventing German rearmament.]

Article 17. Duration of limitations. Each of the military and air clauses of the present Treaty shall remain in force until modified in whole or in part by agreement between the Allied and Associated Powers and Austria or, after Austria becomes a member of the United Nations, by agreement between the Security Council and Austria.

[*Article 18. Repatriation of prisoners of war.*]

[*Article 19. Maintenance of war graves.*]

Part III

Article 20. Withdrawal of Allied forces. ... The forces of the Allied and Associated Powers and members of the Allied Commission for Austria shall be withdrawn from Austria within ninety days from the coming into force of the present Treaty, and in so far as possible not later than 31st December 1955. ...

Part IV · Claims arising out of the war

Article 21. Reparation. No reparation shall be exacted from Austria arising out of the existence of a state of war in Europe after 1st September 1939.

Article 22. German assets in Austria. The Soviet Union, the United Kingdom, the United States of America and France have the right to dispose of all German assets in Austria in accordance with the Protocol of the Berlin Conference of 2nd August 1945.

1. The Soviet Union shall receive for a period of validity of thirty years concessions to oilfields equivalent to 60 per cent of the extraction of oil in Austria for

1947, as well as property rights to all buildings, constructions, equipment, and other property belonging to these oilfields, in accordance with list No. 1 and map No. 1 annexed to the Treaty ... [details of other payments to the Soviet Union].

The United Kingdom, the United States of America and France hereby transfer to Austria all property, rights and interests held or claimed by her on behalf of any of them in Austria as former German assets or war booty.

...

Treaty of Peace with Japan, San Francisco, 8 September 1951

Whereas the Allied Powers and Japan are resolved that henceforth their relations shall be those of nations which, as sovereign equals, cooperate in friendly association to promote their common welfare and to maintain international peace and security, and are therefore desirous of concluding a Treaty of Peace which will settle questions still outstanding as a result of the existence of a state of war between them;

Whereas Japan for its part declares its intention to apply for membership in the United Nations and in all circumstances to conform to the principles of the Charter of the United Nations; to strive to realize the objectives of the Universal Declaration of Human Rights; to seek to create within Japan conditions of stability and well-being as defined in Articles 55 and 56 of the Charter of the United Nations and already initiated by post-surrender Japanese legislation; and in public and private trade and commerce to conform to internationally accepted fair practices;

Whereas the Allied Powers welcome the intentions of Japan set out in the foregoing paragraph;

The Allied Powers and Japan have

therefore determined to conclude the present Treaty of Peace, and have accordingly appointed the undersigned plenipotentiaries, who, after presentation of their full powers, found in good and due form, have agreed on the following provisions:

Chapter I: Peace

Article 1. (a) The state of war between Japan and each of the Allied Powers is terminated as from the date on which the present Treaty comes into force between Japan and the Allied Power concerned as provided for in Article 23.

(b) The Allied Powers recognize the full sovereignty of the Japanese people over Japan and its territorial waters.

Chapter II: Territory

Article 2. (a) Japan, recognizing the independence of Korea, renounces all right, title and claim to Korea, including the islands of Quelpart, Port Hamilton and Dagelet.

(b) Japan renounces all right, title and claim to Formosa and the Pescadores.

(c) Japan renounces all rights, title and claim to the Kurile islands, and to that portion of Sakhalin and the islands adjacent to it over which Japan acquired sovereignty as a consequence of the Treaty of Portsmouth of September 5, 1905.

(d) Japan renounces all right, title and claim in connection with the League of Nations Mandate System, and accepts the action of the United Nations Security Council of April 2, 1947, extending the trusteeship system to the Pacific islands formerly under mandate to Japan.

(e) Japan renounces all claim to any right or title to or interest in connection with any part of the Antarctic area, whether deriving from the activities of Japanese nationals or otherwise.

(f) Japan renounces all right, title and claim to the Spratly islands and to the Paracel islands.

Article 3. Japan will concur in any proposal of the United States to the United Nations to place under its trusteeship system, with the United States as the sole administering authority. . . .

Chapter III: Security

Article 5. (a) Japan accepts the obligations set forth in Article 2 of the Charter of the United Nations, and in particular the obligations

(i) to settle its international disputes by peaceful means in such a manner that international peace and security, and justice, are not endangered;

(ii) to refrain in its international relations from the threat or use of force against the territorial integrity or political independence of any State or in any other manner inconsistent with the Purposes of the United Nations;

(iii) to give the United Nations every assistance in any action it takes in accordance with the Charter and to refrain from giving assistance to any State against which the United Nations may take preventive or enforcement action.

(b) The Allied Powers confirm that they will be guided by the principles of Article 2 of the Charter of the United Nations in their relations with Japan.

(c) The Allied Powers for their part recognize that Japan as a sovereign nation possesses the inherent right of individual or collective self-defense referred to in Article 51 of the Charter of the United Nations and that Japan may voluntarily enter into collective security arrangements.

Article 6. (a) All occupation forces of the Allied Powers shall be withdrawn from Japan as soon as possible after the coming into force of the present Treaty, and in any case not later than ninety days thereafter. Nothing in this provision shall, however, prevent the stationing or retention of foreign armed forces in Japanese territory under or in consequence of any bilateral or multilateral agreements which have been or may be made between one or more of the Allied Powers, on the one hand, and Japan on the other.

(b) The provisions of Article 9 of the Potsdam Proclamation of July 26, 1945, dealing with the return of Japanese military forces to their homes, to the extent not already completed, will be carried out.

(c) All Japanese property for which compensation has not already been paid, which was supplied for the use of the occupation forces. . . .

Chapter IV: Political and economic clauses

• • •

Article 10. Japan renounces all special rights and interests in China, including all benefits and privileges resulting from the provisions of the final Protocol signed at Peking on September 7, 1901, and all annexes, notes and documents supplementary thereto, and agrees to the abrogation in respect to Japan of the said Protocol, annexes, notes and documents.

Article 11. Japan accepts the judgements of the International Military Tribunal for the Far East and of other Allied War Crimes Courts both within and outside Japan, and will carry out the sentences imposed thereby upon Japanese nationals imprisoned in Japan. The power to grant clemency, to reduce sentences and to parole with respect to such prisoners may not be exercised except on the decision of the Government or Governments which imposed the sentence in each instance, and on the recommendation of Japan. In the case of persons sentenced by the International Military Tribunal for the Far East, such power may not be exercised except on the decision of a majority of the Governments represented on the Tribunal, and on the recommendation of Japan.

Article 12. [Trade arrangements.] (c) In respect to any matter, however, Japan shall be obliged to accord to an Allied Power national treatment, or most-favored-nation treatment, only to the extent that the Allied Power concerned accords Japan national treatment or most-favored-nation treatment, as the case may be, in respect of the same matter.

Chapter V: Claims and property

Article 14. (a) It is recognized that Japan should pay reparations to the Allied Powers for the damage and suffering caused by it during the war. Nevertheless it is also recognized that the resources of Japan are not presently sufficient, if it is to maintain a viable economy, to make complete reparation for all such damage and suffering and at the same time meet its other obligations.

Therefore,

(i) Japan will promptly enter into negotiations with Allied Powers so desiring, whose present territories were occupied by Japanese forces and damaged by Japan, with a view to assisting to compensate those countries for the cost of repairing the damage done, by making available the services of the Japanese people in production, salvaging and other work for the Allied Powers in question. Such arrangements shall avoid the imposition of additional liabilities on other Allied Powers, and, where the manufacturing of raw materials is called for, they shall be supplied by the Allied Powers in question, so as not to throw any foreign exchange burden upon Japan....

(b) Except as otherwise provided in the present Treaty, the Allied Powers waive all reparations claims of the Allied Powers, other claims of the Allied Powers and their nationals arising out of any actions taken by Japan and its nationals in the course of the prosecution of the war, and claims of the Allied Powers for direct military costs of occupation.

. . .

Article 16. As an expression of its desire to indemnify those members of the armed forces of the Allied Powers who suffered undue hardships while prisoners of war of Japan, Japan will transfer its assets and those of its nationals in countries which were neutral during the war, or which were at war with any of the Allied Powers, or, at its option, the equivalent of such assets, to the International Committee of the Red Cross which shall liquidate such assets and distribute the resultant fund to appropriate national agencies, for the benefit of former prisoners of war and their families on such basis as it may determine to be equitable....

Chapter VII: Final clauses

Article 23. (a) The present Treaty shall be ratified by the States which sign it, including Japan, and will come into force for all the States which have then ratified it, when instruments of ratification have been deposited by Japan and by a majority, including the United States of America as the principal occupying Power....

. . .

Article 26. Japan will be prepared to conclude with any State which signed or adhered to the United Nations Declaration of January 1, 1942, and which is at war with Japan, or with any State which previously formed a part of the territory of a State named in Article 23, which is not a signatory of the present Treaty, a bilateral treaty of peace on the same or substantially the same terms as are provided for in the present Treaty, but this obligation on the part of Japan will expire three years after the first coming into force of the present Treaty. Should Japan make a peace settlement or war claims settlement with any State granting that State greater advantages than those provided by the present Treaty, those same advantages shall be extended to the parties to the present Treaty.

Security Treaty between the United States and Japan, 8 September 1951

Japan has this day signed a Treaty of Peace with the Allied Powers. On the coming into force of that Treaty, Japan will not have the effective means to exercise its inherent right of self-defense because it has been disarmed.

There is danger to Japan in this situation because irresponsible militarism has not yet been driven from the world. Therefore Japan desires a Security Treaty with the United States of America to come into force simultaneously with the Treaty of Peace between the United States of America and Japan.

The Treaty of Peace recognizes that Japan as a sovereign nation has the right to enter into collective security arrangements, and further, the Charter of the United Nations recognizes that all nations possess an inherent right of individual and collective self-defense.

In exercise of these rights, Japan desires, as a provisional arrangement for its defense, that the United States of America should maintain armed forces of its own in and about Japan so as to deter armed attack upon Japan.

The United States of America, in the interest of peace and security, is presently willing to maintain certain of its armed forces in and about Japan, in the expectation, however, that Japan will itself increasingly assume responsibility for its own defense against direct and indirect aggression, always avoiding any armament which could be an offensive threat or serve other than to promote peace and security in accordance with the purposes and principles of the United Nations Charter.

Accordingly, the two countries have agreed as follows:

Article I. Japan grants, and the United States of America accepts, the right, upon the coming into force of the Treaty of Peace and of this Treaty, to dispose United States land, air and sea forces in and about Japan. Such forces may be utilized to contribute to the maintenance of international peace and security in the Far East and to the security of Japan against armed attack from without, including assistance given at the express request of the Japanese Government to put down large-scale internal riots and disturbances in Japan, caused through instigation or intervention by an outside Power or Powers.

Article II. During the exercise of the right referred to in Article I, Japan will not grant, without the prior consent of the United States of America, any bases or any rights, powers or authority whatsoever, in or relating to bases or the right of garrison or of maneuver or transit of ground, air or naval forces to any third Power.

Article III. The conditions which shall govern the disposition of armed forces of the United States of America in and about Japan shall be determined by administrative agreements between the two Governments.

Article IV. This Treaty shall expire whenever in the opinion of the Governments of the United States of America and Japan there shall have come into force such United Nations arrangements or such alternative individual or collective security dispositions as will satisfactorily provide for the maintenance by the United Nations or otherwise of international peace and security in the Japan area.

Article V. This Treaty shall be ratified by the United States of America and Japan and will come into force when instruments of ratification thereof have been exchanged by them at Washington.

...

Note: The Japanese Constitution

Chapter II: Renunciation of war

Article 9. Aspiring sincerely to an international peace based on justice and order, the Japanese people forever renounce war as a sovereign right of the nation and the threat or use of force as means of settling international disputes.

In order to accomplish the aim of the preceding paragraph, land, sea, and air forces, as well as other war potential, will never be maintained. The right of belligerency of the State will not be recognized.

Treaty of Mutual Cooperation and Security between the United States and Japan, 19 January 1960

...

Article I. The parties undertake, as set forth in the Charter of the United Nations, to settle any international disputes in which they may be involved by peaceful means in such a manner that international peace and security and justice are not endangered and to refrain in their international relations from the threat or use of force against the territorial integrity or political independence of any State, or in any other manner inconsistent with the purposes of the United Nations.

The parties will endeavor in concert with other peace-loving countries to strengthen the United Nations so that its mission of maintaining international peace and security may be discharged more effectively.

Article II. The parties will contribute toward the further development of peaceful and friendly international relations by strengthening their free institutions, by bringing about a better understanding of the principles upon which these institutions are founded, and by promoting conditions of stability and well-being. They will seek to eliminate conflict in their international economic policies and will encourage economic collaboration between them.

Article III. The parties, individually and in cooperation with each other, by means of continuous and effective self-help and mutual aid, will maintain and develop, subject to their constitutional provisions, their capacities to resist armed attack.

Article IV. The parties will consult together from time to time regarding the implementation of this Treaty, and, at the request of either party, whenever the security of Japan or international peace and security in the Far East is threatened.

Article V. Each party recognizes that an armed attack against either party in the territories under the administration of Japan would be dangerous to its own peace and safety and declares that it would act to meet the common danger in accordance with its constitutional provisions and processes.

Any such armed attack and all measures taken as a result thereof shall be immediately reported to the Security Council of the United Nations in accordance with the provisions of Article 51 of the Charter. Such measures shall be terminated when the Security Council has taken the measures necessary to restore and maintain international peace and security.

Article VI. For the purpose of contributing to the security of Japan and the maintenance of international peace and security in the Far East, the United States of America is granted the use by its land, air and naval forces of facilities and areas in Japan.

The use of these facilities and areas as well as the status of United States armed forces in Japan shall be governed by a separate agreement, replacing the Administrative Agreement under Article III of the Security Treaty between the United States of America and Japan, signed at Tokyo on February 28, 1952, as amended, and by such other arrangements as may be agreed upon.

Article VII. This Treaty does not affect and shall not be interpreted as affecting in any way the rights and obligations of the parties under the Charter of the United Nations or the responsibility of the United Nations for the maintenance of international peace and security.

Article VIII. This Treaty shall be ratified by the United States of America and Japan in accordance with their respective constitutional processes. . . .

Article IX. The Security Treaty between the United States of America and Japan signed at the city of San Francisco on September 8, 1951 shall expire upon the entering into force of this Treaty.

Article X. This Treaty shall remain in force until in the opinion of the Governments of the United States of America and Japan there shall have come into force such United Nations arrangements as will satisfactorily provide for the maintenance of international peace and security in the Japan area.

However, after the Treaty has been in force for ten years, either party may give notice to the other party of its intention to terminate the Treaty, in which case the Treaty shall terminate one year after such notice has been given. . . .

Agreed Minute to the Treaty of Mutual Cooperation and Security

Japanese plenipotentiary:
While the question of the status of the islands administered by the United States under Article 3 of the Treaty of Peace with Japan has not been made a subject of discussion in the course of treaty negotiations, I would like to emphasize the strong concern of the Government and people of Japan for the safety of the people of these islands since Japan possesses residual sovereignty over these islands. If an armed attack occurs or is threatened against these islands, the two countries will of course consult together closely under Article IV of the Treaty of Mutual Cooperation and Security. In the event of an armed attack, it is the intention of the Government of Japan to explore with the United States measures which it might be able to take for the welfare of the islanders.
United States plenipotentiary:
In the event of an armed attack against these islands, the United States Government will consult at once with the Government of Japan and intends to take the necessary measures for the defense of these islands, and to do its utmost to secure the welfare of the islanders.

Exchanges of Notes between Japan and the United States

WASHINGTON, *January 19, 1960*
EXCELLENCY:
I have the honour to refer to the Treaty of Mutual Cooperation and Security between Japan and the United States of America signed today, and to inform Your Excellency that the following is the

understanding of the Government of Japan concerning the implementation of Article VI thereof:

Major changes in the deployment into Japan of United States armed forces, major changes in their equipment, and the use of facilities and areas in Japan as bases for military combat operations to be undertaken from Japan other than those conducted under Article V of the said Treaty, shall be the subjects of prior consultation with the Government of Japan.

I should be appreciative if Your Excellency would confirm on behalf of your Government that this is also the understanding of the Government of the United States of America.

I avail myself of this opportunity to re-new to Your Excellency the assurance of my highest consideration.

Agreement under Article VI

Article 2.... 2. At the request of either Government, the Governments of the United States and Japan shall review such arrangements and may agree that such facilities and areas shall be returned to Japan or that additional facilities and areas may be provided.

3. The facilities and areas used by the United States armed forces shall be returned to Japan whenever they are no longer needed for purposes of this Agreement, and the United States agrees to keep the needs for facilities and areas under continual observation with a view toward such return....

Statement by the Governments of the United States of America, the United Kingdom, the Union of Soviet Socialist Republics, and the Provisional Government of the French Republic on zones of occupation in Germany, 5 June 1945

1. Germany, within her frontiers as they were on 31 December 1937, will, for the purposes of occupation, be divided into four zones, one to be allotted to each Power as follows:

an eastern zone to the Union of Soviet Socialist Republics;
a north-western zone to the United Kingdom;
a south-western zone to the United States of America;
a western zone to France.

The occupying forces in each zone will be under a Commander-in-Chief desig-nated by the responsible Power. Each of the Four Powers may, at its discretion, include among the forces assigned to oc-cupation duties under the command of its Commander-in-Chief, auxiliary contin-gents from the forces of any other Allied Power which has actively participated in military operations against Germany.

2. The area of 'Greater Berlin' will be occupied by forces of each of the Four Powers. An Inter-Allied Governing Auth-ority (in Russian, *Komendatura*) consist-ing of four Commandants, appointed by their respective Commanders-in-Chief, will be established to direct jointly its administration.

Statement by the Governments of the United States of America, the United Kingdom, the Union of Soviet Socialist Republics, and the Provisional Government of the French Republic on control machinery in Germany, 5 June 1945

. . .

In the period when Germany is carrying out the basic requirements of unconditional surrender, supreme authority in Germany will be exercised, on instructions from their Governments, by the British, United States, Soviet and French Commanders-in-Chief, each in his own zone of occupation, and also jointly, in matters affecting Germany as a whole. The four Commanders-in-Chief will together constitute the Control Council. Each Commander-in-Chief will be assisted by a Political Adviser.

2. The Control Council, whose decisions shall be unanimous, will ensure appropriate uniformity of action by the Commanders-in-Chief in their respective zones of occupation and will reach agreed decisions on the chief questions affecting Germany as a whole.

3. Under the Control Council there will be a permanent Coordinating Committee composed of one representative of each of the four Commanders-in-Chief, and a Control Staff organized in the following Divisions (which are subject to adjustment in the light of experience): Military; Naval; Air; Transport; Political; Economic; Finance; Reparation, Deliveries and Restitution; Internal Affairs and Communications; Legal; Prisoners of War and Displaced Persons; Manpower. There will be four heads of each Division, one designated by each Power. The staffs of the Divisions may include civilian as well as military personnel, and may also in special cases include nationals of other United Nations appointed in a personal capacity.

4. The functions of the Coordinating Committee and of the Control Staff will be to advise the Control Council, to carry out the Council's decisions and to transmit them to, the appropriate German organs, and to supervise and control the day-to-day activities of the latter.

5. Liaison with the other United Nations Governments chiefly interested will be established through the appointment by such Governments of military missions (which may include civilian members) to the Control Council. These missions will have access through the appropriate channels to the organs of control.

6. United Nations organizations will, if admitted by the Control Council to operate in Germany, be subordinate to the Allied control machinery and answerable to it.

7. The administration of the 'Greater Berlin' area will be directed by an Inter-Allied Governing Authority, which will operate under the general direction of the Control Council, and will consist of four Commandants, each of whom will serve in rotation as Chief Commandant. They will be assisted by a technical staff which will supervise and control the activities of the local German organs.

8. The arrangements outlined above will operate during the period of occupation following German surrender, when Germany is carrying out the basic requirements of unconditional surrender. Arrangements for the subsequent period will be the subject of a separate agreement.

Minutes of the Thirteenth Meeting of the Control Council approving the establishment of air corridors between the American and British zones of Germany and Berlin, Berlin, 30 November 1945

...

110. Proposed air routes for inter-zonal flights

The Meeting had before them CONL/P (45) 63.

Marshal Zhukov recalled that the Co-ordinating Committee had approved the establishing of three air corridors, namely, Berlin–Hamburg, Berlin–Bückeburg and Berlin–Frankfurt-on-Main.

Field Marshal Montgomery expressed the hope that in due course the question of establishing the remaining air corridors would be settled satisfactorily.

General Koenig approved the paper in principle and shared the opinion of Field Marshal Montgomery.

Marshal Zhukov expressed himself confident that in due course the other air corridors would be opened. He added that he would like to make a proposal on this paper. He assumed that his colleagues would give the Soviet military authorities the right to fly along these air corridors into the Western zones and would consent to put at their disposal appropriate airfields for landing Soviet aircraft, or at least allow Soviet ground staffs on terminal and intermediate airfields along the proposed air corridors to facilitate the servicing of Soviet aircraft. The reason which Marshal Zhukov gave for the necessity of establishing Soviet airfields in the Western zones was the work of dismantling plants for deliveries on account of reparations when it comes to sending Soviet experts to organize that work.

Field Marshal Montgomery stated that in his zone he would afford every facility for Soviet aircraft.

Marshal Zhukov said that he would like to clarify his declaration: namely, he proposed that appropriate airfields should be placed at the disposal of the Soviet authorities in the Western zones, or that permission should be given for Soviet ground crews for the servicing of Soviet aircraft to be stationed at these airfields.

Field Marshal Montgomery proposed to refer the proposal made by the head of the Soviet delegation to the Air Directorate for examination. He asked whether his understanding was correct that the question of the three air corridors from the Western zones to Berlin was settled and that the organization of these air corridors could be started immediately, without awaiting the results of the examination of the Soviet proposal.

Marshal Zhukov observed that he considered the paper accepted and expressed the hope that the proposal of the Soviet delegation on placing airfields in the Western zones at the disposal of the Soviet authorities would meet with full sympathy on the part of his colleagues.

The Meeting

(110) (a) approved the establishment of three air corridors from Berlin to the Western zones as defined in CONL/P (45) 63;

(b) agreed to refer proposal of the Soviet delegation on the placing of airfields at the disposal of the Soviet authorities or the setting up of Soviet ground crews in the Western zones to the Air Directorate for study.

...

Agreement between Poland and the German Democratic Republic, 6 July 1950

The President of the Republic of Poland and the President of the Democratic Republic of Germany,

Desirous of proving their will to consolidate universal peace and wishing to contribute their share to the great work of harmonious cooperation carried on by peace-loving nations,

Considering that this cooperation between the Polish people and the German people has become possible, thanks to the defeat of German fascism by the U.S.S.R. and to the progressive development of democratic forces in Germany, and

Wishing to create – after the tragic experiences of Hitlerism – unshakeable foundations for a peaceful and good-neighbour relationship between the two nations,

Wishing to stabilize and strengthen mutual relations on the basis of the Potsdam Agreement, which established the frontiers along the Odra and Nysa Luzycka rivers,

Executing the decisions contained in the Warsaw Declaration by the Government of the Republic of Poland and the Delegation of the Provisional Government of the Democratic Republic of Germany on June 6, 1950,

Recognizing the established and existing frontier as the inviolable frontier of peace and friendship, which does not divide but unites both nations. . . .

Article 1. The High Contracting Parties jointly declare that the established and existing frontier running from the Baltic Sea along the line west of Swinoujscie and along the Odra river to the place where the Nysa Luzycka river flows into the Odra river and then along the Nysa Luzycka river to the Czechoslovak frontier, constitutes the State frontier between Poland and Germany.

[*Articles 2–7*. Concern Demarcation Commission, airspace and ratification.]

Declaration of the Government of the Soviet Union concerning the assumption of full sovereignty by the German Democratic Republic, 25 March 1954 (translated by J. A. S. Grenville)

[A similar declaration was made by the Government of the German Democratic Republic on 27 March 1954.]

The Government of the Union of the Soviet Socialist Republics continues undeviatingly to strive to go on regulating the German problem in conformity with the interests of strengthening peace and of safeguarding the national reunion of Germany on the basis of democracy.

These aims are served by practical steps to bring closer East and West Germany, by the holding of free elections throughout Germany and the conclusion of a peace treaty with Germany.

Regardless of the efforts of the Union of the Soviet Socialist Republic, no steps were taken at the recent Berlin Conference of the Foreign Ministers of the Four Powers towards the restoration of German unity and towards the conclusion of a peace treaty.

In view of this situation and in consequence of negotiations between the Soviet Government and the Government of the German Democratic Republic, the Government of the Soviet Union considers it necessary, at this time, before Germany is unified and before the peace treaty, to take further steps which are in the interests of the German people, namely:

1. The Union of Soviet Socialist Republics will take up relations with the German Democratic Republic on the same basis as with other sovereign nations. The German Democratic Republic will have the freedom to decide in accordance with its own judgement on domestic and foreign questions including relations with West Germany.

2. The Union of Soviet Socialist Republics retains in the German Democratic Republic those functions which are related to guaranteeing security and which result from the obligations of the Soviet Union arising from Four Power agreements. The Government of the Soviet Union takes note of the declaration of the Government of the German Democratic Republic that it will fulfil the obligations arising for the German Democratic Republic from the Potsdam Agreements concerning the development of Germany as a democratic and peace-loving State, as well as the obligations which are related to the present (*zeitweiligen*) stay of Soviet troops in the German Democratic Republic.

3. The supervision of the activities of the State organs of the German Democratic Republic, which hitherto has been exercised by the High Commissioner of the Soviet Union, will be given up. In conformity with the foregoing, the function of the High Commissioner of the Soviet Union in Germany will be restricted to the range of questions which are related to the above-mentioned guarantee of security, and of the maintenance of the relevant agreements concluded with the representatives of the occupation authorities of the United States, Great Britain and France in all German questions as well as to obligations which arise from the negotiated agreements of the Four Powers concerning Germany ...

Treaty between the Federal Republic of Germany and the Soviet Union, Moscow, 12 August 1970 (translated by J. A. S. Grenville)

The High Contracting Parties, striving to contribute to the strengthening of peace and security in Europe and in the world,

In the conviction that the peaceful co-operation of States on the basis of the aims and principles of the Charter of the United Nations corresponds to the ardent wishes of the people and is in the general interests of international peace,

In appreciation of the fact that their previous agreements which have been carried out, especially the agreement of 13 September 1955 to take up diplomatic relations, have created favourable conditions for the taking of new important steps leading to the further development and strengthening of their mutual relations,

In the desire to give expression in a contractual form to their determination to bring about the improvement and widening of their cooperation including their economic relations and scientific, technical and cultural contacts in the interests of both States, have agreed as follows:

Article 1. The Federal German Republic and the Union of Soviet Socialist Republics consider it as an important objective of their policy to maintain international peace and to bring about a relaxation of tension.

They declare their intention to further the normalization of the situation in Europe and the development of peaceful relations between all European States, and regard as the starting point the reality of the situation as it exists in this region.

Article 2. The Federal Republic of Germany and the Union of Soviet Socialist Republics will be guided in their relations with each other as well as in questions guaranteeing the European and international peace by the principles and objectives of the Charter of the United Nations. Accordingly they will resolve disputes between them only by peaceful means and they undertake to abstain from the threat of force or the use of force, in accordance with Article 2 of the Charter of the United Nations, in dealing with questions involving the security of Europe and international security.

Article 3. In conformity with the objectives and principles set out in the previous articles the Federal German Republic and the Union of Soviet Socialist Republics are in agreement in recognizing that peace in Europe can only be maintained if no one attempts to violate the present frontiers.

They undertake to respect without reservation the territorial integrity of all States in Europe in their present frontiers.

They declare that they have no territorial claims against anyone and will not raise such in the future.

They consider the frontiers of all States in Europe as inviolable, in the present and the future, as demarcated on the day of signature of this Treaty, including the Oder–Neisse line as forming the western frontier of the People's Republic of Poland and the frontier between the Federal German Republic and the German Democratic Republic.

Article 4. This Treaty between the Federal Republic of Germany and the Union of Soviet Socialist Republics does not affect the bilateral or multilateral treaties and agreements earlier concluded by the two parties.

[*Article 5.* Ratification.]

Accompanying letter from German Foreign Minister, Walter Scheel, to Soviet Foreign Minister, 12 August 1970

With respect to today's signature of the Treaty, the Federal German Republic has the honour to affirm that this Treaty is not in contradiction to the political objective of the German Federal Republic to contribute to conditions of peace in which the German people will regain their unity in free self-determination.

Treaty between the Federal Republic of Germany and Poland concerning the bases for the normalization of their relations, Warsaw, 7 December 1970 (translated by J. A. S. Grenville)

• • •

Considering that more than twenty-five years have elapsed since the end of the Second World War, whose first victim was Poland and which brought grievous injury to all the peoples of Europe,

Considering that in both countries meantime a new generation has grown up to whom a peaceful future should be assured,

Wishing to establish lasting bases of peace and to develop normal and good relations between them,

Attempting to strengthen the peace and security in Europe, and

Conscious that the inviolability of the frontiers and the respect for the territorial integrity and sovereignty of all States of Europe in their present frontiers is a fundamental condition for peace,

Have agreed as follows:

Article 1. 1. The Federal Republic of Germany and the People's Republic of Poland mutually agree on the fact that the present frontier, which was laid down in section VIII of the decisions of the Potsdam Conference of 2 August 1945, and which runs from the Baltic immediately to the west of Swinemünde, and from there along the river Oder up to the point where it joins the Lemnitzer Neisse, and then along the Lemnitzer Neisse river to the frontier of Czechoslovakia, constitutes the western State Frontier of the People's Republic of Poland.

2. They confirm the inviolability of their existing frontiers for the present and for the future, and undertake without reservation to respect each other's territorial integrity.

3. They declare that they have no claims of territory to make on each other and that they will not raise any in the future.

Article 2. 1. The Federal Republic of Germany and the People's Republic of Poland undertake to be guided by the aims and principles which are embodied in the United Nations Charter in their relations with each other as well as in questions guaranteeing security in Europe and in the world.

2. Accordingly they will resolve all their disputes only by peaceful means in accordance with Articles 1 and 2 of the United Nations Charter, and they undertake to abstain from the threat of force or the use of force in dealing with questions concerning European or international security as well as in their relations with each other.

Article 3. 1. The Federal Republic of Germany and the People's Republic of Poland will undertake further steps toward the complete normalization and the widest development of their mutual relations, based on the firm foundations of this Treaty.

2. They are agreed that the expansion of their cooperation in areas of economic, scientific, technological, cultural and other fields is to their mutual interest.

Article 4. This Treaty does not affect the bilateral or unilateral treaties and agreements earlier concluded or involving the two parties.

[*Article 5*. Ratification.]

Four Power Declaration by the United States, Britain, France and the Soviet Union on membership of the Federal Republic of Germany and the German Democratic Republic in the United Nations, released 9 November 1972

The Governments of the United Kingdom of Great Britain and Northern Ireland, the French Republic, the Union of Soviet Socialist Republics and the

United States of America, having been represented by their Ambassadors who held a series of meetings in the building formerly occupied by the Allied Control

Council, are in agreement that they will support the applications for membership in the United Nations when submitted by the Federal Republic of Germany and the German Democratic Republic, and affirm in this connection that this membership shall in no way affect the rights and responsibilities of the Four Powers and the corresponding, related quadripartite agreements, decisions and practices.

Treaty on the bases of relations between the German Democratic Republic and the Federal Republic of Germany, Berlin, 21 December 1972

The High Contracting Parties, mindful of their responsibility for the preservation of peace; endeavouring to make a contribution to *détente* and security in Europe; recognizing that the inviolability of frontiers and respect for the territorial integrity and sovereignty of all States in Europe within their present frontiers are a basic condition of peace; in the knowledge that therefore the two German States in their relations must refrain from the threat or the use of force; proceeding from historical realities and notwithstanding the different views of the Federal Republic of Germany and the German Democratic Republic on fundamental issues, including the national question; desirous of creating conditions for co-operation between the Federal Republic of Germany and the German Democratic Republic; have agreed as follows:

Article 1. The Federal Republic of Germany and the German Democratic Republic shall develop good neighbourly relations towards each other on the basis of equal rights.

Article 2. The Federal Republic of Germany and the German Democratic Republic shall be guided by the aims and principles of the United Nations Charter, especially in regard to the sovereign equality of all States, respect for their independence and territorial integrity, their right to self-determination, and the preservation of human rights and non-discrimination.

Article 3. In accordance with the United Nations Charter the Federal Republic of Germany and the German Democratic Republic will solve their disputes only by peaceful means and will not threaten or use force.

They affirm the inviolability of the existing frontier between them now and in the future, and undertake to respect without reservation each other's territorial integrity.

Article 4. The Federal Republic of Germany and the German Democratic Republic proceed from the consideration that neither one of the two States can represent or act in the name of the other in international affairs.

Article 5. The Federal Republic of Germany and the German Democratic Republic will promote peaceful relations between the European States and will contribute to cooperation and security in Europe.

They support efforts for a reduction of armed forces and armaments in Europe, provided that this is not permitted to adversely affect the security of the participants.

The Federal Republic of Germany and the German Democratic Republic will support efforts which have as their objective general and complete disarmament under effective international control to contribute to international security, especially in the field of nuclear weapons and other weapons of mass destruction.

Article 6. The German Federal Republic and the German Democratic Republic proceed from the principle that the sovereign power of each of the two States is limited to its own territory. They respect the independence of each of the two States in its internal and external affairs.

Article 7. The Federal Republic of Germany and the German Democratic Republic declare their willingness as a part of the normalization of their relations to regulate practical and humanitarian questions. They will conclude agreements to develop and promote cooperation, on the basis of this Treaty and to the benefit of both parties, in the fields of the economy, science and technology, traffic, legal relations, posts and telecommunications, health, culture, sports, protection of the environment and in other areas.

Article 8. The Federal Republic of Germany and the German Democratic Republic will exchange permanent representatives. They will be established at the seat of the respective Governments. Practical questions which are related to the establishment of the representations will be settled additionally.

Article 9. The Federal Republic of Germany and the German Democratic Republic are agreed that bilateral and multilateral international treaties and agreements concluded earlier by them or concerning them are not affected by this Treaty.

Article 10. This Treaty is subject to ratification and enters into force on the day following the Exchange of Notes to this effect.
[Signed] Egon Bahr, Dr Michael Kohl.

Additional documents

[The treaty was accompanied by a number of additional detailed agreements, protocols and statements concerning the delimitation of the frontier between the two States (reference to Article 3), trade (reference to Article 7), postal affairs, regulation of passenger traffic, improving the movements of people across frontiers and solving the problem of separated families and legal questions.

The two German Governments took note of the pact that each in accordance with its own laws would apply for membership of the United Nations, and they promised to keep each other informed.

The two signatories also exchanged letters noting that the D.D.R. would communicate the following text to the ambassadors of the U.S.S.R. (and the Federal German Republic to the British, French and American ambassadors):

The Federal Republic of Germany and the German Democratic Republic, with reference to Article 9 of the Treaty on the bases of relations between the two, state that the rights and responsibilities of the Four Powers and the respective quadripartite agreements, decisions and practices shall not be affected by this Treaty.]

XII · The alliances and alignments of the United States

When the war came to an end the United States alone among the victorious Great Powers faced the future without alliance commitments to any single Power or separate group of Powers. Even during the course of the war Roosevelt had concluded no formal alliances but signed executive agreements not requiring a two-thirds majority of the Senate for approval. Thus the United States, for instance, was bound to its allies by only an executive agreement as one of the signatories of the *Declaration by the United Nations, 1 January 1942* (p. 212), whose obligations ceased with the end of the war. In 1945 the United States administration tried to return to its 'normal' peacetime diplomacy, rejecting exclusive alliances which, it was feared, would once again divide the world into hostile groupings. In the place of alliances, the U.S. had become a principal advocate and founder of the United Nations. But the objectives of American policy in 1945 remained global, based on the expectation of continued cooperation among the 'Big Three', Britain, the Soviet Union and the United States.

The United States and Latin America

At the same time as adopting the global approach to foreign policy, the States maintained its tradition of claiming special rights and responsibilities in the Western hemisphere as embodied in the Monroe Doctrine (1923). In practice this has meant that the United States, whilst recognizing how varied the twenty Latin American Republics are, and how much of the time their interests have conflicted with each other, has also claimed that they form part of an American system. American Presidents have claimed the right to intervene unilaterally, if need be, if the vital interests of the United States were held

4 The Americas

to be endangered – vital interests which were declared to be equally in the interests of the American Republics as a whole. This might happen if a Latin American Republic developed close ties with a State potentially hostile to the United States and especially, as in Cuba, where foreign military bases or weapons were involved. Geographically, U.S. intervention has been confined in the main to the strategically vital Caribbean region; the United States possesses Guantanamo naval base in Cuba and controls the Panama Canal. Until Franklin D. Roosevelt proclaimed the Good Neighbor policy in 1933, United States armed intervention had been frequent, especially in Cuba, Panama, Nicaragua, Mexico, Haiti and the Dominican Republic, despite the attempts of inter-American conferences to prevent United States military action.

Eight international conferences of the American States met before the end of the Second World War: the first took place in Washington during 1889 and 1890, and since then numerous other special inter-American conferences have also been convened. They have produced many treaties, declarations and enunciations of principles, but the gap between these aspirations and practical achievements has been a wide one. Fervent expressions of faith in the principles of democracy have rung especially hollow when ascribed to by dictatorships that exist and continue to flourish in some of the Latin American Republics. Nor have the political, economic and international objectives of the Governments of the twenty Latin American Republics always coincided with those of the much more powerful United States; the twenty Republics are also divided on many issues among each other.

The International American Conferences have been concerned with four basic aspects of inter-American relations: (i) establishing the independence and sovereignty of each State, thus ensuring non-intervention by any other State especially by the United States; (ii) hemispheric security; (iii) inter-American cooperation in many fields, economic and social, which frequently entails attempting to secure favourable trading conditions and economic aid from the United States; (iv) establishing effective machinery for settling inter-American disputes peacefully.

Inter-American solidarity was not prominently in evidence during the First World War. After the war, *the Fifth International Conference of American States, meeting in Santiago, 25 March–3 May 1923*, was notable for the conclusion of a *Treaty to Avoid or Prevent Conflicts*, generally known as the *Gondra Treaty*; this provided for a commission to investigate disputes and a six-months cooling-off period. At a special conference of American States, held in Washington, *10 December 1928–5 January 1929*, two treaties were adopted, the *General Convention of Inter-American Conciliation* and the *General Treaty of Inter-American*

Arbitration; but the weakness of the latter treaty was that both parties to a dispute would have to agree to setting up arbitration machinery. A special commission of American jurists, appointed after the Sixth International Conference at Havana (1928), drew up a *Convention Defining the Rights and Duties of States* which was adopted by the *Seventh International Conference of American States at Montevideo, 3–26 December 1933*; according to Article 8 of this convention, no State had the right to intervene in the internal or external affairs of another. The United States ratified the convention in June 1934, but Franklin Roosevelt in practice interpreted Article 8 as referring only to armed intervention. On 29 May 1934 Roosevelt abrogated the *Platt Amendment* under which the United States enjoyed special rights in Cuba.

A large number of resolutions and conventions were agreed and signed at a special *Inter-American Conference for the Maintenance of Peace, held in Buenos Aires, December 1936*. This conference also led to the conclusion in treaty form of acceptance of the principle of non-intervention in the *Non-Intervention Additional Protocol between the United States and Other American Republics, 23 December 1936* (p. 320). Two years later, at the *Eighth International Conference of American States at Lima, December 1938*, one of many declarations (no. 109) provided for periodic consultations of the Foreign Ministers of the American Republics and affirmed the continental solidarity of the American Republics in case the peace, security or territorial integrity of any one of them was threatened. But despite the many treaties and convention resolutions from 1890 to 1938 the actual degree of inter-American cooperation and solidarity remained limited, and the machinery for settling disputes in the Americas peacefully was far from effective. The twenty Republics had not succeeded in achieving complete security from undue United States influence in their affairs, although Roosevelt's Good Neighbor policy brought about a great improvement in their relationship. Nor had the United States secured complete security through the establishment of the kind of inter-American cooperation that would have induced all the Latin American Republics to give priority to relations with America as against relations with European States.

With the outbreak of war in Europe in September 1939, inter-American cooperation was strengthened. The first meeting of the Foreign Ministers of the Republics took place in *Panama, 23 September–3 October 1939*. This conference adopted the *Act of Panama*, a multilateral executive agreement, which included a general declaration of neutrality; an agreement on the setting-up of a committee of experts for the duration of the war to study and make recommendations on problems of neutrality; a declaration that a neutral zone was established on the high seas 300 miles from the shores of the Republics; and, most important of all, a resolution that if any region in the Americas belonging to a European State should change sovereignties, thereby endangering the security of the Americas, a consultive meeting should be called urgently. The German conquests of the Netherlands and of France brought about a danger of the kind contemplated at Panama, and the Foreign Ministers therefore met again in *Havana, 21–30 July 1940*, and adopted the *Act of Havana* (p. 324). It stated that should a change of sovereignty be threatened in the case of the European colonies, then the American Republics would create a committee to administer them; but should the emergency arise before a committee could act, then one State could take action alone, which in practice meant the United States. Another resolution declared that aggression against one of the Republics would be regarded as aggression against all, though they were only bound to consult in that event on measures of common defence. The United States concluded many bilateral agreements with individual American States during the Second World War, providing credit, purchasing raw materials and securing rights of bases.

When shortly after Pearl Harbor the *third consultive meeting of American Foreign Ministers took place in Rio de Janeiro, 15–28 January 1942*, nine Central American and Caribbean States had declared war on the Axis and eleven Latin American States either broke off diplomatic relations or declared non-belligerency. But inter-American military cooperation remained far from wholehearted, with the Argentine being sympathetic to the Axis, and only by the time war was drawing to a close in 1945 had all the American Republics declared war on Germany and Japan. The future relations of the American Republics and inter-American cooperation in the post-war world which would see established the United Nations was the principal subject of the *Inter-American Conference on Problems of War and Peace, in Mexico City, 21 February–8 March 1945*. The conference was more concerned with post-war problems, and especially with the United Nations organization, than with problems of wartime alliance. The *Dumbarton Oaks* proposals (p. 241) were generally endorsed, but resolutions were also passed urging adequate representation for Latin American States on the proposed Security Council; in general the Latin American Republics wished to reduce the dominant role of the Great Powers. Agreement was reached on the *Act of Chapultepec* (Resolution 8) which provided for sanctions and appropriate regional action in the event of an American or non-American State committing aggression against another American State, but with the additional proviso that such action would need to be consistent with the purpose of the world international organization when established. The Act of Chapultepec only remained in force whilst the war continued; it was intended that a new treaty should replace it later in time of peace. Other resolutions called upon the next American conference to agree on measures to strengthen inter-American collaboration in the economic and other fields. At the *San Francisco Conference* establishing the United Nations (p. 242), the United States and the Latin American States secured an important modification of the Dumbarton Oaks proposals. It emerged as Article 51 of the Charter, which permitted groups of States to make treaties for collective self-defence to meet an armed attack. But this right is limited to the point of time when the Security Council takes what action it deems appropriate. It is nevertheless an important safeguard where the Security Council is deadlocked or where one of the permanent members uses its veto against any enforcement action (p. 242). Article 51 is further limited by Articles 53 to 54, which state that whilst the Security Council may authorize some regional action for 'enforcement action', no such action may be taken without the authorization of the Security Council; the Security Council also has to be kept fully informed of any action in contemplation. Thus Article 51 only confers a right of self-defence in case of armed attack, not of enforcement against a State that is more vaguely accused of aggression or aggressive intent before an armed attack has occurred.

The Ninth Inter-American Conference for the Maintenance of Continental Peace and Security met near Rio de Janeiro, 15 August–2 September 1947, under the shadow of the 'cold war'; their deliberations concluded with the signature of the *Inter-American Treaty of Reciprocal Assistance, 2 September 1947* (p. 325), also known as the *Pact of Rio*, which became effective after ratification by two-thirds of the signatories on 3 December 1948. It was signed by nineteen American Republics, that is all except Nicaragua and Ecuador. In March 1960 Cuba withdrew from the treaty. The Pact of Rio established an inter-American alliance of collective defence against armed attack as permitted by Article 51 of the U.N. Charter; it was also a regional agreement laying down the procedures to be followed in the event of any other act, or threat of aggression. Although Canada was not a party to the treaty, Article 4 defined the region covered as all of North and South America, and included Canada and Greenland and a part of Antarctica. The treaty left it to each signatory to act immediately as it considered necessary after an armed attack had taken place, until by a two-thirds majority the members of the pact decided on what future action was required. But if 'indirect aggression' was claimed to have taken place, such as the support of revolution in one State by another (many Latin American Republics shared United States fears of communist subversion), then no automatic right of intervention was allowed to any one State or a group of States; in such an event members of the treaty would meet to decide on what joint measures to take. According to Article 53 of the U.N. Charter, any 'enforcement action' then decided on would require the Security Council's authorization.

The Rio treaty made hemispheric defence the joint responsibility of the American Republics, but did not supersede the Monroe Doctrine or the claim of the United States to act unilaterally in defence of its own vital interests. The Rio treaty was significant in another respect, for it provided the model for other regional treaties to which the United States was a party, especially the North Atlantic Treaty (p. 335).

The second treaty, complementing the Rio pact, which reorganized the inter-American system in the post Second World War years, was the *Charter of the Organization of American States, 30 April 1948* (p. 328), signed by all twenty-one American Republics. Trinidad joined in February 1967, and Barbados in October 1967, but Cuba was later expelled in February 1962. This treaty emerged from the negotiations at the *Ninth International Conference of American States at Bogotá, 30 March–2 May 1948*. The Charter of the Organization of American States (O.A.S.) comprises 112 articles. It places the inter-American system on a permanent treaty basis within the U.N. framework. Articles 32 to 101 define the structure and functions of the O.A.S. The supreme organ of the O.A.S. is the Inter-American Conference, which in ordinary session meets every five years, though at the request of two-thirds of the members a special conference may be convened. The old Pan-American Union at Washington becomes the permanent central organ and general secretariat of O.A.S. Its council is composed of a representative from each Member State. The council acts as a consultative body in the event of an act of aggression; it also decides by majority to call a consultative meeting of Foreign Ministers when requested by one member. The council works through three organs: the Inter-American Economic and Social Council, the Inter-American Council of Jurists and the Inter-American Cultural Council. In addition, some twelve specialized organizations, commissions and agencies work within the framework of the O.A.S. The charter sets out the purpose, principles, duties and rights of the O.A.S.; the purpose of the organization is to facilitate the pacific settlements of disputes, to strengthen inter-American solidarity and to raise economic, social and cultural standards.

The third treaty on which post-war inter-American relations were to be based was the *American Treaty on Pacific Settlement, 30 April 1948*, known as the *Pact of Bogotá* (p. 330). Its purpose was to coordinate treaties signed at earlier conferences to ensure that disputes between American States would be settled by peaceful means. Although the treaty provided for compulsory arbitration (Article 46) and for the compulsory jurisdiction of the International Court (Article 32), reservations made to the pact at the time of signature by seven American Republics, including the United States, have made these compulsory procedures, wherein the main strength of the pact lies, inoperative in practice.

It is a characteristic of all these treaties that no State is automatically bound to offer armed assistance to any other signatory; also important is the fact that the United States is not prevented from acting in accordance with the treaty, if it decides to do so, by the possible opposition of one or more of the Latin American Republics.

The 'Cold War' in Europe and American policy, 1947–50

As has already been noted, the wartime alliance commitments of the United States ceased with the end of the war in 1945. But the American determination before 1947 to avoid new exclusive alliance commitments outside the Americas in peacetime, other than the general obligations of the United Nations Charter, was replaced by a search for reliable allies after 1947 in the new era of East–West relations that became known as the 'cold war'. It is not possible to date the origin of this 'cold war' in the same way as the origins of a shooting war. In a sense it goes back to the Bolshevik Revolution, for the mutual suspicions then aroused were never overcome, not even during the years of alliance in the Second World War. At the end of that war Soviet influence and military power had tremendously increased in Europe, and Stalin treated the region of Central and Eastern Europe as belonging to the Soviet communist sphere of influence. This attitude precluded the restoration of Poland and the Balkan States to their pre-war independence; and it also introduced to these countries, to some gradually and to others immediately, the suppression of individual political freedom, the secret police, imprisonment without trial and the 'purge'. In 1946 Churchill characterized the self-imposed isolation of communist-dominated Europe as an 'iron curtain'. Genuine Allied cooperation in the Government of Germany as a whole proved a pipedream. In Germany, and in the United Nations at the Security Council, the Soviet Union clashed with the policies of the Western Powers.

There was no sharing of the secrets of the atomic bomb; faced with a huge preponderance of Soviet armies in Europe whilst the West had demobilized, sole possession of the atomic bomb, the West believed, could alone restore the balance and deter Stalin from further expansion. That this was his intention Britain and the United States deduced from Soviet pressure on Turkey and from the Soviet Union's unwillingness to withdraw from Iran in accordance with wartime agreements; after U.S. protests, the Soviet Union in March 1946 did announce its withdrawal from Iran. In Greece, communist neighbours were aiding the Greek guerrillas in the Greek civil war. Truman saw these communist efforts as part of a general Soviet strategy to spread communist power under the direction of the Soviet Union, and responded with an address to Congress broadcast to the nation which contained the passage that became known as the *Truman Doctrine, 12 March 1947.*

The Truman Doctrine. The immediate need to help Greece was placed by Truman in the wider context of helping free peoples everywhere to maintain their institutions and their national integrity against aggressive movements that attempted to impose on them totalitarian government. He warned that such direct or indirect aggression, if successful, would undermine the foundations of international peace. American help, Truman advised, should be primarily extended through economic and financial aid. Greece and Turkey received American help. This was only a beginning. A few months later the *Marshall Plan*, originally proposed by the Secretary of State on *5 June 1947*, provided massive economic support to the countries of Western Europe (p. 379).

Until the spring of 1948 the United States continued to rely primarily on granting economic support and on diplomacy to prevent the extension of Soviet and communist influence and power. But communist successes and pressures in 1948 and 1949 led to a reappraisal of American policies. In Europe the Czech Communists gained complete control of Czechoslovakia in February 1948. Soon after, in April 1948, the divergence of Soviet and Western policies over Germany decided Stalin to put pressure on the Western Powers by impeding Western land and water communications with Berlin. By 1 July 1948 the Russians had imposed a complete land and sea blockade in breach of Allied agreements, but they desisted from interfering with the air corridors.

The Western Powers responded to events in Czechoslovakia and to Soviet hostility in Germany with a military alliance, the *Brussels Treaty*, and later pursued a policy which would lead to the creation of a rehabilitated sovereign and rearmed West German State (p. 386). In Washington, the *Vandenberg Resolution*, adopted by Senate on *11 June 1948*, gave bi-partisan Congressional support for an American alliance policy within the U.N. framework to meet any military communist threat; the resolution did not actually use the word 'alliance', but instead referred to 'collective arrangements'. It stated that the United States Government should pursue 'regional and other collective arrangements for individual and collective self-defense', and sanctioned the 'Association of the United States by constitutional process' with such arrangements as affected American security. By 'constitutional process' was meant the necessary consent of Senate to any alliance treaty as required by the constitution. The resolution also required that any treaty engagements entered into should be mutual in their application, i.e. if the United States undertook to aid another country to meet aggression, that country would be bound to aid the United States in similar conditions.

The Vandenberg Resolution made possible the association of the United States (and Canada) with the West European States in an Atlantic military alliance, the *North Atlantic Treaty, 4 April 1949* (p. 335). This treaty involved no automatic commitment on the part of the United States to go to war. The key article is no. 5; it stipulates that an armed attack against one or more signatories would be regarded as an attack on all, but only required the other signatories to assist the victim of an attack by such action as each deemed necessary. Article 6 defined the area covered by the treaty, which included the territory of the Federal Republic of Germany and West Berlin since the troops of the signatories were stationed there. The practical expectation that an attack on one signatory would in fact entail war with all was brought much closer eighteen months after signature when, in accordance with Article 3 (which required the signatories to develop their collective capacity to resist), agreement was reached that NATO would establish an integrated defence force. An integrated command structure with a Supreme Commander was developed. The supreme command has so far (up to 1973) always been held by an American General. Of great importance in the development of NATO has been the question of nuclear capacity and its control.

From 1957 to 1960 the United States signed agreements concerning 'cooperation' in atomic weapons with Britain, Canada, France, the German Federal Republic, Greece, the Netherlands and Italy. NATO since 1957 has had nuclear capacity, but its actual use is subject to the consent of the President of the United States. A Nuclear Planning Committee is intended to provide for consultation. Britain, a NATO signatory, has independent nuclear capacity and so has France, but it is small compared to the capacity of the United States. Under an agreement with the United States signed in December 1962, Britain has received from the United States Polaris missiles. Only the stock of American atomic weapons and missiles, however, is capable of matching the capacity for nuclear attack of the Soviet Union. (On NATO see also p. 383.)

A significant article of the NATO treaty from the American, or more precisely the Senate's point of view, is Article 11, which required that the treaty be ratified by each country according to its own 'constitutional processes'. This meant that ratification would be required by a two-thirds majority of Senate. The NATO treaty was duly ratified by Senate on 21 July 1949. There existed at that time an understanding between leaders of Congress on the one hand, and the President and his administration on the other, that treaties involving military collaboration against communism should contain a clause requiring ratification by 'constitutional process', that is by the Senate.

Supplementing the United States participation with Western Europe, Congress passed the *Mutual Defense Act, 6 October 1949*, which permitted the administration to sign bilateral treaties to aid and rearm countries for broad political reasons, or for the sake of the security of the United States. Huge sums were expended in such aid. Bilateral treaties were concluded with each of the European NATO allies in Europe on 27 January 1950, with Iran on 23 May 1950, and in Asia with South Korea on 26 January 1950.

The conflict in Asia since 1950

The communist victory in China during the summer of 1949, the conclusion of the Sino-Soviet Treaty in February 1950 (p. 370), the American awareness that the Soviet Union also had exploded an atomic bomb in September 1949 – all these events led to changes in U.S. policy in the Pacific. American military strength and political influence in eastern Asia was founded on the occupation of Japan, and the establishment of military bases in Japan and on Okinawa in the Ryukus. In the Philippines the United States had secured bases by a *Philippine–United States Treaty, 14 March 1947*. With Nationalist China impotent on *Taiwan (Formosa)*, the administration's advisers in Washington began to reconsider during the winter months of 1949 and 1950 whether a signature of a Japanese peace treaty and an American withdrawal from Japan was any longer desirable. A strategy for Asia now began to take shape which had its parallel in America's policy towards Western Germany; the objective of the policy was to transform a defeated and occupied enemy into an ally. Hence the United States took the lead in negotiating a generous Japanese peace treaty with or without Soviet approval, and simultaneously concluded an American–Japanese alliance permitting the continued presence of U.S. forces. The outbreak of the Korean War in June 1950 both confirmed the existing objectives of American foreign policy and led to new commitments and policies.

The new elements of American policy after the outbreak of war in Korea were, firstly, the decision to commit American naval and air forces to fight in South Korea on the Asian mainland; and secondly, the decision to interpose the Seventh Fleet between the Chinese mainland and Taiwan (Formosa), thus intervening in the Chinese Civil War. This latter decision was reached by Truman on 26 June 1950, and meant that each side was forbidden to attack the other, though clearly the danger was seen to arise from a communist attack on Taiwan; Truman declared that in the new circumstances this 'would be a direct threat to the Pacific area and to the United States forces performing their lawful and necessary functions there'. (It should be noted that before the outbreak of the conflict Truman had stated in January 1950 that the United States would not 'pursue a course which will lead to involvement in the civil conflict in China'.) On 29 and 30 June 1950 Truman committed U.S. ground forces in South Korea as well (p. 449).

The Korean War, with its varying military fortunes, and especially with Communist Chinese intervention in late October 1950, changed the emphasis of America's China policy. During the months preceding the Korean War, the United States had refused to recognize Mao Tse-tung's proclaimed People's Republic of China (1 October 1949) as the Government of China. After the outbreak of the Korean War, the United States gradually decided to give full support to Chiang Kai-shek's Republic of China established in Taiwan. The possibility of a more flexible policy towards mainland China was abandoned for some years.

During the period from 1950 to 1954 the United States administration concluded that the threat to stability and peace arising from the possibility of communist direct attack or subversion was increasing and could only be met by throwing the military weight of America behind Asian and European allies willing to resist aggression. The objective was deterrence. The cohesion of the European NATO alliance was accordingly strengthened with substantial American and German military contributions. In Asia a search for new allies was intensified in 1950. But in Asia there was no continuous ring of developed nations that could be formed among China's neighbours. Running from north to south (see map on p. 432) Japan, South Korea, Taiwan, and the Philippines formed an unbroken flank, but in the South China Sea, Malaysia and Indonesia kept aloof; south of Indonesia and far removed from China were Australia and New Zealand; these two joined the United States alliance groupings. On the mainland of Asia, Thailand and South Vietnam were associated in alliances; Cambodia and Laos were never securely brought in; Burma, India and Ceylon refused to join an anti-communist alliance, but Pakistan in 1954 did so; the American arc of defensive alliances against the Soviet Union continued unbroken thereafter through Iran to Turkey and Greece.

Two further important points need to be noted: firstly, the European anti-Soviet grouping of NATO is a separate alliance system which is not directly linked to the alliances of Asia. The only link is provided by the United States as a member of all these alliances in both Asia and Europe; Britain and (nominally) France are also involved in one Asian alliance, SEATO as well as in NATO. Secondly, the Asian allies have not undertaken to defend each other collectively but their commitment is limited to the particular treaty which they have signed. Only the United States is committed to all as the signatory of all the treaties.

The Asian alliances which the United States negotiated were of necessity a patchwork rather than a unified system, since each Asian ally was often as

concerned, if not more concerned, with its own regional problems and conflicts as with general opposition to communist expansion. Australia and New
Zealand desired assurances of American support against any renewal of a
threat from a revived Japan. The Philippines were involved in disputes with
Indonesia and Malaysia; Chiang Kai-shek proclaimed intentions of reconquer-
ing the Chinese mainland; Pakistan has periodically remained in conflict with
India especially over Kashmir; and the South Koreans refused to abandon
hopes of unification. The key to American policy in the western Pacific was
Japan.

To overcome the obstacles to a Japanese peace treaty and to strengthen the
defences of southern Asia, *the United States concluded a Security Treaty with
Australia and New Zealand, 1 September 1951 (ANZUS)* (p. 337), and also at
the same time the *Philippine–American Security Treaty, 30 August 1951*. Both
treaties had the same joint defence clause which bound each signatory to act
against any armed attack on either signatories in the Pacific; such action would
be taken in accordance with each country's 'constitutional processes'. The
signatories undertook by self-help and mutual aid to develop their collective
capacity to resist armed attack. In the case of the Philippine treaty no joint
consultative machinery was established (until the Philippine Mutual Defense
Board in 1958), but American forces continued to be stationed in the Philippines as provided for in the treaty of 1947. The ANZUS treaty established a
Consultative Council of Foreign Ministers, which has met and undertaken
coordinating work. Neither treaty involved any automatic commitments to go
to war though their language certainly implied a moral commitment.

The third Pacific treaty to be concluded on the same occasion was the
Japanese–United States Security Treaty, 8 September 1951 (p. 286). This treaty
was signed on the same day as the *Japanese Peace Treaty* (p. 283). In the preamble of the Japanese–American Security Treaty, its purpose is described as a
'provisional arrangement' for the defence of Japan in the absence of its own
means to provide for self-defence; the United States in order to promote
peace and security declared itself willing to maintain its armed forces in
and about Japan in the expectation that Japan would increasingly assume
responsibility for its own defence against 'direct and indirect aggression'.
Articles 1 and 2 are the most important as they granted bases to the United
States exclusively, and no other Power was to be granted bases without
American consent; American forces would be used to further the security of
Japan and the Far East, and could also be used internally as a police force at
the Japanese Government's request, to 'put down large-scale internal riots'.
Notes which accompanied the treaty bound the United States to consult with
the Japanese Government concerning the stationing of nuclear weapons in

Japan and the deployment of American troops from Japanese bases. All these three Pacific treaties ratified by the Senate on 20 March 1952 came into force as follows: the Philippine–American Treaty, 27 August 1952; the American–Japanese Security Treaty, 28 April 1952; and ANZUS on 29 April 1952. The next treaty followed the signature of the Korean armistice, 27 July 1953 *The Mutual Defense Treaty between Korea and the United States, 10 October 1953* (p. 339), reassured South Korea and was the price paid by America for South Korean acceptance of the armistice, and especially for abandoning a policy of reunification by force. This treaty permitted the stationing of American troops in and about Korea; it took effect on 17 November 1954, the Senate in a reservation underscoring that the United States was only committed to come to the aid of South Korea 'in case of an external armed attack ... against territory which has been recognized by the United States as lawfully brought under the administrative control of the Republic of Korea'.

During the year following the Korean armistice, in 1954, the Chinese Communists launched a bombardment of two small islands, Quemoy and Matsu, close to the mainland of China but held by nationalist garrisons. The United States committed itself to the defence of nationalist-held Taiwan (Formosa) and the Pescadores islands, but allowed itself latitude whether or not to defend Quemoy and Matsu. *A Mutual Defense Treaty between the United States and China, 2 December 1954* (p. 340), was concluded on terms similar to the other American defence treaties in Asia. It involved a promise to act to meet armed attack in accordance with each State's constitutional processes. But in approving the treaty the United States Senate added three understandings of importance: the ultimate legal title to Formosa and the Pescadores was not affected by the treaty, thus the United States was not committed ultimately to the claims of sovereignty of either side in the Chinese Civil War; secondly, the United States would only act if the nationalists were forced to fight in self-defence; finally, there was to be no extension territorially of the U.S. commitment without the prior consent of Senate.

Mao Tse-tung's victory had brought Communist China to the borders of Indo-China in 1949. The opportunity for spreading communism throughout Indo-China seemed favourable. Ho Chi Minh and his supporters had been fighting the French army since December 1946 after abortive negotiations with the French Fourth Republic for the independence of Vietnam. Subsequently, in 1949, France recognized the independence of Vietnam, Laos and Cambodia, but within the French Union and in practice under leadership acceptable to the French, i.e. ready to oppose Ho Chi Minh and the communists. Ho Chi Minh continued to fight. Strengthened by Chinese help, the Vietminh army began to strike at French garrisons in October 1950. The United States by then had

become involved in granting aid and supplies to the French-led armies, a consequence of a decision taken by Truman the previous May. Truman acted on
the conviction that there was a threat of communism spreading throughout
south-east Asia and that the loss of this whole region, coming after the loss of
mainland China, would undermine the global defences of the West. The out-
outbreak of the Korean War intensified this sense of threat, and American aid
to the French-led armies in Vietnam was increased. Despite this aid the French
were losing the struggle, and on 6 May 1954, when the Vietminh overran the
French defences at Dien Bien Phu, a conference at Geneva had already been
convened to work out an armistice and a settlement of the Indo-Chinese
conflicts. The French Government had lost heart in the struggle and at the
Geneva Conference, 26 April–21 July 1954 (p. 441) agreed to a settlement in
Indo-China which restricted their influence to South Vietnam, with the
possibility of losing even that if elections (if held) in 1956 should favour Ho
Chi Minh.

Although the French had received massive economic support from the
United States, and the Eisenhower administration in the spring of 1954 had
even considered supporting the French with ground forces (provided this was
a joint action with allies Britain, France and Australia and, if possible, Thailand and the Philippines), the French Government preferred to end the first
phase of the Indo-Chinese war on the terms of the Geneva settlement.

John Foster Dulles, Secretary of State in the Eisenhower administration,
disapproved of the Geneva settlement; the United States would not sign it but
in a declaration promised not to upset these arrangements. Dulles continued to
strengthen opposition to the spread of communism in southern Asia in the
face of the French military disaster. He conducted negotiations for an alliance
of collective defence among the major Powers interested in this region, Britain,
France, Australia and New Zealand, together with such Asian States as would
join in the grouping. The new treaty would thus extend and complement
ANZUS. The outcome of the negotiations was the *South-East Asia Collective
Defense Treaty (SEATO), in Manila on 8 September 1954* (p. 341), together with a
Pacific Charter (p. 343) of principles. The eight signatories were the United
States, Britain, France, Australia, New Zealand, and the three Asian States,
Pakistan, Thailand and the Philippines. It followed the general structure of
other United States defence treaties in that the signatories bound themselves
separately and jointly by self-help and mutual aid to develop their individual
and collective capacity to resist armed attack or subversion (Article 2);
an armed attack on one signatory was recognized as contributing a danger to
all, and the signatories agreed to 'act to meet the common danger in accordance
with its own constitutional processes'; the signatories further would consult

together if the integrity or independence of a signatory, or of any State designated in the treaty, were threatened by other than armed attack or 'by any fact or situation which might endanger the peace of the area'. A number of provisions, however, rendered the treaty rather vague or flexible in its possible application. The treaty area as geographically defined in Article 8 excluded Hong Kong and Taiwan. Pakistan as a signatory was included, but the position of India was left uncertain. In the event, when China fought India in 1962 (p. 435) SEATO did not concern itself as a treaty organization. An additional Protocol designated Cambodia, Laos, and the 'free territory under the jurisdiction of the State of Vietnam' as falling within the treaty area for the purposes of Article 4. Cambodia rejected the protection of SEATO in 1956. From 1954 to 1961 SEATO's capacity for providing effective aid in Laos and Vietnam was not tested; but the renewal of conflict in South Vietnam by the Vietcong and North Vietnamese in 1960, and in Laos by the Pathet Lao forces, raised the question at SEATO's ministerial council which met in Bangkok in March 1961. In the event neither France nor Britain would support military action in Laos. Laos was neutralized in 1962 (p. 462). Nor have all the SEATO Powers acting within the framework of the treaty provided collective support for South Vietnam. Instead, a number of SEATO Powers have given armed support 'separately' as provided for by Article 2, but without calling upon SEATO machinery. During the Laos crisis of 1962, the United States, principally with British, New Zealand and Australian support, moved forces and established bases in north-eastern Thailand to reassure Thailand. The United States provided unilateral support for the neutralist régime in Laos after 1962. SEATO was further weakened in the 1960s by Pakistan's concern over its conflict with India. A specific American and Australian reservation had excluded the application of the treaty to such a conflict. Pakistan drew closer to China; the United States and Britain rushed arms to India during and after the Indian–Chinese border conflict of 1962 (p. 435), which also strengthened India against Pakistan and caused bitter resentment in Pakistan, a SEATO ally. France became increasingly opposed to United States involvement in Vietnam during the 1960s and withdrew from active SEATO membership. In the Vietnamese conflict, Britain refused active military cooperation, and since 1968 has run down its bases east of Suez. Of the SEATO Powers only Australia and the Philippines contributed small forces. SEATO had been conceived as providing United States, British and French 'Big Power' support to the States of Asia willing to contain the threat of communism and Chinese expansion, i.e. Thailand, Pakistan, New Zealand, Australia, the Philippines and the three Indo-Chinese States, by providing military and economic assistance. The weaknesses resulting from a lack of British and French support, from Pakistan's virtual withdrawal and the changing policies of the United States in south-east Asia, became very apparent in 1972. SEATO has not proved very effective in providing 'collective' armed support. Yet the loose SEATO alliance grouping remains in consultative being as these countries of Asia continue to search for a counterbalance to threats arising in Asia.

During the 1960s American–Japanese treaty relations were modified. The *American–Japanese Treaty of Mutual Cooperation and Security, 19 January 1960* (p. 287), restored sovereign rights to Japan which it had lost in the earlier 1957 treaty. It implicitly acknowledged that Japanese forces would only be used in self-defence as the signatories promise to help each other 'subject to their constitutional provisions', and hence also in accordance with the Japanese constitution. Article 5 limits the obligation to act to an armed attack on either party 'in the territories under the administration of Japan'. Specifically the American forces could no longer be used to put down internal riots as in the 1951 treaty. (See also p. 271 for the later developments 1970–2.)

In addition to the treaties of alliance already outlined, the United States signed a number of executive agreements under the Mutual Security Program under the *Mutual Defense Assistance Act, approved by Congress 6 October 1949*, and the *Mutual Security Act, approved by Congress 10 October 1951*. The 1949 Mutual Defense Act supplied the NATO allies with economic aid for rearmament through a series of bilateral agreements concluded in 1950 and 1951. The act of 1951 extended the programme of 'mutual defense and self-help' and technical assistance to all areas of the world, requiring the President to lay down the terms of assistance to strengthen the defences of the country to which such aid was granted. These agreements were not supposed to involve definite political treaty commitments of support. They were signed with the allies of the United States associated in various security treaties; but assistance agreements were also concluded with countries not in a formal alliance treaty relationship with the United States. Thus, for instance, a Mutual Defense and Assistance Agreement was concluded on 26 September 1953 between Spain and the United States, providing assistance to Spain and securing bases for the United States in that country. Among the many countries with which bilateral aid, military, economic, and technical assistance agreements have been concluded, and which are not political allies of the United States, are several African States: Congo (Zaire), 1963; Dahomey, 1962; Ethiopia, 1953; Guinea, 1965; Liberia, 1951; Mali, 1961; Niger, 1962; Senegal, 1962; South Africa, 1951; and a number of Middle Eastern States: Israel, 1952; Lebanon, 1957; Libya, 1954; and Saudi Arabia, 1953. The actual pattern of this aid changes from time to time with the political development of the area concerned.

In Asia, the United States signed mutual defence and assistance agreements under the 1949 act with Cambodia, Laos and Vietnam, and France in December 1950. Further agreements were concluded for military and economic aid under the U.S. Mutual Security Act of 1951 with Laos and Vietnam. In 1955 the United States signed agreements for direct assistance with South Vietnam and Laos. A further agreement between South Vietnam and the United States was concluded in 1961.

Conflict within South Vietnam was renewed in 1959 and brought with it increasing North Vietnamese and United States involvement. The United States first sent military advisers to stiffen the South Vietnamese army, and supported the South Vietnamese leader Ngo Dinh Diem who refused to hold all-Vietnamese elections in 1956 and to carry out this aspect of the Geneva Agreement of 1954 (p. 454). United States involvement escalated step by step until the introduction of large-scale American forces in 1965; the air war was extended over all Vietnam and American forces took over a large share of the fighting in South Vietnam. In 1964 President Johnson's administration sought the approval of Congress 'to take all necessary steps including the use of armed force', in defence of any member or protocol State of the SEATO treaty system, when reporting to Congress that on 2 August and 4 August 1964 North Vietnamese torpedo boats had carried out an unprovoked attack on two American destroyers in the international waters of the Gulf of Tonkin. The *Gulf of Tonkin Resolution, 7 August 1964,* drafted in collaboration with Congressional leaders, called for support of military action by the United States within the SEATO framework; it allowed the widest discretion to the President in the following passage:

...

The United States regards as vital to its national interest and to world peace the maintenance of international peace and security in south-east Asia. Consonant with the Constitution of the United States and the Charter of the United Nations and in accordance with its obligations under the South-east Asia Collective Defense Treaty, the United States is, therefore, prepared, as the President determines, to take all necessary steps, including the use of armed force, to assist any member or protocol State of the South-east Asia Collective Defense Treaty requesting assistance in defense of its freedom.

The Joint Resolution was adopted by the Senate and by the House of Representatives on 7 August 1964.

[For the later stages of American involvement in the wars of Vietnam, Laos and Cambodia, see pp. 440–6.]

United States treaty relations in the Middle East

Two unrelated conflicts involved the United States in the Middle East: firstly, the tension between the Soviet Union on the one hand and its Middle Eastern neighbours, Turkey and Iran, on the other; and secondly, the foundation of Israel and the continuing conflict between Israel and the Arab States. United States policy sought both to strengthen anti-Soviet and anti-communist alignments, and to give support to the State of Israel sufficient to ensure its survival among the hostile Arab States. Beginning in about 1955 these two separate strands, the 'cold war' and 'Arab-Israeli' conflicts, began to intertwine and cause much perplexity to American policy-makers.

The first post-war involvement of the United States was to provide economic, diplomatic and military aid to *Iran* and *Turkey* (and *Greece*) to withstand the Soviet Union and communist expansion (Truman Doctrine, p. 306). Aid to these three countries continued throughout the 1950s on a growing scale based on the Mutual Defense Program begun in 1949.

When Israel was proclaimed on 14 May 1948, the United States under the Truman administration expressed its moral support by recognizing the Provisional Government on 22 June 1948. The armistice of February 1949 established temporary boundaries for the State of Israel, which the Arabs refused to accept as permanent; indeed, the Arab States would not accept a State of Israel as permanent. But the United States joined with Britain and France in the *Tripartite Declaration, 25 May 1950*, which expressed their opposition to an arms race between Israel and the Arab States and declared that if any of the States should prepare to violate the armistice lines or the frontier, they would in these circumstances immediately take action. This declaration in effect supported Israel's right to exist within the frontiers established by force of arms pending a peace treaty. The United States signed a Mutual Defense Assistance Agreement with Israel in July 1952 and has provided economic aid and military equipment to Israel since that year.

The second phase of the Middle Eastern crisis developed in 1956. Again two strands of conflict intermingled: Britain and France versus Egypt, especially over the issue of Nasser's nationalization of the Suez Canal (July 1956); and rising tensions between Israel on the one hand and Egypt, whose leaders called for a united Arab effort to destroy Israel, on the other. On 31 October 1956 Britain and France launched their attack on Egypt – first by bombing airfields and then on 5 November by landing troops on the western end of the Suez Canal. The United States, not informed in advance of the Anglo-French attack, worked for a ceasefire and for an Israeli, French and British withdrawal. The ceasefire went into force on 6 November and Britain and France withdrew in December 1956. The Soviet Union (which had supplied Egypt with arms) together with the United States supported Egypt, and gained much credit in Arab eyes (see also p. 500).

The growing influence of the Soviet Union in Egypt and Syria, and a possible spread of communist influence after Suez and the 1956 war, alarmed the American administration and led to a Joint Resolution of Congress, signed by the President, which became known as the *Eisenhower Doctrine, 5 January 1957*. It pledged American support for the independence and integrity of Middle Eastern States as a vital American interest; American armed support was promised to resist armed aggression 'from any country controlled by international communism', provided the President regarded it as necessary, and provided such armed support was requested. In accordance with this resolution the United States supported Jordan in April 1957 and sent increased arms to Lebanon, Turkey and Iraq. When in July 1958 the pro-Western Government of Iraq was overthrown and King Faisal was murdered, Jordan and Lebanon requested American help. American marines were landed in the Lebanon immediately (British troops went to the assistance of Jordan). *On 28 July 1958, by executive agreements with Britain, Turkey, Iran and Pakistan, the United States* (p. 500) linked herself to these States of the *Baghdad Pact*. The pact was renamed the *Central Treaty Organization, CENTO*, after the formal withdrawal of Iraq in 1959.

A decade of uneasy peace and rival armaments deals elapsed before the third Israeli–Arab war. 'The Six Day War' began with an Israeli air strike on 5 June 1967. The United Arab Republic was rapidly defeated and Israeli troops reached the Suez Canal. A ceasefire between the United Arab Republic and Israel came into operation on 8 June 1967, and fighting also ceased with Syria. The United States had declared itself neutral and entered into no new treaty commitments.

The United States and the Americas since 1950

The United States administration endeavoured to draw the attention of the Latin American States to the dangers of international communism during the early 1950s, but without much response. The election of President Arbeñz in Guatemala in 1950 alarmed the administration, which regarded him as sympathetic to communist policies. At the *Tenth International Conference of American States at Caracas, 1–28 March 1954*, Secretary of State Dulles secured the passage of a resolution directed against the control of the political institutions of any American State by the 'international communist movement'; but no resolution specifically allowed for any joint intervention in the affairs of an American

State. In June 1954 Guatemala was invaded from Honduras, and Arbeñz was overthrown. It was widely believed that the United States was chiefly responsible and that the Central Intelligence Agency was involved in the invasion. Latin American fears of a return by the United States to a policy of intervention, and dissatisfaction with the economic policies of the United States, made the 1950s a bleak decade in relations between the United States and its South American neighbours. The decade ended with Castro's successful Cuban Revolution. The United States broke off diplomatic relations with Castro in 1961. Cuba's communist alignments represented a major challenge to United States leadership in the Americas. An attempt to bring about Castro's fall by aiding Cuban exiles to land in the Bay of Pigs and to raise a revolt ended in a fiasco in April 1961. This setback to inter-American relations was counterbalanced by President Kennedy's initiative in launching the 'Alliance for Progress'.

A special meeting of the *Inter-American Economic and Social Council held in Punta del Este, Uruguay, 5-17 August 1961, adopted the Charter of Punta del Este, establishing an Alliance for Progress* (p. 346). The United States undertook to provide 20 billion dollars, mainly from public funds, over a period of ten years. But these vast funds were not to be applied in the normal way of foreign aid. They were to be utilized to transform society in Latin America. Latin American Governments pledged themselves to carry through far-reaching social reforms 'to permit a fair distribution of the fruits of economic and social progress'. These provisional reforms ranged from better use of land, housing, and education, to the elimination of corruption and to economic collaboration. The results in Latin America have been disappointing during the 1960s in terms of the objectives set out in the Alliance for Progress.

The United States continued to show itself ready to act unilaterally when it believed its vital interests were threatened. When Russian missiles were being erected in Cuba, Kennedy secured their removal in his confrontation with Khrushchev during the thirteen days of the *Cuban Missile Crisis in October 1962*. But the United States also received a measure of support from the American States when the O.A.S. adopted a resolution on 23 October which sanctioned the use of armed force if necessary against Cuba under the terms of the Rio treaty (p. 325). Three years later, in April 1965, President Johnson intervened in the Dominican Republic where a revolution threatened to establish a Government judged by his administration to be controlled by communists. The United States again acted unilaterally in the Caribbean since it believed its most vital interests threatened by a hostile Government which, as in Cuba, might have linked itself with the Soviet Union. This intervention was motivated by fears of another Castro-type régime developing in the Caribbean.

The Latin American Republics have formed among themselves a number of associations designed to lead to greater prosperity through free trade and the integration of economic policies. Draft treaties to establish a *Central American Common Market* (*C.A.C.M.*) were signed on 10 June 1958 by El Salvador, Guatemala, Honduras and Nicaragua, and in 1962 by Costa Rica. Subsequently a *General Treaty of Central American Economic Integration* was concluded by the same four Central American Republics on *13 December 1960*. The Dominican Republic later became a full member, and Panama an associate member. Integration proceeded successfully in the 1960s. A *Latin American Free Trade Association* (*LAFTA*) came into existence with the signature of the *Montevideo Treaty, 18 February 1960*. Its members are Argentina, Bolivia, Brazil, Chile, Colombia, Ecuador, Mexico, Paraguay, Peru, Uruguay and Venezuela. LAFTA has made disappointingly little progress; but some success has been achieved in economic cooperation and tariff reduction by the smaller grouping of the *Andean Pact* countries, Colombia, Chile, Peru, Bolivia and Ecuador, who concluded the treaty forming the pact on *26 May 1969*. On 13 February 1973 Venezuela became the sixth member and Mexico describes its association not as membership but as a 'working partner'. The *Caribbean Free Trade Association* was formed in *December 1968* by Antigua, Barbados and Guyana, and later Trinidad and Tobago, Dominica, Grenada, St Kitts–Nevis–Anguilla, St Lucia, St Vincent, Jamaica and Montserrat joined this group. Barbados, Guyana, Jamaica and Trinidad and Tobago established an *Economic Community by a treaty concluded on 4 July 1973*. This treaty is designed to strengthen the *Caribbean Free Trade Association*. Cooperation in economic, educational and health spheres is envisaged; it is also envisaged in foreign policy to counterbalance the power of the United States.

With Canada, its northern neighbour, the United States has established close defence cooperation for the security of the North American continent. In 1940 a Permanent Joint Board of Defence was first established, and in 1947 the Canadian and American Governments agreed to continue it indefinitely. In 1951 and 1955 agreements were signed establishing across Canada radar warning systems linking the western Alaskan islands to the eastern Canadian shore. Canada, with the United States, is a founder member of NATO. The air defences of North America have been coordinated in a joint command (NORAD) since 1958. In 1959 agreement was reached for establishing a ballistic missile early warning system. Numerous other agreements exist on questions of joint defence with the United States but, as a member of the Commonwealth, Canada has held aloof from Pan-American organizations.

Convention between the United States of America and other American Republics concerning the fulfillment of existing treaties between the American States, Buenos Aires, 23 December 1936

The Governments represented at the Inter-American Conference for the Maintenance of Peace,

Animated by a desire to promote the maintenance of general peace in their mutual relations;

Appreciating the advantages derived and to be derived from the various agreements already entered into condemning war and providing methods for the pacific settlement of international disputes;

Recognizing the need for placing the greatest restrictions upon resort to war; and

Believing that for this purpose it is desirable to conclude a new convention to coordinate, extend, and assure the fulfillment of existing agreements, have ... agreed upon the following provisions:

Article 1. Taking into consideration that, by the Treaty to Avoid and Prevent Conflicts between the American States, signed at Santiago, May 3, 1923 (known as the Gondra Treaty), the High Contracting Parties agree that all controversies which it has been impossible to settle through diplomatic channels or to submit to arbitration in accordance with existing treaties shall be submitted for investigation and report to a Commission of Inquiry;

That by the Treaty for the Renunciation of War, signed at Paris on August 28, 1928 (known as the Kellogg–Briand Pact, or Pact of Paris), the High Contracting Parties solemnly declare in the names of their respective peoples that they condemn recourse to war for the solution of international controversies and renounce it as an instrument of national policy in their relations with one another;

That by the General Convention of Inter-American Conciliation, signed at Washington, January 5, 1929, the High Contracting Parties agree to submit to the procedure of conciliation all controversies between them, which it may not have been possible to settle through diplomatic channels, and to establish a 'Commission of Conciliation' to carry out the obligations assumed in the Convention;

That by the General Treaty of Inter-American Arbitration, signed at Washington, January 5, 1929, the High Contracting Parties bind themselves to submit to arbitration, subject to certain exceptions, all differences between them of an international character, which it has not been possible to adjust by diplomacy and which are juridical in their nature by reason of being susceptible of decision by the application of the principles of law, and moreover, to create a procedure of arbitration to be followed; and

That by the Treaty of Non-Aggression and Conciliation, signed at Rio de Janeiro, October 10, 1933 (known as the Saavedra Lamas Treaty), the High Contracting Parties solemnly declare that they condemn wars of aggression in their mutual relations or in those with other States and that the settlement of disputes or controversies between them shall be effected only by pacific means which have the sanction of international law, and also declare that as between them territorial questions must not be settled by violence, and that they will not recognize any territorial arrangement not obtained by pacific means, nor the validity of the occupation or acquisition of territories brought about by force of arms, and, moreover, in a case of non-compliance with these obligations, the Contracting States undertake to adopt, in their character as neutrals, a common and solidary attitude and to exercise the political, juridical, or economic means authorized by international law, and to bring the influence of public opinion to bear, without, however, resorting to intervention, either diplomatic or armed, subject nevertheless to the attitude that may be incumbent upon them by virtue of their collective treaties; and, furthermore, undertake to create a procedure of conciliation;

The High Contracting Parties reaffirm the obligations entered into to settle, by pacific means, controversies of an international character that may arise between them.

Article 2. The High Contracting Parties, convinced of the necessity for the cooperation and consultation provided for in the Convention for the Maintenance, Preservation and Re-establishment of Peace signed by them on this same day, agree that in all matters which affect peace on the continent, such consultation and cooperation shall have as their object to assist, through the tender of friendly good offices and of mediation, the fulfillment by the American Republics of existing obligations for pacific settlement, and to take counsel together, with full recognition of their juridical equality, as sovereign and independent States, and of their general right to individual liberty of action, when an emergency arises which affects their common interest in the maintenance of peace.

Article 3. In case of threat of war, the High Contracting Parties shall apply the provisions contained in Articles 1 and 2 of the Convention for the Maintenance, Preservation, and Re-establishment of Peace, above referred to, it being understood that, while such consultation is in progress and for a period of not more than six months, the parties in dispute will not have recourse to hostilities or take any military action whatever.

Article 4. The High Contracting Parties further agree that, in the event of a dispute between two or more of them, they will seek to settle it in a spirit of mutual regard for their respective rights, having recourse for this purpose to direct diplo-

matic negotiations or to the alternative procedures of mediation, commissions of inquiry, commissions of conciliation, tribunals of arbitration, and courts of justice, as provided in the treaties to which they may be parties; and they also agree that, should it be impossible to settle the dispute by diplomatic negotiation and should the States in dispute have recourse to the other procedures provided in the present Article, they will report this fact and the progress of the negotiations to the other signatory States. These provisions do not affect controversies already submitted to a diplomatic or juridical procedure by virtue of special agreements.

Article 5. The High Contracting Parties agree that, in the event that the methods provided by the present Convention or by agreements previously concluded should fail to bring about a pacific settlement of differences that may arise between any two or more of them, and hostilities should break out between two or more of them, they shall be governed by the following stipulations;

(a) They shall, in accordance with the terms of the Treaty of Non-Aggression and Conciliation (Saavedra Lamas Treaty), adopt in their character as neutrals a common and solidary attitude; and shall consult immediately with one another, and take cognizance of the outbreak of hostilities in order to determine, either jointly or individually, whether such hostilities shall be regarded as constituting a state of war so as to call into effect the provisions of the present Convention.

(b) It is understood that, in regard to the question whether hostilities actually in progress constitute a state of war, each of the High Contracting Parties shall reach a prompt decision. In any event, should hostilities be actually in progress between two or more of the Contracting Parties, or between two or more signatory States not at the time parties to this Convention by reason of failure to ratify it, each Contracting Party shall take notice of the situation and shall adopt such an attitude as would be consistent with other multilateral treaties to which it is a party or in accordance with its municipal legislation. Such action shall not be deemed an unfriendly act on the part of any State affected thereby.

Article 6. Without prejudice to the universal principles of neutrality provided for in the case of an international war outside of America and without affecting the duties contracted by those American States, members of the League of Nations, the High Contracting Parties reaffirm their loyalty to the principles enunciated in the five agreements referred to in Article 1, and they agree that in the case of an outbreak of hostilities or threat of an outbreak of hostilities between two or more of them, they shall, through consultation, immediately endeavor to adopt in their character as neutrals a common and solidary attitude, in order to discourage or prevent the spread or prolongation of hostilities.

With this object, and having in mind the diversity of cases and circumstances, they may consider the imposition of prohibitions or restrictions on the sale or shipment of arms, munitions and implements of war, loans or other financial help to the States in conflict, in accordance with the municipal legislation of the High Contracting Parties, and without detriment to their obligations derived from other treaties to which they are or may become parties.

Article 7. Nothing contained in the present Convention shall be understood as affecting the rights and duties of the High Contracting Parties which are at the same time members of the League of Nations.

Article 8. The present Convention shall be ratified by the High Contracting Parties in accordance with their constitutional procedures. The original Convention and the instruments of ratification shall be deposited with the Ministry of Foreign Affairs of the Argentine Republic, which shall communicate the ratifica-

tions to the other signatory States. It shall come into effect when ratifications have been deposited by not less than eleven signatory States.

The Convention shall remain in force indefinitely; but it may be denounced by any of the High Contracting Parties, such denunciation to be effective one year after the date upon which such notification has been given. Notices of denunciation shall be communicated to the Ministry of Foreign Affairs of the Argentine Republic which shall transmit copies thereof to the other signatory States. Denunciation shall not be regarded as valid if the party making such denunciation shall be actually in a state of war, or shall be engaged in hostilities without fulfilling the provisions established by this Convention.

In witness whereof, the plenipotentiaries above-mentioned have signed this Treaty in English, Spanish, Portuguese, and French, and have affixed thereto their respective seals, in the City of Buenos Aires, Capital of the Argentine Republic, this twenty-third day of December of the year 1936.

RESERVATIONS

Reservation of the Argentine Delegation: (1) In no case, under Article 6, can foodstuffs or raw materials destined for the civil populations of belligerent countries be considered as contraband of war, nor shall there exist any duty to prohibit credits for the acquisition of said foodstuffs or raw materials which have the destination indicated.

With reference to the embargo on arms, each nation may reserve freedom of action in the face of a war of aggression.

Reservation of the Delegation of Paraguay: (2) In no case, under Article 6, can foodstuffs or raw materials destined for the civil populations of belligerent countries be considered as contraband of war, nor shall there exist any duty to prohibit credits for the acquisition of said foodstuffs or raw materials which have the destination indicated.

With reference to the embargo on arms,

each nation may reserve freedom of action in the face of a war of aggression.

Reservation of the Delegation of El Salvador: (3) With reservation with respect to the idea of continental solidarity when confronted by foreign aggression.

Reservation of the Delegation of Colombia: (4) In signing this Convention, the Delegation of Colombia understands that the phrase 'in their character as neutrals', which appears in Articles 5 and 6, implies a new concept of international law which allows a distinction to be drawn between the aggressor and the attacked, and to treat them differently. At the same time, the Delegation of Colombia considers it necessary, in order to assure the full and effective application of this Pact, to set down in writing the following definition of the aggressor:

That State shall be considered as an aggressor which becomes responsible for one or several of the following acts:

(a) That its armed forces, to whatever branch they may belong, illegally cross the land, sea, or air frontiers of other States. When the violation of the territory of a State has been effected by irresponsible bands organized within or outside of its territory and which have received direct or indirect help from another State, such violation shall be considered equivalent, for the purposes of the present Article, to that effected by the regular forces of the State responsible for the aggression;

(b) That it has intervened in a unilateral or illegal way in the internal or external affairs of another State;

(c) That it has refused to fulfill a legally given arbitral decision or sentence of international justice.

No consideration of any kind, whether political, military, economic, or of any other kind, may serve as an excuse or justification for the aggression here anticipated.

...

United States Senate Resolution when ratifying the Convention, 29 June 1937

The United States of America holds that the reservations of this Convention do not constitute an amendment to the text, but that such reservations, interpretations, and definitions by separate Governments are solely for the benefit of such respective Governments and are not intended to be controlling upon the United States of America.

Additional Protocol between the United States of America and other American Republics concerning non-intervention, Buenos Aires, 23 December 1936

The Governments represented at the Inter-American Conference for the Maintenance of Peace,

Desiring to assure the benefits of peace in their mutual relations and in their relations with all the nations of the earth, and to abolish the practice of intervention; and

Taking into account that the Convention on Rights and Duties of States, signed at the Seventh International Conference of American States, December 26, 1933, solemnly affirmed the fundamental principle that 'no State has the right to intervene in the internal or external affairs of another',

Have resolved to reaffirm this principle through the negotiation of the following Additional Protocol ...

Article 1. The High Contracting Parties declare inadmissible the intervention of any one of them, directly or indirectly, and for whatever reason, in the internal or external affairs of any other of the parties.

The violation of the provisions of this Article shall give rise to mutual consultation, with the object of exchanging views and seeking methods of peaceful adjustment.

Article 2. It is agreed that every question concerning the interpretation of the present Additional Protocol, which it has not been possible to settle through diplomatic channels, shall be submitted to the procedure of conciliation provided for in the agreements in force, or to arbitration, or to judicial settlement.

Article 3. The present Additional Protocol shall be ratified by the High Contracting Parties in conformity with their respective constitutional procedures. The original instrument and the instruments of ratification shall be deposited in the Ministry of Foreign Affairs of the Argentine Republic which shall communicate the ratifications to the other signatories. The Additional Protocol shall come into effect between the High Contracting Parties in the order in which they shall have deposited their ratifications.

Article 4. The present Additional Protocol shall remain in effect indefinitely but may be denounced by means of one year's notice after the expiration of which period the Protocol shall cease in its effects as regards the party which denounces it, but shall remain in effect for the remaining signatory States. ...

Convention on the provisional administration of European colonies and possessions in the Americas, Havana, 30 July 1940

The Governments represented at the Second Meeting of Ministers of Foreign Affairs of the American Republics,

Considering ...

That as a result of the events which are taking place in the European continent situations may develop in the territories of the possessions which some of the belligerent nations have in the Americas which may extinguish or materially impair the sovereignty which they exercise over them, or leave their Government without a leader, thus creating a state of danger to the peace of the continent and a state of affairs in which the rule of law, order, and respect for life, liberty and the property of inhabitants may disappear ...

That any transfer, or attempted transfer, of the sovereignty, jurisdiction, possession of any interest in or control over any such region to another non-American State, would be regarded by the American Republics as against American sentiments and principles and the rights of American States to maintain their security and political independence ...

That the American Republics, through their respective Government agencies, reserve the right to judge whether any transfer or attempted transfer of sovereignty, jurisdiction, cession or incorporation of geographic regions in the Americas, possessed by European countries up to September 1, 1939, has the effect of impairing their political independence even though no formal transfer or change in the status of such region or regions shall have taken place;

... Being desirous of protecting their

peace and safety and of promoting the interests of any of the regions herein referred to which may fall within the purview of the foregoing recitations, have resolved to conclude the following convention:

Article I. If a non-American State shall directly or indirectly attempt to replace another non-American State in the sovereignty or control which it exercised over any territory located in the Americas, thus threatening the peace of the continent, such territory shall automatically come under the provisions of this Convention and shall be submitted to a provisional administrative régime.

Article II. The administration shall be exercised, as may be considered advisable in each case, by one or more American States, with their previous approval.

Article III. When the administration shall have been established for any region it shall be exercised in the interests of the security of the Americas and for the benefit of the region under administration, with a view to its welfare and progress, until such time as the region is in a position to govern itself or is restored to its former status, whenever the latter is compatible with the security of the American Republics.

...

Article XVI. A Commission to be known as the 'Inter-American Commission for Territorial Administration' is hereby established, to be composed of a representative from each one of the States which ratifies this Convention; it shall be the international organization to which this Convention refers. Once this Convention has become effective, any country which ratifies it may convoke the first meeting proposing the city in which it is to be held. The Commission shall elect its chairman, complete its organization and fix its definitive seat. Two-thirds of the members of the Commission shall constitute a quorum and two-thirds of the members present may adopt decisions.

Article XVII. The Commission is authorized to establish a provisional administration in the regions to which the present Convention refers; allow such administration to be exercised by the number of States which it may determine in each case, and supervise its exercise under the terms of the preceding Articles.

Inter-American Treaty of Reciprocal Assistance, Rio de Janeiro, 2 September 1947

In the name of their Peoples, the Governments represented at the Inter-American Conference for the Maintenance of Continental Peace and Security, desirous of consolidating and strengthening their relations of friendship and good neighborliness, and

Considering...

That the High Contracting Parties reiterate their will to remain united in an Inter-American System consistent with the purposes and principles of the United Nations, and reaffirm the existence of the agreement which they have concluded concerning those matters relating to the maintenance of international peace and security which are appropriate for regional action;

That the High Contracting Parties reaffirm their adherence to the principles of inter-American solidarity and cooperation, and especially to those set forth in the preamble and declarations of the Act of Chapultepec, all of which should be understood to be accepted as standards of their mutual relations and as the juridical basis of the Inter-American System ...

That the obligation of mutual assistance and common defense of the American Republics is essentially related to their democratic ideals and to their will to cooperate permanently in the fulfillment of the principles and purposes of a policy of peace ...

Have resolved, in conformity with the objectives stated above, to conclude the following Treaty, in order to assure peace, through adequate means, to provide for effective reciprocal assistance to meet armed attacks against any American State, and in order to deal with threats of aggression against any of them:

Article 1. The High Contracting Parties formally condemn war and undertake in their international relations not to resort to the threat or the use of force in any manner inconsistent with the provisions of the Charter of the United Nations or of this Treaty.

Article 2. As a consequence of the principle set forth in the preceding Article, the High Contracting Parties undertake to submit every controversy which may arise between them to methods of peaceful settlement and to endeavour to settle any such controversy among themselves by means of the procedures in force in the Inter-American System before referring it to the General Assembly or the Security Council of the United Nations.

Article 3. 1. The High Contracting Parties agree that an armed attack by any State against an American State shall be considered as an attack against all the American States and, consequently, each one of the said Contracting Parties undertakes to assist in meeting the attack in the exercise of the inherent right of individual or collective self-defense recognized by Article 51 of the Charter of the United Nations.

2. On the request of the State or States directly attacked and until the decision of the Organ of Consultation of the Inter-American System, each one of the Contracting Parties may determine the immediate measures which it may individually take in fulfillment of the obligation contained in the preceding paragraph and in accordance with the principle of continental solidarity. The Organ of Consultation shall meet without delay for the purpose of examining those measures and agreeing upon the measures of a collective character that should be taken.

3. The provisions of this Article shall be applied in case of any armed attack which takes place within the region described in Article 4 or within the territory of an American State. When the attack takes place outside of the said areas, the provisions of Article 6 shall be applied.

4. Measures of self-defense provided for under this Article may be taken until the Security Council of the United Nations has taken the measures necessary to maintain international peace and security.

Article 4. The regions to which this Treaty refers are the North and South American continents and Greenland and an area of Antarctica.

Article 5. The High Contracting Parties shall immediately send to the Security Council of the United Nations, in conformity with Articles 51 and 54 of the Charter of the United Nations, complete information concerning the activities undertaken or in contemplation in the exercise of the right of self-defense or for the purpose of maintaining inter-American peace and security.

Article 6. If the inviolability or the integrity of the territory or the sovereignty or political independence of any American State should be affected by an aggression which is not an armed attack or by an extra-continental or intra-continental conflict, or by any other fact or situation that might endanger the peace of America, the Organ of Consultation shall meet immediately in order to agree on the measures which must be taken in case of aggression to assist the victim of the aggression or, in any case, the measures which should be taken for the common defense and for the maintenance of the peace and security of the continent.

Article 7. In the case of a conflict between two or more American States, without prejudice to the right of self-defense in conformity with Article 51 of the Charter of the United Nations, the High Contracting Parties meeting in consultation shall call upon the contending States to suspend hostilities and restore matters to the *status quo ante bellum*, and shall take in addition all other necessary measures to re-establish or maintain inter-American peace and security and for the solution of the conflict by peaceful means. The rejection of the pacifying action will be considered in the determination of the aggressor and in the application of the measures which the consultative meeting may agree upon.

[*Article 8.* Sanctions ranged from breaking off diplomatic relations, to economic sanctions, to the use of armed force.]

Article 9. In addition to other acts which the Organ of Consultation may characterize as aggression, the following shall be considered as such:
(a) Unprovoked armed attack by a State against the territory, the people, or the land, sea or air forces of another State;
(b) Invasion, by the armed forces of a State, of the territory of an American State, through the trespassing of boundaries demarcated in accordance with a treaty, judicial decision, or arbitral award, or, in the absence of frontiers thus demarcated, invasion affecting a region which is under the effective jurisdiction of another State.

Article 10. None of the provisions of this Treaty shall be construed as impairing the rights and obligations of the High Contracting Parties under the Charter of the United Nations.

Article 11. The consultations to which this Treaty refers shall be carried out by means of the Meetings of Ministers of Foreign Affairs of the American Republics which have ratified the Treaty, or in the manner or by the organ which in the future may be agreed upon.

Article 12. The Governing Board of the Pan-American Union may act provisionally as an organ of consultation until the meeting of the Organ of Consultation referred to in the preceding Article takes place.

Article 13. The consultations shall be initiated at the request addressed to the Governing Board of the Pan-American Union by any of the signatory States which has ratified the Treaty.

Article 14. In the voting referred to in this Treaty only the representatives of the signatory States which have ratified the Treaty may take part.

Article 15. The Governing Board of the Pan-American Union shall act in all matters concerning this Treaty as an organ of liaison among the signatory States which have ratified this Treaty and between these States and the United Nations.

Article 16. The decisions of the Governing Board of the Pan-American Union referred to in Articles 13 and 15 above shall be taken by an absolute majority of the members entitled to vote.

Article 17. The Organ of Consultation shall take its decisions by a vote of two-thirds of the signatory States which have ratified the Treaty.

Article 18. In the case of a situation or dispute between American States, the parties directly interested shall be excluded from the voting referred to in two preceding Articles.

Article 19. To constitute a quorum in all the meetings referred to in the previous Articles, it shall be necessary that the number of States represented shall be at least equal to the number of votes necessary for the taking of the decision.

Article 20. Decisions which require the application of the measures specified in Article 8 shall be binding upon all the signatory States which have ratified this Treaty, with the sole exception that no State shall be required to use armed force without its consent.

Article 21. The measures agreed upon by the Organ of Consultation shall be executed through the procedures and agencies now existing or those which may in the future be established.

[*Articles 22-4.* Ratification and Registration. Ratification by two-thirds of signatories necessary.]

Article 25. This Treaty shall remain in force indefinitely, but may be denounced by any High Contracting Party by a notification in writing to the Pan-American Union, which shall inform all the other High Contracting Parties of each notification of denunciation received.

After the expiration of two years from the date of the receipt by the Pan-American Union of a notification of denunciation by any High Contracting Party, the present Treaty shall cease to be in force and with respect to such State, but shall remain in full force and effect with respect to all the other High Contracting Parties.

Article 26. The principles and fundamental provisions of this Treaty shall be incorporated in the Organic Pact of the Inter-American System.

RESERVATION OF HONDURAS

[Concerning Honduras–Nicaraguan boundary.]

Charter of the Organization of American States, Bogotá, 30 April 1948

IN THE NAME OF THEIR PEOPLES, THE STATES REPRESENTED AT THE NINTH INTERNATIONAL CONFERENCE OF AMERICAN STATES,

Convinced that the historic mission of America is to offer to man a land of liberty, and a favorable environment for the development of his personality and the realization of his just aspirations;

Conscious that that mission has already inspired numerous agreements, whose essential value lies in the desire of the American peoples to live together in peace, and, though their mutual understanding and respect for the sovereignty of each one, to provide for the betterment of all, in independence, in equality and under law;

Confident that the true significance of American solidarity and good neighborliness can only mean the consolidation on this continent, within the framework of democratic institutions, of a system of individual liberty and social justice based on respect for the essential rights of man;

Persuaded that their welfare and their contribution to the progress and the civilization of the world will increasingly require intensive continental cooperation;

Resolved to persevere in the noble undertaking that humanity has conferred upon the United Nations, whose principles and purposes they solemnly reaffirm;

Convinced that juridical organization is a necessary condition for security and peace founded on moral order and on justice; and

In accordance with Resolution IX of the Inter-American Conference on Problems of War and Peace, held at Mexico City,

Have agreed upon the following CHARTER OF THE ORGANIZATION OF AMERICAN STATES

Part One

Chapter I: Nature and purposes

Article 1. The American States establish by this Charter the international organization that they have developed to achieve an order of peace and justice, to promote their solidarity, to strengthen their collaboration, and to defend their sovereignty, their territorial integrity and their independence. Within the United Nations, the Organization of American States is a regional agency.

. . .

Article 4. The Organization of American States, in order to put into practice the principles on which it is founded and to fulfill its regional obligations under the Charter of the United Nations, proclaims the following essential purposes:

a) To strengthen the peace and security of the continent;

b) To prevent possible causes of difficulties and to ensure the pacific settlement of disputes that may arise among the Member States;

c) To provide for common action on the part of those States in the event of aggression;

d) To seek the solution of political, juridical and economic problems that may arise among them; and

e) to promote, by cooperative action, their economic, social and cultural development.

Chapter II: Principles

[*Article 5.* These affirm good faith, condemn aggression, aspire to social justice and economic cooperation.]

Chapter III: Fundamental rights and duties of States

Article 6. States are juridically equal, enjoy equal rights and equal capacity to exercise these rights, and have equal duties. The rights of each State depend not upon its power to ensure the exercise thereof, but upon the mere fact of its existence as a person under international law.

[*Articles 7–14.* Set out the rights and duties.]

Article 15. No State or group of States has the right to intervene, directly or indirectly, for any reason whatever, in the internal or external affairs of any other State. The foregoing principle prohibits not only armed force but also any other form of interference or attempted threat against the personality of the State or against its political, economic and cultural elements.

Article 16. No State may use or encourage the use of coercive measures of an economic or political character in order to force the sovereign will of another State and obtain from it advantages of any kind.

Article 17. The territory of a State is inviolable; it may not be the object, even temporarily, of military occupation or of other measures of force taken by another State, directly or indirectly, on any grounds whatever. No territorial acquisitions or special advantages obtained either by force or by other means of coercion shall be recognized.

Article 18. The American States bind themselves in their international relations not to have recourse to the use of force, except in the case of self-defense in accordance with existing treaties or in fulfillment thereof.

Article 19. Measures adopted for the maintenance of peace and security in accordance with existing treaties do not constitute a violation of the principles set forth in Articles 15 and 17.

Chapter IV: Pacific settlement of disputes

Article 20. All international disputes that may arise between American States shall be submitted to the peaceful procedures set forth in this Charter, before being referred to the Security Council of the United Nations.

[*Articles 21–3.* Briefly set out the peaceful procedures.]

Chapter V: Collective security

Article 24. Every act of aggression by a State against the territorial integrity or the inviolability of the territory or against the sovereignty or political independence of an American State shall be considered an act of aggression against the other American States.

Article 25. If the inviolability or the integrity of the territory or the sovereignty or political independence of any American State should be affected by an armed attack or by an act of aggression that is not an armed attack, or by an extra-continental conflict, or by a conflict between two or more American States, or by any other fact or situation that might endanger the peace of America, the American States, in furtherance of the principles of continental solidarity or collective self-defense, shall apply the measures and procedures established in the special treaties on the subject.

Chapter VI: Economic standards

[*Articles 26–7.*]

Chapter VII: Social standards

[*Articles 28–9.*]

Chapter VIII: Cultural standards

[*Articles 30–1.*]

American Treaty on Pacific Settlement (Pact of Bogotá), Bogotá, 30 April 1948

In the name of their peoples, the Governments represented at the Ninth International Conference of American States have resolved, in fulfillment of Article XXIII of the Charter of the Organization of American States, to conclude the following Treaty:

Chapter One: General obligation to settle disputes by pacific means

Article I. The High Contracting Parties, solemnly reaffirming their commitments made in earlier international conventions and declarations, as well as in the Charter of the United Nations, agree to refrain from the threat or the use of force, or from any other means of coercion for the settlement of their controversies, and to have recourse at all times to pacific procedures.

Article II. The High Contracting Parties recognize the obligation to settle international controversies by regional pacific procedures before referring them to the Security Council of the United Nations.

Consequently, in the event that a controversy arises between two or more signatory States which, in the opinion of the parties, cannot be settled by direct negotiations through the usual diplomatic channels, the parties bind themselves to use the procedures established in the present Treaty, in the manner and under the conditions provided for in the following Articles, or, alternatively, such special procedures as, in their opinion, will permit them to arrive at a solution.

Article III. The order of the pacific procedures established in the present Treaty does not signify that the parties may not have recourse to the procedure which they consider most appropriate in each case, or that they should use all these procedures, or that any of them have preference over others except as expressly provided.

Article IV. Once any pacific procedure has been initiated, whether by agreement between the parties or in fulfillment of the present Treaty or a previous pact, no other procedure may be commenced until that procedure is concluded.

Article V. The aforesaid procedures may not be applied to matters which, by their nature, are within the domestic jurisdiction of the State. If the parties are not in agreement as to whether the controversy concerns a matter of domestic jurisdiction, this preliminary question shall be submitted to decision by the International Court of Justice, at the request of any of the parties.

Article VI. The aforesaid procedures, furthermore, may not be applied to matters already settled by arrangement between the parties, or by arbitral award or by decision of an international court, or which are governed by agreements or treaties in force on the date of the conclusion of the present Treaty.

Article VII. The High Contracting Parties bind themselves not to make diplomatic representations in order to protect their nationals, or to refer a controversy to a court of international jurisdiction for that purpose, when the said nationals have had available the means to place their case before competent domestic courts of the respective State.

Article VIII. Neither recourse to pacific means for the solution of controversies, nor the recommendation of their use, shall, in the case of an armed attack, be ground for delaying the exercise of the right of individual or collective self-defense, as provided for in the Charter of the United Nations.

Chapter Two: Procedures of good offices and mediation

Article IX. The procedure of good offices consists in the attempt by one or more American Governments not parties to the controversy, or by one or more eminent citizens of any American State which is not a party to the controversy, to bring the parties together, so as to make it possible for them to reach an adequate solution between themselves. [Procedures detailed in Articles X–XIV.]

Chapter Three: Procedure of investigation and conciliation

Article XV. The procedure of investigation and conciliation consists in the submission of the controversy to a Commission of Investigation and Conciliation, which shall be established in accordance with the provisions established in subsequent Articles of the present Treaty, and which shall function within the limitations prescribed therein.

...

Article XVIII. Without prejudice to the provisions of the foregoing Article, the Pan-American Union shall draw up a permanent panel of American conciliators, to be made up as follows:

(a) Each of the High Contracting Parties shall appoint, for three-year periods, two of their nationals who enjoy the highest reputation for fairness, competence and integrity;

(b) The Pan-American Union shall request of the candidates notice of their formal acceptance, and it shall place on the panel of conciliators the names of the persons who so notify it;

(c) The Governments may, at any time, fill vacancies occurring among their appointees; and they may reappoint their members.

Article XIX. In the event that a controversy should arise between two or more American States that have not appointed the Commission referred to in Article XVII, the following procedure shall be observed:

(a) Each party shall designate two members from the permanent panel of American conciliators, who are not of the same nationality as the appointing party;

(b) These four members shall in turn choose a fifth member, from the permanent panel, not of the nationality of either party;

(c) If, within a period of thirty days following the notification of their selection, the four members are unable to agree upon a fifth member, they shall each separately list the conciliators composing the permanent panel, in order of their preference, and upon comparison of the lists so prepared, the one who first receives a majority of votes shall be declared elected. The person so elected shall perform the duties of chairman of the Commission.

Article XX. In convening the Commission of Investigation and Conciliation, the Council of the Organization of American States shall determine the place where the Commission shall meet....

[*Articles XX–XXVI.* Procedure of Commission.]

Article XXVII. If an agreement is reached by conciliation, the final report of the Commission shall be limited to the text of the agreement and shall be published after its transmittal to the parties, unless the parties decide otherwise. If no agreement is reached, the final report shall contain a summary of the work of the Commission; it shall be delivered to the parties, and shall be published after the expiration of six months unless the parties decide otherwise. In both cases, the final report shall be adopted by a majority vote.

Article XXVIII. The reports and conclusions of the Commission of Investigation and Conciliation shall not be binding upon the parties, either with respect to the statement of facts or in regard to questions of law, and they shall have no other character than that of recommendations submitted for the consideration of the parties in order to facilitate a friendly settlement of the controversy.

• • •

Chapter Four: Judicial procedure

Article XXXI. In conformity with Article 36, paragraph 2, of the Statute of the International Court of Justice, the High Contracting Parties declare that they recognize in relation to any other American State, the jurisdiction of the Court as compulsory *ipso facto*, without the neces-

sity of any special agreement so long as the present Treaty is in force, in all disputes of a juridical nature that arise among them concerning:

(a) The interpretation of a treaty;

(b) Any question of international law;

(c) The existence of any fact which, if established, would constitute the breach of an international obligation;

(d) The nature or extent of the reparation to be made for the breach of an international obligation.

Article XXXII. When the conciliation procedure previously established in the present Treaty or by agreement of the parties does not lead to a solution, and the said parties have not agreed upon an arbitral procedure, either of them shall be entitled to have recourse to the International Court of Justice in the manner prescribed in Article 40 of the Statute thereof. The Court shall have compulsory jurisdiction in accordance with Article 36, paragraph 1, of the said Statute.

Article XXXIII. If the parties fail to agree as to whether the Court has jurisdiction over the controversy, the Court itself shall first decide that question.

Article XXXIV. If the Court, for the reasons set forth in Articles V, VI and VII of this Treaty, declares itself to be without jurisdiction to hear the controversy, such controversy shall be declared ended.

Article XXXV. If the Court for any other reason declares itself to be without jurisdiction to hear and adjudge the controversy, the High Contracting Parties obligate themselves to submit it to arbitration, in accordance with the provisions of Chapter Five of this Treaty.

• • •

Chapter Five: Procedure of arbitration

Article XXXVIII. Notwithstanding the provisions of Chapter Four of this Treaty, the High Contracting Parties may, if they so agree, submit to arbitration differences of any kind, whether juridical or not, that have arisen or may arise in the future between them.

[*Articles XXXIX–XLV*. Details of procedure of selecting arbiters or arbiter either by the Council of the Organization from nominations of parties in dispute, or the parties may by mutual agreement establish the Arbitration Tribunal in the manner they deem most appropriate.]

Article XLVI. The award shall be accompanied by a supporting opinion, shall be adopted by a majority vote, and shall be published after notification thereof has been given to the parties. The dissenting arbiter or arbiters shall have the right to state the grounds for their dissent.

The award, once it is duly handed down and made known to the parties, shall settle the controversy definitively, shall not be subject to appeal, and shall be carried out immediately.

Article XLVII. Any differences that arise in regard to the interpretation or execution of the award shall be submitted to the decision of the Arbitral Tribunal that rendered the award.

. . .

Chapter Six: Fulfillment of decisions

Article L. If one of the High Contracting Parties should fail to carry out the obligations imposed upon it by a decision of the International Court of Justice or by an arbitral award, the other party or parties concerned shall, before resorting to the Security Council of the United Nations, propose a Meeting of Consultation of Ministers of Foreign Affairs to agree upon appropriate measures to ensure the fulfillment of the judicial decision or arbitral award.

Chapter Seven: Advisory opinions

Article LI. The parties concerned in the solution of a controversy may, by agreement, petition the General Assembly or the Security Council of the United Nations to request an advisory opinion of the International Court of Justice on any juridical question.

The petition shall be made through the Council of the Organization of American States.

. . .

Article LVI. The present Treaty shall remain in force indefinitely, but may be denounced upon one year's notice, at the end of which period it shall cease to be in force with respect to the State denouncing it, but shall continue in force for the remaining signatories. The denunciation shall be addressed to the Pan-American Union, which shall transmit it to the other Contracting Parties.

The denunciation shall have no effect with respect to pending procedures initiated prior to the transmission of the particular notification.

. . .

RESERVATIONS

Argentina. The Delegation of the Argentine Republic, on signing the American Treaty on Pacific Settlement (Pact of Bogotá), makes reservations in regard to the following Articles, to which it does not adhere:

1. VII, concerning the protection of aliens;

2. Chapter Four (Articles XXXI to XXXVII), Judicial procedure;

3. Chapter Five (Articles XXXVIII to XLIX), Procedure of arbitration;

4. Chapter Six (Article L), Fulfillment of decisions.

Arbitration and judicial procedure have, as institutions, the firm adherence of the Argentine Republic, but the Delegation cannot accept the form in which the procedures for their application have been regulated, since, in its opinion, they should have been established only for controversies arising in the future and not originating in or having any relation to causes, situations or facts existing before the signing of this instrument. The compulsory execution of arbitral or judicial decisions and the limitation which prevents the States from judging for themselves in regard to matters that pertain to their domestic jurisdiction in accordance with Article V are contrary to

Argentine tradition. The protection of aliens, who in the Argentine Republic are protected by its Supreme Law to the same extent as the nationals, is also contrary to that tradition.

Bolivia. The Delegation of Bolivia makes a reservation with regard to Article VI, inasmuch as it considers that pacific procedures may also be applied to controversies arising from matters settled by arrangement between the parties, when the said arrangement affects the vital interests of a State.

Ecuador. The Delegation of Ecuador, upon signing this Pact, makes an express reservation with regard to Article VI and also every provision that contradicts or is not in harmony with the principles proclaimed by or the stipulations contained in the Charter of the United Nations, the Charter of the Organization of American States, or the Constitution of the Republic of Ecuador.

United States of America. 1. The United States does not undertake as the complainant State to submit to the International Court of Justice any controversy which is not considered to be properly within the jurisdiction of the Court.

2. The submission on the part of the United States of any controversy to arbitration, as distinguished from judicial settlement, shall be dependent upon the conclusion of a special agreement between the parties to the case.

3. The acceptance by the United States of the jurisdiction of the International Court of Justice as compulsory *ipso facto* and without special agreement, as provided in this Treaty, is limited by any jurisdictional or other limitations contained in any Declaration deposited by the United States under Article 36, paragraph 4, of the Statute of the Court, and in force at the time of the submission of any case.

4. The Government of the United States cannot accept Article VII relating to diplomatic protection and the exhaustion of remedies. For its part, the Government of the United States maintains the rules of diplomatic protection, including the rule of exhaustion of local remedies by aliens, as provided by international law.

Paraguay. The Delegation of Paraguay makes the following reservation:

Paraguay stipulates the prior agreement of the parties as a prerequisite to the arbitration procedure established in this Treaty for every question of a non-juridical nature affecting national sovereignty and not specifically agreed upon in treaties now in force.

Peru. The Delegation of Peru makes the following reservations:

1. Reservation with regard to the second part of Article V, because it considers that domestic jurisdiction should be defined by the State itself.

2. Reservation with regard to Article XXXIII and the pertinent part of Article XXXIV, inasmuch as it considers that the exceptions of *res judicata*, resolved by settlement between the parties or governed by agreements and treaties in force, determine, in virtue of their objective and peremptory nature, the exclusion of these cases from the application of every procedure.

3. Reservation with regard to Article XXXV, in the sense that, before arbitration is resorted to, there may be, at the request of one of the parties, a meeting of the Organ of Consultation, as established in the Charter of the Organization of American States.

4. Reservation with regard to Article XLV, because it believes that arbitration set up without the participation of one of the parties is in contradiction with its constitutional provisions.

Nicaragua. The Nicaraguan Delegation, on giving its approval to the American Treaty on Pacific Settlement (Pact of Bogotá) wishes to record expressly that no provisions contained in the said Treaty may prejudice any position assumed by the Government of Nicaragua with respect to arbitral decisions the validity of which it has contested on the basis of the principles of international law, which clearly permit arbitral decisions to be attacked when they are adjudged to be null or invalidated. Consequently, the signature of the Nicaraguan Delegation to the Treaty in question cannot be alleged as an acceptance of any arbitral decisions that Nicaragua has contested and the validity of which is not certain.

Hence the Nicaraguan Delegation reiterates the statement made on the 28th of the current month on approving the text of the above-mentioned Treaty in Committee III.

North Atlantic Treaty between Belgium, Canada, Denmark, France, Iceland, Italy, Luxembourg, the Netherlands, Norway, Portugal, Britain and the United States, Washington, 4 April 1949

The parties to this Treaty reaffirm their faith in the purposes and principles of the Charter of the United Nations and their desire to live in peace with all peoples and all Governments.

They are determined to safeguard the freedom, common heritage and civilization of their peoples, founded on the principles of democracy, individual liberty and the rule of law.

They seek to promote stability and well-being in the North Atlantic area.

They are resolved to unite their efforts for collective defence and for the preservation of peace and security.

They therefore agree to this North Atlantic Treaty:

Article 1. The parties undertake, as set forth in the Charter of the United Nations, to settle any international disputes in which they may be involved by peaceful means in such a manner that international peace and security and justice are not endangered, and to refrain in their international relations from the threat or use of force in any manner inconsistent with the purposes of the United Nations.

Article 2. The parties will contribute toward the further development of peaceful and friendly international relations by strengthening their free institutions, by bringing about a better understanding of the principles upon which these institutions are founded, and by promoting conditions of stability and well-being. They will seek to eliminate conflict in their international economic policies and will encourage economic collaboration between any or all of them.

Article 3. In order more effectively to achieve the objectives of this Treaty, the parties, separately and jointly, by means of continuous and effective self-help and mutual aid, will maintain and develop their individual and collective capacity to resist armed attack.

Article 4. The parties will consult together whenever, in the opinion of any of them, the territorial integrity, political independence or security of any of the parties is threatened.

Article 5. The parties agree that an armed attack against one or more of them in Europe or North America shall be considered an attack against them all; and consequently they agree that, if such an armed attack occurs, each of them in exercise of the right of individual or collective self-defence recognized by Article 51 of the Charter of the United Nations, will assist the party or parties so attacked by taking forthwith, individually and in concert with the other parties, such action as it deems necessary, including the use of armed force, to restore and maintain the security of the North Atlantic area.

Any such armed attack and all measures taken as a result thereof shall immediately be reported to the Security Council. Such measures shall be terminated when the Security Council has taken the measures necessary to restore and maintain international peace and security.

Article 6. For the purpose of Article 5 an armed attack on one or more of the parties is deemed to include an armed attack on the territory of any of the parties in Europe or North America, on the Algerian Departments of France, on the occupation forces of any party in Europe, on the islands under the jurisdiction of any party in the North Atlantic area north of the Tropic of Cancer, or on the vessels or aircraft in this area of any of the parties.

Article 7. This Treaty does not affect, and shall not be interpreted as affecting, in any way the rights and obligations under the Charter of the parties which are members of the United Nations, or the primary responsibility of the Security Council for the maintenance of international peace and security.

Article 8. Each party declares that none of the international engagements now in force between it and any other of the parties or any third State is in conflict with the provisions of this Treaty, and undertakes not to enter into any international engagement in conflict with this Treaty.

Article 9. The parties hereby establish a Council, on which each of them shall be represented, to consider matters concerning the implementation of this Treaty. The Council shall be so organized as to be able to meet promptly at any time. The Council shall set up such subsidiary bodies as may be necessary; in particular it shall establish immediately a Defence Committee which shall recommend measures for the implementation of Articles 3 and 5.

Article 10. The parties may, by unanimous agreement, invite any other European State in a position to further the principles of this Treaty and to contribute to the security of the North Atlantic area to accede to this Treaty. Any State so invited may become a party to the Treaty by depositing its instrument of accession with the Government of the United States of America. The Government of the United States of America will inform each of the parties of the deposit of each such instrument of accession.

Article 11. This Treaty shall be ratified and its provisions carried out by the parties in accordance with their respective constitutional processes. The instruments of ratification shall be deposited as soon as possible with the Government of the United States of America, which will notify all the other signatories of each deposit. The Treaty shall enter into force between the States which have ratified it as soon as the ratifications of the majority of the signatories, including the ratifications of Belgium, Canada, France, Luxembourg, the Netherlands, the United Kingdom and the United States, have been deposited, and shall come into effect with respect to other States on the date of the deposit of their ratifications.

Article 12. After the Treaty has been in force for ten years, or at any time thereafter, the parties shall, if any of them so requests, consult together for the purpose of reviewing the Treaty, having regard for the factors then affecting peace and security in the North Atlantic area, including the development of universal as well as regional arrangements under the Charter of the United Nations for the maintenance of international peace and security.

Article 13. After the Treaty has been in force for twenty years, any party may cease to be a party one year after its notice of denunciation has been given to the Government of the United States of

America, which will inform the Governments of the other parties of the deposit of each notice of denunciation.

Article 14. This Treaty, of which the English and French texts are equally authentic, shall be deposited in the archives of the Government of the United States of America. Duly certified copies thereof will be transmitted by that Government to the Governments of the other signatories.

Agreement between the United States and Korea to establish a Military Advisory Group, Seoul, 26 January 1950

Preamble. In conformity with the request of the Government of the Republic of Korea to the Government of the United States, the President of the United States has authorized the establishment of the United States Military Advisory Group to the Republic of Korea (hereinafter referred to as the Group), under the terms and conditions specified below :

Article I. The purpose of the Group will be to develop the Security Forces of the Republic of Korea within the limitations of the Korean economy by advising and assisting the Government of the Republic of Korea in the organization, administration and training of such forces. [U.S. advisers not to exceed 500.]

Article II. This Agreement may be terminated at any time :
1. By either Government, provided that six months' written notice is given to the other Government;
2. By recall of the Group when either Government deems such recall to be in its public interest and shall have so notified the other Government without necessity of compliance with provision (1) of this Article. However, termination of this Agreement by recall does not relieve the Government of the Republic of Korea from its obligations arising under this Agreement during such time, not exceeding three months, reasonably necessary to permit the Group to terminate its functions and physically depart from Korea.

Article III. The functions of the Group shall be to provide such advice and assistance to the Government of the Republic of Korea on military and related matters as may be necessary to accomplish the purposes set forth in Article I of this Agreement....

Security Treaty between Australia, New Zealand and the United States (ANZUS), San Francisco, 1 September 1951

The parties to this Treaty,
Reaffirming their faith in the purposes and principles of the Charter of the United Nations and their desire to live in peace with all peoples and all Governments, and desiring to strengthen the fabric of peace in the Pacific area,
Noting that the United States already

has arrangements pursuant to which its armed forces are stationed in the Philippines, and has armed forces and administrative responsibilities in the Ryukyus, and upon the coming into force of the Japanese Peace Treaty may also station armed forces in and about Japan to assist in the preservation of peace and security in the Japan area,

Recognizing that Australia and New Zealand as members of the British Commonwealth of Nations have military obligations outside as well as within the Pacific area,

Desiring to declare publicly and formally their sense of unity, so that no potential aggressor could be under the illusion that any of them stand alone in the Pacific area, and

Desiring further to coordinate their efforts for collective defense for the preservation of peace and security pending the development of a more comprehensive system of regional security in the Pacific area,

Therefore declare and agree as follows:

Article I. The parties undertake, as set forth in the Charter of the United Nations, to settle any international disputes in which they may be involved by peaceful means in such a manner that international peace and security and justice are not endangered and to refrain in their international relations from the threat or use of force in any manner inconsistent with the purposes of the United Nations.

Article II. In order more effectively to achieve the objective of this Treaty the parties separately and jointly by means of continuous and effective self-help and mutual aid will maintain and develop their individual and collective capacity to resist armed attack.

Article III. The parties will consult together whenever in the opinion of any of them the territorial integrity, political independence or security of any of the parties is threatened in the Pacific.

Article IV. Each party recognizes that an armed attack in the Pacific area on any of the parties would be dangerous to its own peace and safety and declares that it would act to meet the common danger in accordance with its constitutional processes.

Any such armed attack and all measures taken as a result thereof shall be immediately reported to the Security Council of the United Nations. Such measures shall be terminated when the Security Council has taken the measures necessary to restore and maintain international peace and security.

Article V. For the purpose of Article IV, an armed attack on any of the parties is deemed to include an armed attack on the metropolitan territory of any of the parties, or on the island territories under its jurisdiction in the Pacific or on its armed forces, public vessels or aircraft in the Pacific.

Article VI. This Treaty does not affect and shall not be interpreted as affecting in any way the rights and obligations of the parties under the Charter of the United Nations or the responsibility of the United Nations for the maintenance of international peace and security.

Article VII. The parties hereby establish a Council, consisting of their Foreign Ministers or their Deputies, to consider matters concerning the implementation of this Treaty. The Council should be so organized as to be able to meet at any time.

Article VIII. Pending the development of a more comprehensive system of regional security in the Pacific area and the development by the United Nations of more effective means to maintain international peace and security, the Council, established by Article VII, is authorized to maintain a consultative relationship with States, Regional Organizations, Associations of States or other authorities in the Pacific area in a position to further the purposes of this Treaty and to contribute to the security of that area.

Article IX. This Treaty shall be ratified by the parties in accordance with their respective constitutional processes....

Article X. This Treaty shall remain in force indefinitely. Any party may cease to be a member of the Council established by Article VII one year after notice has been given to the Government of Australia, which will inform the Governments of the other parties of the deposit of such notice.

[*Article XI.* Certified copies and deposit.]

Mutual Defense Treaty between the United States and Korea (South), Washington, 10 October 1953

The parties to this Treaty . . . have agreed as follows:

Article I. The parties undertake to settle any international disputes in which they may be involved by peaceful means . . .

Article II. The parties will consult together whenever, in the opinion of either of them, the political independence or security of either of the parties is threatened by external armed attack. Separately and jointly, by self-help and mutual aid, the parties will maintain and develop appropriate means to deter armed attack and will take suitable measures in consultation and agreement to implement this Treaty and to further its purposes.

Article III. Each party recognizes that an armed attack in the Pacific area on either of the parties in territories now under their respective administrative control, or hereafter recognized by one of the parties as lawfully brought under the administrative control of the other, would be dangerous to its own peace and safety and declares that it would act to meet the common danger in accordance with its constitutional processes.

Article IV. The Republic of Korea grants, and the United States of America accepts, the right to dispose United States land, air and sea forces in and about the territory of the Republic of Korea as determined by mutual agreement.

Article V. This Treaty shall be ratified by the United States of America and the Republic of Korea in accordance with their respective constitutional processes . . .

Article VI. This Treaty shall remain in force indefinitely. Either party may terminate it one year after notice has been given to the other party.

[The United States ratified the Treaty on 17 November 1954 subject to the following understanding:

It is the understanding of the United States that neither party is obligated, under Article III of the above Treaty, to come to the aid of the other except in case of an external armed attack against such party; nor shall anything in the present Treaty be construed as requiring the United States to give assistance to Korea except in the event of an armed attack against territory which has been recognized by the United States as lawfully brought under the administrative control of the Republic of Korea.]

Mutual Defense Treaty between the United States and China, Washington, 2 December 1954

The parties to this Treaty,

Reaffirming their faith in the purposes and principles of the Charter of the United Nations and their desire to live in peace with all peoples and all Governments, and desiring to strengthen the fabric of peace in the West Pacific area,

Recalling with mutual pride the relationship which brought their two peoples together in a common bond of sympathy and mutual ideals to fight side by side against imperialist aggression during the last war,

Desiring to declare publicly and formally their sense of unity and their common determination to defend themselves against external armed attack, so that no potential aggressor could be under the illusion that either of them stands alone in the West Pacific area, and

Desiring further to strengthen their present efforts for collective defense for the preservation of peace and security pending the development of a more comprehensive system of regional security in the West Pacific area,

Have agreed as follows:

Article I. The parties undertake, as set forth in the Charter of the United Nations, to settle any international dispute in which they may be involved by peaceful means in such a manner that international peace, security and justice are not endangered and to refrain in their international relations from the threat or use of force in any manner inconsistent with the purposes of the United Nations.

Article II. In order more effectively to achieve the objective of this Treaty, the parties separately and jointly by self-help and mutual aid will maintain and develop their individual and collective capacity to resist armed attack and communist subversive activities directed from without against their territorial integrity and political stability.

Article III. The parties undertake to strengthen their free institutions and to cooperate with each other in the development of economic progress and social well-being and to further their individual and collective efforts toward these ends.

Article IV. The parties, through their Foreign Ministers or their deputies, will consult together from time to time regarding the implementation of this Treaty.

Article V. Each party recognizes that an armed attack in the West Pacific area directed against the territories of either of the parties would be dangerous to its own peace and safety and declares that it would act to meet the common danger in accordance with its constitutional processes.

Any such armed attack and all measures taken as a result thereof shall be immediately reported to the Security Council of the United Nations. Such measures shall be terminated when the Security Council has taken the measures necessary to restore and maintain international peace and security.

Article VI. For the purposes of Articles II and V, the terms 'territorial' and 'territories' shall mean in respect of the Republic of China, Taiwan and the Pescadores; and in respect of the United States of America, the island territories in the West Pacific under its jurisdiction. The provisions of Articles II and V will be applicable to such other territories as may be determined by mutual agreement.

Article VII. The Government of the Republic of China grants, and the Government of the United States of America accepts, the right to dispose such United States land, air and sea forces in and about Taiwan and the Pescadores as may be required for their defense, as determined by mutual agreement.

Article VIII. This Treaty does not affect and shall not be interpreted as affecting in any way the rights and obligations of the parties under the Charter of the United Nations or the responsibility of the United Nations for the maintenance of international peace and security.

Article IX. This Treaty shall be ratified by the United States of America and the Republic of China in accordance with their respective constitutional processes ...

Article X. This Treaty shall remain in force indefinitely. Either party may terminate it one year after notice has been given to the other party ...

South-East Asia Collective Defense Treaty (SEATO), Manila, 8 September 1954

The parties to this Treaty,

Recognizing the sovereign equality of all the parties,

Reiterating their faith in the purposes and principles set forth in the Charter of the United Nations and their desire to live in peace with all peoples and all Governments,

Reaffirming that, in accordance with the Charter of the United Nations, they uphold the principle of equal rights and self-determination of peoples, and declaring that they will earnestly strive by every peaceful means to promote self-government and to secure the independence of all countries whose peoples desire it and are able to undertake its responsibilities,

Desiring to strengthen the fabric of peace and freedom and to uphold the principles of democracy, individual liberty and the rule of law, and to promote the economic well-being and development of all peoples in the treaty area,

Intending to declare publicly and formally their sense of unity, so that any potential aggressor will appreciate that the parties stand together in the area, and

Desiring further to coordinate their efforts for collective defense for the preservation of peace and security,

Therefore agree as follows:

Article I. The parties undertake, as set forth in the Charter of the United Nations, to settle any international disputes in which they may be involved by peaceful means in such a manner that international peace and security and justice are not endangered, and to refrain in their international relations from the threat or use of force in any manner inconsistent with the purposes of the United Nations.

Article II. In order more effectively to achieve the objectives of this Treaty, the parties, separately and jointly, by means of continuous and effective self-help and mutual aid will maintain and develop their individual and collective capacity to resist armed attack and to prevent and counter subversive activities directed from without against their territorial integrity and political stability.

Article III. The parties undertake to strengthen their free institutions and to cooperate with one another in the further development of economic measures, including technical assistance, designed both to promote economic progress and social well-being and to further the individual and collective efforts of Governments toward these ends.

Article IV. 1. Each party recognizes that aggression by means of armed attack in the treaty area against any of the parties or against any State or territory which the parties by unanimous agreement may hereafter designate, would endanger its own peace and safety, and agrees that it will in that event act to meet the common danger in accordance with its constitutional processes. Measures taken under this paragraph shall be immediately reported to the Security Council of the United Nations.

2. If, in the opinion of any of the parties, the inviolability or the integrity of the territory or the sovereignty or political independence of any party in the treaty area or of any other State or territory to which the provisions of paragraph 1 of this Article from time to time apply is threatened in any way other than by armed attack or is affected or threatened by any fact or situation which might endanger the peace of the area, the parties shall consult immediately in order to agree on the measures which should be taken for the common defense.

3. It is understood that no action on the territory of any State designated by unanimous agreement under paragraph 1 of this Article or on any territory so designated shall be taken except at the invitation or with the consent of the Government concerned.

Article V. The parties hereby establish a Council, on which each of them shall be represented, to consider matters concerning the implementation of this Treaty. The Council shall provide for consultation with regard to military and any other planning as the situation obtaining in the treaty area may from time to time require. The Council shall be so organized as to be able to meet at any time.

Article VI. This Treaty does not affect and shall not be interpreted as affecting in any way the rights and obligations of any of the parties under the Charter of the United Nations or the responsibility of the United Nations for the maintenance of international peace and security.

Each party declares that none of the international engagements now in force between it and any other of the parties or any third party is in conflict with the provisions of this Treaty, and undertakes not to enter into any international engagement in conflict with this Treaty.

Article VII. Any other State in a position to further the objectives of this Treaty and to contribute to the security of the area may, by unanimous agreement of the parties, be invited to accede to this Treaty. . . .

Article VIII. As used in this Treaty, the 'treaty area' is the general area of southeast Asia, including also the entire territories of the Asian parties, and the general area of the south-west Pacific not including the Pacific area north of 21 degrees 30 minutes north latitude. The parties may, by unanimous agreement, amend this Article to include within the treaty area the territory of any State acceding to this Treaty in accordance with Article VII or otherwise to change the treaty area.

Article IX. . . . The Treaty shall be ratified and its provisions carried out by the parties in accordance with their respective constitutional processes . . .

Article X. This Treaty shall remain in force indefinitely, but any party may cease to be a party one year after notice of denunciation has been given . . .

[*Article XI*. Languages of authentic texts.]

UNDERSTANDING OF THE UNITED STATES OF AMERICA

The United States of America in executing the present Treaty does so with the understanding that its recognition of the effect of aggression and armed attack and its agreement with reference thereto in Article IV, paragraph 1, apply only to communist aggression but affirms that in the event of other aggression or armed attack it will consult under the provisions of Article IV, paragraph 2.

Protocol to the South-East Asia Collective Defense Treaty signed at Manila on 8 September 1954

DESIGNATION OF STATES AND TERRITORY AS TO WHICH PROVISIONS OF ARTICLE IV AND ARTICLE III ARE TO BE APPLICABLE

The parties to the South-east Asia Collective Defense Treaty unanimously designate for the purposes of Article IV of the Treaty the States of Cambodia and Laos and the free territory under the jurisdiction of the State of Vietnam.

The parties further agree that the above-mentioned States and territory shall be eligible in respect of the economic measures contemplated by Article III.

This Protocol shall enter into force simultaneously with the coming into force of the Treaty.

In witness whereof, the undersigned plenipotentiaries have signed this Protocol to the South-east Asia Collective Defense Treaty.

Done at Manila, this eighth day of September, 1954.

Pacific Charter, Manila, 8 September 1954

The Delegates of Australia, France, New Zealand, Pakistan, the Republic of the Philippines, the Kingdom of Thailand, the United Kingdom of Great Britain and Northern Ireland, and the United States of America,

Desiring to establish a firm basis for common action to maintain peace and security in south-east Asia and the south-west Pacific,

Convinced that common action to this end, in order to be worthy and effective, must be inspired by the highest principles of justice and liberty,

Do hereby proclaim:

First, in accordance with the provisions of the United Nations Charter, they uphold the principle of equal rights and self-determination of peoples and they will earnestly strive by every peaceful means to promote self-government and to secure

the independence of all countries whose peoples desire it and are able to undertake its responsibilities;

Second, they are each prepared to continue taking effective practical measures to ensure conditions favorable to the orderly achievement of the foregoing purposes in accordance with their constitutional processes;

Third, they will continue to cooperate in the economic, social and cultural fields in order to promote higher living standards, economic progress and social well-being in this region;

Fourth, as declared in the South-east Asia Collective Defense Treaty, they are determined to prevent or counter by appropriate means any attempt in the treaty area to subvert their freedom or to destroy their sovereignty or territorial integrity.

Treaty of Mutual Cooperation and Security between the United States of America and Japan, 19 January 1960

The United States of America and Japan,

Desiring to strengthen the bonds of peace and friendship traditionally existing between them, and to uphold the principles of democracy, individual liberty, and the rule of law;

Desiring further to encourage closer economic cooperation between them and to promote conditions of economic stability and well-being in their countries;

Reaffirming their faith in the purposes and principles of the Charter of the United Nations, and their desire to live in peace with all peoples and all Governments;

Recognizing that they have the inherent right of individual or collective self-defense as affirmed in the Charter of the United Nations;

Considering that they have a common concern in the maintenance of international peace and security in the Far East;

Having resolved to conclude a Treaty of Mutual Cooperation and Security;

Therefore agree as follows:

Article I. The parties undertake, as set forth in the Charter of the United Nations, to settle any international disputes in which they may be involved by peaceful means in such a manner that international peace and security and justice are not endangered and to refrain in their international relations from the threat or use of force against the territorial integrity or political independence of any State, or in any other manner inconsistent with the purposes of the United Nations.

The parties will endeavor in concert with other peace-loving countries to strengthen the United Nations so that its mission of maintaining international peace and security may be discharged more effectively.

Article II. The parties will contribute toward the further development of peaceful and friendly international relations by strengthening their free institutions, by bringing about a better understanding of the principles upon which these institutions are founded, and by promoting conditions of stability and well-being. They will seek to eliminate conflict in their international economic policies and will encourage economic collaboration between them.

Article III. The parties, individually and in cooperation with each other, by means of continuous and effective self-help and mutual aid will maintain and develop, subject to their constitutional provisions, their capacities to resist armed attack.

Article IV. The parties will consult together from time to time regarding the implementation of this Treaty, and, at the request of either party, whenever the security of Japan or international peace and security in the Far East is threatened.

Article V. Each party recognizes that an armed attack against either party in the territories under the administration of Japan would be dangerous to its own peace and safety and declares that it would act to meet the common danger in accordance with its constitutional provisions and processes.

Any such armed attack and all measures taken as a result thereof shall be immediately reported to the Security Council of the United Nations in accordance with the provisions of Article 51 of the Charter. Such measures shall be terminated when the Security Council has taken the measures necessary to restore and maintain international peace and security.

Article VI. For the purpose of contributing to the security of Japan and the maintenance of international peace and security in the Far East, the United States of America is granted the use by its land, air and naval forces of facilities and areas in Japan.

The use of these facilities and areas as well as the status of United States armed forces in Japan shall be governed by a separate agreement, replacing the Administrative Agreement under Article III of the Security Treaty between the United States of America and Japan, signed at Tokyo on February 28, 1952, as amended, and by such other arrangements as may be agreed upon.

Article VII. This Treaty does not affect and shall not be interpreted as affecting in any way the rights and obligations of the parties under the Charter of the United Nations or the responsibility of the United Nations for the maintenance of international peace and security.

Article VIII. This Treaty shall be ratified by the United States of America and Japan in accordance with their respective constitutional processes and will enter into force on the date on which the instruments of ratification thereof have been exchanged by them in Tokyo.

Article IX. The Security Treaty between the United States of America and Japan signed at the city of San Francisco on September 8, 1951, shall expire upon the entering into force of this Treaty.

Article X. This Treaty shall remain in force until in the opinion of the Governments of the United States of America and Japan there shall have come into force such United Nations arrangements as will satisfactorily provide for the maintenance of international peace and security in the Japan area.

However, after the Treaty has been in force for ten years, either party may give notice to the other party of its intention to terminate the Treaty, in which case the Treaty shall terminate one year after such notice has been given. . . .

Agreement of Cooperation between Iran and the United States, 5 March 1959

. . .

[Similar treaties were concluded between the United States and Pakistan, and Turkey.]

Article I. The Imperial Government of Iran is determined to resist aggression. In case of aggression against Iran, the Government of the United States of America, in accordance with the Constitution of the United States of America, will take such appropriate action, including the use of armed forces, as may be mutually agreed upon and as is envisaged in the Joint Resolution to Promote Peace and Stability in the Middle East, in order to assist the Government of Iran at its request.

Article II. The Government of the United States of America, in accordance with the Mutual Security Act of 1954, as amended, and related laws of the United States of America, and with applicable agreements heretofore or hereafter entered into between the Government of the United States of America and the Government of Iran, reaffirms that it will continue to furnish the Government of Iran such military and economic assistance as may be mutually agreed upon between the Government of the United States of America and the Government of Iran, in order to assist the Government of Iran in the preservation of its national independence and integrity and in the effective promotion of its economic development.

Article III. The Imperial Government of Iran undertakes to utilize such military and economic assistance as may be provided by the Government of the United States of America in a manner consonant with the aims and purposes set forth by the Governments associated in the Declaration signed at London on July 28, 1958, and for the purpose of effectively promoting the economic development of Iran and of preserving its national independence and integrity.

Article IV. The Government of the United States of America and the Government of Iran will cooperate with the other Governments associated in the Declaration signed at London on July 28, 1958, in order to prepare and participate in such defensive arrangements as may be mutually agreed to be desirable, subject to the other applicable provisions of this Agreement.

Article V. The provisions of the present Agreement do not affect the cooperation between the two Governments as envis-

aged in other international agreements or arrangements.

Article VI. This Agreement shall enter into force upon the date of its signature and shall continue in force until one year after the receipt by either Government of written notice of the intention of the the other Government to terminate the Agreement.

The Charter of Punta Del Este establishing an Alliance for Progress, 17 August 1961

Declaration to the Peoples of America

Assembled in Punta del Este, inspired by the principles consecrated in the Charter of the Organization of American States, in Operation Pan-America and in the Act of Bogotá, the representatives of the American Republics hereby agree to establish an Alliance for Progress: a vast effort to bring a better life to all the peoples of the continent.

This Alliance is established on the basic principle that free men working through the institution of representative democracy can best satisfy man's aspirations, including those for work, home and land, health and schools. No system can guarantee true progress unless it affirms the dignity of the individual which is the foundation of our civilization.

Therefore the countries signing this Declaration in the exercise of their sovereignty have agreed to work toward the following goals during the coming years:

To improve and strengthen democratic institutions through application of the principle of self-determination by the people.

To accelerate economic and social development, thus rapidly bringing about

a substantial and steady increase in the average income in order to narrow the gap between the standard of living in Latin American countries and that enjoyed in the industrialized countries.

To carry out urban and rural housing programs to provide decent homes for all our people.

To encourage, in accordance with the characteristics of each country, programs of comprehensive agrarian reform, leading to the effective transformation, where required, of unjust structures and systems of land tenure and use; with a view to replacing *latifundia* and dwarf holdings by an equitable system of property so that, supplemented by timely and adequate credit, technical assistance and improved marketing arrangements, the land will become for the man who works it the basis of his economic stability, the foundation of his increasing welfare, and the guarantee of his freedom and dignity.

To assure fair wages and satisfactory working conditions to all our workers; to establish effective systems of labor–management relations and procedures for consultation and cooperation among government authorities, employers' associations, and trade unions in the interests of social and economic development.

To wipe out illiteracy; to extend, as

quickly as possible, the benefits of primary education to all Latin Americans; and to provide broader facilities, on a vast scale, for secondary and technical training and for higher education.

To press forward with programs of health and sanitation in order to prevent sickness, combat contagious disease, and strengthen our human potential.

To reform tax laws, demanding more from those who have most, to punish tax evasion severely, and to redistribute the national income in order to benefit those who are most in need, while, at the same time, promoting savings and investment and reinvestment of capital.

To maintain monetary and fiscal policies which, while avoiding the disastrous effects of inflation or deflation, will protect the purchasing power of the many, guarantee the greatest possible price stability, and form an adequate basis for economic development.

To stimulate private enterprise in order to encourage the development of Latin American countries at a rate which will help them to provide jobs for their growing populations, to eliminate unemployment, and to take their place among the modern industrialized nations of the world.

To find a quick and lasting solution to the grave problem created by excessive price fluctuations in the basic exports of Latin American countries on which their prosperity so heavily depends.

To accelerate the integration of Latin America so as to stimulate the economic and social development of the continent. This process has already begun through the General Treaty of Economic Integration of Central America and, in other countries, through the Latin American Free Trade Association.

This Declaration expresses the conviction of the nations of Latin America that these profound economic, social, and cultural changes can come about only through the self-help efforts of each country. Nonetheless, in order to achieve the goals which have been established with the necessary speed, domestic efforts must be reinforced by essential contributions of external assistance.

The United States, for its part, pledges its efforts to supply financial and technical cooperation in order to achieve the aims of the Alliance for Progress. To this end, the United States will provide a major part of the minimum of twenty billion dollars, principally in public funds, which Latin America will require over the next ten years from all external sources in order to supplement its own efforts.

The United States will provide from public funds, as an immediate contribution to the economic and social progress of Latin America, more than one billion dollars during the twelve months which began on March 13, 1961, when the Alliance for Progress was announced.

The United States intends to furnish development loans on a long-term basis, where appropriate running up to fifty years and in general at very low or zero rates of interest.

For their part, the countries of Latin America agree to devote a steadily increasing share of their own resources to economic and social development, and to make the reforms necessary to assure that all share fully in the fruits of the Alliance for Progress.

Further, as a contribution to the Alliance for Progress, each of the countries of Latin America will formulate a comprehensive and well-conceived national program for the development of its own economy.

Independent and highly qualified experts will be made available to Latin American countries in order to assist in formulating and examining national development plans.

Conscious of the overriding importance of this Declaration, the signatory countries declare that the inter-American community is now beginning a new era when it will supplement its institutional, legal, cultural and social accomplishments with immediate and concrete actions to secure a better life, under freedom and democracy, for the present and future generations.

The Charter of Punta del Este

Establishing an Alliance for Progress within the framework of Operation Pan-America

Preamble. We, the American Republics, hereby proclaim our decision to unite in a common effort to bring our people accelerated economic progress and broader social justice within the framework of personal dignity and political liberty.

Almost two hundred years ago we began in this hemisphere the long struggle for freedom which now inspires people in all parts of the world. Today, in ancient lands, men moved to hope by the revolutions of our young nations search for liberty. Now we must give a new meaning to that revolutionary heritage. For America stands at a turning point in history. The men and women of our hemisphere are reaching for the better life which today's skills have placed within their grasp. They are determined for themselves and their children to have decent and ever more abundant lives, to gain access to knowledge and equal opportunity for all, to end those conditions which benefit the few at the expense of the needs and dignity of the many. It is our inescapable task to fulfill these just desires – to demonstrate to the poor and forsaken of our countries, and of all lands, that the creative powers of free men hold the key to their progress and to the progress of future generations. And our certainty of ultimate success rests not alone on our faith in ourselves and in our nations but on the indomitable spirit of free man which has been the heritage of American civilization.

Inspired by these principles, and by the principles of Operation Pan-America and the Act of Bogotá, the American Republics hereby resolve to adopt the following program of action to establish and carry forward an Alliance for Progress.

[TITLE I. The Treaty sets out the objectives of the alliance in conformity with the Declaration to the Peoples of America.]

TITLE II

[Economic and social development: requirements, National Development Programs, immediate and short-term measures.]

• • •

Chapter IV: External assistance in support of National Development Programs

1. The economic and social development of Latin America will require a large amount of additional public and private financial assistance on the part of capital-exporting countries, including the members of the Development Assistance Group and international lending agencies. The measures provided for in the Act of Bogotá and the new measures provided for in this Charter, are designed to create a framework within which such additional assistance can be provided and effectively utilized.

2. The United States will assist those participating countries whose development programs establish self-help measures and economic and social policies and programs consistent with the principles of this Charter. To supplement the domestic efforts of such countries, the United States is prepared to allocate resources which, along with those anticipated from other external sources, will be of a scope and magnitude adequate to realize the goals envisaged in this Charter. Such assistance will be allocated to both social and economic development and, where appropriate, will take the form of grants or loans on flexible terms and conditions. The participating countries will request the support of other capital-exporting countries and appropriate institutions so that they may provide assistance for the attainment of these objectives.

3. The United States will help in the financing of technical assistance projects proposed by a participating country or by the General Secretariat of the Organization of American States for the purpose of:

(a) Providing experts contracted in agreement with the Governments to work under their direction and to assist them in the preparation of specific investment projects and the strengthening of national mechanisms for preparing projects, using specialized engineering firms where appropriate;

(b) Carrying out, pursuant to existing agreements for cooperation among the General Secretariat of the Organization of American States, the Economic Commission for Latin America, and the Inter-American Development Bank, field investigations and studies, including those relating to development problems, the organization of national agencies for the preparation of development programs, agrarian reform and rural development, health, cooperatives, housing, education and professional training, and taxation and tax administration; and

(c) Convening meetings of experts and officials on development and related problems.

The Governments or above-mentioned organizations should, when appropriate, seek the cooperation of the United Nations and its specialized agencies in the execution of these activities.

4. The participating Latin American countries recognize that each has in varying degree a capacity to assist fellow Republics by providing technical and financial assistance. They recognize that this capacity will increase as their economies grow. They therefore affirm their intention to assist fellow Republics increasingly as their individual circumstances permit.

Chapter V: Organization and procedures

1. In order to provide technical assistance for the formulation of development programs, as may be requested by participating nations, the Organization of American States, the Economic Commission for Latin America, and the Inter-American Development Bank will continue and strengthen their agreements for coordination in this field, in order to have available a group of programming experts whose service can be used to facilitate the implementation of this Charter. The participating countries will also seek an intensification of technical assistance from the specialized agencies of the United Nations for the same purpose.

2. The Inter-American Economic and Social Council, on the joint nomination of the Secretary-General of the Organization of American States, the President of the Inter-American Development Bank, and the Executive Secretary of the United Nations Economic Commission for Latin America, will appoint a panel of nine high-level experts, exclusively on the basis of their experience, technical ability, and competence in the various aspects of economic and social development. The experts may be of any nationality, though if of Latin American origin an appropriate geographical distribution will be sought. They will be attached to the Inter-American Economic and Social Council, but will nevertheless enjoy complete autonomy in the performance of their duties. They may not hold any other remunerative position. The appointment of these experts will be for a period of three years, and may be renewed.

3. Each Government, if it so wishes, may present its program for economic and social development for consideration by an *Ad hoc* Committee, composed of no more than three members drawn from the panel of experts referred to in the preceding paragraph together with an equal number of experts not on the panel. The experts who compose the *Ad hoc* Committee will be appointed by the Secretary-General of the Organization of American States at the request of the interested Government and with its consent.

4. The Committee will study the development program, exchange opinions with the interested Government as to possible modifications and, with the consent of the Government, report its conclusions to the Inter-American Development Bank and to other Governments and institutions that may be prepared to extend external financial and technical assistance in connection with the execution of the program.

. . .

[7. A Government whose program has been approved by the *Ad hoc* Committee with respect to external financial requirements may submit the program to the Inter-American Development Bank so that the Bank may negotiate the finance.

8. The Inter-American Economic and Social Council will review progress of development programs and submit recommendations to the Council of the O.A.S.]

[TITLE III. Dealt with economic integration of Latin America.]

[TITLE IV. Basic export commodities.]

XIII · The Soviet alliances, 1945–71

Soviet alliances in Europe, *1945–71*

From 1939 to 1945 Stalin sought to regain for the Soviet Union the territory that had once constituted the Tsarist Russian Empire in 1914 with two exceptions: Poland and Finland. Although accepting separate Polish and Finnish States, Stalin was not prepared to recognize as final their frontiers as established after the First World War, nor their right to follow policies of enmity to the Soviet Union. The twin impulses of expanding Soviet power for its own sake and of creating a 'buffer' of greater security against the West motivated Soviet policies from 1939 to 1945. Stalin regarded both 'Fascist' and 'democratic' Europe as basically hostile to the Soviet Union; if the 'capitalists' were divided, the Soviet Union, still weaker than the capitalist world, should seek advantage and safety from any capitalist conflicts. Its policy towards them would be governed by the opportunism of Soviet self-interest. From 1939 to 1940 Stalin achieved his territorial objectives in alliance with Hitler.

In September 1939 the Soviet Union occupied eastern Poland and incorporated this territory some weeks later in the Soviet Union. As a result of the Winter War with Finland (November 1939–March 1940) the Soviet Union annexed Finnish territory of strategic importance, especially the Karelian isthmus and, in the extreme north of Finland, Petsamo and its district which gave the Soviet Union a common frontier with Norway in the Arctic. In June 1940, Rumania under Soviet pressure and on German 'advice' returned Bessarabia; in August 1940 Lithuania, Latvia and Estonia were incorporated in the Soviet Union. In 1945, the Soviet Union retained all these gains of 1939–40 and added further relatively small but strategically important areas: Ruthenia, or what was called by the Soviet leaders the Subcarpathian Ukraine, was acquired from Czechoslovakia, and thereby the Soviet Union regained a common frontier with Hungary which had been lost after the First World War. The Soviet Union also administered the northern half of German East Prussia, the southern half being administered by Poland.

A complementary aspect of Soviet policy was to ensure that those independent post-Versailles States on her borders still surviving should be friendly to the Soviet Union and closely linked to her politically, economically and culturally. Before 1939 only Czechoslovakia had pursued a policy of friendship and alliance with the Soviet Union. Stalin was determined that the Soviet Union's neighbours should become a source of strength and not of weakness for the Soviet Union, and that the revival of a German military threat be delayed as long as possible. Stalin's diplomatic methods were foreshadowed in the *Soviet–Czechoslovak Treaty of Friendship, 12 December 1943* (p. 215). By friendly neighbours Stalin meant States which would be bound by political treaties to the Soviet alliance, whose military resources would be dominated by the Soviet Union and which would permit the stationing or entry of Soviet troops for mutual protection. In the evaluating of these 'political' treaties it must be remembered that additional 'economic' agreements were just as important in the relationship. 'Friendly' also meant that the economies of Russia's allies would more or less follow the communist pattern; during the Stalinist period these economies were shaped mainly in the interests of the Soviet Union. Whilst in Poland and Czechoslovakia the political leadership at first did not have to be entirely communist in appearance and 'united front' Governments were formed, the economic reorganization and the Soviet presence ensured that real political power lay in the hands of the Soviet Union and with the communist leadership of these countries, most of whom had been trained in Moscow.

The Soviet Union signed alliances with Poland on 21 April 1945 (p. 361), *and with Yugoslavia on 11 April 1945* (p. 363), in addition to the Czech alliance already cited. These followed a common pattern in that the States agreed to collaborate in the event of any renewed aggression on the part of Germany specifically, or in the event of any other State attacking the territorial integrity of the signatories; an agreement on the part of the signatories was included stating that they would not join in alliances directed against the other signatories. The agreement that close political, economic, social and cultural ties would be promoted meant in fact that these States within a few years became dependent on the Soviet Union; clauses in the treaty promising non-interference in the domestic affairs of the neighbours of the Soviet Union were in practice not observed. Only Finland and Yugoslavia were allowed some genuine measure of domestic independence.

During the first six months of 1945, under the aegis of the Red Army, communist-controlled Governments were set up in Rumania and Bulgaria. In Poland and Hungary 'united front' Governments were permitted with some non-communist participation until the summer of 1947. In 1948 Czechoslovakia came under complete communist control. In Yugoslavia Marshal Tito had established his communist Government without Russian help. Denounced in June 1948 for national deviationism by Stalin, Tito successfully resisted all Soviet pressure.

The Soviet Union concluded alliance treaties with Rumania on 4 February 1948 (p. 364), *with Hungary on 18 February and Bulgaria on 18 March 1948.* A few months earlier in *September 1947* the *Communist Information Bureau, Cominform,* had been established with headquarters in Belgrade but with nothing really to do. Tito's successful defiance of Stalin's accusations, which Stalin had delivered through the Cominform, soon made the Cominform totally ineffective, though as an organization it remained formally in being until 1956. Tito's assertion of Yugoslav independence led to Soviet-inspired purges in Hungary, Bulgaria, Albania, Poland, Rumania and Czechoslovakia. Soviet policy was laid down by the Party and backed by Soviet Army units, which could be used as a last resort. Whilst Stalin decided not to attack Yugoslavia he was all the more determined to prevent a spread of a revived Balkan 'nationalism' whether communist or of any other kind.

These developments in Eastern and Central Europe were related to the growing conflict between the Western wartime allies and the Soviet Union which became known as the cold war. Western policies were viewed by Stalin as attempts under the leadership of the United States to revive in a new form a capitalist coalition of States, which would encircle the Soviet Union. Stalin saw in the same light Western protests over Russian policy in the Soviet zone of Germany and in Central and Eastern Europe. For Stalin, 20 million Russian war casualties and the destruction of much of European Russia justified and necessitated a post-war policy that would ensure Soviet security and material reparations. Experience during the Second World War of the extent of Allied solidarity did not lessen his deep-rooted fear that in the post-war world an isolated Soviet Russia was facing a more powerful Western coalition possessing the atom bomb.

Stalin interpreted the Marshall Plan (p. 379) and American economic aid as attempts to revive capitalism among Russia's neighbours to the detriment of the security of the Soviet Union. But the event which most alarmed Central and Eastern Europe was the creation of the Federal Republic of Germany and German rearmament (p. 381). The Soviet response was to form an alliance of communist States, ostensibly among equals, with joint responsibilities and mutual decision-making organs giving the appearance of equality. *The Council of Mutual Economic Assistance (Comecon) established in January 1949* was set up as the Soviet counterpart to the *Organization for European Economic Cooperation* created in April 1948 (see p. 381). But Comecon was little more than a paper organization until the death of Stalin on 5 March 1953; it had only met twice before the Dictator's death.

In June 1953 the first of a series of upheavals among Russia's satellites was crushed in East Germany. In January–February 1954 the Foreign Ministers of the Big Four met again in Berlin, but could not agree on a solution for a divided Germany. From April to July 1954 the Geneva Conference convened to discuss the problems of Asia (p. 441). The post-Stalin period of flexibility over Germany drew to a close with the signature by the Western allies of the Paris Agreements, 23 October 1954, which came into force in May 1955 and which restored sovereignty to the German Federal Republic and provided for her entry into NATO (p. 387). The Soviet response was to convene a conference in Moscow from 29 November–2 December 1954 attended by Albania, Bulgaria, Czechoslovakia, the German Democratic Republic, Hungary, Poland and Rumania and the Soviet Union. They jointly declared that if the Paris Agreements were ratified they would adopt measures to safeguard their security. On 6 May 1955, the day after the ratification of the Paris Agreements, the Soviet Union denounced the Anglo-Soviet Alliance Treaty of 1942 (see p. 212). On *14 May 1955* the same eight communist States signed the *Treaty of Friendship, Cooperation and Mutual Assistance* known as the *Warsaw Pact* (p. 365).

The Warsaw Pact is the most important multilateral treaty between the communist States under Soviet leadership both militarily and politically, but little is known about its institutional structure; the treaty refers to a political consultative committee which has the power to set up auxiliary bodies. Militarily it formalized arrangements for Soviet control dating probably three years earlier to about August 1952, when a decision was taken to re-equip the satellite armies and place them under Soviet command. In accordance with the agreement reached in May 1955, the following January a United Military Command was established with headquarters in Moscow. A Soviet officer, Marshal Konev, became commander-in-chief, and the Defence Ministers of participating countries were to be deputy commanders-in-chief. Joint military exercises have been held in member countries since the autumn of 1961.

At first the Asian communist countries – China, North Korea and North Vietnam – sent observers to the Warsaw Pact, but they withdrew by 1962. Albania was excluded and withdrew after 1961, siding with China in the Sino-Soviet conflict. Of the Asian countries only Mongolia has remained a member since 1959.

Following the momentous Twentieth Congress of the Communist Party of the Soviet Union in February 1956, when Khrushchev attacked the mistakes and cruelty of Stalin's dictatorship, Poland and Hungary sought more independence from Soviet control. Outright Soviet military intervention was only just avoided in Poland; but in October and November 1956 Soviet troops crushed Hungarian resistance after the Hungarian Nagy Government on 1 November 1956 had seceded from the Warsaw Pact. The Soviet Union moved back into Hungary just as the Western Suez involvement was reaching its culmination (p. 494). Khrushchev emerged as the principal Soviet leader in 1956–8. He sought to normalize relations within the Soviet alliance.

Comecon from May 1956 increasingly began to take joint decisions and set up standing commissions. After 13 April 1960, when a formal Comecon Charter came into force setting out its purpose and institutions, the organization became more genuinely international, respecting some measure of independence of its members. In June 1962 an Executive Committee consisting of the Deputy Premiers of Member Governments was created. Increasing Rumanian economic independence has hampered the development of Comecon since 1964. The treaty relationships between the Soviet Union and her East European allies gradually became less one-sided.

The limitations of independence and apparent equality of the Soviet Union and other States were, however, exposed when on 21 August 1968 the Soviet Union and the other European Warsaw Pact countries (except Rumania), acting as socialist allies, invaded Czechoslovakia, itself a member of the Warsaw Pact. According to *Pravda*, the 'allied socialist' troops together with the Soviet Union, i.e. the Warsaw Pact countries, had 'a solemn commitment – to stand up in defence of the gains of socialism'. All participants of the Warsaw Treaty Organization were involved, for to tolerate a breach in this organization would contradict the vital interests of all the member countries, including the Soviet Union. Although the Czech Government denounced the invasion as illegal and Rumania also condemned it, Czechoslovakia by the end of August 1968 was occupied and forced to submit. The Soviet justification on the basis of limited sovereignty within the socialist community became known as the Brezhnev Doctrine.

Bilateral treaties were concluded between the *Soviet Union and Poland, 17 December 1956*, the *Soviet Union and the German Democratic Republic, 12 March 1957*, the *Soviet Union and Rumania, 15 April 1957*, and the *Soviet Union and Hungary, 27 May 1957*, in the aftermath of the Polish troubles and the Hungarian uprising, to normalize and improve relations, limit Soviet supervision and direct interference, and above all to justify the stationing of Soviet troops ostensibly to fulfil the needs of the Warsaw Pact. The treaty with Poland more specifically stated that the 'temporary stay' of Soviet troops in Poland neither could affect Polish sovereignty nor lead to any interference in the domestic affairs of Poland, and that no Soviet troop movements outside specified areas in Poland would be permitted without Polish authorization. Despite the bilateral treaty signed between the *Soviet Union and Rumania, 15 April 1957*, all Soviet troops were withdrawn in 1958. These treaties were supplemented by a network of bilateral treaties between the East European States. But these Soviet treaty assurances about respecting the sovereignty of her Warsaw Pact allies lost credibility with the invasion of Czechoslovakia in August 1968. *In October 1968 a new treaty was signed between Czechoslovakia and the Soviet Union*, formally ending the occupation but granting to Soviet troops the right to remain in Czechoslovakia for an indefinite time without any of the restrictions in the Hungarian or Polish treaties of 1957.

Relations with Czechoslovakia and Rumania were placed on a more 'friendly' footing by the conclusion of a *Treaty of Friendship, Cooperation and Mutual Aid between the Soviet Union and Czechoslovakia, 6 May 1970* (p. 374), and a *Treaty of Friendship, Cooperation and Mutual Aid between the Soviet Union and Rumania, 7 July 1970*.

Towards Finland the Soviet Union followed a conciliatory policy, not attempting to exert the same degree of control over internal Finnish policy as over those Central and East European States in the Soviet orbit. A *Soviet–Finnish Mutual Assistance Treaty was concluded, 6 April 1948* (p. 369), which was extended a further twenty years on 19 September 1955. This treaty provides that if Finland or the Soviet Union are attacked by Germany or any State allied to Germany, Finland will repulse the aggressor, acting within her boundaries with the assistance in case of need of the Soviet Union, or jointly with the Soviet Union (Article 1). Finland does not have to come to the assistance of the Soviet Union if attacked or at war in any other region. The treaty does ensure that Finland will not join in any alliance or alliance treaty organization of which the Federal Republic of Germany is a member.

Soviet treaty relations in the Middle East, Africa and Cuba, 1955–71

Before 1955 the States of the Middle East viewed the Soviet Union with hostility and suspicion, and a number of them joined in a defensive alliance with the West (p. 499). In 1955–6 tensions among the Arab States, the continuing hostility between Israel and her neighbours and the crisis over Suez culminating in the Anglo-French landing in November 1956, offered the Soviet Union opportunities for penetrating the Middle East. Egypt became the focal point of Soviet efforts. An agreement to deliver arms to Egypt from Czechoslovakia was concluded in September 1955. These did not save Egypt from a catastrophic defeat when Israel attacked on 29 October 1956, followed by the Anglo-French Suez landings (p. 498). The Soviet Union pledged full support to Egypt during the crisis which ended with the Anglo-French withdrawal and a truce with Israel. Relations between the Soviet Union and Egypt became increasingly cordial from 1956 to 1964, though Nasser continued to maintain normal relations with the United States. Soviet support for both Syria (since February 1966) and Egypt made these countries increasingly dependent on Soviet economic and military assistance. The Soviet support was extended as well to Yemen and Algeria.

The third Arab–Israeli military conflict which became the 'Six Day War' broke out on 5 June 1967 and ended in the rapid defeat of Egypt, Syria and Jordan; on 8 June 1967 the armistice between Egypt (U.A.R.) and Israel came into force and left the Israelis in control of the Sinai desert and along the length of the east bank of the Suez Canal. Other territorial gains were made at Jordan's expense, i.e. the territory lying on the west bank of the Jordan river, and Israel also occupied the Syrian Golan heights. The Soviet Union began replacing Egyptian losses with new arms and economic aid, was granted the use of Egyptian naval and air bases, and increasingly sent Soviet technical advisers to ensure that Soviet armaments including missiles could be effectively used. President Podgorny visited Cairo from 25 to 28 May 1971. A *Soviet–Egyptian Treaty of Friendship, 27 May 1971* was concluded on this occasion. Although an accompanying communiqué stigmatized Israeli 'aggression', the twelve articles of the treaty itself emphasized that its purpose was defensive. Soviet arms and training were to be applied to strengthening defence. Consultation was to take place to avert threats of war actually leading to conflict. The treaty has a duration of fifteen years.

Soviet involvement in Africa has been comparatively minor, though for a time close relations were established between the Soviet Union and Ghana until Nkrumah's fall in 1966. The International Communist Conference held in Moscow had concluded with a declaration in December 1960 which pledged support to national liberation revolutions in Asia, Africa and Latin America.

It was Soviet policy in Latin America, or more precisely in Cuba, that led in the autumn of 1962 to a grave confrontation between the atomic Superpowers, the Soviet Union and the United States. Fidel Castro had taken power in Cuba in 1959. The American-supported attempt to overthrow Castro at the time of the abortive Bay of Pigs landing in April 1961 strengthened Soviet–Cuban ties. The Soviet Union provided economic aid; in late 1961 or early 1962 Khrushchev decided to install a missile base in Cuba. The discovery on 16 October 1962 by U.S. reconnaisance aircraft that Soviet medium range nuclear surface-to-surface missiles were being deployed in Cuba, despite earlier Soviet denials, marked the beginning of the Cuban Missile Crisis. When news of Khrushchev's undertaking (28 October 1962) to withdraw the missiles and dismantle the sites reached Washington, the Cuban Missile Crisis of thirteen days was past. Castro, disenchanted with the Soviet climbdown, thereafter turned for support to Peking whilst continuing his links with Moscow.

Soviet treaty relations in Asia, 1941–71

THE SOVIET UNION AND CHINA

Concern for the security of the Soviet Union's frontier in Asia has been a constant preoccupation of Soviet leaders. The importance of Asia in Soviet thinking has at times been overlooked by Western diplomats. Stalin was seriously worried by Japanese ascendancy in Manchuria, and armed conflicts occurred on the frontiers of Mongolia and Manchuria in 1939 (p. 185). But the growing European dangers led the Soviet Union to conciliate Japan, a new policy marked by the signature of the *Soviet–Japanese Neutrality Pact, 13 April 1941*. The Soviet Union ceased to aid Nationalist China in resisting Japanese aggression. As the Germans advanced through Greece and Yugoslavia, Stalin sought security on his Asian frontiers through a policy of friendship with Japan, and signed the extensive *Soviet–Japanese Commercial Agreement, 11 June 1941*, providing for exchange of goods and reciprocal most-favoured-nation treatment. With the German attack on the Soviet Union on 22 June 1941, the Soviet Union first became Britain's ally in the war in Europe and later that of the United States also. But Stalin did not extend the Grand Alliance to Asia where Britain and the United States were also allied with China in the war against Japan. Relations between China and the Soviet Union steadily deteriorated from June 1941 to the spring of 1945. Nationalist China by October 1943 had forced Soviet influence out of the Chinese province of Sinkiang, where Stalin hoped to build up a strong economic base. The Soviet Union continued to pursue friendly relations with Japan and concluded another *Soviet–Japanese Agreement on 30 March 1944*, whereby Japan returned to Russia the oil and coal concession in northern Sakhalin which she had secured from Russia in 1925, and the Soviet Union renewed the Fisheries Convention and undertook to pay Japan an annual sum of 5 million roubles and to deliver 50,000 metric tons of oil. In Europe Soviet armies continued their advance; in China Japan resumed her offensive, and both offensives proved to be successful in 1944. The war against Germany was drawing to its close in the new year of 1945; Britain and the United States would soon be able to devote all their energies to the certain defeat of Japan; Stalin prepared the way for switching sides and exacting a price for doing so.

At the *Yalta Conference in February 1945* (p. 230) a secret agreement was reached between Britain, the United States and the Soviet Union; the Soviet Union would enter the war against Japan two or three months after the surrender of Germany; the Soviet Union also promised to conclude an alliance with the Nationalist Government of China; in return the Soviet Union was to secure extensive rights in Chinese Manchuria similar to those Tsarist Russia had once enjoyed before the Russo-Japanese war of 1904-5. The agreement about Russian rights in China was made subject to Chiang Kai-shek's concurrence since he had not been consulted, but the President of the United States promised to 'take measures in order to obtain this concurrence on advice from Marshal Stalin'. The agreement was kept secret until February 1946, but Stalin's breach with Japan became public when on 5 April 1945 he unilaterally denounced the Russo-Japanese Neutrality Pact. On 8 August 1945 Russia declared war on Japan shortly after the atomic bomb had been dropped on Hiroshima.

The Soviet Union was only one week at war before the unconditional surrender of Japan on 14 August 1945. On the same day the *Soviet–Chinese Treaty of Alliance and Friendship, 14 August 1945* (p. 237), was signed. The treaty had lost its purpose as a wartime alliance, but fears of a Japanese military revival remained strong in Asia for some time. For the Soviet Union the treaty gave her those rights in China promised at Yalta. The Nationalist Chinese also valued the treaty, for in the summer of 1945 the Nationalist Government of Chiang Kai-shek was faced not only with the problem of regaining control over the Japanese-occupied regions of China, but also with the Communist Chinese rival bid for power in North China; and a third difficulty was the continued unrest and doubtful Chinese control of the province of Sinkiang. The treaty with Russia held out hope of support in all these problems. The Soviet Union undertook to pursue a friendly policy toward the Nationalist Government and to aid the nationalists alone (and not the communists); the treaty contained a Soviet recognition of sovereignty over all the regions of China occupied by Japan. Though extensive rights were granted to the Soviet Union, actual occupation of Chinese territory by Soviet troops was to last for a limited period of time and ostensibly Chinese sovereignty was not thereby diminished. The Chinese Nationalist Government for their part in an exchange of notes agreed to recognize the independence of Outer Mongolia after the wishes of the Mongolian people had been tested. Formal Chinese recognition, and with it a renunciation of earlier suzerain claims, was accorded by the Nationalist Chinese Government on 5 January 1946; *on*

27 February 1946 the Soviet Union and the Outer Mongolian Republic signed a new alliance treaty.

Despite the alliance treaty relations between Nationalist China and the Soviet Union soon became acrimonious. There were disputes over the delayed Soviet evacuation of northern China, over Soviet expropriation of Manchurian industry as war booty, and there were charges of Soviet help to the communists in violation of the Soviet–Chinese treaty.

The victory of the Chinese Communists in 1949 under Mao Tse-tung's leadership opened a new chapter in Sino-Soviet relations. In December 1949 Mao Tse-tung led a delegation to Moscow to negotiate another alliance treaty with the Soviet Union. *A Treaty of Friendship, Alliance and Mutual Assistance and a number of associated agreements were signed on 14 February 1950* (p. 370). The Sino-Soviet Alliance of 14 August 1945 was declared null and void, but Chinese recognition of the independence of Outer Mongolia was reaffirmed. The alliance was directed to resisting any renewed Japanese aggression and extended to any State collaborating with Japan. This reflected the new realities of the cold war and Soviet–American hostility. The Soviet Union also abandoned many of her rights in northern China acquired in 1945. (The actual transfer of the Manchurian railway to China occurred in 1952 and of Port Arthur by 1955.) The Soviet Union extended a credit to China and promised economic aid. Whilst the 1950 treaty changed the Sino-Soviet relationship, the Soviet Union continued to retain a privileged position in China and was the acknowledged leader of the communist world movement for the next decade. Until 1956 the Soviet Union and Communist China acted in close collaboration internationally and domestically. After 1956 the growing Sino-Soviet rift soon turned into open conflict and hostility during the 1960s (p. 447).

The conflicts of Asia in the 1950s and 1960s created opportunities for the Soviet Union to counter the efforts of the United States for allies in Asia. The Soviet Union has signed treaties of *Friendship, Cooperation and Mutual Assistance with North Korea, 6 July 1961*, and *Economic Aid Agreements with North Vietnam in 1965 and 1966.* The precise nature of all these agreements is not known. The Soviet Union and China, whilst both supporting Communist 'liberation movements' in Asia, do not pursue common policies in Asia. This rift became especially evident on the Indian subcontinent where on 9 August 1971 the *Soviet Union and India signed a Treaty of Peace, Friendship and Cooperation* (p. 435). (For a more detailed analysis of Asian conflicts see Chapter XV.)

Agreement regarding Friendship, Mutual Assistance and Post-War Cooperation between the Soviet Union and the Polish Republic, Moscow, 21 April 1945

The President of the National Council of the Homeland and the Presidium of the Supreme Council of the Union of Socialist Soviet Republics moved by an unshaken determination to bring, in a common effort, the war with the German aggressors to a complete and final victory;

Wishing to consolidate the fundamental change in the history of the Polish-Soviet relations in the direction of friendly cooperation, which has taken place in course of a common fight against the German imperialism;

Trusting that a further consolidation of good neighbourly relations and friendship between Poland and her direct neighbour – the U.S.S.R. – is vital to the interests of the Polish and Soviet peoples;

Confident that friendship and close cooperation between the Polish people and the Soviet people will serve the cause of successful economic development of both countries during the war as well as after the war;

Wishing to support after the war by all possible means the cause of peace and security of peoples;

Have resolved to conclude this agreement and have ... appointed as their plenipotentiaries:

the President of the National Council of the Homeland – Edward Osóbka-Morawski, the President of the Council of Ministers and the Minister of Foreign Affairs of the Polish Republic,

The Presidium of the Supreme Council of the Union of Socialist Soviet Republics – Joseph Vissarionovitch Stalin, Chairman of the Council of People's Commissars of the U.S.S.R.;

Who, after exchange of full powers which were recognized as being in order and drawn up in due form, have agreed as follows:

Article 1. The High Contracting Parties jointly with all United Nations will continue the fight against Germany until final victory. In that fight the High Contracting Parties undertake to give one another mutual military and other assistance using all the means at their disposal.

Article 2. The High Contracting Parties, in a firm belief that in the interest of security and successful development of the Polish and Soviet peoples it is necessary to preserve and to strengthen lasting and unshaken friendship during the war as well as after the war, will strengthen the friendly cooperation between the two countries in accordance with the principles of mutual respect for their independence and sovereignty and non-interference in the internal affairs of the other Government.

Article 3. The High Contracting Parties further undertake that even after the end of the present war they will jointly use all the means at their disposal in order to eliminate every possible menace of a new aggression on the part of Germany or on the part of any other Government whatsoever which would be directly or in any other manner allied with Germany.

For this purpose the High Contracting Parties will, in a spirit of most sincere collaboration, take part in all international activities aiming at ensuring peace and security of peoples and will contribute their full share to the cause of realization of these high ideals.

The High Contracting Parties will execute this Agreement in compliance with the international principles in the establishment of which both Contracting Parties took part.

Article 4. If one of the High Contracting Parties during the post-war period should become involved in war operations against Germany in case she should resume aggressive policy or against any other Government whatsoever which would be allied with Germany directly or in any other form in such a war the other High Contracting Party will immediately extend to the other Contracting Party which is involved in military operations military and other support with all the means at its disposal.

Article 5. The High Contracting Parties undertake not to sign without mutual consent an armistice or a peace treaty with the Hitlerite Government or any other authority in Germany which menaces or may menace the independence, territorial integrity or security of either of the two High Contracting Parties.

Article 6. Each of the High Contracting Parties undertakes not to enter into any alliance or to take part in any coalition directed against the other High Contracting Party.

Article 7. The High Contracting Parties will cooperate in a spirit of friendship also after the end of the present war for the purpose of developing and strengthening the economic and cultural relations between the two countries and will give mutual assistance in the economic reconstruction of the two countries.

Article 8. This Agreement comes into force from the moment of signing and is liable to ratification within the shortest possible period. Exchange of ratifying documents will take place in Warsaw as soon as possible.

This Agreement will remain in force for twenty years after the moment of signing.

If one of the High Contracting Parties does not make a statement twelve months before the expiration of the twenty years period to the effect that it wishes to give notice, this Agreement will remain in force for a further period of five years and so on until one of the High Contracting Parties makes a statement in writing twelve months before the expiration of a successive five years period to the effect that it intends to give notice of the Agreement.

In witness whereof the mandatories have signed this Agreement and have apposed their seals thereto.

Drawn up in Moscow on April 21, 1945, in duplicate, each copy in Polish and in Russian, both texts being equally binding.

By authority of the President of the National Council of the Homeland
OsÓBKA-MORAWSKI

By authority of the Presidium of the Supreme Council of the U.S.S.R.
J. STALIN

After consideration this Agreement has been recognized equitable in its whole as well as in individual provisions contained therein; it is, therefore, announced that it has been accepted, ratified and approved and will be strictly complied with.

In witness whereof this Act has been issued with the seal of the Polish Republic duly apposed thereto.

WARSAW, September 19, 1945

President of the National Council of the Homeland
BOLESLAW BIERUT

President of the Council of Ministers
EDWARD OsÓBKA-MORAWSKI

Vice-Minister of Foreign Affairs
p.p. Z. MODZELEWSKI

Treaty of Friendship, Mutual Aid and Post-War Cooperation between the Soviet Union and Yugoslavia. Moscow, 11 April 1945

The Presidium of the Supreme Soviet of the Union of Soviet Socialist Republics and the Regency Council of Yugoslavia,

Resolved to bring the war against the German aggressors to its final conclusion; desirous still further to consolidate the friendship existing between the peoples of the Soviet Union and Yugoslavia, which together are fighting against the common enemy – Hitlerite Germany; desirous to ensure close cooperation between the peoples of the two countries and all United Nations during the war and in peacetime, and to make their contribution to the post-war organization of security and peace; convinced that the consolidation of friendship between the Soviet Union and Yugoslavia corresponds to the vital interests of the two peoples, and best serves the further economic development of the two countries, have ... agreed on the following:

Article 1. Each of the Contracting Parties will continue the struggle in cooperation with one another and with all the United Nations against Germany until final victory. The two Contracting Parties pledge themselves to render each other military and other assistance and support of every kind.

Article 2. If one of the Contracting Parties should in the post-war period be drawn into military operations against Germany, which would have resumed her aggressive policy, or against any other State which would have joined Germany either directly or in any other form in a war of this nature, the other Contracting Party shall immediately render military or any other support with all the means available.

Article 3. The two Contracting Parties state that they will participate, in the spirit of closest cooperation, in all international activities designed to ensure peace and security of peoples, and will make their contribution for attaining these lofty purposes.

The Contracting Parties state that the application of the present Treaty will be in accordance with international principles in the acceptance of which they have participated.

Article 4. Each of the Contracting Parties undertakes not to conclude any alliance and not to take part in any coalition directed against the other party.

Article 5. The two Contracting Parties state that after the termination of the present war they will act in a spirit of friendship and cooperation for the purpose of further developing and consolidating the economic and cultural ties between the peoples of the two countries.

Article 6. The present Treaty comes into force immediately it is signed and is subject to ratification in the shortest possible time. The exchange of ratification documents will be effected in Belgrade as early as possible.

The present Treaty will remain in force for a period of twenty years. If one of the Contracting Parties at the end of this twenty years period does not, one year before the expiration of this term, announce its desire to renounce the Treaty, it will remain in force for the following five years, and so on each time until one of the Contracting Parties gives written notice of its desire to terminate the efficacy of the Treaty one year before the termination of the current five-year period.

Treaty of Friendship, Collaboration and Mutual Assistance between the Rumanian People's Republic and the Soviet Union, Moscow, 4 February 1948

[A treaty in similar terms was concluded between Bulgaria and the Soviet Union, 18 March 1948; and between Hungary and the Soviet Union, 18 February 1948.]

The Praesidium of the Rumanian Popular Republic and the Praesidium of the Supreme Soviet of the Union of Soviet Socialist Republics,

Desirous of consolidating friendly relations between Rumania and the Soviet Union;

Desirous of keeping-up close collaboration, with a view to consolidating peace and general security, in accordance with the purposes and principles of the United Nations Organization;

Convinced that the keeping up of friendship and good neighbourliness between Rumania and the Soviet Union is in accordance with the vital interests of the peoples of both States, and will bring the best possible contribution to their economic development;

Have decided to conclude this Treaty, and have to that end full powers:

Article 1. The High Contracting Parties undertake to take jointly all measures in their power to remove any threat of repeated aggression on the part of Germany, or of any State allying itself with Germany directly or in any other way.

The High Contracting Parties state that it is their intention to participate with full sincerity in any international action aimed at ensuring the peace and security of nations, and that they will fully contribute to the carrying out of these great tasks.

Article 2. Should one of the High Contracting Parties be involved in armed conflict with Germany, attempting to renew her policy of aggression, or with any other State allying itself with Germany, directly or in any other way, in her aggressive policy, the other High Contracting Party will lose no time in giving the High Contracting Party involved in a conflict military or other aid with all the means at its disposal.

This Treaty will be applied in accordance with the principles of the United Nations Charter.

Article 3. Each of the High Contracting Parties undertakes to conclude no alliance and to participate in no coalition, action or measures directed against the other High Contracting Party.

Article 4. The High Contracting Parties will consult with regard to all important international issues concerning the interests of the two countries.

Article 5. The High Contracting Parties state that they will act in a spirit of friendship and collaboration, with a view to further developing and strengthening economic and cultural relations between the two States, with due regard for the principles of mutual respect for their independence and sovereignty, and of non-interference in the internal affairs of the other State.

Article 6. This Treaty will remain in force for twenty years, as from the date of its signing. If, one year before the expiry of the twenty years, none of the High Contracting Parties expresses the wish to cancel the Treaty, it will remain in force another five years, and so on, until one of the High Contracting Parties, one year before the expiry of the current five-year period, announces in writing its intention to put an end to the validity of the Treaty....

Treaty between the Soviet Union and Poland concerning the frontier and mutual assistance in frontier matters, Moscow, 15 February 1951

The Government of the Union of Soviet Socialist Republics and the Government of the Polish People's Republic, desiring to determine measures conducive to the maintenance in good order of the régime of the State frontier between the Union of Soviet Socialist Republics and the Polish People's Republic and to the settlement of frontier questions in a spirit of cooperation and mutual assistance, have decided to conclude this Treaty for that purpose and have accordingly appointed as their plenipotentiaries ... who have agreed as follows:

Chapter I: Course of the frontier line, frontier marks, marking and maintenance of the frontier

Article I. 1. The State frontier line between the Union of Soviet Socialist Republics and the Polish People's Republic established by the Treaty between the

Union of Soviet Socialist Republics and the Polish Republic concerning the Soviet-Polish State frontier, signed on 16 August 1945, the Treaty between the Union of Soviet Socialist Republics and the Polish Republic concerning the exchange of sectors of their State territories, together with the annexes thereto, signed on 15 February 1951, the Treaty between the Union of Soviet Socialist Republics and the Polish People's Republic concerning the demarcation of the existing Soviet-Polish State frontier in the sector adjoining the Baltic Sea, signed on 5 March 1957, and the Protocol between the Government of the Union of Soviet Socialist Republics and the Government of the Polish People's Republic concerning the delimitation of Soviet and Polish territorial waters in the Gulf of Gdansk of the Baltic Sea, signed on 18 March 1958, shall follow on the ground the course defined in....

Treaty of Friendship, Cooperation and Mutual Assistance between Albania, Bulgaria, Hungary, the German Democratic Republic, Poland, Rumania, the Soviet Union and Czechoslovakia (Warsaw Pact), Warsaw, 14 May 1955

The Contracting Parties,

Reaffirming their desire to create a system of collective security in Europe based on the participation of all European States, irrespective of their social and political structure, whereby the said States may be enabled to combine their efforts in the interests of ensuring peace in Europe;

Taking into consideration, at the same time, the situation that has come about in Europe as a result of the ratification of the Paris Agreements, which provide for the constitution of a new military group in the form of a 'West European Union', with the participation of a remilitarized West Germany and its inclusion in the North Atlantic bloc, thereby increasing the danger of a new war and creating a threat to the national security of peace-loving States;

Being convinced that in these circumstances the peace-loving States of Europe must take the necessary steps to safeguard their security and to promote the maintenance of peace in Europe;

Being guided by the purposes and principles of the Charter of the United Nations;

In the interests of the further strengthening and development of friendship, cooperation and mutual assistance in accordance with the principles of respect for the independence and sovereignty of States and of non-intervention in their domestic affairs;

Have resolved to conclude the present Treaty of Friendship, Cooperation and Mutual Assistance and have appointed as their plenipotentiaries ... who have agreed as follows:

Article 1. The Contracting Parties undertake, in accordance with the Charter of the United Nations, to refrain in their international relations from the threat or use of force and to settle their international disputes by peaceful means in such a manner that international peace and security are not endangered.

Article 2. The Contracting Parties declare that they are prepared to participate, in a spirit of sincere cooperation, in all international action for ensuring international peace and security and will devote their full efforts to the realization of these aims.

In this connection, the Contracting Parties shall endeavour to secure, in agreement with other States desiring to cooperate in this matter, the adoption of effective measures for the general reduction of armaments and the prohibition of atomic, hydrogen and other weapons of mass destruction.

Article 3. The Contracting Parties shall consult together on all important international questions involving their common interests, with a view to strengthening international peace and security.

Whenever any one of the Contracting Parties considers that a threat of armed attack on one or more of the States parties to the Treaty has arisen, they shall consult together immediately with a view to providing for their joint defence and maintaining peace and security.

Article 4. In the event of an armed attack in Europe on one or more of the States parties to the Treaty by any State or group of States, each State party to the Treaty shall, in the exercise of the right of individual or collective self-defence, in accordance with Article 51 of the United Nations Charter, afford the State or States so attacked immediate assistance, individually and in agreement with the other States parties to the Treaty, by all the means it considers necessary, including the use of armed force. The States parties to the Treaty shall consult together immediately concerning the joint measures necessary to restore and maintain international peace and security.

Measures taken under this Article shall be reported to the Security Council in accordance with the provisions of the United Nations Charter. These measures shall be discontinued as soon as the Security Council takes the necessary action to restore and maintain international peace and security.

Article 5. The Contracting Parties have agreed to establish a Unified Command, to which certain elements of their armed forces shall be allocated by agreement between the parties, and which shall act in accordance with jointly established principles. The parties shall likewise take such other concerted action as may be necessary to reinforce their defensive strength, in order to defend the peaceful labour of their peoples, guarantee the inviolability of their frontiers and territories and afford protection against possible aggression.

Article 6. For the purpose of carrying out the consultations provided for in the present Treaty between the States parties thereto, and for the consideration of matters arising in connection with the application of the present Treaty, a Political Consultative Committee shall be established, in which each State party to the Treaty shall be represented by a member of the Government or by some other specially appointed representative.

The Committee may establish such auxiliary organs as may prove to be necessary.

Article 7. The Contracting Parties undertake not to participate in any coalitions or alliances, and not to conclude any agreements, the purposes of which are incompatible with the purposes of the present Treaty.

The Contracting Parties declare that their obligations under international treaties at present in force are not incompatible with the provisions of the present Treaty.

Article 8. The Contracting Parties declare that they will act in a spirit of friendship and cooperation to promote the further development and strengthening of the economic and cultural ties among them, in accordance with the principles of respect for each other's independence and sovereignty and of non-intervention in each other's domestic affairs.

Article 9. The present Treaty shall be open for accession by other States, irrespective of their social and political structure, which express their readiness by participating in the present Treaty, to help in combining the efforts of the peace-loving States to ensure the peace and security of the peoples. Such accessions shall come into effect with the consent of the States parties to the Treaty after the instruments of accession have been deposited with the Government of the Polish People's Republic.

Article 10. The present Treaty shall be subject to ratification, and the instruments of ratification shall be deposited with the Government of the Polish People's Republic.

The Treaty shall come into force on the date of deposit of the last instrument of ratification. The Government of the Polish People's Republic shall inform the other States parties to the Treaty of the deposit of each instrument of ratification.

Article 11. The present Treaty shall remain in force for twenty years. For Contracting Parties which do not, one year before the expiration of that term, give notice of termination of the Treaty to the Government of the Polish People's Republic, the Treaty shall remain in force for a further ten years.

In the event of the establishment of a system of collective security in Europe and the conclusion for that purpose of a General European Treaty concerning collective security, a goal which the Contracting Parties shall steadfastly strive to achieve, the present Treaty shall cease to have effect as from the date on which the General European Treaty comes into force.

Done at Warsaw, this fourteenth day of May 1955, in one copy, in the Russian, Polish, Czech and German languages, all the texts being equally authentic. Certified copies of the present Treaty shall be transmitted by the Government of the Polish People's Republic to all the other parties to the Treaty.

Treaty of Alliance, Political Cooperation and Mutual Assistance between Greece, Turkey and Yugoslavia, Bled, 9 August 1954

...

Article I. The Contracting Parties undertake to settle any international dispute in which they may become involved by peaceful means in conformity with the provisions of the Charter of the United Nations ...

Article II. The Contracting Parties agree that any armed aggression against one or more of them on any part of their territory shall be deemed to constitute aggression against all of them, and the Contracting Parties, exercising the right of individual or collective self-defence recognized by Article 51 of the Charter of the United Nations, shall accordingly, individually and collectively assist the attacked party or parties by immediately taking, by common agreement, all measures, including the use of armed force, which they consider necessary for effective defence.

Without prejudice to Article VII of this Treaty, the Contracting Parties bind themselves not to conclude peace or to make any other arrangement with the aggressor without prior common agreement among themselves.

[*Article III.* Mutual assistance to strengthen capacity for defence.]

[*Article IV.* Permanent Ministerial Council to meet twice a year and cooperation of General Staffs.]

Article V. If the situation referred to in Article II of this Treaty should arise, the Contracting Parties shall forthwith consult with one another and the Permanent Council shall meet without delay to determine what measures, in addition to those already adopted in pursuance of Article II above, should be taken jointly to deal with the situation.

Article VI. In the event of a serious deterioration of the international situation, particularly in regions in which such a deterioration might directly or indirectly have an adverse effect on security in their region, the Contracting Parties shall consult with one another with a view to studying the situation and determining their position.

The Contracting Parties, aware that armed aggression against a country other than their own may, if extended, directly or indirectly threaten the security and integrity of one or more of their number, hereby agree as follows:

In the event of armed aggression against a country towards which one or more of the Contracting Parties owes or owe, at the time of the signature of this Treaty, an obligation to render mutual assistance, the Contracting Parties shall consult with one another concerning what measures should be taken, in conformity with the purposes of the United Nations, to deal with the situation thereby created in their region.

It is understood that the consultations contemplated in this Article may include an emergency meeting of the Council.

[*Article VII.* Inform U.N. of conflict or defensive measures.]

Article VIII. The Contracting Parties reaffirm their determination not to participate in any coalition directed against any one of them and not to enter into any commitment incompatible with the provisions of this Treaty.

[*Article IX.* U.N. obligations not impaired.]

...

Article XIII. This Treaty shall remain in effect for a period of twenty years.

If not denounced by one of the Contracting Parties one year before its expiry the Treaty shall be automatically renewed for the ensuing year and so on thereafter until it is denounced by one of the Contracting Parties.

[*Article XIV.* Ratification.]

Treaty of Friendship, Cooperation and Mutual Assistance between the Soviet Union and the Finnish Republic, Moscow, 6 April 1948

The Presidium of the Supreme Soviet of the Union of Soviet Socialist Republics and the President of the Finnish Republic,

With the object of further promoting friendly relations between the U.S.S.R. and Finland;

Convinced that consolidation of good-neighbourly relations and cooperation between the Union of Soviet Socialist Republics and the Finnish Republic meets the vital interests of both countries;

Considering Finland's aspiration to stand aside from the contradictions of interests of the Great Powers, and

Expressing their unswerving aspiration to cooperate in the interests of the preservation of international peace and security in conformity with the aims and principles of the United Nations Organization;

Have decided to conclude for these ends the present Treaty, and ... have appointed as their plenipotentiaries:

for the Presidium of the Supreme Soviet of the Union of Soviet Socialist Republics – Vyacheslav Mikhailovich Molotov, vice-chairman of the Council of Ministers and Minister of Foreign Affairs of the U.S.S.R.;

for the President of the Finnish Republic – Mauno Pekkala, Prime Minister of the Finnish Republic,

Who upon exchanging their credentials, found in due form and full order, have agreed upon the following:

Article I. In the event of Finland or the Soviet Union, across the territory of Finland, becoming the object of military aggression on the part of Germany or any State allied to the latter, Finland, loyal to her duty as an independent State, will fight to repulse the aggression. In doing so, Finland will direct all the forces at her disposal to the defence of the inviolability of her territory on land, on sea and in the air, acting within her boundaries in accordance with her obligations under the present Treaty, with the assistance, in case of need, of the Soviet Union or jointly with the latter.

In the cases indicated above, the Soviet Union will render Finland the necessary assistance, in regard to the granting of which the parties will agree between themselves.

Article II. The High Contracting Parties will consult each other in the event of a threat of military attack envisaged in Article I being ascertained.

Article III. The High Contracting Parties affirm their intention to participate most sincerely in all actions aimed at preserving international peace and security in conformity with the aims and principles of the United Nations Organization.

Article IV. The High Contracting Parties reaffirm the undertaking, contained in

Article III of the Peace Treaty signed in Paris on 10 February 1947, not to conclude any alliance and not to take part in coalitions aimed against the other High Contracting Party.

Article V. The High Contracting Parties affirm their determination to act in the spirit of cooperation and friendship with the object of further promoting and consolidating the economic and cultural ties between the Soviet Union and Finland.

Article VI. The High Contracting Parties undertake to observe the principles of mutual respect for their State sovereignty and independence as well as non-interference in the domestic affairs of the other State.

Article VII. Implementations of the present Treaty will conform to the principles of the United Nations Organization.

Article VIII. The present Treaty is subject to ratification, and will be valid for ten years as from the day of its coming into force. The Treaty will come into force as from the day of the exchange of ratification instruments, which will be effected in Helsinki within the shortest possible time.

Unless either of the High Contracting Parties denounces the Treaty one year before the expiration of the above-mentioned ten-year term, it will remain in force for each of the next five-year terms until either of the High Contracting Parties gives notice in writing of its intention to terminate the operation of the Treaty.

Treaty of Friendship, Alliance and Mutual Assistance between the People's Republic of China and the Soviet Union, Moscow, 14 February 1950

The Central People's Government of the People's Republic of China and the Presidium of the Supreme Soviet of the Union of Soviet Socialist Republics, fully determined to prevent jointly, by strengthening friendship and cooperation between the People's Republic of China and the Union of Soviet Socialist Republics, the revival of Japanese imperialism and the resumption of aggression on the part of Japan or any other State that may collaborate in any way with Japan in acts of aggression; imbued with the desire to consolidate lasting peace and universal security in the Far East and throughout the world in conformity with the aims and principles of the United Nations; profoundly convinced that the consolidation of good neighbourly relations and friendship between the People's Republic of China and the Union of Soviet Socialist

Republics meets the vital interests of the peoples of China and the Soviet Union, have towards this end decided to conclude the present Treaty and have appointed as their plenipotentiary representatives: Chou En-lai, Premier of the Government Administration Council and Minister of Foreign Affairs, acting for the Central People's Government of the People's Republic of China; and Andrei Yanuaryevich Vyshinsky, Minister of Foreign Affairs of the U.S.S.R., acting for the Presidium of the Supreme Soviet of the Union of Soviet Socialist Republics. Both plenipotentiary representatives having communicated their full powers found them in good and due form, have agreed upon the following:

Article 1. Both Contracting Parties undertake jointly to adopt all necessary measures at their disposal for the purpose of preventing the resumption of aggression and violation of peace on the part of Japan or any other State that may collaborate with Japan directly or indirectly in acts of aggression. In the event of one of the Contracting Parties being attacked by Japan or any State allied with her and thus being involved in a state of war, the other Contracting Party shall immediately render military and other assistance by all means at its disposal.

The Contracting Parties also declare their readiness to participate in a spirit of sincere cooperation in all international actions aimed at ensuring peace and security throughout the world and to contribute their full share to the earliest implementation of these tasks.

Article 2. Both Contracting Parties undertake in a spirit of mutual agreement to bring about the earliest conclusion of a peace treaty with Japan jointly with other Powers which were allies in the Second World War.

Article 3. Each Contracting Party undertakes not to conclude any alliance directed against the other Contracting Party and not to take part in any coalition or in any actions or measures directed against the other Contracting Party.

Article 4. Both Contracting Parties, in the interests of consolidating peace and universal security, will consult with each other in regard to all important international problems affecting the common interests of China and the Soviet Union.

Article 5. Each Contracting Party undertakes, in a spirit of friendship and cooperation and in conformity with the principles of equality, mutual benefit and mutual respect for the national sovereignty and territorial integrity and non-interference in the internal affairs of the other Contracting Party, to develop and consolidate economic and cultural ties between China and the Soviet Union, to render the other all possible economic assistance and to carry out necessary economic cooperation.

Article 6. The present Treaty shall come into force immediately after its ratification; the exchange of instruments of ratification shall take place in Peking.

The present Treaty shall be valid for thirty years. If neither of the Contracting Parties gives notice a year before the expiration of this term of its intention to denounce the Treaty, it shall remain in force for another five years and shall be further extended in compliance with this provision.

Done in Moscow on 14 February 1950, in two copies, each in the Chinese and Russian languages, both texts being equally valid.

On the authorization of the Central People's Government of the People's Republic of China

Chou En-lai

On the authorization of the Presidium of the Supreme Soviet of the Union of Soviet Socialist Republics

A. Y. Vyshinsky

Agreement between the People's Republic of China and the Union of Soviet Socialist Republics on the Chinese Changchun Railway, Port Arthur and Dairen

The Central People's Government of the People's Republic of China and the Presidium of the Supreme Soviet of the Union of Soviet Socialist Republics record that since 1945, fundamental changes have occurred in the situation in the Far East, namely: imperialist Japan has suffered defeat; the reactionary Kuomintang Government has been overthrown; China has become a People's Democratic Republic; a new People's Government has been established in China which has unified the whole of China, has carried out a policy of friendship and cooperation with the Soviet Union and has proved its ability to defend the national independence and territorial integrity of China and the national honour and dignity of the Chinese people.

The Central People's Government of the People's Republic of China and the Presidium of the Supreme Soviet of the Union of Soviet Socialist Republics consider that this new situation permits a new approach to the question of the Chinese Changchun Railway, Port Arthur and Dairen.

In conformity with these new circumstances the Central People's Government of the People's Republic of China and the Presidium of the Supreme Soviet of the Union of Soviet Socialist Republics have decided to conclude the present Agreement on the Chinese Changchun Railway, Port Arthur and Dairen:

Article 1. Both Contracting Parties agree that the Soviet Government transfer without compensation to the Government of the People's Republic of China all its rights to joint administration of the Chinese Changchun Railway with all the property belonging to the Railway. The transfer shall be effected immediately after the conclusion of a peace treaty with Japan, but not later than the end of 1952.

Pending the transfer, the existing Sino-Soviet joint administration of the Chinese Changchun Railway shall remain unchanged. After this Agreement becomes effective, posts (such as manager of the Railway, chairman of the Central Board, etc.) will be periodically alternated between representatives of China and the U.S.S.R.

As regards concrete methods of effecting the transfer, they shall be agreed upon and determined by the Governments of both Contracting Parties.

Article 2. Both Contracting Parties agree that Soviet troops be withdrawn from the jointly utilized naval base Port Arthur, and that the installations in this area be handed over to the Government of the People's Republic of China immediately on the conclusion of a peace treaty with Japan, but not later than the end of 1952. The Government of the People's Republic of China will compensate the Soviet Union for expenses which it has incurred in restoring and constructing installations since 1945.

For the period pending the withdrawal of Soviet troops and the transfer of the above-mentioned installations the Governments of China and the Soviet Union will each appoint an equal number of military representatives to form a joint Chinese-Soviet Military Commission which will be alternately presided over by each side and which will be in charge of military affairs in the area of Port Arthur; concrete measures in this sphere will be drawn up by the joint Chinese-Soviet Military Commission within three months after the present Agreement becomes effective and shall be put into force upon approval of these measures by the Governments of both countries.

The civil administration in the aforementioned area shall be under the direct authority of the Government of the People's Republic of China. Pending the withdrawal of Soviet troops, the zone for billeting Soviet troops in the area of Port Arthur will remain unaltered in conformity with existing frontiers.

In the event of either of the Contracting Parties becoming the victim of aggression on the part of Japan or any State that may collaborate with Japan, and as a result thereof becoming involved in hostilities, China and the Soviet Union may, on the proposal of the Government of the People's Republic of China and with the agreement of the Government of the U.S.S.R., jointly use the naval base Port Arthur for the purpose of conducting joint military operations against the aggressor.

Article 3. Both Contracting Parties agree that the question of Dairen harbour be further considered on the conclusion of a peace treaty with Japan. As regards the administration of Dairen, it is in the hands of the Government of the People's Republic of China. All the property in Dairen now temporarily administered by or leased to the Soviet Union, shall be taken over by the Government of the People's Republic of China. To carry out the transfer of the aforementioned property, the Governments of China and the Soviet Union shall appoint three representatives each to form a Joint Commission which, within three months after the present Agreement comes into effect, shall draw up concrete measures for the transfer of the property; and these measures shall be fully carried out in the course of 1950 after their approval by the Governments of both countries upon the proposal of the Joint Commission.

[*Article 4*. Ratification.]

Agreement between the Central People's Government of the People's Republic of China and the Government of the Union of Soviet Socialist Republics on the granting of credit to the People's Republic of China

In connection with the consent of the Government of the Union of Soviet Socialist Republics to grant the request of the Central People's Government of the People's Republic of China for a credit to pay for the equipment and other materials which the Soviet Union has agreed to deliver to China, both Governments have agreed upon the following:

Article 1. The Government of the Union of Soviet Socialist Republics grants to the Central People's Government of the People's Republic of China a credit which in terms of American dollars, amounts to U.S. $300,000,000, taking 35 American dollars to one ounce of fine gold.

In view of the extraordinary devastation of China as a result of prolonged hostilities on its territory, the Soviet Government has agreed to grant the credit at the favourable rate of interest of 1 per cent per annum.

...

Article 3. The Central People's Government of the People's Republic of China shall repay the credit mentioned in Article

1, together with the interest thereon, in deliveries of raw materials, tea, gold and American dollars. Prices for raw materials and tea and their quantities and dates of delivery shall be determined by special agreement, with prices to be determined on the basis of prices on the world markets.

The credit shall be repaid in ten equal annual instalments ...

...

[In the communiqué issued at the time of the signature of the treaty the following statements were made.]

...

In connection with the signing of the Treaty of Friendship, Alliance and Mutual Assistance, and the Agreement on the Chinese Changchun Railway, Port Arthur and Dairen, Chou En-lai, Premier and Minister of Foreign Affairs, and A. Y. Vyshinsky, Minister of Foreign Affairs, exchanged notes to the effect that the respective Treaty and Agreements concluded on August 14, 1945, between China and the Soviet Union are now null and void, and also that both Governments affirm that the independent status of the Mongolian People's Republic is fully guaranteed as a result of the plebiscite of 1945 and the establishment with it of diplomatic relations by the People's Republic of China.

At the same time, A. Y. Vyshinsky, Minister of Foreign Affairs, and Chou En-lai, Premier and Minister of Foreign Affairs, also exchanged notes on the decision of the Soviet Government to transfer without compensation to the Government of the People's Republic of China the property acquired in Manchuria from Japanese owners by Soviet economic organizations, and also on the decision of the Soviet Government to transfer without compensation to the Government of the People's Republic of China all the buildings in the former military compound in Peking ...

Treaty of Friendship, Cooperation and Mutual Aid between the Union of Soviet Socialist Republics and the Czechoslovak Socialist Republic, Prague, 6 May 1970

The Union of Soviet Socialist Republics and the Czechoslovak Socialist Republic,

Affirming their fidelity to the aims and principles of the Soviet-Czechoslovak Treaty of Friendship, Mutual Aid and Post-War Cooperation, concluded on December 12, 1943, and extended on November 27, 1963, a treaty that played a historic role in the development of friendly relations between the peoples of the two States and laid a solid foundation for the further strengthening of fraternal friendship and all-round cooperation between them;

Profoundly convinced that the indestructible friendship between the Union of Soviet Socialist Republics and the Czechoslovak Socialist Republic, which was cemented in the joint struggle against Fascism and has received further deepening in the years of the construction of socialism and communism, as well as the fraternal mutual assistance and all-round cooperation between them, based on the teachings of Marxism-Leninism and the immutable principles of socialist internationalism, correspond to the fundamental interests of the peoples of both countries and of the entire socialist commonwealth;

Affirming that the support, strengthening and defence of the socialist gains achieved at the cost of the heroic efforts and selfless labour of each people are the common internationalist duty of the socialist countries;

Consistently and steadfastly favouring the strengthening of the unity and solidarity of all countries of the socialist commonwealth, based on the community of their social systems and ultimate goals;

Firmly resolved strictly to observe the obligations stemming from the May 14, 1955, Warsaw Treaty of Friendship, Cooperation and Mutual Aid;

Stating the economic cooperation between the two States facilitates their development, as well as the further improvement of the international socialist division of labour and socialist economic integration within the framework of the Council for Mutual Economic Aid;

Expressing the firm intention to promote the cause of strengthening peace and security in Europe and throughout the world, to oppose imperialism, revanchism and militarism;

Guided by the goals and principles proclaimed in the United Nations Charter;

Taking into account the achievements of socialist and communist construction in the two countries, the present situation and the prospects for all-round cooperation, as well as the changes that have taken place in Europe and throughout the world since the conclusion of the Treaty of December 12, 1943;

Have agreed on the following:

Article 1. In accordance with the principles of socialist internationalism, the High Contracting Parties will continue to strengthen the eternal, indestructible friendship between the peoples of the Union of Soviet Socialist Republics and the Czechoslovak Socialist Republic, to develop all-round cooperation between the two countries and to give each other fraternal assistance and support, basing their actions on mutual respect for State sovereignty and independence, on equal rights and non-interference in one another's internal affairs.

Article 2. The High Contracting Parties will continue, proceeding from the principles of friendly mutual assistance and the international socialist division of labour, to develop and deepen mutually advantageous bilateral and multilateral economic, scientific and technical co-operation with the aim of developing their national economies, achieving the highest possible scientific and technical level and efficiency of social production, and increasing the material well-being of the working people of their countries.

The two sides will promote the further development of economic ties and co-operation and the socialist economic integration of the member countries of the Council for Mutual Economic Aid.

Article 3. The High Contracting Parties will continue to develop and expand co-operation between the two countries in the fields of science and culture, education, literature and the arts, the press, radio, motion pictures, television, public health, tourism and physical culture and in other fields.

Article 4. The High Contracting Parties will continue to facilitate the expansion of cooperation and direct ties between the bodies of State authority and the public organizations of the working people, with the aim of achieving a deeper mutual familiarization and a closer drawing together between the peoples of the two States.

Article 5. The High Contracting Parties, expressing their unswerving determination to proceed along the path of the construction of socialism and communism, will take the necessary steps to defend the socialist gains of the peoples and the security and independence of the two countries, will strive to develop all-round relations among the States of the socialist commonwealth, and will act in a spirit of the consolidation of the unity, friendship and fraternity of these States.

Article 6. The High Contracting Parties proceed from the assumption that the Munich Pact of September 29, 1938, was signed under the threat of aggressive war and the use of force against Czechoslovakia, that it was a component part of Hitler Germany's criminal conspiracy against peace and was a flagrant violation of the basic norms of international law, and hence was invalid from the very outset, with all the consequences stemming therefrom.

Article 7. The High Contracting Parties, consistently pursuing a policy of the peaceful coexistence of States with different social systems, will exert every effort for the defence of international peace and the security of the peoples against encroachments by the aggressive forces of imperialism and reaction, for the relaxation of international tension, the cessation of the arms race and the achievement of general and complete disarmament, the final liquidation of colonialism in all its forms and manifestations, and the giving of support to countries that have been liberated from colonial domination and are marching along the path of strengthening national independence and sovereignty.

Article 8. The High Contracting Parties will jointly strive to improve the situation and to ensure peace in Europe, to strengthen and develop cooperation among the European States, to establish good-neighbour relations among them and to create an effective system of European security on the basis of the collective efforts of all European States.

Article 9. The High Contracting Parties declare that one of the main preconditions for ensuring European security is the immutability of the State borders that were formed in Europe after the Second World War. They express their firm resolve, jointly with the other Member States of the May 14, 1955, Warsaw Treaty of Friendship, Cooperation and Mutual Aid and in accordance with this Treaty, to ensure the inviolability of the borders of the Member States of this Treaty and to take all necessary steps to prevent aggression on the part of any forces of militarism and revanchism and to rebuff the aggressor.

Article 10. In the event that one of the High Contracting Parties is subjected to an armed attack by any State or group of States, the other Contracting Party, regarding this as an attack against itself, will immediately give the first party all possible assistance, including military aid, and will also give it support with all means at its disposal, by way of implementing the right to individual or collective self-defence in accordance with Article 51 of the United Nations Charter.

The High Contracting Parties will without delay inform the United Nations Security Council of steps taken on the basis of this Article, and they will act in accordance with the provisions of the United Nations Charter.

Article 11. The High Contracting Parties will inform each other and consult on all important international questions affecting their interests and will act on the basis of common positions agreed upon in accordance with the interests of both States.

Article 12. The High Contracting Parties declare that their obligations under existing international treaties are not at variance with the provisions of this Treaty.

Article 13. This Treaty is subject to ratification and will enter into force on the day of the exchange of instruments of ratification, which will be conducted in Moscow in a very short time.

Article 14. This Treaty is concluded for a period of twenty years and will be automatically extended every five years thereafter, if neither of the High Contracting Parties gives notice that it is denouncing the Treaty twelve months before the expiration of the current period.

[Signed] L. BREZHNEV and A. KOSYGIN, G. HUSAK and L. STROUGAL.

XIV · West European integration, 1947–72

Among the major international changes in the world that have taken place since the Second World War the developing integration of Western Europe is one of the most important. The onset of the 'cold war' and the break-up of Allied unity led to the realignment of European Powers and the rehabilitation of West Germany much earlier than anyone anticipated in 1945. The economic success of collaboration and the lessening of destructive nationalist feelings provided positive and fresh idealistic goals for greater West European unity. The first condition of European unity was in fact the 'iron curtain' and the division into East and West.

The first phase, 1947–50: the split of Europe into East and West

During the first five years following the defeat of Germany some basic characteristics of European integration began to emerge. First and most important, these years marked the political division of Europe, which made possible a separate evolution of Western Europe.

As one by one the interrelationships of Western Europe's economic, political, social and international problems were perceived by the National Governments of Western Europe, by German leaders (who to begin with had no Government of their own) and by the American administration anxious to aid West European recovery and the Western capacity for self defence, so varied solutions were found to deal with these problems. The variety of the solutions, in several complex treaties and in the setting up of numerous apparently overlapping institutions, reveal the different attitudes towards European integration adopted by the West European States.

In reconstructing post-war Europe, the political leaders of the wartime

377

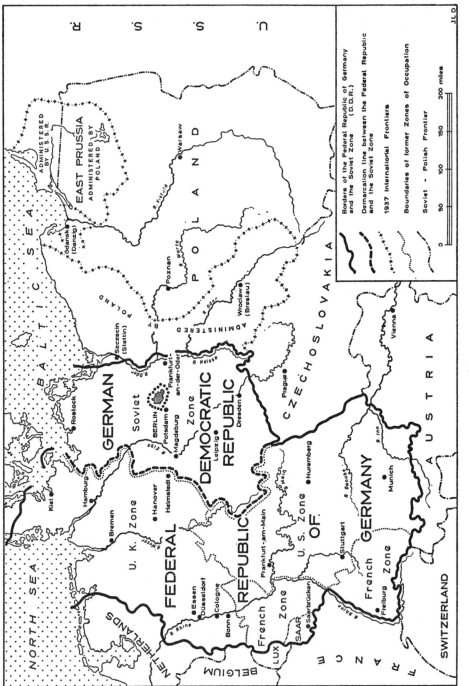

5 Germany, 1972

alliance were faced with a number of immediate problems for which they had no clear-cut answers during the first two years after the war. First and foremost was the question of the policy to be adopted towards Germany. Would Allied cooperation lead eventually to a restored united Germany? The considerations applying to Germany's future to a lesser extent also applied to Austria. With the onset of the 'cold war' a new relationship was established between the occupying Allied authorities in Western Germany and the German political leaders. Efforts to bring about European economic recovery too were dependent on the policies to be adopted towards the great industrial complexes in West Germany's Ruhr valley. During the years from 1945 to 1950, many uncertainties on these issues gave way to settled policies.

The changing attitudes of these years are exemplified by French thinking, which to begin with was dominated by a traditional fear of German revival and renewed aggression. *The Treaty of Dunkirk concluded between Britain and France, 4 March 1947* (p. 398), bound the two signatories to come to each other's aid if attacked by Germany, and pledged them to common action if Germany should fail to fulfil her economic obligations. The treaty also looked forward to a new Europe with provisions for Anglo-French economic cooperation. It became characteristic of later alliances that they were not purely military but also provided for economic and social cooperation and political consultation. The breakdown of Allied cooperation in Germany, the Berlin blockade, and the onset of the cold war (p. 383) outdated the ordering of defence priorities that lay behind the making of the Treaty of Dunkirk.

In the new realities of politics and power as perceived from 1947 to 1950, a programme for West European, including West German, economic recovery was launched. A process leading eventually to the full restoration of West German sovereignty was started, Western European defence was coordinated and brought into association with the United States and Canada, and the first vital steps taken that were to lead to the close association of the six continental Powers in the European Economic Community.

Lack of Allied progress in settling the German question from 1945 to 1947, the Western response to Soviet policies in Central and Eastern Europe, and civil war in Greece, all led the United States into commitments to provide more military and economic aid to Governments in conflict with communism within their States, and to strengthen their capacity to resist attack from without; this was the purpose of the *Truman Doctrine, 12 March 1947* (p. 306). It was followed by the Harvard speech of the Secretary of State, George C. Marshall, on 5 June 1947 in which he first offered a massive programme of United States economic aid to all Europe (including Germany but excepting Spain). The resulting programme became known as the *Marshall Plan*. The prime condition on which such aid would be made available, Marshall had stated, was that the joint aid programme should be agreed to by a number of, if not all, European nations. The thinking behind American policy at the time confidentially set out by George Kennan, the head of a planning staff advising Marshall, was that American aid to Europe should be directed not to combating communism as such but to the restoration of the economic health and vigour of European society. If this could be achieved it would remedy the European economic distress which was believed to be making European society vulnerable to communism and totalitarian exploitation. The Marshall Plan intentionally provided a powerful stimulus to West European cooperation, since American aid was to be furnished not for individual national economic programmes but for a programme agreed to by West European Governments acting together.

Ernest Bevin, Britain's Foreign Secretary, took the lead in response, and together with Georges Bidault, the French Foreign Minister, invited twenty-two European nations (but not Spain) to a conference to work out a recovery programme. The Western European States accepted the invitation to the conference, and Poland and Czechoslovakia also wished to attend. Molotov, on behalf of the Soviet Union, agreed to meet Bevin and Bidault in Paris beforehand to work out the agenda and procedure for the conference. These tripartite discussions soon broke down and Molotov condemned the principle of a 'European plan'; he insisted on separate and bilateral negotiations between European States and the United States for American aid. The Soviet Union *together* with Poland and Czechoslovakia and the States within the Soviet sphere refused to cooperate on the basis of the American proposal after Molotov's departure from Paris.

This marked an irrevocable breach between the post-war economic development of Eastern and Western Europe. Separate development was dictated by political and ideological considerations. It also meant that the United Nations' *Economic Commission for Europe*, set up in Geneva in 1947 and concerned with Europe as a whole, would be stillborn. Separate organizations were set up to handle the economic policies of Communist Europe and of Western Europe. In Western Europe the organization required to handle American aid and the recovery programme was fashioned at a conference of Western Powers held in Paris during the summer of 1947.

The Paris Conference, 12 July–22 September 1947, was attended by sixteen nations: Austria, Belgium, Britain, Denmark, France, Greece, Iceland, Ireland, Italy, Luxembourg, the Netherlands, Norway, Portugal, Sweden, Switzerland and Turkey. The main result of the conference was the report of the *Committee of Economic Cooperation, 22 September 1947,* which outlined a four-year European recovery programme and proposed the creation of a permanent organization of the sixteen participating nations. At a *second Conference in Paris, 15-16 March 1948*, a working party was set up by the representatives of the same sixteen nations together with the military representatives of the Anglo-American and French zones of Germany, to draft the convention for economic cooperation which led in turn to the treaty setting up the *Organization for European Economic Cooperation (O.E.E.C.), 16 April 1948*. In October 1949, the German Federal Republic acceded to O.E.E.C. as a full member. Associated with the work of the O.E.E.C. are the following countries: the United States, Canada, Yugoslavia and Finland.

The O.E.E.C. worked out programmes for the participating States which were submitted for approval to the *United States Economic Cooperation Administration* (set up by Congress in 1948). Between 1948 and 1952 American aid to Western Europe amounted to $13,812 million, in addition to technical and administrative assistance. Successful as the O.E.E.C. proved to be in channelling American aid to Western Europe, this aid was applied essentially to support the individual economies of the participating States. Little Western European economic integration was achieved.

West European recovery was intimately dependent on West German recovery. At a number of conferences held in London in 1948, Britain, France and the Benelux countries reached agreement by the end of that year on the steps that were to lead to a Federal West German constitution, the fusion of all three Western zones of occupation and the establishment of an International Authority for the Ruhr. The lessening of tension with the Soviet Union after the raising of the Berlin blockade (12 May 1949) did not divert the three Western allies from steps towards setting up a West German State. In May 1949 the three Allied Military Governors approved the Federal West German constitutional draft entitled the *Basic Law*; in addition the *Occupation Statute* laid down the new relationship between the Western occupying Powers, the rights they reserved to themselves and the jurisdiction to be granted to a West German Federal Government; finally the French zone of occupation was merged with the Anglo-American 'Bizone'. On 21 September 1949 Western Germany passed from Allied Military Government to a supervised West German democracy, when the Western allies assumed their new function as the Allied High Commission on the basis of the Occupation Statute, and a Federal German Government headed by Chancellor Konrad Adenauer was inaugurated.

Simultaneously with the changing relationship between the three Western Powers and West Germany, the Western European States placed their military, political and economic cooperation on a new footing. Bevin, in a speech on

24 January 1948, launched a plan to expand the Anglo-French partnership established by the Treaty of Dunkirk into a more comprehensive Western union. The communist takeover in Czechoslovakia in February 1948 lent urgency to the discussions. Negotiations in Brussels in March 1948 between Britain, France and the Benelux countries (the Netherlands, Belgium and Luxembourg, formed by treaty on 5 September 1944) were brought to a conclusion with the signature of the *Brussels Treaty, 17 March 1948* (p. 399). The military alliance between the signatories was no longer solely directed against the possibility of renewed German aggression but provided for defence against any aggressor. The signatories also pledged themselves to collaborate in economic, social and cultural fields. A Consultative Council of the five Foreign Ministers was established, but it had no supranational powers; it was a body which would make recommendations to individual Governments. The European movement aimed at much closer European political union. Their resolutions were considered by the Consultative Council of the Brussels Treaty Powers, who in January 1949 agreed that a *Council of Europe* should be established consisting of a Ministerial Committee meeting in private and a Consultative Body meeting in public. At the conclusion of a conference in London, the five Brussels Treaty Powers, the Benelux countries, Britain and France, joined by Denmark, Ireland, Italy, Norway and Sweden, agreed on the *Statute of the Council of Europe, 5 May 1949* (p. 401), as the constitution of the Council of Europe was entitled. The constitution did not provide for the merging of national sovereignties in the political and economic fields as many of the sponsors of the European movement hoped. The Committee of Ministers (the Council's Executive Organ) could consult, cooperate and discuss, but it could only recommend action to Member Governments for decision, the Council itself could not reach binding decisions. An assembly consisting of Parliamentarians had little real power. This assembly was not to be elected by direct European elections but in practice was composed of delegations sent by member National Parliaments. Among the most important agreements reached subsequently by the Council of Europe was the European Convention for the *Protection of Human Rights, 4 November 1950*, which was made a condition of membership. When the Greek Government was found to have violated the convention, Greece resigned in 1969. Cooperation has been achieved by committees of experts in cultural and social fields. A *European Social Charter was concluded on 18 October 1961*, and came into effect on 26 February 1965. In addition to the ten founding members of the Council of Europe – Belgium, Britain, Denmark, France, Irish Republic, Italy, Luxembourg, the Netherlands, Norway and Sweden – the following countries have joined: Greece, August 1949; Turkey, August 1949; Iceland, March 1950; German Federal Republic, March

1951; Austria, April 1956; Cyprus, April 1961; Switzerland, May 1965 and Malta, January 1965.

For the military defence of Europe the help of a non-European State, the United States, was indispensable. The Vandenberg Resolution, adopted by the United States Senate on 11 June 1948, made possible effective American support for European collective security. The Soviet military authorities had been progressively stopping communications between West Berlin and West Germany since April 1948. On 24 June 1948 in response to currency reforms in the Western zones of Germany, designed as part of a programme to re-habilitate Western Germany economically and politically, the Soviet military authorities began the full land blockade of Western Berlin. It lasted until 12 May 1949. This necessitated a dramatic airlift by the West which heightened public awareness of the crisis. Against this background of tension, with the Western Powers certain that only a firm Allied stand would lead to their reduction and the safeguarding of the West, the negotiations for consolidating a military Atlantic partnership culminated in the signature in Washington of the *North Atlantic Treaty, 4 April 1949* (p. 335). The negotiations were initially conducted between the European members of the Brussels Treaty, and in addition the United States and Canada. Later in Washington, Norway, Denmark, Iceland, Italy and Portugal were invited to join, and become original signatories of the treaty. Thus the twelve original signatories were: Belgium, Britain, Canada, Denmark, France, Iceland, Italy, Luxembourg, the Netherlands, Norway, Portugal and the United States. The core of the alliance treaty was Article 5. It stated that an armed attack against one or more of the signatories in Europe or North America would be considered an attack on all. Unlike the Brussels Treaty it did not provide for any automatic commitment of military assistance. A decision to provide armed help would be taken by each individual Government to the extent it deemed necessary. The formulation of this article had caused much difficulty as the Senate of the United States wished to safeguard its constitutional right to declare war by a majority vote, and not to be bound by such a treaty commitment beforehand. Article 6 specifically defined the territories of the allies that fell within the scope of the treaty: besides the European and American territories of the signatories the area was extended to the Algerian *Département* of France in North Africa, and the islands north of the Tropic of Cancer belonging to Portugal, that is Madeira and the Azores; it also extended to any attack on the occupation forces of any of the signatories in Europe and thereby included West Germany, West Berlin, the western sectors of Austria, and the Western forces in Vienna. When Greece and Turkey became members in February 1952, the alliance extended to the Mediterranean flank. In October 1954 the Federal

Republic of Germany acceded (p. 387). A NATO Council was set up in accordance with Article 9 of the treaty and held its first meeting in September 1949. Various committees were also created. In December 1950 agreement was reached on the setting up of an integrated defence force under centralized control and command, to which all participating Governments would contribute. The supreme headquarters of Allied Powers in Europe was established in Paris during the years from 1951 to 1967. French forces were withdrawn from the integrated command finally in 1966, and thereafter the NATO headquarters moved to Mons, Belgium. In 1952 an international secretariat with a Secretary-General was created, and the NATO organization grew greatly in size.

Article 2 of NATO extended cooperation to the economic relations of the signatories, but it never found much application except in the field of defence expenditure. Although the NATO treaty does not automatically guarantee military assistance to help a signatory that has been attacked, NATO remains the cornerstone of Western defence in Europe.

There was no fusion of sovereignty provided for by any of the treaties of European and North Atlantic cooperation signed during the period 1945 to 1950; to that extent, the enthusiasm of the European movement, inaugurated at the Hague in 1948, had not succeeded in achieving one of its main objectives, which was to create a Government and Parliament responsible to and responsible for Western Europe.

The second phase, 1951–5: Western Europe divides

The Brussels Treaty and NATO provided the military alliance shield for Western Europe. The Council of Europe and the O.E.E.C. represented the degree of economic and cultural cooperation on which the Western European States could agree. In March 1951 France and Germany took another decisive step forward. They began negotiations for an integration of economic policies which envisaged a transfer of national decision-making to an international authority. Such a diminution of sovereignty was unacceptable to Britain and some other European States. The States which became known as the Six proceeded without Britain. *The Paris Treaty of 18 April 1951*, signed by France, the Federal (West) German Republic, Italy, Belgium, Luxembourg and the Netherlands, embodied their agreement to set up a *European Coal and Steel Community* (*E.C.S.C.*, p. 405). The negotiations were based on the initiative taken by the French Foreign Minister, Maurice Schuman, who at a press conference on 9 May 1950 had outlined a French Government plan 'to place all Franco-German coal and steel production under a common High Authority, in an organization open to the participation of the other countries of Europe'. The adoption of such a plan would be the first step towards European federation, Schuman declared, and would 'change the destiny of regions that have long been devoted to the production of war armaments of which they themselves have been the constant victims'. Schuman's objective was primarily political in that he wished to transform Franco-German relations, to bring to an end their hostility by making war impossible between them, since coal and steel essential for war production would cease to be under national control. The adoption of the plan transformed the problems associated with the future of the Saar, the control of the Ruhr, German rearmament and the status of the German Federal Republic, which now became an equal member of the European Coal and Steel Community. The blueprint for the Schuman plan had been worked out by Jean Monnet and a few close collaborators in the offices of the Commissariat du Plan de Modernisation et d'Equipment. It represented the approach of the 'functionalists' who believed the political union of the European States was too high a hurdle to overcome immediately and wished to proceed step by step. A beginning would be made by pooling some aspects of sovereignty to international institutions with limited functions but real power. The Paris Treaty emphasized the supranational aspect of the E.C.S.C., and its organization was deliberately designed to serve as a model for future European institutions. After ratification by the six National Parliaments the treaty came into force on 25 July 1952 and Monnet was made the first president of E.C.S.C. Britain held aloof. One important link that was maintained between the Europe of the Council of Europe and the Europe of the Six, the E.C.S.C., was that the Assembly of the E.C.S.C. would be composed of the parliamentary representatives of the six who sat in the Assembly of the Council of Europe; but neither parliamentary bodies had much practical control over policy-making by the Ministers of the Council of Europe, or over the decisions taken by the Commissioners of the High Authority of the E.C.S.C.

The formation of the E.C.S.C. from 1950 to 1952 was a crucial part of a Western policy supported by France, of restoring Western German sovereignty provided a West German Republic remained closely tied by treaty to Western Europe. Additional safeguards were sought from Britain and the United States so that no revived West German State would either be able to dominate Western Europe or be able to play off East against West in following an independent policy towards the Soviet Union. The West German Government for their part was ready to accept this new West European role. Adenauer believed that only by identifying Western Germany loyally with the West could Germany be secured from the threat of Soviet domination. Only if he could gain the trust of Germany's wartime enemies would it be possible to end the Allied occupation of West Germany.

With the communist takeover in Czechoslovakia in February 1948, the Berlin blockade 1948-9, and the outbreak of the Korean War in June 1950, the administration of the United States became so alarmed at this evidence of aggressiveness of world communism that it took the lead in arguing the necessity of German rearmament as an indispensable condition of West European defence (p. 306). These strands, the European and the American, came together in the signature of two treaties between West Germany and her former enemies, signed on successive days in Bonn and Paris. The *Bonn Agreements, 26 May 1952,* consisted of a number of treaties which provided for the ending of the Occupation Statute, the abolition of the High Commission, and the restoration of German sovereignty subject to new contractual agreements between the Allies and West Germany. But the ratification or coming into force of the Bonn Agreements depended on the ratification of another treaty signed on the following day in Paris, 27 May 1952, establishing the European Defence Community which allowed for a German military contribution within the framework of the combined defensive efforts of the Six.

On 24 October 1950 the French Prime Minister, René Pleven, had proposed to the French Assembly the creation of a European army linked to political institutions of a united Europe. Negotiations concerning the rearming of Germany, and the incorporation of German divisions in a European army, proved especially difficult, but in the end accord was reached in Paris on a *Treaty establishing the European Defence Community (E.D.C.), 27 May 1952,* between Belgium, France, West Germany, the Netherlands, Italy and Luxembourg. A number of agreements particularly designed to reassure the French accompanied the treaty. First there was a Three Power agreement between France, Britain and the United States concerning stationing of their troops in Europe; it stated that any threat to the security of the E.D.C. would be regarded as a threat to their own security. Secondly, although Britain was not prepared to fuse its defence entirely with Western Europe's, the British Government signed an agreement with the six E.D.C. countries stating that while Britain was a member of NATO it would render all military and other aid in its power to any signatory of the E.D.C. which became the victim of an armed attack in Europe. Another protocol to the treaty promised reciprocal aid as between members of NATO or E.D.C. if attacked. A year later, in March 1953, a draft treaty was signed establishing a political community between them to which the E.D.C. would be subject. But throughout this period no French Government could be sure of securing the necessary majority in the French Assembly to secure ratification of the E.D.C. treaty, involving as it did the abandonment of an independent French army in Europe under exclusive French command. Although the Benelux countries and West Germany had secured parliamentary ratification of the treaties, the French National Assembly rejected it on 30 August 1954. This meant that the *Bonn Agreements* of 1952 ending the Allied occupation of Western Germany and bringing about the restoration of West German sovereignty could not be ratified. It also meant that the contribution of a revived but controlled German armaments industry and reconstituted West German armed forces could not be made available for the mutual defence of Western Europe through the planned supranational arrangements of the Six in alliance with the other NATO Powers. If a West German contribution was regarded as essential for the defence of Western Europe then an entirely new treaty framework had to be found to replace the many-sided commitments of the Paris Treaty of 1952. The West European States found this framework in the Brussels Treaty Alliance of 17 March 1948 (p. 399).

On Britain's initiative, the Brussels Treaty, which complemented but in military significance had been superseded by NATO was revived in the autumn of 1954 and expanded. Multilateral negotiations were conducted at the Nine Power *London Conference, 28 September–3 October 1954*, attended by Belgium, Britain, Canada, France, the German Federal Republic, Italy, Luxembourg, the Netherlands and the United States. Mendés-France, for France, insisted that West German rearmament and the accession of West Germany to NATO would only be assented to by France if Britain and the United States undertook to maintain their troops in Europe, if German rearmament were controlled, and if an agreement could be reached on the Saar. At the London Conference it was agreed that at a subsequent conference in Paris a comprehensive set of agreements were to be drawn up in binding legal form. After further negotiations, the *Paris Agreements, 23 October 1954, were signed* (p. 411). The Brussels Treaty Organization was renamed and reconstituted as the *West European Union* by four Protocols.

Protocol I. The German Federal Republic and Italy were admitted to the original Brussels Treaty Powers (the Six and Britain). The Consultative Council of the Brussels Treaty became the Council of Western European Union.

Protocol II. This laid down the maximum strength of land and air forces to be maintained in time of peace by each signatory of the W.E.U. under the command of the supreme command of NATO. Britain undertook to maintain in Europe a stated minimum of four divisions together with tactical air support which would not be withdrawn without the consent of the majority of the W.E.U.

Protocol III. This consisted of resolutions concerning the control of West

German armaments; the German Federal Republic was forbidden to manufacture atomic, biological or chemical weapons, and other limitations were also
placed on German rearmament.

Protocol IV. This set up an agency for the control of West German armament.

The W.E.U. was headed by a Council consisting of the Foreign Ministers of
Member States, a Permanent Council consisting of the Ambassadors of
Member States and a Secretariat. An Assembly was added consisting of the
representatives of the W.E.U. at the Consultative Assembly of the Council of
Europe. The Agency for the Control of Armaments was attached to the
Secretariat responsible to the Council. The W.E.U. gave the Assembly no real
powers and the Council was a conference of allied Foreign Ministers whose
decisions depended on individual Government policies and approval. The
W.E.U. thus lacked the supranational character of E.S.C.S. and the rejected
E.D.C. The military functions of W.E.U. came to be exercised in practice by
NATO. Economic questions and negotiations were conducted by other
specialized organizations like the E.E.C., and so the W.E.U. did little to bridge
the gap developing between the Six on the one hand and Britain and the remaining West European States on the other. Subsequent attempts to use the W.E.U.
as a West European political forum were not successful. The most important
later decisions of the W.E.U. were those that lifted many of the restrictions on
the rearmament of the Federal German Republic after 1959. The importance
of the W.E.U. lies in the fact that it established a treaty framework making
possible West German rearmament and the restoration of German sovereignty.

The *Paris Agreements, 23 October 1954* (p. 411), thus restored the objectives
of the abortive *Bonn Agreements of 1952*, abrogating the Occupation Statute and
abolishing the Allied High Commission. The three wartime allies, Britain,
France and the United States, retained their rights regarding Berlin, German
reunification and the eventual German peace treaty. In a declaration, Britain,
France and the United States recognized the Government of the German
Federal Republic as the only legitimate one entitled to speak for the whole of
Germany; the Federal German Republic for their part agreed never to use
force to alter the frontiers of the Federal German Republic or to bring about
the reunification of Germany, and promised to solve by peaceful means all
international differences. The Federal German Republic at the same time was
admitted to membership of NATO in the winter of 1954. Finally Germany and
France signed an agreement covering the Saar. After the ratification of the
Paris Agreements by the Member States, including the French Assembly and
the Bundestag, they entered into force on 5 May 1955. On that day the Federal
German Republic regained its sovereignty with the ending of the occupation
by Britain, France and the United States.

The third phase, 1955–72: I. The Six establish the Common Market (E.E.C.)

The success of the European Coal and Steel Community (E.C.S.C.) from 1955–7 and the unprecedented growth of economic recovery among the Six stimulated new efforts to take further the integration of the Six. At a meeting of the Foreign Ministers of the Six at Messina a resolution was adopted on 3 June 1955 pledging their determination to work 'toward the establishment of a United Europe, through the development of common institutions, the gradual merger of national economies, the creation of a common market and increasing harmonization of social policies'. Support for this policy was given by the European Movement which had been founded at the Hague in 1948 to mobilize public opinion. Strong support too was provided by the parliamentarians of the Six who were members of the Common Assembly of the E.C.S.C.

1. The treaties

After lengthy negotiations extending over nearly two years, the *Treaty of Rome was signed, 25 March 1957* (p. 412) by the Six, namely Belgium, France, the Federal Republic of Germany, Italy, Luxembourg and the Netherlands. The Treaty of Rome established the *European Economic Community* (*E.E.C.*). On the same day, also in Rome, the Six signed the *Euratom Treaty* creating the *European Atomic Energy Community*. Euratom was designed to develop the peaceful uses only of nuclear energy; it was regarded by the Six as of great future importance in building up European union. In practice it failed to develop as anticipated. Nuclear work for military purposes became a national enterprise in France (as in Britain, a non-signatory), and despite expensive budgets for research centres in the 1950s and 1960s, national policies, even in the non-military nuclear field, predominated over cooperative joint efforts. By the close of the 1960s Euratom was bypassed and its members could no longer agree on expensive budgets. A great drawback for Euratom from the very start was that the one European State with an advanced nuclear technology, Britain, was not a member. The *European Economic Community*, by way of contrast, although Britain would not join at its inception, successfully did, in the words of the preamble to the treaty, 'establish the foundations of an ever closer union among the European peoples'.

2. The objectives of the treaties

The Treaty of Rome is based on the objective of achieving freedom of market and competition within the Member States and a common external tariff with the rest of the world. In some respects the treaty was precise. It set out time-tables for the reduction of internal tariffs, for the removal of quotas internally and for the creation of a common external tariff. These objectives were all achieved in July 1968 ahead of the timetable of the Treaty of Rome. Other objectives of the Rome Treaty which are set out in Articles 2 and 3 are to lead the Six to complete economic integration; these remain to be realized. To this group of activities belong many questions of economic and social policy which have continued to be dealt with on a national basis. A common monetary policy has proved an especially thorny problem, involving as it does supra-national regulation of those financial policies by which individual Govern-ments attempt to regulate their employment, balance of payments and inflation. The E.E.C. agreed in principle in June 1970 on the 'Werner Plan' designed to achieve an economic and monetary union by 1980. The Council of the E.E.C. decided to reach this goal in two stages, 1 January 1971–31 December 1973 and from 1 January 1974 to 1980. The critical decision requiring transfer of national sovereignty to an E.E.C. supranational body will have to be made in 1973 if the plan is adhered to.

Besides iron and steel and atomic energy, dealt with in separate treaties, the Treaty of Rome also set out guidelines and objectives for establishing certain common policies, but did not provide detailed means or precise timetables for their achievement – the practical policies were to be worked out subsequently by the community of the E.E.C. (the Common Agricultural Policy was to be finalized in unspecified stages by 1 January 1970). The areas of common policy thus defined are transport, energy and agriculture. Progress on evolving agreed common policies in the fields of transport and energy have been slow, though the pace of agreement on these questions has quickened since 1968. The E.E.C. was able to progress despite this, but the evolution of an agreed Common Agricultural Policy from the first proved of more critical importance, and the existence of E.E.C. seemed to depend on finding satisfactory solutions.

3. The Common Agricultural Policy

The Treaty of Rome represented compromises of national interests on the part of the signatories. For France the Common Agricultural Policy (C.A.P.) spelt the chief economic advantage to be placed against the possible economic dis-advantages of a common market without trade barriers. The progressive implementation of the C.A.P. presented the Community with several crises; a French boycott from July 1965 to January 1966 was partly precipitated by the agricultural problem, but it also proved the Community's basic strength in that agreement was reached in the end. The essential features of the Com-munity's C.A.P. are that prices are established for agricultural products which are designed to give a proper return to the European farmer. But the prices have been generally well above world market prices for these commodities which hitherto could be imported at the lower world price, so the Community raised a protective barrier against imports from non-members. A Farm Fund was established to implement financially the C.A.P. Member States contributed a fixed proportion of the Fund from their national budgets. The common Farm Fund's purpose is threefold: to support buying when the market price is about to fall below that fixed by the Commission, secondly to provide export subsidies to lower the Community's price when selling abroad and finally to finance modernization and retraining schemes. This policy led to an over-production at the prices fixed, as for example by creating an enormous stock-piled 'butter mountain'. The costs of the Farm Fund escalated beyond what had been anticipated. 'Reform' proved difficult. France, the chief beneficiary, wished to safeguard its position. In December 1969 the E.E.C. reached a fundamental agreement for the continuation of C.A.P. and changes in its financing. Funds for the Farm Fund would after 1971 no longer be contributed through the national budgets of the members, but the Community would receive them automatically from the duties levied on agricultural imports together with a fixed percentage of the Value Added Tax levied within each Member State. The importance of the C.A.P. can be gauged from the fact that it has accounted for more than 90 per cent of the total Community's expenditure.

4. Accession of other States

The Treaty of Rome provided for other States joining as full members or being associated with E.E.C. Only European States could apply to become full members of the Community according to Article 237 on the basis of which Britain, Ireland, Norway and Denmark applied. But special agreements and forms of association with non-European States and territories are set out in Articles 131–6. At the time of the signature of the Treaty of Rome it was agreed to grant associate status to French African territories and other overseas dependencies. As many of these territories became independent the *Yaoundé Convention was signed, 20 July 1963*, covering eighteen associated States in Africa, and this convention was extended to include some other overseas territories of France and the Netherlands. They comprise Burundi, Cameroon, the Central African Republic, Chad, Zaire, Congo, Dahomey, Gabon, Upper Volta, Ivory Coast, Madagascar, Mali, Mauritania, Niger, Rwanda, Senegal, Somalia, Togo, Surinam, Netherlands Antilles and French overseas *Départements* and territories. An association treaty was signed with Nigeria in 1966 but not ratified. In 1968 partial association agreements were signed with Kenya,

Tanzania and Uganda, and in 1969 with Morocco and Tunisia, and in 1971 with Malta. Various special trade agreements have been signed with Lebanon, Israel, Iran, Spain and one East European Communist State, Yugoslavia, some of which which could lead to associate status. European States which have negotiated associate membership are: Greece in 1962, but the establishment of the military régime in 1967 led to the virtual freezing of policies of harmonization; Turkey in 1964; six EFTA members, Austria, Switzerland, Sweden, Portugal, Finland and Iceland in July 1972, have successfully concluded negotiations with the Community on the eventual creation of a Free Trade Zone in industrial goods by July 1977.

European States applying for full membership have been Britain, Ireland and Denmark in August 1961 and Norway in May 1962. Subsequently Austria, Sweden and Switzerland applied separately for association. These negotiations were indefinitely adjourned after President de Gaulle's 'veto' in January 1963. In May 1967 Britain renewed her applicatiom for membership followed by Denmark, Ireland and Norway. These negotiations too came to a standstill in December of that year, due to French objections. The resignation of General de Gaulle in 1969 opened the way for renewal of negotiations in June 1970 and these were completed in June 1971. The British Parliament completed ratification of the Treaty of Accession on 20 September 1972. Denmark and Ireland also completed ratification before the close of 1972. *The Treaty of Accession to the Community of Denmark, Ireland, Norway and the United Kingdom was signed on 22 January 1972.* A referendum in Norway subsequently rejected the treaty. The three countries which have joined obtained a number of special concessions.

5. British terms of accession

Britain obtained the following terms: a transitional period of five years for adjustment to E.E.C. tariffs and rules and to the agreed common policies including the Common Agricultural Policy, calculated from Britain's date of joining the Community on 1 January 1973. The stages of harmonization were also agreed. Britain agreed to meet the Budget costs of the Community on a rising scale from 8·64 per cent in 1973 to 18·92 per cent in 1977, whereafter with some safeguards in 1978 and 1979 the new automatic financing of the Budget come into force as agreed under the Common Agricultural Policy. These percentages may have to be raised marginally in view of Norway's rejection of membership. Special quantitative guarantees for New Zealand exports in dairy products have been granted until 1978; thereafter, except for cheese, new arrangements are to be agreed. Less definite assurances were secured for Commonwealth sugar after 1974, but a gentleman's agreement promises to negotiate reasonable terms after 1974. On the question of the position of the independent Commonwealth countries, it was agreed that they could negotiate a form of association similar to the Yaoundé Convention or conclude a commercial agreement. British dependent territories, with the exception of Hong Kong and Gibraltar, are eligible for association. A Generalized Preference Scheme will apply to Hong Kong, India, Pakistan, Ceylon, Malaysia and Singapore, and suitable agreements will be offered to Cyprus and Gibraltar.

6. The decision-making process of the E.E.C.

In 1967 a treaty was signed declaring the intention of the Six to merge the three separate institutions which are the European Coal and Steel Community, Euratom and E.E.C. The supranational core of the European Economic Community is the *Commission*, supported by its own civil service several thousand strong. It has its headquarters in Brussels. When the Treaty of Accession entered into force in 1973 admitting the three new members, the number of Commissioners was increased from nine to thirteen. At least one Commissioner (and not more than two) must be a national of each Member State. The Commissioners are to be appointed for four years by the common agreement of all Member States, and the appointment is renewable. The treaty lays down that the Commissioners shall act in the Community's interest and are not to be influenced by the Government of a Member State. The Commission has considerable powers. It can initiate proposals for legislation, and its duty is to implement the treaty as supplemented by policy agreements. It can impose fines on individual firms judged in default of the terms of the treaty. The *European Community Court of Justice* sitting in Luxembourg gives final rulings when appealed to by Member States, by individual firms or by the Commission, concerning the application of the Treaty of Rome. So fines imposed by the Commission, for instance, can be appealed against before the Court of Justice. Both the Commission and Member States have brought a number of cases against each other before the Court.

The Commission submits proposals to the *Council of Ministers*. It is in the *Council* that final decisions are made. The Council is not supranational but consists of one Minister sent by each National Government that is a Member State. The voting system of the Council is complicated: on most issues it is supposed to proceed on a 'qualified majority' principle, having passed on from the first stage where unanimity was required. The question of voting was one of the principal causes of conflict between France and the Commission in 1965. In practice since 1966 unanimity has been required whenever a Member State regards the issue of sufficient importance to it. This allows each State to exercise a veto on Commission proposals it regards as important and inimical to its national interests. The Council of Ministers has been supported since 1967 by a *Committee of the Permanent Diplomatic Representatives* of the Six in Brussels who meet regularly, represent national viewpoints and act as liaison between the E.E.C. institutions and their Governments. Like the Council of Ministers, whom they advise, the individual representatives are answerable to their Governments and cannot be dismissed by any means open to the E.E.C. The Commission, on the other hand, is theoretically answerable to the *European Parliament* meeting in Strasbourg. The *European Parliament* is not composed of members elected directly by popular suffrage but of delegates sent by the Parliaments of member countries. So far the European Parliament has enjoyed little real power but has been a valuable forum for discussion. The 'theory' and 'practice' of Community decision-making differ markedly. With strong pressure from France especially, the Council of Ministers, continuing to act mainly on a unanimity principle, has enjoyed increasing real power at the expense of the *Commission*. In this way national policy-making has been emphasized as against supranationalism. The operation of the enlarged Community may come to differ during the course of the 1970s. There is likely to be a continuing debate between the supporters of the policy of giving more real power to the *European Parliament* and of placing emphasis on Community decision-making, and the supporters of a policy of lessening the supranationalism of European institutions.

7. Financial aid for development

Such aid has been given mostly to overseas countries which were formerly colonial possessions of Member States. The aid of the Six has been on a comparatively large scale. In 1969 its total from official and private sources amounted to $5,196 million. In 1969, by way of comparison, the United States provided $4,645 million and Britain $1,068 million. The *European Investment Bank* was established by the Rome treaty and has granted loans to the European associates Greece and Turkey; it has also financed loans for projects in the less developed regions of Member States. This has been of particular benefit to Italy. Finally, a *European Social Fund* has paid out aid to help finance industrial adaptation as a result of the impact of the E.E.C., especially to retrain redundant workers.

The new relationship of France and Germany within the Western Europe of the 1960s was strengthened by the *Franco-German Treaty of Cooperation, 22 January 1963,* which provided for regular consultations between the two Heads of State and other Ministers especially on questions of defence, foreign policy and cultural policies.

The third phase, 1955-72: II. The O.E.C.D. and W.E.U.: the 'Outer Seven' establish the European Free Trade Area (EFTA)

The Organization for European Economic Cooperation (O.E.E.C.) had been set up under a convention signed by sixteen European nations to facilitate the economic recovery of Western Europe with the help of aid offered by the Marshall Plan (p. 379). The membership reached eighteen when the German Federal Republic joined in October 1949 and Spain in July 1959. Yugoslavia participated in some activities, Finland sent observers to some committees, and the United States and Canada participated as associate members.

In 1960 members of the O.E.E.C. decided that the objectives of the Marshall Plan had been reached and that cooperation between Western Europe and North America should be continued to meet new and pressing problems. After conferences in Paris in May 1960 and July 1960, representatives of the eighteen members of O.E.E.C., of the E.E.C., of the United States and Canada, agreed on a new convention to replace O.E.E.C. *The Convention of the Organization for Economic Cooperation and Development, 14 December 1960*, was signed by the eighteen full members of O.E.E.C. and by Canada and the U.S., now full members of the new organization. It entered into force on 30 September 1961. Japan acceded as a full member on 28 April 1964. Special forms of partial association in some of the work of the O.E.C.D. have also been worked out with Yugoslavia, Finland and Australia. The O.E.C.D. thus represents the most important trading nations of the 'developed' Western world. The objectives of O.E.C.D. are set out in the preamble and in Article 1: '(a) to achieve the highest sustainable economic growth and employment and a rising standard of living in member countries, while maintaining financial stability, and thus to contribute to the development of the world economy; (b) to contribute to sound economic expansion in member – as well as non-member – countries in the process of economic development; and (c) to contribute to the expansion of world trade on a multilateral, non-discriminatory basis, in accordance with international obligations.' The convention provides for consultation and cooperation to attain these objectives. A Council was set up composed of all members and a Secretary-General with a Secretariat appointed by the Council and responsible to it. Decisions are made by the Council acting on the principle of unanimity. The O.E.C.D., whose basic objectives are freeing exchange and liberalizing trade, has been active in the monetary field to attempt to promote orderly and stable currency exchange rates. It set up a European Fund and Multilateral Clearing System under the *European Monetary Agreement, 27 December 1958*, to supersede the earlier European Payments Union established in 1950. Its purpose was to help members in temporary balance-of-payment difficulties. In its global aims the O.E.C.D.'s achievements have so far (by 1973) been limited, the financial interest of blocks of powers such as the E.E.C., the United States and Japan have been frequently in disagreement with each other. The Development Assistance Committee was set up to coordinate aid to undeveloped countries and to examine many aspects of aid programmes. Research on these questions and the training of senior officials from developing nations is the function of the O.E.C.D. Development Centre. But the fundamental financial and trading interests of the 'rich' and 'poor' nations remain in basic conflict. O.E.C.D. provides a continuing forum for negotiation among the most formidable financial powers of the Western world; negotiations for a reform of the monetary system in the 1970s have been conducted in O.E.C.D. with a view to finding a way of bridging the serious differences between the U.S.A. and other members on balance of payments and trade questions.

The *West European Union* has continued to function in the period 1955–72, although most military questions are dealt with in NATO and economic and social issues largely in E.E.C. For a time in the 1960s the W.E.U. acted as liaison between the E.E.C. and the European Free Trade Association. The need for liaison disappeared once negotiations between the new applicants to E.E.C. got seriously underway in 1970. The W.E.U. continues to embody the European alliance commitments of the original Treaty of Brussels (p. 399) and to act as a watchdog over the degree of permissible rearmament of the Federal German Republic.

The *European Free Trade Association* (EFTA) was established by the *Treaty of Stockholm, 4 January 1960 and ratified 3 May 1960* (p. 428), by Austria, Britain, Denmark, Norway, Portugal and Switzerland. Finland became an associate member in 1961. Its establishment marks the split of the Western European States into two distinct groups. The E.E.C. has been developing integrated economic policies among its six members and has been moving towards 'European union', with some institutions such as the original High Authority of the European Coal and Steel Community and the Commission of the E.E.C. possessing supranational characteristics. During the 1950s, which saw the creation of the E.E.C. and the working together of the six continental European Powers, Britain emphasized her separate world position as the centre of the Commonwealth, enjoying a special relationship with the U.S. Britain regarded herself as a Great Power with global responsibilities, and successive Governments before 1960 rejected Britain's submitting her economic and defence policies to any supranational European bodies. With strong economic Commonwealth links and trading with the United States, the policy of a common external tariff for agricultural and industrial goods did not appear advantageous to British Governments. The Scandinavian countries, especially Finland and Sweden, as well as Switzerland and Austria, did not wish to or could not compromise their political neutrality by joining a Western group of nations. Attempts at meetings of the O.E.E.C. in 1957 and 1958 to create a European industrial free trade area to exist parallel with E.E.C. failed. Subsequent rounds of negotiations among the 'Outer Seven' (Austria, Britain, Denmark, Norway, Portugal, Sweden and Switzerland) from December 1958 to December 1959 led to the establishment of EFTA. Its objectives were limited. With headquarters in Geneva, a small Secretariat and a Council of representatives from Member States acting unanimously where decisions involving new obligations are concerned, the machinery lacked supranational decision-making institutions. It established by progressive reduction of tariffs between members on industrial goods a common market in industrial goods. This progress was in fact accelerated so that with few exceptions these tariffs had been entirely removed by 1 January 1967. There was, however no attempt to apply an agreed common external tariff to non-EFTA members. (The common external tariff is an essential feature of the E.E.C.) Each EFTA State regulates tariffs with non-members according to its individual trade policies. EFTA succeeded in expanding trade between its members during the 1960s; but the applications of Britain, Denmark, Norway and Ireland to join the E.E.C. in 1961 and 1967 underlined the 'temporary' nature of EFTA, which was always seen as a first step to a larger European grouping With the success of these applications in 1971–2, negotiations were begun between the E.E.C. and the EFTA members who were not willing to join, that is Switzerland, Austria, Finland, Portugal and Iceland. These were conducted bilaterally and separately by the Commission with each of the five States. They were successfully concluded in *a series of trade treaties between the five remaining EFTA States and the E.E.C. and signed in Brussels on 22 July 1972.* These treaties taken together will create a *European Free Trade Area* in most industrial goods covering all fifteen countries comprising EFTA and E.E.C. The position of Norway remains to be clarified – it is an EFTA member but will need to negotiate a treaty with the E.E.C. after 1972. Tariffs for industrial goods *within* EFTA and E.E.C. no longer exist; the key to the new agreements is that tariffs *between* E.E.C. and individual EFTA States in industrial goods will be abolished step by step during a five-year transitional period from 1 April 1973 to July 1977. Exceptions with each EFTA State in which free trade would hurt the economy of that country unduly, or in which the application of the E.E.C. agricultural external tariff would injure that country deeply, have led to special agreements. For instance, Iceland may sell fish duty-free in Europe (though fish are not industrial); Portugal gained special arrangements for its fruit, vegetables and wine exports; Finland won a longer transitional period for paper products.

The nations of the new European Free Trade Area account for nearly half the world's trade and have a population of about 300 million people. During the transitional period EFTA will continue to function. But it is important to note that the enlarged E.E.C. is not merged with EFTA. Both the common external tariff, important mainly in agricultural goods, and economic and political integration are an essential aspect of the Western Europe being developed by the E.E.C. States. EFTA members, by choice, are not participating in these political and economic policies.

For the Scandinavian countries the *Nordic Council* acts as a bridge between former and present EFTA members. It was inaugurated in February 1953 and its members are Denmark, Finland, Iceland, Norway and Sweden. It is advisory and consultative, decisions being taken by Member Governments and not the Nordic Council. The Nordic Council seeks to promote Scandinavian regional cooperation in culture, law, social policy and economic policy.

Treaty of Alliance and Mutual Assistance between Britain and France (Treaty of Dunkirk), 4 March 1947

... Determined to collaborate in measures of mutual assistance in the event of any renewal of German aggression, while considering most desirable the conclusion of a Treaty between all the Powers having responsibility for action in relation to Germany with the object of preventing Germany from becoming again a menace to peace;

Having regard to the Treaties of Alliance and Mutual Assistance which they have respectively concluded with the Union of Soviet Socialist Republics;

Intending to strengthen the economic relations between the two countries to their mutual advantage and in the interests of general prosperity;

Have decided to conclude a Treaty with these objects ...

Article I. Without prejudice to any arrangements that may be made, under any

Treaty concluded between all the Powers having responsibility for action in relation to Germany under Article 107 of the Charter of the United Nations, for the purpose of preventing any infringements by Germany of her obligations with regard to disarmament and demilitarization and generally of ensuring that Germany shall not again become a menace to peace, the High Contracting Parties will, in the event of any threat to the security of either of them arising from the adoption by Germany of a policy of aggression or from action by Germany designed to facilitate such a policy, take, after consulting with each other and where appropriate with the other Powers having responsibility for action in relation to Germany, such agreed action (which so long as the said Article 107 remains operative shall be action under that Article) as is best calculated to put an end to this threat.

Article II. Should either of the High Contracting Parties become again involved in hostilities with Germany, either in consequence of an armed attack, within the meaning of Article 51 of the Charter of the United Nations, by Germany against that party, or as a result of agreed action taken against Germany under Article I of this Treaty, or as a result of enforcement action taken against Germany by the United Nations Security Council, the other High Contracting Party will at once give the High Contracting Party so involved in hostilities all the military and other support and assistance in his power.

Article III. In the event of either High Contracting Party being prejudiced by the failure of Germany to fulfil any obligation of an economic character imposed on her as a result of the Instrument of Surrender or arising out of any subsequent settlement, the High Contracting Parties will consult with each other and where appropriate with the other Powers having responsibility for action in relation to Germany, with a view to taking agreed action to deal with the situation.

Article IV. Bearing in mind the interests of the other members of the United Nations, the High Contracting Parties will by constant consultation on matters affecting their economic relations with each other take all possible steps to promote the prosperity and economic security of both countries and thus enable each of them to contribute more effectively to the economic and social objectives of the United Nations.

Article V. 1. Nothing in the present Treaty should be interpreted as derogating in any way from the obligations devolving upon the High Contracting Parties from the provisions of the Charter of the United Nations or from any special agreements concluded in virtue of Article 43 of the Charter.

2. Neither of the High Contracting Parties will conclude any alliance or take part in any coalition directed against the other High Contracting Party; nor will they enter into any obligation inconsistent with the provisions of the present Treaty.

Article VI. 1. The present Treaty is subject to ratification and the instruments of ratification will be exchanged in London as soon as possible.

2. It will come into force immediately on the exchange of the instruments of ratification and will remain in force for a period of fifty years... [Thereafter in perpetuity unless one year's notice of the desire to end the Treaty is given by one of the signatories.]

Treaty between Belgium, France, Luxembourg, the Netherlands and Britain (Brussels Treaty), Brussels, 17 March 1948

... Resolved

To reaffirm their faith in fundamental human rights, in the dignity and worth of the human person and in the other ideals proclaimed in the Charter of the United Nations;

To fortify and preserve the principles of democracy, personal freedom and political liberty, the constitutional traditions and the rule of law, which are their common heritage;

To strengthen, with these aims in view, the economic, social and cultural ties by which they are already united;

To cooperate loyally and to coordinate their efforts to create in Western Europe a firm basis for European economic recovery;

To afford assistance to each other, in accordance with the Charter of the United Nations, in maintaining international peace and security and in resisting any policy of aggression;

To take such steps as may be held to be necessary in the event of a renewal by Germany of a policy of aggression;

To associate progressively in the pursuance of these aims other States inspired by the same ideals and animated by the like determination;

Desiring for these purposes to conclude a Treaty for collaboration in economic, social and cultural matters and for collective self-defence ...

Article I. Convinced of the close community of their interests and of the necessity of uniting in order to promote the economic recovery of Europe, the High Contracting Parties will so organize and coordinate their economic activities as to produce the best possible results, by the elimination of conflict in their economic policies, the coordination of production and the development of commercial exchanges.

The cooperation provided for in the preceding paragraph, which will be effected through the Consultative Council referred to in Article VII as well as through other bodies, shall not involve any duplication of, or prejudice to, the work of other economic organizations in which the High Contracting Parties are or may be represented but shall on the contrary assist the work of those organizations.

Article II. The High Contracting Parties will make every effort in common, both by direct consultation and in specialized agencies, to promote the attainment of a higher standard of living by their peoples and to develop on corresponding lines the social and other related services of their countries.

The High Contracting Parties will consult with the object of achieving the earliest possible application of recommendations of immediate practical interest, relating to social matters, adopted with their approval in the specialized agencies.

They will endeavour to conclude as soon as possible conventions with each other in the sphere of social security.

Article III. The High Contracting Parties will make every effort in common to lead their peoples towards a better understanding of the principles which form the basis of their common civilization and to promote cultural exchanges by conventions between themselves or by other means.

Article IV. If any of the High Contracting Parties should be the object of an armed attack in Europe, the other High Contracting Parties will, in accordance with the provisions of Article 51 of the Charter of the United Nations, afford the Party so attacked all the military and other aid and assistance in their power.

Article V. All measures taken as a result of the preceding Article shall be immediately reported to the Security Council. They shall be terminated as soon as the Security Council has taken the measures necessary to maintain or restore international peace and security.

The present Treaty does not prejudice in any way the obligations of the High Contracting Parties under the provisions of the Charter of the United Nations. It shall not be interpreted as affecting in any way the authority and responsibility of the Security Council under the Charter to take at any time such action as it deems necessary in order to maintain or restore international peace and security.

Article VI. The High Contracting Parties declare, each so far as he is concerned, that none of the international engagements now in force between him and any other of the High Contracting Parties or any third State is in conflict with the provisions of the present Treaty.

None of the High Contracting Parties will conclude any alliance or participate in any coalition directed against any other of the High Contracting Parties.

Article VII. For the purpose of consulting together on all the questions dealt with in the present Treaty, the High Contracting Parties will create a Consultative Council, which shall be so organized as to be able to exercise its functions continuously. The Council shall meet at such times as it shall deem fit.

At the request of any of the High Contracting Parties, the Council shall be immediately convened in order to permit the High Contracting Parties to consult with regard to any situation which may constitute a threat to peace, in whatever area this threat should arise; with regard to the attitude to be adopted and the steps to be taken in case of a renewal by Germany of an aggressive policy; or with regard to any situation constituting a danger to economic stability.

[*Article VIII.* Provisions for settling disputes among signatories by peaceful means.]

Article IX. The High Contracting Parties may, by agreement, invite any other State to accede to the present Treaty on condition to be agreed between them and the State so invited....

[*Article X.* Ratification.]

Statute of the Council of Europe, London, 5 May 1949

The Governments of the Kingdom of Belgium, the Kingdom of Denmark, the French Republic, the Irish Republic, the Italian Republic, the Grand Duchy of Luxembourg, the Kingdom of the Netherlands, the Kingdom of Norway, the Kingdom of Sweden and the United Kingdom of Great Britain and Northern Ireland;

Convinced that the pursuit of peace based upon justice and international co-operation is vital for the preservation of human society and civilization;

Reaffirming their devotion to the spiritual and moral values which are the common heritage of their peoples and the true source of individual freedom, political liberty and the rule of law, principles which form the basis of all genuine democracy;

Believing that, for the maintenance and further realization of these ideals and in the interests of economic and social progress, there is need of a closer unity between all like-minded countries of Europe;

Considering that, to respond to this need and to the expressed aspirations of their peoples in this regard, it is necessary forthwith to create an organization which will bring European States into closer association;

Have in consequence decided to set up a Council of Europe consisting of a Committee of representatives of Governments and of a Consultative Assembly, and have for this purpose adopted the following Statute:

Chapter I: Aim of the Council of Europe

Article 1. (a) The aim of the Council of Europe is to achieve a greater unity between its Members for the purpose of safeguarding and realizing the ideals and principles which are their common heritage and facilitating their economic and social progress.

(b) This aim shall be pursued through the organs of the Council by discussion of questions of common concern and by agreements and common action in economic, social, cultural, scientific, legal and administrative matters and in the maintenance and further realization of human rights and fundamental freedoms.

(c) Participation in the Council of Europe shall not affect the collaboration of its Members in the work of the United Nations and of other international organizations or unions to which they are parties.

(d) Matters relating to National Defence do not fall within the scope of the Council of Europe.

Chapter II: Membership

Article 2. The Members of the Council of Europe are the parties to this Statute.

Article 3. Every Member of the Council of Europe must accept the principles of the rule of law and of the enjoyment by all persons within its jurisdiction of human rights and fundamental freedoms, and collaborate sincerely and effectively in the realization of the aim of the Council as specified in Chapter I.

Article 4. Any European State, which is deemed to be able and willing to fulfil the provisions of Article 3, may be invited to become a Member of the Council of Europe by the Committee of Ministers. Any State so invited shall become a Member on the deposit on its behalf with the Secretary-General of an instrument of accession to the present Statute.

...

[*Article 7.* Member States may withdraw after formal notification.]

Article 8. Any Member of the Council of Europe, which has seriously violated Article 3, may be suspended from its rights of representation and requested by the Committee of Ministers to withdraw under Article 7. If such Member does not comply with this request, the Committee may decide that it has ceased to be a Member of the Council as from such date as the Committee may determine.

Article 9. The Committee of Ministers may suspend the right of representation on the Committee and on the Consultative Assembly of a Member which has failed to fulfil its financial obligation, during such period as the obligation remains unfulfilled.

Chapter III: General

Article 10. The organs of the Council of Europe are:
    (i) the Committee of Ministers;
    (ii) the Consultative Assembly.

Both these organs shall be served by the Secretariat of the Council of Europe.

Article 11. The seat of the Council of Europe is at Strasbourg.

Article 12. The official languages of the Council of Europe are English and French. The rules of procedure of the Committee of Ministers and of the Consultative Assembly shall determine in what circumstances and under what conditions other languages may be used.

Chapter IV: Committee of Ministers

Article 13. The Committee of Ministers is the organ which acts on behalf of the Council of Europe in accordance with Articles 15 and 16.

Article 14. Each Member shall be entitled to one representative on the Committee of Ministers and each representative shall be entitled to one vote. Representatives on the Committee shall be the Ministers for Foreign Affairs. When a Minister for Foreign Affairs is unable to be present or in other circumstances where it may be desirable, an alternate may be nominated to act for him, who shall, whenever possible, be a member of his Government.

Article 15. (a) On the recommendation of the Consultative Assembly or on its own initiative, the Committee of Ministers shall consider the action required to further the aim of the Council of Europe, including the conclusion of conventions or agreements and the adoption by Governments of a common policy with regard to particular matters. Its conclusions shall be communicated to Members by the Secretary-General.

(b) In appropriate cases, the conclusions of the Committee may take the form of recommendations to the Governments of Members, and the Committee may request the Governments of Members to inform it of the action taken by them with regard to such recommendations.

Article 16. The Committee of Ministers shall, subject to the provisions of Articles 24, 28, 30, 32, 33 and 35, relating to the powers of the Consultative Assembly, decide with binding effect all matters relating to the internal organization and arrangements of the Council of Europe. For this purpose the Committee of Ministers shall adopt such financial and administrative regulations as may be necessary.

Article 17. The Committee of Ministers may set up advisory and technical committees or commissions for such specific purposes as it may deem desirable.

Article 18. The Committee of Ministers shall adopt its rules of procedure which shall determine amongst other things:
  (i) the quorum;
  (ii) the method of appointment and term of office of its President;
  (iii) the procedure for the admission of items to its agenda, including the giving of notice of proposals for resolutions; and
  (iv) the notifications required for the nomination of alternates under Article 14.

Article 19. At each session of the Consultative Assembly the Committee of Ministers shall furnish the Assembly with statements of its activities, accompanied by appropriate documentation.

Article 20. (a) Resolutions of the Committee of Ministers relating to the following important matters, namely:
  (i) recommendations under Article 15 (b);
  (ii) questions under Article 19;
  (iii) questions under Article 21 (a) (i) and (b);
  (iv) questions under Article 33;
  (v) recommendations for the amendment of Articles 1 (d), 7, 15, 20 and 22; and
  (vi) any other question which the Committee may, by a resolution passed under (d) *below*, decide should be

subject to a unanimous vote on account of its importance
require the unanimous vote of the representatives casting a vote, and of a majority of the representatives entitled to sit on the Committee.

(b) Questions arising under the rules of procedure or under the financial and administrative regulations may be decided by a simple majority vote of the representatives entitled to sit on the Committee.

(c) Resolutions of the Committee under Articles 4 and 5 require a two-thirds majority of all the representatives entitled to sit on the Committee.

(d) All other resolutions of the Committee, including the adoption of the Budget, of rules of procedure and of financial and administrative regulations, recommendations for the amendment of Articles of this Statute, other than those mentioned in paragraph (a) (v) above, and deciding in case of doubt which paragraph of this Article applies, require a two-thirds majority of the representatives casting a vote and of a majority of the representatives entitled to sit on the Committee.

Article 21. (a) Unless the Committee decides otherwise, meetings of the Committee of Ministers shall be held:
  (i) in private, and
  (ii) at the seat of the Council.

(b) The Committee shall determine what information shall be published regarding the conclusions and discussions of a meeting held in private.

(c) The Committee shall meet before and during the beginning of every session of the Consultative Assembly and at such other times as it may decide.

Chapter V: The Consultative Assembly

Article 22. The Consultative Assembly is the deliberative organ of the Council of Europe. It shall debate matters within its competence under this Statute and present its conclusions, in the form of recommendations, to the Committee of Ministers.

Article 23 [as amended in May 1951]. (a) The Consultative Assembly may discuss and make recommendations upon any matter within the aim and scope of the Council of Europe as defined in Chapter I. It shall also discuss and may make recommendations upon any matter referred to it by the Committee of Ministers with a request for its opinion.

(b) The Assembly shall draw up its Agenda in accordance with the provisions of paragraph (a) above. In so doing, it shall have regard to the work of other European inter-Governmental organizations to which some or all of the Members of the Council are parties.

(c) The President of the Assembly shall decide, in case of doubt, whether any question raised in the course of the Session is within the Agenda of the Assembly.

Article 24. The Consultative Assembly may, with due regard to the provisions of Article 38 (d), establish committees or commissions to consider and report to it on any matter which falls within its competence under Article 23, to examine and prepare questions on its agenda and to advise on all matters of procedure.

Article 25 [as amended in May 1951]. (a) The Consultative Assembly shall consist of representatives of each Member elected by its Parliament or appointed in such manner as that Parliament shall decide, subject, however, to the right of each Member Government to make any additional appointments necessary when the Parliament is not in session and has not laid down the procedure to be followed in that case. Each representative must be a national of the Member whom he represents, but shall not at the same time be a member of the Committee of Ministers.

(b) No representative shall be deprived of his position as such during a session of the Assembly without the agreement of the Assembly.

(c) Each representative may have a substitute who may, in the absence of the representative, sit, speak and vote in his place. The provisions of paragraph (a) above apply to the appointment of substitutes.

Article 26 [as amended in May 1951]. Members shall be entitled to the number of representatives given below:

Belgium	7
Denmark	5
France	18
Germany (Federal Republic)	18
Greece	7
Iceland	3
Ireland	4
Italy	18
Luxembourg	3
Netherlands	7
Norway	5
Saar	3
Sweden	6
Turkey	10
United Kingdom of Great Britain and Northern Ireland	18

Article 27 [as amended in May 1951]. The conditions under which the Committee of Ministers collectively may be represented in the debates of the Consultative Assembly, or individual representatives on the Committee or their alternates may address the Assembly, shall be determined by such rules of procedure on this subject as may be drawn up by the Committee after consultation with the Assembly.

Article 28. (a) The Consultative Assembly shall adopt its rules of procedure and shall elect from its members its President, who shall remain in office until the next ordinary session....

. . .

Article 32. The Consultative Assembly shall meet in ordinary session once a year, the date and duration of which shall be determined by the Assembly so as to avoid as far as possible overlapping with parliamentary sessions of Members and with sessions of the General Assembly of the United Nations. In no circumstances shall the duration of an ordinary session exceed one month unless both the Assembly and the Committee of Ministers concur.

Article 34 [as amended in 1951]. The Consultative Assembly may be convened in extraordinary sessions upon the initiative either of the Committee of Ministers or of the President of the Assembly after agreement between them, such agreement also to determine the date and place of the sessions.

...

Chapter VI: The Secretariat

Article 36. (a) The Secretariat shall consist of a Secretary-General, a Deputy Secretary-General and such other staff as may be required....

...

Chapter VII: Finance

Article 38. (a) Each Member shall bear the expenses of its own representation in the Committee of Ministers and in the Consultative Assembly.

(b) The expenses of the Secretariat and all other common expenses shall be shared between all Members in such proportions as shall be determined by the Committee on the basis of the population of Members.

The contributions of an Associate Member shall be determined by the Committee.

(c) In accordance with the financial regulations, the Budget of the Council shall be submitted annually by the Secretary-General for adoption by the Committee.

(d) The Secretary-General shall refer to the Committee requests from the Assembly which involve expenditure exceeding the amount already allocated in the Budget for the Assembly and its activities.

(e) The Secretary-General shall also submit to the Committee of Ministers an estimate of the expenditure to which the implementation of each of the recommendations presented to the Committee would give rise. Any resolution the implementation of which requires additional expenditure shall not be considered as adopted by the Committee of Ministers unless the Committee has also approved the corresponding estimates for such additional expenditure.

Article 39. The Secretary-General shall each year notify the Government of each Member of the amount of its contribution, and each Member shall pay to the Secretary-General the amount of its contribution, which shall be deemed to be due on the date of its notification, not later than six months after that date.

Chapter VIII: Privileges and immunities

...

Treaty instituting the European Coal and Steel Community, Paris, 18 April 1951

...

Considering that world peace may be safeguarded only by creative efforts equal to the dangers which menace it;

Convinced that the contribution which an organized and vital Europe can bring to civilization is indispensable to the maintenance of peaceful relations;

Conscious of the fact that Europe can be built only by concrete actions which create a real solidarity and by the establishment of common bases for economic development;

Desirous of assisting through the expansion of their basic production in raising the standard of living and in furthering the works of peace;

Resolved to substitute for historic rivalries a fusion of their essential interests;

to establish, by creating an economic community, the foundation of a broad and independent community among peoples long divided by bloody conflicts; and to lay the bases of institutions capable of giving direction to their future common destiny;

Have decided to create a European Coal and Steel Community. . . .

TITLE ONE: The European Coal and Steel Community

Article 1. By the present Treaty the HIGH CONTRACTING PARTIES institute among themselves a EUROPEAN COAL AND STEEL COMMUNITY, based on a common market, common objectives, and common institutions.

Article 2. The mission of the European Coal and Steel Community is to contribute to economic expansion, the development of employment and the improvement of the standard of living in the participating countries through the institution, in harmony with the general economy of the Member States, of a common market as defined in Article 4.

The Community must progressively establish conditions which will in themselves assure the most rational distribution of production at the highest possible level of productivity, while safeguarding the continuity of employment and avoiding the creation of fundamental and persistent disturbances in the economies of the Member States.

Article 3. Within the framework of their respective powers and responsibilities and in the common interest, the institutions of the Community shall:

(a) see that the common market is regularly supplied, taking account of the needs of third countries;

(b) assure to all consumers in comparable positions within the common market equal access to the sources of production;

(c) seek the establishment of the lowest prices which are possible without requiring any corresponding rise either in the prices charged by the same enterprises in other transactions or in the price level as

a whole in another period, while at the same time permitting necessary amortization and providing normal possibilities of remuneration for capital invested;

(d) see that conditions are maintained which will encourage enterprises to expand and improve their ability to produce and to promote a policy of rational development of natural resources, avoiding inconsiderate exhaustion of such resources;

(e) promote the improvement of the living and working conditions of the labour force in each of the industries under its jurisdiction so as to make possible the equalization of such conditions in an upward direction;

(f) further the development of international trade and see that equitable limits are observed in prices charged on external markets;

(g) promote the regular expansion and the modernization of production as well as the improvement of its quality, under conditions which preclude any protection against competing industries except where justified by illegitimate action on the part of such industries or in their favour.

Article 4. The following are recognized to be incompatible with the common market for coal and steel, and are, therefore, abolished and prohibited within the Community in the manner set forth in the present Treaty:

(a) import and export duties, or charges with an equivalent effect, and quantitative restrictions on the movement of coal and steel;

(b) measures or practices discriminating among producers, among buyers or among consumers, specifically as concerns prices, delivery terms and transportation rates, as well as measures or practices which hamper the buyer in the free choice of his supplier;

(c) subsidies or State assistance, or special charges imposed by the State, in any form whatsoever;

(d) restrictive practices tending towards the division of markets or the exploitation of the consumer.

Article 5. The Community shall accomplish its mission, under the conditions provided for in the present Treaty, with limited direct intervention.

To this end, the Community will:

enlighten and facilitate the action of the interested parties by collecting information, organizing consultations and defining general objectives;

place financial means at the disposal of enterprises for their investments and participate in the expenses of readaptation;

assure the establishment, the maintenance and the observance of normal conditions of competition and take direct action with respect to production and the operation of the market only when circumstances make it absolutely necessary;

publish the justifications for its action and take the necessary measures to ensure observance of the rules set forth in the present Treaty.

The institutions of the Community shall carry out these activities with as little administrative machinery as possible and in close cooperation with the interested parties.

Article 6. The Community shall have juridical personality....

TITLE TWO: The institutions of the Community

Article 7. The institutions of the Community shall be as follows:

a HIGH AUTHORITY, assisted by a *Consultative Committee*;

a COMMON ASSEMBLY, hereafter referred to as 'the Assembly';

a SPECIAL COUNCIL, composed of MINISTERS, hereafter referred to as 'the Council';

a COURT OF JUSTICE, hereafter referred to as 'the Court'.

Chapter I: The High Authority

Article 8. The High Authority shall be responsible for assuring the fulfilment of the purposes stated in the present Treaty under the terms thereof.

Article 9. The High Authority shall be composed of nine members designated for six years and chosen for their general competence.

A member shall be eligible for reappointment. The number of members of the High Authority may be reduced by unanimous decision of the Council.

Only nationals of the Member States may be members of the High Authority.

The High Authority may not include more than two members of the same nationality.

The members of the High Authority shall exercise their functions in complete independence, in the general interest of the Community. In the fulfilment of their duties, they shall neither solicit nor accept instructions from any Government or from any organization. They will abstain from all conduct incompatible with the supranational character of their functions.

Each Member State agrees to respect this supranational character and to make no effort to influence the members of the High Authority in the execution of their duties.

The members of the High Authority may not exercise any business or professional activities, paid or unpaid, nor acquire or hold, directly or indirectly, any interest in any business related to coal and steel during their term of office or for a period of three years thereafter.

Article 10. The Governments of the Member States shall designate eight members of the High Authority by agreement among themselves. These eight members will elect a ninth member, who shall be deemed elected if he receives at least five votes.

The members thus designated will remain in office for six years following the date of the establishment of the common market.

In case a vacancy should occur during this first period for one of the reasons set forth in Article 12, it will be filled under the provisions of the third paragraph of that Article, by common agreement among the Governments of the Member States....

Article 11. The President and the Vice President of the High Authority shall be designated from among the membership of the High Authority for two years, in accordance with the procedure provided for the designation of the members of the High Authority by the Governments of the Member States. They may be re-elected.

Except in the case of a complete redesignation of the membership of the High Authority, the designation of the President and Vice President shall be made after consultation with the High Authority.

Article 12. In addition to the provisions for regular redesignation, the terms of office of a member of the High Authority may be terminated by death or resignation....

Article 13. The High Authority shall act by vote of a majority of its membership.

Its quorum shall be fixed by its rules of procedure. However, this quorum must be greater than one-half of its membership.

Article 14. In the execution of its responsibilities under the present Treaty and in accordance with the provisions thereof, the High Authority shall issue decisions, recommendations and opinions.

Decisions shall be binding in all their details.

Recommendations shall be binding with respect to the objectives which they specify but shall leave to those to whom they are directed the choice of appropriate means for attaining these objectives.

Opinions shall not be binding.

When the High Authority is empowered to issue a decision, it may limit itself to making a recommendation.

Article 15. The decisions, recommendations and opinions of the High Authority shall state the reasons therefor, and shall take note of the opinions which the High Authority is required to obtain.

When such decisions and recommendations are individual in character, they shall be binding on the interested party upon their notification to him.

In other cases, they shall take effect automatically upon publication.

The High Authority shall determine the manner in which the provisions of the present Article are to be carried out.

Article 16. The High Authority shall take all appropriate measures of an internal nature to assure the functioning of its services....

Article 17. The High Authority shall publish annually, at least a month before the meeting of the Assembly, a general report on the activities of the Community and on its administrative expenditures.

Article 18. There shall be created a Consultative Committee, attached to the High Authority. It shall consist of not less than thirty and not more than fifty-one members, and shall include producers, workers and consumers and dealers in equal numbers.

The members of the Consultative Committee shall be appointed by the Council.

As concerns producers and workers, the Council shall designate the representative organizations among which it shall allocate the seats to be filled. Each organization shall be asked to draw up a list comprising twice the number of seats allocated to it. Designations shall be made from this list.

The members of the Consultative Committee shall be designated in their individual capacity. They shall not be bound by any mandate or instruction from the organizations which proposed them as candidates.

A President and officers shall be elected for one-year terms by the Consultative Committee from its own membership. The Committee shall fix its own rules of procedure.

The allowances of members of the Consultative Committee shall be determined by the Council on proposal by the High Authority.

Article 19. The High Authority may consult the Consultative Committee in any case it deems proper. It shall be required to do so whenever such consultation is prescribed by the present Treaty.

The High Authority shall submit to the Consultative Committee the general objectives and programme established under the terms of Article 46, and shall keep the Committee informed of the broad lines of its action under the terms of Articles 54, 65 and 66.

If the High Authority deems it necessary, it shall give the Consultative Committee a period in which to present its opinion of not less than ten days from the date of the notification to that effect addressed to the President of the Committee.

The Consultative Committee shall be convoked by its President, either at the request of the High Authority or at the request of a majority of its members, for the purpose of discussing a given question.

The minutes of the meetings shall be transmitted to the High Authority and to the Council at the same time as the opinions of the Committee.

Chapter II: The Assembly

Article 20. The Assembly, composed of representatives of the peoples of the Member States of the Community, shall exercise the supervisory powers which are granted to it by the present Treaty.

Article 21. The Assembly shall be composed of delegates whom the Parliaments of each of the Member States shall be called upon to designate once a year from among their own membership, or who shall be elected by direct universal suffrage, according to the procedure determined by each respective High Contracting Party.

The number of delegates is fixed as follows:

Germany	18
Belgium	10
France	18
Italy	18
Luxembourg	4
Netherlands	10

The representatives of the people of the Saar are included in the number of delegates attributed to France.

Article 22. The Assembly shall hold an annual session. It shall convene regularly on the second Tuesday in May. Its session may not last beyond the end of the then current fiscal year.

The Assembly may be convoked in extraordinary session on the request of the Council in order to state its opinion on such questions as may be put to it by the Council.

It may also meet in extraordinary session on the request of a majority of its members or of the High Authority.

Article 23. The Assembly shall designate its President and officers from among its membership.

The members of the High Authority may attend all meetings. The President of the High Authority or such of its members as it may designate shall be heard at their request.

The High Authority shall reply orally or in writing to all questions put to it by the Assembly or its members.

The members of the Council may attend all meetings and shall be heard at their request.

Article 24. The Assembly shall discuss in open session the general report submitted to it by the High Authority.

If a motion of censure on the report is presented to the Assembly, a vote may be taken thereon only after a period of not less than three days following its introduction, and such vote shall be by open ballot.

If the motion of censure is adopted by two-thirds of the members present and voting, representing a majority of the total membership, the members of the High Authority must resign in a body. They shall continue to carry out current business until their replacement in accordance with Article 10.

Article 25. The Assembly shall fix its own rules of procedure, by vote of a majority of its total membership.

The acts of the Assembly shall be published in a manner to be prescribed in such rules of procedure.

Chapter III: The Council

Article 26. The Council shall exercise its functions in the events and in the manner provided in the present Treaty in particular with a view to harmonizing the action of the High Authority and that of the Governments, which are responsible for the general economic policy of their countries.

To this end, the Council and the High Authority shall consult together and exchange information.

The Council may request the High Authority to examine all proposals and measures which it may deem necessary or appropriate for the realization of the common objectives.

Article 27. The Council shall be composed of representatives of the Member States. Each State shall designate thereto one of the members of its Government.

The Presidency of the Council shall be exercised for a term of three months by each member of the Council in rotation in the alphabetical order of the Member States.

Article 28. Meetings of the Council shall be called by its President on the request of a State or of the High Authority.

When the Council is consulted by the High Authority, it may deliberate without necessarily proceeding to a vote. The minutes of its meetings shall be forwarded to the High Authority.

Wherever the present Treaty requires the concurrence of the Council, this concurrence shall be deemed to have been granted if the proposal submitted by the High Authority is approved:

– by an absolute majority of the representatives of the Member States, including the vote of the representative of one of the States which produces at least 20 per cent of the total value of coal and steel produced in the Community;

– or, in case of an equal division of votes, and if the High Authority maintains its proposal after a second reading, by the representatives of two Member States, each of which produces at least 20 per cent of the total value of coal and steel in the Community.

Wherever the present Treaty requires a unanimous decision or unanimous concurrence, such decision or concurrence will be adopted if supported by the votes of all of the members of the Council.

The decisions of the Council, other than those which require a qualified majority or a unanimous vote, will be taken by a vote of the majority of the total membership. This majority shall be deemed to exist if it includes the absolute majority of the representatives of the Member States including the vote of the representative of one of the States which produces at least 20 per cent of the total value of coal and steel produced in the Community.

In case of a vote, any member of the Council may act as proxy for not more than one other member.

The Council shall communicate with the Member States through the intermediary of its President.

The acts of the Council shall be published under a procedure which it shall establish.

Article 29. The Council shall fix the salaries, allowances and pensions of the President of the High Authority, and of the President, the Judges, the Court Advocates and the Clerk of the Court.

Article 30. The Council shall establish its own rules of procedure.

Chapter IV: The Court

Article 31. The function of the Court is to ensure the rule of law in the interpretation and application of the present Treaty and of its implementing regulations.

Article 32. The Court shall be composed of seven Judges, appointed for six years by agreement among the Governments of the Member States from among persons of recognized independence and competence.

A partial change in membership of the

Court shall occur every three years, affecting alternatively three members and four members. The three members whose terms expire at the end of the first period of three years shall be designated by lot.

Judges shall be eligible for reappointment.

The number of Judges may be increased by unanimous vote of the Council on proposal by the Court.

Protocol between Britain, the United States, France, and the Federal Republic of Germany on the termination of the occupation régime, Paris, 23 October 1954

The United States of America, the United Kingdom of Great Britain and Northern Ireland, the French Republic and the Federal Republic of Germany agree as follows:

Article 1. The Convention on Relations between the Three Powers and the Federal Republic of Germany, the Convention on the Rights and Obligations of Foreign Forces and their Members in the Federal Republic of Germany, the Finance Convention, the Convention on the Settlement of Matters arising out of the War and the Occupation, signed at Bonn on 26 May 1952, the Protocol signed at Bonn on 27 June 1952 to correct certain textual errors in the aforementioned Conventions, and the Agreement on the Tax Treatment of the Forces and their Members signed at Bonn on 26 May 1952, as amended by the Protocol signed at Bonn on 26 July 1952, shall be amended in accordance with the five Schedules to the present Protocol and as so amended shall enter into force (together with subsidiary documents agreed by the signatory States relating to any of the aforementioned instruments) simultaneously with it.

Article 2. Pending the entry into force of the arrangements for the German Defence Contribution, the following provisions shall apply:
1. The rights heretofore held or exercised by the United States of America,

the United Kingdom of Great Britain and Northern Ireland and the French Republic relating to the fields of disarmament and demilitarization shall be retained and exercised by them, and nothing in any of the instruments mentioned in Article 1 of the present Protocol shall authorize the enactment, amendment, repeal or deprivation of effect of legislation or, subject to the provisions of paragraph 2 of this Article, executive action in those fields by any other authority.

2. On the entry into force of the present Protocol, the Military Security Board shall be abolished (without prejudice to the validity of any action or decisions taken by it) and the controls in the fields of disarmament and demilitarization shall thereafter be applied by a Joint Four-Power Commission to which each of the signatory States shall appoint one representative and which shall take its decisions by majority vote of the four members.

3. The Governments of the signatory States will conclude an administrative agreement which shall provide, in conformity with the provisions of this Article, for the establishment of the Joint Four-Power Commission and its staff and for the organization of its work.

Article 3. 1. The present Protocol shall be ratified or approved by the signatory States in accordance with their respective constitutional procedures. The Instruments of Ratification or Approval shall be deposited by the signatory States with the Government of the Federal Republic of Germany.

2. The present Protocol and subsidiary documents relating to it agreed between the signatory States shall enter into force upon the deposit by all the signatory States of the instruments of ratification or approval as provided in paragraph 1 of this Article.

3. The present Protocol shall be deposited in the Archives of the Government of the Federal Republic of Germany, which will furnish each signatory State with certified copies thereof and notify each State of the date of entry into force of the present Protocol.

[Signed] Dulles, Eden, Mendès-France, Adenauer.

Treaty between Belgium, the Federal Republic of Germany, France, Italy, Luxembourg and the Netherlands establishing the European Economic Community (Treaty of Rome), 25 March 1957

Part One · Principles

Article 1. By this Treaty, the High Contracting Parties establish among themselves a European Economic Community.

Article 2. The Community shall have as its task, by establishing a common market and progressively approximating the economic policies of Member States, to promote throughout the Community a harmonious development of economic activities, a continuous and balanced expansion, an increase in stability, an accelerated raising of the standard of living and closer relations between the States belonging to it.

Article 3. For the purposes set out in Article 2, the activities of the Community shall include, as provided in this Treaty and in accordance with the timetable set out therein:

(a) the elimination, as between Member States, of customs duties and of quantitative restrictions on the import and export of goods, and of all other measures having equivalent effect;

(b) the establishment of a common customs tariff and of a common commercial policy towards third countries;

(c) the abolition, as between Member States, of obstacles to freedom of movement for persons, services and capital;

(d) the adoption of a common policy in the sphere of agriculture;

(e) the adoption of a common policy in the sphere of transport;

(f) the institution of a system ensuring that competition in the common market is not distorted;

(g) the application of procedures by which the economic policies of Member States can be coordinated and disequilibria in their balances of payments remedied;

(h) the approximation of the laws of Member States to the extent required for the proper functioning of the common market;

(i) the creation of a European Social Fund in order to improve employment opportunities for workers and to contribute to the raising of their standard of living;

(j) the establishment of a European Investment Bank to facilitate the economic expansion of the Community by opening up fresh resources;

(k) the association of the overseas countries and territories in order to increase trade and to promote jointly economic and social development.

Article 4. 1. The tasks entrusted to the Community shall be carried out by the following institutions:

an Assembly,
a Council,
a Commission,
a Court of Justice.

Each institution shall act within the limits of the powers conferred upon it by this Treaty.

2. The Council and the Commission shall be assisted by an Economic and Social Committee acting in an advisory capacity.

Article 5. Member States shall take all appropriate measures, whether general or particular, to ensure fulfilment of the obligations arising out of this Treaty or resulting from action taken by the institutions of the Community. They shall facilitate the achievement of the Community's tasks.

They shall abstain from any measure which could jeopardize the attainment of the objectives of this Treaty.

Article 6. 1. Member States shall, in close cooperation with the institutions of the Community, coordinate their respective economic policies to the extent necessary to attain the objectives of this Treaty.

2. The institutions of the Community shall take care not to prejudice the internal and external financial stability of the Member States.

Article 7. Within the scope of application of this Treaty, and without prejudice to any special provisions contained therein, any discrimination on grounds of nationality shall be prohibited.

The Council may, on a proposal from the Commission and after consulting the Assembly, adopt, by a qualified majority, rules designed to prohibit such discrimination.

Article 8. 1. The common market shall be progressively established during a transitional period of twelve years. [Note: this period in practice was shortened to 1 July 1968.]

This transitional period shall be divided into three stages of four years each; the length of each stage may be altered in accordance with the provisions set out below.

2. To each stage there shall be assigned a set of actions to be initiated and carried through concurrently....

Part Two · Foundations of the Community

TITLE I: Free movement of goods

Article 9. 1. The Community shall be based upon a customs union which shall cover all trade in goods and which shall involve the prohibition between Member States of customs duties on imports and exports and of all charges having equivalent effect, and the adoption of a common customs tariff in their relations with third countries.

2. The provisions of Chapter 1, Section 1, and of Chapter 2 of this Title shall apply to products originating in Member States and to products coming from third countries which are in free circulation in Member States.

Article 10. 1. Products coming from a third country shall be considered to be in free circulation in a Member State if the import formalities have been complied with and any customs duties or charges having equivalent effect which are payable have been levied in that Member State, and if they have not benefited from a total or partial drawback of such duties or charges....

Article 11. Member States shall take all appropriate measures to enable Governments to carry out, within the periods of time laid down, the obligations with regard to customs duties which devolve upon them pursuant to this Treaty.

Chapter 1: The Customs Union

SECTION I · ELIMINATION OF CUSTOMS
DUTIES BETWEEN MEMBER STATES

Article 12. Member States shall refrain from introducing between themselves any new customs duties on imports or exports or any charges having equivalent effect, and from increasing those which they already apply in their trade with each other.

Article 13. 1. Customs duties on imports in force between Member States shall be progressively abolished by them during the transitional period in accordance with Articles 14 and 15....

[*Article 14*. Sets out timetable of reductions.]

• • •

SECTION 2 · SETTING UP OF THE
COMMON CUSTOMS TARIFF

Article 18. The Member States declare their readiness to contribute to the development of international trade and the lowering of barriers to trade by entering into agreements designed, on a basis of reciprocity and mutual advantage, to reduce customs duties below the general level of which they could avail themselves as a result of the establishment of a customs union between them.

[*Articles 19–28*. Provide for the setting up of an external trade barrier between the Common Market and the rest of the world – the common external tariff – and these articles also set out the detailed provisions of the tariffs.]

Article 29. In carrying out the tasks entrusted to it under this Section the Commission shall be guided by:

(a) the need to promote trade between Member States and third countries;

(b) developments in conditions of competition within the Community in so far as they lead to an improvement in the competitive capacity of undertakings;

(c) the requirements of the Community as regards the supply of raw materials and semi-finished goods; in this connec-

tion the Commission shall take care to avoid distorting conditions of competition between Member States in respect of finished goods;

(d) the need to avoid serious disturbances in the economies of Member States and to ensure rational development of production and an expansion of consumption within the Community.

Chapter 2: Elimination of quantitative restrictions between Member States

Article 30. Quantitative restrictions on imports and all measures having equivalent effect shall, without prejudice to the following provisions, be prohibited between Member States.

Article 31. Member States shall refrain from introducing between themselves any new quantitative restrictions or measures having equivalent effect.

This obligation shall, however, relate only to the degree of liberalization attained in pursuance of the decisions of the Council of the Organisation for European Economic Cooperation of 14 January 1955. Member States shall supply the Commission, not later than six months after the entry into force of this Treaty, with lists of the products liberalized by them in pursuance of these decisions. These lists shall be consolidated between Member States.

Article 32. In their trade with one another Member States shall refrain from making more restrictive the quotas and measures having equivalent effect existing at the date of the entry into force of this Treaty.

These quotas shall be abolished by the end of the transitional period at the latest. During that period, they shall be progressively abolished in accordance with the following provisions. [These are set out in Articles 33 to 36.]

Article 37. 1. Member States shall progressively adjust any State monopolies of a commercial character so as to ensure that when the transitional period has ended no discrimination regarding the conditions under which goods are procured and marketed exists between nationals of Member States....

TITLE II: Agriculture

Article 38. 1. The common market shall extend to agriculture and trade in agricultural products. 'Agricultural products' means the products of the soil, of stock-farming and of fisheries and products of first-stage processing directly related to these products....

Article 39. 1. The objectives of the common agricultural policy shall be:

(a) to increase agricultural productivity by promoting technical progress and by ensuring the rational development of agricultural production and the optimum utilization of the factors of production, in particular labour;

(b) thus to ensure a fair standard of living for the agricultural community, in particular by increasing the individual earnings of persons engaged in agriculture;

(c) to stabilize markets;

(d) to assure the availability of supplies;

(e) to ensure that supplies reach consumers at reasonable prices.

2. In working out the common agricultural policy and the special methods for its application, account shall be taken of:

(a) the particular nature of agricultural activity, which results from the social structure of agriculture and from structural and natural disparities between the various agricultural regions;

(b) the need to effect the appropriate adjustments by degrees;

(c) the fact that in the Member States agriculture constitutes a sector closely linked with the economy as a whole.

Article 40. 1. Member States shall develop the common agricultural policy by degrees during the transitional period and shall bring it into force by the end of that period at the latest.

2. In order to attain the objectives set out in Article 39 a common organiza-tion of agricultural markets shall be established....

...

Article 42. The provisions of the Chapter relating to rules on competition shall apply to production of and trade in agricultural products only to the extent determined by the Council within the framework of Article 43 (2) and (3) and in accordance with the procedure laid down therein, account being taken of the objectives set out in Article 39.

The Council may, in particular, authorize the granting of aid:

(a) for the protection of enterprises handicapped by structural or natural conditions;

(b) within the framework of economic development programmes.

[*Article 43.* Details of procedural steps to be taken by the Commission and Council to create the Common Agricultural Policy and to form the common agricultural market.]

Article 44. 1. In so far as progressive abolition of customs duties and quantitative restrictions between Member States may result in prices likely to jeopardize the attainment of the objectives set out in Article 39, each Member State shall, during the transitional period, be entitled to apply to particular products, in a non-discriminatory manner and in substitution for quotas and to such an extent as shall not impede the expansion of the volume of trade provided for in Article 45 (2), a system of minimum prices below which imports may be either:

temporarily suspended or reduced; or allowed, but subjected to the condition that they are made at a price higher than the minimum price for the product concerned.

In the latter case the minimum prices shall not include customs duties.

2. Minimum prices shall neither cause a reduction of the trade existing between Member States when this Treaty enters into force nor form an obstacle to progressive expansion of this trade. Mini-

mum prices shall not be applied so as to form an obstacle to the development of a natural preference between Member States.

3. As soon as this Treaty enters into force the Council shall, on a proposal from the Commission, determine objective criteria for the establishment of minimum price systems and for the fixing of such prices.

These criteria shall in particular take account of the average national production costs in the Member State applying the minimum price, of the position of the various undertakings concerned in relation to such average production costs, and of the need to promote both the progressive improvement of agricultural practice and the adjustments and specialization needed within the common market....

Article 45. 1. Until national market organizations have been replaced by one of the forms of common organization referred to in Article 40 (2), trade in products in respect of which certain Member States:

have arrangements designed to guarantee national producers a market for their products; and

are in need of imports,

shall be developed by the conclusion of long-term agreements or contracts between importing and exporting Member States.

These agreements or contracts shall be directed towards the progressive abolition of any discrimination in the application of these arrangements to the various producers within the Community.

Such agreements or contracts shall be concluded during the first stage; account shall be taken of the principle of reciprocity.

2. As regards quantities, these agreements or contracts shall be based on the average volume of trade between Member States in the products concerned during the three years before the entry into force of this Treaty and shall provide for an increase in the volume of trade within the limits of existing requirements, ac-

count being taken of traditional patterns of trade.

As regards prices, these agreements or contracts shall enable producers to dispose of the agreed quantities at prices which shall be progressively approximated to those paid to national producers on the domestic market of the purchasing country.

This approximation shall proceed as steadily as possible and shall be completed by the end of the transitional period at the latest.

Prices shall be negotiated between the parties concerned within the framework of directives issued by the Commission for the purpose of implementing the two preceding sub-paragraphs....

Article 46. Where in a Member State a product is subject to a national market organization or to internal rules having equivalent effect which affect the competitive position of similar production in another Member State, a countervailing charge shall be applied by Member States to imports of this product coming from the Member State where such organization or rules exist, unless that State applies a countervailing charge on export.

The Commission shall fix the amount of these charges at the level required to redress the balance; it may also authorize other measures, the conditions and details of which it shall determine.

Article 47. As to the functions to be performed by the Economic and Social Committee in pursuance of this Title, its agricultural section shall hold itself at the disposal of the Commission to prepare, in accordance with the provisions of Articles 197 and 198, the deliberations of the Committee.

TITLE III: Free movement of persons, services and capital

Chapter 1: Workers

Article 48. 1. Freedom of movement for workers shall be secured within the Community by the end of the transitional period at the latest.

2. Such freedom of movement shall entail the abolition of any discrimination based on nationality between workers of the Member States as regards employment, remuneration and other conditions of work and employment.

3. It shall entail the right, subject to limitations justified on grounds of public policy, public security or public health:

(a) to accept offers of employment actually made;

(b) to move freely within the territory of Member States for this purpose;

(c) to stay in a Member State for the purpose of employment in accordance with the provisions governing the employment of nationals of that State laid down by law, regulation or administrative action;

(d) to remain in the territory of a Member State after having been employed in that State, subject to conditions which shall be embodied in implementing regulations to be drawn up by the Commission.

4. The provisions of this Article shall not apply to employment in the public service.

Article 49. As soon as this Treaty enters into force, the Council shall, acting on a proposal from the Commission and after consulting the Economic and Social Committee, issue directives or make regulations setting out the measures required to bring about, by progressive stages, freedom of movement for workers, as defined in Article 48, in particular:

(a) by ensuring close cooperation between national employment services;

(b) by systematically and progressively abolishing those administrative procedures and practices and those qualifying periods in respect of eligibility for available employment, whether resulting from national legislation or from agreements previously concluded between Member States, the maintenance of which would form an obstacle to liberalization of the movement of workers;

(c) by systematically and progressively abolishing all such qualifying periods and other restrictions provided for either under national legislation or under agreements previously concluded between Member States as impose on workers of other Member States conditions regarding the free choice of employment other than those imposed on workers of the State concerned;

(d) by setting up appropriate machinery to bring offers of employment into touch with applications for employment and to facilitate the achievement of a balance between supply and demand in the employment market in such a way as to avoid serious threats to the standard of living and level of employment in the various regions and industries.

Article 50. Member States shall, within the framework of a joint programme, encourage the exchange of young workers.

Article 51. The Council shall, acting unanimously on a proposal from the Commission, adopt such measures in the field of social security as are necessary to provide freedom of movement for workers; to this end, it shall make arrangements to secure for migrant workers and their dependants:

(a) aggregation, for the purpose of acquiring and retaining the right to benefit and of calculating the amount of benefit, of all periods taken into account under the laws of the several countries;

(b) payment of benefits to persons resident in the territories of Member States.

Chapter 2: Right of establishment

Article 52. Within the framework of the provisions set out below, restrictions on the freedom of establishment of nationals of a Member State in the territory of another Member State shall be abolished by progressive stages in the course of the transitional period. Such progressive abolition shall also apply to restrictions on the setting up of agencies, branches or subsidiaries by nationals of any Member State established in the territory of any Member State.

Freedom of establishment shall include

the right to take up and pursue activities as self-employed persons and to set up and manage undertakings, in particular companies of firms within the meaning of the second paragraph of Article 58, under the conditions laid down for its own nationals by the law of the country where such establishment is effected, subject to the provisions of the Chapter relating to capital.

[*Articles 53–8*. Set out details of implementation.]

Chapter 3: Services

Article 59. Within the framework of the provisions set out below, restrictions on freedom to provide services within the Community shall be progressively abolished during the transitional period in respect of nationals of Member States who are established in a State of the Community other than that of the person for whom the services are intended.

The Council may, acting unanimously on a proposal from the Commission, extend the provisions of this Chapter to nationals of a third country who provide services and who are established within the Community.

[*Articles 60–6*. Set out details of implementation.]

Chapter 4: Capital

Article 67. 1. During the transitional period and to the extent necessary to ensure the proper functioning of the common market, Member States shall progressively abolish between themselves all restrictions on the movement of capital belonging to persons resident in Member States and any discrimination based on the nationality or on the place of residence of the parties or on the place where such capital is invested.

[*Articles 68–72*. Set out details of implementation.]

Article 73. 1. If movements of capital lead to disturbances in the functioning of the capital market in any Member State, the Commission shall, after consulting the Monetary Committee, authorize that State to take protective measures in the field of capital movements, the conditions and details of which the Commission shall determine.

The Council may, acting by a qualified majority, revoke this authorization or amend the conditions or details thereof.

2. A Member State which is in difficulties may, however, on grounds of secrecy or urgency, take the measures mentioned above, where this proves necessary, on its own initiative. The Commission and the other Member States shall be informed of such measures by the date of their entry into force at the latest. In this event the Commission may, after consulting the Monetary Committee, decide that the State concerned shall amend or abolish the measures.

TITLE IV: Transport

[*Articles 74–84*. Set out objectives and means of implementing a common transport policy covering road, rail, waterways and air transport.]

Part Three · Policy of the Community

TITLE I: Common rules

Chapter 1: Rules on competition

Section 1 · Rules applying to undertakings

Article 85. 1. The following shall be prohibited as incompatible with the common market: all agreements between undertakings, decisions by associations of undertakings and concerted practices which may affect trade between Member States and which have as their object or effect the prevention, restriction or distortion of competition within the common market, and in particular those which:

(a) directly or indirectly fix purchase or selling prices or any other trading conditions;

(b) limit or control production, markets, technical development, or investment;

(c) share markets or sources of supply. . . .

Article 86. Any abuse by one or more undertakings of a dominant position within the common market or in a substantial part of it shall be prohibited as incompatible with the common market in so far as it may affect trade between Member States. Such abuse may, in particular, consist in:

(a) directly or indirectly imposing unfair purchase or selling prices or other unfair trading conditions;

(b) limiting production, markets or technical development to the prejudice of consumers ...

Article 87. 1. Within three years of the entry into force of this Treaty the Council shall, acting unanimously on a proposal from the Commission and after consulting the Assembly, adopt any appropriate regulations or directives to give effect to the principles set out in Articles 85 and 86. ...

[*Articles 89–90.* Commission's powers of supervision and control.]

[*Article 91.* Commission's powers of supervision of injurious practices of dumping.]

SECTION 3 · AIDS GRANTED BY STATE

Article 92. 1. Save as otherwise provided in this Treaty, any aid granted by a Member State or through State resources in any form whatsoever which distorts or threatens to distort competition by favouring certain undertakings or the production of certain goods shall, in so far as it affects trade between Member States, be incompatible with the common market. ... [Exceptions are set out such as disaster aid and aid to promote economic development where standards of living are exceptionally low.]

Article 93. 1. The Commission shall, in cooperation with Member States, keep under constant review all systems of aid existing in those States. It shall propose to the latter any appropriate measures required by the progressive development or by the functioning of the common market ...

3. The Commission shall be informed, in sufficient time to enable it to submit its comments, of any plans to grant or alter aid. If it considers that any such plan is not compatible with the common market having regard to Article 92, it shall without delay initiate the procedure provided for in paragraph 2. The Member State concerned shall not put its proposed measures into effect until this procedure has resulted in a final decision.

Article 94. The Council may, acting by a qualified majority on a proposal from the Commission, make any appropriate regulations for the application of Articles 92 and 93 and may in particular determine the conditions in which Article 93 (3) shall apply and the categories of aid exempted from this procedure.

Chapter 2: Tax provisions

Article 95. No Member State shall impose, directly or indirectly, on the products of other Member States any internal taxation of any kind in excess of that imposed directly or indirectly on similar domestic products.

Furthermore, no Member State shall impose on the products of other Member States any internal taxation of such a nature as to afford indirect protection to other products.

Member States shall, not later than at the beginning of the second stage, repeal or amend any provisions existing when this Treaty enters into force which conflict with the preceding rules.

Article 96. Where products are exported to the territory of any Member State, any repayment of internal taxation shall not exceed the internal tax imposed on them, whether directly or indirectly.

[*Articles 97–9.* Details concerning introduction of value added tax.]

Chapter 3: Approximation of laws

Article 100. The Council shall, acting unanimously on a proposal from the Commission, issue directives for the approximation of such provisions laid down by law, regulation or administrative action in Member States as directly affect the establishment or functioning of the common market.

The Assembly and the Economic and Social Committee shall be consulted in the case of directives whose implementation would, in one or more Member States, involve the amendment of legislation.

Article 101. Where the Commission finds that a difference between the provisions laid down by law, regulation or administrative action in Member States is distorting the conditions of competition in the common market and that the resultant distortion needs to be eliminated, it shall consult the Member States concerned.

If such consultation does not result in an agreement eliminating the distortion in question, the Council shall, on a proposal from the Commission, acting unanimously during the first stage and by a qualified majority thereafter, issue the necessary directives. The Commission and the Council may take any other appropriate measures provided for in this Treaty.

...

TITLE II: Economic policy

Chapter 1: Conjunctural policy

Article 103. 1. Member States shall regard their conjunctural policies as a matter of common concern. They shall consult each other and the Commission on the measures to be taken in the light of the prevailing circumstances. ...

Chapter 2: Balance of payments

Article 104. Each Member State shall pursue the economic policy needed to ensure the equilibrium of its overall balance of payments and to maintain confidence in its currency, while taking care to ensure a high level of employment and a stable level of prices.

Article 105. 1. In order to facilitate attainment of the objectives set out in

Article 104, Member States shall coordinate their economic policies. They shall for this purpose provide for cooperation between their appropriate administrative departments and between their central banks.

The Commission shall submit to the Council recommendations on how to achieve such cooperation. ...

[*Article 106.* Abolition of restrictions on transfers of currency.]

Article 107. 1. Each Member State shall treat its policy with regard to rates of exchange as a matter of common concern.

2. If a Member State makes an alteration in its rate of exchange which is inconsistent with the objectives set out in Article 104 and which seriously distorts conditions of competition, the Commission may, after consulting the Monetary Committee, authorize other Member States to take for a strictly limited period the necessary measures, the conditions and details of which it shall determine, in order to counter the consequences of such alteration.

Article 108. 1. Where a Member State is in difficulties or is seriously threatened with difficulties as regards its balance of payments either as a result of an overall disequilibrium in its balance of payments, or as a result of the type of currency at its disposal, and where such difficulties are liable in particular to jeopardize the functioning of the common market or the progressive implementation of the common commercial policy, the Commission shall immediately investigate the position of the State in question and the action which, making use of all the means at its disposal, that State has taken or may take in accordance with the provisions of Article 104. The Commission shall state what measures it recommends the State concerned to take. ... [The Commission may authorize the State in difficulties to take protective measures.]

Article 109. 1. Where a sudden crisis in the balance of payments occurs and a decision within the meaning of Article

108 (2) is not immediately taken, the Member State concerned may, as a precaution, take the necessary protective measures. Such measures must cause the least possible disturbance in the functioning of the common market and must not be wider in scope than is strictly necessary to remedy the sudden difficulties which have arisen. . . .

3. After the Commission has delivered an opinion and the Monetary Committee has been consulted, the Council may, acting by a qualified majority, decide that the State concerned shall amend, suspend or abolish the protective measures referred to above.

Chapter 3: Commercial policy

Article 110. By establishing a customs union between themselves Member States aim to contribute, in the common interest, to the harmonious development of world trade, the progressive abolition of restrictions on international trade and the lowering of customs barriers.

The common commercial policy shall take into account the favourable effect which the abolition of customs duties between Member States may have on the increase in the competitive strength of undertakings in those States.

[*Articles 111–12.* Implementation.]

Article 113. 1. After the transitional period has ended, the common commercial policy shall be based on uniform principles, particularly in regard to changes in tariff rates, the conclusion of tariff and trade agreements, the achievement of uniformity in measures of liberalization, export policy and measures to protect trade such as those to be taken in case of dumping or subsidies.

2. The Commission shall submit proposals to the Council for implementing the common commercial policy.

3. Where agreements with third countries need to be negotiated, the Commission shall make recommendations to the Council, which shall authorize the Commission to open the necessary negotiations.

The Commission shall conduct these negotiations in consultation with a special committee appointed by the Council to assist the Commission in this task and within the framework of such directives as the Council may issue to it.

4. In exercising the powers conferred upon it by this Article, the Council shall act by a qualified majority.

Article 114. The agreements referred to in Article 111 (2) and in Article 113 shall be concluded by the Council on behalf of the Community, acting unanimously during the first two stages and by a qualified majority thereafter.

...

TITLE III: Social policy

Chapter 1: Social provisions

Article 117. Member States agree upon the need to promote improved working conditions and an improved standard of living for workers, so as to make possible their harmonization while the improvement is being maintained.

They believe that such a development will ensue not only from the functioning of the common market, which will favour the harmonization of social systems, but also from the procedures provided for in this Treaty and from the approximation of provisions laid down by law, regulation or administrative action.

Article 118. Without prejudice to the other provisions of this Treaty and in conformity with its general objectives, the Commission shall have the task of promoting close cooperation between Member States in the social field. . . .

Article 119. Each Member State shall during the first stage ensure and subsequently maintain the application of the principle that men and women should receive equal pay for equal work. . . .

...

Chapter 2: The European Social Fund

Article 123. In order to improve employment opportunities for workers in the common market and to contribute thereby to raising the standard of living, a European Social Fund is thereby established in accordance with the provisions set out below; it shall have the task of rendering the employment of workers easier and of increasing their geographical and occupational mobility within the Community.

Article 124. The Fund shall be administered by the Commission.

The Commission shall be assisted in this task by a Committee presided over by a member of the Commission and composed of representatives of Governments, trade unions and employers' organizations.

. . .

TITLE IV: The European Investment Bank

Article 129. A European Investment Bank is hereby established; it shall have legal personality.

The members of the European Investment Bank shall be the Member States.

The Statute of the European Investment Bank is laid down in a Protocol annexed to this Treaty.

Article 130. The task of the European Investment Bank shall be to contribute, by having recourse to the capital market and utilizing its own resources, to the balanced and steady development of the common market in the interest of the Community. For this purpose the Bank shall, operating on a non-profit-making basis, grant loans and give guarantees which facilitate the financing of the following projects in all sectors of the economy:

(a) projects for developing less developed regions;

(b) projects for modernizing or converting undertakings or for developing fresh activities called for by the progressive establishment of the common market, where these projects are of such a size or nature that they cannot be entirely

financed by the various means available in the individual Member States;

(c) projects of common interest to several Member States which are of such a size or nature that they cannot be entirely financed by the various means available in the individual Member States.

Part Four · Association of the overseas countries and territories

Article 131. The Member States agree to associate with the Community the non-European countries and territories which have special relations with Belgium, France, Italy and the Netherlands. These countries and territories (hereinafter called 'the countries and territories') are listed in Annex IV to this Treaty.

The purpose of association shall be to promote the economic and social development of the countries and territories and to establish close economic relations between them and the Community as a whole.

In accordance with the principles set out in the Preamble to this Treaty, association shall serve primarily to further the interests and prosperity of the inhabitants of these countries and territories in order to lead them to the economic, social and cultural development to which they aspire.

. . .

Part Five · Institutions of the Community

TITLE I: Provisions governing the institutions

Chapter 1: *The institutions*

SECTION I · THE ASSEMBLY

Article 137. The Assembly, which shall consist of representatives of the peoples of the States brought together in the Community, shall exercise the advisory and supervisory powers which are conferred upon it by this Treaty.

Article 138. 1. The Assembly shall consist of delegates who shall be designated by the respective Parliaments from among their members in accordance with the procedure laid down by each Member State.

When the Treaty of Accession enters into force the number of delegates to the Assembly will be as follows [but note that since Norway has not joined an adjustment needs to be made] :

Belgium	14
Denmark	10
Germany	36
France	36
Ireland	10
Italy	36
Luxembourg	6
Netherlands	14
(Norway	10)
United Kingdom	36

[*Articles 139-43.* Procedures of Assembly.]

Article 144. If a motion of censure on the activities of the Commission is tabled before it, the Assembly shall not vote thereon until at least three days after the motion has been tabled and only by open vote.

If the motion of censure is carried by a two-thirds majority of the votes cast, representing a majority of the members of the Assembly, the members of the Commission shall resign as a body. They shall continue to deal with current business until they are replaced in accordance with Article 158.

Article 145. To ensure that the objectives set out in this Treaty are attained, the Council shall, in accordance with the provisions of this Treaty:

ensure coordination of the general economic policies of the Member States; have power to take decisions.

Article 146. The Council shall consist of representatives of the Member States. Each Government shall delegate to it one of its members.

The office of president shall be held for a term of six months by each member of the Council in turn ...

Article 147. The Council shall meet when convened by its President on his own initiative or at the request of one of its members or of the Commission.

Article 148. 1. Save as otherwise provided in this Treaty, the Council shall act by a majority of its members.

2. Where the Council is required to act by a qualified majority, the votes of its members shall be weighted as follows:

Belgium	2
Germany	4
France	4
Italy	4
Luxembourg	1
Netherlands	2

For their adoption, acts of the Council shall require at least:

twelve votes in favour where this Treaty requires them to be adopted on a proposal from the Commission, twelve votes in favour, cast by at least four members, in other cases.

3. Abstentions by members present in person or represented shall not prevent the adoption by the Council of acts which require unanimity.

[With the Accession Treaty in force the weighting of votes as provided for by that treaty are as follows – but note that since Norway has not joined an adjustment needs to be made:

Belgium	5
Denmark	3
Germany	10
France	10
Ireland	3
Italy	10
Luxembourg	2
Netherlands	5
(Norway	3)
United Kingdom	10]

Article 149. Where, in pursuance of this Treaty, the Council acts on a proposal from the Commission, unanimity shall be required for an act constituting an amendment to that proposal.

As long as the Council has not acted,

the Commission may alter its original proposal, in particular where the Assembly has been consulted on that proposal.

...

Article 155. In order to ensure the proper functioning and development of the common market, the Commission shall:

ensure that the provisions of this Treaty and the measures taken by the institutions pursuant thereto are applied;
formulate recommendations or deliver opinions on matters dealt with in this Treaty, if it expressly so provides or if the Commission considers it necessary;
have its own power of decision and participate in the shaping of measures taken by the Council and by the Assembly in the manner provided for in this Treaty;
exercise the powers conferred on it by the Council for the implementation of the rules laid down by the latter.

...

Article 157 [as revised by Article 10 of the Merger Treaty]. 1. The Commission shall consist of nine members, who shall be chosen on the grounds of their general competence and whose independence is beyond doubt.

The number of members of the Commission may be altered by the Council, acting unanimously.

Only nationals of Member States may be members of the Commission.

The Commission must include at least one national of each of the Member States, but may not include more than two members having the nationality of the same State.

2. The members of the Commission shall, in the general interest of the Communities, be completely independent in the performance of their duties.

In the performance of these duties, they shall neither seek nor take instructions from any Government or from any body. They shall refrain from any action incompatible with their duties. Each Member State undertakes to respect this principle and not to seek to influence the members of the Commission in the performance of their tasks.

The members of the Commission may not, during their term of office, engage in any other occupation, whether gainful or not. When entering upon their duties they shall give a solemn undertaking that, both during and after their term of office, they will respect the obligations arising therefrom and in particular their duty to behave with integrity and discretion as regards the acceptance, after they have ceased to hold office, of certain appointments or benefits. In the event of any breach of these obligations, the Court of Justice may, on application by the Council or the Commission, rule that the member concerned be, according to the circumstances, either compulsorily retired in accordance with the provisions of Article 13 or deprived of his right to a pension or other benefits in its stead.

[The Treaty of Accession increased the number of Commissioners from nine to fourteen, but at that time Norway was included in the calculation. In fact there are thirteen members of the Commission.]

Article 158. The members of the Commission shall be appointed by common accord of the Governments of the Member States.

Their term of office shall be four years. It shall be renewable.

...

Article 163. The Commission shall act by a majority of the number of members provided for in Article 157.

A meeting of the Commission shall be valid only if the number of members laid down in its rules of procedure is present.

SECTION 4 · THE COURT OF JUSTICE

Article 164. The Court of Justice shall ensure that in the interpretation and application of this Treaty the law is observed.

Article 165. The Court of Justice shall consist of seven Judges ... [The Treaty of Accession increased this number to eleven, but Norway was included.]

Article 166. The Court of Justice shall be assisted by two Advocates-General.

It shall be the duty of the Advocate-General, acting with complete impartiality and independence, to make, in open court, reasoned submissions on cases brought before the Court of Justice, in order to assist the Court in the performance of the task assigned to it in Article 164. . . .

Article 167. The Judges and Advocates-General shall be chosen from persons whose independence is beyond doubt and who possess the qualifications required for appointment to the highest judicial offices in their respective countries or who are jurisconsults of recognized competence; they shall be appointed by common accord of the Governments of the Member States for a term of six years. . . .

. . .

Article 169. If the Commission considers that a Member State has failed to fulfil an obligation under this Treaty, it shall deliver a reasoned opinion on the matter after giving the State concerned the opportunity to submit its observations.

If the State does not comply with the opinion within the period laid down by the Commission, the latter may bring the matter before the Court of Justice.

Article 170. A Member State which considers that another Member State has failed to fulfil an obligation under this Treaty may bring the matter before the Court of Justice.

Before a Member State brings an action against another Member State for an alleged infringement of an obligation under this Treaty, it shall bring the matter before the Commission.

The Commission shall deliver an opinion after each of the States concerned has been given the opportunity to submit its own case and its observations on the other party's case both orally and in writing.

If the Commission has not delivered an opinion within three months of the date on which the matter was brought before it, the absence of such opinion shall not prevent the matter being brought before the Court of Justice.

Article 171. If the Court of Justice finds that a Member State has failed to fulfil an obligation under this Treaty, the State shall be required to take the necessary measures to comply with the judgement of the Court of Justice.

Article 172. Regulations made by the Council pursuant to the provisions of this Treaty may give the Court of Justice unlimited jurisdiction in regard to the penalties provided for in such regulations.

Article 173. The Court of Justice shall review the legality of acts of the Council and the Commission other than recommendations or opinions. It shall for this purpose . . .

. . .

Article 175. Should the Council or the Commission, in infringement of this Treaty, fail to act, the Member States and the other institutions of the Community may bring an action before the Court of Justice to have the infringement established . . .

. . .

Article 177. The Court of Justice shall have jurisdiction to give preliminary rulings concerning:

(a) the interpretation of this Treaty;

(b) the validity and interpretation of acts of the institutions of the Community;

(c) the interpretation of the statutes of bodies established by an act of the Council, where those statutes so provide. . . .

. . .

Article 182. The Court of Justice shall have jurisdiction in any dispute between Member States which relates to the subject matter of this Treaty if the dispute is submitted to it under a special agreement between the parties.

...

Chapter 2: Provisions common to several institutions

Article 189. In order to carry out their task the Council and the Commission shall, in accordance with the provisions of this Treaty, make regulations, issue directives, take decisions, make recommendations or deliver opinions.

A regulation shall have general application. It shall be binding in its entirety and directly applicable in all Member States.

A directive shall be binding, as to the result to be achieved, upon each Member State to which it is addressed, but shall leave to the national authorities the choice of form and methods.

A decision shall be binding in its entirety upon those to whom it is addressed.

Recommendations and opinions shall have no binding force.

...

Article 192. Decisions of the Council or of the Commission which impose a pecuniary obligation on persons other than States shall be enforceable.

Enforcement shall be governed by the rules of civil procedure in force in the State in the territory of which it is carried out.

Chapter 3: The Economic and Social Committee

Article 193. An Economic and Social Committee is hereby established. It shall have advisory status.

The Committee shall consist of representatives of the various categories of economic and social activity, in particular, representatives of producers, farmers, carriers, workers, dealers, craftsmen, professional occupations and representatives of the general public.

...

Article 198. The Committee must be consulted by the Council or by the Commission where this Treaty so provides. The Committee may be consulted by these institutions in all cases in which they consider it appropriate. ...

TITLE II: Financial provisions

Article 199. All items of revenue and expenditure of the Community, including those relating to the European Social Fund, shall be included in estimates to be drawn up for each financial year and shall be shown in the budget.

The revenue and expenditure shown in the budget shall be in balance.

Article 200. 1. The budget revenue shall include, irrespective of any other revenue, financial contributions of Member States on the following scale:

Belgium	7·9
Germany	28·0
France	28·0
Italy	28·0
Luxembourg	0·2
Netherlands	7·9

2. The financial contributions of Member States to cover the expenditure of the European Social Fund, however, shall be determined on the following scale:

Belgium	8·8
Germany	32·0
France	32·0
Italy	20·0
Luxembourg	0·2
Netherlands	7·0

3. The scales may be modified by the Council, acting unanimously.

...

Part Six · General and final provisions

[*Articles 210-40.* These include provisions for regulations covering officials and servants of the Community and official languages.]

Article 228. 1. Where this Treaty provides for the conclusion of agreements between the Community and one or more States or an international organization, such agreements shall be negotiated by the Commission. Subject to the powers vested in the Commission in this field, such agreements shall be concluded by the Council, after consulting the Assembly where required by this Treaty. . . .

. . .

Article 236. The Government of any Member State or the Commission may submit to the Council proposals for the amendment of this Treaty.

If the Council, after consulting the Assembly and, where appropriate, the Commission, delivers an opinion in favour of calling a conference of representatives of the Governments of the Member States, the conference shall be convened by the President of the Council for the purpose of determining by common accord the amendments to be made to this Treaty.

The amendments shall enter into force after being ratified by all the Member States in accordance with their respective constitutional requirements.

Article 237. Any European State may apply to become a member of the Community. It shall address its application to the Council, which shall act unanimously after obtaining the opinion of the Commission.

The conditions of admission and the adjustments to this Treaty necessitated thereby shall be the subject of an agreement between the Member States and the applicant State. This agreement shall be submitted for ratification by all the contracting States in accordance with their respective constitutional requirements.

Article 238. The Community may conclude with a third State, a union of States or an international organization agreements establishing an association involving reciprocal rights and obligations, common action and special procedures.

These agreements shall be concluded by the Council, acting unanimously after consulting the Assembly.

Where such agreements call for amendments to this Treaty, these amendments shall first be adopted in accordance with the procedure laid down in Article 236.

. . .

[*Articles 247–8.* Ratification by High Contracting Parties in accordance with their respective constitutional requirements. Dutch, French, German and Italian equally authentic languages of original treaty.]

In witness whereof, the undersigned plenipotentiaries have signed this Treaty.

Done at Rome this twenty-fifth day of March in the year one thousand nine hundred and fifty-seven.

P. H. Spaak
Adenauer
Pineau
Antonio Segni
Bech
J. Luns
J. Ch. Snoy et d'Oppuers
Hallstein
M. Faure
Gaetano Martino
Lambert Schaus
J. Linthorst Homan

Convention establishing the European Free Trade Association (EFTA), Stockholm, 4 January 1960

[Austria, Denmark, Norway, Portugal, Sweden, Switzerland and Britain ...]

Having regard to the Convention for European Economic Cooperation of 16th April 1948, which established the Organization for European Economic Cooperation;

Resolved to maintain and develop the cooperation instituted within that organization;

Determined to facilitate the early establishment of a multilateral association for the removal of trade barriers and the promotion of closer economic cooperation between the Members of the Organization for European Economic Cooperation, including the Members of the European Economic Community;

Having regard to the General Agreement on Tariffs and Trade;

Resolved to promote the objectives of that Agreement;

Have agreed as follows:

Article 1: The Association. 1. An international organization to be known as the European Free Trade Association, hereinafter referred to as 'the Association', is hereby established.

2. The Members of the Association, hereinafter referred to as 'Member States', shall be the States which ratify this Convention and such other States as may accede to it.

3. The Area of the Association shall be the territories to which this Convention applies.

4. The Institutions of the Association shall be a Council and such other organs as the Council may set up.

Article 2: Objectives. The objectives of the Association shall be

(a) to promote in the Area of the Association and in each Member State a sustained expansion of economic activity, full employment, increased productivity and the rational use of resources, financial stability and continuous improvement in living standards,

(b) to secure that trade between Member States takes place in conditions of fair competition,

(c) to avoid significant disparity between Member States in the conditions of supply of raw materials produced within the Area of the Association, and

(d) to contribute to the harmonious development and expansion of world trade and to the progressive removal of barriers to it.

Article 3: Import duties. 1. Member States shall reduce and ultimately eliminate, in accordance with this Article, customs duties and any other charges with equivalent effect, except duties notified in accordance with Article 6 and other charges which fall within that Article, imposed on or in connection with the importation of goods which are eligible for Area tariff treatment in accordance with Article 4. Any such duty or other charge is hereinafter referred to as an 'import duty'.

2. (a) On and after each of the following dates, Member States shall not apply an import duty on any product at a level exceeding the percentage of the basic duty specified against that date [reducing from 80 per cent on 1 July 1960 to 10 per cent on 1 January 1969].

(b) On and after 1st January 1970, Member States shall not apply any import duties. . . .

[*Articles 4-29.* Cooperation, trading practices etc.]

Article 30: Economic and financial policies. Member States recognize that the economic and financial policies of each of them affect the economies of other Member States and intend to pursue those policies in a manner which serves to promote the objectives of the Association. They shall periodically exchange views on all aspects of those policies. In so doing, they shall take into account the corresponding activities within the Organization for European Economic Cooperation and other international organizations. The Council may make recommendations to Member States on matters relating to those policies to the extent necessary to ensure the attainment of the objectives and the smooth operation of the Association.

Article 31: General consultations and complaints procedures. 1. If any Member considers that any benefit conferred upon it by this Convention or any objective of the Association is being or may be frustrated and if no satisfactory settlement is reached between the Member States concerned, any of those Member States may refer the matter to the Council.

2. The Council shall promptly, by majority vote, make arrangements for examining the matter. Such arrangements may include a reference to an examining committee constituted in accordance with Article 33. Before taking action under paragraph 3 of this Article, the Council shall so refer the matter at the request of any Member State concerned. Member States shall furnish all information which they can make available and shall lend their assistance to establish the facts.

3. When considering the matter, the Council shall have regard to whether it has been established that an obligation under the Convention has not been fulfilled, and whether and to what extent any benefit conferred by the Convention or any objective of the Association is being or may be frustrated. In the light of this consideration and of the report of any examining committee which may have been appointed, the Council may, by majority vote, make to any Member State such recommendations as it considers appropriate.

4. If a Member State does not or is un-able to comply with a recommendation made in accordance with paragraph 3 of this Article and the Council finds, by majority vote, that an obligation under this Convention has not been fulfilled, the Council may, by majority decision, authorize any Member State to suspend to the Member State which has not complied with the recommendation the application of such obligations under this Convention as the Council considers appropriate.

5. Any Member State may, at any time while the matter is under consideration, request the Council to authorize, as a matter of urgency, interim measures to safeguard its position. If it appears to the Council that the circumstances are sufficiently serious to justify interim action, and without prejudice to any action which it may subsequently take in accordance with the preceding paragraphs of this Article, the Council may, by majority decision, authorize a Member State to suspend its obligations under this Convention to such an extent and for such a period as the Council considers appropriate.

Article 32: The Council. 1. It shall be the responsibility of the Council

(a) to exercise such powers and functions as are conferred upon it by this Convention,

(b) to supervise the application of this Convention and keep its operation under review, and

(c) to consider whether further action should be taken by Member States in order to promote the attainment of the objectives of the Association and to facilitate the establishment of closer links with other States, unions of States or international organizations.

2. Each Member State shall be represented in the Council and shall have one vote.

3. The Council may decide to set up such organs, committees and other bodies as it considers necessary to assist it in accomplishing its tasks.

4. In exercising its responsibility under

paragraph 1 of this Article, the Council may take decisions which shall be binding on all Member States and may make recommendations to Member States.

5. Decisions and recommendations of the Council shall be made by unanimous vote, except in so far as this Convention provides otherwise. Decisions or recommendations shall be regarded as unanimous unless any Member State casts a negative vote. Decisions and recommendations which are to be made by majority vote require the affirmative vote of four Member States.

6. If the number of the Member States changes, the Council may decide to amend the number of votes required for decisions and recommendations which are to be made by majority vote.

[*Article 33*. Composition of Examining Committees to be appointed by the Council.]

[*Article 34*. Administrative arrangements of the Association.]

[*Article 35*. Legal capacity, privileges and immunities.]

[*Article 36*. Relations with international organizations.]

[*Article 37*. Obligations under other international agreements.]

[*Articles 39-40*. Ratification and entry into force.]

Article 41: Accession and association. 1. Any State may accede to this Convention, provided that the Council decides to approve its accession, on such terms and conditions as may be set out in that decision. The instrument of accession shall be deposited with the Government of Sweden which shall notify all other Member States. This Convention shall enter into force in relation to an acceding State on the date indicated in that decision.

2. The Council may negotiate an agreement between the Member States and any other State, union of States or international organization, creating an association embodying such reciprocal rights and obligations, common actions and special procedures as may be appropriate. Such an agreement shall be submitted to the Member States for acceptance and shall enter into force provided that it is accepted by all Member States. Instruments of acceptance shall be deposited with the Government of Sweden which shall notify all other Member States.

Article 42: Withdrawal. Any Member State may withdraw from this Convention provided that it gives twelve months' notice in writing to the Government of Sweden which shall notify all other Member States.

[*Article 43*. Territorial application.]

[*Article 44*. Amendments require agreement of all Member States.]

XV · The conflicts and alignments of Asia, 1945-73

Since 1945, warfare has never ceased in one or more of the regions of Asia. Internal civil wars, conflicts between the new Nation States of Asia, the Great Power involvement in the 'cold war' – all of these, often interrelated and occurring simultaneously have made Asia an area of intense conflict in world diplomacy. In categorizing the conflicts of Asia after the defeat of Japan, over-lapping geographical regions and phases of time can be distinguished.

South and south-eastern Asia, with the exception of the Philippines (U.S.), once formed part of the European empires principally of Britain (India, Ceylon, Burma, the Malay States and Straits Settlement), of the Netherlands (Nether-land East Indies), and of France (Indo-China). Thailand was the only sizeable independent Asian State in this part of the world. During the years from 1946 to 1957 European control ceased and was replaced by Asian National States. The Philippines gained independence in July 1946, India and Pakistan in August 1947, Burma in January 1948, Ceylon in February 1948, and Indonesia in December 1949. Indo-China, which the French left in the period 1954-6, has been the scene of continued conflict. Malaya gained independence in August 1957.

The zone of eastern and north-eastern Asia comprises mainland China, Taiwan, Japan, Korea and the Soviet Union. Finally, the great landmass of Central Asia is dominated by China, Mongolia, Afghanistan, Chinese Tibet and the Soviet Union (see map on p. 432).

India, Pakistan and the problems of Kashmir; the Chinese border since 1947

The transfer of power in the Indian subcontinent to the independent States of Pakistan and India on midnight 14-15 August 1947 was marred by large-scale

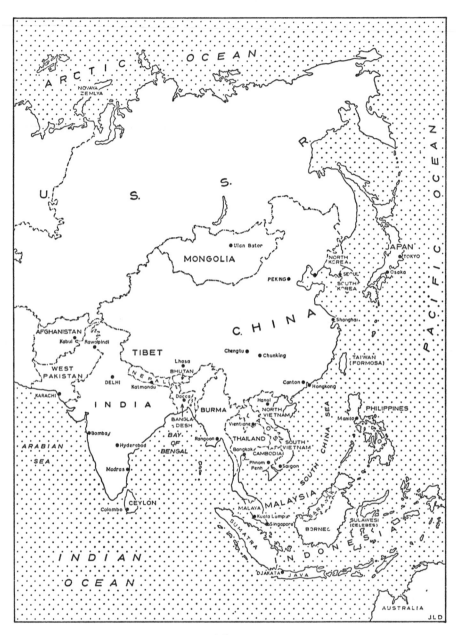

6 Asia, 1972

bloodshed as Hindu and Moslem minorities were attacked and many killed. Britain accepted the claims that a separate Muslim State should be created and that the Muslims could not all be incorporated in an Indian Government. Thus Pakistan as a nation owed its existence to the separate national right of Muslims. The State carved out of the areas of Muslim majorities in India comprised one region in the west separated by more than 1,000 miles from another region in the east. Despite large population movements fleeing in fear of their lives at the time of independence, large Hindu minorities remained in what became Pakistan, and millions of Muslims became Indian citizens, India rejecting religion as a basis of nationality. The rulers of the 562 Indian States, who had ruled under British paramountcy before 1947, were advised by the British to choose to accede to either Pakistan or India. This process was carried through with surprisingly few complications, except for three States: Hyderabad and Junagarh, both occupied by Indian forces, and the State of Kashmir and Jammu, whose unresolved relationship to India and Pakistan became a dominant issue and cause of conflict between India and Pakistan.

The Maharaja of Kashmir was a Hindu ruling over a population which was predominantly Muslim. He made no choice for either State as in the partition months of August and September 1947 communal strife, armed insurrection and massacres by bands crossing Kashmir, occurred. In October 1947 Pathan tribesmen invaded Kashmir from the territory of Pakistan. This brought the Maharaja's rule to the verge of collapse. In return for Indian military help, *the Maharaja on 26 October 1947 signed a Treaty of Accession with India*. It was accepted, but Nehru at the time promised that the ultimate future fate of Kashmir and Jammu would be left for the people of Kashmir to decide when law and order had been restored. From 1947 to 1948 India and Pakistan fought in Kashmir. On 1 January 1949 a ceasefire was agreed upon and a ceasefire line established in Kashmir on 27 July 1949. But the unresolved dispute continued to embitter and dominate the relations between India and Pakistan, and to influence the relations and alignments of Pakistan and India with the Great Powers contesting influence in Asia from Korea to Afghanistan.

Pakistan joined the Western anti-communist alliances of SEATO and CENTO in 1954, and received arms and economic assistance from the United States intended for anti-communist use, to strengthen its defences against China and the Soviet Union. With the deterioration of Chinese–Indian relations and the outbreak of fighting over the dispute of the Sino-Indian border (p. 434), Pakistan drew closer to China as an ally against India, and thus ceased to be regarded as a firm ally of the West. On 14 July 1972 President Bhutto declared Pakistan had withdrawn from SEATO but would reactivate its membership of CENTO.

Indian foreign policy was only partly shaped to meet the threat of conflict with the smaller Pakistan. Nehru in the 1950s espoused the cause of non-aligned nations, neutrals in the conflict between the Western Powers and the Soviet Union, and freedom from colonial rule; he also sought a combination of the less developed African and Asian nations so that they might assert themselves in a world dominated by Great Powers. *The Bandung Conference, April 1955*, attended by the representatives of twenty-nine African and Asian States, meant different things to different participants. To some, including Chou En-lai who attended the conference, it symbolized anti-Western nationalism. For Nehru it symbolized non-aligned Asian nationalism and Asian cooperation internationally with non-aligned African States (six African States attended), and so became the prototype of later Afro-Asian solidarity conferences. Subsequent conferences of unaligned nations have been held in Belgrade in September 1961, Cairo in October 1964 and Belgrade in 1969, but to date the impact of a concerted non-aligned block of Powers on international relations has been limited.

India's espousal of positive neutralism was also illustrated in *April 1954* with the signature of a *Chinese–Indian Commercial Treaty* which recognized Chinese suzerainty over Tibet (occupied by China in 1950). To this treaty were attached the Five Principles of Coexistence. Nehru established better relations with both the Soviet Union and China. Khrushchev's and Bulganin's visit to India in 1955 was utilized to demonstrate Soviet support for India's position in Pakistan. But Pakistan had by then joined the anti-Soviet alliances of SEATO and CENTO. Thus the 'cold war' and Kashmir dispute became intertwined as each State attempted to utilize this conflict to further its own objectives.

Fighting broke out again in the autumn of 1962, not over the Kashmir dispute as such but over the still unsettled frontiers of India and Kashmir with China. This frontier, running through some of the most desolate regions of the world, has not been entirely delimited or demarcated during the period of British rule or since independence. Legally the issue is exceedingly complex, rival maps making rival claims. The most serious dispute concerned the frontiers of north-eastern Kashmir in a region known as Aksai Chin, through which the Chinese were building a road connecting Chinese Tibet and Sinkiang; the second frontier in dispute lies between Kashmir and Nepal; the third, a very small area, is the Sikkim frontier between Nepal and Bhutan; the fourth and largest area lies between Bhutan and Burma in the Assam Himalayas.

The good relations between China and India began deteriorating after 1959 for several reasons: rivalry between Chinese and Indian influence developed in the independent State of Nepal (the two other Himalayan States, Bhutan and Sikkim, are under Indian control); the Dalai Lama found refuge in India after the Tibetan revolt of 1959 which drew world attention to Chinese subjugation in Tibet; finally, conflict developed over the disputed sections of the Indo-Chinese borders. A Chinese military demonstration in strength in Assam routed the defending Indian troops in October and November 1962, and China invaded India before withdrawing. A ceasefire between China and India was arranged in December 1962. Pakistan signed a border agreement with China in March 1963. The Chinese invasion led to Indian military reorganization and Britain and the United States sent military equipment and aid to India.

In August 1965 renewed tension along the Indian–West Pakistan frontier erupted into full-scale war in Kashmir, and on other sectors of the front between India and Pakistan in September 1965. Neither side could win a decisive victory and both accepted a U.N. 'demand' for a ceasefire which came into force on 23 September 1965. With the Soviet Union acting as mediator, Kosygin invited Shastri (India) and Ayub Khan (Pakistan) to *a conference at Tashkent, 3 January–10 January 1966*, which resulted in an agreement. The *Tashkent Declaration, 10 January 1966*, placed the Kashmir dispute on ice, restored normal Indian–Pakistan relations, and provided that the armies of both sides would withdraw to the positions they had occupied before the fighting began in August 1965; discussions were to be continued on all differences. *India signed a Treaty of Peace and Friendship and Cooperation with the Soviet Union, 9 August 1971*, which strengthened its position faced with a new crisis in relations with Pakistan. The concrete terms of the treaty were 'negative' in character. The two signatories undertook not to join any military alliances directed against each other (Article 8), and not to provide assistance to any other State engaged in armed conflict with one of the signatories, but immediately to consult with each other if one of the signatories is attacked or under threat of attack (Article 9). Thus neither signatory is committed to come to the aid of its treaty partner. The remaining articles deal with principles of cooperation in various spheres, and the Soviet Union expresses its support of the Indian policy of non-alignment.

Civil War in Pakistan between the eastern and western parts of the State began in March 1971, and was the cause of the third outbreak of war between Pakistan and India. The Muslims, who formed the Bengali population of Eastern Pakistan, had been to the forefront in 1947 in demanding a separate Muslim Pakistan State and secession from India. But the Bengalis of East Pakistan soon resented the imposition of rule by the Urdu-speaking West Pakistanis, whose population was smaller than that of East Pakistan but whose share of wealth and area of land was greater. On 25 March 1971 the West Pakistani army began ruthless military operations in East Pakistan to suppress an incipient independence movement. Some ten million refugees fled to India during the course of the following nine months, whilst among the Bengali East Pakistan population, bands of guerrilla freedom-fighters were formed. The Pakistan army, who were supported by some Urdu-speaking Bihari Moslems (the Biharis had originally left India in 1947 to escape Hindu domination), attempted to suppress Bengali nationalism savagely. India meantime housed the refugees and gave increasing support to the Bengali Government in exile – the Bangladesh Government. Pakistan launched air attacks on India, and on 6 December 1971 Pakistan and India were at war. In East Pakistan Indian forces were entirely victorious, and a new State of *Bangladesh* emerged on 16 December 1971 as the third State on the Indian subcontinent. India and Pakistan agreed to a ceasefire on 17 December 1971. Six months later, at the *Simla Conference, 28 June–2 July 1972*, President Bhutto of Pakistan and Mrs Gandhi, Prime Minister of India, reached an agreement. Indian and Pakistani armed forces were to be withdrawn each to their side of the pre-war (5 December 1971) frontier. This was a considerable concession to Pakistan as India was holding far more West Pakistan territory than the Indian territory the Pakistanis were occupying. But the agreement concerning Kashmir and Jammu stated that 'the line of control resulting from the ceasefire line of *December 17, 1971*, shall be respected by both sides without prejudice to the recognized position of either side'. The exchange of prisoners of war was one of several difficult questions which it was agreed should be left to later negotiations, since Bangladesh has demanded war crimes trials and Pakistan refuses to recognize Bangladesh (April 1973). The prisoners held by India and Pakistan captured on India's western front have been exchanged, but some 90,000 Pakistani prisoners removed by India from Bangladesh remain in camps in India in April 1973. The Kashmir and Jammu dispute also awaits a final settlement.

Indian troops withdrew from Bangladesh on 12 March 1972 and a week later *India and Bangladesh signed a Treaty of Friendship and Cooperation, 19 March 1972*, which looked forward to cooperation and which contained the undertaking that neither signatory would join alliances directed against the other or give assistance to an aggressor. In the event of an attack, or threatened attack, both signatories would immediately consult together.

Ceylon gained its independence on 4 February 1948, but in foreign policy has followed the Indian lead in non-alignment during the 1950s. At the time of independence Ceylon entered into defence agreements with Britain, but these were terminated in 1956 and 1957.

South-east Asia: Burma, the Philippines, Malaysia and Indo-China

Burma gained independence on 4 January 1948. Like Ceylon, Burma was determined not to become involved in the 'cold war'. After years of tension, communist insurgency, separatist movements and Nationalist Chinese insurgency, when the Burmese army faced a variety of internal enemies, Burma's international position has been strengthened by the agreement reached in 1960 on the Chinese–Burmese boundary. Relations with China and the Soviet Union are maintained at a cautious level, and aid is received from both as well as limited aid from the United States. Burma is staunchly neutralist and seeks to isolate itself from international conflicts, but Chinese threats against Thailand have jeopardized good relations with Burma.

The independent Republic of the Philippines was inaugurated on 4 July 1946. The Philippines have retained close links with the United States, leasing bases and concluding defence and assistance treaties with the United States in 1947 and 1951 and as a member of the multilateral SEATO alliance in 1954 (p. 341). The independent Philippine Government was the first to face a communist-inspired military resistance from the Filipino Communist Party's 'People's Anti-Japanese Resistance Army', 'Huk' for short. A state of incipient civil war existed between the Huk and American anti-guerrilla forces during the Japanese occupation. After participating in post-war Filipino politics, the Huks decided on armed action on a large scale in 1950, utilizing 12,000 guerrillas in order to seize power and in protest at corruption in elections; by 1954 the Huk revolutionary movement had become ineffective in the face of Government action.

In Malaya during the closing stages of the Japanese occupation, the Malayan Communists planned to gain power, but failed when the British returned in 1945. In June 1948 the Chinese Communists launched a new insurrection which was not mastered by the British troops until 1954. The insurrection delayed the granting of Malayan independence until 31 August 1957. Malay misgivings delayed further the incorporation of Singapore, with its predominantly Chinese population, in the new State of Malaya. The final agreement, which set up a greater Malaya consisting of Malaya, Singapore, Sarawak and Sabah, was signed in London in July 1963, and on 16 September 1963 the Federation of Malaysia came into being. The defence of Malaya, Singapore and Borneo, and later Malaysia, from 1957 to 1971 was the joint responsibility of Britain, Australia and New Zealand. But in March 1968 the British Government declared its intention to withdraw British garrisons from south-east Asia, including Singapore, by 1971. The involvement of large numbers of British troops in the confrontation with Indonesia 1963–6 (see below) was replaced by new defence arrangements between Malaysia and Singapore (independent since 1965). Australia, New Zealand and Britain provide a small Commonwealth force (ANZUK), based in Singapore, to back up the defence capacity of Malaysia and Singapore.

Two days after the Japanese surrender to the Allies, on 7 August 1945, Indonesian nationalist leaders proclaimed an independent Republic with Sukarno as President. The Netherlands refused to accept this declaration and attempted to regain control over the whole of their former Netherlands East Indian Empire. In December 1949 they agreed to pass sovereignty to an independent Indonesia. Conflict with the Netherlands continued in the dispute over the sovereignty of Western New Guinea, whose incorporation became Indonesia's dominant foreign concern. An *Indonesian–Netherlands Agreement, 16 August 1962*, after a brief interim period allowed Western New Guinea to pass under Indonesian sovereignty.

In mid-September 1963, Indonesian hostility to the creation of Malaysia and specifically to the incorporation of the two British States of North Borneo, Sarawak and Sabah, led to a state of undeclared war between Malaysia and Indonesia. The overthrow of Sukarno in 1966 was accompanied by a change in Indonesian foreign policy and the ending of the conflict with Malaysia. The incorporation of Sabah also caused tension between Malaysia and the Philippines, which claimed Sabah.

The foundation of the *Association of South-East Asian Nations (ASEAN), 8 August 1967*, has created a loose regional alliance between Indonesia, Malaysia, the Philippines, Singapore and Thailand. There is no secretariat but ASEAN provides a treaty framework for annual consultations among the members' Foreign Ministers and for some cultural, technical and economic cooperation. Some members of ASEAN continue to belong to alliance groupings with non-Asian Powers, but a sense of regional south-east Asian cooperation is fostered.

South-east Asia: Thailand, Laos, Cambodia and the war in Vietnam

Vietnam, Laos and Cambodia have been a battleground for the greater part of the twenty-eight years since the Second World War. A number of stages in this continuing conflict can be distinguished.

1. THE ORIGINS OF CONFLICT IN VIETNAM

Indo-China as one colonial unit ceased to exist when the Japanese removed the Vichy French administration in March 1945. The Japanese next induced Vietnam, Laos and Cambodia to proclaim independence. Before Nationalist

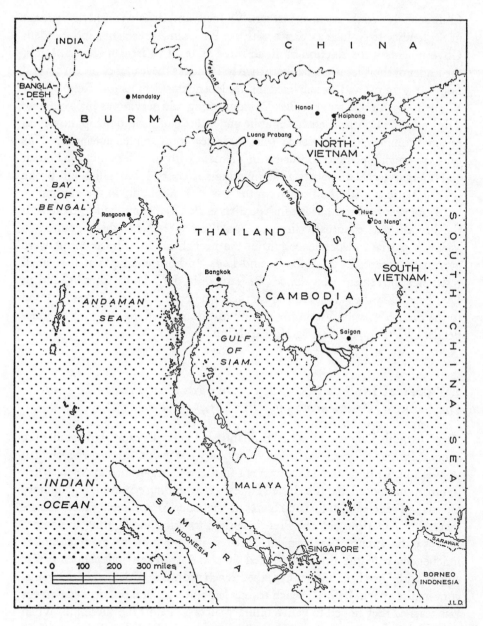

7 Indo-China, 1972

Chinese forces could occupy northern Vietnam and Britain southern Vietnam in September 1945, in accordance with the Potsdam Agreements, independent Governments were functioning in all three States. In Vietnam Ho Chi Minh, the leader of the Vietminh, had returned to Hanoi as the leader of one of several political groups and proclaimed an independent democratic Republic of Vietnam, with the Emperor Bao Dai abdicating and serving as his 'Supreme Adviser'. The Fourth French Republic under de Gaulle's leadership, however, rejected complete independence, offering instead only limited autonomy. This caused a crucial split and confusion in Vietnam with the Vietminh, the French and Vietnamese Nationalists all competing for control. Ho Chi Minh broke off negotiations with the French on the basis of autonomy in the autumn of 1946 and prepared to fight for independence. Bao Dai continued to treat with the French, and eventually in 1949 signed an agreement which granted to Vietnam partial independence within the French union. Similar terms were eventually accepted by Cambodia and Laos. In both countries at first small resistance movements developed: in Cambodia the Khmer Issaraks, and in Laos eventually the Pathet Lao. By far the most important of the forces opposed to the French was the Vietminh, communist dominated, fighting for an independent Vietnam, and led by Ho Chi Minh.

2. The first Indo-China war, fought by the Vietminh against the French, December 1946–July 1954

The Vietminh fought a long and brilliantly led guerrilla campaign against the French forces, coupled with a revolutionary campaign among the civilian population. United States involvement in the war began in May 1950, when Truman announced that the United States was extending economic and military aid to the French and associated States in Vietnam. After several years, despite increasing American aid, the French wished to bring the fighting to an end. In 1953 the French Government declared its intention to grant complete independence to the three associated States. A treaty of independence was signed with Laos in October 1953; the French promised to defend Laos against communist attack. Before French troops left and a general political settlement was reached they hoped to gain a military success against the Vietminh. When the Foreign Ministers of the Four Powers met in Berlin in February 1954 it was the French, with strong British support, who insisted that Indo-China should be placed on the agenda of the Geneva Conference, which was to meet two months later, so that a negotiated settlement could be reached.

The first *Geneva Conference, 26 April–21 July 1954*, was attended by representatives from nine States – France, Britain, the United States, the Soviet Union, the People's Republic of China, the Democratic Republic of Vietnam, the State of Vietnam, Laos and Cambodia – some of which did not recognize each other: for instance, the United States did not recognize the People's Republic of China, and the French did not recognize the Vietminh. Ten documents comprise the various accords reached by the close of the conference: three military agreements, six unilateral declarations, and a *Final Declaration of the Geneva Conference* (p. 454); but two participants, the State of Vietnam (South Vietnam) and the United States, in unilateral declarations repudiated important parts of this Final Declaration. Instead of negotiating from a position of strength, with the fall of Dien Bien Phu on 7 May, the French Government became anxious to end its own direct military involvement as soon as possible. An armistice throughout Indo-China was agreed to at the conference. It took the form of three military documents signed on 20 and 21 July 1954 between the French High Command and the Vietminh High Command, dealing separately with Vietnam, Cambodia and Laos. The following are the main provisions of the Vietnam military agreement: a demilitarized zone and ceasefire line was established close to the 17th parallel; agreements were reached on a mutual exchange of prisoners, cessation of hostilities, on a period of 300 days during which each side would regroup and withdraw its troops to its own side of the ceasefire line; no fresh troops or bases were to be established, and no alliances would be permitted with outside Powers. A French–Vietnamese Armistice Commission (India, Canada and Poland) was also established; most controversially, elections were to be held throughout Vietnam after two years to determine the final status of Vietnam. In unilateral declarations the State of Vietnam (recognized by France) protested against many aspects of the armistice terms agreed to by the French High Command without reference to the Vietnamese Government, especially the date of the proposed elections, and reserved to itself full liberty of action. The United States in its unilateral declaration took note of the three armistice agreements and the Final Declaration, and promised to refrain from the threat of force to disturb them, but declared its view that free elections should be supervised by the U.N. (and not the proposed International Supervisory Commission); it also supported the declaration of the State of Vietnam that the people of Vietnam are entitled to determine their own future. The United States indicated its dissociation from the Geneva Agreements not only by its declaration, but by the return to Washington in May of Dulles, the Secretary of State, when the conference agenda reached Indo-China, though a deputy continued as U.S. representative. The United States refused to sign any of the agreements or the Final Declaration. The Geneva Agreements as they applied to Laos accorded sovereignty over the whole of Laos to the Royal Government, rejecting claims of a communist Pathet Lao Government in exile; but the Pathet Lao were permitted temporary control of two provinces, a base from which the conflict was later renewed.

The Geneva Agreements are a collection of documents but contain no actual treaty binding all the participants, indeed no *political* treaties were signed. Judged by treaty standards the agreements are unusual, perhaps even unique in modern times. The three military agreements imposed military obligations which were carried out; but they also brought about political changes such as the division of Vietnam into two parts with the Democratic Republic (recognized only by the Soviet Union and China) in *de facto* control of the north and the State of Vietnam able to exercise authority only in the south. They also provided for elections in 1956, a political and not a military matter. The State of Vietnam (finally granted full independence by France on 4 June 1954) was not a signatory of the armistice agreement. The controversial Final Declaration was signed by none of the delegates but merely listed the participants in a preamble. It consisted of nine paragraphs taking note of or concurring with agreements and declarations made during the course of the conference, of one paragraph (8) interpreting the military agreements, of paragraph (9) imposing certain duties on authorities of both zones and (12) and (13) imposing certain duties on members of the conference, two of whom unilaterally declared that they would not feel bound by them. The Geneva Agreements did end the fighting between the French and Vietminh, the partition did occur and Cambodia and Laos gained independence; but the major provisions concerning Vietnam expressed the intents and desires of some participants whilst being opposed by others. The Final Declaration does not bind all the participants in commitments towards each other.

3. THE CONSOLIDATION OF NORTH AND SOUTH VIETNAM, AUGUST 1954-9

The Geneva Agreements brought fighting to an end in Indo-China between the opposing French-led and Vietminh armies. But in Laos the Pathet Lao continued to maintain their independent position and retain control of the two northern provinces with Vietminh help. After the conclusion of the Geneva Conference, the *SEATO Alliance was signed, 8 September 1954*, which extended its scope to cover Cambodia, Laos and South Vietnam (p. 343). However, both Cambodia and Laos, after Laos became neutral in 1962, declined SEATO protection.

In South Vietnam the French continued to attempt to assert their influence, and the United States to provide aid. The Government was headed by Ngo Dinh Diem, who turned the State of Vietnam into the Republic of Vietnam in 1955; American influence began to replace the French, who finally withdrew in May 1956 stating that they no longer accepted any special responsibility concerning the application of the Geneva Agreements. The date for holding elections as set out in the Geneva Agreements (July 1956) passed, but neither North or South Vietnam proceeded to take any military action against the other. The United States Military Assistance Advisory Group, a small mission not exceeding in number that authorized by the International Control Commission, advised the South Vietnamese forces. In 1958 a Vietcong insurrection began with the assassination of provincial officials. In May 1959 the Central Committee of the Vietnamese Communist Party decided to renew fighting and to support the Vietcong. This decision made itself felt seriously in South Vietnam during the winter of 1959-60.

4. THE SECOND INDO-CHINA WAR, FOUGHT BY THE VIETCONG AND BY NORTH VIETNAM AGAINST SOUTH VIETNAM AND THE UNITED STATES, 1960-73

With the active support of North Vietnam the strength of the Vietcong, which set up a 'Nationalist Front for the Liberation of South Vietnam', increased rapidly in 1960 and 1961. During the same period northern and most of central Laos was overrun by the communist Pathet Lao, with the help of a 'neutralist' faction and of the Vietminh and with Soviet supplies. In May 1961 a second Geneva Conference was convened to deal with the Laos crisis, and fourteen months later the delegates from fourteen nations reached the *Geneva Agreement on Laos, 23 July 1962* (p. 462). A Laotian Government of national union was formed from the three warring factions, and Laos was neutralized. This proved to be largely a paper settlement. An uneasy political and military balance between the factions continued but Laos was not neutralized. Its territory played an important role in the Vietnam war as the supply route from North to South Vietnam, the Ho Chi Minh trail, runs through eastern Laos.

Thailand, a member of SEATO, was alarmed at SEATO's inability to act in neighbouring Laos in 1960 and 1961. Thailand also faced its own insurgency problems in the north-east in the region bordering on Laos. To reassure Thailand, a joint U.S.-Thailand statement was issued in Washington on 6 March 1962, indicating that the U.S. regarded the SEATO treaty commitment as involving individual as well as collective responsibility in the event of communist aggression in Thailand. In May 1962 the U.S. sent combat forces to Thailand, later followed by small British, Australian, New Zealand and Philippine contingents. From 1965 to 1973, the U.S. has utilized bases in Thailand for bombing missions in Vietnam, and U.S. troops have been stationed in Thailand. The U.S. has promised to defend Thailand against communist attack.

In South Vietnam, as the situation worsened for Diem's Government, the new Kennedy administration in May 1961 approved of more (partly open, partly secret) support for the South Vietnamese Government. From the autumn of 1961 until the death of Kennedy two years later, American military personnel in South Vietnam increased to more than 16,000 men. This growing American commitment of U.S. 'advisers' in South Vietnam was made at a time of unstable internal Vietnamese politics which followed the overthrow of the Diem régime (November 1963). When Johnson followed Kennedy in the White House in 1963 he was determined to continue earlier American support for the South Vietnamese Government against the Vietcong and the North Vietnamese, who had sent their troops south of the ceasefire line in support of the Vietcong.

In August 1964 the attack by North Vietnamese warships on U.S. warships engaged on an intelligence mission in the Gulf of Tonkin persuaded Congress, at Johnson's request, to permit the President to take such counter-measures against the North as he thought necessary (p. 315). In February 1965 Johnson took a crucial further step, escalating U.S. involvement in order to deter the North Vietnamese from continuing to support the Vietcong; he authorized the bombing of North Vietnam. On 1 April 1965 Johnson took his second crucial decision when he authorized the commitment of U.S. combat troops in the South. From then on both the North Vietnamese and the United States committed ever larger resources and troops to the struggle in South Vietnam, until American forces rose to more than half a million men. Contingents from Australia, New Zealand, the Philippines, Thailand, and sizeable forces from South Korea supported the American–South Vietnamese military effort. General Thieu emerged in South Vietnam as President and a strong leader in the war against the Vietcong and North Vietnam.

From 1970 to March 1973 the Nixon administration steadily decreased the participation of American ground forces, leaving the ground fighting to the South Vietnamese army, but continued the air war in South and North Vietnam.

In May 1968 peace talks were begun in Paris between the United States and North Vietnam, later joined by Vietcong and South Vietnamese delegates, whilst the war continued. The Nixon administration persevered with both the

Paris talks and the war, extending the latter to Vietcong supply lines in Cambodia. The peace talks were broken off in May 1972 but resumed in July. They were conducted on the American side by Dr Henry Kissinger and on the North Vietnamese side by Le Duc Tho, with Mrs Nguyen Thi Binh representing the Vietcong. These talks were deadlocked by 13 December 1972, in part owing to the opposition of the South Vietnamese President Thieu. From 18 December 1972 until mid-January 1973 the United States resumed heavy bombing, including attacks on Hanoi. *The Agreement to end the Vietnam war was signed in Paris on 27 January 1973 between the Vietcong, South Vietnam, the United States and North Vietnam* (p. 465). Despite the ceasefire fighting has continued in South Vietnam between the Vietnamese contestants endeavouring to gain and hold the maximum territory before a political solution is found by the Vietnamese. Exchanges of prisoners of war have, however, proceeded, and the last United States combat soldier had left Vietnam by the end of March 1973. The United States has left advisers and a bomber force stationed in Thailand.

The end of March 1973 thus marks the end of direct military involvement by the United States in Vietnam, though it retains a capacity for renewing conflict from the air and the sea. The administration of the ceasefire became the responsibility of the South Vietnamese and Vietcong as North Vietnamese and American officials left. *On 2 March 1973 the International Conference on Vietnam, held in Paris, concluded a Declaration between Canada, the People's Republic of China, the United States, France, the Vietcong, South Vietnam, Hungary, Indonesia, Poland, North Vietnam, Britain and the Soviet Union* (p. 472). It commits all twelve States to upholding the Paris Peace Agreement on Vietnam signed on 27 January 1973 between the two Vietnamese States, the Vietcong and the United States; it also endorses the responsibilities of Canada, Hungary, Indonesia and Poland, who make up the *International Commission of Control and Supervision*, to supervise the ceasefire terms and the fragile peace.

In Laos an *Agreement to end the war was concluded between the Laotian Government and the Pathet Lao on 21 February 1973*. It provides for an end to a conflict that has lasted two decades. The agreement stipulates that a new Coalition Government is to be formed within thirty days, that all foreign forces are to withdraw within ninety days and that all Laotian forces are to remain in place. A Council of National Union is to be set up, with half of the members nominated by the Pathet Lao, to assist the Government and to supervise general elections at a time to be arranged. All prisoners of war, including Americans, are to be released within ninety days.

In Cambodia fighting continues in November 1973, and the capital, Phnom Penh, is surrounded by communist forces, partly Cambodian and partly North

Vietnamese. The South Vietnamese and Americans are providing help for the Cambodian Government.

Eastern and North-eastern Asia: the wars of China and Korea

CHINA

The war in China, during the period of the wider global conflict of 1941 to 1945, was fought on three fronts: Nationalist Chinese, Communist Chinese and Japanese. All American efforts to bring about a collaboration of communist and nationalist war efforts against Japan failed. Whereas the United States gave first priority to the defeat of Japan, Chiang Kai-shek and Mao Tse-tung looked beyond the war to the struggle for the control of China, involving the defeat and subordination of either the nationalist or communist cause. Internationally, Chiang Kai-shek's Government was bolstered by the recognition and the support of all the Western Powers, by a permanent seat for China on the Security Council of the U.N. and by the *Sino-Soviet Treaty of 14 August 1945* (p. 237). Mao Tse-tung continued to build up communist strength after the defeat of Japan; time was gained by both sides when General Marshall, on a mediating mission in China, helped to arrange a ceasefire in January 1946. Several months of uneasy truce and apparent communist–nationalist co-operation ended in November 1946, and a full scale Chinese Civil War ensued.

The Chinese Civil War from 1946 to 1949 involved huge armies on each side (at the outset of the war 1 million communist troops against 3 million nationalist troops), and ended on the mainland of China with the collapse of the nationalist armies on several fronts in the autumn of 1949. *On 1 October 1949 Mao Tse-tung proclaimed the People's Republic of China.* The military takeover in mainland China took longer to complete, and authority over all mainland China was not established by the communists until May 1950.

The Nationalist Government of Chiang Kai-shek settled on Taiwan (Formosa). It claimed to speak for all China and received sufficient international recognition to continue to hold the Chinese seat on the Security Council until 1971. After June 1950 the United States protected Taiwan from any possible communist attack by Truman's decision to interpose the American Seventh Fleet in the Taiwan Straits, to prevent both nationalists and communists from attacking each other. Increasing American aid for Chiang Kai-shek was followed by treaty commitments with the signature of the *Mutual Defense Treaty between the United States and China, 2 December 1954* (p. 340). United States–Chinese relations remained frozen in mutual hostility until an international ping-pong match was utilized as a signal for a new relationship, the foundations of which were laid by Mao Tse-tung, Chou En-lai and Nixon during Nixon's visit to China in February 1972.

The People's Republic of China as its first task wished to establish sovereign authority over all territories it regarded as rightly forming part of China. It has thus asserted Chinese sovereignty over Taiwan and all nationalist-held islands, and will not accept a 'two China' solution which would grant separate State-hood to the parts of China over which Chiang Kai-shek has established control – Taiwan, the Pescadores, Quemoy and Matsu. Nationalist China also rejects the two China solution by its claim to be the sole legitimate representative of China, and as such represented China on the Security Council until expelled from membership of the U.N. in 1971.

The People's Republic of China succeeded in reasserting its control over mainland China gradually. Mao Tse-tung replaced the terms of the *Sino-Soviet Treaty of 14 August 1945* (p. 237), which was declared void, by negotiating in Moscow, after much hard bargaining, a new treaty, the *Treaty of Friendship, Alliance and Mutual Assistance, 14 February 1950* (p. 370). In this treaty China reaffirmed the independence of Outer Mongolia, but Mao Tse-tung secured the consent of the Soviet Union to abandon many of the rights the Soviet Union had acquired under the treaty of 1945 in northern China. The Man-churian Railway was transferred to China in 1952 and Port Arthur in 1953. The alliance was directed against Japan or any Power associated with Japan (the most obvious candidate being the United States). The Soviet Union promised aid and credits.

The reassertion of Chinese sovereignty over the borderlands brought China into conflict with some of her neighbours. Tibet was invaded in 1950, and despite a Sino-Indian Agreement in 1954 the dispute over the frontier between China and India (which in part involved Chinese claims for territory of Tibetan suzerainty) led to brief fighting in October and November 1962 (p. 435). Disputes over the Chinese–Soviet frontier in 1963 also became an important factor in the rift which had been developing between the Soviet Union and China beginning in 1956, three years after the death of Stalin.

During the early 1950s the Soviet Union had provided China with technical, military and economic assistance, but at the price of increased Soviet influence and partial control of joint enterprises. After 1956 Mao Tse-tung increasingly decried the pre-eminence of the Soviet Union in the international communist movement and the ideological split widened. The Soviet Union in 1958 and 1959 would not provide nuclear assistance to China on terms acceptable to the Chinese leaders. In August 1960 Soviet technicians were withdrawn, an indica-tion of how far Sino-Soviet relations had worsened. The Chinese denounced

Khrushchev's efforts to improve relations with the United States in a new era of Soviet–United States 'coexistence'. The Chinese equally resented Soviet military and economic aid to India which continued despite the Sino-Indian armed conflict of 1962.

In March 1963 the Chinese publicly described the treaties signed by Imperial China with Tsarist Russia – the treaties of Aigun (1858), Peking (1860) and St Petersburg (1881) – as among the 'unequal treaties' imposed by imperialists on China. Mao Tse-tung added that they raised outstanding issues that ought to be settled by peaceful negotiation. The Soviet Union denied the Chinese claim challenging the Russian–Chinese frontiers settled by these treaties, but was ready to negotiate on specific points. These negotiations broke down in 1964.

The Sino-Soviet border can be divided into three sections: the Sinkiang sector running from the disputed frontier regions of the Pamirs where Afghanistan, Russia and Kashmir meet, northward to Mongolia; the Mongolian sector, strictly speaking not a Soviet frontier but the frontier between the Mongolian Republic allied to the Soviet Union and China; and thirdly, the Manchurian sector running in a great arc from the Mongolian frontier to North Korea, along the banks of the rivers Argun and Amur and down the Ussuri to Lake Khank (see map on p. 432).

Chinese efforts to place Sinkiang firmly under Chinese administration led to conflict with India in 1962. The *Treaty of St Petersburg, 24 February 1881*, established the Russian–Chinese boundary which was later demarcated in 1882–5 and 1895. Northern China has suspected the Soviet Union of wishing to change the status of Sinkiang itself and of substituting Soviet influence and predominance for Chinese sovereignty. In the 1960s the Sino-Russian border on the Ili has been the scene of many 'incidents'. The Chinese have accused the Russians of 'unbridled subversive activities' in China's borderland among the non-Chinese minorities, about whose loyalty the Chinese are especially sensitive.

The independence of Outer Mongolia recognized in the Sino-Soviet treaties of 1945 and 1950 continues to rankle with the Chinese. Despite these treaties Mao Tse-tung in July 1964 mentioned the question of Outer Mongolia as open to further discussion. On the other hand in 1962 a Sino-Mongolian boundary treaty was signed, and China made numerous territorial concessions to Mongolia. The independent status of Outer Mongolia is not in serious dispute.

The third section of the Sino-Russian frontier, also settled by what the Chinese claim are the unequal treaties of *Aigun, 16 May 1858*, and *Peking, 14 November 1860*, separates Manchuria from Russia. The Ussuri river and some islands in it became the scene of incidents culminating in some violence in March 1969. But this frontier has followed the natural boundaries of the rivers Argun, Amur and Ussuri for a century and is not territorially seriously in dispute.

The conflict of the Sino-Soviet frontier from the Pamirs to Korea appears to be mainly a conflict of principle with the Chinese, requiring from the Soviet Union an admission that the 'unequal' treaties are not valid and that only freely negotiated treaties between the Soviet Union and China can be made valid. The Soviet claim to these frontiers is founded on orthodox international law relating to the Russian period of possession and effective occupation. The Sino-Soviet frontier disputes are, in the last resort, more a symptom of Sino-Soviet relations than a cause of their conflict. Since the winter of 1969 secret negotiations to settle the Sino-Soviet frontier (and other differences) have been in progress, and in the autumn of 1972 there were signs that these negotiations might be successful, but by November 1973 no progress was recorded.

As a result of other 'unequal treaties', two European possessions remain on mainland China: Hong Kong, as a British colony, and Portuguese Macao. Hong Kong Island was annexed in 1841, the mainland peninsula of Kowloon in 1860, and a lease of more Chinese territory obtained on a ninety-nine year lease in 1898 expiring in 1997. Communist China has made no moves to acquire these two European outposts.

KOREA

From 1905 to 1945 Korea was under Japanese rule. During the Second World War at the Cairo Conference in 1943 Korea was promised independence 'in due course', a promise confirmed at the Potsdam Conference in 1945, which also contained the agreement that Soviet troops should accept the surrender of Japanese forces in North Korea whilst South Korea should be occupied first by American military forces. The demarcation between the two zones became the 38th parallel. This demarcation soon became a *de facto* political frontier as all negotiations for free elections in the whole of Korea failed. In South Korea, the Republic of Korea came into being on 15 August 1948, and in North Korea a communist State, the Korean People's Republic, was established in September 1948.

On 25 June 1950 the North Korean army invaded South Korea in strength. Because of the international date-line it was 24 June in Washington. The day after the invasion, 26 June in Korea, 25 June in the United States, the Security Council met, passed its first resolution stating that the North Korean attack constituted a 'breach of peace', and called for an immediate end to hostilities and a withdrawal of North Korean forces to their own side of the border. In the absence of the Soviet representative (owing to Soviet protest at the seating of the Nationalist Chinese representative), this resolution was adopted by a vote of 9–0 with Yugoslavia abstaining. The United States decision to provide the South Korean forces south of the 38th parallel with all-out air and naval support was taken by Truman on the evening of 26 June, and orders were issued at once. On the afternoon of 27 June the Security Council adopted a second and stronger resolution calling upon members to give all possible help to the Republic of Korea to repel the invasion and to restore peace and security in the area. On this resolution Yugoslavia dissented and Egypt and India abstained. President Truman announced his order to the United States air and sea forces to support the South Korean Government, and also that he had ordered the Seventh Fleet to prevent any attack on Formosa (p. 308). On 29 and 30 June, Truman decided to commit the United States ground forces in Korea. The United States' call for help was supported by sixteen nations including the British Commonwealth and Turkey, which sent contingents of armed forces, and many more nations sent civilian aid. The bulk of the fighting force was South Korean and American, which formed the United Nations Command under an American general appointed to lead it.

The Korean War passed through five major phases: 25 June–14 September 1950, when North Korean forces occupied all South Korea but for the Pusan perimeter; 15 September–30 September 1950, when U.N. forces defeated the North Korean troops in the south after the success of the Inchon landing; 25 October 1950, when U.N. forces crossed the 38th parallel and advanced towards the Chinese and Russian frontier; 26 October 1950–25 January 1951, when U.N. forces continued to advance but were defeated as a result of Chinese intervention, and pulled back south of the 38th parallel where a stable line of defence was established; February 1951–July 1953, when heavy fighting north and south of the 38th parallel finally left the U.N. troops almost all along the front to the north of the 38th parallel, and the ceasefire line was finally established on 27 July 1953. The Korean War was a major war involving North Korean and Chinese armies of more than 1 million, whilst some 700,000 men served with the United Nations Command; casualties on both sides, civilian and military, were very heavy. Negotiations for a truce began in Kaesong in July 1951 whilst fighting continued. These negotiations, suspended several times, led two years later to the *Armistice Agreement signed at Panmunjon, 27 July 1953* (p. 464), providing for a ceasefire line, the suspension of hostilities, and the exchange of prisoners of war voluntarily wishing to return.

A note on international development aid for Asia

Since the Second World War economic development in Asia has been supported by international aid on a large scale to meet the huge problems of Asia. This aid has been provided in part through the machinery of international organizations, but mainly directly between nations. The relative scale of aid can be seen from the following figures (Dr Werner Klatt in the *Asia Handbook*, ed. Guy Wint, Harmondsworth, Penguin, 1969 edn, pp. 722–5, should be consulted for detailed statistics). *The World Bank and International Development Association* has made loans and granted credits from 1944 to 1966 to the total of 3,750 million dollars. *The United Nations* has provided expert technical assistance and training programmes. More than 10,000 experts have been sent out and more than 20,000 training fellowships have been provided. *The Colombo Plan* for cooperative economic development in south and south-east Asia was initiated by the British Commonwealth, and set out detailed development programmes for India, Pakistan, Ceylon, Malaya, Singapore, North Borneo and Sarawak. Published in November 1950, it went into operation in July 1951. It was joined by a non-Commonwealth member, the United States, which provided the largest share of the funds, and extended in application to non-Commonwealth Asian members, Afghanistan, Burma, Nepal, Bhutan, Cambodia, Laos, South Vietnam, Thailand and the Philippines. Members outside the region are the United States, Britain, Australia, New Zealand, Canada and Japan. The plan also provides for the employment of experts and training facilities, which during the decade 1951–61 cost some 250 million dollars.

In terms of money, the largest amount of aid is provided directly by one nation to another and not through international institutions. The United States has granted by far the largest share of bilateral aid. Assistance, including military assistance, has been given through Mutual Defense Assistance Treaties (p. 307) and in several other ways. United States economic and military aid from 1946 to 1966 has almost totalled 38,000 million dollars, that is rather more than twice as much as was made available to Western Europe by the Marshall Plan in the shorter period 1948–52 (p. 379). Rather more than two-thirds of this aid has been for economic development and just under one-third for military purposes. Two-thirds of the aid was made in grants which are not repayable and only a third in loans. During the two decades 1946–66 India has received about one-fifth of the total, 6,770 million dollars, and Korea about the same amount; Taiwan and South Vietnam more than 4,500 million dollars each; Japan nearly 4,000 million dollars and Pakistan 3,000 million dollars; the Philippines close to 2,000 million dollars and Thailand 1,000 million dollars;

other Asian countries including Indonesia, Laos, Cambodia and Afghanistan have received less than 1,000 million dollars each.

Soviet aid, and later the aid from the communist bloc, was first granted to China on a large scale in 1950. The *Chinese–Soviet Treaty, 14 February 1950* (p. 370), provided a credit of 300 million dollars. With subsequent credits total Soviet aid to China has been estimated at 1,550 million dollars. In addition, until their withdrawal in 1960 the Soviet Union had some 1,400 technical experts working in China and had trained many thousand Chinese experts. Soviet bloc aid to Asian countries has been granted in the form of credits. During the ten years since 1954 it has exceeded 1,200 million dollars in the amount of loans used by countries other than China; three times that amount was actually offered for projects but not accepted. Soviet bloc aid in Asia has probably amounted to rather less than one-tenth of United States aid; accurate figures are impossible to establish.

British economic aid and technical assistance in roughly the same period, 1945–67, has totalled 517 million dollars, of which half was provided for India and the remainder principally to Malaysia, Burma and Pakistan. It is small in comparison, but has played a valuable role.

A combination of population increases and natural and man-made disasters have not enabled the peoples of Asia, as a whole, to narrow the gap between the rich and the poor, despite aid programmes. The developing nations of Asia devote much of their limited wealth to arms. Trade and world finance remains in the control of the rich nations which are urged by the poor to devote a higher percentage of their gross national product for the poor of the world, so far (1973) without much positive response.

A note on the Commonwealth of Nations

In Asia, Africa, the Americas and Australasia, a number of former British territories on attaining independence have continued as members of the Commonwealth, together with Britain, in what is an association of independent sovereign States. Republics with their own Heads of State may be members of the Commonwealth recognizing the Queen as Head of the Commonwealth; Australia, Canada and New Zealand regard the Queen as both the Head of State and the Head of the Commonwealth.

Membership of the Commonwealth involves no treaty commitments; the Commonwealth has no constitution. States may leave whenever they choose to. No Commonwealth country has been formally 'expelled', though the South African Republic left in 1961 when other members of the Commonwealth condemned the policy of apartheid.

The practical independence of the Dominions can be dated to the years following the First World War. The Inter-Imperial Relations Committee of the 1926 Imperial Conference defined the 'autonomous communities within the British Empire' as 'equal in status, in no way subordinate one to another in any aspect of their domestic or external affairs, though united by a common allegiance to the Crown and freely associated as Members of the British Commonwealth of Nations'. The legal supremacy of the British Parliament was removed by the *Statute of Westminster* (11 December 1931). The Dominions were no longer bound to go to war when Britain became engaged in war, a question of importance in the 1930s. Although Britain's declaration of war in September 1939 was accepted by New Zealand and Australia as committing them, South Africa only declared war after a change of Government, and Canada after parliamentary debate. India's decision to become a Republic in 1949 redefined the common allegiance to the Crown; the Prime Ministers at the 1949 conference agreed that the King had to be accepted only as a 'symbol of the free association', which paved the way for Republics to become members of the Commonwealth and for other variations.

Commonwealth consultations over questions of foreign policy have been sporadic rather than obligatory. During the Suez crisis of 1956 there was a clear lack of consultation by Britain of the views of other members of the Commonwealth. But Prime Ministers of the Commonwealth States hold periodic meetings. The Prime Ministers' Meeting constitutes the most important political advisory or consultative body of the Commonwealth, but its advice when given is not binding on members. The Prime Ministers' Meeting has been supported by the Commonwealth Secretariat since 1965. The Secretariat is divided into Departments of International Affairs, Economic Affairs and Administration.

There are a number of Commonwealth organizations whose purpose is to further cooperation and consultation in the fields of education and scientific, agricultural and medical research, as well as in communications and transport. But the ties binding the Commonwealth have loosened since 1945. The rights once enjoyed by Commonwealth citizens, for example, free entry to Britain, have been drastically curtailed since the Second World War. Economic and financial preferences and arrangements between Commonwealth countries, once important, have greatly diminished, especially since Britain's entry into the European Community on 1 January 1973. The *Colombo Plan*, however, remains a major commitment to economic development in Asia by Commonwealth members together with other States. In 1972 there were thirty-two member countries of the Commonwealth: Australia, Barbados, Botswana, Canada, Ceylon, Cyprus, Fiji, Gambia, Ghana, Guyana, India, Jamaica, Kenya,

Lesotho, Malawi, Malaysia, Malta, Mauritius, Nauru, New Zealand, Nigeria, Pakistan, Sierre Leone, Singapore, Swaziland, Tanzania, Tonga, Trinidad and Tobago, Uganda, the United Kingdom of Great Britain and Northern Ireland, Western Samoa and Zambia. But Pakistan withdrew in January 1972 and Bangladesh joined in April 1972. In addition to these full members, there are a number of dependent countries for whom Britain or other Commonwealth countries are responsible.

[For a note on Commonwealth defence agreements and cooperation, see pp. 549–51.]

The Geneva Agreements, 21 July 1954

Extracts from verbatim record of Eighth Plenary Session

The Chairman (Mr Eden): As I think my colleagues are aware, agreement has now been reached on certain documents. It is proposed that this Conference should take note of these agreements. I accordingly propose to begin by reading out a list of the subjects covered by the documents, which I understand every delegation has in front of them.

First, agreement on the cessation of hostilities in Viet Nam; second, agreement on the cessation of hostilities in Laos; third, agreement on the cessation of hostilities in Cambodia. I would draw particular attention to the fact that these three agreements now incorporate the texts which were negotiated separately concerning the supervision of the Armistice in the three countries by the International Commission and the joint committees.

I should also like to draw the attention of all delegations to a point of some importance in connection with the Armistice Agreements and the related maps and documents on supervision. It has been agreed among the parties to each of these Agreements that none of them shall be made public for the present, pending further agreement among the parties. The reason for this, I must explain to my colleagues, is that these Armistice terms come into force at different dates. And it is desired that they should not be made public until they have come into force.

The further documents to which I must draw attention, which are in your possession, are: fourth, declaration by the Government of Laos on elections; fifth, declaration by the Government of Cambodia on elections and integration of all citizens into the national community; sixth, declaration by the Government of Laos on the military status of the country; seventh, declaration by the Government of Cambodia on the military status of the country; eighth, declaration by the Government of the French Republic on the withdrawal of troops from the three countries of Indochina.

Finally, gentlemen, there is the Draft Declaration by the Conference, which takes note of all these documents. I think all my colleagues have copies of this Draft Declaration before them. I will ask my colleagues in turn to express themselves upon this Declaration.

The Representative of France.

M. Mendès-France (France): Mr Chairman, the French Delegation approves the terms of this Declaration.

The Chairman: The Representative of Laos.

Mr Phoui Sananikone (Laos): The Delegation of Laos has no observations to make on this text.

The Chairman: The Representative of the People's Republic of China.

Mr Chou En-Lai (People's Republic of China): We agree.

The Chairman: On behalf of Her Majesty's Government in the United Kingdom, I associate myself with the Final Declaration of this Conference.

The Union of Soviet Socialist Republics.

M. Molotov (U.S.S.R.): The Soviet Delegation agrees.

The Chairman: The Representative of Cambodia.

Mr Tep Pham (Cambodia): The Delegate of Cambodia wishes to state that, among the documents just listed, one is missing. This is a Cambodian Declaration which we have already circulated to all delegations. Its purport is as follows: Paragraphs 7, 11 and 12 of the Final Declaration stipulate respect for the territorial integrity of Viet Nam. The Cambodian Delegation asks the Conference to consider that this provision does not imply the abandonment of such legitimate rights and interests as Cambodia might assert with regard to certain regions of South Viet Nam, about which Cambodia has made express reservations, in particular at the time of the signature of the Franco-Khmer Treaty of November 8, 1949, on relations between Cambodia and France and at the time the French law which linked Cochinchina to Viet Nam was passed. Faithful to the ideal of peace, and to the international principle of non-interference, Cambodia has no intention of interfering in the internal affairs of the State of Viet Nam and associates herself fully with the principle of respect for its integrity, provided certain adjustments and regularizations be arrived at with regard to the borders between this State and Cambodia, borders which so far have been fixed by a mere unilateral act of France.

In support of this Declaration, the Cambodian Delegation communicates to all members of this Conference a note on Cambodian lands in South Viet Nam.

The Chairman: If this Declaration was not inscribed on the agenda on the list of documents I have read out, it is because it has only at this instant reached me. I do not think it is any part of the task of this Conference to deal with any past controversies in respect of the frontiers between Cambodia and Viet Nam.

The Representative of the Democratic Republic of Viet Nam.

Mr Pham van Dong (Democratic Republic of Viet Nam): Mr Chairman. I agree completely with the words pronounced by you. In the name of the Government of the Democratic Republic of Viet Nam we make the most express reservations regarding the statement made by the Delegation of Cambodia just now. I do this in the interests of good relations and understanding between our two countries.

The Chairman: I think the Conference can take note of the statements of the Delegation of Cambodia just circulated and of the statement of the Representative of the Democratic Republic of Viet Nam.

I will continue calling upon countries to speak on the subject of the Declaration. I call upon the United States of America.

Mr Bedell Smith (United States): Mr Chairman, Fellow Delegates, as I stated to my colleagues during our meeting on July 18, my Government is not prepared to join in a Declaration by the Conference such as is submitted. However, the United States makes this Unilateral Declaration of its position in these matters:

DECLARATION

The Government of the United States being resolved to devote its efforts to the strengthening of peace in accordance with the principles and purposes of the United Nations

Takes Note

of the Agreements concluded at Geneva on July 20 and 21, 1954, between (a) the Franco-Laotian Command and the Command of the People's Army of Viet Nam; (b) the Royal Khmer Army Command and the Command of the People's Army of Viet Nam; (c) Franco-Vietnamese

Command and the Command of the People's Army of Viet Nam, and of paragraphs 1 to 12 of the Declaration presented to the Geneva Conference on July 21, 1954.

The Government of the United States of America

Declares with regard to the aforesaid Agreements and paragraphs that (i) it will refrain from the threat or the use of force to disturb them, in accordance with Article 2 (Section 4) of the Charter of the United Nations dealing with the obligation of Members to refrain in their international relations from the threat or use of force; and (ii) it would view any renewal of the aggression in violation of the aforesaid Agreements with grave concern and as seriously threatening international peace and security.

In connection with the statement in the Declaration concerning free elections in Viet Nam, my Government wishes to make clear its position which it has expressed in a Declaration made in Washington on June 29, 1954, as follows:

In the case of nations now divided against their will, we shall continue to seek to achieve unity through free elections, supervised by the United Nations to ensure that they are conducted fairly.

With respect to the statement made by the Representative of the State of Viet Nam, the United States reiterates its traditional position that peoples are entitled to determine their own future and that it will not join in an arrangement which would hinder this. Nothing in its declaration just made is intended to or does indicate any departure from this traditional position.

We share the hope that the agreement will permit Cambodia, Laos and Viet Nam to play their part in full independence and sovereignty, in the peaceful community of nations, and will enable the peoples of that area to determine their own future.

Thank you, Mr Chairman.

The Chairman: The Conference will, I think, wish to take note of the statement of the Representative of the United States of America.

I call on the Representative of the State of Viet Nam.

Mr Tran van Do (State of Viet Nam): Mr Chairman, as regards the Final Declaration of the Conference, the Vietnamese Delegation requests the Conference to incorporate in this Declaration after Article 10, the following text:

The Conference takes note of the Declaration of the Government of the State of Viet Nam undertaking:

to make and support every effort to re-establish a real and lasting peace in Viet Nam;

not to use force to resist the procedures for carrying the ceasefire into effect, in spite of the objections and reservations that the State of Viet Nam has expressed, especially in its final statement.

The Chairman: I shall be glad to hear any views that my colleagues may wish to express. But, as I understand the position, the Final Declaration has already been drafted and this additional paragraph has only just now been received; indeed, it has been amended since I received the text a few minutes ago. In all the circumstances, I suggest that the best course we can take is that the Conference should take note of the Declaration of the State of Viet Nam in this respect. If any of my colleagues has a contrary view, perhaps they would be good enough to say so. (None.) If none of my colleagues wishes to make any other observations, may I pass to certain other points which have to be settled before this Conference can conclude its labours?

The first is that, if it is agreeable to our colleagues, it is suggested that the two Chairmen should at the conclusion of this meeting address telegrams to the Governments of India, Poland and Canada to ask them if they will undertake the duties of supervision which the Conference has invited them to discharge. Is that agreeable? (Agreed.) Thank you.

The last is perhaps the least agreeable chapter of all our work. Certain costs arise from the decisions which the Conference has taken. It is suggested that it should be left here to your Chairmen as their parting gift to try to put before you some proposal in respect of those costs. I only wish to add in that connection that, as this Conference is peculiar in not having any Secretariat in the usual sense of the term, the two Chairmen with considerable reluctance are prepared to undertake this highly invidious task. The costs to which I refer are not our own but those of the International Commission.

Does any delegate wish to make any further observation? (None.)

Gentlemen, perhaps I may say a final word as your Chairman for this day. We have now come to the end of our work. For a number of reasons it has been prolonged and intricate. The cooperation which all delegates have given to your two Chairmen has enabled us to overcome many procedural difficulties. Without that cooperation, we could not have succeeded in our task. The Agreements concluded today could not, in the nature of things, give complete satisfaction to everyone. But they have made it possible to stop a war which has lasted for eight years and brought suffering and hardship to millions of people. They have also, we hope, reduced international tension at a point of instant danger to world peace. These results are surely worth our many weeks of toil. In order to bring about a ceasefire, we have drawn up a series of agreements. They are the best that our hands could devise. All will now depend upon the spirit in which those agreements are observed and carried out.

Gentlemen, before we leave this hospitable town of Geneva I'm sure you would wish your Chairmen to give a message of gratitude to the United Nations and its able staff who have housed and helped us in our work.

And lastly let me express our cordial thanks to the Swiss Government and to the people and authorities of Geneva who have done so much to make our stay here pleasant as well as of service to the cause of peace.

The Representative of the United States of America.

Mr Bedell Smith (U.S.A.): If I presume to speak for my fellow delegates, it is because I know that they all feel as I do. I hope that they join me in expressing our thanks to the two Chairmen of this Conference. Their patience, their tireless efforts, and their goodwill have done a great deal to make this settlement possible. We owe them our sincere thanks.

The Chairman: The Representative of the Union of Soviet Socialist Republics.

M. Molotov (U.S.S.R.): Mr Chairman, as one of the Chairmen at the Geneva Conference, I would like to reply to the remarks just made by Mr Bedell Smith, who spoke highly of the work done by the Chairmen. Naturally I must stress the outstanding services and the outstanding role played by our Chairman of today, Mr Eden, whose role in the Geneva Conference cannot be exaggerated. And I would also like to reply and thank Mr Bedell Smith for his warm words of today.

The Chairman: Has any other delegate anything else they want to say?

The Representative of Viet Nam.

Mr Tran van Do (State of Viet Nam): Mr Chairman, I expressed the view of the Delegation of the State of Viet Nam in my statement and I would have this Conference take note of it in its final act.

The Chairman: As I think I explained, we cannot now amend our final act, which is the statement of the Conference as a whole, but the Declaration of the Representative of the State of Viet Nam will be taken note of.

Any other observations? (None.)

I would like to be allowed to add my thanks for what General Bedell Smith has said and also to thank M. Molotov for his words. Both were undeserved, but even if things are not true, if they are nice things it's pleasant to hear them said.

But I do want to close this Conference

with this one sentence: I'm quite sure that each one of us here hopes that the work which we have done will help to strengthen the forces working for peace.

Final Declaration of the Geneva Conference on the problem of restoring peace in Indo-China, in which the representatives of Cambodia, the Democratic Republic of Viet Nam, France, Laos, the People's Republic of China, the State of Viet Nam, the Union of Soviet Socialist Republics, the United Kingdom and the United States of America took part

1. The Conference takes note of the agreements ending hostilities in Cambodia, Laos and Viet Nam and organizing international control and the supervision of the execution of the provisions of these agreements.

2. The Conference expresses satisfaction at the ending of hostilities in Cambodia, Laos and Viet Nam; the Conference expresses its conviction that the execution of the provisions set out in the present Declaration and in the agreements on the cessation of hostilities will permit Cambodia, Laos and Viet Nam henceforth to play their part, in full independence and sovereignty, in the peaceful community of nations.

3. The Conference takes note of the declarations made by the Governments of Cambodia and of Laos of their intention to adopt measures permitting all citizens to take their place in the national community, in particular by participating in the next general elections, which, in conformity with the constitution of each of these countries, shall take place in the course of the year 1955, by secret ballot and in conditions of respect for fundamental freedoms.

4. The Conference takes note of the clauses in the agreement on the cessation of hostilities in Viet Nam prohibiting the introduction into Viet Nam of foreign troops and military personnel as well as of all kinds of arms and munitions. The Conference also takes note of the declarations made by the Governments of Cambodia and Laos of their resolution not to request foreign aid, whether in war material, in personnel or in instructors except for the purpose of the effective defence of their territory and, in the case of Laos, to the extent defined by the agreements on the cessation of hostilities in Laos.

5. The Conference takes note of the clauses in the agreement on the cessation of hostilities in Viet Nam to the effect that no military base under the control of a foreign State may be established in the regrouping zones of the two parties, the latter having the obligation to see that the zones allotted to them shall not constitute part of any military alliance and shall not be utilized for the resumption of hostilities or in the service of an aggressive policy. The Conference also takes note of the declarations of the Governments of Cambodia and Laos to the effect that they will not join in any agreement with other States if this agreement includes the obligation to participate in a military alliance not in conformity with the principles of the Charter of the United Nations or, in the case of Laos, with the principles of the agreement on the cessation of hostilities in Laos or, so long as their security is not threatened, the obligation to establish bases on Cambodian or Laotian territory for the military forces of foreign Powers.

6. The Conference recognizes that the essential purpose of the agreement relating to Viet Nam is to settle military questions with a view to ending hostilities and that the military demarcation line is provisional and should not in any way be interpreted as constituting a political or territorial boundary. The Conference expresses its conviction that the execution of the provisions set out in the present Declaration and in the agreement on the cessation of hostilities creates the necessary basis for the achievement in the near future of a political settlement in Viet Nam.

7. The Conference declares that, so far as Viet Nam is concerned, the settlement of political problems, effected on the basis of respect for the principles of independence, unity and territorial integrity, shall permit the Vietnamese people to enjoy the fundamental freedoms, guaranteed by democratic institutions established as a result of free general elections by secret ballot. In order to ensure that sufficient progress in the restoration of peace has been made, and that all the necessary conditions obtain for free expression of the national will, general elections shall be held in July 1956, under the supervision of an international commission composed of representatives of the Member States of the International Supervisory Commission, referred to in the agreement on the cessation of hostilities. Consultations will be held on this subject between the competent representative authorities of the two zones from July 20, 1955, onwards.

8. The provisions of the agreements on the cessation of hostilities intended to ensure the protection of individuals and of property must be most strictly applied and must, in particular, allow everyone in Viet Nam to decide freely in which zone he wishes to live.

9. The competent representative authorities of the Northern and Southern zones of Viet Nam, as well as the authorities of Laos and Cambodia, must not permit any individual or collective reprisals against persons who have collaborated in any way with one of the parties during the war, or against members of such persons' families.

10. The Conference takes note of the declaration of the Government of the French Republic to the effect that it is ready to withdraw its troops from the territory of Cambodia, Laos and Viet Nam, at the request of the Governments concerned and within periods which shall be fixed by agreement between the parties except in the cases where, by agreement between the two parties, a certain number of French troops shall remain at specified points and for a specified time.

11. The Conference takes note of the declaration of the French Government to the effect that for the settlement of all the problems connected with the re-establishment and consolidation of peace in Cambodia, Laos and Viet Nam, the French Government will proceed from the principle of respect for the independence and sovereignty, unity and territorial integrity of Cambodia, Laos and Viet Nam.

12. In their relations with Cambodia, Laos and Viet Nam, each member of the Geneva Conference undertakes to respect the sovereignty, the independence, the unity and the territorial integrity of the above-mentioned States, and to refrain from any interference in their internal affairs.

13. The members of the Conference agree to consult one another on any question which may be referred to them by the International Supervisory Commission, in order to study such measures as may prove necessary to ensure that the agreements on the cessation of hostilities in Cambodia, Laos and Viet Nam are respected.

DOCUMENT NO. 3: Agreement on the cessation of hostilities in Cambodia, 20 July 1954

Chapter I: Principles and conditions governing execution of the ceasefire

Article 1. As from twenty-third July, 1954, at 0800 hours (Peking mean time) complete cessation of all hostilities throughout Cambodia shall be ordered and enforced by the Commanders of the Armed Forces of the two parties for all troops and personnel of the land, naval and air forces under their control.

Article 2. In conformity with the principle of a simultaneous ceasefire throughout Indo-China, there shall be a simultaneous cessation of hostilities throughout Cambodia, in all the combat areas and for all the forces of the two parties.

To obviate any mistake or misunderstanding and to ensure that both the ending of hostilities and all other operations arising from cessation of hostilities are in fact simultaneous ...

NHIEK TIOULONG,
General

For the Commander-in-Chief of the Units of the Khmer Resistance Forces and for the Commander-in-Chief of the Vietnamese Military Units:

TA-QUANG-BUU,
Vice-Minister of National Defence of the Democratic Republic of Viet Nam

DOCUMENT NO. 4: Agreement on the cessation of hostilities in Laos, 20 July 1954

...

For the Commander-in-Chief of the forces of the French Union Forces in Indo-China:

DELTEIL,
Brigader-General

For the Commander-in-Chief of the fighting units of 'Pathet-Laos' and for the Commander-in-Chief of the People's Army of Viet Nam:

TA-QUANG-BUU,
Vice-Minister of National Defence of the Democratic Republic of Viet Nam

DOCUMENT NO. 5: Agreement on the cessation of hostilities in Viet Nam, 20 July 1954

Chapter I: Provisional military demarcation line and demilitarized zone

Article 1. A provisional military demarcation line shall be fixed, on either side of which the forces of the two parties shall be regrouped after their withdrawal, the forces of the People's Army of Viet Nam to the north of the line and the forces of the French Union to the south.

The provisional military demarcation line is fixed as shown on the map attached ...

It is also agreed that a demilitarized zone shall be established on either side of the demarcation line, to a width of not more than 5 km from it, to act as a buffer zone and avoid any incidents which might result in the resumption of hostilities.

Article 2. The period within which the movement of all forces of either party into the regrouping zone on either side of the provisional military demarcation line shall be completed shall not exceed three hundred (300) days from the date of the present Agreement's entry into force.

...

Chapter III: Ban on the introduction of fresh troops, military personnel, arms and munitions. Military bases

Article 16. With effect from the date of entry into force of the present Agreement, the introduction into Viet Nam of any troop reinforcements and additional military personnel is prohibited.

...

Article 18. With effect from the date of entry into force of the present Agreement, the establishment of new military bases is prohibited throughout Viet Nam territory.

Article 19. With effect from the date of entry into force of the present Agreement, no military base under the control of a foreign State may be established in the regrouping zone of either party; the two parties shall ensure that the zones assigned to them do not adhere to any military alliance and are not used for the resumption of hostilities or to further an aggressive policy.

...

Article 25. The Commanders of the Forces of the two parties shall afford full protection and all possible assistance and cooperation to the Joint Commission and its joint groups and to the International Commission and its inspection teams in the performance of the functions and tasks assigned to them by the present Agreement.

...

Article 27. The signatories of the present Agreement and their successors in their functions shall be responsible for ensuring the observance and enforcement of the terms and provisions thereof. The Commanders of the Forces of the two parties shall, within their respective commands, take all steps and make all arrangements necessary to ensure full compliance with all the provisions of the present Agreement by all elements and military personnel under their command.

The procedures laid down in the present Agreement shall, whenever necessary, be studied by the Commanders of the two parties and, if necessary, defined more specifically by the Joint Commission.

Chapter VI: Joint Commission and International Commission for supervision and control in Viet Nam

Article 28. Responsibility for the execution of the agreement on the cessation of hostilities shall rest with the parties.

Article 29. An International Commission shall ensure the control and supervision of this execution.

Article 30. In order to facilitate, under the condition shown below, the execution of provisions concerning joint actions by the two parties, a Joint Commission shall be set up in Viet Nam.

For the Commander-in-Chief of the French Union Forces in Indo-China:
DELTEIL,
Brigadier-General

For the Commander-in-Chief of the People's Army of Viet Nam:
TA-QUANG-BUU,
Vice-Minister of National Defence

. . .

DOCUMENT NO. 6: Declaration by the Royal Government of Cambodia, 21 July 1954

(Reference: Article 3 of the Final Declaration)

The Royal Government of Cambodia.
In the desire to ensure harmony and agreement among the peoples of the Kingdom,

Declares itself resolved to take the necessary measures to integrate all citizens, without discrimination, into the national community and to guarantee them the enjoyment of the rights and freedoms for which the Constitution of the Kingdom provides:

DOCUMENT NO. 7: Declaration by the Royal Government of Laos, 21 July 1954

(Reference: Article 3 of the Final Declaration)

The Royal Government of Laos,
In the desire to ensure harmony and agreement among the peoples of the Kingdom,

Declares itself resolved to take the necessary measures to integrate all citizens, without discrimination, into the national community and to guarantee them the enjoyment of the rights and freedoms for which the Constitution of the Kingdom provides;

Affirms that all Laotian citizens may freely participate as electors or candidates in general elections by secret ballot . . .

DOCUMENT NO. 8: Declaration by the Royal Government of Cambodia, 21 July 1954

(Reference: Articles 4 and 5 of the Final Declaration)

The Royal Government of Cambodia is resolved never to take part in an aggressive policy and never to permit the territory of Cambodia to be utilized in the service of such a policy.

The Royal Government of Cambodia will not join in any agreement with other States, if this agreement carries for Cambodia the obligation to enter into military alliance not in conformity with the principles of the Charter of the United Nations, or, as long as its security is not threatened, the obligation to establish bases on Cambodian territory for the military forces of foreign Powers.

The Royal Government of Cambodia

is resolved to settle its international disputes by peaceful means, in such a manner as not to endanger peace, international security and justice.

During the period which will elapse between the date of the cessation of hostilities in Viet Nam and that of the final settlement of political problems in this country, the Royal Government of Cambodia will not solicit foreign aid in war material, personnel or instructors except for the purpose of the effective defence of the territory.

DOCUMENT NO. 9: Declaration by the Royal Government of Laos, 21 July 1954

(Reference: Articles 4 and 5 of the Final Declaration)

The Royal Government of Laos is resolved never to pursue a policy of aggression and will never permit the territory of Laos to be used in furtherance of such a policy.

The Royal Government of Laos will never join in any agreement with other States if this agreement includes the obligation for the Royal Government of Laos to participate in a military alliance not in conformity with the principles of the Charter of the United Nations or with the principles of the agreement on the cessation of hostilities or, unless its security is threatened, the obligation to establish bases on Laotian territory for military forces of foreign Powers.

The Royal Government of Laos is resolved to settle its international disputes by peaceful means so that international peace and security and justice are not endangered.

During the period between the cessation of hostilities in Viet Nam and the final settlement of that country's political problems, the Royal Government of Laos will not request foreign aid, whether in war material, in personnel or in instructors, except for the purpose of its effective territorial defence and to the extent defined by the agreement on the cessation of hostilities.

DOCUMENT NO. 10: Declaration by the Government of the French Republic, 21 July 1954

(Reference: Article 10 of the Final Declaration)

The Government of the French Republic declares that it is ready to withdraw its troops from the territory of Cambodia, Laos and Viet Nam, at the request of the Governments concerned and within a period which shall be fixed by agreement between the parties, except in the cases where, by agreement between the two parties, a certain number of French troops shall remain at specified points and for a specified time.

DOCUMENT NO. 11: Declaration by the Government of the French Republic, 21 July 1954

(Reference: Article 11 of the Final Declaration)

For the settlement of all the problems connected with the re-establishment and consolidation of peace in Cambodia, Laos and Viet Nam, the French Government will proceed from the principle of respect for the independence and sovereignty, the unity and territorial integrity of Cambodia, Laos and Viet Nam.

Declaration on the neutrality of Laos, Geneva, 23 July 1962

The Governments of the Union of Burma, the Kingdom of Cambodia, Canada, the People's Republic of China, the Democratic Republic of Viet Nam, the Republic of France, the Republic of India, the Polish People's Republic, the Republic of Viet Nam, the Kingdom of Thailand, the Union of Soviet Socialist

Republics, the United Kingdom of Great Britain and Northern Ireland and the United States of America, whose representatives took part in the International Conference on the Settlement of the Laotian Question, 1961-2;

Welcoming the presentation of the statement of neutrality by the Royal Government of Laos of July 9, 1962, and taking note of this statement, which is, with the concurrence of the Royal Government of Laos, incorporated in the present Declaration as an integral part thereof, and the text of which is as follows:

THE ROYAL GOVERNMENT OF LAOS,

Being resolved to follow the path of peace and neutrality in conformity with the interests and aspirations of the Laotian people, as well as the principles of the Joint Communiqué of Zurich dated June 22, 1961, and of the Geneva Agreements of 1954, in order to build a peaceful, neutral, independent, democratic, unified and prosperous Laos,

Solemnly declares that:

1. It will resolutely apply the five principles of peaceful coexistence in foreign relations, and will develop friendly relations and establish diplomatic relations with all countries, the neighbouring countries first and foremost, on the basis of equality and of respect for the independence and sovereignty of Laos;

2. It is the will of the Laotian people to protect and ensure respect for the sovereignty, independence, neutrality, unity, and territorial integrity of Laos;

3. It will not resort to the use or threat of force in any way which might impair the peace of other countries, and will not interfere in the internal affairs of other countries;

4. It will not enter into any military alliance or into any agreement, whether military or otherwise, which is inconsistent with the neutrality of the Kingdom of Laos; it will not allow the establishment of any foreign military base on Laotian territory, nor allow any country to use Laotian territory for military purposes or for the purposes of interference

in the internal affairs of other countries, nor recognize the protection of any alliance or military coalition, including SEATO;

5. It will not allow any foreign interference in the internal affairs of the Kingdom of Laos in any form whatsoever;

6. Subject to the provisions of Article 5 of the Protocol, it will require the withdrawal from Laos of all foreign troops and military personnel, and will not allow any foreign troops or military personnel to be introduced into Laos;

7. It will accept direct and unconditional aid from all countries that wish to help the Kingdom of Laos build up an independent and autonomous national economy on the basis of respect for the sovereignty of Laos;

8. It will respect the treaties and agreements signed in conformity with the interests of the Laotian people and of the policy of peace and neutrality of the Kingdom, in particular the Geneva Agreements of 1962, and will abrogate all treaties and agreements which are contrary to those principles. ...

[The above-mentioned countries ...]

2. Undertake, in particular, that

(a) they will not commit or participate in any way in any act which might directly or indirectly impair the sovereignty, independence, neutrality, unity or territorial integrity of the Kingdom of Laos;

(b) they will not resort to the use or threat of force or any other measure which might impair the peace of the Kingdom of Laos;

(c) they will refrain from all direct or indirect interference in the internal affairs of the Kingdom of Laos;

(d) they will not attach conditions of a political nature to any asistance which they may offer or which the Kingdom of Laos may seek;

(e) they will not bring the Kingdom of Laos in any way into any military alliance or any other agreement, whether military or otherwise, which is inconsistent with her neutrality, nor invite or encourage her to enter into any such alliance or to conclude any such agreement;

(f) they will respect the wish of the Kingdom of Laos not to recognize the protection of any alliance or military coalition, including SEATO;

(g) they will not introduce into the Kingdom of Laos foreign troops or military personnel in any form whatsoever, nor will they in any way facilitate or connive at the introduction of any foreign troops or military personnel;

(h) they will not establish nor will they in any way facilitate or connive at the establishment in the Kingdom of Laos of any foreign military base, foreign strong point or other foreign military installation of any kind;

(i) they will not use the territory of the Kingdom of Laos for interference in the internal affairs of other countries;

(j) they will not use the territory of any country, including their own for interference in the internal affairs of the Kingdom of Laos.

...

4. Undertake, in the event of a violation or threat of violation of the sovereignty, independence, neutrality, unity or territorial integrity of the Kingdom of Laos, to consult jointly with the Royal Government of Laos and among themselves in order to consider measures which might prove to be necessary to ensure the observance of these principles and the other provisions of the present Declaration.

...

Military armistice in Korea, Panmunjon, 27 July 1953

... in the interest of stopping the Korean conflict, with its great toll of suffering and bloodshed on both sides, and with the objective of establishing an armistice which will insure a complete cessation of hostilities and of all acts of armed force in Korea until a final peaceful settlement is achieved, do individually collectively, and mutually agree to ...

Article I: Military demarcation line and demilitarized zone. 1. A military demarcation line shall be fixed and both sides shall withdraw two (2) kilometres from this line so as to establish a demilitarized zone between the opposing forces. A demilitarized zone shall be established as a buffer zone to prevent the occurrence of incidents which might lead to a resumption of hostilities.

2. The military demarcation line is located as indicated on the attached map ...

...

24. The general mission of the Military Armistice Commission shall be to supervise the implementation of this Armistice Agreement and to settle through negotiations any violations of this Armistice Agreement.

...

[36. A Neutral Nations Supervisory Commission established.]

Article III: Arrangements relating to prisoners of war. 51. The release and repatriation of all prisoners of war held in the custody of each side at the time this Armistice Agreement becomes effective shall be effected in conformity with the following provisions agreed upon by both sides prior to the signing of this Armistice Agreement.

(a) Within sixty (60) days after this Armistice Agreement becomes effective, each side shall, without offering any hindrance, directly repatriate and hand over in groups all those prisoners of war in its custody who insist on repatriation to the side to which they belonged at the time of capture. Repatriation shall be accomplished in accordance with the related provisions of this Article. In order to expedite the repatriation process of such personnel, each side shall, prior to the signing of the Armistice Agreement, exchange the total numbers, by nationalities, of personnel to be directly repatriated. Each group of prisoners of war delivered to the other side shall be accompanied by rosters, prepared by nationality, to include name, rank (if any) and internment or military serial number.

(b) Each side shall release all those remaining prisoners of war, who are not directly repatriated, from its military control and from its custody and hand them over to the Neutral Nations Repatriation Commission for disposition in accordance with the provisions in the Annex hereto: 'Terms of Reference for Neutral Nations Repatriation Commission'....

Article IV: Recommendation to the Governments concerned on both sides. 60. In order to ensure the peaceful settlement of the Korean question, the Military Commanders of both sides hereby recommend to the Governments of the countries concerned on both sides that, within three (3) months after the Armistice Agreement is signed and becomes effective, a political conference of a higher level of both sides be held by representatives appointed respectively to settle through negotiation the questions of the withdrawal of all foreign forces from Korea, the peaceful settlement of the Korean question, etc.

...

Agreement to end the Vietnam war, Paris, 27 January 1973

The parties participating in the Paris Conference on Vietnam, with a view to ending the war and restoring peace in Vietnam on the basis of respect for the Vietnamese people's fundamental national rights and the South Vietnamese people's right to self-determination, and to contributing to the consolidation of peace in Asia and the world, have agreed on the following provisions and undertake to respect and to implement them:

Chapter I: The Vietnamese people's fundamental national rights

Article 1. The United States and all other countries respect the independence, sovereignty, unity and territorial integrity of Vietnam as recognized by the 1954 Geneva Agreements on Vietnam.

Chapter II: Cessation of hostilities—withdrawal of troops

Article 2. A ceasefire shall be observed throughout South Vietnam as of 24.00 hours GMT, on January 27, 1973.

At the same hour, the United States will stop all its military activities against the territory of the Democratic Republic of Vietnam by ground, air and naval forces, wherever they may be based, and end the mining of the territorial waters, ports, harbours, and waterways of the Democratic Republic of Vietnam.

The United States will remove, permanently deactivate or destroy all the mines in the territorial waters, ports, harbours, and waterways of North Vietnam as soon as this Agreement goes into effect.

The complete cessation of hostilities mentioned in this Article shall be durable and without limit of time.

Article 3. The parties undertake to maintain the ceasefire and to ensure a lasting and stable peace.

As soon as the ceasefire goes into effect:

(a) The United States forces and those of the other foreign countries allied with the United States and the Republic of Vietnam shall remain in place pending the implementation of the plan of troop withdrawal. The Four Party Joint Military Commission described in Article 16 shall determine the modalities.

(b) The armed forces of the two South Vietnamese parties shall remain in place. The Two-Party Joint Military Commission described in Article 17 shall determine the areas controlled by each party and the modalities of stationing.

(c) The regular forces of all services and arms and the irregular forces of the parties in South Vietnam shall stop all offensive activities against each other and shall strictly abide by the following stipulations:

All acts of force on the ground, in the air, and on the sea shall be prohibited;

All hostile acts, terrorism and reprisals by both sides will be banned.

Article 4. The United States will not continue its military involvement or intervene in the internal affairs of South Vietnam.

Article 5. Within sixty days of the signing of this Agreement, there will be a total withdrawal from South Vietnam of troops, military advisers, and military personnel, including technical military personnel and military personnel associated with the pacification programmes, armaments, munitions and war material of the United States and those of the other foreign countries mentioned in Article 3 (a). Advisers from the above-mentioned countries to all paramilitary organizations and the police force will also be withdrawn within the same period of time.

Article 6. The dismantlement of all military bases in South Vietnam of the United States and of the other foreign countries mentioned in Article 3 (a) shall be completed within sixty days of the signing of this Agreement.

Article 7. From the enforcement of the ceasefire to the formation of the Government provided for in Articles 9 (b) and 14 of this Agreement, the two South Vietnamese parties shall not accept the introduction of troops, military advisers, and military personnel including technical military personnel, armaments, munitions, and war material into South Vietnam.

The two South Vietnamese parties shall be permitted to make periodic replacement of armaments, munitions and war material which have been destroyed, damaged, worn out or used up after the ceasefire, on the basis of piece-for-piece, of the same characteristics and properties, under the supervision of the Joint Military Commission of the two South Vietnamese parties and of the International Commission of Control and Supervision.

Chapter III: The return of captured military personnel and foreign civilians, and captured and detained Vietnamese civilian personnel

Article 8. (a) The return of captured military personnel and foreign civilians of the parties shall be carried out simultaneously with and completed not later than the same day as the troop withdrawal mentioned in Article 5. The parties shall exchange complete lists of the above-mentioned captured military personnel and foreign civilians on the day of the signing of this Agreement.

(b) The parties shall help each other to get information about those military personnel and foreign civilians of the parties missing in action, to determine the location and take care of the graves of the dead so as to facilitate the exhumation and repatriation of the remains, and to take any such other measures as may be required to get information about those still considered missing in action.

(c) The question of the return of Vietnamese civilian personnel captured and detained in South Vietnam will be resolved by the two South Vietnamese parties on the basis of the principles of Article 21 (b) of the Agreement on the cessation of hostilities in Vietnam of July 20, 1954.

The two South Vietnamese parties will do so in a spirit of national reconciliation and accord, with a view to ending hatred and enmity, in order to ease suffering and to reunite families. The two South Vietnamese parties will do their utmost to resolve this question within ninety days after the ceasefire comes into effect.

Chapter IV: The exercise of the South Vietnamese people's right of self-determination

Article 9. The Government of the United States of America and the Government of the Democratic Republic of Vietnam undertake to respect the following principles for the exercise of the South-Vietnamese people's right to self-determination:

(a) The South Vietnamese people's right to self-determination is sacred, inalienable, and shall be respected by all countries.

(b) The South Vietnamese people shall decide themselves the political future of South Vietnam through genuinely free and democratic elections under international supervision.

(c) Foreign countries shall not impose any political tendency or personality on the South Vietnamese people.

Article 10. The two South Vietnamese parties undertake to respect the ceasefire and maintain peace in South Vietnam, settle all matters of contention through negotiations, and avoid all armed conflict.

Article 11. Immediately after the ceasefire, the two South Vietnamese parties will:

Achieve national reconciliation and concord, end hatred and enmity, prohibit all acts of reprisal and discrimination against individuals or organizations that have collaborated with one side or the other;

Ensure the democratic liberties of the people: personal freedom, freedom of speech, freedom of the press, freedom of meeting, freedom of organization, freedom of political activities, freedom of belief, freedom of movement, freedom of residence, freedom of work, right to property ownership and right to free enterprise.

Article 12. (a) Immediately after the ceasefire, the two South Vietnamese parties shall hold consultations in a spirit of national reconciliation and concord, mutual respect and mutual nonelimination to set up a National Council of National Reconciliation and Concord of three equal segments.

The Council shall operate on the principle of unanimity. After the National Council of National Reconciliation and Concord has assumed its functions, the two South Vietnamese parties will consult about the formation of councils at lower levels.

The two South Vietnamese parties shall sign an agreement on the internal matters of South Vietnam as soon as possible and do their utmost to accomplish this within ninety days after the ceasefire comes into effect, in keeping with the South Vietnamese people's aspirations for peace, independence and democracy.

(b) The National Council of National Reconciliation and Concord shall have the task of promoting the two South Vietnamese parties' implementation of this Agreement, achievement of national reconciliation and concord and ensurance of democratic liberties.

The National Council of National Reconciliation and Concord will organize the free and democratic general elections provided for in Article 9 (b) and decide the procedures and modalities of these general elections.

The institutions for which the general elections are to be held will be agreed upon through consultations between the two South Vietnamese parties. The National Council of National Reconciliation and Concord will also decide the procedures and modalities of such local elections as the two South Vietnamese parties agree upon.

Article 13. The question of Vietnamese armed forces in South Vietnam shall be settled by the two South Vietnamese parties in a spirit of national reconciliation and concord, equality and mutual respect, without foreign interference, in accordance with the post-war situation.

Among the questions to be discussed by the two South Vietnamese parties are steps to reduce their military effectives and to demobilize the troops being reduced. The two South Vietnamese parties will accomplish this as soon as possible.

Article 14. South Vietnam will pursue a foreign policy of peace and independence. It will be prepared to establish relations with all countries irrespective of their political and social systems on the basis of mutual respect for independence and sovereignty, and accept economic and technical aid from any country with no political conditions attached.

The acceptance of military aid by South Vietnam in the future shall come under the authority of the Government set up after the general elections in South Vietnam provided for in Article 9 (b).

Chapter V: The reunification of Vietnam and the relationship between North and South Vietnam

Article 15. The reunification of Vietnam shall be carried out step by step through peaceful means on the basis of discussion and agreements between North and South Vietnam, without coercion or annexation by either part, and without foreign interference. The time for reunification will be agreed upon by North and South Vietnam.

Pending the reunification:

(a) The military demarcation line between the two zones at the seventeenth parallel is only provisional and not a political or territorial boundary, as provided for in paragraph 6 of the Final Declaration of the 1954 Geneva Conference.

(b) North and South Vietnam shall respect the demilitarized zone on either side of the provisional military demarcation line.

(c) North and South Vietnam shall promptly start negotiations with a view to re-establishing normal relations in various fields. Among the questions to be negotiated are the modalities of civilian movement across the provisional military demarcation line.

(d) North and South Vietnam shall not join any military alliance or military block and shall not allow foreign Powers to maintain military bases, troops, military advisers, and military personnel on their respective territories, as stipulated in the 1954 Geneva Agreements on Vietnam.

Chapter VI: The Joint Military Commissions, the International Commission of Controls and Supervision, the International Conference

Article 16. (a) The parties participating in the Paris Conference on Vietnam shall immediately designate representatives to form a Four Party Joint Military Commission with the task of ensuring joint action by the parties in implementing the following provisions of this Agreement:

The first paragraph of Article 2, regarding the enforcement of the ceasefire throughout South Vietnam:

Article 3 (a), regarding the ceasefire by United States forces and those of the other foreign countries referred to in that Article;

Article 3 (c), regarding the ceasefire between all parties in South Vietnam;

Article 5, regarding the withdrawal from South Vietnam of United States troops and those of the other foreign countries mentioned in Article 3 (a);

Article 6, regarding the dismantlement of military bases in South Vietnam of the United States and those of the other foreign countries mentioned in Article 3 (a);

Article 8 (a), regarding the return of captured military personnel and foreign civilians of the parties;

Article 8 (b), regarding the mutual assistance of the parties in getting information about those military personnel and foreign civilians of the parties missing in action.

(b) The Four Party Joint Military Commission shall operate in accordance with the principle of consultations and unanimity. Disagreements shall be referred to the International Commission of Control and Supervision.

(c) The Four Party Joint Military Commission shall begin operating immediately after the signing of this Agreement and end its activities in sixty days, after the completion of the withdrawal of United States troops and those of the other foreign countries mentioned in Article 3 (a) and the completion of the return of captured military personnel and foreign civilians of the parties.

(d) The four parties shall agree immediately on the organization, the working procedure, means of activity, and expenditures of the Four Party Joint Military Commission.

Article 17. (a) The two South Vietnamese parties shall immediately designate representatives to form a Two Party Joint Military Commission with the task of ensuring joint action by the two South Vietnamese parties in implementing the following provisions of this Agreement:

The first paragraph of Article 2, regarding the enforcement of the ceasefire throughout South Vietnam, when the Four Party Joint Military Commission has ended its activities;

Article 3 (b), regarding the ceasefire between the two South Vietnamese parties;

Article 3 (c), regarding the ceasefire between all parties in South Vietnam, when the Four Party Joint Military Commission has ended its activities;

Article 7, regarding the prohibition of the introduction of troops into South Vietnam and all other provisions of this Article;

Article 8 (c) regarding the question of the return of Vietnamese civilian personnel captured and detained in South Vietnam;

Article 13, regarding the reduction of the military effectives of the two South Vietnamese parties and the demobilization of the troops being reduced.

(b) Disagreements shall be referred to the International Commission of Control and Supervision.

(c) After the signing of this Agreement the Two Party Joint Military Commission shall agree immediately on the measures and organization aimed at enforcing the ceasefire and preserving peace in South Vietnam.

Article 18. (a) After the signing of this Agreement, an International Commission of Control and Supervision shall be established immediately.

(b) Until the International Conference provided for in Article 19 makes definitive arrangements, the International Commission of Control and Supervision will report to the four parties on matters concerning the control and supervision of the implementation of the following provisions of this Agreement:

The first paragraph of Article 2, regarding the enforcement of the ceasefire through South Vietnam;

Article 3 (a), regarding the ceasefire by United States forces and those of the other foreign countries referred to in that Article;

Article 3 (c), regarding the ceasefire between all the parties in South Vietnam;

Article 5, regarding the withdrawal from South Vietnam of United States troops and those of the other foreign countries mentioned in Article 3 (a);

Article 6, regarding the dismantlement of military bases in South Vietnam of the United States and those of the other foreign countries mentioned in Article 3 (a);

Article 8 (a), regarding the return of captured military personnel and foreign civilians of the parties.

The International Commission of Control and Supervision shall form control teams for carrying out its tasks. The four parties shall agree immediately on the location and operation of these teams. The parties will facilitate their operation.

(c) Until the International Conference makes definitive arrangements, the International Commission of Control and Supervision will report to the two South Vietnamese parties on matters concerning the control and supervision of the implementation of the following provisions of this Agreement:

The first paragraph of Article 2, regarding the enforcement of the ceasefire throughout South Vietnam, when the Four Party Joint Military Commission has ended its activities;

Article 3 (b), regarding the ceasefire between the two South Vietnamese parties;

Article 3 (c), regarding the ceasefire between all parties in South Vietnam, when the Four Party Joint Military Commission has ended its activities;

Article 7, regarding the prohibition of the introduction of troops into South Vietnam and all other provisions of this Article;

Article 8 (c), regarding the question of the return of Vietnamese civilian personnel captured and detained in South Vietnam;

Article 9 (b), regarding the free and democratic general elections in South Vietnam;

Article 13, regarding the reduction of the military effectives of the two South Vietnamese parties and the demobilization of the troops being reduced.

The International Commission of Control and Supervision shall form control teams for carrying out its tasks. The two South Vietnamese parties shall agree immediately on the location and operation of these teams. The two South Vietnamese parties will facilitate their operations.

(d) The International Commission of Control and Supervision shall be composed of representatives of four countries: Canada, Hungary, Indonesia and Poland. The chairmanship of this commission will rotate among the members for specific periods to be determined by the commission.

(e) The International Commission of Control and Supervision shall carry out its tasks in accordance with the principle of respect for the sovereignty of South Vietnam.

(f) The International Commission of Control and Supervision shall operate in accordance with the principle of consultations and unanimity.

(g) The International Commission of Control and Supervision shall begin operating when a ceasefire comes into force in Vietnam. As regards the provisions in Article 18 (b) concerning the four parties, the International Commission of Control and Supervision shall end its activities when the commission's tasks of control and supervision regarding these provisions have been fulfilled.

As regards the provisions in Article 18 (c) concerning the two South Vietnamese parties, the International Commission of Control and Supervision shall end its activities on the request of the Government formed after the general elections in South Vietnam provided for in Article 9 (b).

(h) The four parties shall agree immediately on the organization, means of activity, and expenditures of the International Commission of Control and Supervision. The relationship between the International Commission and the International Conference will be agreed upon by the International Commission and the International Conference.

Article 19. The parties agree on the convening of an International Conference within thirty days of the signing of this Agreement to acknowledge the signed agreements; to guarantee the ending of the war, the maintenance of peace in Vietnam, the respect of the Vietnamese people's fundamental national rights, and the South Vietnamese people's right to self-determination; and to contribute to and guarantee peace in Indo-China.

The United States and the Democratic Republic of Vietnam, on behalf of the parties participating in the Paris Conference on Vietnam, will propose to the following parties that they participate in this International Conference: the People's Republic of China, the Republic of France, the Union of Soviet Socialist Republics, the United Kingdom, the four countries of the International Commission of Control and Supervision, and the Secretary-General of the United Nations, together with the parties participating in the Paris Conference on Vietnam.

Chapter VII: Regarding Cambodia and Laos

Article 20. (a) The parties participating in the Paris Conference on Vietnam shall strictly respect the 1954 Geneva Agreements on Cambodia and the 1962 Geneva Agreements on Laos, which recognized the Cambodian and the Laos people's fundamental national rights, i.e. the independence, sovereignty, unity and territorial integrity of these countries. The parties shall respect the neutrality of Cambodia and Laos.

The parties participating in the Paris Conference on Vietnam undertake to refrain from using the territory of Cambodia and the territory of Laos to encroach on the sovereignty and security of one another and of other countries.

(b) Foreign countries shall put an end to all military activities in Cambodia and Laos, totally withdraw from and refrain from reintroducing into these two countries troops, military advisers and military personnel, armaments, munitions and war material.

(c) The internal affairs of Cambodia and Laos shall be settled by the people of each of these countries without foreign interference.

(d) The problems existing between the Indo-Chinese countries shall be settled by the Indo-Chinese parties on the basis of respect for each other's independence, sovereignty and territorial integrity and non-interference in each other's internal affairs.

Chapter VIII: The relationship between the United States and the Democratic Republic of Vietnam

Article 21. The United States anticipates that this Agreement will usher in an era of reconciliation with the Democratic Republic of Vietnam as with all the peoples of Indo-China. In pursuance of its traditional policy, the United States will contribute to healing the wounds of war and to post-war reconstruction of the Democratic Republic of Vietnam and throughout Indo-China.

Article 22. The ending of the war, the restoration of peace in Vietnam, and the strict implementation of this Agreement will create conditions for establishing a new, equal and mutually beneficial relationship between the United States and the Democratic Republic of Vietnam on the basis of respect for each other's independence and sovereignty, and non-interference in each other's internal affairs. At the same time, this will ensure stable peace in Vietnam and contribute to the preservation of lasting peace in Indo-China and South-east Asia.

Chapter IX: Other provisions

Article 23. This Agreement shall enter into force upon signature by plenipotentiary representatives of the parties participating in the Paris Conference on Vietnam. All the parties concerned shall strictly implement this Agreement and its Protocols.

Done in Paris this twenty-seventh day of January, one thousand nine hundred and seventy-three, in Vietnamese and English. The Vietnamese and English texts are officially and equally authentic.

For the Government of the United States of America: William P. Rogers, Secretary of State.

For the Government of the Republic of Vietnam: Tran Van Lam, Minister for Foreign Affairs.

For the Government of the Democratic Republic of Vietnam: Nguyen Duy Trinh, Minister for Foreign Affairs.

For the Provisional Revolutionary Government of the Republic of South Vietnam: Nguyen Thi Binh, Minister for Foreign Affairs.

Declaration of the International Conference on Vietnam, Paris, 2 March 1973

The Government of Canada, the Government of the People's Republic of China, the Government of the United States of America, the Government of the French Republic, the Provisional Revolutionary Government of the Republic of South Vietnam, the Government of the Hungarian People's Republic, the Government of the Republic of Indonesia, the Government of the Polish People's Republic, the Government of the Democratic Republic of Vietnam, the Government of the United Kingdom of Great Britain and Northern Ireland, the Government of the Republic of Vietnam, and the Government of the Union of Soviet Socialist Republics in the presence of the Secretary-General of the United Nations,

With a view to acknowledging the signed agreements guaranteeing the ending of the war, the maintenance of peace in Vietnam, the respect of the Vietnamese people's fundamental national rights, and the South Vietnamese people's right to self-determination, and contributing to and guaranteeing peace in Indochina,

Have agreed on the following provisions, and undertake to respect and implement them:

Article 1. The parties to this Act solemnly acknowledge, express their approval of and support the Paris Agreement on Ending the War and Restoring Peace in Vietnam signed in Paris on January 27, 1973, and the four Protocols to the Agreement signed on the same date (hereinafter referred to respectively as the Agreement and the Protocols).

Article 2. The Agreement responds to the aspirations and fundamental national rights of the Vietnamese people, i.e. the independence, sovereignty, unity, and territorial integrity of Vietnam, to the right of the South Vietnamese people to self-

determination, and to the earnest desire for peace shared by all countries in the world. The Agreement constitutes a major contribution to peace, self-determination, national independence, and the improvement of relations among countries. The Agreement and the Protocols should be strictly respected and scrupulously implemented.

Article 3. The parties to this Act solemnly acknowledge the commitments by the parties to the Agreement and the Protocols to strictly respect and scrupulously implement the Agreement and the Protocols.

Article 4. The parties to this Act solemnly recognize and strictly respect the fundamental national rights of the Vietnamese people, i.e. the independence, sovereignty, unity, and territorial integrity of Vietnam, as well as the right of the South Vietnamese people to self-determination. The parties to this Act shall strictly respect the Agreement and the Protocols by refraining from any action at variance with their provisions.

Article 5. For the sake of a durable peace in Vietnam, the parties to this Act call on all countries to strictly respect the fundamental national rights of the Vietnamese people, i.e. the independence, sovereignty, unity, and territorial integrity of Vietnam, and the right of the South Vietnamese people to self-determination, and to strictly respect the Agreement and the Protocols by refraining from any action at variance with their provisions.

Article 6. (a) The four parties to the Agreement or the two South Vietnamese parties may, either individually or through joint action, inform the other parties to this Act about the implementation of the Agreement and the Protocols. Since the reports and views submitted by the International Commission of Control and Supervision concerning the control and supervision of the implementation of those provisions of the Agreement and the Protocols which are within the tasks of the commission will be sent to either the four parties signatory to the Agreement or to the two South Vietnamese parties, those parties shall be responsible, either individually or through joint action, for forwarding them promptly to the other parties to this Act.

(b) The four parties to the Agreement or the two South Vietnamese parties shall also, either individually or through joint action, forward this information and these reports and views to the other participant in the International Conference on Vietnam for his information.

Article 7. (a) In the event of a violation of the Agreement or the Protocols which threatens the peace, the independence, sovereignty, unity, or territorial integrity of Vietnam, or the right of the South Vietnamese people to self-determination, the parties signatory to the Agreement and the Protocols shall, either individually or jointly, consult with the other parties to this Act with a view to determining necessary remedial measures.

(b) The International Conference on Vietnam shall be reconvened upon a joint request by the Government of the United States of America and the Government of the Democratic Republic of Vietnam on behalf of the parties signatory to the Agreement or upon a request by six or more of the parties to this Act.

Article 8. With a view to contributing to and guaranteeing peace in Indo-China, the parties to this Act acknowledge the commitment of the parties to the Agreement to respect the independence, sovereignty, unity, territorial integrity, and neutrality of Cambodia and Laos as stipulated in the Agreement, agree also to respect them and to refrain from any action at variance with them, and call on other countries to do the same.

Article 9. This Act shall enter into force upon signature by plenipotentiary representatives of all twelve parties and shall be strictly implemented by all the parties. Signature of this Act does not constitute recognition of any party in any case in which it has not previously been accorded.

Done in twelve copies in Paris this second day of March, 1973, in English, French, Russian, Vietnamese and Chinese. All texts are equally authentic.

XVI · The conflicts and alignments of Africa, 1945–72

The continent of Africa south of the Sahara has, on the whole, remained outside the main stream of world rivalries and alignments; the 'cold war' has passed by the greater part of Africa. The Soviet Union has provided aid to a small number of African States and has sought in general to capitalize on its stand against 'colonialism' and 'racism'. The interest and influence of the United States in Africa is most in evidence through the provision of financial aid by way of international U.N. programmes. The United States 'Peace Corps' seeks to create goodwill in some twenty-three African countries through personal service. The United States has also signed Defense Pacts with Liberia (1959) providing military aid and promising to consult in case of aggression. Like the Soviet Union, the United States has condemned apartheid in South Africa, the Unilateral Declaration of Independence in Rhodesia, and colonialism in general. France remains influential among the independent West African States forming the French community, and Britain retains some influence around the independent States forming the Commonwealth. China established a spectacular 'bridgehead' of influence in Tanzania through technical and economic assistance. As the decade of the 1960s drew to a close, it became apparent that the Soviet Union and China were rivals for influence in Somalia and Ethiopia, and China has replaced Soviet influence in the Sudan. But the African States, some leaning towards socialism, others conservative and opposed to socialism, are non-aligned in terms of global international relations.

North of the Sahara lie the Arab Muslim States of Morocco, Algeria, Tunisia, Libya and Egypt. Although these States play a role in African affairs and have supported African solidarity, their international policies are more frequently subordinated to the interests, conflicts and alignments of the Middle East and

8 The emergence of independence in Africa, 1970

the Mediterranean. In this area Soviet and American and Western policies have been in opposition for much of the time since the Second World War. Oil, and the continuing Israeli–Arab state of war, make this region one of importance in global international affairs. It needs to be considered separately from the rest of Africa (see Chapter XVII).

The emergence of African independence since 1957

The partition of Africa, largely completed during the last quarter of the nineteenth century, and only modified after the First World War with the distribution of Germany's colonies, brought international peace to the continent based on the agreed boundaries of the European empires. Within these empires the degree of European control varied: colonies were completely dependent, so were African territories such as Portuguese Angola and Mozambique or French Algeria, which were simply regarded as overseas provinces of the motherland; hardly distinguishable was the nominal autonomy of the Sultan of Morocco within the French Protectorate. But between the wars of 1914 and 1939, there is an example of a measure of progress to independence. The relationship between Britain and Egypt changed during these years as Egypt progressed from a Protectorate to the qualified independence granted by the treaty of 1922, and to the much greater independence bestowed by the treaty of 1936, which still, however, permitted Britain to garrison and defend the Suez Canal. Southern Rhodesia came close to independence in 1923 when granted responsible government without Dominion status. The Union of South Africa, created in 1909, was recognized as enjoying complete sovereign rights by the Statute of Westminster in 1931. It was the only part of Africa, once colonized, which during the years from 1900–50 had gained independence. Only two African States escaped the partition process of the later nineteenth century and maintained their independence: Liberia and Ethiopia, though the latter was occupied by Italy from 1936–41. The emergence of African independence has been a continuing process since 1957 and has taken place at an uneven pace. From this circumstance have sprung some of the major problems of international relations in the continent.

Britain took the lead before 1939 in granting South African independence and Rhodesian self-government, thus creating the most intractable problem in present-day African politics since power was transferred to minorities of European descent. In West Africa after the Second World War, the colony of the Gold Coast was the first to be granted independence as Ghana on 6 March 1957; the small U.N. trusteeship territory of British Togoland voted to integrate with Ghana. Next followed Nigeria, with a population of about 55 million, attaining independence on 1 October 1960; Sierra Leone on 27 April 1961; and the small colony of Gambia on 18 February 1965.

In East Africa, Uganda was accorded independence on 9 October 1962; Tanganyika, a U.N. trusteeship territory, attained independence on 9 December 1961, and after the union with Zanzibar on 26 April 1964 became the United Republic of Tanganyika and Zanzibar, renamed Tanzania, on 29 October 1964.

Independence was a more difficult process for Kenya where a powerful community of white settlers had been accustomed to authority over the Africans. Strong nationalist feelings led some of the Kikuyu into the secret Mau Mau society, which in the years 1952–6 resorted to violent guerilla activities directed against the white settlers. A period of repression was followed by further progress towards independence. Kenya finally became independent on 12 December 1963. The British Protectorate of Somali became independent in June 1960 and joined Somalia to form one State in July 1960. The small island of Mauritius was given independence in 1968. In South Central Africa the process of independence proved the most difficult of all, and the support of independent Africa for the African majority in Rhodesia remains a focal point of international conflict. The powerful community of European settlers in Southern Rhodesia had gained the status of a self-governing colony in 1923, a time when European Governments regarded the African majority rule as a far-off prospect, if realistically attainable at all. The administrations of North and South Rhodesia and Nyasaland had been loosely coordinated since 1944 until a closer union was formed with the creation of the Central African Federation in August 1953. It lasted ten years. The African Nationalists sought independence and African majority rule in Northern Rhodesia and Nyasaland, as well as in Southern Rhodesia. Northern Rhodesia was acknowledged to have the right to secede from the Federation in 1963, and became independent on 24 October 1964 taking the name of Zambia. Nyasaland gained independence a few weeks earlier on 6 July 1964 and took the name of Malawi. In Southern Rhodesia complete independence, which would follow from Britain's readiness to relinquish its 'reserved powers' over legislation that could be condemned as racially discriminatory, was prevented by the Southern Rhodesian Government's insistence of the continuation of predominant settler rule in the foreseeable future. The Southern Rhodesian Smith Government, unable to secure a British grant of independence in November 1965, declared independence unilaterally (U.D.I.).

In Southern Africa, the former Protectorate of Bechuanaland became the independent Republic of Botswana on 30 September 1966, and Lesotho and Swaziland, enclaves in South Africa, gained independence on 4 October 1966 and 6 September 1968 respectively.

France granted self-government and independence to its former West and Central African colonies together in 1960 as part of a coordinated policy. General de Gaulle's Constitution of 1958 replaced the French Union by the concept of the French Community, which permitted the French overseas territories full internal self-government but left defence, foreign policy and general economic planning in French hands, with the President of France acting as Chairman of a Council of Prime Ministers from the countries of the Community. Only Guinea voted against this constitution, and after being granted independence on 2 October 1958 it was penalized by being immediately deprived of French aid and technical assistance. Guinea turned for help – and received it – from communist States during the early years of independence. It signed agreements with China but has also received aid from the United States. The remaining African members of the French Community were not all satisfied with their status and worked for complete independence. This was granted by France, and independence was proclaimed on 26 June 1960 in Madagascar, which took the name of Malagasy Republic; in Chad on 1 August 1960; the Central African Republic, 13 August 1960; Congo-Brazzaville, 15 August 1960; and Gabon, 17 August 1960. These States became fully independent, but decided to remain in the French Community and concluded Cooperation and Mutual Defence Agreements with France. The following States on attaining independence remained outside the Community: Dahomey, 1 August 1960; Niger, 2 August 1960; Upper Volta, 5 August 1960; Ivory Coast, 6 August 1960; and Mauritania, 27 November 1960. The short-lived Mali Federation on 20 June 1960 attained independence, but in August 1960 Senegal seceded, was granted French recognition on 11 September 1960, and remained inside the Community whilst Mali left it. The powers of the French Community itself were altered in 1961; France in effect conceded the full exercise of sovereignty to the African States. French aid, and in some instances as in Chad, military support, has remained an important influence.

In North Africa the attainment of independence was only achieved after fierce fighting in Algeria, where a large number of European Frenchmen resisted the handing over of power to an Arab majority. France granted independence to Morocco on 2 March 1956, faced with the threat of an armed insurrection. Spain followed suit but retained some small territories: Ceuta, Melilla and Ifni; Tangier was integrated into Morocco. Tunisia was granted independence in the same month on 20 March 1956. Algeria, which was not a colony or Protectorate but constitutionally a part of metropolitan France, faced a bitter struggle before independence. In 1954 the Algerian Arab Nationalists, who had formed the F.L.N., began an insurrection against France. After increasingly bitter fighting between the F.L.N., the French army, and the French extremist O.A.S. determined to keep Algeria French, the civil war came to an end on 18 March 1962 when at the second *Evian Conference* a cease-fire was agreed. In July 1962 Algeria became fully independent. *Spain* granted independence to one of its Spanish possessions in Africa, Equatorial Guinea, on 12 October 1968.

The United Nations has been ultimately responsible for several African territories. The former North African colonies of Italy were united and formed the independent State of Libya which was granted independence in 1951. In British and French administered Togoland (pre-1914 German colonial possession), 'British' Togoland integrated with Ghana in March 1957, and

'French' Togoland became independent as Togo on 27 April 1960. 'French' Cameroons achieved independence as the Republic of Cameroon on 1 January 1960; after plebiscites, 'British' Cameroons was divided, the north in June 1961 joining Nigeria, and the south joining the Republic of Cameroon. Somaliland, which had been placed under Italian administration by the U.N., became independent on 1 July 1960 as Somalia, which included the British Protectorate of Somaliland. Tanganyika achieved independence in December 1961. Belgian administered Ruanda-Urundi became two independent States in July 1962, Rwanda and Burundi. South-west Africa is not a U.N. trusteeship territory but under the 'supervision' of the U.N. South Africa was given the mandate of this former German colony by the League of Nations after the First World War, and wished to incorporate the territory. After the Second World War, it refused to place the territory under U.N. trusteeship, and since then has opposed U.N. efforts to make its supervision effective and to accord to the people of this territory independence. The policy of *apartheid* and the defiance of the U.N. led in 1963 to the passing of resolutions calling on members to impose an arms embargo. The question of 'south-west Africa' continues. The U.N. have revoked the mandate (October 1966) and have taken direct control of Namibia, the name given to this territory; but South Africa refuses to hand over its administration and withdraw.

Belgium's most important African colony was the second largest country in Africa, the Congo. With its production of industrial diamonds, cobalt and coppers, its mineral wealth is of world importance. The Congo was ill-prepared for independence, which was granted on 30 June 1960; within a month law and order in the various regions broke down, atrocities were committed, the Congolese army mutinied, and the mineral-rich province of Katanga seceded on 11 July proclaiming its independence. Belgian troops returned to the Congo claiming to protect its nationals. The Congolese leaders on 12 July 1960 asked the U.N. for urgent military assistance. The Security Council authorized the Secretary-General to provide technical and military assistance as necessary. On 15 July the first U.N. military forces landed. (They were eventually to reach 20,000.) In August 1960, Katanga accepted them but the Secretary-General refused to end secession by force. Not until December 1962 was the Congo question ameliorated with the reunification of Katanga in the Congo. The Secretary of the U.N., Dag Hammarskjöld, had been mainly responsible for the energetic U.N. response; but in September 1961, while engaged in an attempt to prevent the outbreak of renewed fighting, he and seven staff members of the U.N. lost their lives in a plane crash. The U.N. military operations were controversial: the Soviet Union condemned the policy of the Secretary-General and refused to contribute towards the cost, nearly half of which was paid for by the United States. Internationally the U.N. Congo operation was dragged into the 'cold war' confrontation. The Congo took the name of Zaire.

African territories remaining under European control

Only three European States retain African territories; France, Spain and Portugal. France is still responsible for a small neighbour of Somalia on the shores of the Red Sea, the territory of the Afars and Issas, whose population voted in March 1967, by a majority, to stay associated with France. Its main town is Djibouti.

Spain continues to exercise its sovereignty over Ceuta, Melilla and enclaves in Morocco, and over the large territory of the Spanish Sahara on the Atlantic coast. It is sparsely inhabited by about 50,000 Saharans, 8,000 Spanish civilians and several thousand troops. Its importance lies in its large phosphate deposits, among the biggest in the world. Morocco has claimed all these territories as belonging to it.

Portugal possesses by far the largest European empire in Africa, and continues to maintain its hold over territories which it claims are an integral part of greater Portugal. The size of its combined African population of about 11 million exceeds the population of Portugal in Europe. Portugal's African territories comprise Mozambique in south-east Africa, Angola in south-west Africa, Portuguese Guinea in north-west Africa, and also the islands of Cape Verde, São Tomé and Principe. Portugal has been and continues to be engaged in fighting African nationalist insurrections in Mozambique, Angola and Guinea with a large Portuguese army of some 130,000 troops, without being able to defeat the forces of the African Nationalists which are supported by the Organization of African Unity (p. 484).

African conflicts

The frontiers of the independent African States are for the most part based on the nineteenth century frontiers of the era of European partition. They reflect as often as not the European balance of power and were the outcome of conquest or the result of European diplomatic bargains of a bygone age. Frontiers frequently cut across ethnic and tribal African entities. In the era of independence this has led to many instances of African irredentism and even endangered the unity of a number of African States.

In Nigeria the secession of the Ibo Eastern Region on 30 May 1967 and the proclamation of Biafra was the beginning of a bitter civil war, which only ended with the conquest of Biafra by the Federal Nigerian army in January 1970.

Ghana's relations and border disputes with its neighbours Upper Volta and Togo have been strained at times; Somalia's conflict with both Kenya and Ethiopia over territory with Somali populations incorporated in these States led to open fighting, and was finally ameliorated by agreement in 1967. Ethiopia faced an insurrectionary movement in Eritrea incorporated with Ethiopia. The suppression by the Sudanese of the insurgent southern provinces has strained relations between the Sudan and her southern African neighbours. The frontier between Morocco and Algeria is disputed and led to conflict in 1963. Fighting broke out between Tanzania and Uganda in September 1972. Disputes, including sporadic fighting, for territorial and other causes have frequently occurred in parts of Africa each year; but there have also been some notable efforts of cooperation and regional organization.

Regional organization: the Organization of African Unity

Pan-Africanism has its roots in the early twentieth century, and is in part a reaction to European nationalism which in its relationship with Africa involved the assertion of white superiority. African nationalism thus found a common cause in unequal treatment of the African, and it appeals to a revival of African pride, the realization of an independent African unity and consciousness. Its leaders were mainly American and West Indian until the Second World War. When Ghana achieved independence Kwame Nkrumah championed Pan-Africanism and invited the independent African States to a conference in Accra in December 1958. But soon after, they split into competing groups differing in the sides they supported in the Congo conflict and the Nigerian Civil War; they differed also in their 'European' cultural backgrounds and were divided by personal rivalries. Many groupings proved temporary, such as the union of Ghana–Guinea and Mali from 1959 to 1963, which it was intended should form the nucleus of a wider African political union and was inspired by Nkrumah. Among the more successful groupings was that between Kenya, Uganda and Tanzania; the three States signed the *Treaty for East African Cooperation, 6 June 1967*, which established an *East African Economic Community*. This came into force on *1 December 1967*, and established links with the E.E.C. (see p. 391, for links between the African States and the E.E.C.). Since the autumn of 1972, however, cooperation has been interrupted by the conflict between Tanzania and Uganda. The frequency of political coups in some African States diminished the stability of some of the regional groupings, but *the Organization of African Unity* is probably the most important international grouping of African States, and the most successful.

The Organization of African Unity (O.A.U.), 25 May 1963 (p. 484), was set up by a conference of African Heads of State and Government, which had convened in Addis Ababa in May 1963. Of the thirty-two independent African States then in existence, thirty States attended; all signed except South Africa, which did not attend, and subsequent independent African States have acceded to it. Rhodesian independence is not recognized.

The O.A.U. is an organization within the definition of Article 51 of the United Nations Charter. Its purposes, which are set out in Article 2 of its own Charter, are to 'promote the unity and solidarity of African States'; to promote and intensify collaboration to 'achieve a better life for the peoples of Africa'; to defend their sovereignty, territorial integrity and independence; to 'eradicate all forms of colonialism from Africa'; and to promote international cooperation with due regard to the Charter of the U.N. and the Universal Declaration of Human Rights. From these purposes derive the institutions and policies of the O.A.U., set out as 'principles' in Article 3. They include 'peaceful settlement of disputes by negotiation, mediation, conciliation or arbitration'; the condemnation of all forms of subversive activities, political assassination or interference by any State in the internal affairs of another State; the 'absolute dedication to the total emancipation of the African territories which are still dependent'; and the affirmation of a policy of 'non-alignment with regard to all blocs'.

The Assembly of Heads of State and Government is the supreme organ of the O.A.U. and meets at least once a year. Each Member State has one vote, procedural questions are decided by simple majority and resolutions are approved by two-thirds majority.

A Council of Ministers, frequently Foreign Ministers, meets for consultative purposes, and is required to do so at least twice a year. It is responsible to the Assembly of the Heads of State and Government.

An Administrative Secretary-General of the Organization, who directs the affairs of the Secretariat, is appointed by the Assembly of the Heads of State and Government.

There are five specialized commissions dealing with economic and social problems, educational and cultural affairs, health and sanitation and nutrition, defence, and scientific, technical and research problems. A separate Protocol of the Commission of Mediation, Conciliation and Arbitration establishes the composition and function of these commissions, the duties of members of the O.A.U., and the procedures to be followed.

One of the crucial functions of the O.A.U. is to facilitate the settlement of disputes between its members. 'Mediation' can only be undertaken with the consent of the parties concerned (Article XX of the Protocol); 'conciliation' can be initiated by one party to a dispute provided the other is notified, but the President of the Bureau of the Commission of Mediation, Conciliation and Arbitration is required on receipt of the request to establish a Board of Conciliators 'in agreement with the parties'. Arbitration may be resorted to by agreement of the parties, and 'shall be regarded as submission in good faith to the award of the Arbitral Tribunal' (Article XXVIII). Thus the procedures of mediation and arbitration require the consent of all parties to the dispute; conciliation can be initiated by one party but it clearly cannot be brought to a successful conclusion without the cooperation of all the parties. There is no provision for any enforcement action against a Member State (compare with Organization of American States, p. 328). The emphasis is on peaceful conciliation. The 'resolutions' of the O.A.U. are also advisory.

The O.A.U. has played a helpful role in a number of disputes, notably in the border conflict between Somalia, Kenya and Ethiopia in 1967. A resolution, adopted at the O.A.U. meeting in July 1964, declared that all Member States 'pledge themselves to respect the frontiers existing on their achievement of national independence'. In regard to the Nigerian conflict a resolution of the O.A.U. during the September meeting in 1967 declared that it was for Nigeria to settle it, but the O.A.U. expressed its confidence in the Federal Government and supported its unity and territorial integrity. Thus the O.A.U. has not been sympathetic to 'tribal' secessions. At its meetings racial discrimination and apartheid have been vehemently condemned. Action has been coordinated at the U.N.; at the Addis Ababa meeting in May 1963 members were called on to boycott South African goods, and a Committee for the Liberation Movement of Africa was set up. At the November O.A.U. meeting of 1966, the 'British racist minority settlers' together with the 'hypocritical attitude and vacillation of the British Government' were condemned, and members were called on to help and support the 'Zimbabwe Freedom Fighters' more effectively. Similarly, by another resolution in November 1966 support was pledged to the peoples of south-west Africa to rid themselves of South African occupation. Support too has been accorded to African Nationalists fighting in the African territories of Portugal. The material influence of these policies is difficult to assess as the Governments of South Africa and Southern Rhodesia in 1972, despite sanctions imposed by the U.N. in 1966, remain secure in their control of these countries. The combined military strength of Portugal, Southern Rhodesia and South Africa exceeds what the independent African States theoretically can muster. Nor can South Africa's neighbours economically and militarily afford a policy of outright opposition. South Africa's position internationally in trade and finance is strong, and Britain and the United States among other Powers are opposed to sanctions against South Africa and do not accept the argument that apartheid as such constitutes a threat to peace.

Charter of the Organization of African Unity, Addis Ababa, 25 May 1963

We, the Heads of African and Malagasy States and Governments assembled in the City of Addis Ababa, Ethiopia;

Convinced that it is the inalienable right of all people to control their own destiny;

Conscious of the fact that freedom, equality, justice and dignity are essential objectives for the achievement of the legitimate aspirations of the African peoples;

Conscious of our responsibility to harness the natural and human resources of our continent for the total advancement of our peoples in spheres of human endeavour;

Inspired by a common determination to promote understanding among our peoples and cooperation among our States in response to the aspirations of our peoples for brotherhood and solidarity, in a larger unity transcending ethnic and national differences;

Convinced that, in order to translate this determination into a dynamic force in the cause of human progress, conditions for peace and security must be established and maintained;

Determined to safeguard and consolidate the hard-won independence as well as the sovereignty and territorial integrity of our States, and to resist neo-colonialism in all its forms;

Dedicated to the general progress of Africa;

Persuaded that the Charter of the United Nations and the Universal Declaration of Human Rights, to the principles of which we reaffirm our adherence, provide a solid foundation for peaceful and positive cooperation among States;

Desirous that all African States should henceforth unite so that the welfare and well-being of their peoples can be assured;

Resolved to reinforce the links between our States by establishing and strengthening common institutions;

Have agreed to the present Charter.

ESTABLISHMENT

Article I. 1. The High Contracting Parties do by the present Charter establish an Organization to be known as the '*Organization of African Unity*'.

2. The Organization shall include the Continental African States, Madagascar and other Islands surrounding Africa.

PURPOSES

Article II. 1. The Organization shall have the following purposes:

(a) To promote the unity and solidarity of the African States;

(b) To coordinate and intensify their collaboration and efforts to achieve a better life for the peoples of Africa;

(c) To defend their sovereignty, their territorial integrity and independence;

(d) To eradicate all forms of colonialism from Africa; and

(e) To promote international cooperation, having due regard to the Charter of the United Nations and the Universal Declaration of Human Rights.

2. To these ends, the Member States shall coordinate and harmonize their general policies, especially in the following fields:

(a) Political and diplomatic cooperation;

(b) Economic cooperation, including transport and communications;

(c) Educational and cultural cooperation;

(d) Health, sanitation, and nutritional cooperation;

(e) Scientific and technical cooperation; and

(f) Cooperation for defence and security.

PRINCIPLES

Article III. The Member States, in pursuit of the purposes stated in Article II, solemnly affirm and declare their adherence to the following principles:

1. The sovereign equality of all Member States;

2. Non-interference in the internal affairs of States;

3. Respect for the sovereignty and territorial integrity of each State and for its inalienable right to independent existence;

4. Peaceful settlement of disputes by negotiation, mediation, conciliation or arbitration;

5. Unreserved condemnation, in all its forms, of political assassination as well as of subversive activities on the part of neighbouring States or any other States;

6. Absolute dedication to the total emancipation of the African territories which are still dependent;

7. Affirmation of a policy of non-alignment with regard to all blocs.

MEMBERSHIP

Article IV. Each independent sovereign African State shall be entitled to become a Member of the Organization.

RIGHTS AND DUTIES OF MEMBER STATES

Article V. All Member States shall enjoy equal rights and have equal duties.

Article VI. The Member States pledge themselves to observe scrupulously the principles enumerated in Article III of the present Charter.

INSTITUTIONS

Article VII. The Organization shall accomplish its purposes through the following principal institutions;

1. The Assembly of Heads of State and Government;

2. The Council of Ministers;

3. The General Secretariat;

4. The Commission of Mediation, Conciliation and Arbitration.

THE ASSEMBLY OF HEADS OF STATE AND GOVERNMENT

Article VIII. The Assembly of Heads of State and Government shall be the supreme organ of the Organization. It shall, subject to the provisions of this Charter, discuss matters of common concern to Africa with a view to coordinating and harmonizing the general policy of the Organization. It may in addition review the structure, functions and acts of all the organs and any specialized agencies which may be created in accordance with the present Charter.

Article IX. The Assembly shall be composed of the Heads of State and Government or their duly accredited representatives and it shall meet at least once a year. At the request of any Member State and on approval by a two-thirds majority of the Member States, the Assembly shall meet in extraordinary session.

Article X. 1. Each Member State shall have one vote.

2. All resolutions shall be determined by a two-thirds majority of the Members of the Organization.

3. Questions of procedure shall require a simple majority. Whether or not a question is one of procedure shall be determined by a simple majority of all Member States of the Organization.

4. Two-thirds of the total membership of the Organization shall form a quorum at any meeting of the Assembly.

Article XI. The Assembly shall have the power to determine its own rules of procedure.

THE COUNCIL OF MINISTERS

Article XII. 1. The Council of Ministers shall consist of Foreign Ministers or such other Ministers as are designated by the Governments of Member States.

2. The Council of Ministers shall meet at least twice a year. When requested by any Member State and approved by two-thirds of all Member States, it shall meet in extraordinary session.

Article XIII. 1. The Council of Ministers shall be responsible to the Assembly of Heads of State and Government. It shall be entrusted with the responsibility of preparing conferences of the Assembly.

2. It shall take cognisance of any matter referred to it by the Assembly. It shall be entrusted with the implementation of the decisions of the Assembly of Heads of State and Government. It shall coordinate inter-African cooperation in accordance with the instructions of the Assembly and in conformity with Article II (2) of the present Charter.

Article XIV. 1. Each Member State shall have one vote.

2. All resolutions shall be determined by a simple majority of the members of the Council of Ministers.

3. Two-thirds of the total membership of the Council of Ministers shall form a quorum for any meeting of the Council.

Article XV. The Council shall have the power to determine its own rules of procedure.

GENERAL SECRETARIAT

Article XVI. There shall be an Administrative Secretary-General of the Organization, who shall be appointed by the Assembly of Heads of State and Government. The Administrative Secretary-General shall direct the affairs of the Secretariat.

Article XVII. There shall be one or more Assistant Secretaries-General of the Organization, who shall be appointed by the Assembly of Heads of State and Government.

Article XVIII. The functions and conditions of services of the Secretary-General, of the Assistant Secretaries-General and other employees of the Secretariat shall be governed by the provisions of this Charter and the regulations approved by the Assembly of Heads of State and Government.

1. In the performance of their duties the Administrative Secretary-General and his staff shall not seek or receive instructions from any Government or from any other authority external to the Organization. They shall refrain from any action which might reflect on their position as international officials responsible only to the Organization.

2. Each Member of the Organization undertakes to respect the exclusive character of the responsibilities of the Administrative Secretary-General and the Staff and not seek to influence them in the discharge of their responsibilities.

COMMISSION OF MEDIATION, CONCILIATION AND ARBITRATION

Article XIX. Member States pledge to settle all disputes among themselves by peaceful means and, to this end, decide to establish a Commission of Mediation, Conciliation and Arbitration, the composition of which and conditions of service shall be defined by a separate Protocol to be approved by the Assembly of Heads of State and Government. Said Protocol shall be regarded as forming an integral part of the present Charter.

SPECIALIZED COMMISSIONS

Article XX. The Assembly shall establish such Specialized Commissions as it may deem necessary, including the following:

1. Economic and Social Commission;
2. Educational and Cultural Commission;
3. Health, Sanitation, and Nutrition Commission;
4. Defence Commission;

5. Scientific, Technical and Research Commission.

Article XXI. Each Specialized Commission referred to in Article XX shall be composed of the Ministers concerned or other Ministers or plenipotentiaries designated by the Governments of the Member States.

Article XXII. The functions of the Specialized Commissions shall be carried out in accordance with the provisions of the present Charter and of the regulations approved by the Council of Ministers.

THE BUDGET

Article XXIII. The budget of the Organization prepared by the Administrative Secretary-General shall be approved by the Council of Ministers. The budget shall be provided by contributions from Member States in accordance with the scale of assessment of the United Nations; provided, however, that no Member State shall be assessed an amount exceeding 20 per cent of the yearly regular budget of the Organization. The Member States agree to pay their respective contributions regularly.

SIGNATURE AND RATIFICATION OF CHARTER

Article XXIV. 1. This Charter shall be open for signature to all independent sovereign African States and shall be ratified by the signatory States in accordance with their respective constitutional processes.

2. The original instrument, done if possible in African languages, in English and French, all texts being equally authentic, shall be deposited with the Government of Ethiopia which shall transmit certified copies thereof to all independent sovereign African States.

3. Instruments of ratification shall be deposited with the Government of Ethiopia, which shall notify all signatories of each such deposit.

ENTRY INTO FORCE

Article XXV. This Charter shall enter into force immediately upon receipt by the Government of Ethiopia of the instruments of ratification from two-thirds of the signatory States.

REGISTRATION OF THE CHARTER

Article XXVI. This Charter shall, after due ratification, be registered with the Secretariat of the United Nations through the Government of Ethiopia in conformity with Article 102 of the Charter of the United Nations.

INTERPRETATION OF THE CHARTER

Article XXVII. Any question which may arise concerning the interpretation of this Charter shall be decided by a vote of two-thirds of the Assembly of Heads of State and Government of the Organization.

ADHESION AND ACCESSION

Article XXVIII. 1. Any independent sovereign African State may at any time notify the Administrative Secretary-General of its intention to adhere or accede to this Charter.

2. The Administrative Secretary-General shall, on receipt of such notification, communicate a copy of it to all the Member States. Admission shall be decided by a simple majority of the Member States. The decision of each Member State shall be transmitted to the Administrative Secretary-General, who shall, upon receipt of the required number of votes, communicate the decision to the State concerned.

MISCELLANEOUS

Article XXIX. The working languages of the Organization and all its institutions shall be, if possible, African languages, English and French.

Article XXX. The Administrative Secretary-General may accept on behalf of the Organization gifts, bequests and other donations made to the Organization, provided that this is approved by the Council of Ministers.

Article XXXI. The Council of Ministers shall decide on the privileges and immunities to be accorded to the personnel of the Secretariat in the respective territories of the Member States.

CESSATION OF MEMBERSHIP

Article XXXII. Any State which desires to renounce its membership shall forward a written notification to the Administrative Secretary-General. At the end of one year from the date of such notification, if not withdrawn, the Charter shall cease to apply with respect to the renouncing State, which shall thereby cease to belong to the Organization.

AMENDMENT TO THE CHARTER

Article XXXIII. This Charter may be amended or revised if any Member State makes a written request to the Administrative Secretary-General to that effect; provided, however, that the proposed amendment is not submitted to the Assembly for consideration until all the Member States have been duly notified of it and a period of one year has elapsed. Such an amendment shall not be effective unless approved by at least two-thirds of all the Member States.

IN FAITH WHEREOF, We, the Heads of African State and Government, have signed this Charter.

Protocol of the Commission of Mediation, Conciliation and Arbitration, Cairo, 21 July 1964

Part I · Establishment and organization

Article I. The Commission of Mediation, Conciliation and Arbitration established by Article XIX of the Charter of the Organization of African Unity shall be governed by the provisions of the present Protocol.

Article II. 1. The Commission shall consist of twenty-one Members elected by the Assembly of Heads of State and Government.

2. No two Members shall be nationals of the same State.

3. The Members of the Commission shall be persons with recognized professional qualifications.

4. Each Member State of the Organization of African Unity shall be entitled to nominate two candidates.

5. The Administrative Secretary-General shall prepare a list of the candidates nominated by Member States and shall submit it to the Assembly of Heads of State and Government.

[*Articles III–X.* Composition and election of members of the Board.]

Article XI. The Seat of the Commission shall be at Addis Ababa, Ethiopia.

Part II · General provisions

Article XII. The Commission shall have jurisdiction over disputes between States only.

Article XIII. 1. A dispute may be referred to the Commission jointly by the parties concerned, by a party to the dispute, by the Council of Ministers or by the Assembly of Heads of State and Government.

2. Where a dispute has been referred to the Commission as provided in paragraph 1, and one or more of the parties have refused to submit to the jurisdiction of the Commission, the Bureau shall refer the matter to the Council of Ministers for consideration.

Article XIV. The consent of any party to a dispute to submit to the jurisdiction of the Commission may be evidenced by:

(a) a prior written undertaking by such party that there shall be recourse to Mediation, Conciliation, or Arbitration;

(b) reference of a dispute by such party to the Commission; or

(c) submission by such party to the jurisdiction in respect of a dispute referred to the Commission by another State, by the Council of Ministers, or by the Assembly of Heads of State and Government.

Article XV. Member States shall refrain from any act or omission that is likely to aggravate a situation which has been referred to the Commission.

...

Article XVIII. Where, in the course of Mediation, Conciliation, or Arbitration, it is deemed necessary to conduct an investigation or inquiry for the purpose of elucidating facts or circumstances relating to a matter in dispute, the parties concerned and all other Member States shall extend to those engaged in any such proceedings the fullest cooperation in the conduct of such investigation or inquiry.

Article XIX. In case of a dispute between Member States, the parties may agree to resort to any one of these modes of settlement: Mediation, Conciliation, and Arbitration.

Part III · Mediation

Article XX. When a dispute between Member States is referred to the Commission for Mediation, the President shall, with the consent of the parties, appoint one or more Members of the Commission to mediate the dispute.

Article XXI. 1. The role of the mediator shall be confined to reconciling the views and claims of the parties.

2. The mediator shall make written proposals to the parties as expeditiously as possible.

3. If the means of reconciliation proposed by the mediator are accepted, they shall become the basis of a protocol of arrangement between the parties.

Part IV · Conciliation

Article XXII. 1. A request for the settlement of a dispute by conciliation may be submitted to the Commission by means of a petition addressed to the President by one or more of the parties to the dispute.

2. If the request is made by only one of the parties, that party shall indicate that prior written notice has been given to the other party.

3. The petition shall include a summary explanation of the grounds of the dispute.

Article XXIII. 1. Upon receipt of the petition, the President shall, in agreement with the parties, establish a Board of Conciliators, of whom three shall be appointed by the President from among the Members of the Commission, and one each by the parties.

...

Article XXVI. 1. At the close of the proceedings, the Board shall draw up a report stating either:

(a) that the parties have come to an agreement and, if the need arises, the terms of the agreement and any recommendations for settlement made by the Board; or

(b) that it has been impossible to effect a settlement.

2. The Report of the Board of Conciliators shall be communicated to the parties and to the President of the Commission without delay and may be published only with the consent of the parties.

Part V · Arbitration

Article XXVII. 1. Where it is agreed that arbitration should be resorted to, the Arbitral Tribunal shall be established in the following manner:

(a) each party shall designate one arbitrator from among the Members of the Commission having legal qualifications;

(b) the two arbitrators thus designated shall, by common agreement, designate from among the Members of the Commission a third person who shall act as Chairman of the Tribunal;

(c) where the two arbitrators fail to agree, within one month of their appointment, in the choice of the person to be Chairman of the Tribunal, the Bureau shall designate the Chairman.

2. The President may, with the agreement of the parties, appoint to the Arbitral Tribunal two additional Members who need not be Members of the Commission but who shall have the same powers as the other Members of the Tribunal.

3. The arbitrators shall not be nationals of the parties, or have their domicile in the territories of the parties, or be employed in their service, or have served as mediators or conciliators in the same dispute. They shall all be of different nationalities.

Article XXVIII. Recourse to arbitration shall be regarded as submission in good faith to the award of the Arbitral Tribunal.

Article XXIX. 1. The parties shall, in each case, conclude a *compromis* which shall specify:

(a) the undertaking of the parties to go to arbitration, and to accept as legally binding, the decision of the Tribunal;

(b) the subject matter of the controversy; and

(c) the seat of the Tribunal.

2. The *compromis* may specify the law to be applied by the Tribunal and the power, if the parties so agree, to adjudicate *ex aequo et bono*, the time limit within which the award of the arbitrators shall be given, and the appointment of agents and counsel to take in the proceedings before the Tribunal.

Article XXX. In the absence of any provision in the *compromis* regarding the applicable law, the Arbitral Tribunal shall decide the dispute according to treaties concluded between the parties, International Law, the Charter of the Organization of African Unity, the Charter of the United Nations and, if the parties agree, *ex aequo et bono*.

Article XXXI. 1. Hearings shall be held *in camera* unless the arbitrators decide otherwise.

2. The record of the proceedings signed by the arbitrators and the Registrar shall alone be authoritative.

3. The arbitral award shall be in writing and shall, in respect of every point decided, state the reasons on which it is based.

. . .

XVII · The conflicts and alignments of the Middle East, 1945–72

Between the two world wars Britain and France had enjoyed a position of pre-dominance in the Middle East. Britain controlled the Suez Canal and with France nearly all the important strategic bases. Italy was the only other Colonial Power of importance, occupying Abyssinia, Eritrea, Italian Somaliland and Libya. Italy was forced to renounce her colonies in the peace treaty of 1947. British and French predominance lasted little more than a decade longer than Italy's.

The international relations of the Middle East after 1945 were not a 'repeat' of the inter-war years, for the United States and the Soviet Union replaced Britain and France as the most important external Powers. With independence came profound internal changes in many of the Middle Eastern States where conservative Monarchies were swept away by revolutionary Republican Governments. New discoveries of oil and its constantly increasing use by de-veloped industrial nations transformed the pattern of economic relationships. Finally, the creation of the Jewish State of Israel, enjoying the support of the Western Powers, made a decisive impact and coloured all Arab relations with the outside world.

France's and Britain's attempts to retain, and subsequent decision to abandon, their power positions based on military superiority, 1945–58

France and Britain did not reconcile themselves immediately after the Second World War to the loss of military power in the Middle East. Nevertheless the defeat of France in 1940 had weakened France's position as a Colonial Power. North Africa, the Lebanon and Syria had remained in Vichy hands in 1940. In Syria and the Lebanon Vichy France's weakness strengthened the nationalist

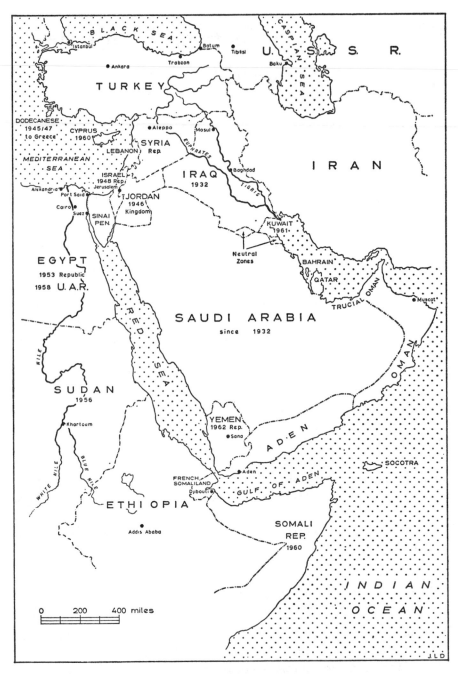

9 The Middle East, 1960–2

movements, and both the Vichy French authorities and the British Free-French administration, which took over in 1941, promised to make Syria and the Lebanon free sovereign States. British pressure on the French led to independence being granted during the course of the Second World War; it was confirmed in 1946 when the United Nations demanded the withdrawal of British and French troops still stationed in the Levant. The era of the French mandates was past, and Britain had played an important role in their ending.

Although Britain had helped to ease France out of its colonial-type control of Syria and the Lebanon, British Governments were not prepared to liquidate Britain's Middle Eastern position of power. There was a readiness to change the relationship, provided interests regarded vital to Britain were safeguarded. Thus the continued control of the oil industries of Iran through the Anglo-Iranian Oil Company, of Iraq through the Iraqi Petroleum Company (though European and American oil interests also held important shares in these enterprises) and the maintenance of British predominance over the 'imperial' arteries now believed vital economically as well, namely the Persian Gulf and the Suez Canal, were considered essential. Finally, Britain until May 1947 shouldered the 'Great Power' humanitarian responsibility of maintaining law and order in Palestine and leading this mandatory country to independence.

As the Second World War drew to a close, Britain favoured the growth of an Arab unity where Arab Governments favourable to Britain would have a pre-dominance. The *Arab Unity Conference held in Alexandria, Egypt, in September and October 1944*, led to the formation of the *Pact establishing the Arab League, 22 March 1945* (p. 502). Its founder members were Egypt, Iraq, Syria, Lebanon, Transjordan, Saudi Arabia and Yemen. Rivalries and tensions between members of the Arab League have weakened and often made impossible the adoption of common policies. The supreme body of the Arab League is the Council, which can lend its good offices to mediate: but in the case of aggression or threat of aggression between Member States it can only act on a unanimous vote with the aggressor having no vote; similarly if a Member State is attacked by another State not a member, complete unanimity is necessary for action. The League and its Secretary-General has its headquarters in Cairo. The lack of military and political coordination was revealed in the first Arab–Israeli war of 1948–9 (p. 496). The Arab League did not become the ally Britain hoped for; under Egyptian influence it was used to develop common attitudes directed against the continued British and French military presence in the Middle East, and against Zionism and Israel, but not with complete success.

Britain and Transjordan concluded an alliance on 15 March 1948 (p. 504). They promised to come to each other's aid if engaged in war; in fulfilment of this pledge Transjordan made available bases for British forces, and permitted the stationing of these forces in Transjordan 'until such a time . . . that the state of the world renders such measures unnecessary'. The treaty was to last at least twenty years. But negotiations with Egypt and Iraq in 1948 which would have permitted British bases failed. In the same year, in May 1948, Britain withdrew from Palestine.

Israel's success and identification with the Western Powers made Britain's continued presence in the Suez Canal zone increasingly difficult. The Egyptian revolution of July 1952 which brought Nasser to power (after some months delay) led to a settlement over the Canal zone between Nasser and Britain embodied in an *Agreement regarding the Suez Canal Base, signed on 19 October 1954.* Britain agreed to remove its troops within twenty months, but with the proviso that Egypt continued to offer to Britain 'such facilities as may be necessary in order to place the Base (in the Canal zone) on a war footing and to operate it effectively' if any outside State attacked a member of the Arab League or Turkey. The Anglo-Egyptian differences over the future of the Sudan had been resolved a year earlier in February 1953, which left the choice to the Sudanese. Sudan opted for independence and became a sovereign State in 1956.

The Suez Crisis of the summer of 1956, with Britain and France resorting to the use of force in October 1956 to uphold their rights, marks the turning point of Britain's and France's position of power in the Middle East. After bombing airfields on 31 October 1956, Britain and France landed at the western end of the Suez Canal on 5 November 1956 and rapidly proceeded to occupy the Canal zone. This military action followed Nasser's decision to nationalize the Suez Canal on 26 July 1956, a few days after the United States, Britain and the World Bank had withdrawn their earlier offers to provide financial aid to build the High Dam at Aswan. The British Government since the spring of 1956 had blamed Nasser for his efforts to undermine Britain's position in the Middle East, especially in Jordan, Iraq and the Suez Canal. The summer's tensions brought no solution nearer over the disputes concerning the Suez Canal. Simultaneously, growing tension between Israel and the Arab States culminated in the attack by Israel on 29 October 1956 which marked the opening of the second Israeli–Arab war. On 31 October Britain and France bombed Egyptian airfields. According to French and Israeli sources a secret Franco-British–Israeli Agreement had been concluded on 23 and 24 October 1956 for some concerted action against Egypt, but Prime Minister Eden and Foreign Secretary Selwyn Lloyd in the House of Commons rejected all charges of 'collusion'. In 1973 the documents are not available for a definitive treatment of this question. At the time the stated reason for the invasion by France and

Britain was the necessity of protecting the Canal zone from war. On 30 October 1956 the British and French Governments delivered an ultimatum to Egypt and Israel to withdraw to lines 10 miles each side of the Canal, which British and French troops would occupy. Egypt rejected the ultimatum and resisted the landings on 5 November 1956. Only a day later, on 6 November, Britain agreed to a ceasefire and France was obliged to follow. At the United Nations, the United States and the Soviet Union had acted together to stop the Anglo-French military action. By 23 December 1956 British and French troops had withdrawn and a United Nations force taken over.

Elsewhere in the Middle East British military power through alliances and bases greatly diminished during the decade after the Second World War. In Iraq the staunchly pro-British and Western Royal Government was bitterly opposed to Nasser's republican Egypt. Popular nationalism, however, prevented this Government from concluding an alliance with Britain on the model of Jordan in 1948. Instead an *Exchange of Notes in April 1955* promised to maintain and develop peace and friendship between the two States. Iraq was also with Turkey a founder member of the *Baghdad Pact* (p. 507). The overthrow of the Iraqi Monarchy and Government in July 1958 ended Britain's special influence. With Iran, Britain enjoyed good relations, except for the period from 1951–3 when the nationalization of the Anglo-Iranian Oil Company brought about a rupture of these relations. In 1954, by the Anglo-Iranian Agreement, Britain accepted nationalization and received agreed compensation. In 1955 the Shah of Iran aligned Iran with the West and also joined the Baghdad Pact. Britain's special position in Jordan was weakened on 13 March 1957 with the agreement between the two countries to terminate the alliance of 1948. But little more than a year later, in July 1958, Britain at Jordan's request sent troops, at the time of the revolution and murder of King Faisal of Iraq, to support the Jordanian Hashemite royal family.

During the decade of the 1960s Britain and France relinquished practically all their remaining military positions in the Middle East. In North Africa, Moroccan and Tunisian nationalist opposition to continued French rule led to independence for Morocco on 2 March 1956 and for Tunisia on 20 March 1956. But France retained control of the naval base at Bizerta, which France did not evacuate (after a Tunisian appeal to the Security Council) until October 1965. The French conflict in North Africa was most serious in Algeria. Algeria was a part of France, not a colony or protected territory, and more than a million Frenchmen, originally from the mainland and concentrated in the towns, regarded Algeria as their French home. Faced with mounting violence and terror, the French army being unable to overcome the nationalist forces, de Gaulle decided to grant Algeria independence. At the *Second*

Evian Conference a ceasefire was agreed on 18 March 1962, and Algeria became a sovereign State on 3 July 1962. In fighting French 'imperialism' the Algerian National Liberation Front (F.L.N.) forged links with the Soviet Union and later Communist China. But in the 1960s good relations developed between France and independent Algeria. By the end of 1968 France had evacuated all its land bases in Algeria and the naval base at Mers-el-Kebir, but it retains an airforce base. France extends financial and technical aid to Algeria. With its neighbour Morocco, Algeria was involved in serious frontier disputes, which were settled in 1969. In the international tensions of the Middle East, Algeria is active in the Arab conflict with Israel.

The pace of British withdrawal did not slacken during the 1960s. Britain relinquished control of Cyprus, which became independent in August 1960, though retaining sovereignty over two military bases. The British alliance with Libya ended when in 1969 Colonel Gaddafi overthrew King Idris, and Britain withdrew from her extensive air and military training base. Britain gave up the Aden base on the Red Sea, useless since the closure of the Suez Canal, in 1967 and 1971; the Trucial States on the Persian Gulf, which had for so long enjoyed British protection, were left to arrange their own international security when Britain withdrew. Britain retains naval facilities with her NATO allies in independent Malta and exercises sovereignty in Gibraltar, despite Spanish endeavours to 'negotiate' about the future of the base.

The Arab–Israeli wars: 1948–9, 1956, 1967

Unwilling to continue to take responsibility as the mandatory authority in Palestine in the face of growing Arab and Zionist conflict, and with the Jewish survivors of Hitler's concentration camps seeking entrance without restriction, the British Government announced in 1947 that British troops would be withdrawn by 15 May 1948 and that the solution of Palestine would be left to the United Nations.

The United Nations devised a partition plan which was rejected by the Arabs. *On 14 May 1948, the Jewish State of Israel was proclaimed.* On the following day, military forces from Egypt, Jordan and Iraq began to advance into Palestine. The Arab forces were weak and divided, and in a series of battles during the two phases of the war from 1948–9, the Israelis enlarged the territory allotted to them by the division devised by the U.N. Only the Transjordanian troops had any success. They crossed the river Jordan and occupied the Palestinian West Bank and half of Jerusalem. After the armistice of the spring of 1949 they retained the West Bank, and the country renamed itself Jordan. Some 700,000 Arabs fled from their homes in Israeli-held Pales-

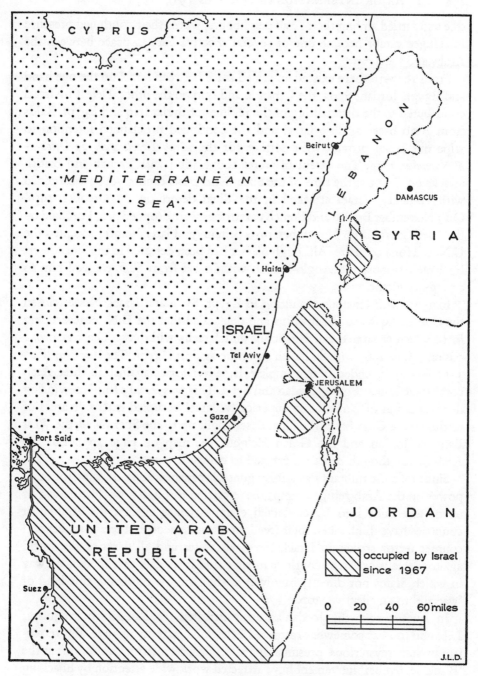

10 Israel and the Arab States

tine and settled among their Arab neighbours, where their continued presence in refugee camps became one of several effective bars to peace between the Arabs and the Jews.

From 1949–56 there existed an armed truce between Israel on the one hand and Egypt, Jordan, Syria, the Lebanon and Iraq on the other. Defeat by Israel contributed to the discrediting of the régimes of Syria, Iraq and Egypt. Raids from Arab bases against Israel and the continued proclaimed intention to wipe out Israel provided the setting for the *Arab–Israeli war, 29 October– 6 November 1956*. The extent of secret cooperation with French and British attacks on Egypt at the time of the Suez Canal crisis cannot yet be ascertained with certainty. Israel attacked in the Sinai desert on 29 October 1956. On 5 November British and French paratroops were dropped near Port Said on the Suez Canal. On 6 November 1956 Britain (and later France) accepted the U.N. call for a ceasefire. Although Nasser had been defeated in the Sinai desert by Israeli troops, the Anglo-French withdrawal from Suez enabled him to emerge as victor.

In 1967, with tensions mounting in Egypt, Syria and Israel, Nasser closed the Gulf of Aqaba to Israeli ships and demanded that the U.N. peacekeeping force which separated the Egyptians and Israelis withdraw. The war broke out on 5 June 1967 with an Israeli air-strike against Egypt. The *Six Day War, 5–10 June 1967*, ended with complete Israeli victories against all three Arab combatant States: Egypt, Jordan and Syria. This was Israel's third convincing demonstration of her military superiority. Israel occupied extensive areas of territory: the Gaza Strip, the Sinai desert right up to the Suez Canal, the West Bank of Jordan and the Golan Heights (see map on page 497). But the Arab States, though defeated, refused to conclude peace.

Since 1967 the militant Palestinian guerrilla organizations, drawing for manpower on the Arab refugee camps, have carried through a worldwide war of terror and raids into Israel. Israeli counter-strikes against the Arab host countries have diminished their freedom of movement; but terror strikes and counter terror strikes in Israel, the Arab States and all parts of the world against Israelis or Arabs continue in 1973, and it appears that there is no way in which States not directly involved in the struggle can bring this kind of 'warfare' to an effective stop.

In August 1970 the Jordanian army defeated the Palestinian irregulars; Lebanon too has somewhat restricted Palestinian activity in 1972. But terrorism by such mysterious, presumably Palestinian, terrorist organizations as the 'Black September' movement have attracted worldwide attention by hijacking airliners, by sending letter bombs and by the attack on the Israeli participants during the Munich Olympic Games in 1972. Libya has emerged as the most extreme supporter of these terror tactics. The bitterness and hostility of the Arab States against Israel continues undiminished. Israel has also demonstrated its will to retaliate in kind: in April 1973, it struck against leaders of Palestinian terror organizations by gunning them down in their homes in the Lebanon. Only Israeli relations with Jordan are more nearly normal.

Alliance groupings in the Middle East

The Arab League, though not the force of unity and strength intended by its founders, continues to represent the closest alignment of which the Arab States are capable. But the Arab monarchical countries, Saudi-Arabia and Jordan, continue to be wary of Arab socialism and nationalism as represented by Egypt and Syria. From 1958 to 1961 Egypt and Syria (with Yemen for a short time) formed the United Arab Republic. In the summer of 1972 Libya and Egypt announced that they would form a union. Attempts at Arab union have generally been short-lived.

INTERNATIONAL ALLIANCES: THE UNITED STATES AND THE SOVIET UNION IN THE MIDDLE EAST

The rivalries of the Arab States made any attempt to incorporate them together in an alliance cordon against the Soviet Union impossible in the era of the 'cold war'. The United States made every effort to create a 'northern tier' of alliances in 1953 for the defence of Turkey, Iran, Iraq, Afghanistan and Pakistan. This was the application of Foster Dulles's (the American Secretary of State) policy of containment. In April 1954 Pakistan and Turkey signed a bilateral treaty of friendship. The *Baghdad Pact* developed from a series of regional alliances: *the Treaty of Alliance between Iraq and Turkey, 24 February 1955; Britain acceded to this alliance on 4 April 1955; Pakistan acceded on 23 September 1955 and Iran in October 1955* (p. 507). Thus the Baghdad Pact had become a Five Power alliance of Britain, Iran, Iraq, Turkey and Pakistan. Iraq, the one Arab State in this 'Western alliance', by joining it exposed itself to the enmity of other Arab States, especially Egypt. Jordan, whose Hashemite royal dynasty wished to align the State with the fellow Hashemite kingdom of Iraq, would also have joined the Baghdad Pact but for the nationalist Arab opposition in Jordan inspired by Nasser's Egypt. The United States was ready to aid with money and arms, but was not willing to assume treaty commitments in the Middle East at this time. The security of this region was still left in the hands of the British alliance partners in 1955.

With Suez and the Arab–Israeli war of 1956, Britain's position in the

Middle East was gravely weakened, and her chief Arab ally, Iraq, shared in the Western discredit. The United States began now to replace Britain as the chief Western outside Power in the Middle East; this deeper involvement became clear with the pronouncement of the *Eisenhower Doctrine, which became law in March 1957* (p. 317). The crisis for the Western diplomatic alignment broke in July 1958. Revolution overthrew the royal Iraq dynasty and its pro-Western conservative Government of Nuri al-Said on 14 July 1958. Fearing revolution in their country, the Lebanese asked for United States protection, and the United States Sixth Fleet landed marines in the Lebanon; Britain sent troops to Jordan responding to the appeal of King Hussein. In March 1959 Iraq formally left the Baghdad Pact, which was now renamed as the Central Treaty Organization (CENTO), with new headquarters in Ankara. To strengthen the alliance, the United States linked herself to each of the four remaining Powers of CENTO by executive agreements on 28 July 1958, two weeks after the revolution in Iraq. Pakistan's participation in CENTO was largely determined by her desire to strengthen her position against India rather than the Soviet Union; thus Pakistan was not an active partner, but since the third Pakistan–Indian war (p. 435) has expressed renewed interest. CENTO during the 1960s proved of importance not only militarily but also economically to Turkey, the recipient of American and British aid. With the thaw in the 'cold war' Soviet relations with two CENTO Powers, Iran and Turkey, became more friendly and relaxed, and the Soviet Union also began to extend economic aid to Turkey though not on the scale of Western aid and trade.

Soviet power in the Mediterranean has greatly increased since the Suez Crisis of 1956. The Soviet Union focused its efforts on providing supports for Egypt, and re-equipped the Egyptian army after its two defeats in 1956 and 1967. In 1972, disappointed with the restraints of dependence on the Soviet Union, Egypt asked Soviet military and technical personnel to leave the country. A policy of exclusive reliance on the Soviet Union was thus on the wane (p. 357).

Since the late 1960s Soviet warships have made their presence felt, though they are much weaker than the American Sixth Fleet. The Soviet Union has to utilize the bases of its allies and friends in the Mediterranean: its fleet enjoys facilities principally in Syria at Ladhiqijah and in Egypt at Port Said and Alexandria, as well as anchorages on points of the North African coastline. *The Montreux Convention of 1936* (p. 83) permits the passage of Soviet warships from the Black Sea to the Mediterranean with few restrictions.

Oil and the Middle East

Oil has been of importance in the international relations of the Middle East since the 1920s, and a major factor since the Second World War. In known oil reserves the Middle East still dominates the world, and has provided Europe with relatively cheap resources of power. The concessions once controlled mainly by France and Britain are now more international, with five of the seven great international companies being American. Until the mid-1950s this oil came mainly from Iran, Kuwait and Iraq. The discovery and phenomenal expansion of oil production in the Arabian peninsula and North Africa has made Europe less dependent on traditional Middle Eastern sources, though Iran, Kuwait, Iraq and the Trucial States produce rather more than half of the oil of the region; by 1970 Saudi Arabia and Libya had each become as great producers of oil as Iran and Kuwait, and both States exceeded the production of Iraq. Those Middle Eastern States which lack sizeable oil resources also lack financial resources. The 'poor' Arab States of the Middle East are Egypt, Syria and Jordan. The oil-rich States provide some help. For the rest, Egypt, Syria and Jordan rely on foreign financial assistance especially from the Soviet Union, and in Jordan's case from the United States.

The oil-producing countries have struggled to gain a larger share of profits from the great international companies, and to raise the cost of oil. Nationalizing the physical assets of the oil companies operating in their own country was the most common form of pressure applied, and was tried in Iran in 1951. But so far only the international oil companies have had the capacity to finance the oil operation and market the oil. However, the balance of power was moving towards the Middle Eastern States in 1972–3.

To redress the balance of power which had favoured the oil companies backed by their Governments, five oil-producing States, Iran, Iraq, Kuwait, Saudi Arabia and Venezuela, *in 1960 formed the Organization of Petroleum Exporting Countries (OPEC)*. During the course of the 1960s Qatar, Indonesia, Libya, Abu Dhabi and Algeria joined. These States account for some 85 per cent of the world's total oil exports outside the Soviet bloc. In *December 1967*, after the Israeli war, the Arab Oil States of Kuwait, Libya, Saudi Arabia, Abu Dhabi, Bahrain, Dubai and Qatar and Algeria also formed the *Organization of Arab Petroleum Exporting Countries (OAPEC)*. The success of the Middle Eastern Oil States acting together, coupled with the rising energy needs of the developed world – even the United States can no longer cover its oil needs from domestic production – foreshadows in the 1970s renewed efforts on the part of the oil-consuming nations to put pressure on the Oil States to conclude arrangements regarded as reasonable by the West.

Pact of the Arab League, Cairo, 22 March 1945

[Syria, Transjordan, Iraq, Saudi Arabia, Lebanon, Egypt and Yemen]
... Desirous of strengthening the close relations and numerous ties which link the Arab States;

And anxious to support and stabilize these ties upon a basis of respect for the independence and sovereignty of these States, and to direct their efforts towards the common good of all the Arab countries, the improvement of their status, the security of their future, the realization of their aspirations and hopes;

And responding to the wishes of Arab public opinion in all Arab lands;

Have agreed to conclude a Pact to that end and ... have agreed upon the following provisions:

Article 1. The League of the Arab States is composed of the independent Arab States which have signed this Pact.

Any independent Arab State has the right to become a member of the League. If it desires to do so, it shall submit a request which will be deposited with the permanent Secretariat-General and submitted to the Council at the first meeting held after submission of the request.

Article 2. The League has as its purpose the strengthening of the relations between the Member States; the coordination of their policies in order to achieve cooperation between them and to safeguard their independence and sovereignty; and a general concern with the affairs and interests of the Arab countries. It has also as its purpose the close cooperation of the Member States, with due regard to the organization and circumstances of each State, on the following matters:

(a) Economic and financial affairs, including commercial relations, customs, currency, and questions of agriculture and industry.

(b) Communications: this includes railroads, roads, aviation, navigation, telegraphs, and posts.

(c) Cultural affairs.

(d) Nationality, passports, visas, execution of judgements, and extradition of criminals.

(e) Social affairs.

(f) Health problems.

Article 3. The League shall possess a Council composed of the representatives of the Member States of the League; each State shall have a single vote, irrespective of the number of its representatives.

It shall be the task of the Council to achieve the realization of the objectives of the League and to supervise the execution of agreements which the Member States have concluded on the questions enumerated in the preceding Article, or on any other questions.

It likewise shall be the Council's task to decide upon the means by which the League is to cooperate with the international bodies to be created in the future in order to guarantee security and peace and regulate economic and social relations.

Article 4. For each of the questions listed in Article 2 there shall be set up a special committee in which the Member States of the League shall be represented. These committees shall be charged with the task of laying down the principles and extent of cooperation. Such principles shall be formulated as draft agreements, to be presented to the Council for examination preparatory to their submission to the aforesaid States.

Representatives of the other Arab countries may take part in the work of the aforesaid committees. The Council shall determine the conditions under which these representatives may be permitted to participate and the rules governing such representation.

Article 5. Any resort to force in order to resolve disputes arising between two or more Member States of the League is prohibited. If there should arise among them a difference which does not concern a State's independence, sovereignty, or territorial integrity, and if the parties to the dispute have recourse to the Council for the settlement of the difference, the decision of the Council shall then be enforceable and obligatory.

In such a case, the States between whom the difference has arisen shall not participate in the deliberations and decisions of the Council.

The Council may lend its good offices for the settlement of all differences which threaten to lead to war between two Member States, or a Member State and a third State, with a view to bringing about their reconciliation.

Decisions of arbitration and mediation shall be taken by majority vote.

Article 6. In case of aggression or threat of aggression by one State against a Member State, the State which has been attacked or threatened with aggression may demand the immediate convocation of the Council.

The Council shall by unanimous decision determine the measures necessary to repulse the aggression. If the aggressor is a Member State, his vote shall not be counted in determining unanimity.

If, as a result of the attack, the Government of the State attacked finds itself unable to communicate with the Council, that State's representative in the Council shall have the right to request the convocation of the Council for the purpose indicated in the foregoing paragraph. In the event that this representative is unable to communicate with the Council, any Member State of the League shall have the right to request the convocation of the Council.

Article 7. Unanimous decisions of the Council shall be binding upon all Member States of the League; majority decisions shall be binding only upon those States which have accepted them.

In either case the decisions of the Council shall be enforced in each Member State according to its respective fundamental laws.

Article 8. Each Member State shall respect the systems of government established in the other Member States and regard them as exclusive concerns of those States. Each shall pledge to abstain from any action calculated to change established systems of government.

Article 9. States of the League which desire to establish closer cooperation and stronger bonds than are provided by this Pact may conclude agreements to that end.

Treaties and agreements already concluded or to be concluded in the future between a Member State and another State shall not be binding or restrictive upon other members.

Article 10. The permanent seat of the League of Arab States is established in Cairo. The Council may, however, assemble at any other place it may designate.

Article 11. The Council of the League shall convene in ordinary session twice a year, in March and in October. It shall convene in extraordinary session upon the request of two Member States of the League whenever the need arises.

Article 12. The League shall have a permanent Secretariat-General which shall consist of a Secretary-General, Assistant Secretaries, and an appropriate number of officials.

The Council of the League shall appoint the Secretary-General by a majority of two-thirds of the States of the League. The Secretary-General, with the approval of the Council, shall appoint the Assistant Secretaries and the principal officials of the League.

• • •

Article 16. Except in cases specifically indicated in this Pact, a majority vote of the Council shall be sufficient to make enforceable decisions on the following matters:

(a) Matters relating to personnel.

(b) Adoption of the budget of the League.

(c) Establishment of the administrative regulations for the Council, the committees, and the Secretariat-General.

(d) Decisions to adjourn the sessions.

(1) Annex regarding Palestine

Since the termination of the last great war the rule of the Ottoman Empire over the Arab countries, among them Palestine, which had become detached from that Empire, has come to an end. She has come to be independent in herself, not subordinate to any other State.

The Treaty of Lausanne proclaimed that her future was to be settled by the parties concerned.

However, even though she was as yet unable to control her own affairs, the Covenant of the League (of Nations) in 1919 made provision for a régime based upon recognition of her independence.

Her international existence and independence in the legal sense cannot, therefore, be questioned, any more than could the independence of the other Arab countries.

Although the outward manifestations of this independence have remained obscured for reasons beyond her control, this should not be allowed to interfere with her participation in the work of the Council of the League.

The States signatory to the Pact of the Arab League are therefore of the opinion that, considering the special circumstances of Palestine, and until that country can effectively exercise its independence, the Council of the League should take charge of the selection of an Arab representative from Palestine to take part in its work.

...

Treaty of Alliance between Britain and Transjordan, 15 March 1948

Article 1. There shall be perpetual peace and friendship between His Britannic Majesty and His Majesty the King of the Hashimite Kingdom of Transjordan.

A close alliance shall continue between the High Contracting Parties in consecration of their friendship, their cordial understanding and their good relations.

Each of the High Contracting Parties undertakes not to adopt in regard to foreign countries an attitude which is inconsistent with the Alliance or might create difficulties for the other party thereto.

Article 2. Should any dispute between either High Contracting Party and a third State produce a situation which would involve the risk of a rupture with that State, the High Contracting Parties will concert together with a view to the settlement of the said dispute by peaceful means in accordance with the provisions of the Charter of the United Nations and of any other international obligations which may be applicable to the case.

Article 3. Should either High Contracting Party notwithstanding the provisions of Article 2 become engaged in war, the other High Contracting Party will, subject always to the provisions of Article 4, immediately come to his aid as a measure of collective defence.

In the event of an imminent menace of hostilities the High Contracting Parties will immediately concert together the necessary measures of defence.

Article 4. Nothing in the present Treaty is intended to, or shall in any way prejudice the rights and obligations which devolve, or may devolve, upon either of the High Contracting Parties under the Charter of the United Nations or under any other existing international agreements, conventions or treaties.

Article 5. The present Treaty of which the Annex is an integral part shall replace the Treaty of Alliance signed in London on 22nd March 1946, of the Christian Era, together with its Annex and all Letters and Notes, interpreting or otherwise exchanged in 1946 in connection therewith, provided however that Article 9 of the said Treaty shall remain in force in accordance with and as modified by the Notes exchanged on this day on this subject.

Article 6. Should any difference arise relative to the application or interpretation of the present Treaty and should the High Contracting Parties fail to settle such difference by direct negotiations, it shall be referred to the International Court of Justice unless the parties agree to another mode of settlement.

Article 7. The present Treaty shall be ratified and shall come into force upon the exchange of instruments of ratification which shall take place at London as soon as possible. It shall remain in force for a period of twenty years from the date of its coming into force. At any time after fifteen years from the date of the coming into force of the present Treaty, the High Contracting Parties will, at the request of either of them, negotiate a revised Treaty which shall provide for the continued cooperation of the High Contracting Parties in the defence of their common interests. The period of fifteen years shall be reduced if a complete system of security agreements under Article 43 of the Charter of the United Nations is concluded before the expiry of this period. At the end of twenty years, if the present Treaty has not been revised it shall remain in force until the expiry of one year after notice of termination has been given by either High Contracting Party

to the other through the diplomatic channel.

Annex

Article 1. (a) The High Contracting Parties recognize that, in the common interests of both, each of them must be in a position to discharge his obligations under Article 3 of the Treaty.

(b) In the event of either High Contracting Party becoming engaged in war, or of a menace of hostilities, each High Contracting Party will invite the other to bring to his territory or territory controlled by him the necessary forces of all arms. Each will furnish to the other all the facilities and assistance in his power, including the use of all means and lines of communication, and on financial terms to be agreed upon.

(c) His Majesty the King of the Hashimite Kingdom of Transjordan will safeguard, maintain and develop as necessary the airfields, ports, roads and other means and lines of communication in and across the Hashimite Kingdom of Transjordan as may be required for the purposes of the present Treaty and its Annex, and will call upon His Britannic Majesty's assistance as may be required for this purpose.

(d) Until such time as the High Contracting Parties agree that the state of world security renders such measures unnecessary, His Majesty the King of the Hashimite Kingdom of Transjordan invites His Britannic Majesty to maintain units of the Royal Air Force at Amman and Mafrak airfields. His Majesty the King of the Hashimite Kingdom of Transjordan will provide all the necessary facilities for the accommodation and maintenance of the units mentioned in this paragraph, including facilities for the storage of their ammunition and supplies and the lease of any land required.

Article 2. In the common defence interests of the High Contracting Parties a permanent joint advisory body will be set up immediately on the coming into force of the present Treaty to coordinate defence matters between the Governments of the High Contracting Parties within the scope of the present Treaty.

This body, which will be known as the Anglo-Transjordan Joint Defence Board, will be composed of competent military representatives of the Governments of the High Contracting Parties in equal numbers ...

Alliance Treaty between Libya and Britain, 29 July 1953

...

Article 1. There shall be peace and friendship and a close alliance between the High Contracting Parties in consecration of their cordial understanding and their good relations.

Each of the High Contracting Parties undertakes not to adopt in regard to foreign countries an attitude which is inconsistent with the alliance or which might create difficulties for the other party thereto.

Article 2. Should either High Contracting Party become engaged in war or armed conflict, the other High Contracting Party will, subject always to the provisions of Article 4, immediately come to his aid as a measure of collective defence. In the event of an imminent menace of hostilities involving either of the High Contracting Parties they will immediately concert together the necessary measures of defence.

Article 3. The High Contracting Parties recognize that it is in their common interest to provide for their mutual defence and to ensure that their countries are in a position to play their part in the maintenance of international peace and security. To this end each will furnish to the other all the facilities and assistance in his power on terms to be agreed upon. In return for facilities provided by His Majesty The King of Libya for British armed forces in Libya on conditions to be agreed upon, Her Britannic Majesty will provide financial assistance to His Majesty

The King of Libya, on terms to be agreed upon as aforesaid.

Article 4. Nothing in the present Treaty is intended to, or shall in any way prejudice the rights and obligations which devolve, or may devolve, upon either of the High Contracting Parties under the Charter of the United Nations or under any other existing international agreements, conventions or treaties including, in the case of Libya, the Covenant of the League of Arab States.

Article 5. This Treaty shall be ratified and shall come into force upon the exchange of instruments of ratification which shall take place as soon as possible.

Article 6. This Treaty shall remain in force for a period of twenty years except in so far as it may be revised or replaced by a new Treaty during that period by agreement of both the High Contracting Parties, and it shall in any case be reviewed at the end of ten years. Each of the High Contracting Parties agrees in this connection to have in mind the extent to which international peace and security can be ensured through the United Nations. Before the expiry of a period of nineteen years either High Contracting Party may give to the other through the diplomatic channel notice of termination at the end of the said period of twenty years. If the Treaty has not been so terminated and subject to any revision or replacement thereof, it shall continue in force after the period of twenty years until the expiry of one year after notice of termination has been given by either High Contracting Party to the other through the diplomatic channel.

Article 7. Should any difference arise relative to the application or interpretation of the present Treaty and should the High Contracting Parties fail to settle such difference by direct negotiations, it shall be referred to the International Court of Justice unless the parties agree to another mode of settlement.

...

Pact of Mutual Cooperation between Iraq and Turkey (Baghdad Pact), February–October 1955

Whereas the friendly and brotherly relations existing between Iraq and Turkey are in constant progress, and in order to complement the contents of the Treaty of Friendship and Good Neighbourhood concluded between His Majesty the King of Iraq and His Excellency the President of the Turkish Republic signed in Ankara on the 29th of March 1946, which recognized the fact that peace and security between the two countries is an integral part of the peace and security of all the nations of the world and in particular the nations of the Middle East, and that it is the basis for their foreign policies.

Whereas Article 11 of the Treaty of Joint Defence and Economic Cooperation between the Arab League States provides that no provision of that Treaty shall in any way affect, or is designed to affect, any of the rights and obligations accruing to the Contracting Parties from the United Nations Charter;

And having realized the great responsibilities borne by them in their capacity as members of the United Nations concerned with the maintenance of peace and security in the Middle East region which necessitate taking the required measures in accordance with Article 51 of the United Nations Charter ... have agreed as follows:

Article 1. Consistent with Article 51 of the United Nations Charter the High Contracting Parties will cooperate for their security and defence. Such measures as they agree to take to give effect to this cooperation may form the subject of special agreements with each other.

Article 2. In order to ensure the realization and effect application of the cooperation provided for in Article 1 above, the competent authorities of the High Contracting Parties will determine the measures to be taken as soon as the present Pact enters into force. These measures will become operative as soon as they have been approved by the Governments of the High Contracting Parties.

Article 3. The High Contracting Parties undertake to refrain from any interference whatsoever in each other's internal affairs. They will settle any dispute between themselves in a peaceful way in accordance with the United Nations Charter.

Article 4. The High Contracting Parties declare that the dispositions of the present Pact are not in contradiction with any of the international obligations contracted by either of them with any third State or States. They do not derogate from, and cannot be interpreted as derogating from, the said international obligations. The High Contracting Parties undertake not to enter into any international obligation incompatible with the present Pact.

Article 5. This Pact shall be open for accession to any Member State of the Arab League or any other State actively concerned with the security and peace in this region and which is fully recognized by both of the High Contracting Parties. Accession shall come into force from the date on which the instrument of accession of the State concerned is deposited with the Ministry of Foreign Affairs of Iraq.

Any acceding State party to the present Pact may conclude special agreements in accordance with Article 1, with one or more States parties to the present Pact. The competent authority of any acceding State may determine measures in accordance with Article 2. These measures will become operative as soon as they have been approved by the Governments of the parties concerned.

Article 6. A Permanent Council at ministerial level will be set up to function within the framework of the purposes of this Pact when at least four Powers become parties to the Pact.

The Council will draw up its own rules of procedure.

Article 7. This Pact remains in force for a period of five years, renewable for other five-year periods. Any Contracting Party may withdraw from the Pact by notifying the other parties in writing of its desire to do so, six months before the expiration of any of the above-mentioned periods, in which case the Pact remains valid for the other parties.

[*Article 8.* Ratification.]

XVIII · The reduction of international tension and the problem of arms control, 1960–72

During the height of the cold war period in the 1950s and 1960s, the Western Powers on the one hand and the Communist Powers on the other tended to view every international conflict among smaller States in terms of a global struggle between the 'Free World' and the 'Communist World'. The neutral stance of States calling themselves the 'Third World' was regarded with suspicion by both sides. But a more traditional division in international relations often loosely referred to as the 'balance of power' was never quite lost sight of. It made itself felt in the mutual recognition by the 'Great Powers', especially the 'Superpowers', the United States and the Soviet Union, that as Great Powers they shared some common interests in their relations with other States. The most fundamental of these interests is to diminish the possibility of bypassing Washington and Moscow when decisions are being taken on questions of war and peace by other States. Such 'Superpower' control remains imperfect. Neither the United States nor the U.S.S.R. wishes to be dragged into conflicts not of their choosing and forced into positions created by the independent policies of other States. Above all, the United States and the Soviet Union are not prepared to risk a nuclear war of destruction between them as a result of decisions taken outside the White House and the Kremlin. But the 'special relationship' between the United States and the Soviet Union has not entailed the abandonment of Western and communist alliance groupings or removed mutual fears. On the contrary, alliances are still a prominent feature of international relations.

The American–Soviet dialogue has been highlighted by personal meetings between the Soviet leaders and the President of the United States. *An agreement was reached regarding the establishment of a direct communications link, and signed in Geneva, 20 June 1963*; it established the so-called 'hot line' between

Moscow and Washington for use in urgent situations, to enable the President of the United States and the Soviet leaders to communicate directly. A number of agreements have been concluded between the United States and the Soviet Union on cooperation in space, including the 'moon and celestial bodies'. With some of these agreements Britain has been a third partner, although lacking the capacity to reach celestial bodies. The most important area of American–Soviet collaboration has been concerned with achieving arms control and preventing the spread of nuclear weapons.

From 1945 until September 1949 the United States enjoyed a nuclear monopoly. The secret Anglo-American wartime executive agreements in Quebec, 19 August 1943, and Hyde Park, U.S.A., September 1944, did not survive Roosevelt, and cooperation and the sharing of atomic information with Britain ceased with the enacting of the United States' Atomic Energy Act (the McMahon Act) in August 1946. But the United States could not prevent the spread of atomic weaponry. Efforts in the United Nations to secure international control and inspection over the manufacture of atomic energy failed as the U.S.S.R. was determined to make its own bomb and to catch up on the U.S. lead. The U.S.S.R. became the second Atomic Power in the autumn of 1949. Britain was equally determined to attain the status of Atomic Power (the post-1945 equivalent of 'Great Power' status) and reached its goal in October 1952. By this time, November 1952, the U.S. had tested the first hydrogen bomb. France, excluded by the United States and Britain from a share in nuclear weapon technology, succeeded in making its own atomic bomb in 1960.

Meantime, British collaboration with the United States was resumed in 1957, the year after Britain had independently made its own hydrogen bomb. In March 1957 at Bermuda, President Eisenhower agreed in principle to provide guided missiles for Britain's nuclear warheads. An amendment to the Atomic Energy Act gave the President discretion to exchange atomic information with any ally making substantial and material contributions to U.S. defence. Britain accepted U.S. missile bases, though their use in an emergency was to be a joint decision. In return for the close alliance relationship, the U.S. in February 1958 agreed to exchange atomic information, which in practice meant help and cooperation in developing a missile for delivery of the nuclear warhead. The intended missile 'Skybolt' was cancelled, but Macmillan and Kennedy concluded the *Nassau Agreement, December 1962*, whereby Polaris missiles would be placed in British-built submarines. The missile submarines were to be used for Western defence, but the British Government retained the ultimate control of these ships. Thus the Polaris submarines, though dependent on a U.S. rocket, gave Britain an independent nuclear deterrent, albeit a small one.

De Gaulle rejected dependence on the U.S. for missiles and developed a small independent nuclear capacity. He also vetoed Britain's application to join the E.E.C. on the ground that Britain preferred a junior partnership with the U.S. to Western European alignment (p. 392).

During the early 1960s Britain enjoyed a special position. Although not a Superpower, Britain engaged in Superpower diplomacy. When the Soviet Union and the United States conducted arms control negotiations, Britain acted as a third negotiating partner. The nuclear Power not invited was de Gaulle's France. China was also left out when the Communist Chinese succeeded in their first atomic test in October 1964. Both France and China have refused to accept the terms of arms control worked out in the treaties sponsored by the United States, the Soviet Union and Britain. The Soviet Union had apparently promised help in nuclear manufacture to China in 1957, but after 1960 this assistance came to a virtual halt. Thus both the United States and the Soviet Union, whilst establishing bases among allies, did not share atomic secrets with these allies (except to a limited extent with Britain). Thus in practice both Superpowers followed a non-proliferation policy. Simultaneously they have engaged in a nuclear armaments race whilst doing their best to prevent other States from acquiring nuclear weapon technology.

The first treaty of arms control to be concluded by the United States, the Soviet Union and Britain was the *Limited Nuclear Test Ban, 5 August 1963* (p. 515); it banned all nuclear testing in the atmosphere and elsewhere, except underground. The effect of this treaty was not to hinder the research programmes of the advanced nuclear Powers, the U.S. and the Soviet Union; the less advanced nuclear or near-nuclear Powers, such as France and China, have refused to accede to it and continue atmospheric testing.

The treaty on principles governing the activities of States in the exploration and use of outer space including the moon and other celestial bodies, 27 January 1967, signed by the United States, the Soviet Union and Britain, banned nuclear warheads in space (Article 4). But its arms control value is limited since satellites capable of carrying warheads may be tested without them, and the presence of warheads cannot be verified in any case. The Soviet Union is believed to have a capacity for launching nuclear weapons from orbiting satellites. The *treaty on the prohibition of the emplacement of nuclear weapons and other weapons of mass destruction on the sea bed and ocean floor, December 1970*, does not curb armaments since there appears to be no longer a sound military reason for anchoring nuclear weapons to the sea bed, although at the time this seemed possible; the mobile submarine with nuclear missiles is not banned. The earlier *Antarctic Treaty, 1 December 1959* prohibits nuclear explosions on Antarctica. A *treaty for the prohibition of nuclear weapons in Latin America was signed in Mexico on 14*

February 1967 by fourteen Latin American States, and the United States acceded to it on 12 May 1971.

The agreement which best exemplifies the mutual interests of the two Superpowers is the *Treaty on the non-proliferation of nuclear weapons, 1 July 1968* (p. 516), which was concluded after several years of negotiations. The Soviet Union and the United States both wish to prevent the spread to other States of the capacity to make atomic weapons. The treaty is not likely to prove a very effective instrument for achieving this objective; just as the United States monopoly broke down, so nuclear weapon technology has spread to five States without aid from the more advanced nuclear predecessors. Nuclear States France and China have refused to sign this treaty. Independent nations cannot be made to sign and ratify it, and, until the world has become a permanently safer place, few of those nations which have the future capacity for making atomic bombs are likely to take the final step of irrevocably committing themselves never to make such weapons. A major difficulty is that the peaceful use of nuclear power provides the potential for making weapons. More than twenty-five countries by the mid-1970s will be operating nuclear reactors for electric power and thus producing the plutonium necessary for atomic bombs. Only seventy-one nations had ratified the treaty by mid-1972, including two with the capacity in the near future for making a bomb, Canada and Sweden. The Federal Republic of Germany, Japan, Italy, Egypt, Israel, India, Brazil, Argentina and South Africa, all possible 'near-nuclear Powers', had not ratified the treaty by that date, and the last-named five have not signed it either. Careful analysis of the wording of the treaty text has also revealed important loopholes and ambiguities. Nor does the treaty prevent the deployment of nuclear warheads on the territory of non-nuclear States, provided they remain under the control of a nuclear Power. Thus nuclear warheads are available to NATO on air bases from Britain to Turkey.

None of the arms treaties of the 1960s actually reduced nuclear armaments. They do *not* represent any progress in disarmament. On the contrary, the 1960s were a decade of an unprecedented nuclear armaments race. Since the Cuban Missile Crisis of October 1962 the Soviet Union has rapidly expanded its missiles and nuclear arsenal, and both Superpowers have nuclear stocks believed to provide a margin of 'safety' beyond that necessary to completely destroy each other. But efforts to secure some reduction of the accelerating future costs imposed by this armaments race were begun by the Superpowers with the start of the *Strategic Arms Limitations Talks in November 1969 (SALT)*. Technological advances, more specifically the space satellite, have overcome one of the principal obstacles to armaments control: how to verify that agreed limitations are observed, in the face of the Soviet Union's refusal since the Second World

War to permit inspections on the ground (i.e. in the Soviet Union and the U.S.) judged as adequate by the United States. The U2 spy plane, which allowed observation from the air, and whose presence wrecked the Paris Summit Conference of 1960, has been replaced by unmanned spy satellites capable of relaying back information concerning large land-based missile sites, launchings and tests. Their acceptance was one of the breakthroughs making possible the signature on the occasion of Nixon's Moscow visit of a *treaty on the limitation of antiballistic missile systems, 26 May 1972*, which set up future ceilings for each Power of 200 defensive nuclear missiles. A companion *agreement on certain measures with respect to the limitation of strategic offensive arms, 26 May 1972*, is termed not a full treaty but an 'interim agreement' for five years. It limits the ceiling of intercontinental ballistic missiles (I.C.B.M.s) to those now under construction or already deployed. It allows the Soviet Union a higher ceiling than the U.S. for land-based and submarine missiles, but the multiple warheads of certain American missiles give the United States the lead in total numbers of nuclear warheads. The Antiballistic Missile Treaty is much more tightly drafted; it has no time limit, but permits one Power to withdraw after six months' notice if it regards its 'supreme interests are jeopardized'; it is clear that the failure to negotiate a comprehensive treaty would justify in American eyes withdrawal from the A.B.M. Treaty. Thus the treaties and agreements of May 1972 should be seen mainly as limited declarations of faith in the outcome of the new round of ongoing SALT negotiations which may lead to a comprehensive treaty covering all aspects of nuclear armaments.

Seen in perspective the earlier U.S.–Soviet agreements of the 1960s concerning nuclear weapons and space, although mainly environmental and scientific in their beneficial effect rather than effective as disarmament measures, built the 'bridges' leading to the more substantive disarmament negotiations of SALT. Britain, it should be noted, has dropped out of the direct negotiations between the Superpowers. The extent to which these bilateral negotiations are coordinated and related to the needs of defence of the Warsaw Pact alliance and NATO is ultimately dependent on the attitudes and policies of the Soviet Union and the United States, each to its alliance partners.

There have been other American–Soviet agreements all pointing to the emergence of a changed relationship. Two agreements were signed on 30 September 1971, one improving the 'hot line' link, the other on 'Measures to Reduce Risk of War between the United States of America and the Union of Soviet Socialist Republics'. A year later, on 18 October 1972, the United States and the Soviet Union signed a comprehensive trade agreement to run initially for three years. This reduces discriminatory tariffs against Soviet imports to the United States, and is expected to triple the Soviet–U.S. trade; the Soviet

Union also agreed to pay 921 million dollars by July 2001 in a debt settlement for aid amounting to more than 11,000 million dollars received from the U.S. during the Second World War.

The framework for the development of practical cooperation between the United States and the Soviet Union was set out in the *United States–Soviet Declaration, 29 May 1972* (p. 522), and the *Joint Communiqué* issued by the two Powers also on 29 May 1972 to mark the end of the Nixon visit to Moscow (p. 522).

A fundamental change in U.S. policy towards the Chinese People's Republic was also publicly proclaimed when Nixon visited Peking in February 1972. No treaties or agreements were signed. *A Chinese–United States Joint Communiqué, 27 February 1972* (p. 524), was issued at the end of Nixon's visit. Unlike the U.S.–Soviet communiqué three months later, important parts of the Chinese–U.S. joint communiqué are not joint at all, each side stating its own case. The very fact that the visit took place at all is, however, evidence that both countries wish to normalize their relations, an objective set out in the joint communiqué. U.S. recognition of the Republic of China established in Taiwan is one of the principal obstacles to normal relations between the two States, as both the Taiwan Chinese Republic and the People's Republic of China on the mainland claim to be the legitimate Government of the whole of China. The Chinese statement in the joint communiqué affirmed that the People's Republic of China is the sole legal Government of China and that Taiwan is a province of China; that its 'liberation' was entirely an internal Chinese affair in which no outside Power had the right to interfere; that all U.S. forces should be withdrawn from Taiwan. The United States in its statement would only acknowledge the fact that 'all Chinese on either side of the Taiwan Strait maintain, there is but one China'. The United States also reaffirmed its interest in a peaceful settlement by the Chinese themselves. The United States declared it would ultimately withdraw all U.S. forces from Taiwan and progressively reduce its forces as tension in the area diminished. The communiqué added no timetable for this withdrawal. Elsewhere in the communiqué the U.S. for its part, also without a timetable, declared that it would ultimately withdraw its forces from Indo-China 'consistent with the aim of self-determination for each country of Indo-China'. In Korea the U.S. would work for a relaxation of tension and would support peace in South Asia, a region which should not become an area of Great Power rivalry. Statements of differences and the desire for better relations without binding commitments characterize the measure of agreement reached by the United States and the Soviet Union.

In 1972 a worldwide reduction of tension took place among the 'Great Powers', and a desire to take practical steps which are intended to bring some immediate benefits was manifested. In Europe, the Berlin Agreement and the relationship being established between the Government of East Germany and the Federal Republic of West Germany was made possible by Chancellor Brandt's pursuit of a constructive Eastern policy supported by the Four Powers, who are still responsible by treaty for Germany as a whole. Preparations were made in 1972 and 1973 for a European Security Conference, which if it takes place will have as one of its principal tasks the negotiation of an agreement of mutual and balanced force reduction. In Asia, President Nixon's policy of Vietnamization is being brought to the logical conclusion of U.S. withdrawal and an agreement to leave the political solution to the Vietnamese. But in 1972 there was little progress towards settling the fundamental conflicts of the Middle East and Africa.

In the important field of international finance the structure of Bretton Woods, created in 1944–5, is seen some twenty-seven years later to be in need of urgent revision and change. This too has come to be accepted as necessary in 1973. No immediate agreed solutions are in sight which will enable the Third World of developing nations to close the gap between the poor and the rich. Aid to the poor nations continues to be negotiated mainly by bilateral agreements on conditions acceptable to the rich nations. The poor nations continue to urge larger aid granted by international machinery 'without strings attached'. With a lessening emphasis on military confrontation, economic and trade issues are becoming more central to international relationhips in 1973.

The treaties and agreements of 1972, some closing old problems and others looking tentatively forward to new solutions, seem to mark the end of a distinct period of international relations that began in 1945 in the aftermath of the Second World War.

Treaty banning nuclear weapon tests in the atmosphere in outer space and under water, Moscow, 5 August 1963

The Governments of the United States of America, the United Kingdom of Great Britain and Northern Ireland, and the Union of Soviet Socialist Republics, hereinafter referred to as the 'original parties',

Proclaiming as their principal aim the speediest possible achievement of an agreement on general and complete disarmament under strict international control in accordance with the objectives of the United Nations which would put an end to the armaments race and eliminate the incentive to the production and testing of all kinds of weapons, including nuclear weapons,

Seeking to achieve the discontinuance of all test explosions of nuclear weapons for all time, determined to continue negotiations to this end, and desiring to put an end to the contamination of man's environment by radioactive substances,

Have agreed as follows:

Article I. 1. Each of the parties to this Treaty undertakes to prohibit, to prevent, and not to carry out any nuclear weapon test explosion, or any other nuclear explosion, at any place under its jurisdiction or control:

(a) in the atmosphere; beyond its limits, including outer space; or under water, including territorial waters or high seas; or

(b) in any other environment if such explosion causes radioactive debris to be present outside the territorial limits of the State under whose jurisdiction or control such explosion is conducted. It is understood in this connection that the provisions of this sub-paragraph are without prejudice to the conclusion of a treaty resulting in the permanent banning of all nuclear test explosions, including all such explosions underground, the conclusion of which, as the parties have stated in the Preamble to this Treaty, they seek to achieve.

2. Each of the parties to this Treaty undertakes furthermore to refrain from causing, encouraging, or in any way participating in, the carrying out of any nuclear weapon test explosion, or any other nuclear explosion, anywhere which would take place in any of the environments described, or have the effect referred to, in paragraph 1 of this Article.

[*Article II.* Amendments require a majority of all signatories including the assent of all the original signatories.]

Article III. This Treaty shall be open to all States for signature ...

Article IV. This Treaty shall be of unlimited duration.

Each party shall in exercising its national sovereignty have the right to withdraw from the Treaty if it decides that extraordinary events, related to the subject matter of this Treaty, have jeopardized the supreme interest of its country. It shall give notice of such withdrawal to all other parties to the Treaty three months in advance.

...

[Signed] Rusk, Home, Gromyko.

Treaty on the non-proliferation of nuclear weapons, 1 July 1968

The States concluding this Treaty, hereinafter referred to as the 'parties to the Treaty',

Considering the devastation that would be visited upon all mankind by a nuclear war and the consequent need to make every effort to avert the danger of such a war and to take measures to safeguard the security of peoples;

Believing that the proliferation of nuclear weapons would seriously enhance the danger of nuclear war;

In conformity with resolutions of the United Nations General Assembly calling for the conclusion of an agreement on the prevention of wider dissemination of nuclear weapons;

Undertaking to cooperate in facilitating the application of International Atomic Energy Agency safeguards on peaceful nuclear activities;

Expressing their support for research, development and other efforts to further the application, within the framework of the International Atomic Energy Agency safeguards system, of the principle of safeguarding effectively the flow of source and special fissionable materials by use of instruments and other techniques at certain strategic points;

Affirming the principle that the benefits of peaceful applications of nuclear technology, including any technological by-products which may be derived by nuclear-weapon States from the development of nuclear explosive devices, should be available for peaceful purposes to all parties to the Treaty, whether nuclear-weapon or non-nuclear-weapon States;

Convinced that, in furtherance of this principle, all parties to the Treaty are entitled to participate in the fullest possible exchange of scientific information for, and to contribute alone or in cooperation with other States to, the further development of the applications of atomic energy for peaceful purposes;

Declaring their intention to achieve at the earliest possible date the cessation of the nuclear arms race and to undertake effective measures in the direction of nuclear disarmament;

Urging the cooperation of all States in the attainment of this objective;

Recalling the determination expressed by the parties to the 1963 treaty, banning nuclear weapon tests in the atmosphere in outer space and under water, in its Preamble to seek to achieve the discontinuance of all test explosions of nuclear weapons for all time and to continue negotiations to this end;

Desiring to further the easing of international tension and the strengthening of trust between States in order to facilitate the cessation of the manufacture of nuclear weapons, the liquidation of all their existing stockpiles, and the elimination from national arsenals of nuclear weapons and the means of their delivery pursuant to a treaty on general and complete disarmament under strict and effective international control;

Recalling that, in accordance with the Charter of the United Nations, States must refrain in their international relations from the threat or use of force against the territorial integrity or political independence of any State, or in any other manner inconsistent with the purposes of the United Nations, and that the establishment and maintenance of international peace and security are to be promoted with the least diversion for armaments of the world's human and economic resources;

Have agreed as follows:

Article I. Each nuclear-weapon State party to the Treaty undertakes not to transfer to any recipient whatsoever nuclear weapons or other nuclear explosive devices or control over such weapons or explosive devices directly, or indirectly; and not in any way to assist, encourage, or induce any non-nuclear-weapon State to manufacture or otherwise acquire nuclear weapons or other nuclear explosive devices, or control over such weapons or explosive devices.

Article II. Each non-nuclear-weapon State party to the Treaty undertakes not to receive the transfer from any transferor whatsoever of nuclear weapons or other nuclear explosive devices or of control over such weapons or explosive devices directly, or indirectly; not to manufacture or otherwise acquire nuclear weapons or other nuclear explosive devices; and not to seek or receive any assistance in the manufacture of nuclear weapons or other nuclear explosive devices.

Article III. 1. Each non-nuclear-weapon State party to the Treaty undertakes to accept safeguards, as set forth in an agreement to be negotiated and concluded with the International Atomic Energy Agency in accordance with the Statute of the International Atomic Energy Agency and the Agency's safeguards system, for the exclusive purpose of verification of the fulfilment of its obligations assumed under this Treaty with a view to preventing diversion of nuclear energy from peaceful uses to nuclear weapons or other nuclear explosive devices. Procedures for the safeguards required by this Article shall be followed with respect to source or special fissionable material whether it is being produced, processed or used in any principal nuclear facility or is outside any such facility. The safeguards required by this Article shall be applied on all source or special fissionable material in all peaceful nuclear activities within the territory of such State, under its jurisdiction, or carried out under its control anywhere.

2. Each State party to the Treaty undertakes not to provide: (a) source of special fissionable material, or (b) equipment or material especially designed or prepared for the processing, use or production of special fissionable material, to any non-nuclear-weapon State for peaceful purposes, unless the source of special fissionable material shall be subject to the safeguards required by this Article.

3. The safeguards required by this Article shall be implemented in a manner designed to comply with Article IV of this Treaty, and to avoid hampering the economic or technological development of the parties or international cooperation in the field of peaceful nuclear activities, including the international exchange of nuclear material and equipment for the processing, use or production of nuclear material for peaceful purposes in accordance with the provisions of this Article and the principle of safeguarding set forth in the Preamble of the Treaty.

4. Non-nuclear-weapon States party to the Treaty shall conclude agreements with the International Atomic Energy Agency to meet the requirements of this Article either individually or together with other States in accordance with the Statute of the International Atomic Energy Agency. Negotiation of such agreements shall commence within 180 days from the original entry into force of this Treaty. For States depositing their instruments of ratification or accession after the 180-day period, negotiation of such agreements shall commence not later than the date of such deposit. Such agreements shall enter into force not later than eighteen months after the date of initiation of negotiations.

Article IV. 1. Nothing in this Treaty shall be interpreted as affecting the inalienable right of all the parties to the Treaty to develop research, production and use of nuclear energy for peaceful purposes without discrimination and in conformity with Articles I and II of this Treaty.

2. All the parties to the Treaty undertake to facilitate, and have the right to participate in, the fullest possible exchange of equipment, materials and scientific and technological information for the peaceful uses of nuclear energy. Parties to the Treaty in a position to do so shall also cooperate in contributing alone or together with other States or international organizations to the further development of the applications of nuclear energy for peaceful purposes, especially in the territories of non-nuclear-weapon States party to the Treaty, with due consideration for the needs of the developing areas of the world.

Article V. Each party to the Treaty undertakes to take appropriate measures to ensure that, in accordance with this Treaty, under appropriate international observation and through appropriate international procedures, potential benefits from any peaceful applications of nuclear explosions will be made available to non-nuclear-weapon States party to the Treaty on a non-discriminatory basis and that the charge of such parties for the explosive devices used will be as low as possible and exclude any charge for research and development. Non-nuclear-weapon States party to the Treaty shall be able to obtain such benefits, pursuant to a special international agreement or agreements, through an appropriate international body with adequate representation of non-nuclear-weapon States. Negotiations on this subject shall commence as soon as possible after the Treaty enters into force. Non-nuclear-weapon States party to the Treaty so desiring may also obtain such benefits pursuant to bilateral agreements.

Article VI. Each of the parties to the Treaty undertakes to pursue negotiations in good faith on effective measures relating to cessation of the nuclear arms race at an early date and to nuclear disarmament, and on a treaty on general and complete disarmament under strict and effective international control.

Article VII. Nothing in this Treaty affects the right of any group of States to conclude regional treaties in order to assure the total absence of nuclear weapons in their respective territories.

Article VIII. 1. Any party to the Treaty may propose amendments to this Treaty. The text of any proposed amendment shall be submitted to the Depositary Governments which shall circulate it to all parties to the Treaty. Thereupon, if requested to do so by one-third or more of the parties to the Treaty, the Depositary Governments shall convene a conference, to which they shall invite all the parties to the Treaty, to consider such an amendment.

2. Any amendment to this Treaty must be approved by a majority of the votes of all the parties to the Treaty, including the votes of all nuclear-weapon States party to the Treaty and all other parties which, on the date the amendment is circulated, are members of the Board of Governors of the International Atomic Energy Agency. The amendment shall enter into force for each party that deposits its instrument of ratification of the amendment upon the deposit of such instruments of ratification by a majority of all the parties, including the instruments of ratification of all nuclear-weapon States party to the Treaty and all other parties which, on the date the amendment is circulated, are members of the Board of Governors of the International Atomic Energy Agency. Thereafter, it shall enter into force for any other party upon the deposit of its instrument of ratification of the amendment.

3. Five years after the entry into force of this Treaty, a conference of parties to the Treaty shall be held in Geneva, Switzerland, in order to review the operation of this Treaty with a view to assuring that the purposes of the Preamble and the provisions of the Treaty are being realized. At intervals of five years thereafter,

a majority of the parties to the Treaty may obtain, by submitting a proposal to this effect to the Depositary Governments, the convening of further conferences with the same objective of reviewing the operation of the Treaty.

Article IX. 1. This Treaty shall be open to all States for signature. Any State which does not sign the Treaty before its entry into force in accordance with paragraph 3 of this Article may accede to it at any time.

2. This Treaty shall be subject to ratification by signatory States. Instruments of ratification and instruments of accession shall be deposited with the Governments of the United States of America, the United Kingdom of Great Britain and Northern Ireland and the Union of Soviet Socialist Republics, which are hereby designated the Depositary Governments.

3. This Treaty shall enter into force after its ratification by the States, the Governments of which are designated Depositaries of the Treaty, and forty other States signatory to this Treaty and the deposit of their instruments of ratification. For the purposes of this Treaty, a nuclear-weapon State is one which has manufactured and exploded a nuclear weapon or other nuclear explosive device prior to January 1, 1967.

4. For States whose instruments of ratification or accession are deposited subsequent to the entry into force of this Treaty, it shall enter into force on the date of the deposit of their instruments of ratification or accession.

5. The Depositary Governments shall promptly inform all signatory and acceding States of the date of each signature, the date of deposit of each instrument of ratification or of accession, the date of the entry into force of this Treaty, and the date of receipt of any requests for convening a conference or other notices.

6. This Treaty shall be registered by the Depositary Governments pursuant to Article 102 of the Charter of the United Nations.

Article X. 1. Each party shall in exercising its national sovereignty have the right to withdraw from the Treaty if it decides that extraordinary events, related to the subject matter of this Treaty, have jeopardized the supreme interests of its country. It shall give notice of such withdrawal to all other parties to the Treaty and to the United Nations Security Council three months in advance. Such notice shall include a statement of the extraordinary events it regards as having jeopardized its supreme interests.

2. Twenty-five years after the entry into force of the Treaty, a conference shall be convened to decide whether the Treaty shall continue in force indefinitely, or shall be extended for an additional fixed period or periods. This decision shall be taken by a majority of the parties to the Treaty.

[*Article XI.* Authentic texts.]

Joint Declaration by the United States and Soviet Union on basic principles of relations between them, Moscow, 29 May 1972

The United States of America and the Union of Soviet Socialist Republics,

Guided by their obligations under the Charter of the United Nations and by a desire to strengthen peaceful relations with each other and to place these relations on the firmest possible basis;

Aware of the need to make every effort to remove the threat of war and to create conditions which promote the reduction of tensions in the world and the strengthening of universal security and international cooperation;

Believing that improvement of United States–Soviet relations and their mutually advantageous development in such areas as economics, science and culture will meet these objectives and contribute to better mutual understanding and businesslike cooperation, without in any way prejudicing the interests of third countries;

Conscious that these objectives reflect the interests of the peoples of both countries;

Have agreed as follows:

First. They will proceed from the common determination that in the nuclear age there is no alternative to conducting their mutual relations on the basis of peaceful coexistence. Differences in ideology and in the social systems of the U.S.A. and the U.S.S.R. are not obstacles to the bilateral development of normal relations based on the principles of sovereignty, equality, non-interference in internal affairs and mutual advantage.

Second. The U.S.A. and the U.S.S.R. attach major importance to preventing the development of situations capable of causing a dangerous exacerbation of their relations. Therefore, they will do their utmost to avoid military confrontations and to prevent the outbreak of nuclear war. They will always exercise restraint in their mutual relations, and will be prepared to negotiate and settle differences by peaceful means. Discussions and negotiations on outstanding issues will be conducted in a spirit of reciprocity, mutual accommodation and mutual benefit.

Both sides recognize that efforts to obtain unilateral advantage at the expense of the other, directly or indirectly ... are inconsistent with these objectives. The prerequisites for maintaining and strengthening peaceful relations between the U.S.A. and the U.S.S.R. are the recognition of the security interests of the parties based on the principle of equality and the renunciation of the use or threat of force.

Third. The U.S.A. and the U.S.S.R. have a special responsibility ... as do other countries which are permanent members of the United Nations Security Council, to do everything in their power so that conflicts or situations will not arise which would serve to increase international tensions. Accordingly they will seek to promote conditions in which all countries will live in peace and security and will not be subject to outside interference in their internal affairs.

Fourth. The U.S.A. and the U.S.S.R. intend to widen the juridical basis of their mutual relations and to exert the necessary efforts so that bilateral agreements which they have concluded and multilateral treaties and agreements to which they are jointly parties are faithfully implemented.

Fifth. The U.S.A. and the U.S.S.R. reaffirm their readiness to continue the practice of exchanging views on problems of mutual interest and, when necessary, to conduct such exchanges at the highest level, including meetings between leaders of the two countries.

The two Governments welcome and will facilitate an increase in productive contacts between representatives of the legislative bodies of the two countries.

Sixth. The parties will continue their efforts to limit armaments on a bilateral as well as on a multilateral basis. They will continue to make special efforts to limit strategic armaments. Whenever possible, they will conclude concrete agreements aimed at achieving these purposes.

The U.S.A. and the U.S.S.R. regard as the ultimate objective of their efforts the achievement of general and complete disarmament and the establishment of an effective system on international security in accordance with the purposes and principles of the United Nations.

Seventh. The U.S.A. and the U.S.S.R. regard commercial and economic ties as an important and necessary element in the strengthening of their bilateral relations and thus will actively promote the growth of such ties. They will facilitate cooperation between the relevant organizations and enterprises of the two countries and the conclusion of appropriate agreements and contracts, including long-term ones.

The two countries will contribute to the improvement of maritime and air communications between them.

Eighth. The two sides consider it timely and useful to develop mutual contacts and cooperation in the fields of science and technology. Where suitable, the U.S.A. and the U.S.S.R. will conclude appropriate agreements dealing with concrete cooperation in these fields.

Ninth. The two sides reaffirm their intention to deepen cultural ties with one another and to encourage fuller familiarization with each other's cultural values. They will promote improved conditions for cultural exchanges and tourism.

Tenth. The U.S.A. and the U.S.S.R. will seek to ensure that their ties and cooperation in all the above-mentioned fields and in any others in their mutual interest are built on a firm and long-term basis. To give a permanent character to these efforts, they will establish in all fields where this is feasible joint commissions or other joint bodies.

Eleventh. The U.S.A. and the U.S.S.R. make no claim for themselves and would not recognize the claims of anyone else to any special rights or advantages in world affairs. They recognize the sovereign equality of all States.

The development of United States–Soviet relations is not directed against third countries and their interests.

Twelfth. The basic principles set forth in this Document do not affect any obligations with respect to other countries earlier assumed by the U.S.A. and the U.S.S.R.

Joint Communiqué by the Soviet Union and United States, Moscow, 29 May 1972

The discussions covered a wide range of questions of mutual interest and were frank and thorough.

I · Bilateral relations

As a result of progress made in negotiations which preceded the summit meeting, and in the course of the meeting itself, a number of significant agreements were reached.

LIMITATION OF STRATEGIC ARMAMENTS

The two sides gave primary attention to the problem of reducing the danger of nuclear war.

The two sides attach great importance to the treaty on the limitation of anti-ballistic systems and the interim agreement on certain measures with respect to the limitation of strategic offensive arms concluded between them.

These agreements, which were concluded as a result of the negotiations in Moscow, constitute a major step towards curbing and ultimately ending the arms race.

The two sides intended to continue active negotiations for the limitation of strategic offensive arms and to conduct them in a spirit of goodwill, respect for each other's legitimate interests and observance of the principle of equal security.

COMMERCIAL AND ECONOMIC RELATIONS

Both sides agreed on measures designed to establish more favourable conditions for developing commercial and other economic ties between the U.S.A. and the U.S.S.R.

MARITIME MATTERS: INCIDENTS AT SEA

The two sides agreed to continue the negotiations aimed at reaching an agreement on maritime and related matters.

An agreement was concluded between the two sides on measures to prevent incidents at sea and in air space over it between vessels and aircraft of the United States and Soviet navies. By providing agreed procedures for ships and aircraft of the two navies operating in close proximity, this agreement will diminish the chances of dangerous accidents.

COOPERATION IN SCIENCE AND TECHNOLOGY

The two sides signed an agreement for cooperation in the fields of science and technology. A United States–Soviet Joint Commission on Scientific and Technical Cooperation will be created for identifying and establishing cooperation programmes.

COOPERATION IN SPACE

The two sides agreed to make suitable arrangements to permit the docking of American and Soviet spacecraft and stations. The first joint docking experiment of the two countries' piloted spacecraft, with visits by astronauts and cosmonauts to each other's spacecraft, is contemplated for 1975.

COOPERATION IN THE FIELD OF HEALTH

The two sides concluded an agreement on health cooperation which marks a fruitful beginning of sharing knowledge about, and collaborative attacks on, the common enemies, disease and disability.

ENVIRONMENT COOPERATION

The two sides agreed to initiate a programme of cooperation in the protection and enhancement of man's environment.

EXCHANGES IN THE FIELD OF SCIENCE, TECHNOLOGY, EDUCATION AND CULTURE

The two sides have agreed to expand the areas of cooperation, as reflected in new agreements concerning space, health, the environment and science and technology.

II · International issues

EUROPE

In the course of the discussions on the international situation, both sides took note of favourable developments in the relaxation of tensions in Europe.

Recognizing the importance to world peace of developments in Europe ... the U.S.A. and the U.S.S.R. intend to make further efforts to ensure a peaceful future for Europe, free of tensions, crises and conflicts. They agree that the territorial integrity of all States in Europe should be respected.

Both sides view the September 3, 1971, quadripartite agreement relating to the Western sectors of Berlin as a good example of fruitful cooperation between the States concerned, including the U.S.A. and the U.S.S.R.

Both sides welcomed the treaty between the U.S.S.R. and the Federal Republic of Germany signed on August 12, 1970.

The U.S.A. and the U.S.S.R. are in accord that multilateral consultations looking towards a conference on security and cooperation in Europe could begin after the signature of the final quadripartite protocol of the agreement of September 3, 1971.

The two Governments agree that the conference should be carefully prepared in order that it may concretely consider specific problems of security and cooperation and thus contribute to the progressive reduction of the underlying causes of tension in Europe. This conference should be convened at a time to be agreed by the countries concerned, but without undue delay.

Both sides believe that the goal of ensuring stability and security in Europe would be served by a reciprocal reduction of armed forces and armaments, first of all in Central Europe.

THE MIDDLE EAST

The two sides ... reaffirm their support for a peaceful settlement in the Middle East in accordance with Security Council Resolution 242.

Noting the significance of constructive cooperation of the parties concerned with the special representative of the United Nations Secretary-General, Ambassador Jarring, the U.S.A. and the U.S.S.R. confirm their desire to contribute to his mission's success and also declare their readiness to play their part in bringing about a peaceful settlement in the Middle East.

INDO-CHINA

Each side set forth its respective standpoint with regard to the continuing war in Vietnam and the situation in the area of Indo-China as a whole.

The United States side emphasizes the need to bring an end to the military conflict as soon as possible and reaffirmed its commitment to the principle that the political future of South Vietnam should be left for the South Vietnamese people to decide for themselves, free from outside interference.

The United States reiterated its willingness to enter into serious negotiations with the North Vietnamese side to settle the war in Indo-China on a basis just to all.

The Soviet side stressed its solidarity with the just struggle of the peoples of Vietnam, Laos and Cambodia for their freedom, independence and social progress.

DISARMAMENT ISSUES

The two sides note that in recent years their joint and parallel actions have facilitated the working out and conclusion of treaties which curb the arms race or ban some of the most dangerous types of weapons.

Both sides regard the convention on the prohibition of the development and stockpiling of bacteriological (biological) and toxic weapons, and on their destruction, as an essential disarmament measure.

Along with Great Britain, they are the depositories for the convention which was recently opened for signature by all States. The U.S.A. and the U.S.S.R. will continue their efforts to reach an international agreement regarding chemical weapons.

The U.S.A. and the U.S.S.R. will actively participate in negotiations aimed at working out new measures designed to curb and end the arms race. The ultimate purpose is general and complete disarmament, including nuclear disarmament, under strict international control. A world disarmament conference could play a role in this process at an appropriate time.

STRENGTHENING THE UNITED NATIONS

Both sides will strive to strengthen the effectiveness of the United Nations on the basis of strict observance of the United Nations Charter.

Both sides emphasized that agreements and understandings reached in the negotiations in Moscow, as well as the contents and nature of these negotiations, are not in any way directed against any other country.

Both sides believe that positive results were accomplished in the course of the talks at the highest level.

Both sides expressed the desire to continue close contact on a number of issues that were under discussion. They agreed that regular consultations on questions of mutual interest, including meetings at the highest level, would be useful.

In expressing his appreciation for the hospitality accorded him in the Soviet Union, President Nixon invited General Secretary L. I. Brezhnev, Chairman N. V. Podgorny, and Chairman A. N. Kosygin to visit the United States at a mutually convenient time. This invitation was accepted.

Joint U.S.–Chinese Communiqué, Shanghai, 27 February 1972

President Richard Nixon of the United States of America visited the People's Republic of China at the invitation of Premier Chou En-lai of the People's Republic of China from February 21 to February 28, 1972. Accompanying the President were Mrs Nixon, United States Secretary of State William Rogers, Assistant to the President Dr Henry Kissinger, and other American officials.

President Nixon met with Chairman Mao Tse-tung of the Communist Party of China on February 21. The two leaders had a serious and frank exchange of views on Sino–United States relations and world affairs.

During the visit, extensive, earnest and frank discussions were held between President Nixon and Premier Chou En-lai on the normalization of relations between

the United States of America and the People's Republic of China, as well as on other matters of interest to both sides. In addition, Secretary of State William Rogers and Foreign Minister Chi Peng-fei held talks in the same spirit.

President Nixon and his party visited Peking and viewed cultural, industrial and agricultural sites, and they also toured Hangchow and Shanghai where, continuing discussions with Chinese leaders, they viewed similar places of interest.

The leaders of the People's Republic of China and the United States of America found it beneficial to have this opportunity, after so many years without contact, to present candidly to one another their views on a variety of issues. They reviewed the international situation, in which important changes and great upheavals are taking place, and expounded their respective positions and attitudes.

The United States side stated: Peace in Asia and peace in the world requires efforts both to reduce immediate tensions and to eliminate the basic causes of conflict. The United States will work for a just and secure peace: just, because it fulfils the aspirations of peoples and nations for freedom and progress; secure, because it removes the danger of foreign aggression. The United States supports individual freedom and social progress for all the peoples of the world, free of outside pressure or intervention.

The United States believes that the effort to reduce tensions is served by improving communication between countries that have different ideologies so as to lessen the risks of confrontation through accident, miscalculation or misunderstanding. Countries should treat each other with mutual respect and be willing to compete peacefully, letting performance be the ultimate judge. No country should claim infallibility and each country should be prepared to re-examine its own attitudes for the common good.

The United States stressed that the peoples of Indo-China should be allowed to determine their destiny without outside intervention; its constant primary objective has been a negotiated solution; the eight-point proposal put forward by the Republic of Vietnam and the United States on January 27, 1972, represents a basis for the attainment of that objective; in the absence of a negotiated settlement the United States envisages the ultimate withdrawal of all United States forces from the region consistent with the aim of self-determination for each country of Indo-China.

The United States will maintain its close ties with and support for the Republic of Korea; the United States will support efforts of the Republic of Korea to seek a relaxation of tension and increased communication in the Korean peninsula.

The United States places the highest value on its friendly relations with Japan; it will continue to develop the existing close bonds.

Consistent with the United Nations Security Council Resolution of December 21, 1971, the United States favours the continuation of the ceasefire between India and Pakistan and the withdrawal of all military forces to within their own territories and to their own sides of the ceasefire line in Jammu and Kashmir; the United States supports the right of the peoples of South Asia to shape their own future in peace, free of military threat, and without having the area become the subject of Great Power rivalry.

The Chinese side stated: Wherever there is oppression, there is resistance. Countries want independence, nations want liberation and the people want revolution – this has become the irresistible trend of history. All nations, big or small, should be equal; big nations should not bully the small and strong nations should not bully the weak. China will never be a Superpower and it opposes hegemony and power politics of any kind.

The Chinese side stated that it firmly supports the struggles of all the oppressed people and nations for freedom and liberation and that the people of all countries have the right to choose their social systems, according to their own wishes, and the right to safeguard the independence, sovereignty and territorial integrity of their own countries and oppose foreign aggression, interference, control and subversion. All foreign troops should be withdrawn to their own countries.

The Chinese side expressed its firm support to the peoples of Vietnam, Laos and Cambodia in their efforts for the attainment of their goal and its firm support to the seven-point proposal of the Provisional Revolutionary Government of the Republic of South Vietnam and the elaboration of February this year on the two key problems in the proposal, and to the Joint Declaration of the summit conference of the Indo-Chinese peoples.

It firmly supports the eight-point programme for the peaceful unification of Korea put forward by the Government of the Democratic People's Republic of Korea on April 12, 1971, and the stand for the abolition of the 'United Nations Commission for the unification and rehabilitation of Korea'.

It firmly opposes the revival and outward expansion of Japanese militarism and firmly supports the Japanese people's desire to build an independent, democratic, peaceful and neutral Japan.

It firmly maintains that India and Pakistan should, in accordance with the United Nations resolutions on the India–Pakistan question, immediately withdraw all their forces to their respective territories and to their own sides of the cease-fire line in Jammu and Kashmir, and firmly supports the Pakistan Government and people in their struggle to preserve their independence and sovereignty and the people of Jammu and Kashmir in their struggle for the right of self-determination.

There are essential differences between China and the United States in their social systems and foreign policies. However, the two sides agreed that countries, regardless of their social systems, should conduct their relations on the principles of respect for the sovereignty and territorial integrity of all States, non-aggression against other States, non-interference in the internal affairs of other States, equality and mutual benefit, and peaceful coexistence.

International disputes should be settled on this basis, without resorting to the use or threat of force. The United States and the People's Republic of China are prepared to apply these principles to their mutual relations.

With these principles of international relations in mind, the two sides stated that: Progress towards the normalization of relations between China and the

United States is in the interests of all countries.

Both wish to reduce the danger of international military conflict.

Neither should seek hegemony in the Asia–Pacific region and each is opposed to efforts by any other country or group of countries to establish such hegemony.

Neither is prepared to negotiate on behalf of any third party or to enter into agreements or understandings with the other directed at other States.

Both sides are of the view that it would be against the interests of the peoples of the world for any major country to collude with another against other countries, or for major countries to divide up the world into spheres of interest.

The two sides reviewed the long-standing serious disputes between China and the United States.

The Chinese side reaffirmed its position: The Taiwan question is the crucial question obstructing the normalization of relations between China and the United States; the Government of the People's Republic of China is the sole legal Government of China; Taiwan is a province of China which has long been returned to the motherland; the liberation of Taiwan is China's internal affair in which no other country has the right to interfere; and all United States forces and military installations must be withdrawn from Taiwan.

The Chinese Government firmly opposes any activities which aim at the creation of 'one China, one Taiwan', 'one China, two Governments', 'two Chinas' and 'independent Taiwan', or advocate that 'the status of Taiwan remains to be determined'.

The United States side declared: The United States acknowledges that all Chinese on either side of the Taiwan Strait maintain there is but one China and that Taiwan is a part of China. The United States Government does not challenge that position. It reaffirms its interest in a peaceful settlement of the Taiwan question by the Chinese themselves.

With this prospect in mind, it affirms the ultimate objective of the withdrawal of all United States forces and military installations from Taiwan. In the meantime, it will progressively reduce its forces and military installations on Taiwan as the tension in the area diminishes.

The two sides agreed that it is desirable to broaden the understanding between the two peoples. To this end, they discussed specific areas in such fields as science, technology, culture, sports and journalism, in which people-to-people contacts and exchanges would be mutually beneficial. Each side undertakes to facilitate the further development of such contacts and exchanges.

Both sides view bilateral trade as another area from which mutual benefit can be derived, and agreed that economic relations based on equality and mutual benefit are in the interest of the peoples of the two countries. They agree to facilitate the progressive development of trade between their two countries.

The two sides agreed that they will stay in contact through various channels, including the sending of a senior United States representative to Peking from time to time for concrete consultations to further the normalization of relations between the two countries and continue to exchange views on issues of common interest.

The two sides expressed the hope that the gains achieved during this visit would open up new prospects for the relations between the two countries. They believe that the normalization of relations between the two countries is not only in the interest of the Chinese and American peoples but also contributes to the relaxation of tension in Asia and the world.

President Nixon, Mrs Nixon and the American party expressed their appreciation for the gracious hospitality shown them by the Government and people of the People's Republic of China.

XIX · The major international conflicts, treaties and agreements of 1973

Many of the new trends in international affairs evident during 1972 have persisted through 1973. That is not to say that it can be safely predicted that they will continue to do so in the long term or even in the immediate future. There are many variables: the 'decision-makers' themselves, and the conditions in which they function, may suddenly change in a way unforeseen. For example, the 'Watergate' crisis involving the American presidency during 1972 and 1973 may affect the conduct of American foreign policy.

In the Soviet Union, the balance of power among the leadership of the *Politburo* is always liable to shift and change and remains unpredictable. On a smaller scale Labour Governments in Australia and New Zealand have led to the re-examination of previously held tenets of foreign policy in these countries. In Britain the nature of the relationship within the European Economic Community remains in doubt and lacks a political consensus of agreement. These are but a few examples. In every country of the world policies change, and perhaps quite rapidly, so that no formula can be worked out, or cyclical theory of international relations postulated, which, interpreting the past and analysing the present, will predict the future course of events.

The *détente* between the Soviet Union and the United States, and China and the United States, and the nuclear armaments rivalry

Both the Soviet Union and the United States regard the *détente* relationship from the point of view of national interests and the interests of its allies (at times interpreted for them). In 1972 there was also common ground between the two countries. Neither Superpower seriously considers that a solution of its global problems can be achieved by a successful first strike in a nuclear war.

In theory, nuclear security can only be attained by possessing the capacity to deliver a devastating nuclear attack on the enemy in *all circumstances*. The circumstances can be categorized from the most disastrous, where all that is left of a country is its capacity to counterstrike with missiles with the certainty of sufficient of them getting through (e.g. from submarines in the ocean after an enemy nuclear attack, or from missiles underground which have escaped an enemy attack), to the 'best' circumstance that permits a successful first or second retaliatory strike against an enemy with the certainty of no more than 'acceptable' damage resulting from an enemy's first strike or second retaliatory strike. Categorizing missile systems as 'offensive' and 'defensive' loses much of its meaning when it comes to the sophistry of arguments about nuclear missile rivalry. A country possessing acceptable nuclear defensive capacity with anti-missile systems is not only sure of being able to survive an enemy's attack, but also has the capacity to attack since it need not be deterred by the enemy's counterstrike. Thus antiballistic missile systems can be classified both as 'offensive' and 'defensive' weapons. Similarly, the capacity to wipe out with certainty all the enemy's capacity to strike a counterblow, and the enemy's recognition of this power, would enable the country possessing it to exert nuclear 'blackmail'. Fortunately for humanity, in the nuclear arms race no country has been able to convince itself so far that it can be certain that the results achieved will approximate the theoretical absolute concepts which would make a nuclear attack worthwhile, and that nuclear warfare, however begun, would not expose *both* contestants to devastation so unacceptable that there could be neither victors nor vanquished. This provides the basis for U.S.–Soviet attempts to control nuclear developments and to limit the huge capital resources that could be spent in fruitless attempts to reach the absolute. With the stakes so high, and the possible consequences of miscalculation so incalculable, practical progress is slow.

The *SALT I* negotiations and agreements did not call a halt to the *qualitative* nuclear arms race. The successful testing by the U.S.S.R. of multiple independently-targeted re-entry vehicle systems (MIRVS), announced by the American Defence Secretary in August 1973, has shown once again how technological progress by one Power can undo the 'balance' believed to have been achieved by an earlier agreement such as SALT I.

During the visit of Leonid Brezhnev to Washington in June 1973 the eleven agreements signed included a nuclear arms agreement, the *United States–Soviet Agreement on limiting strategic arms, 21 June 1973* (p. 540). The principles and aims set out in this agreement are intended to serve as the basis for the forthcoming second phase of the SALT negotiations, which are meant to lead to permanent and more complete agreements on the limitation of strategic offensive arms. The text is ambiguous as to whether this limitation is to be both qualitative as well as quantitative. The Russians are anxious to close the technological missile gap (if it exists). The Soviet Union and the United States also signed an *Agreement on the prevention of nuclear war, 22 June 1973* (p. 541). In the coming months, perhaps years, the words of these treaties may be translated into practical steps. So far they express intentions rather than reflect concrete results.

The Nixon–Brezhnev Washington summit ranged widely over international questions and bilateral relations. *The text of the final communiqué, 25 June 1973*, refers to agreements reached on bilateral cooperation in trade and in space as well as on other questions (p. 542). It does not by itself suddenly end U.S.–Soviet confrontation despite its cordial language. The *détente* framework appears to have limited the danger of a clash through involvement in the Arab–Israeli war, October 1973, and has contributed to finding a basis of minimal U.S.–Soviet cooperation despite the different objectives of their policies in the Middle East (see pp. 537–40).

The changing emphases of United States–Soviet and Sino–American relations have had worldwide repercussions on the relations of the two Superpowers with other States. Competition for the goodwill and support of the 'Third World' has been sustained. The United States' relations with Japan are being re-examined. The Soviet Union is also adopting a friendlier attitude to Japan. But at the same time as the U.S.–Soviet *détente*, a *détente* between East and West Europe has taken place.

Europe

Chancellor Willy Brandt's *Ostpolitik*, the policy of *détente* he has pursued with the Warsaw Pact Powers, could not have been successfully carried through without the support and approval of the Soviet Union (for the earlier phases of this policy see pp. 275–6). In May 1973 Brezhnev visited Bonn. The German Federal Republic is the Soviet Union's largest Western supplier. Plans for large-scale industrial and economic cooperation were discussed. The basis of a framework had been established by a treaty in the previous year, the *Federal German–Soviet Trade and Economic Agreement of 5 July 1972*. On 19 May 1973 further agreements on economic, industrial and technical cooperation were signed. One difficulty revolved around the relationship of the Federal Republic and West Berlin and the Federal German claim to represent West Berlin. The Soviet Union has sought to limit the extent of this representation, and the difficulty was not entirely removed by a communiqué which affirmed 'the strict observance and full application' of the Four Power Agreement on Berlin.

The agreements of 19 May 1973 were also extended to cover West Berlin. However, later in the year this issue caused difficulty in finalizing a treaty with Czechoslovakia (see below).

The German Federal Republic and the German Democratic Republic completed the ratification of the general relations treaty between the two States on 20 June 1973 (p. 296). But the Federal German Government insists that this treaty does not impede the eventual unification of Germany in any way. The Federal Republic continues with a temporary constitution, the Basic Law, and has not officially abandoned the expectation of eventually concluding a formal peace treaty between the Allies of the Second World War on the one hand and a unified Germany on the other. On 20 June 1973 the text of a *Treaty on mutual relations between the Federal Republic of Germany and Czechoslovakia* was also initialled. One of the principal causes of difficulty in these negotiations concerned the validity of the Munich Agreement of September 1938 (p. 176). Complex legal difficulties concerning the status of Sudeten Germans from 1938 to 1945 and the validity of legal transactions during these years was one reason that made the West German negotiators hesitate to declare the Munich treaty null and void. In the end the Czech–German treaty text avoided the issue. Practical legal difficulties were overcome by the exemptions specified in Article II. In Article I the Munich Agreement was declared void with regard to the current and future relations of the two countries; in the preamble the Federal German Government agreed that the Munich settlement had been imposed on Czechoslovakia by the Nazi régime under the threat of force. The Federal German Government has specifically undertaken not only to accept the present frontiers but also to raise no territorial claims in the future. A further difficulty had been the reluctance of the Czechoslovak Government to accept the Federal German Republic's claim to fully represent West Berlin. A compromise appears to have been reached on this issue, and Chancellor Brandt visited Prague on *11 December 1973* to sign this treaty. On 21 December 1973 the German Federal Republic re-established diplomatic relations with Bulgaria and Hungary, thus normalizing its relations with all European States, except Albania, twenty-eight years after the end of the Second World War, but the freer movement of peoples between the two Germanies has not been realized in 1973. The border guards of the German Democratic Republic continue to fire on their own citizens who attempt unauthorized crossings of the frontier into the Federal Republic.

The freer movement of peoples and ideas is one of the points on the agenda of the *European Security Conference*. The weakness at the heart of the *détente* policy lies in the establishment of 'normal' relations between East and West when the public in the West is daily reminded of the denial of basic human rights in the Soviet Union and in some of the States of its allies.

The most elaborate show of *détente* in Europe was the assembly of the *European Security Conference in Helsinki, 3-7 July 1973*, attended by thirty-five Foreign Ministers from all European States and Principalities including Monaco, San Marino, the Holy See, Malta, Cyprus, two non-European countries, members of NATO, Canada and the United States. Agreement on an agenda for a second stage of the conference, which opened in Geneva on 18 September 1973, was reached. An elaborate agenda was adopted covering questions relating to European security, including the sovereign equality of all nations and respect for sovereign rights; respect for human rights and fundamental freedoms; equal rights of States and peoples; the peaceful settlement of disputes and non-intervention in internal affairs; cooperation in the fields of economics, science and technology; expanding human contacts; freer information and cultural exchanges; and guarantees of East–West security. If the enunciation of principles and diplomatic language could be accepted as corresponding to actuality, which patently is not the case, then the 'Brezhnev doctrine' which justified the Soviet invasion of Czechoslovakia could not be repeated, and human rights would be assured in the Soviet Union and throughout Europe. But the gap between language and present reality is so wide that the real question confronting the negotiators in Geneva is whether any bargain can be struck between East and West that will allow some concrete realization of some points on the agenda. In return for a recognition by the Western Powers of post-war frontiers and a tacit acceptance of Soviet hegemony over the Warsaw Pact allies, and increased trade, can a greater degree of human rights or freer human contact between East and West and a lowering of barriers be assured? In 1973 it is difficult to foresee quick and substantial progress in Geneva on these fundamental issues. There is no time limit to the second stage of the conference. Hopefully, it is to be followed by a third stage, a 'summit conference', to ratify any agreements reached at Geneva.

A month later, on 30 October, nineteen NATO and Soviet bloc nations of the Warsaw Pact met in Vienna to begin negotiations at the *Conference on the Mutual Reduction of Forces in Central Europe*. No agenda could be agreed on after five months of preparatory talks; however, it was agreed that negotiations should begin and that, on Soviet insistence, the word 'balanced' should be dropped from the title of the conference, as 'mutual balanced reduction' would imply proportional reductions by each side, thus larger reductions by the Warsaw Pact nations than by NATO. This question is one of several that remain to be negotiated.

Thus the hard bargaining, leading possibly to some effective realization of the *détente*, is still to come in the interrelated web of negotiations which began in the autumn of 1973: *SALT II*, the *Conference on the Mutual Reduction of Forces in Central Europe*, and the second phase of the *European Security Conference*; in addition numerous bilateral negotiations on trade and other topics including those between the Soviet Union and the United States are to be pursued.

The enlargement of the European Economic Community to nine members has taken place administratively during 1973. Major internal and external questions have been raised but little more than the opening shots of the coming arguments have been fired on the reform of the Common Agricultural Policy, the size of a fund for regional aid, and, above all, trade relations with the United States. There was no decided response to the American Secretary of State's call for a new 'Atlantic Charter' or a written 'set of principles' to establish the purposes of the Atlantic partnership and to adapt NATO and other Atlantic institutions to what are conceived, by Kissinger, as the needs of the 1970s and 1980s. From a European, more especially French, point of view, the objectionable aspect of the proposed approach would be to link questions of economic policy, defence and foreign affairs within a broad political framework, for this raises the possibility of 'bargaining' economic concessions in U.S. relations with the E.E.C. for U.S. military support within NATO. Compromises on the various attitudes may well be made as long as the overriding mutual interest in maintaining good 'Atlantic' relations persists, the *détente* with the Soviet Union notwithstanding. The Middle East Arab–Israeli War in October 1973 sharply accentuated the different attitudes of the United States and its European NATO allies. Kissinger openly expressed dissatisfaction with Europe's 'neutral' policy and fear of Arab oil sanctions. In Europe there was alarm at apparent American 'brinkmanship' and the American failure to consult its NATO allies.

The E.E.C. in June 1973 agreed on the principles of trade relations with the Mediterranean States, Israel, Spain, Algeria, Morocco and Tunisia allowing these countries duty-free or low tariff exports to the E.E.C. up to a quantitative ceiling; these States are not 'associated' with the E.E.C. A significant agreement under the generalized preference system was also signed by the Ministers of the Nine of the E.E.C. in June 1973, with Rumania (which had applied in February 1972) becoming the first member of the Warsaw Pact to have negotiated a special economic relationship with the E.E.C.

In a different category of relationship to the E.E.C. are the nineteen mainly French-speaking African States associated with the Community under the Yaoundé Convention, and the nineteen Commonwealth countries in Africa, the Pacific and the Caribbean considered to be 'associable' under Protocol 22 of Britain's Treaty of Accession. The French-speaking associates are Burundi, Cameroon, the Central African Republic, Congo, Ivory Coast, Dahomey,

Gabon, Upper Volta, Madagascar, Mali, Mauritania, Niger, Rwanda, Senegal, Somalia, Chad, Togo, Zaire and Mauritius. The Commonwealth countries are Kenya, Uganda, Tanzania, Botswana, The Gambia, Ghana, Lesotho, Malawi, Swaziland, Nigeria, Sierra Leone, Zambia, Barbados, Guyana, Jamaica, Trinidad and Tobago, Tonga, Fiji and Western Samoa. The two-day conference in Brussels on 25–26 July 1973 was attended by thirty-eight States associated and associable, and representatives from Ethiopia, Liberia, the Sudan, as well as observers from Egypt, Morocco and Tunisia. Substantive negotiations on the future relationships between the E.E.C. and these States, leading to new agreements which are to become effective on 1 February 1975, commenced in Brussels on 17 October 1973. The pattern of aid and trade relations between the E.E.C. and these developing nations of the Third World will have to be agreed and settled since existing treaties and arrangements will run out in the new year of 1975.

The conflict over fishing rights between Iceland and, principally, Britain (though other States are also affected) known as the 'Cod War' became more serious in 1973, but a compromise settlement was reached between Iceland and Britain in November. Iceland claims national fishery control for fifty miles beyond the coastline. There is a general consensus of agreement at the U.N. that the twelve-mile fishing limit should be extended, but not by how much. This problem will be the subject of the *Conference on the Law of the Sea* which is scheduled to open in Caracas in the summer of 1974. The increasing exploitation of the sea bed for minerals (oil and gas) will also lead to a re-examination of international law as codified in the *Conventions of the Law of the Sea* adopted by the U.N. conference in 1958. These conventions provided for a twelve-mile territorial limit on the seas, and special procedures for the preservation of the stock of fish beyond twelve miles. On the sea bed, that is the continental shelf, coastal States are entitled to exploit natural resources as far out as technology permits, and where two coastal States face each other along a median line of division agreed by them.

Iceland in June 1973 also asked for a revision of the 1951 defence treaty under which American forces are stationed on the Keflavik air base which at present plays an important role in NATO's Atlantic defence zone.

A *Comecon* summit meeting convened in Prague in June 1973 was attended mainly by the Prime Ministers of the nine communist members: the Soviet Union, Poland, Hungary, Bulgaria, Rumania, Czechoslovakia, German Democratic Republic, Mongolia and Cuba (which joined in 1972); Yugoslavia sent an observer. The meeting was held in secrecy. The trading conditions created by East–West economic plans and agreements reached in 1972 and 1973 meant that Comecon was faced with major decisions including the possibility of understandings with the E.E.C. In addition decisions were taken on plans of coordination for 1976-80.

Africa

The *Organization of African Unity* held its tenth anniversary meeting in Addis Ababa in May 1973. Collaboration was marred by Somalia's raising of territorial claims against Ethiopia and Libya's general dissatisfaction, which expressed itself in proposals to move the headquarters from Addis Ababa. A pacific settlement was patched up in the dispute between General Amin of Uganda and President Nyerere of Tanzania. A number of resolutions and declarations were approved, including a demand for withdrawal by Israel from occupied Arab territory, a declaration of the O.A.U.'s intention to continue to work for the liberation of alien-controlled African territories, and an economic declaration committing their countries to 'act collectively in multilateral trade negotiations' such as with the E.E.C.

Asia

So far, the terms of the Paris Agreement on the Vietnam ceasefire in January 1973 (p. 465) have only been partially carried out. The scale of fighting between the rival Vietnamese forces has been reduced, but fighting in many areas of Vietnam has continued. The International Commission of Control and Supervision (I.C.C.S.), consisting of Canadians, Poles, Hungarians and Indonesians, became deadlocked and on 31 July 1973 Canada formally withdrew leaving the rest of the I.C.C.S. in suspension. It was agreed that Iran should replace Canada. Meanwhile the United States did stop all military action and U.S. prisoners of war were repatriated. Large numbers of American civilians remain to support the South Vietnamese Government. A fresh attempt to make the ceasefire more effective was agreed in Paris on 13 June 1973, with no better results. Representatives of the South Vietnamese Government and the Provisional Revolutionary Government set up by the Vietcong in South Vietnam have been unable to make any progress on a political settlement for South Vietnam. In the absence of any progress both the South Vietnamese forces and the Vietcong seek to improve their position in the country by military and all other available means. But during the course of 1973 the United States withdrew from any further direct military involvement. There is stalemate. Neither the Saigon Government or the Provisional Revolutionary Government showed signs of collapse internally or militarily during 1973, and neither opponent is ready to make the concessions demanded from the other.

In Laos there was relative peace in the summer of 1973. The Pathet Lao reached a political and military *modus vivendi* with the Laotian Government of Prince Souvanna Phouma. On *14 September 1973 the Pathet Lao and Laotian Government signed a Peace Agreement* intended to settle the military and political future of Laos. It followed the ceasefire accord concluded on 21 February 1973 and takes the form of protocols to the earlier ceasefire accord. It provides for a new Coalition Government by 10 October under the premiership of Prince Souvanna, with two deputies – one from each side – and a division of cabinet posts, five to Pathet Lao, five to the present Laotian Government and two to the neutralists. Other provisions of the agreement cover the demarcation of territory and the terms for the neutralization of the two capitals, Vientiane (administrative) and Luang Prabang (royal). A joint police force of 1,000 and a battalion from each side are to be stationed in Vientiane. Pathet Lao forces will participate with the present Laotian Government forces in maintaining security, controlling immigration and defending airports and supply depots through-out Laos. All these provisions will need to be put into practice in an agreed way before peace can be assured in Laos after more than two decades of conflict.

In Cambodia fighting continued between the rival factions during 1973. By December no settlement had been reached, but the cessation of American military support in the air for the Government of Lon Nol had been hastened by Congressional action in Washington. On 15 August 1973 direct U.S. military involvement ceased also in Cambodia, and the United States began to withdraw air units from Thailand, the principal base from which the air offensive in Indo-China had been mounted. In 1973, the countries of south-east Asia faced the problem of working out fresh policies in the new realities of politics and power brought about by the continuation of conflict in Cambodia and South Vietnam, the military withdrawal of the United States, and the *détente* between China and the United States. But the conflict between the Soviet Union and China continued. In 1973 tension developed between the Mongolian People's Republic, closely allied to the Soviet Union, and China.

India, Pakistan and Bangladesh came a step nearer to a peace settlement and normalization of their relations, broken by the 1971 war, when the *Repatriation Agreement was concluded by India and Pakistan on 28 August 1973*. The key provisions of this accord concern the repatriation of the 90,000 Pakistani prisoners of war and civilian internees held in India, to 'commence with the utmost dispatch as soon as logistic arrangements are completed and from a date to be settled by mutual agreement'. The stumbling-block of the 195 Pakistani prisoners of war in India whom Bangladesh wishes to bring to trial for war crimes is covered by the agreement; they are to remain in India, their future is to be discussed and settled by Bangladesh, Pakistan and India, and it was specifically agreed that no trials may take place during the entire period of repatriation. From Pakistan, the 150,000–200,000 Bengalis, including 30,000 troops, will be permitted to leave for Bangladesh. From Bangladesh, Pakistan has agreed in principle to accept a substantial number of non-Bengalis who wish to emigrate to Pakistan, without specifying precise numbers. The agreement implies a time sequence for the recognition of Bangladesh by Pakistan, and when implemented provides for a major peaceful exchange of populations between the States.

The Middle East: the Seventeen Day Arab–Israeli War and the oil crisis

During the six years that followed the Arab–Israeli War of 1967 (p. 498) all efforts to reach a peaceful settlement of Arab–Israeli differences failed, despite the intensive mediating efforts principally of the U.N. The chief stumbling-blocks were on the one hand the continued Israeli occupation of all the Arab territories captured by Israel in 1967, and on the other the refusal of the Arab States, especially Egypt and Syria, to negotiate a peace settlement directly with Israel. The Arab States insist that Israel should implement *U.N. Resolution 242*, passed unanimously by the Security Council on 22 November 1967, according to the Arab interpretation of that resolution; they demand that Israel should withdraw from all Arab territories captured in the 1967 war. The Israelis interpret the U.N. resolution to mean that their right to safe and secure frontiers, and therefore the extent of withdrawal from occupied Arab territories, is a matter for peace negotiations between Israel and the Arab States at war which should be entered into by both sides directly without preconditions of any kind. Since the resolution also requires that an Israeli withdrawal, an end to the state of belligerency, freedom of shipping, and the mutual recognition of the sovereignty and integrity of all the States involved, should form the essential components of a general settlement, a 'peace conference' is essential. Meanwhile Israel has been unwilling to withdraw partially or wholly before a conference has met to settle all the issues raised in the U.N. resolution. Syria rejected the resolution and Egypt and Syria refused to negotiate directly with Israel; Jordan was secretly more accommodating but King Hussein dared not openly break with his former allies. The disputed U.N. resolution, moreover, was worded with deliberate ambiguity so that the Soviet Union and the United States could both express their agreement with it, at the same time making it clear that they differed on the actual meaning of the resolution! The U.N. resolution could thus later be cited by both contestants to justify their points of view.

The Palestinian political organizations are a third factor in the complex diplomacy of the Middle East. They have been frequently at 'war' both with

Israel and their Arab hosts, first in Jordan from where the militants were expelled, then during 1973 in the Lebanon, which has suffered from retaliatory Israeli raids directed against these militant Palestinian organizations. It is difficult to assess the commitment of Syrians and Egyptians to the Palestinians, their first commitment being the recovery of their own territories lost to Israel, the Sinai desert and the Golan Heights. In 1967 Jordan lost the West Bank territories originally acquired during the first Arab–Israeli War in 1948–9 (p. 496).

The Soviet Union and the United States have played a crucial role in the Middle East. The Soviet Union has militarily equipped Egypt and Syria and Israel relies heavily on the United States. But diplomatically, the American Secretary of State, Henry Kissinger, achieved recognition by both Egyptians and Israelis as a 'peacemaker' in November 1973.

The Seventeen Day Arab–Israeli War began on 6 October 1973 with a simultaneous attack by the Syrians on the Golan Heights and the Egyptians across the Suez Canal. The date was chosen to coincide with the Day of Atonement or Yom Kippur, the most holy of the Jewish religious days. The Israelis were taken by surprise and lost territory in Sinai and on the Golan Heights during the early days of the war. In contrast to the 1967 war, Israeli casualties in 1973 were heavy as during the next seventeen days they sought to stabilize the frontiers and then move over to the offensive. Britain and the principal European States declared themselves neutral and Britain imposed an arms embargo on 'both sides'. Meantime the Soviet Union sent in massive arms to the Arabs, and the United States came to the help of Israel with vital supplies without gaining the cooperation of Britain, France or the Federal Republic of Germany. Angered by this aloofness, Secretary of State Kissinger questioned the effectiveness of the alliance partnership. In the Middle East, Iraq, Morocco and other Arab States offered assistance, and Jordan, whilst maintaining peace on its own frontier with Israel, sent some armoured units to Syria where they joined Syrian and Iraqi forces defending the road to Damascus.

At the United Nations, after more than two weeks of negotiation and disagreement, the *Security Council on 21 October 1973 agreed on a draft ceasefire resolution* proposed by the United States and the Soviet Union. The text of this resolution ran as follows: the Security Council (1) calls upon all parties to the present fighting to cease all fighting and terminate all military activity immediately, no later than twelve hours after the moment of the adoption of this decision, in the positions they now occupy; (2) calls upon the parties concerned to start immediately after the ceasefire the implementation of Security Council Resolution 242 (1967) in all its parts; (3) decides that immediately and concurrently with the ceasefire, negotiations will start between the parties concerned under appropriate auspices aimed at establishing a just and durable peace in the Middle East.

Israel accepted the ceasefire provided all Arab States fighting did so. Egypt and Jordan accepted it, Iraq rejected the ceasefire and Syria accepted it after some delay. On 22 October, when the ceasefire was to come into force, the Israelis had recaptured the Golan Heights and in addition were in possession of Syrian territory on the road to Damascus. Along the Suez Canal, the Egyptians held a stretch of the east bank of the Suez Canal (Sinai) north of the Bitter Lake, but the Israelis established a bridgehead on the west bank of the Suez Canal south of the Bitter Lake. Subsequent to the coming into force of the ceasefire, fighting was renewed on the west bank and the Israelis rapidly thrust past Suez, thereby completely cutting off the Egyptian Third Army still on the east bank. Fighting only came to an end on 24 October 1973.

At the U.N., after a brief Soviet–U.S. crisis, the Superpowers agreed on 25 October on a new resolution of the Security Council, put forward by eight non-aligned members – Guinea, India, Indonesia, Kenya, Panama, Peru, Sudan and Yugoslavia. This demanded an immediate and complete ceasefire and a return to the positions occupied on 22 October 1973; it also authorized the setting-up of a United Nations Emergency Force to be drawn from members of the U.N. but excluding the permanent members of the Security Council. This resolution removed the danger of the Soviet–U.S. confrontation threatened by the possible despatch of Soviet troops or observers to Egypt, which had led to a global alert of U.S. military forces. With the help of Kissinger acting as mediator, on 11 November 1973 Israel and Egypt signed a six-point agreement to stabilize the ceasefire under U.N. auspices. It was the first treaty signed by Israel and an Arab State since 1949 and was intended as an initial step towards meaningful peace negotiations.

After the fighting was over, Western Europe, the United States and Japan continued to be affected by the Middle East crisis because of the decision of the Arab States early in October 1973 to use their oil as a lever of pressure on the West. States regarded as having a friendly attitude to Israel were threatened with oil embargoes. But in November 1973, Britain, Spain, France, Malaysia and Pakistan, together with Lebanon, Tunisia and Egypt, were promised their full oil supplies by Saudi Arabia for their correct or helpful attitude to the Arab cause. The Arab oil-producing States have promised supplies to 'friendly' countries. The United States and the Netherlands are totally embargoed. There have been cutbacks of oil production and further cutbacks were threatened. The effect is to limit severely oil shipments to other countries not on the 'favoured' list, such as Japan, West Germany and Italy. So far (December 1973) the tactic of splitting former customers into 'haves' and 'have nots' has not resulted in any determined and united Western response, although the United States has urged such a response. On the contrary, Arab policy caused dissension within the E.E.C. and with the United States. The Arab oil producers threatened to continue their embargoes and to reduce production until Israeli withdrawal from occupied Arab territory had actually taken place. Paradoxically, in November 1973 Egypt relied heavily on the United States to arrange the ceasefire and to bring the parties at war to a peace conference. The restoration of U.S.–Egyptian diplomatic relations (broken off in 1967) showed that the policy of not relying on Soviet support alone continues to be followed by Egypt.

The new militancy of the Arab oil-producing States had already been exemplified in August 1973 by Colonel Gaddafi, who had decreed unilaterally a takeover of 51 per cent of foreign-held Libyan oil properties. Since the outbreak of the Israeli–Arab War, Arab oil-producing States have similarly acted unilaterally in substantially raising the price of their oil and other world oil-producing States have followed suit.

The Middle East Peace Conference assembled at Geneva *on 21 December 1973* attended by Israel, Egypt, Jordan, the U.S. and the U.S.S.R. in the presence of the Secretary-General of the U.N. Syria refused to participate. The first phase quickly ended with an agreement to set up a military working group to implement the disengagement of Israeli and Egyptian forces on the Suez front. On 31 December 1973 the belligerents were still talking. The future oil policy of the Arab States also remained uncertain.

Agreement by the United States and Soviet Union on limiting strategic arms, Washington, 21 June 1973

The President of the United States of America, Richard Nixon, and the General Secretary of the Central Committee of the C.P.S.U., L. I. Brezhnev.

Having thoroughly considered the question of the further limitation of strategic arms, and the progress already achieved in the current negotiations.

Reaffirming their conviction that the earliest adoption of further limitations of strategic arms would be a major contribution in reducing the danger of an outbreak of nuclear war and in strengthening international peace and security.

First. The two sides will continue active negotiations in order to work out a permanent agreement on more complete measures on the limitation of strategic offensive arms, as well as their subsequent reduction, proceeding from the basic principles of relations between the United States of America and the Union of Soviet Socialist Republics signed in Moscow on May 29, 1972, and from the interim agreement between the United States of America and the Union of Soviet Socialist Republics of May 26, 1972, on certain measures with respect to the limitation of strategic offensive arms.

Over the course of the next year the two sides will make serious efforts to work out the provisions of the permanent agreement on more complete measures on the limitation of strategic offensive arms with the objective of signing it in 1974.

Second. New agreements on the limitation of strategic offensive armaments will be based on the principles of the American–Soviet documents adopted in Moscow in May 1972 and the agreements reached in Washington in June 1973, and in particular, both sides will be guided by the recognition of each other's equal security interests and by the recognition that efforts to obtain unilateral advantage, directly or indirectly, would be inconsistent with the strengthening of peaceful relations between the United States of America and the Union of Soviet Socialist Republics.

Third. The limitations placed on strategic offensive weapons can apply both to their quantitative aspects as well as to their qualitative improvement.

Fourth. Limitations on strategic offensive arms must be subject to adequate verification by national technical means.

Fifth. The modernization and replacement of strategic offensive arms would be permitted under conditions which will be formulated in the agreements to be concluded.

Sixth. Pending the completion of a permanent agreement on more complete measures of strategic offensive arms limitation, both sides are prepared to reach agreements on separate measures to supplement the existing interim agreement of May 26, 1972.

Seventh. Each side will continue to take necessary organizational and technical measures for preventing accidental or unauthorized use of nuclear weapons under its control in accordance with the agreement of September 30, 1971 between the United States of America and the Union of Soviet Socialist Republics.

Agreement by the Soviet Union and United States on the prevention of nuclear war, Washington, 22 June 1973

The United States of America and the Union of Soviet Socialist Republics, hereinafter referred to as the parties:

Guided by the objectives of strengthening world peace and international security;

Conscious that nuclear war would have devastating consequences for mankind;

Proceeding from the desire to bring about conditions in which the danger of an outbreak of nuclear war anywhere in the world would be reduced and ultimately eliminated;

Proceeding from their obligations under the Charter of the United Nations regarding the maintenance of peace, refraining from the threat or use of force, and the avoidance of war, and in conformity with the agreements to which either party has subscribed;

Proceeding from the basic principles of relations between the United States of America and the Union of Soviet Socialist Republics signed in Moscow on May 29, 1972;

Reaffirming that the development of relations between the U.S.A. and the U.S.S.R. is not directed against other countries and their interests, have agreed as follows:

Article I. The United States and the Soviet Union agree that an objective of their policies is to remove the danger of nuclear war and of the use of nuclear weapons.

Accordingly, the parties agree that they will act in such a manner as to prevent the development of situations capable of causing a dangerous exacerbation of their relations, as to avoid military confrontations, and as to exclude the outbreak of nuclear war between them and between either of the parties and other countries.

Article II. The parties agree, in accordance with Article I and to realize the objective stated in that Article, to proceed from the premise that each party will refrain from the threat or use of force against the other party, against the allies of the other party and against other countries, in circumstances which may endanger international peace and security. The parties agree that they will be guided by these considerations in the formulation of their foreign policies and in their actions in the field of international relations.

Article III. The parties undertake to develop their relations with each other and with other countries in a way consistent with the purposes of this Agreement.

Article IV. If at any time relations between the parties or between either party and other countries appear to involve the risk of a nuclear conflict, or if relations between countries not parties to this Agreement appear to involve the risk of nuclear war between the U.S.A. and the U.S.S.R. or between either party and other countries, the United States and the Soviet Union, acting in accordance with the provisions of this Agreement, shall immediately enter into urgent consultations with each other and make every effort to avert this risk.

Article V. Each party shall be free to inform the Security Council of the United Nations, the Secretary-General of the United Nations and the Governments of allied or other countries of the progress and outcome of consultations initiated in accordance with Article IV of this Agreement.

Article VI. Nothing in this Agreement shall affect or impair:

(a) The inherent right of individual or collective self-defense as envisaged by Article 51 of the Charter of the United Nations;

(b) The provisions of the Charter of the United Nations, including those relating to the maintenance or restoration of international peace and security; and

(c) The obligations undertaken by either party towards its allies or other countries in treaties, agreements and other appropriate documents.

Article VII. This Agreement shall be of unlimited duration.

Article VIII. This Agreement shall enter into force upon signature.

Done at the City of Washington, D.C., on June 22, 1973, in two copies, each in the English and in the Russian languages, both texts being equally authentic.

For the United States of America: Richard Nixon, President of the United States of America; for the Union of Soviet Socialist Republics: Leonid Brezhnev, General Secretary of the Central Committee of the C.P.S.U.

Joint Communiqué by the United States and Soviet Union, San Clemente, 25 June 1973

At the invitation of the President of the United States, Richard Nixon, extended during his official visit to the Soviet Union in May 1972, and in accordance with a subsequent agreement, the General Secretary of the Central Committee of the Communist Party of the Soviet Union, Mr Leonid Brezhnev, paid an official visit to the United States from June 18 to June 25.

Mr Brezhnev was accompanied by A. A. Gromyko, Minister of Foreign Affairs of the U.S.S.R., member of the Politburo of the Central Committee, C.P.S.U.; N. S. Patolichev, Minister of Foreign Trade; B. P. Bugayev, Minister of Civil Aviation; G. E. Tsukanov and A. M. Aleksandrov, assistants to the General Secretary of the Central Committee, C.P.S.U.; L. I. Zamyatin, general director of Tass; E. I. Chazov, Deputy Minister of Public Health of the U.S.S.R.; G. M. Korniyenko, member of the Collegium of the Ministry of Foreign Affairs of the U.S.S.R.; G. A. Arbatov, director of the U.S. Institute of the Academy of Sciences of the U.S.S.R.

... President Nixon and General Secretary Brezhnev held thorough and constructive discussions on the progress achieved in the development of U.S.-Soviet relations and on a number of major international problems of mutual interest.

Also taking part in the conversations, held in Washington, Camp David and San Clemente, were:

On the American side, William P. Rogers, Secretary of State; George P. Shultz, Secretary of the Treasury; Dr Henry A. Kissinger, assistant to the President for national security affairs.

On the Soviet side, A. A. Gromyko, Minister of Foreign Affairs, member of the Politburo of the Central Committee, C.P.S.U.; A. F. Dobrynin, Soviet Ambassador to the U.S.A.; N. S. Patolichev, Minister of Foreign Trade; B. P. Bugayev, Minister of Civil Aviation; A. M. Aleksandrov and G. E. Tsukanov, assistants to the General Secretary of the Central Committee, C.P.S.U.; G. M. Korniyenko, member of the Collegium of the Ministry of Foreign Affairs of the U.S.S.R.

I · The general state of United States–Soviet relations

Both sides expressed their mutual satisfaction with the fact that the American-Soviet summit meeting in Moscow in May 1972 and the joint decisions taken there have resulted in a substantial advance in the strengthening of peaceful relations between the United States and the Soviet Union and have created the basis for the further development of broad and mutually beneficial cooperation in various fields of mutual interest to the peoples of both countries and in the interests of all mankind. They noted their satisfaction with the mutual effort to implement strictly and fully the treaties and agreements concluded between the United States and the Soviet Union and to expand areas of cooperation.

They agreed that the process of reshaping relations between the United States and the Soviet Union on the basis of peaceful coexistence and equal security, as set forth in the basic principles of relations between the United States and the Soviet Union signed in Moscow on May 29, 1972, is progressing in an encouraging manner. They emphasized the great importance that each side attaches to these basic principles. They reaffirmed their commitment to the continued scrupulous implementation and to the enhancement of the effectiveness of each of the provisions of that document.

Both sides noted with satisfaction that the outcome of the American–Soviet meeting in Moscow in May 1972 was welcomed by other States and by world opinion as an important contribution to strengthening peace and international security, to curbing the arms race and to developing businesslike cooperation among States with different social systems.

Both sides viewed the return visit to the United States of the General Secretary of the Central Committee of the C.P.S.U., L. I. Brezhnev, and the talks held during the visit as an expression of their mutual determination to continue the course towards a major improvement in American–Soviet relations.

Both sides are convinced that the discussions they have just held represent a further milestone in the constructive development of their relations.

Convinced that such a development of American–Soviet relations serves the interests of both of their peoples and all of mankind, it was decided to take further major steps to give these relations maximum stability and to turn the development of friendship and cooperation between their peoples into a permanent factor for worldwide peace.

II · The prevention of nuclear war and the limitation of strategic armaments

Issues related to the maintenance and strengthening of international peace were a central point of the talks between President Nixon and General Secretary Brezhnev.

Conscious of the exceptional importance for all mankind of taking effective measures to that end, they discussed ways in which both sides could work toward removing the danger of war, and especially nuclear war, between the United States and the Soviet Union, and between either party and other countries.

Consequently, in accordance with the Charter of the United Nations and the basic principles of relations of May 29, 1972, it was decided to conclude an agreement between the United States and the Soviet Union on the prevention of nuclear war. That agreement was signed by the President and the General Secretary on June 22, 1973. The text has been published separately.

The President and the General Secretary, in appraising this agreement, believe that it constitutes a historical landmark in Soviet–American relations and substantially strengthens the foundations of international security as a whole. The United States and the Soviet Union state their readiness to consider additional ways of strengthening peace and removing for ever the danger of war, and particularly nuclear war.

In the course of the meetings, intensive discussions were held on questions of strategic arms limitation. In this connection both sides emphasized the fundamental importance of the treaty on the limitation of anti-ballistic missile systems and the interim agreement on certain measures with respect to the limitation of strategic offensive arms, signed between the United States and the Soviet Union in May 1972, which, for the first time in history, placed actual limits on the most modern and most formidable types of armaments.

Having exchanged views on the progress in the implementation of these agreements, both sides reaffirmed their intention to carry them out and their readiness to move ahead jointly towards an agreement on the further limitation of strategic arms.

Both sides noted that progress has been made in the negotiations that resumed in November 1972, and that the prospects for reaching a permanent agreement on more complete measures limiting strategic offensive armaments are favorable.

Both sides agreed that the progress made in the limitation of strategic armaments is an exceedingly important contribution to the strengthening of American–Soviet relations and to world peace.

On the basis of their discussions, the President and the General Secretary signed on June 21, 1973, basic principles of negotiations on the further limitation of strategic offensive arms. The text has been published separately.

The United States and the Soviet Union attach great importance to joining with all States in the cause of strengthening peace, reducing the burden of armaments and reaching agreements on arms limitation and disarmament measures.

Considering the important role which an effective international agreement with respect to chemical weapons would play, the two sides agreed to continue their efforts to conclude such an agreement in cooperation with other countries.

The two sides agree to make every effort to facilitate the work of the committee on disarmament which has been meeting in Geneva. They will actively participate in negotiations aimed at working out new measures to curb and end the arms race.

They reaffirm that the ultimate objective is general and complete disarmament, including nuclear disarmament, under strict international control. A world disarmament conference could play a role in this process at an appropriate time.

III · International questions: the reduction of tensions and strengthening of international security

President Nixon and General Secretary Brezhnev reviewed the major questions of the current international situation. They gave special attention to the developments which have occurred since the time of the United States–Soviet summit meeting in Moscow.

It was noted with satisfaction that positive trends are developing in international relations towards the further relaxation of tensions and the strengthening of cooperative relations in the interests of peace. In the opinion of both sides, the current process of improvement in the international situation creates new and favorable opportunities for reducing tensions, settling outstanding international issues and creating a permanent structure of peace.

The two sides expressed their deep satisfaction at the conclusion of the agreement on ending the war and restoring peace in Vietnam, and also at the results of the international conference on Vietnam, which approved and supported that agreement.

The two sides are convinced that the conclusion of the agreement on ending the war and restoring peace in Vietnam, and the subsequent signing of the agreement on restoring peace and achieving national concord in Laos, meet the fundamental interests and aspirations of the peoples of Vietnam and Laos and open up a possibility for establishing a lasting peace in Indo-China based on respect for the independence, sovereignty, unity and territorial integrity of the countries of that area. Both sides emphasized that these agreements must be strictly implemented.

They further stressed the need to bring an early end to the military conflict in Cambodia in order to bring peace to the entire area of Indo-China. They also reaffirmed their stand that the political futures of Vietnam, Laos and Cambodia should be left to the respective peoples to determine, free from outside interference.

In the course of the talks both sides noted with satisfaction that in Europe the process of relaxing tensions and developing cooperation is actively continuing and thereby contributing to international stability.

The two sides expressed satisfaction with the further normalization of relations among European countries resulting from treaties and agreements signed in recent years, particularly between the Soviet Union and the Federal Republic of Germany. They also welcome the coming into force of the quadripartite agreement of September 3, 1971. They share the conviction that strict observance of the treaties and agreements that have been concluded will contribute to the security and well-being of all parties concerned.

They also welcome the prospect of United Nations membership this year for the Federal Republic of Germany and the German Democratic Republic and recall, in this connection, that the United States, the Soviet Union, United Kingdom and France have signed the quadripartite declaration of November 9, 1972, on this subject.

The United States and the Soviet Union reaffirm their desire, guided by the appropriate provisions of the joint American–Soviet Union communiqué adopted in Moscow in May 1972, to continue their separate and joint contributions to strengthening peaceful relations in Europe. Both sides affirm that ensuring a lasting peace in Europe is a paramount goal of their policies.

In this connection satisfaction was expressed with the fact that as a result of common efforts by many States, including the United States and the Soviet Union, the preparatory work has been successfully completed for the conference on security and cooperation in Europe, which will be convened on July 3, 1973. The United States and the Soviet Union hold the view that the conference will enhance the possibilities for strengthening European security and developing cooperation among the participating States. The United States and the Soviet Union will conduct their policies so as to realize the goals of the conference and bring about a new era of good relations in this part of the world.

Reflecting their continued positive attitude towards the conference, both sides will make efforts to bring the conference to a successful conclusion at the earliest possible time. Both sides proceed from the assumption that progress in the work of the conference will produce possibilities for completing it at the highest level.

The United States and the Soviet Union believe that the goal of strengthening stability and security in Europe would be further advanced if the relaxation of political tensions were accompanied by a reduction of military tensions in Central Europe. In this respect they attach great importance to the negotiations on the mutual reduction of forces and armaments and associated measures in Central Europe, which will begin on October 30, 1973.

Both sides state their readiness to make, along with other States, their contribution to the achievement of mutually acceptable decisions on the substance of this problem, based on the strict observance of the principle of the undiminished security of any of the parties.

THE MIDDLE EAST

The parties expressed their deep concern with the situation in the Middle East and exchanged opinions regarding ways of reaching a Middle East settlement.

Each of the parties set forth its position on this problem.

Both parties agreed to continue to exert their efforts to promote the quickest possible settlement in the Middle East. This settlement should be in accordance with the interests of all States in the area, be consistent with their independence and sovereignty and should take into due account the legitimate interests of the Palestinian people.

IV · Commercial and economic relations

The President and the General Secretary thoroughly reviewed the status of and prospects for commercial and economic ties between the United States and Soviet Union. Both sides noted with satisfaction the progress achieved in the past year in the normalization and development of commercial and economic relations between them.

They agreed that mutually advantageous cooperation and peaceful relations would be strengthened by the creation of a permanent foundation of economic relationships.

They recall with satisfaction the various agreements on trade and commercial relations signed in the past year. Both sides note that American–Soviet trade has shown a substantial increase, and that there are favourable prospects for a continued rise in the exchange of goods over the coming years.

They believe that the two countries should aim at a total of $2,000 million to $3,000 million of trade over the next three years. The joint American–Soviet Russia commercial commission continues to provide a valuable mechanism to promote the broadscale growth of economic relations. The two sides noted with satisfaction that contacts between American firms and their Soviet counterparts are continuing to expand.

Both sides confirmed their firm intention to proceed from their earlier understanding on measures directed at creating more favorable conditions for expanding commercial and other economic ties between the United States and Soviet Union.

It was noted that as a result of the agreement regarding certain maritime matters signed in October 1972, Soviet and American commercial ships have been calling more frequently at ports of the United States and the Soviet Union, respectively, and since late May of this year a new regular passenger line has started operating between New York and Leningrad.

In the course of the current meeting, the two sides signed a protocol augmenting existing civil air relations between the United States and the Soviet Union providing for direct air services between Washington and Moscow and New York and Leningrad, increasing the frequency of flights and resolving other questions in the field of civil aviation.

In the context of reviewing prospects for further and more permanent economic cooperation, both sides expressed themselves in favour of mutually advantageous long-term projects. They discussed a number of specific projects involving the participation of American companies, including the delivery of Siberian natural gas to the United States. The President indicated that the United States encourages American firms to work out concrete proposals on these projects and will give serious and sympathetic consideration to proposals that are in the interest of both sides.

To contribute to expanded commercial, cultural and technical relations between the United States and the Soviet Union, the two sides signed a tax convention to avoid double taxation on income and eliminate, as much as possible, the need for citizens of one country to become involved in the tax system of the other.

A protocol was also signed on the opening by the end of October 1973 of a trade representation of the Soviet Union

Republic in Washington and a commercial office of the United States in Moscow. In addition, a protocol was signed on questions related to establishing the American–Soviet Chamber of Commerce. These agreements will facilitate the further developments of commercial and economic ties between the United States and the Soviet Union.

V · Further progress in other fields of bilateral cooperation

The two sides reviewed the areas of bilateral cooperation in such fields as environmental protection, public health and medicine, exploration of outer space and science and technology, established by the agreements signed in May 1972 and subsequently. They noted that those agreements are being satisfactorily carried out in practice in accordance with the programmes as adopted. In particular, a joint effort is underway to develop effective means to combat those diseases which are most widespread and dangerous for mankind: cancer, cardio-vascular or infectious diseases and arthritis. The medical aspects of the environmental problems are also subjects of cooperative research.

Preparations for the joint space flight of the Apollo and Soyuz spacecraft are proceeding according to an agreed timetable.

The joint flight of these spaceships for a rendezvous and docking mission, and mutual visits of American and Soviet astronauts in each other's spacecraft, are scheduled for July 1975.

Building on the foundation created in previous agreements, and recognizing the potential of both the United States and the Soviet Union to undertake cooperative measures in current scientific and technological areas, new projects for fruitful joint efforts were identified and appropriate agreements were concluded.

PEACEFUL USES OF ATOMIC ENERGY

Bearing in mind the great importance of satisfying the growing energy demands in both countries and throughout the world, and recognizing that the development of highly efficient energy sources could contribute to the solution of this problem, the President and the General Secretary signed an agreement to expand and strengthen cooperation in the fields of controlled nuclear fusion, fast breeder reactors and research on the fundamental properties of matter. A joint committee on cooperation in the peaceful uses of atomic energy will be established to implement this agreement, which has a duration of ten years.

AGRICULTURE

Recognizing the importance of agriculture in meeting mankind's requirement for food products and the role of science in modern agricultural production, the two sides concluded an agreement providing for a broad exchange of scientific experience in agricultural research and development and of information on agricultural economics. An American–Soviet Union joint committee on agricultural cooperation will be established to oversee joint programmes to be carried out under the agreement.

WORLD OCEAN STUDIES

Considering the unique capabilities and the major interest of both nations in the field of world ocean studies, and noting the extensive experience of United States–Soviet Union oceanographic cooperation, the two sides have agreed to broaden their cooperation and have signed an agreement to this effect. In so doing, they are convinced that the benefits from further development of cooperation in the field of oceanography will accrue not only bilaterally but also to all peoples of the world. An American–Soviet Union joint committee on cooperation in world ocean studies will be established to coordinate the implementation of cooperative programmes.

TRANSPORTATION

The two sides agreed that there are opportunities for cooperation between the United States and the Soviet Union in the solution of problems in the field of transportation. To permit expanded, mutually beneficial cooperation in this field, the two sides concluded an agreement on this subject. The United States and the Soviet Union further agreed that a joint committee on cooperation in transportation would be established.

CONTACTS, EXCHANGES AND COOPERATION

Recognizing the general expansion of United States–Soviet Union bilateral relations and, in particular, the growing number of exchanges in the fields of science, technology, education and culture, and in other fields of mutual interest, the two sides agreed to broaden the scope of these activities under a new general agreement on contacts, exchanges and cooperation, with a duration of six years.

The two sides agreed to this in the mutual belief that it will further promote better understanding between the peoples of the United States and the Soviet Union and will help to improve the general state of relations between the two countries.

Both sides believe that the talks at the highest level, which were held in a frank and constructive spirit, were very valuable and made an important contribution to developing mutually advantageous relations between the United States and the Soviet Union. In the view of both sides, these talks will have a favorable impact on international relations.

They noted that the success of the discussions in the United States was facilitated by the continuing consultation and contacts as agreed in May 1972. They reaffirmed that the practice of consultation should continue. They agreed that further meetings at the highest level should be held regularly.

Having expressed his appreciation to President Nixon for the hospitality extended during the visit to the United States, General Secretary Brezhnev invited the President to visit the Soviet Union in 1974. The invitation was accepted.

Appendix: *A note on Commonwealth defence agreements and cooperation, 1914–73*

The cooperation of the British Dominions and colonies before the outbreak of war in 1914 was informal and flexible, a matter of changing custom rather than the result of treaties or agreements. This flexibility and lack of specific treaty commitments persisted between the two world wars. A degree of coordination was achieved by the Committee of Imperial Defence, strengthened in 1917 and 1918 by the creation of an Imperial War Cabinet. After the First World War the Committee of Imperial Defence continued this tradition, and various Dominion Exchanges provided the means of collaboration. There were some notable examples of practical cooperation such as over the construction of the Singapore naval base. But the simultaneous threat of Germany, Italy and Japan in the 1930s to Britain and the British Commonwealth in the Far East led to the main weight of British defence capability being assigned to Europe. When in 1939 war broke out in Europe, the Dominions by independent decision came to Britain's aid and contributed to the war effort in Europe and the Middle East.

Even before the outbreak of war in the Pacific, Britain and the Dominions recognized that protection against Japan required the alliance of the United States. Canada was the first Dominion to turn for security to the United States. The *Ogdenburg Agreement in 1940*, which provided for the joint defence of the North American continent, began a defence relationship between Canada and the United States which persists to the present (p. 319).

The supreme direction of the war by the Western allies was in the hands of the Combined Chiefs of Staff, British and American. Commonwealth cooperation in strategic planning was of little account. In the Pacific, an attempt to assert the unity of interest of Australia and New Zealand was embodied in the *Canberra Pact, 21 January 1944*. This alliance treaty provides for close cooperation. Elaborate and permanent machinery for collaboration in defence and foreign policy, for industrial, social and missionary policies, was to be established together with a permanent Secretariat; Article 13 declared 'the two Governments agree that, within the framework of a general system of world security, a regional zone of defense comprising the south-west and South Pacific areas shall be established and that this zone should be based on Australia and New Zealand, stretching through the arc of islands north and north-east of Australia, to Western Samoa and the Cook Islands'. Although this elaborate machinery was not set up when it came to actual military operations in South-east Asia, the 'ANZAC' contribution was closely integrated. This trend reached its peak in a totally integrated battalion in South Vietnam. At the same time New Zealand and Australia sought the support of the predominant Pacific Power, the United States, to safeguard their security. Independence and American protection thus became twin poles of a policy not always easy to reconcile.

In the 1950s the United States played a leading role in setting up regional defence treaties directed against the two major communist Powers in Europe and Asia, the Soviet Union and the People's Republic of China. In Europe in 1949 Canada became a partner with Britain and the United States in NATO (p. 307). In Asia in 1951 Australia and New Zealand were partners with the United States in ANZUS (p. 310). Three years later, in 1954, SEATO brought together Britain, Australia, New Zealand and Pakistan (p. 312). A Commonwealth Division (British, Australian, New Zealand and Canadian) fought in the Korean War (p. 309). An Australian–New Zealand force aided the United States in Vietnam (p. 315).

The Dominions of Australia and New Zealand together with Britain have also played a significant role in the defence of Malaysia externally, and internally during the communist insurrection (p. 437). But Britain's policy of withdrawal 'east of Suez' announced by the Labour Government and partially reversed by the Conservative Government has made the extent of future British participation in the 1970s uncertain. In 1971, the *Five Power Defence Arrangements* were concluded between Australia, Britain, Malaysia, New Zealand and Singapore. The coming to power in 1972 of Labour Governments in Australia, under Gough Whitlam, and in New Zealand, under Norman Kirk, has led to a downgrading of military commitments in the Pacific. The Australian Government has declared that most of the Australian ground forces will be withdrawn from Singapore by April 1975. The Pacific Dominions are more inclined to rely on their own resources since America's withdrawal from Indo-China and Australian military commitments to SEATO are in doubt. India and Pakistan have played no active role in Commonwealth defence:

their attitude is dominated by conflict and tension between them (p. 435).

With South Africa, Britain concluded the *Simonstown Agreement* embodied in an exchange of letters and announced in July 1955; South Africa's racial policies, and the U.N. condemnation of them, have made this agreement controversial in the Commonwealth. The British Conservative Government has affirmed its validity; Britain retains a right to use the naval base in peacetime and is guaranteed its use with its allies if Britain (not necessarily South Africa) is at war. The arms Britain is willing to supply to South Africa are for naval defence purposes and for the defence and efficiency of the naval base, and are therefore supposed to be defensive weapons which cannot be used to upport internal racialist policies. Britain and South Africa agreed to cooperate in ensuring the security of a South African maritime zone including sea routes around the Cape. The Simonstown Agreement, or more precisely its interpretation, lacks bi-partisan political support in Britain.

Thus by 1973 the defence collaboration between members of the Commonwealth as a whole had steadily weakened. The more limited role of the Commonwealth in the 1970s was evident during the *Commonwealth Conference in Ottawa* in August 1973. It proved more harmonious than the previous conference in Singapore because less was expected. Thirty-two member nations attended, represented usually by their chief ministers. Rhodesia, and the impediments to majority rule there, proved the most difficult issue: but in general the agreed final communiqué endorsed Britain's policy of seeking a peaceful solution. Wide-ranging discussions took place over economic, monetary, trade, aid and race questions exemplifying the consultative nature of the Commonwealth. Members of the Commonwealth are associated in various regional alliances and association in Europe, the Americas, Asia and Africa. These regional groupings represent the more vital interests of the nations concerned and in practice usually take precedence over the concept of Commonwealth unity.

[For an up-to-date analysis, see W. D. McIntyre, *The Origins and Impact of the Commonwealth of Nations 1869–1971*, Minneapolis, forthcoming.]

Source references for the principal treaties

Treaty texts are usually to be found in several collections. Apart from national treaty series, there are some specialized regional compilations as mentioned in the preface. The forthcoming publication of Peter H. Rohn's *World Treaty Index and Treaty Profiles* in six volumes (Santa Barbara, Calif., Clio Press) will provide the first comprehensive indexing reference guide to more than 20,000 treaties concluded during the period 1920 to 1970. For the publication of contemporary treaty texts, a reliable compilation is provided by *Current Documents*, published as *International Legal Materials* (Washington, D.C.). For the chronological listing of principal treaties below, one major source reference is given in each case; the first number after the abbreviation refers to the volume and the second to the page in the volume. Thus LNTS 19:247 is the reference to the League of Nations Treaty Series, volume 19, page 247. One number after a name refers to the page in the book. The treaty texts reproduced from the *British and Foreign State Papers* and the British and German *Documents on Foreign Policy* are published by kind permission of Her Majesty's Stationery Office.

Key to abbreviations

AD   *Aktuelle Dokumente*, edited by Münch (Berlin, 1971).

BDFP   *Documents on British Foreign Policy 1919–1939*, edited by E. L. Woodward, R. Butler and others (London, 1949–   ).

Bevans *Treaties and Other International Agreements of the United States of America 1776–1949*, compiled by Charles I. Bevans (Washington, D.C., 1968–   ).

BFSP   *British and Foreign State Papers* (London).

DDR   *Dokumente zur Aussenpolitik der Regierung der Deutschen Demokratischen Republik* (Berlin, 1954).

GDFP   *Documents on German Foreign Policy 1918–1945* (Washington, D.C., 1954–).

Hurewitz   *Diplomacy in the Near and Middle East. A Documentary Record*, by J. C. Hurewitz (Princeton, N.J., 1956, 2 vols.).

ILM   *International Legal Materials* (see above).

LNTS   *League of Nations Treaty Series. Treaties and international engagements registered with the Secretariat of the League of Nations* (Lausanne, 205 vols.).

NS   *Nazi–Soviet Relations 1939–41* (Washington, D.C., U.S. Department of State, 1948).

Shapiro   *Soviet Treaties, 1917–1939. A collection of bilateral agreements and conventions etc., concluded between the Soviet Union and foreign Powers*, edited by Leonard Shapiro (Washington, D.C., 1950–5, 2 vols.).

UNTS   *United Nations Treaty Series. Treaties and international agreements registered or filed and recorded with the Secretariat of the United Nations* (New York, 1946–).

UST   *United States Treaties and Other International Agreements* (Washington, D.C.).

Wandycz   *France and her Eastern Allies 1919–25*, by P. S. Wandycz (Minneapolis, 1962).

1914–18

Alliance between Germany and Turkey, 2 August 1914   Hurewitz 2:1

Allied exchange of telegrams concerning the Straits, 4 March–10 April 1915   BDFP (1st ser.) 4:635

Treaty of London, 26 April 1915   BFSP 112:973

Alliance between Bulgaria, Germany and Austria-Hungary, 6 September 1915   LNTS 5:223

McMahon–Hussayn correspondence, July 1915–March 1916   Cmd 5937

Sykes–Picot Agreement, April–October 1916   BDFP (1st ser.) 4:241

Treaty of Brest-Litovsk, 3 March 1918   BFSP 123:727

1919

Treaty of Versailles, 28 June 1919   BFSP 112:1

Minorities Treaty between Allies and Poland, 28 June 1919   BFSP 112:232

Treaty of St Germain, 10 September 1919   BFSP 112:317

Treaty of Neuilly, 27 November 1919   BFSP 112:781

1920

Treaty of Trianon, 4 June 1920   BFSP 113:486
Treaty of Sèvres, 10 August 1920   BFSP 119:502
Treaty of Dorpat, 14 October 1920   LNTS 2:5

1921

Alliance Treaty between France and Poland, 19 February 1921, and Secret Military Convention between France and Poland, 21 February 1921 Wandycz app.:394–5
Treaty between Soviet Russia and Iran, 26 February 1921   LNTS 9:383
Treaty between Soviet Russia and Afghanistan, 28 February 1921   Shapiro 1:96
Polish–Rumanian Alliance, 3 March 1921   LNTS 18:13
Anglo-Soviet Trade Agreement, 16 March 1921   BFSP 118:990
Treaty of Riga, 18 March 1921   LNTS 6:51
Four Power Washington Treaty, 13 December 1921   LNTS 25:84

1922

Limitation of naval armaments, 6 February 1922   BFSP 117:453
Nine Power Treaty, 6 February 1922   LNTS 38:278
Treaty of Rapallo, 16 April 1922   LNTS 19:247

1923

Treaty of Lausanne, 24 July 1923   LNTS 28:11

1924

Alliance Treaty between France and Czechoslovakia, 25 January 1924 Wandycz app.:394–5

1925

Treaty between Japan and Soviet Union, 20 January 1925   LNTS 34:31
Locarno Treaties, 16 October 1925   LNTS 54:289
Alliance Treaty between France and Poland, 16 October 1925   LNTS 54:354
Alliance Treaty between France and Czechoslovakia, 16 October 1925 LNTS 54:361

1926

Treaty of Berlin, 24 April 1926   LNTS 53:387
Treaty between Soviet Union and Lithuania, 28 September 1926   LNTS 60:145

1927

Jedda Treaty, 20 May 1927   BFSP 134:273

1928

Pact of Paris, 27 August 1928   BFSP 128:447

1929

Soviet–German Conciliation Convention, 25 January 1929   LNTS 90:219
Conciliation and Arbitration Convention between American Republics,
    January 1929   Bevans 2:737
Protocol between Soviet Union and her neighbours concerning Pact of Paris,
    9 February 1929   LNTS 89:369

1930

London Naval Treaty, 22 April 1930   LNTS 112:65
Little Entente Treaties, 27 June 1930   LNTS 107:215
Anglo-Iraq Alliance, 30 June 1930   BFSP 134:273

1932

Treaty between Soviet Union and Finland, 21 January 1932   LNTS 157:393
Treaty between Soviet Union and Latvia, 5 February 1932   LNTS 148:114
Treaty between Soviet Union and Estonia, 4 May 1932   LNTS 131:297
Treaty between Soviet Union and Poland, 25 July 1932   LNTS 136:41
Treaty between Soviet Union and France, 29 November 1932   LNTS 157:393

1933

Pact of Organization of Little Entente, 16 February 1933   LNTS 139:235
Treaty between Soviet Union and others defining aggression, 3–4 July 1933
    LNTS 147:67

1934

Balkan Entente between Turkey, Greece, Rumania and Yugoslavia, 9
    February 1934   LNTS 153:155
Baltic Entente, 3 November 1934   LNTS 154:95

1935

Soviet–Japanese Railway Treaty, 23 March 1935   LNTS 139:622
Soviet–French Mutual Assistance Treaty, 2 May 1935   LNTS 167:395
Soviet–Czech Mutual Assistance Treaty, 16 May 1935   LNTS 159:347
Anglo-German Naval Agreement, 18 June 1935   BFSP 139:182

1936

Soviet–Mongolian Alliance Treaty, 12 March 1936   BFSP 138:666
Austro-German Agreement, 11 July 1936   GDFP 1:278,342
Montreux Convention, 20 July 1936   BFSP 140:288
Anglo-Egyptian Alliance, 26 August 1936   BFSP 140:198
Anti-Comintern Pact between Japan and Germany, 26 November 1936
   Papers relating to Foreign Relations of the U.S. and Japan 1934–1941 (Washington, D.C., U.S. Department of State) 2:153
Fulfillment of treaties between American States, 23 December 1936   Bevans
   3:348

1937

Soviet–Chinese Non-Aggression Treaty, 21 August 1937   LNTS 181:101
Nyon Agreement, 14 September 1937   LNTS 181:135

1938

Anglo-Italian Agreement, 16 April 1938   BFSP 142:147
Munich Agreement, 29 September 1938   BDFP (3rd ser.) 3:627
Franco-German Agreement, 6 December 1938   BDFP (3rd ser.) 3:391

1939

Alliance Treaty between Italy and Germany, 22 May 1939   GDFP 6:563
German–Soviet Trade Agreement, 19 August 1939   NS 83
German–Soviet Non-Aggression Pact, 23 August 1939   NS 76
Anglo-Polish Alliance Treaty, 25 August 1939   BFSP 143:301 and 158:393
German–Soviet Boundary Treaty, 28 September 1939   NS 105
Soviet–Estonian Pact, 28 September 1939   GDFP 8:166
Treaty between Britain, France and Turkey, 19 October 1939
   BFSP 151:213
Act of Panama, October 1939   Bevans 3:604

1940

German–Soviet Agreement, 11 February 1940   NS 131
Soviet–Finnish Peace Treaty, 12 March 1940   BFSP 144:383
Armistice between France and Germany, 22 June 1940   GDFP 9:671
Act of Havana, 30 July 1940   Bevans 3:619
Destroyer–Naval Base Agreement, 2 September 1940   BFSP 144:180
Tripartite Pact, 27 September 1940   LNTS 204: 381

1941

Soviet–Japanese Neutrality Pact, 13 April 1941   BFSP 144:839
German–Turkish Non-Aggression Treaty, 18 June 1941   BFSP 144:816
Polish–Soviet Treaty, 30 July 1941   BFSP 144:869
British–Polish Note, 30 July 1941   BFSP 144:642
Atlantic Charter, 14 August 1941   LNTS 204:384

1942

United Nations Declaration, 1 January 1942   BFSP 144:1070
Anglo-Soviet–Iranian Treaty, 29 January 1942   BFSP 144:1017
Anglo-Soviet Alliance, 26 May 1942   BFSP 144:1038

1943

Italian armistice, 8–29 September 1943   Bevans 3:769
Soviet–Czechoslovak Treaty, 12 December 1943   BFSP 145:238

1944

Franco-Soviet Alliance, 10 December 1944   BFSP 149:632

1945

Yalta Conference, 4–11 February 1945   Bevans 3:1005
Act of Chapultepec, 6 March 1945   Bevans 3:1024
Soviet–Yugoslav Alliance, 11 April 1945   BFSP 145:1177
Soviet–Polish Alliance, 21 April 1945   UNTS 12:391
Four Power Declaration, 5 June 1945   Bevans 3:1140
Potsdam Conference, 17 July–2 August 1945   Bevans 3:1207
Sino-Soviet Treaty, 14 August 1945   UNTS 10:334
U.N. Charter   UNTS 1:xvi

1946

Soviet–Mongolian Alliance, 27 February 1946   UNTS 48:177

1947

Italian Peace Treaty, 10 February 1947   UNTS 49:3
Bulgarian Peace Treaty, 10 February 1947   UNTS 41:21
Hungarian Peace Treaty, 10 February 1947   UNTS 41:136
Rumanian Peace Treaty, 10 February 1947   UNTS 42:3
Finnish Peace Treaty, 10 February 1947   UNTS 48:203
Treaty of Dunkirk, 4 March 1947   UNTS 9:187

Inter-American Treaty of Reciprocal Assistance, 2 September 1947　Bevans
　4:559

1948

Soviet–Rumanian Alliance, 4 February 1948　UNTS 48:189
Soviet–Hungarian Alliance, 18 February 1948　UNTS 48:163
Brussels Treaty, 17 March 1948　UNTS 19:51
Soviet–Bulgarian Alliance, 18 March 1948　UNTS 48:135
Soviet–Finnish Treaty, 6 April 1948　UNTS 48:149
Organization for European Economic Cooperation, 16 April 1948　BFSP
　151:278
Charter of the Organization of American States, 30 April 1948　UNTS 119:4
Pact of Bogotá, 30 April 1948　UNTS 30:55

1949

North Atlantic Treaty, 4 April 1949　UNTS 34:243
Statute of Council of Europe, 5 May 1949　UNTS 87:103

1950

U.S. Military Advisory Group in Korea, 26 January 1950　UNTS 178:102
Sino-Soviet Alliance, 14 February 1950　UNTS 226:12
Poland and German Democratic Republic, 6 July 1950　DDR 1:341

1951

Paris Treaty establishing E.C.S.C., 18 April 1951　UNTS 261:140
United States–Philippine Security Treaty, 30 August 1951　UST (1952)
　3:3947
ANZUS Treaty, 1 September 1951　UST (1952) 3:3420
Japanese Peace Treaty, 8 September 1951　UNTS 136:46
Japanese–United States Security Treaty, 8 September 1951　UST (1952)
　3:3329

1952

Bonn Agreements, 26 May 1952　UNTS 331:327
Paris Treaty (abortive), European Defence Community, 27 May 1952　BFSP
　159:516

1953

Panmunjon Armistice, 27 July 1953　UST 4:232
Alliance Treaty between Libya and Britain, 29 July 1953　UNTS 186:185
Defense Treaty between Korea and U.S., 10 October 1953　UNTS 202:1956

1954

Soviet Declaration on restoration of sovereignty of German Democratic Republic, 25 March 1954 DDR 1:303

Geneva Agreements, July 1954 BFSP 161:359; Cmd 9239

Yugoslav–Greek–Turkish Alliance, 9 August 1954 UNTS 211:237

SEATO Alliance, 8 September 1954 UNTS 209:23

Anglo-Egyptian Suez Agreement, 19 October 1954 BFSP 161:75

Paris Agreements, 23 October 1954 UNTS 331:252

Mutual Defense Treaty between U.S. and China, 2 December 1954 UNTS 248:214

1955

Baghdad Pact, 24 February 1955 UNTS 233:199

Warsaw Pact, 14 May 1955 UNTS 219:3

Austrian State Treaty, 15 May 1955 UNTS 217:223

1957

Treaty of Rome, 25 March 1957 UNTS 295:2; H.M.S.O 1972

Soviet–Rumanian Treaty, 15 April 1957 *Izvestia*, 17 April 1957

Soviet–Hungarian Alliance, 27 May 1957 UNTS 407:155

1958

U.S. adhesion to Baghdad Pact, 28 July 1958 UNTS 335:205

1959

U.S. Treaty with Iran, 5 March 1959 UST 10 (part 2):314

Antarctic Treaty, 1 December 1959 UNTS 402:71

1960

Treaty of Stockholm establishing EFTA, 4 January 1960 UNTS 370:3

Japanese–U.S. Security Treaty, 19 January 1960 UST 11:1632, 1652, 2160

Convention of the O.E.C.D., 14 December 1960 UST 12:1728

1961

Alliance for Progress, 17 August 1961 *Organization of American States: Official Record* (Washington, 1961)

1962

Geneva Agreement on Laos, 23 July 1962 UST 14:1104

1963
Organization of African Unity, 25 May 1963   UNTS 479:39
Limited Nuclear Test Ban Treaty, 5 August 1963   UNTS 480:43

1966
Tashkent Declaration, 10 January 1966   UNTS 560:39

1968
Treaty on the non-proliferation of nuclear weapons, 1 July 1968   UST 21:483

1970
Treaty between Soviet Union and Czechoslovakia, 6 May 1970   *Pravda*, 7
   May 1970
Treaty between Soviet Union and Federal German Republic, 12 August 1970
   ILM 9:1026
Treaty between Poland and Federal German Republic, 7 December 1970
   AD 2:103

1971
Soviet–Egyptian Treaty, 27 May 1971   ILM 10:836
Four Power Berlin Agreement, 3 September 1971   ILM 10:895

1972
Treaty of Accession to E.E.C., 22 January 1972   Treaty series (1973), no. 1,
   parts 1 and 2, Cmnd 5179
Agreement on limitation of antiballistic missile systems, 26 May 1972   *The
   Times*, 27 May 1972
Agreement on limitation of strategic offensive arms, 26 May 1972   *The Times*,
   27 May 1972
Treaty between Federal and Democratic Republics of Germany, 21 December
   1972   Official texts

1973
Paris Agreement to end the Vietnam War, 27 January 1973   *The Times*, 25
   January 1973
Declaration of International Conference on Vietnam, 2 March 1973   *The
   Times*, 3 March 1973
U.S.–Soviet Agreement on limiting strategic arms, 21 June 1973   *The Times*,
   22 June 1973

U.S.–Soviet Agreement on the prevention of nuclear war, 22 June 1973 *The Times*, 23 June 1973

Agreement between India and Pakistan, 28 August 1973 *The Times*, 30 August 1973

Laos Peace Agreement, 14 September 1973 *The Times*, 15 September 1973

Treaty on mutual relations between German Federal Republic and Czechoslovakia, 11 December 1973 *Bull. Federal German Republic*, 21 June 1973

Index

Page references in **bold** lettering refer to the texts of the treaties